RISE *of the* MODERN HOSPITAL

RISE *of the* MODERN HOSPITAL

An Architectural History *of* Health *and* Healing, 1870–1940

JEANNE KISACKY

UNIVERSITY *of* PITTSBURGH PRESS

Furthermore:
a program of the J. M. Kaplan Fund

This publication has been supported by a grant from Furthermore:
a program of the J. M. Kaplan Fund.

Published by the University of Pittsburgh Press, Pittsburgh, Pa., 15260
Copyright © 2017, University of Pittsburgh Press
Manufactured in the United States of America
Printed on acid-free paper
10 9 8 7 6 5 4 3 2 1

Cataloging-in-Publication data is available from the Library of Congress

ISBN 13: 978-0-8229-4461-4
ISBN 10: 0-8229-4461-8

Jacket art: Climate Room, at the Chicago Lying-In Hospital, Chicago (Ill.),
Aug. 23, 1949, Photographer—Hedrich-Blessing, Film negative, HB-12537-B,
photo courtesy of Special Collections Research Center, University of
Chicago Library. Copyright permission granted from Chicago History
Museum.

Jacket design by Alex Wolfe

Contents

Acknowledgments

This project has been generously supported by a Grant for Scholarly Works in BioMedicine from the National Library of Medicine as a branch of the National Institutes of Health (Grant G13LM 009479). Without this aid, which allowed me to devote full time to the project and assisted in the acquisition of images for the illustrations, it would never have reached completion. Publication support from Furthermore: A program of the J. M. Kaplan Fund graciously facilitated the inclusion of extensive illustrations.

The project has also benefited from the aid of numerous archives, archivists, collections, and fellow hospital historians. I would like to thank, in particular, Jim Gehrlich, Elizabeth Shepherd, Adele Lerner, and Lisa Mix of the Medical Center Archives of NewYork–Presbyterian/Weill Cornell; Jack Eckert at the Francis A. Countway Library of Medicine of Harvard University, Boston; Arlene Shaner at the New York Academy of Medicine; Miranda Schwartz and Marilyn Kushner at the New York Historical Society; Stephen Greenberg at the National Library of Medicine in Bethesda; Steve Novak of the Archives and Special Collections of the Augustus C. Long Health Sciences Library of Columbia University; Robert Steele, formerly archivist at the Archives Mount Sinai Medical Center, New York City; Kaura Gale and Maria Astifidis of the Beth Israel Hospital; Karen Brewer and Colleen Bradly Sanders at the Ehrman Medical Library, New York University; Rob Roche, archivist at the firm of Shepley Bulfinch, Richardson and Abbott, Boston; and Barbara Opar, Syracuse University Fine Arts Librarian. The outlines of this work began at Cornell University under the able guidance of Christian F. Otto, Mary N. Woods, and Stuart R. Blumin, and I remain thankful for their generous support.

RISE *of the* MODERN HOSPITAL

Introduction

To the well-known saying that "dirt is only matter in the wrong place," may be added another, that disease, and death itself, is but life in the wrong place.

— *American Architect and Building News*, 1882

Hospital: An institution or establishment for the care of the sick or wounded, or of those who require medical treatment.

— *Oxford English Dictionary*

That a hospital—as an institution providing care to sick and injured persons—should be designed to promote the health of its inhabitants is a foregone conclusion. How, exactly, a building design might be expected to facilitate cure or suppress illness is more elusive, and it is the focus of this book.

From the mid-nineteenth to the mid-twentieth century, American hospital designers experimented with a number of competing strategies for the role the building design was to play in the health of its occupants. Designers debated whether the hospital building was a therapy in itself, providing a surrounding that would somehow keep persons in close proximity from sharing their ailments and perhaps even actively instill greater health in its occupants, or whether it was a tool that would organize the activities, materials, and events within the building into an efficient, controlled, therapeutic process.

Over time the questions and the preferred answers changed, reflecting altered medical, social, urban, and architectural circumstances. Mid-nineteenth-century hospital designers overwhelmingly privileged the building's therapeutic potential over its ability to facilitate medical treatments. Mid-twentieth-century hospital designers overwhelmingly privileged the building's potential to facilitate medical actions and interactions over its intrinsic healthiness. This shift from considering the hospital as a therapy to considering it as a tool accompanied drastic institutional transformations. From the last resort of the impoverished urban unwell, hospitals became the first resort of all classes of ailing citizens. From neutral containers of general care, they became active locations in the development of specialized scientific medicine. From charitable institutions organized on an almost familial structure, they became complex organizations modeled on current business structures. From closed institutions into which sick people flowed, they became open institutions out of which health flowed. These multiple, complicated transformations were built into American hospitals as their facilities shifted from low-rise, decentralized pavilion wards to centralized, "modern" high-rises.[1]

Architectural decisions also influenced these transformations. Where a hospital was located in relation to the city, to other hospitals, and to specific neighborhoods affected its patient load and characteristics as directly as the composition of its medical staff. What facilities a hospital contained and how they were arranged could turn it from a warehouse for the sick poor into a location for cutting-edge medicine attracting all classes. The sizes of its inpatient rooms—whether wards (large rooms that housed a number of patients) or single-patient rooms—determined the number of people that could be treated and the extent to which each patient could be isolated from the others, and even delineated who paid for care.

These transformations are relevant today as designers struggle to develop new hospital buildings that are efficient and attractive, and decide which buildings from earlier time periods are worth saving and which are destined only for demolition. The truth is, however, that we know very little in detail about how and why American hospitals shifted from pavilions to high-rises in the crucial period between the end of the Civil War and the beginning of World War II.[2] Many historians of hospital design intentionally avoid this difficult period, ending their discussion at the mid-nineteenth century or beginning it after the mid-twentieth century.[3]

Works that do cover the decades between the 1870s and 1940s often do so in a few pages (or even just a few paragraphs), and touch on the same sequence of examples, moving directly from the internationally famous pavilions of the Johns Hopkins Hospital in Baltimore (1875–1885) to the mature high-rises of the 1930s such as the Columbia-Presbyterian Medical Center in New York City by James Gamble Rogers (1929), the New York Hospital–Cornell Medical Center in New York City by Coolidge Shepley Bulfinch and Abbott (1932), or the Beaujon Hospital in Clichy, France, by Jean Walter (1935). In between these two extremes are given at best a handful of intermediate examples, such as Albert J. Ochsner's 1905 call for vertical hospital design, Arnold Brunner's collaboration with S. S. Goldwater on the new Mount Sinai Hospital in New York City (1901), Goldwater's ideal ward design for cities (1910), or William Henman's Royal Victoria Hospital in Belfast (1903). The detailed sequence of transformation of hospital design between the 1870s and 1930s has become so lost to history that in 1976 Peter Stone could confidently (if erroneously) state that "there had been little literature on the general problem of hospital design since Florence Nightingale's 1863 book *Notes on Hospitals.*"[4]

A few recent works have begun to fill this gap, but each still reveals only a small piece of a much larger story. Jeremy Taylor examines hospital design up to 1914, but he focuses on the transformation of the pavilion-ward type in Britain, not on the development of high-rise, centralized, modern hospital structures. Sven-Olov Wallenstein presents a number of hospitals between the 1900s to the 1930s, but his examples are mostly sanatoria (a specialized type of hospital with design requirements that reduced their height and their centralization) and are chosen for their "modernist" design and designers rather than for their representation as epitomes of hospital planning and function. David Charles Sloane and Beverlie Conant Sloane correlate shifts in the practices and experiences of patients, doctors, and benefactors to the architectural shifts of hospitals from a "home" to a medical workshop to a vertical hospital, but only as a brief prelude to an extended discussion of the transformations of the last half of the twentieth century. In numerous publications, Annmarie Adams has focused on hospital design in the decades between the 1900s and 1940s, but in order "to understand hospital buildings as artifacts of material culture" she has structured her work as a series of thematic essays "rather than a chronology of hospital design." This approach, which studies buildings as historical records in and of themselves, has allowed her to develop a deep knowledge of the social, cultural, and political issues enmeshed in a few hospital designs, but not a broad overview of hospital design in these transitional decades.[5] Her focus on works by hospital architect Edward F. Stevens also limits the story she tells. Stevens was an influential and gifted designer who worked on hospital projects across the globe, but his body of work remained consistently low-rise in comparison to other contemporary practitioners like York and Sawyer or James Gamble Rogers, who pioneered in high-rise hospital designs.

This dearth of a basic historical examination of a crucial developmental period in hospital design inevitably leads to distortions, even misunderstandings of relevant influences, essential chronologies, and critical sequences of change. The architectural history of "aseptic" finishes provides a graphic example. It is typical for modern historians (and practitioners) to assume that "hospital" finishes—hard, impermeable surfaces in hospital white, with rounded corners, no cracks, and no projections—developed in the 1890s and 1900s as a consequence of new aseptic goals of creating germ-free conditions. It is not so straightforward. Hospital finishes were well-established by the first half of the nineteenth century. The materials of choice, however, changed over the years. In the 1850s hard-polished, seamlessly joined varnished wood (which could be intentionally destroyed and replaced for ultimate purification) was popular; in the "antiseptic" designs of the 1880s marble, marble mosaics, and enameled plaster were popular; and in the "aseptic" designs of the 1900s glass, ceramic tile, and metal were popular. Clearly, hospital finishes were not a consequence of asepsis; they were an exaggeration, even a refinement, of an already existing spatial strategy. There is as much evidence to support the argument that these preexisting hygienic hospital finishes influenced the development of germ theory and antiseptic and aseptic practices as there is to support the reverse. This reveals a historical dilemma—a vacillation between whether to consider medicine and culture as an influence on hospital design or hospital design as an influence on medicine and culture.

Many historians have explained the physical transformation of the hospital by treating building form as the consequence of social and medical transformation. John D. Thompson and Grace Goldin, who wrote the most comprehensive available history of hospital design, examine hospitals from antiquity to the twentieth century as a record of social change; they focus on the design of patient spaces as a representation of "the way people were thinking about group housing for the sick at that time and place." More focused considerations of the hospital between the nineteenth and twentieth centuries have emphasized the correlation of medical change to architectural change. According to Henry E. Sigerist regarding the late nineteenth-century hospital, "while the driving forces in the previous periods were social forces, it was the progress of medicine and surgery which now called for a new type of hospital." Lindsay Prior even goes so far as to describe hospital plans as "archaeological records which encapsulate and imprison within themselves a genealogy of medical knowledge." Following this approach, the late nineteenth-century developments of germ theory, antisepsis, and asepsis are frequently posed as critical influences on the early twentieth-century transformations of hospital design.[6]

Other historians have reversed that explanation and examined the consequences of changing hospital design on medical practices. Michel Foucault, for example, discusses how the arrangement of patients into a "clinic" altered the eighteenth-century French doctor's understanding of disease. In her own work and in collaborative work with historians of technology and medical practitioners, Adams traces "the dynamic relationship of architecture and medicine," concluding that at times hospital design "actually slowed medical innovation."[7]

Should architecture be studied as a reflection of sociocultural transformations and aspirations? As a tool? Or as a force in molding and shaping it? As a therapy? At stake in the response to this question is not only what stories can be told of past buildings but how practitioners can understand their role in designing new buildings.

Many studies examine the history of building designs biographically, as the products of the designer's aspirations. This approach illuminates the intentions of designers (whether architects, clients, contractors, or political agencies) and demonstrates design as a conscious action with sociocultural as well as physical consequences. Many of these stories are triumphant tales of progress that create a sense of professional optimism: Designers create the buildings; the buildings shape the society. By studying what has been built, designers create better designs and better designs create better societies. This progression did not (and has not) happened. In fact, the second half of the twentieth century witnessed severe and disillusioning rifts between design intentions and lived realities.

Within the last few decades, buildings have been increasingly studied with the goal of tracing the hidden sociocultural influence of buildings on inhabitants, particularly in terms of "control." Wallenstein, like Foucault before him, looks to hospitals of the past as revelatory of biopolitics—which considers buildings active expressions of (increasingly medicalized) political power structures and controls. Adams examines the gendered nature of designs for the housing of nurses and medical interns and considers the ways in which social categories are reiterated in building partitions (e.g., private patients on upper floors and charity patients on lower floors). Thomas Schlich looks at modern operating room design as revelatory of the culture of control deployed in and by scientific modernity. J. T. H. Connor promotes the study of buildings as material culture, looking at the object itself to tell its history and its importance.[8] These approaches—which look to mute buildings as active influences in shaping actions and society—give voice to the physical artifact. The implicit expectation is that these studies will also empower socially self-aware and culturally critical designers to make informed choices about what to design and how to live in what is designed.

Examining buildings as reflections of personal intentions assigns to the designer the power to shape society without offering any strategies for assessing the actual results of design. Examining buildings as influential artifacts in themselves considers buildings as mechanisms for social suasion, but renders the process of their design mute, almost purposeless, making designers into powerless tools of hidden agendas beyond their control.

I believe that intentions matter. I also believe that design success has to be measured by real consequences, intended and unintended. Every design choice reflects a moment of human existence but it also alters human existence. To reveal this interaction, I examine the history of hospital design in

Figure I.1. "The Hospital of the Twentieth Century." This image depicts the optimism of the 1930s, when a visit to the modern hospital offered a voyage from darkness to light. The patients, in rags and ethnic clothing, crawl, hobble, and are carried into the hospital; they leave upright, vigorous, and dressed in modern middle-class American outfits.

the United States between the Civil War and World War II as both a reflection of its sociocultural milieu and a shape-giving force on its inhabitants. I examine how designer intentions structured a specific building type (one related to health), and at the same time how the resultant experiences in those buildings influenced later choices and possibilities of what occurred within them.

To the extent that I can, I use the concerns and goals of the designers of the time to establish the topics for discussion and the criteria for evaluating the resultant performance and influence of the buildings constructed. Discussions of hospital design deviated in a number of ways from mainstream architectural debates. While nineteenth-century and early twentieth-century architects and architectural publications focused on the various historic styles, contemporary discourses on hospital design downgraded the role of ornament and style to an unnecessary, perhaps even unhygienic addition. Hospital designers emphasized the plan over the facade and developed designs based on massing and circulation rather than decoration and materials.[9] Air flow and air quality were critical aspects of hospital design; this made ventilation and the designed voids (not just the layout of the walls) topics of primary concern. Hospital design also required more than basic architectural expertise—and doctors, lay governors, and consultants as well as architects actively participated in hospital designs. Accordingly, this book presents a history of architecture that focuses on plans; examines ventilation, plumbing, and open spaces in extensive detail; and considers a variety of persons (not just architects) influential in design.

By examining hospital architecture as a "hygienic" rather than "aesthetic" object, this work reveals a fundamental shift not just in the physical form of the hospital buildings but in the basic understanding the designers had of the role the hospital environment would play in health and healing. Up to the late nineteenth century, persons involved in hospital design expected the hospital building, in itself, to participate in the social, moral, and even physiological cure of the inhabitants.[10] In the best light, this therapeutic design provided an orderly, sunlit, well-aired place in which the urban poor could be restored to health (and moral behavior); at worst it provided a relentlessly hygienic space that influenced nonconformist patients to obey new social and medical norms. By the early twentieth century hospital designers increasingly treated the hospital building as a functional backdrop to active medical interventions that were expected to generate a "normal" or healthy physiological condition in the patient. At best, this "modern" hospital design proved an efficient tool for facilitating current medical behaviors and practices; at worst, it provided a cold, off-putting, chaotic space that aggrandized doctors and procedures, fetishized germs, and dehumanized patients. The history of hospital design from the 1870s to the 1940s makes it clear that if the goal is to "design for health," then it is crucial to understand what kind of health is sought, and what role the physical surroundings are expected to play in its acquisition.

Structure and Limitations of This Book

This book is not a comprehensive survey of all hospital buildings in the United States; it is a first attempt to examine a broad variety of selected hospital structures across the United States up to the 1940s and see what conclusions can be drawn from them. I base my analysis and discussion on hospitals that were singled out in the literature of the time as models (whether negative or positive). This selectivity has inevitably left out many worthy hospitals and included many derivative ones. My focus is on new designs of entire hospital facilities and of critical new additions to existing facility designs. While many institutions began in preexisting buildings converted to hospital use, the issues encountered in adapting houses or other building types to hospital use were far different from those encountered when designing a hospital from the ground up.

I have tried to develop a "national" coverage in that I examine hospitals from all states, but larger cities held far more hospitals than did smaller cities, so it is inevitably skewed toward greater representation of hospitals from urban areas of the country. The book has also been deeply influenced by the course of my research. In the early 1990s I set out to write my dissertation on the architectural history of American hospitals (all places, all times). Within a year I reduced the topic to hospitals in New York City, and soon thereafter, to the history of the buildings of the New York Hospital. In 2007 I began work on an architectural history of hospitals in New York City. In 2010, well into the work, I revised the scope to include American hospitals of all states. The project has thus come full circle, but its trajectory is influential. I know a lot about hospital buildings in America; I know the most about hospitals in New York City. I have tried to use the depth of the knowledge I have acquired about hospitals in one particular city as a means of illuminating what happened in other cities, but I have also struggled to keep the New York history from dominating the examples.

While hospitals were a European institution imported to America, this book is almost obsessively about American hospitals. Available histories of hospital design in Europe between the eighteenth and twentieth centuries reveal that the transformation of European hospital design occurred at a different pace and along a different formal trajectory than did the transformation of American hospital design. European hospitals stayed pavilion-ward longer; they also remained charitable in emphasis longer. At the same time, American hospitals underwent extensive transformations that were then exported to other areas of the globe. The goal of this book is to reveal the as yet unwritten history of hospitals in North America during a period of rapid and multiple transformations of the institution, the country, and medicine. Discussions of international hospital designs and issues that were influential on American design are included, as is a minimal discussion of the exportation of American plan hospital designs (particularly in the twentieth century) to other parts of the world. The study of the dissemination of hospital designs between various locales in the nineteenth and twentieth centuries would be the subject of a separate book.

I have limited my focused attention to the period between the 1870s and the 1940s, before the US involvement in World War II. This period saw an epochal shift in hospitals and hospital design. The period between the 1940s and the 1960s saw another sweeping shift, but along a different trajectory—it would require a separate focused study to do it justice. Each chapter covers a different chronological period in American hospital design. Chapter 1 examines the initial cast of American hospitals to 1873, as hospital designers adopted European traditions and embraced the pavilion-ward standards of hospital design, but then struggled to adapt them to local conditions and necessities. After the economic panic of 1873, hospital construction slowed to a trickle, but as chapter 2 reveals, hospital designers then began to examine the possible implications of germ theory on hospital design. From the return of prosperity in 1878 to the next panic of 1897, chapter 3 examines the dilemma American hospital designers faced, between remaining faithful to the established pavilion-ward standard and adapting hospital buildings to the new requirements of asepsis, medical specialization, institutional efficiency, and urban integration. Between 1897 and 1917, the period discussed in chapter 4, intense reconsiderations of the urban and medical role of a hospital and its buildings supported an extensive range of hospital facility designs, from traditional, charitable pavilions to medicalized general hospitals in "stacked" pavilions to medical specialties housed in high-rise structures. Chapter 5 discusses how World War I hospital experiences merged with the new urban postwar culture and established efficient, "vertical" hospital design as the new ideal structure to house a new kind of hospital—a medical rather than a charitable institution. Chapter 6 reveals how, from the Great Depression to the beginning of World War II, economic challenges promoted efficient, economic, and flexible service over "healthy" design. The book concludes with a bibliographic essay, which serves as a broad guide to the secondary literature. The footnotes in the chapters provide the detailed primary and secondary bibliographic sources in support of specific points, topics, or issues, and should be used as a guide to more focused historical inquiries.

CHAPTER 1

The Hospital Building as a Means of Disease Prevention, 1700–1873

"For sixty years the abiding-place of every form of disease and injury to which human flesh is heir, Bellevue Hospital has reached a period of its existence when, in the words of Billroth, the building is a mere slaughter-pen of the wounded.... Medical men take long to learn that plaster, stone, and mortar hold seeds of death most pertinaciously."

— **Thomas K. Cruse, 1872**

The greater number of diseases are . . . more or less preventable. When a preventable disease occurs, some one is to blame—either the subject of it or those who are charged with the duty of providing for his well-being."

— **William Hammond, 1863**

Hospitals are conundrums. Unless practitioners are certain about what causes and spreads disease (and how to prevent it), gathering a number of persons suffering from a variety of ailments into a single building is more likely to breed disease than cure it. In the history of hospital design, certainty about what causes disease has not always correlated with accuracy. American hospital designers of all ages have strongly believed they were designing hospital buildings to participate in the production of health rather than disease; results have not always been consistent with intentions.

In the twenty-first century, medical practitioners are certain that microorganisms cause infectious disease and that they are transferred from a sick individual to a well individual primarily by direct physical contact. More than a century of scientific research and observation supports the accuracy of this understanding, and disease-preventive behaviors based on it have strongly reduced the incidence of contagious diseases but not eliminated it.

Before the development and adoption of germ theory, a majority of Western medical practitioners were certain that sickness was either spread or caused by "corrupted" (dirty, odorous, confined, damp) physical surroundings. That this correlation between environmental quality and sickness was not entirely accurate does not invalidate the doctors' belief in it, nor the actions they took to prevent disease based on their understanding. More than two thousand years of observation and medical writings supported this correlation. Hippocrates wrote about epidemic "airs." Many observed that disease always struck harder in impoverished neighborhoods. Others noticed that sickness spread to persons who came near, but did not touch, other sick persons. Centuries of observations of disease incidence thus pointed to the air as the means of spreading and even causing infectious disease. Given a strong enough concentration of bad air, as occurred in hospitals with their aggregation of sick persons, even building materials could "hold seeds of death most pertinaciously."[1]

In this view, hospitals were inherently unhealthy, even dangerous places that could function as a source of contamination to patients, visitors, practitioners, even to the larger surroundings. Hospital experience supported this fear. A number of dangerous infections (including erysipelas, typhus, hospital gangrene, and other infections) were so much more prevalent in hospitals that they were categorized as "hospital diseases"—ailments generated by the building. An internal outbreak of erysipelas and "hospital gangrene" in more than a dozen patients in the Massachusetts General Hospital in the winter of 1826–1827 provides a graphic example. Attending surgeon George Hayward performed an extensive investigation into the outbreak and concluded that it did not "seem possible in any case to trace it from one patient to another." A month had passed between the initial cases and the next incidence and there was no direct contact between the various patients who contracted it. According to William Hammond, a military surgeon who would become the eleventh surgeon general of the United States, patients gave off foul exhalations that could "cling to the clothing, the furniture, the walls, and especially the bedding." Hayward concluded that the outbreak had been caused and spread by an accumulation of "an atmosphere, capable of producing erysipelas in those predisposed to it . . . [that] was never entirely removed, from the want of sufficient ventilation."[2]

This experience was hardly an isolated incident. In the eighteenth and nineteenth centuries, hospital diseases occurred with a regularity and a severity that is now difficult to comprehend. European and American hospital annual reports regularly counted as many cases of these secondary infections as there were primary ailments. During severe outbreaks, 20 to 40 percent of patients in a hospital might die from diseases they caught *after* admission.

In each incidence, the building itself—its somehow flawed design—was considered the immediate and direct cause of the hospital disease.[3]

Despite this danger, doctors and philanthropists in American and European cities regularly promoted hospitals as a means of dealing with the growing number of sick poor persons. Prospective patients were not as enamored of the idea. According to Paul Starr, "almost no one who had a choice sought hospital care." John Duffy observed that "even as late as 1900 most so-called decent, respectable people expected to be treated at home," whether by family or by medical practitioners. Industrialization and urbanization were rapidly reducing the size of homes, however, making home care burdensome and increasing the number of persons living on the economic edge, without the reserves to afford treatment or even housing through a sickness. In contrast to the poorhouse or almshouse, hospitals offered a temporary way station that would enable the worthy poor incapacitated by sickness to recover health and return to self-sufficiency.[4] But for hospitals to be useful institutions the problem of hospital diseases had to be addressed.

Early American hospital practitioners considered hospital disease to be an Old World problem (the result of crowded chaotic cities) and assumed that it would not occur in New World hospitals. Experience quickly proved them wrong. Not all hospitals were equally affected. Extensive statistical and experiential evidence amassed by European hospital practitioners proved that hospitals on congested urban sites in large cities with hundreds of patients crowded together had the highest rates of hospital disease, while smaller hospitals in natural surroundings with fewer patients had the lowest rates.[5] For European and American practitioners, the conclusion to be drawn seemed obvious: the conditions of the hospital's buildings caused hospital disease.

To prevent disease or to curtail an outbreak in progress, nineteenth-century hospital practitioners ordered architectural alterations and hygienic overhauls of the building. This requires explanation. The word *hygiene*, simply defined, means health-inducing; it encompasses actions and conditions that promote health. In the modern world, in which medicine focuses on germs, *hygiene* has come to evoke ideas of basic cleanliness, both personal and social. In the eighteenth and early nineteenth centuries, in contrast, when health was considered the consequence of orderly, cleanly environments and moral behavior within them, the term evoked a more holistic understanding—inclusive not just of personal habits or predilections but of the conditions of a person's surroundings. In this framework, architecture was an active influence on the healthiness of its occupants. "Curing" hospital disease required first "curing" the building. For example, in response to the 1827 outbreak in the Massachusetts General Hospital, the administrators cleared the wards of all patients, fumigated the wards with chlorine gas to decontaminate the walls and surfaces, left the windows open to the purifying influence of fresh air through most of a Boston January, and overhauled the ventilation system to improve air flow and quality.[6] When the patients were returned to the building, the disease did not (immediately) reappear, and this success was attributed to the architectural renovations.

When it came to new hospital construction, late eighteenth-century hospital designers began to dream of a preventive structure—a building so aerially pure that hospital disease would never develop within its confines. This was a radical departure in hospital design traditions. In many medieval and Renaissance hospitals (like the Ospedale Maggiore in Milan, the Hospital of Santa Maria Nuova in Florence, or Saint John's Hospital in Bruges), cure was as much spiritual as physical, and hospital buildings were designed to allow all the patients to hear religious services from their beds.[7] Large open wards of varying shape and size accommodated multiple rows of beds and interconnected with other spaces, particularly the chapel. In contrast, the hospital designs of late eighteenth-century Europe (like the Stonehouse Naval Hospital in Plymouth or the proposals for a new Hôtel-Dieu in Paris by Bernard Poyet, Antoine Petit, and Jean-Baptiste Leroy) maximized air flow and quality by structuring the hospital as a collection of small buildings, each filled with a narrow, linear room, disconnected from other spaces and surrounded by open air. Inside, at most two rows of beds—each bed aligned to a window—allowed patients to occupy the same room without breathing the same air, thereby preventing aerial transfer of infection. This turned a hospital into a *máchine à guérir*, a healing machine. The healing, or at least the disease prevention, was considered the direct result of the building's success as a self-purifying pneumatic machine.[8]

Adapting European Hospital Ideals to American Requirements

Early American hospital designers borrowed from these European precedents and models, but adapted them to local conditions. The smaller scale of American cities led to hospitals of smaller scale than their European counterparts. As David Charles Sloane and Beverlie Conant Sloane observe, many American hospitals began in or were initially modeled on houses. As American cities increased in size, by the mid-nineteenth century the largest American hospitals had proportions more similar to the grand European institutions. This pushed the limits of the domestic model, and made hospitals far more institutional in scale and appearance.[9]

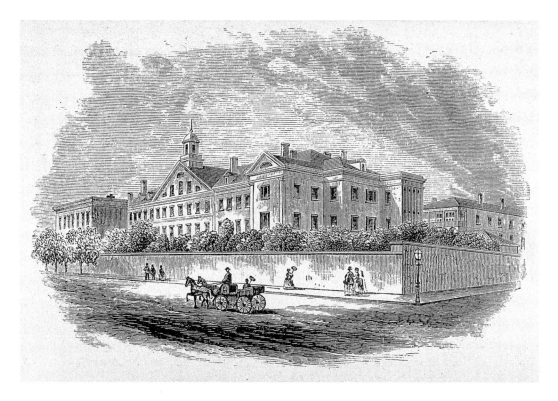

Figure 1.1. View of Charity Hospital, New Orleans, mid-nineteenth century. By the mid-nineteenth century, Charity Hospital held upward of a thousand beds. A surrounding wall, as is depicted in this view, was a prominent feature of early American hospitals, protecting the patients from publicity but also revealing that the inmates were entering a location of control.

Americans founded hospitals with the expectation that they would provide a cost savings over existing outdoor poor-relief expenses. Benjamin Franklin, a driving force in the establishment of the Pennsylvania Hospital (one of the earliest hospitals in the colonies), reckoned that hospital care cost only one-tenth as much as private home care.[10] To achieve this economy, hospital care had to be highly efficient. Although many early hospitals occupied structures adapted from other purposes, a building designed purposely for hospital use was expected to increase economy and efficiency. For example, a building designed with wards sized to hold the greatest number of patients that one nurse could effectively oversee minimized nurse staffing requirements.

In America, as in Europe, hospitals were medical as well as charitable institutions and American doctors were deeply involved in their founding and funding. Medical requirements did not have an enormous influence on hospital design, however. Before the late nineteenth century, medical procedures required little in the way of specialized spaces or expensive equipment—the doctor's black bag still held everything necessary for most treatments. Bleeding and purging remained common treatments for a wide variety of ailments; surgery (done without anesthesia or antiseptics) was a treatment of last resort; and the prescriptive habits of doctors of the time prompted Oliver Wendell Holmes's firm belief "that if the whole materia medica, *as now used*, could be sunk to the bottom of the sea, it would be better for mankind—and all the worse for the fishes." Effective medical treatments did exist for some ailments (bone setting, wound care, simple corrective surgeries), but these tasks did not require specialized spaces. As Morris Vogel observes, "hospitals offered patients no medical advantages not available in the home."[11] They did, however, provide basic nursing care, which was an equally effective part of many a hospital cure, particularly with the increasing popularity of "therapeutic nihilism," which considered the healing power of nature more effective than most medical interventions. This made a hygienically designed hospital—with large windows and open, airy rooms filled with sunlight and fresh air—a treatment in itself, not just a location of care.[12]

The spatial requirements of doctors in hospitals extended beyond the requirements of basic medical care and into the needs of medical education and research. As medical education increasingly emphasized clinical experience (rather than reading lists and attendance at lectures), hospital practice offered doctors and medical students something that could not be gained in private practice and house calls: "a supply of clinical material, adequate for the needs of systematic research in pathology and in therapeutics." Private patients, whom doctors treated on house calls and who paid for their treatments, did not submit to being used in teaching or in medical "experimentation." Hospital patients who received medical care at no charge tacitly paid for their care by serving as this "clinical material"—the subject matter of hands-on education and practical medical development. If a hospital building included spaces that could accommodate specialized research and instruction—such as a laboratory, an autopsy space, a pathological museum, or an operating amphitheater—doctors could maximize the medical benefits drawn from this wealth of clinical material.[13] Such spaces could add extensive, often costly spatial demands to the hospital buildings.

Even without these spaces, hospitals offered doctors clinical control and a spatial structure adapted to focused medical study. According to Judith Leavitt, doctors who treated patients in their homes might have to modify their therapies, while those visiting hospital patients could prescribe treatments without fear of interference from protective family members. Similarly, Starr notes that hospital medical practice made it harder for a patient to ignore or disobey medical instructions, and Ivan Waddington observes that the hospital "provided the ideal structural situation for minimizing resistance to new forms of treatment."[14]

Hospitals also allowed doctors the possibility of grouping patients based on their ailment, thereby providing a spatial structure that contributed to an ongoing transformation of medical focus from seeing the patient to seeing the disease. According to John Harley Warner, in the early nineteenth century, "treatment was to be sensitively gauged not to a disease entity but to such distinctive features of the patient as age, gender, ethnicity, socioeconomic position, and moral status, and to the attributes of place like climate, topography, and population density." By the 1860s doctors focused instead on the detailed physiological course of a disease through various individuals. The removal of the patient from their home environment and into standardized institutional surroundings (which grouped patients by ailment) inevitably played a role in this transformation. Michel Foucault and others have described this transformation as the product of the Parisian "clinic," and have investigated the ways in which hospital ward design supported this new medicine.[15]

Hospitals dispensed more than medical treatment, however. According to historian John Duffy, "it was reasoned that sickness, disease, and poverty resulted from immorality; conversely health, wealth, and happiness were proof of one's adherence to the moral laws." Many of the early American hospitals were founded as much with the intention of providing moral reform as for medical intervention. The managers of the Jews' Hospital in New York City noted that a hospital stay had "been the means, in several instances, of bringing our brethren back to their faith, in rescuing them from public charities, from want and misery, and restoring them to health and the abiding force and truth of Judaism."[16] Practitioners in other denominational institutions expressed similar sentiments. The building design could facilitate this reform by the inclusion of religious worship space or by the creation of an orderly, controlled space that, it was hoped, would itself instill propriety in the inhabitants.

The extent to which hospitals did or did not include these specialized spaces was influenced by local practice but also by institutional specificity. American hospitals were far from standardized institutions; they came in a wide variety, based on their targeted patient clientele, their founding group, and their funding source. General hospitals provided general treatment and care to patients with a wide variety of ailments. Medically specialized hospitals provided care for or by patients with specific ailments. Socially specialized hospitals provided treatments for persons of a specific race, denomination, or nationality.[17]

Figure 1.2. Bellevue Hospital, New York City, in 1879. The main building was the product of sequential construction, with added wings and enlargement of the central pavilion. Later additions of separate wards typically housed patient categories requiring isolation (including, at various times, erysipelas, smallpox, contagious, surgical, phthisis, and psychopathic and alcoholic patients). The medical college building is to the left of the central pavilion.

Municipal general hospitals, funded by public monies, accepted patients regardless of background, ailment (except contagious diseases), or ability to pay; they were the largest and the most crowded institutions. A few, like the Pennsylvania Hospital in Philadelphia, Bellevue Hospital in New York City, Massachusetts General Hospital in Boston, or Charity Hospital in New Orleans, approached the vast scale of their Old World counterparts like Saint Bartholomew's in London, the Hôtel-Dieu in Paris, or the Allgemeines Krankenhaus in Vienna.[18] While many of the larger European hospitals occupied monumental facilities designed according to an overarching plan, the largest of American hospitals up to the early nineteenth century occupied buildings that had started small and been enlarged, one wing or building at a time, until the final product was impressive in scale but a hodgepodge of different periods and changing plans.

"Voluntary" general hospitals, founded and funded by private citizens or philanthropic organizations, typically accepted persons regardless of race, creed, color, or economic class but excluded persons with chronic or contagious diseases and tacitly excluded the "morally vicious." They varied in size (from half a dozen beds to a couple hundred), but were smaller

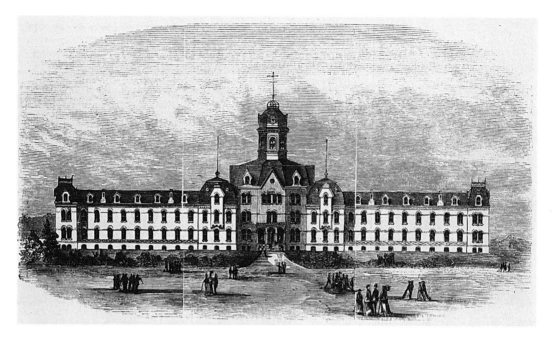

Figure 1.3. German Hospital, New York City, mid-nineteenth century. Designed by German-born architect Carl Pfeiffer and staffed by German doctors, the hospital was both a signpost of the success and a haven for the promotion of German residents of New York City. This image depicts the completed master plan, consisting of four wards and a central administration pavilion, but initially only one ward wing was constructed.

than municipal hospitals.[19] At a time when waves of immigration were turning the largest American cities into socially volatile arenas, hospitals provided a civic presence for their founding group. As Alan M. Kraut has discussed, the conflation of immigration and disease played a tense role in keeping social groups apart and in establishing "healthy," i.e., American, habits as a means of acculturation. Hospitals served as a vital stage upon which this process was carried out. Hospitals founded by prominent social groups served as points of assimilation and cultural hegemony; those founded by marginalized and minority groups offered a haven for the marginalized sick, but also a place for advancement. In the German Hospital in New York City, German-speaking doctors and nurses were the norm. In Saint Vincent's Hospital in New York City and in Charity Hospital in New Orleans, Catholic sisters provided the nursing. In Saint Luke's Hospital in New York City and the Hospital of the Protestant Episcopal Church in Philadelphia, Episcopal sisters did. In the Jews' Hospital in New York City, Jewish doctors provided the care and Jewish traditions were followed in the wards. Rosner has pointed out that the architecture

Figure 1.4. Wills Eye Hospital, Philadelphia, view in 1881. The building opened with seventy beds and included special equipment (including an ophthalmoscope) for treatment.

of these hospitals was as much an expression of the presence and standing of the founding social group within the community as a civic signpost for the needy.[20]

Medically specialized hospitals provided care for patients with difficult-to-treat ailments, vulnerable patients, or groups excluded from other hospitals. The earliest specialized hospitals were for lying-in (obstetric) patients, eye and ear patients, and infectious disease patients. They were usually small institutions, and, as described by Lindsay Granshaw, relatively easy to establish. An interested doctor (or doctors) would start with a few beds in rented facilities but soon might be building a special facility of numerous beds. By the 1850s the New York Eye and Ear Hospital held fifty beds, the Wills Eye Hospital in Philadelphia held seventy, and the Marion Street Maternity Hospital held fifty. Many included design refinements and specialized equipment that tailored the building to the needs of the medical practitioners and practice.[21]

Harriet Richardson, in describing English hospitals of this period, notes that "specialism was the key to the development of hospital architecture, and it is only from an analysis of the different types of hospitals erected that their distinctive appearances can be understood.[22] American hospitals experienced the same forces; their hospital buildings reflected the same differentiations in design.

The Pavilion-Ward Hospital System and Hospital Growth

Given these multiple, at times conflicting, expectations of hospitals, hospital designers struggled to meet design requirements. They had to create a building that was healthy (that would not promote disease), functional (that would provide efficient care, treatment, and reform at a minimum of expense and effort), and suitable for the type of institution it housed (whether general or specialized). In the nineteenth century the first requirement—for a healthy building—eclipsed the other two. Efficiency, economy, and suitability meant little in the face of high rates of cross-infections, hospital diseases, and excess mortality. These dangers played a role in suppressing hospital growth at a time when hospitals could have provided a crucial social safety net in industrializing, urbanizing, and disease-ridden American cities. Waves of epidemics accompanied the waves of immigrants who packed into the tenements and crowded neighborhoods of the seaboard, canal, and railroad cities. Hundreds of accidents occurred in the busy streets and unregulated factories. And yet hospitals remained scarce, marginal institutions within American cities.

This changed after the 1850s, as doctors, philanthropists, and social groups founded dozens of new hospitals in cities across the United States. For example, between 1791 and 1859, seventeen hospital institutions opened in Manhattan while the population increased from 33,131 in 1790 to 813,669 in 1860 (a growth factor of more than 25). Between 1860 and 1870, Manhattan's population increased to 942,292 persons, a growth rate of 116 percent, while between 1860 and 1873 the number of hospitals doubled. This expansion continued into the twentieth century. In 1873 the US Bureau of Education listed 178 hospitals; by 1909, the US Bureau of the Census counted 4,359 hospitals across the United States.[23] From the viewpoint of hospital architecture this rapid expansion clearly coincided with the establishment, popularization, and broad dissemination of a new model of hospital design—the pavilion-ward system—that guaranteed that well-designed and well-administered facilities would not develop hospital disease.

The pavilion-ward hospital was a product of Britain and its colonial expansion; successful hospitals supported successful colonization. After British military hospitals in the Crimea tallied horrendous mortality rates (from diseases and secondary infections as much as battle wounds), Florence Nightingale and a number of volunteer nurses were dispatched to provide aid. In a few short months, the reported mortality rates dropped from 42 percent to 2 percent. Nightingale and her nurses received the credit for this reported improvement, and Nightingale attributed the transformation to better nursing but also to vastly improved hygienic conditions in the wards. Upon her return to England, Nightingale spent the rest of her life advocating for nursing and hospital reform. According to Louise C. Selanders, like the therapeutic nihilists, "it was [Nightingale's] contention that the environment could be altered in such a way as to improve conditions so that nature could act to cure the patient." Nightingale's book, *Notes on Hospitals*, which became the international bible of late nineteenth-century hospital design, correlated hospital mortality rates to hospital layouts as a means of assessing the healthiness of hospital building design. To Nightingale, hospital disease was preventable—the result of choice, not chances—and building hygiene was the means of prevention.[24]

As Grace Goldin, Jeremy Taylor, and Anthony King have pointed out, Nightingale's ideas on hospital design were not original, but they were forcefully and clearly stated and promoted. Pavilion-ward hospital design was not a radical change; it was a systematization of existing strategies. Hospitals before pavilion-ward guidelines had been designed for hygiene—with well-ventilated, easily cleanable spaces—but with varied room sizes, layouts, and functions. The new pavilion-ward design principles transformed those loose guidelines into a quantifiable, standardized, reproducible spatial system. Nightingale's military experiences influenced her plans—she conceptualized wards as barracks.[25]

Nightingale's ideal hospitals comprised a number of separate ward buildings, called pavilions, each functioning independently. Each pavilion took the basic layout developed in the visionary plans of Enlightenment France—one large, narrow ward with windows on all walls and a minimal set of service spaces (in Nightingale's plan these included kitchen, scullery, nurses' office, linen storage, and sanitary facilities). Every type of hospital—municipal, voluntary, general, specialized, small, large—was to follow the same design. The only variation was in scale, measured by the number of pavilions. The result was a "universal" hospital architecture—the same building design was recreated in countries, climates, and locales across the world. That this was an effective adjunct to colonial expansion is obvious. That it also made hospital design requirements widely available and

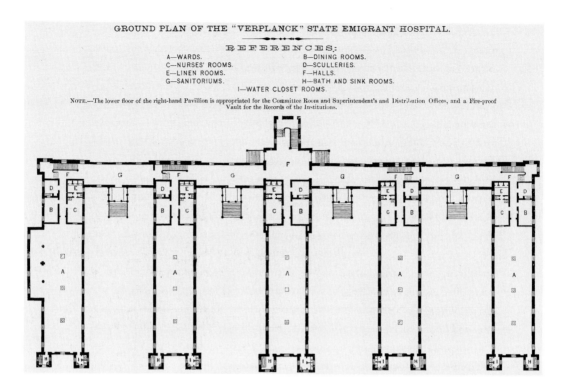

GROUND PLAN OF THE "VERPLANCK" STATE EMIGRANT HOSPITAL.

REFERENCES:

A—WARDS.
C—NURSES' ROOMS.
E—LINEN ROOMS.
G—SANITORIUMS.

B—DINING ROOMS.
D—SCULLERIES.
F—HALLS.
H—BATH AND SINK ROOMS.

I—WATER CLOSET ROOMS.

NOTE.—The lower floor of the right-hand Pavilion is appropriated for the Committee Room and Superintendent's and Distribution Offices, and a Fire-proof Vault for the Records of the Institutions.

Figure 1.5. "Verplanck" State Emigrant Hospital, Ward's Island, New York, 1865. John W. Ritch designed this early pavilion-ward plan hospital. The sanitary towers are the protuberances at the southern extremity of the ward. Though at first built with few services, a central kitchen and laundry were soon added as outbuildings.

was adopted by choice is also obvious. Nightingale's publications, backed by copious statistics and her wealth of hospital experience, functioned as practical how-to manuals, providing a standardized set of design guidelines accessible to anyone who could read. Other texts promoting such improved hospital design soon appeared and further disseminated the information.[26] In a few decades, the pavilion-ward system of hospital design was the ideal in Europe, America, Russia, and most of the colonized world.

America was one of the first countries to build hospitals according to the new ideal. By the 1860s William Hammond even considered the City Hospital in Boston and the Hospital of the Protestant Episcopal Church in Philadelphia "superior to any which have been constructed in any part of the world." The managers of the State Emigrant Hospital in New York City boldly (if erroneously) claimed that the United States predated Europe in the construction of pavilion hospitals, and that Americans were "not the tame imitators of Europe, the mere pupils of her teaching, the followers of her light." During the Civil War, both Union and Confederate armies used Nightingale's publications as a basis for their military hospitals, which were pavilion hospitals on a gargantuan scale. By the early 1870s cities across the United States had new pavilion-ward hospitals; the larger cities had dozens of them.[27]

The pavilion-ward hospital system required undeviating adherence to standardized designs despite the diversity of American hospitals, some of which included extensive facilities for medical education and advancement and others that included extensive facilities for religious reform. Hospital designers had to confront not only the tension between universal solution and specific institutional requirements but how their decisions colored the nature of the institutions that were built.

The Dilemma of Hospital Site Choice

Inevitably, the first task of a hospital building committee (which typically comprised successful lawyers, businessmen, and philanthropists) was to decide where to locate the hospital. This was an often-contentious decision that had long-lasting repercussions for the nature of service.

Hospitals developed where there was a population large enough to justify their expense; they were urban institutions. The ventilation requirements necessary for preventing hospital disease, however, required open landscaped surroundings as a source of fresh air. As Florence Nightingale put it, "to build a hospital in the midst of a crowded neighborhood of narrow streets and high houses, is to ensure a stagnation of the air without, which no ventilation within, no cubic space, however ample, will be able to remedy." But to put a hospital outside the city was to limit its service. A downtown hospital—near busy streets, industries, bustling ports, railroad depots, and densely packed poor neighborhoods—was almost guaranteed to be full of patients with a wide variety of acute conditions requiring medical treatment. Conversely, a more distant hospital often attracted patients with less acute or chronic ailments, who required basic nursing care more than treatment. Accessibility for hospital doctors, benefactors, and patrons was also an issue. An attempt in the 1850s to remove Bellevue Hospital in New York City to a more distant site failed primarily because the doctors claimed it would be inexpedient for them to visit so remote an institution.[28]

In actual practice, American hospitals occupied a variety of locations, ranging from large sites on the urban periphery to single lots in the downtown. Different kinds of hospitals gravitated to different kinds of sites. Managers of specialized hospitals often emphasized accessibility over salubrity. They were typically small-scale institutions and could fit on smaller sites nearer the city center. Medically specialized hospitals, like the Hospital for the Ruptured and Crippled in New York City, were founded by doctors and

EYE AND EAR INFIRMARY.

Figure 1.6. The New York Eye and Ear Infirmary building, New York City, mid-nineteenth century. The building contained a well-equipped operating room and occupied all of its urban site. The corner location was considered a source of light and air.

were typically located at a site convenient to the doctor's home. A few even began as back-office additions. Directors of socially specialized hospitals, like the German Dispensary and Hospital in New York City, selected sites that were near their intended patient clientele. Still, even managers of specialized hospitals experienced the dilemma between a healthy site and an accessible site. Although the directors of Saint Vincent's Hospital in New York City chose a location on the Lower West Side, close to a dense Irish Catholic population, their initial preference was for a large, inexpensive, and well-aired site at distant Turtle Bay.[29]

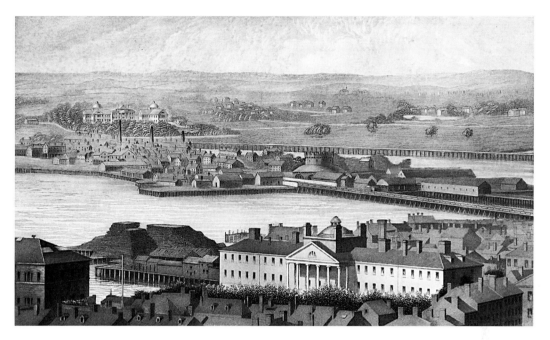

Figure 1.7. Massachusetts General Hospital, Boston, view in 1851. Based on Charles Bulfinch's design, when this municipal hospital was first constructed it was on the city's outskirts. Proximity to the bay allowed for easy delivery of supplies and of patients and an ample supply of water and open air, although it was not always noted for its freshness given the stagnant waters of the bay. The city soon grew to surround the hospital.

When first opened, the large, general municipal hospitals—like the Pennsylvania Hospital in Philadelphia, or Bellevue Hospital in New York City—were regularly located on peripheral sites. These were the largest of American hospitals and required larger sites, which were more available on the periphery. The distance also provided a social buffer between the city and the hospital, which often housed the socially outcast as well as the ill and downtrodden.

Administrators of hospitals that housed vulnerable, persecuted, or contagious patient categories could be sited at quite a distance from the downtown. Contagious disease hospitals, like the Cincinnati Branch Hospital for isolation of contagious cases, were regularly on remote sites, distant from other habitations. Island locations, like the Smallpox Hospital in New York City on Blackwell's Island, were also common in part because they guaranteed a large flow of air to the buildings but also because they provided a form of controlled isolation that could not be defeated by climbing over the hospital wall. Geographical distance could also serve to protect the patients. In 1848 the managers of the Colored Home and Hospital in

New York City located their buildings at Sixty-Fourth to Sixty-Fifth Streets between First Avenue and Avenue A, beyond the easy reach of the persecution that targeted African Americans.

For all kinds of hospitals, larger, newly constructed hospital facilities were almost exclusively undertaken on sites outside the city's developed boundary. This was as much a consequence of urban real estate markets as a positive effort to locate a hospital in open surroundings. Pavilion-ward hospitals required very large sites; downtown sites were expensive, small, and usually already developed. According to the governors of the New York Hospital, "the rapid diminution of large properties under a single ownership in the vicinity of the City" was a hardship for many hospital site searches. To minimize site expenses, hospital building committees often took advantage of municipally donated or leased sites. Such sites were often large (many were full blocks) and were typically on the city's outskirts, but were rarely prime real estate. The municipally acquired site for the Charity Hospital in New Orleans was in a "relatively remote, swampy area at the edge of the city"; for the Woman's Hospital in New York City, it was a former Potter's Field.[30]

Neighborhood opposition could also push new hospitals to undeveloped and undefended peripheral sites. Vogel concludes that "hospitals located where they encountered the least opposition." In 1860, when the directors of the New York Homeopathic Medical College proposed to build a larger building with a hospital at Third Avenue and Twentieth Street in fashionable Gramercy Park, "the protests of such prominent citizenry were enough so that the plan was condemned and the residential status of this 'sacred soil' remained undisturbed." The opposition could also be more subtle. In 1854 the City of Boston purchased the former Boston Lying-In Hospital building and planned to turn it into a new city hospital. "No sooner had they done so than the neighbors sneaked a bill through the legislature making it illegal to maintain a general hospital within 300 feet of a school house, and the City found itself with a white elephant on its hands, for there was a school house next door."[31]

Peripheral sites were not inherently salubrious. Noxious trades, noisy industries, and squatters' settlements also populated the urban fringes. In the late 1860s, according to Dr. Abraham Jacobi, the blocks surrounding the newly built German Hospital in New York City were "a sea of dirty water" laden with garbage and excrement. On paper, the Boston City Hospital's site was lauded for its "open spaces for light and the free circulation of air from the water," but it was on made land (of uncertain composition) and instead of "fresh air," later reports described the open space as providing "malodorous breezes from the putrid South Bay."[32]

Peripheral neighborhoods were also socially volatile, even dangerous. At the Jews' Hospital in New York City, the surrounding tenements created "a neighborhood frequented continually by a number of idle men, women and noisy children, whose disorderly conduct disturbs the rest of our inmates, and often interrupts the solemnity of our devotion and invades the sanctity of our funeral rites." The early days of the Presbyterian Hospital in New York City make the discrepancy between ideal and reality graphically clear. The Presbyterian Hospital's directors lauded the "ample grounds, so near the crowded, bustling city, yet so isolated, retired and accessible as to produce the conviction that a more beautiful and eligible site for the purpose could not have been chosen." In contrast, Dr. David Bryson Delavan, a house doctor at the Presbyterian Hospital in its early years, recalled that "there were no places of respectability anywhere about and the neighborhood was infested with a rough element, lawless under the lack of police protection which had characterized the rule of the Tweed ring."[33]

By the 1850s and 1860s, as the number of hospitals in cities increased rapidly, hospital planners had to take into account the proximity of a prospective site to other hospitals or to densely populated neighborhoods. In most cities, uncoordinated site choices created an uneven, inefficient scattering of facilities. As new hospitals were added, institutions located too close together might have an undersupply of patients and empty beds; those located too far apart might have an oversupply of patients and be overcrowded. In 1871 the president of Saint Luke's Hospital in New York City noted that in the near future the Roosevelt Hospital, Presbyterian Hospital, German Hospital, and Mount Sinai Hospital would all open nearby. He asked, "How are all these Hospitals going to be filled?"[34]

Some believed a more strategic site selection process, one that considered the location of other institutions and population centers, might create a more equitable and efficient distribution of hospitals. In 1870, when considering sites for a new facility for the New York Hospital, the hospital's doctors surveyed the distribution of hospitals across the whole city and concluded that the thickly populated downtown and West Side had few hospitals (1 bed to every 1,800 persons) while the more sparsely populated Upper East Side had many (1 bed to every 284 persons). They argued that any new hospital building should be provided on the West Side, close to downtown, where there was a dearth of beds in relation to the population.[35]

The idea that every neighborhood should have a proportionally similar number of available hospital beds to population, was a simple view of a complex matter. Even if hospitals were spread equally throughout a city, all

Figure 1.8. View of the New York Hospital from Broadway in 1854. The hospital is behind the trees in the center of the image.

beds were not equal. Eye hospitals and lying-in hospitals might provide a number of hospital beds, but they were available to only a small percentage of prospective patients. Municipal hospitals provided a large number of beds, but there was against them, "whether justly or not, a great prejudice, even among the poorer classes."[36]

Many patients voted with their feet—traveling farther to avoid a poorly regarded institution or to reach a more desirable or affordable one. Experiences in the new hospitals in the Upper East Side of New York City demonstrate that factors other than simple geographic proximity influenced a hospital's service. In their first years of operation, Roosevelt and Saint Luke's Hospital stood at least half empty. Conversely, Mount Sinai Hospital and the German Hospital, which catered to specific populations and provided a greater proportion of free care, were regularly full. Rapidly improving public transportation—omnibuses, commuter rail lines, streetcars—increased this mobility. A site near a transportation hub could make a distant hospital readily accessible to numerous neighborhoods. The development in the 1860s of specially designed hospital ambulances, "contrived for the purpose of carrying to the hospital, without jar or exposure, patients unable to endure the motion of ordinary vehicles," further reduced the inconvenience of distant sites. The growth of the city also destabilized site choice. A hospital originally located on the urban periphery, near "salubrious breezes," could soon find itself encompassed by new developments.[37]

The Architectural Consequences of a Building Designed around Air

Whether on a downtown site or a pastoral site, the crucial goal of making the building so full of fresh air that disease would not spread within it differentiated hospital design from other building types. Ventilation requirements determined not only who could design the hospital building but what layouts, materials, and structures were allowable.

Designing the Hospital: A Medical as Much as an Architectural Specialty

Because of the perceived correlation between interior environmental quality and disease incidence in hospital buildings, doctors were as involved in the design of hospital buildings as architects.[38] Architects were trained in the planning of structurally, spatially, or aesthetically complex buildings, but hospital design also required expertise in "architectural hygiene"— how building design (particularly ventilation) might influence health. At the time, ventilation was a peripheral topic for architects who regularly sized and located fireplaces, windows, and chimneys to a room's aesthetic requirements, not according to its heating or ventilating load. Constant client complaints about beautifully designed but uninhabitable rooms and buildings—including smoky chimneys, cold drafts, cold feet, warm heads, and even faintness of breath—reveal the architect's blind spot.[39]

Doctors, on the other hand, could claim knowledge of what created and constituted "bad" air, and they used this knowledge to establish expertise in hospital design, often at the expense of architects. According to Dr. John Aikin, architects tried to accommodate "the greatest number of people in the least possible space," thereby promoting hospital disease. Conversely, medical requirements would "leave as much vacant space, occupied by the fresh air alone circulating freely," as possible. Doctors (and reformers), not architects, penned the majority of European publications on hospital design. These books, which were the basis for the dissemination of pavilion-ward design standards, spoke the language of hygiene, not architecture.[40]

In a few early publications, American doctors reiterated the arguments and approaches of their European counterparts. Dr. John Jones described a hospital that was more air than patients. Dr. William Paul Crillon Barton proposed a far more palatial ideal naval hospital (similar to the Royal Military Hospitals in Haslar and Greenwich, England) with numerous ancillary spaces for services, medicine, therapy, and research. His designs limit-

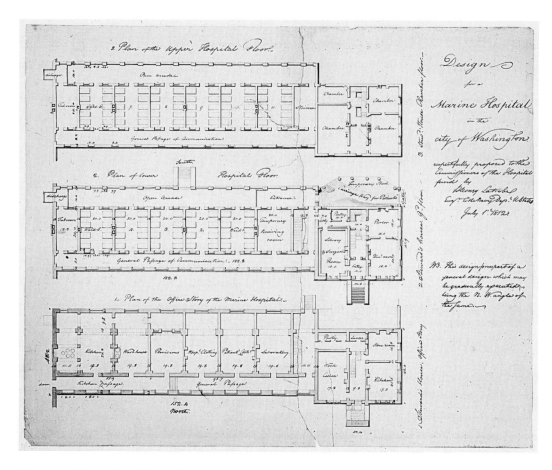

Figure 1.9. Design for a Marine Hospital in the City of Washington, 1821. Benjamin H. Latrobe designed the wards to be small, with windows only on one wall and beds quite close together. The enclosed north passage was intended to protect the patients from the ill influence of cold, damp north-facing walls. The structure was to be vaulted masonry, with pedimented porches and three domes.

ed the number of patients per ward and provided for extensive ventilation by windows, fireplaces, and in-wall air ducts. In contrast, Dr. James Tilton, a military surgeon of the Revolutionary War, proposed an intentionally crude, earth-floored hut of unhewn logs chinked together with clay mortar. It was divided into three small rooms, limiting the numbers of patients in one space, allowing better patient categorization, and controlling air quality by providing abundant window ventilation and fumigation by smoke.[41]

The extent to which architects did indeed bring alternate concerns to hospital design is discernible in a brief report on Marine hospitals for sailors by Benjamin Henry Latrobe (known as the first professional American architect). Latrobe acknowledged the importance of architectural hygiene:

he emphasized ventilation and buffered the patients from exposure to the damp cold of north walls, which, in European hospitals, had proven to prolong illness. Instead of a large open ward he advocated smaller wards of six patients (in beds very close together) with windows only on one wall. Latrobe claimed this layout allowed better categorization and isolation of patients, "reduced the amount of foot traffic through any one ward," and accommodated more patients in less space.[42] Latrobe also extolled the architectural virtues of the vaulted masonry construction that would have made his hospital virtually fireproof but also monumental in features (and cost).

If both architects and doctors could claim expertise relevant to hospital design, in practice doctors and administrators "designed" many of the earliest American hospitals with limited or no input from architects. Samuel Rhoads, a master builder and hospital manager, consulted the Pennsylvania Hospital's physicians and surgeons in the design of the Pennsylvania Hospital. In Ohio, Dr. Daniel Drake not only helped establish the Commercial Hospital in Cincinnati, he "personally drew the plans for the first buildings, for which service he was paid ten dollars by the township authorities."[43]

Given the scarcity of architects in early American settlements, architectural input, even if desired, was not always to be had. The New York Hospital governors sought design advice as far away as New Haven, Connecticut, from Peter Harrison, a wealthy merchant sailing captain who had received some architectural training in Europe and drawn designs for a number of prominent buildings in Rhode Island. As the number of American architects increased in the nineteenth century, architect involvement in American hospital design also increased. Robert Mills (Latrobe's protégé) designed a number of Marine hospitals. Gentleman architect Charles Bulfinch was involved with the Massachusetts General Hospital from its planning stages to his winning design submission. Thomas U. Walter designed the Wills Eye Hospital in Philadelphia. A few architects, like John W. Ritch and James Renwick in New York City, designed more than one hospital.[44]

While competitions were a popular, inexpensive means of acquiring a hospital design, they constrained architect involvement. Anyone could submit a design, whether or not they had architectural training. Even if an architect won the competition, winning did not always bring any further commission or involvement in the project. In the 1850s the architect W. W. Gardiner's drawings won the design competition for a new building for the New York Hospital, but after giving him the prize, the doctors and governors established the building program, traveled to other American hospitals to determine what heating and ventilation system the new building should include, and worked directly with the contractors in constructing the building. The managers of the Hospital of the Protestant Episcopal

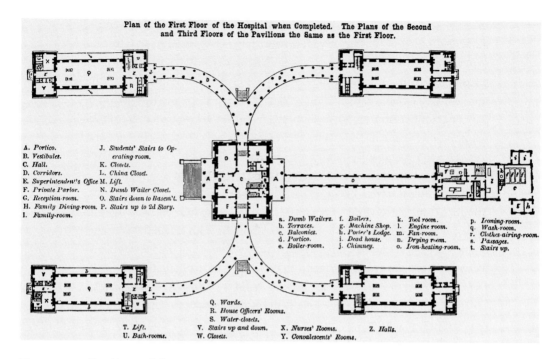

Figure 1.10. City Hospital, Boston, plan, 1865. Gridley Bryant's design was a pavilion plan with widely separated wards connected only by open arcaded walks. The boxes drawn in the ward plans represent risers for heated air. The hospital plan was published and proved influential on a number of other early American hospital designs.

Church in Philadelphia engaged Samuel Sloan, winner of the design competition, to be the architect of the project only after he offered them "extremely liberal terms" for design development of the plans.[45]

By the 1860s informal collaboration between doctors and architects on a hospital design was common. Mr. Boyington, the architect of the new Mercy Hospital in Chicago, based his plans on "suggestions that were offered by Dr. Edmund Andrews, who has spent much time abroad studying the construction and architecture of the most noted European hospitals." In the design competition for the Boston Free City Hospital, Mr. Boyden worked with Dr. John C. Green on an honorable mention entry. For his prizewinning entry in that same competition, Gridley Bryant "had extensively availed himself of the suggestions of Dr. Henry Grafton Clark as to the elevation and general disposition of the pavilions and several apartments." The governors of the Roosevelt Hospital created a more formal collaboration. They hired the architect Carl Pfeiffer to develop the design but also retained local surgeon Dr. Stephen Smith "to study and report to the Board the principles of hospital construction now recognized as most appropriate to the ends to be attained in a public hospital." Smith provided the medical guidelines; Pfeiffer interpreted them into an effective building design. The experience proved influential for both. Smith went on to become an important figure in the development of public health, particularly in cleaning up the urban environment. Pfeiffer went on to argue that architects should pay greater attention to the "sanitary" role that building design played in health, even suggesting that an architect's success should be measured not by the beauty of the buildings but by the health of the occupants.[46]

This emphasis on the hygienic rather than aesthetic influence of buildings made hospitals an atypical architectural problem and offered opportunity for a different kind of practitioner. At a time when American architects were embracing the aesthetic emphasis of France's Beaux-Arts architectural practices, the architects most successful in gaining hospital commissions were those with an engineering or construction background. John W. Ritch was an engineer as well as an architect and adept at developing detailed ventilation designs and hygienic details. Samuel Sloan designed dozens of asylums and a number of hospitals but began his career as a carpenter. Carl Pfeiffer was educated as an engineer with "a considerable amount of architectural study."[47]

The Hygienics of Hospital Layouts

The requirements of architectural hygiene also made hospitals different in overall layout from other urban building types. To maximize the use of expensive urban real estate, offices, stores, and tenements were multistory, compact structures that extended to the lot lines. Even on costly downtown sites, hospital buildings were low-rise, complex, rambling structures with setbacks and partial courtyards. These differences were the result of ventilation strategies. Keeping hospital buildings low maximized wind flow and diminished the possible spread of bad air from floor to floor. The low height was also practical—it reduced the work necessary for the daily delivery of meals and supplies to wards, and it reduced the danger (and discomfort) of carrying bedridden patients up and down stairs. Up to the 1850s hospitals rarely exceeded three or four stories; by the 1860s pavilion-ward advocates established that hospital buildings were "never to be over two stories in height."[48] One-story buildings—which could take advantage of ceiling (or ridge) ventilation—were even better.

The open space between hospital pavilions or wings was not simply leftover space; it was an integral aspect of hospital ventilation strategies. Open land provided a reservoir of fresh air and acted as a buffer to keep the contaminated air from one part of the building from infiltrating another.

Figure 1.11. Mount Sinai Hospital, New York City, view in 1874. This was the second home of the hospital, built to replace an 1855 building that was not considered up to pavilion-ward standards. The widely spaced pavilions, connected only by open arcades, compensated for their four-story height.

Up to the 1850s hospitals often occupied single structures (with complex footprints) sited in the middle of their lots with extensive setbacks. By the 1860s pavilion-ward guidelines broke the hospital into separate buildings, each of which was to be distant from the other buildings by at least twice their height. The amount of open space on hospital sites became an element of pride and competition; the managers of the Mount Sinai Hospital in New York City boasted that at their second building, Griffeth Thomas's design left 125 feet of open land between its pavilions, while other hospitals only had 75 to 100 feet. The open space made many hospitals green oases within the densely crowded urban context, particularly when the hospital

Figure 1.12. Saint Luke's Hospital, New York City, view in 1896. The landscaped hospital grounds and the set-back, widely separated buildings created parklike oases within the increasingly built-up urban context.

administrators developed the grounds into a garden. Saint Luke's Hospital in New York City was surrounded by trees and a lawn interspersed with flowers. At the original Jews' Hospital in New York City (which occupied only two small urban lots), half of the ground was left open and "laid out in beautiful style, as a garden for the invalids."[49] This surrounding open space also turned the simply decorated hospitals into aesthetically prominent buildings within the urban context—a fitting monument to the charity, whether public or private.

The design consequences of these ventilation requirements, coupled with functional divisions within the hospital, pushed hospitals into a few basic layouts. Before the 1850s a number of the smaller or more specialized hospitals occupied a single, centralized structure (e.g., the Commercial Hospital in Cincinnati, the Cleveland City Hospital, the first Jews' Hospital building in New York City, and the New York Eye and Ear Hospital in New York). A majority of early American hospital buildings, however, were arranged into a tripartite layout—including a central administrative

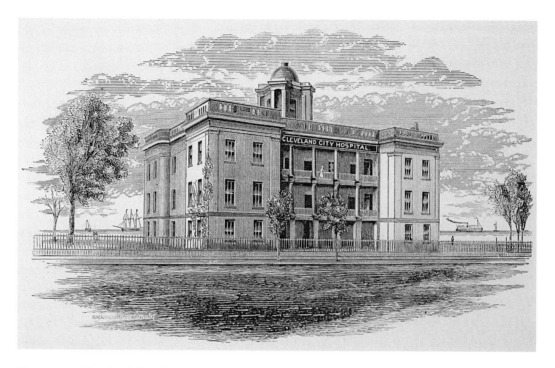

Figure 1.13. Cleveland City Hospital, view in 1876.

section and two adjacent ward wings housing patients. This division was a practical expression of the four basic medical categories of hospital patients: male medical, male surgical, female medical, and female surgical. A hospital with a pair of two-story wings had one ward for each of those categories. Other smaller wards, in basements, attics, outbuildings, or ancillary spaces, could serve overflow patients or additional categories. Although in practice the numbers of patients of each group varied, the spatial equalization—one ward to each category—also regulated medical responsibilities in the hospital (each ward was typically under the charge of a single attending doctor).

Until the 1850s the most common arrangement of these three components was either a squat *H*, a *U*, or a single line. By the 1860s pavilion-ward guidelines demanded multiple separate pavilions. While master plans might include between four and a dozen ward pavilions, initial construction often included only two ward pavilions plus the administration building. Hospitals with more than two planned ward pavilions often opted for "serrated" plans, which used a long open corridor to connect a series of wards that all opened off the same side of the corridor (for example, the Roosevelt Hospital and the State Emigrant Hospital in New York City).

Civil War barracks hospitals, which often held dozens of pavilions, came

Table 1.1. American Hospital Layouts, 1700–1859

Hospital Layouts, 1700–1859	Name of Hospital	Year
H- and U-Shaped Hospitals	Pennsylvania Hospital, Philadelphia	1755
	New York Hospital, New York City (original building)	1791
	Charity Hospital, New Orleans	1834
	Maryland Hospital, Baltimore (began as single building, additions made it an "H")	1798–1819
	New York Nursery and Child's Hospital, New York City	1858
	Island (City) Hospital, New York City	1858
	St. Luke's Hospital, New York City	1859
	Colored Home and Hospital, New York City	1849
Center Building and Two Wings in Line	Massachusetts General Hospital, Boston (later added wings to make it a shallow U)	1821
	Island Hospital, New York City	1851
	Marine Hospital, proposed by Benjamin H. Latrobe	1821
	Marine Hospital, Charleston (Robert Mills, Architect)	1834
Rectangular Buildings (with a Central Hallway)	Commercial Hospital, Cincinnati	1821
	Marion Street Maternity Hospital, New York City	1830
	Wills Eye Hospital, Philadelphia	1834
	Jews' Hospital, New York City	1855
	New York Eye and Ear Infirmary, New York City	1855
	Smallpox Hospital, New York City (later added wings to make an "H")	1856
	City Hospital, St. Louis	1845
Multiple Separate Buildings	Bellevue (original location in two outbuildings behind almshouse)	1816
	New York Hospital (after additions)	1835–1859

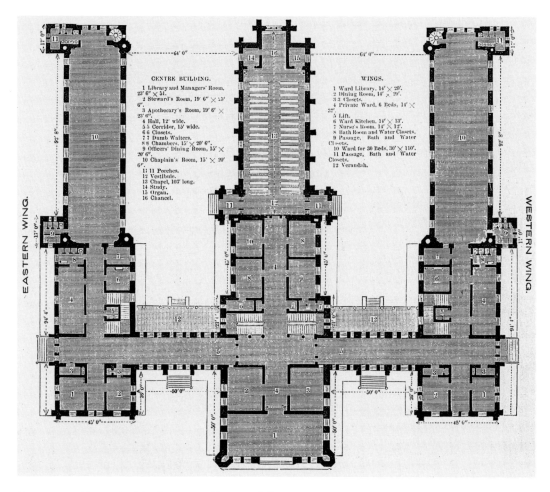

Figure 1.14. Hospital of the Protestant Episcopal Church in Philadelphia, plan in 1859. Initially only one ward wing and the administration wing of Samuel Sloan's master plan were constructed. The wards, which held thirty beds, included corner fireplaces to induce constant air flow up the chimney. The chapel was large, but did not have a direct connection with the wards. Each wing held a small (six-bed) private ward off the hallway, as well as the usual accessory service spaces. The dining room and library across the hall from each ward were for convalescent patients.

in a variety of arrangements ranging from grids to *en echelon* to radial plans (which facilitated distribution of supplies on small railways). Hollow squares (with open corners for air flow) were another common arrangement, as evidenced by the Presbyterian Hospital in New York City, the proposed second building of the Saint Louis City Hospital, the Alexian Brothers Hospital in Chicago, and the Cincinnati General Hospital. Richard Morris Hunt, architect for the Presbyterian Hospital in New York City, promoted the open courtyard layout because it minimized exposure to the cold northerly

Figure 1.15. New Saint Louis City Hospital, Bird's-Eye View in 1874. Though the buildings were still separated by open air corridors, the aerial separation occurred in the middle of the quadrangle, risking the danger of "stagnant" corners decried by Florence Nightingale.

winds and maximized the southern sunlight.[50] A number of hospitals, including the German Hospital and Woman's Hospital in New York City and the Rhode Island Hospital in Providence followed the example of the published plan for the Boston Free City Hospital—a grid of four pavilions with an administrative building centered in the space between them.

Though structured for ventilation, a hospital's facility layout had functional consequences for administrative practices and for what activities a hospital could support. Hospitals built before the 1850s—with multiple ward wings directly connected to a central administrative building—functioned as a single coordinated institution. After the 1850s, according to W. Gill Wylie, "the essential feature of the pavilion construction is that of breaking up hospitals of any size into a number of separate detached parts, having a common administration, but nothing else in common." Each pavilion was, in essence, a complete and independent hospital with its own separate staff, patients, doctors, and nurses.[51] The difference was subtle, but consequential.

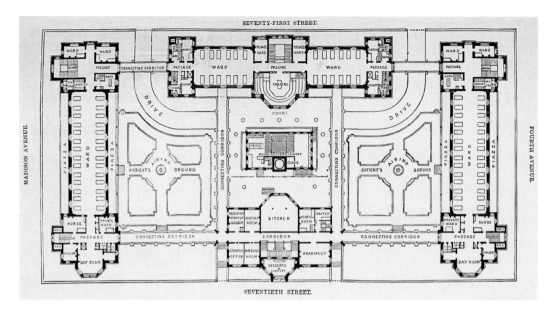

Figure 1.16. Presbyterian Hospital, New York City, first-floor plan, 1872. In Richard M. Hunt's design, the pavilion along Seventy-First Street held the surgical wards, with twelve-bed wards and an integrated amphitheater. The other pavilions were medical wards, each holding one large twenty-eight-bed ward, several smaller separation wards (for ward patients requiring seclusion) and one private ward (for paying patients).

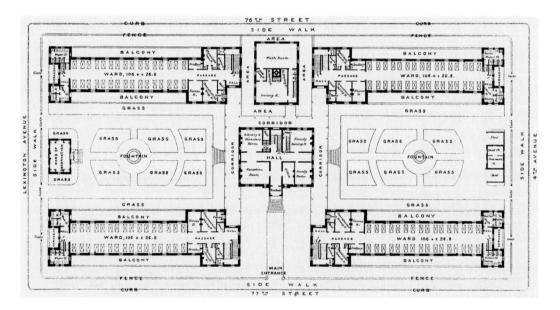

Figure 1.17. German Hospital, New York City, plan, 1866. This hospital plan is one of the few to depict the pathological building (mortuary and dead house) and an observation (isolation) ward separate from the large wards. The extensive gardens were an essential component of the architectural hygiene.

The Pneumatic Structure of the Hospital Ward

All rooms required ventilation, but in most building types ventilation simply consisted of providing openings (doors or windows) for passive air exchange. In hospital rooms that housed sick persons whose exhalations were believed to cause disease, the ultimate goal of ventilation was to prevent one person from breathing air exhaled by another. At a time when the technologies of air movement were at best unreliable, to achieve this control hospital designers structured the hospital ward for ventilation. The size and shape of wards, the placement of architectural openings, and the inclusion of ventilation technologies promoted specific patterns of air flow.

Increasing the open space in a ward diluted the concentration of bad air. This made room size, in correlation to the number and placement of occupants, critical to a hospital's healthiness. Late eighteenth-century calculations of the minimum safe cubic volume of air in a ward varied from five hundred to two thousand or more cubic feet per occupant. Mid-nineteenth-century American hospital wards typically provided between one thousand and two thousand cubic feet of air per patient.[52]

For greatest effectiveness, this air space needed to surround the patient. A high ceiling above densely packed patients did little to ameliorate air quality at floor level. By the nineteenth century, the minimum recommended dimensions of open floor space around each patient ranged between 100 and 120 square feet, with a minimum of three feet between beds.[53] This put each patient in a separate "room" of air.

In addition to volumetric dilution, ward ventilation required constant air exchange to replace the corrupted air with pure fresh air. There were two available means of promoting air exchange—natural and mechanical. Natural ventilation relied on winds and temperature differentials to induce air flow and architectural openings such as windows, doors, and chimneys to direct that air flow in specific patterns. It was inexpensive and straightforward but inconstant. Mechanical ventilation used machines—fans or blowers—to propel the air into ducts and risers and then into rooms. It was relatively expensive and difficult to operate, but constant.

At a time when medical practitioners as well as laypersons saw nature—in the form of sunlight, fresh air, and greenery—as more than a landscape, as a reservoir of invigorating (even divine) healing influence, natural ventilation was preferred. Fears that air mechanically forced through fans and ducts lost some vital principle or gained some deleterious influence in its passage remained potent well into the second half of the nineteenth century. In this uncertainty, early nineteenth-century hospital designers in

Europe and the United States exhibited a preference for natural ventilation, particularly for supply air.[54]

Windows were the primary mechanism for natural ventilation in the hospital ward, and effective window placement generated the basic pavilion ward dimensions and shape. Maximum cross-ventilation occurred when windows were on opposing walls less than thirty feet apart; pavilions were narrow rooms—typically between twenty and thirty-five feet wide—with windows directly opposite each other on the longer walls. Since contemporary expectations were that air flowed in a direct line from window to window, theoretically, a good wind created a moving "wall" of fresh air across the ward, between beds. Unfortunately, on stagnant days no air flowed at all and on windy days foul air exhaled by one patient might be carried directly across the ward to another. To minimize this danger, American and European hospital designers developed features to induce vertical as well as horizontal air flow around each patient, typically through the use of strategically placed exhaust flues or heat sources (which induced an updraft). At the Hospital of the Protestant Episcopal Church in Philadelphia, ventilation grilles directly above each bed opened into vertical flues with steam coils at the top, creating a constant exhaust flow at the point of greatest contamination (the patient's breath). This individualized air flow was even further developed in the Roosevelt Hospital in New York City. Supply grilles under each bed provided fresh air; from there, heat sources (including the patient's own body heat) induced the air to flow upward and then out through individual exhaust ducts located high on the wall above each bed.[55]

Heat sources—fireplaces with chimneys, steam coils, even gas jets— that induced a constant exhaust flow, could be quite dangerous, particularly when installed within the wall or duct. While steam coils were the most common (and relatively safe) heat source, the designers of the New York Nursery and Child's Hospital in New York City placed gas jets inside the exhaust ducts. Since those ducts and the building's structure were wood, the open flames created a grave fire danger. To reduce this danger, some hospital designers specified fireproof materials for ducts. At the Hospital of the Protestant Episcopal Church in Philadelphia the ducts were to be smooth-plastered and slate-encased. In many hospitals the in-duct heat source was a backup system, only turned on when the "amount of air carried off at any time falls below what might be considered desirable."[56] This minimized but did not prevent the danger.

Ventilation in the hospital ward was regularly in conflict with the requirements of comfort. For constant ventilation, windows were open even in the winter and fires were lit in the fireplaces (which functioned as exhaust

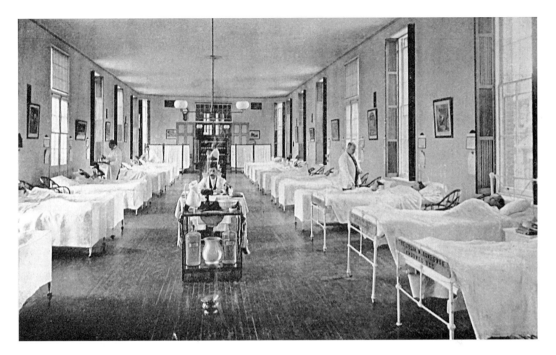

Figure 1.18. Roosevelt Hospital, New York City, view of male ward, 1893. Though a ward was one big open space, the windows determined bed placement both for air flow and maximum sunshine.

ventilators) even in the summer. On the coldest days, patients notoriously closed the windows purposely left open by nurses and doctors. A number of hospital designs included ancillary "natural" ventilators—gratings, siphon ducts, and other contraptions that promoted constant air movement. These were often simply unclosable openings in the building's walls, floors, or ceiling, which increased the building's permeability. As early as 1754, the Pennsylvania Hospital incorporated rooftop "ventilators to carry off the foul Air." The first building of the Jews' Hospital in New York City (1855) included "openings, covered with metallic gratings, from the outside, so that pure air will always flow in, no matter what the state of the weather may be."[57]

Window ventilation, in-wall exhaust, and ventilators made each pavilion pneumatically independent—air exchange occurred between inside and outside, not between rooms. But window ventilation required extensive exterior walls, which created costly, rambling footprints. William Strutt and Charles Sylvester at the Derbyshire Infirmary in England developed a centralized furnace-driven ventilation system that used the heat of the furnace to create a temperature differential that drew fresh air into the building through long underground intake ducts. The air, once heated, rose to

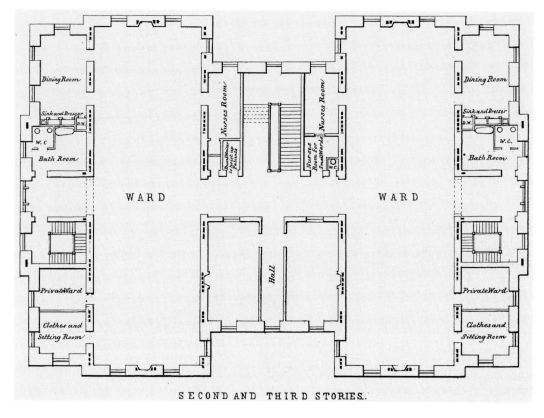

SECOND AND THIRD STORIES.

Figure 1.19. New York Hospital, New York City, plan of new South Building, 1855. The ward ventilation was provided by extensive risers and ducts rather than by windows, allowing the services to be within much greater proximity to the wards and allowing a greater centralization of plan. Built just before the blossoming of pavilion-ward guidelines, the building was soon considered obsolete, if not dangerously poorly ventilated.

the various rooms through extensive supply ducts. Separate exhaust ducts, also heated by the central furnace, drew off expired air. This system was not dependent on windows or window placement, yet it created a constant, controlled movement of air that could keep even physically adjacent rooms aerially independent. As Christine Stevenson points out, this allowed the Derbyshire Infirmary to be constructed in a much more compact and economical (square) plan without fear of compromising the all-essential ventilation.[58] American hospital designers experimented with this centralized hot-air furnace ventilation between the 1820s and 1850s, with the earliest installation possibly at the Massachusetts General Hospital. The compact plan of the new South Building of the New York Hospital (1855) reveals the more centralized plan that could develop when a hospital ward was planned for ducts, rather than windows, to provide the ventilation.

Figure 1.20. Presbyterian Hospital, New York City, view [1876]. The prominent central chimney generated exhaust ventilation for the entire facility. Initial construction included only one out of the three planned ward pavilions.

By the 1860s, with the widespread adoption of the pavilion-ward system, the distance between pavilions made centralized ventilation systems inefficient. Nevertheless, although windows were the primary source of fresh air supply in the pavilions, a number of American hospital designers continued to use a centralized chimney—usually one fed by the hospital's boilers—to create a whole-facility exhaust system. Ducts extended underground from the hospital pavilions to vertical risers around the central chimney. The chimney's heat warmed the surrounding risers and created a suction strong enough to draw the air out forcefully from the distant pavilions. These exhaust-air systems typically provided constant removal of air from the most tainted spaces in the hospital. At the Rhode Island Hospital in Providence, architect A. C. Morse designed "an arrangement by which the draft in the flues of the chimney affords ventilation to the sewers of the establishment." At the Presbyterian Hospital in New York, Richard Morris Hunt included a central hundred-foot-high chimney shaft for the boilers with air chambers around it that provided exhaust suction for the water closets, kitchen, laundry, and dead-rooms.[59]

American hospital designers began to incorporate mechanical propulsion systems for air supply by the late 1850s. The City Hospital in Boston and the Charity Hospital in New York City included large fans to push air into underground supply ducts. Carl Pfeiffer specified a ten-foot-diameter ventilation fan for an unbuilt project for the New York Hospital, while the State Emigrant Hospital on Ward's Island included a fourteen-foot-diameter fan "by which a current of air is created which commands the respect of all who approach, as hats are never seen to be worn in its presence." According to the records of the Roosevelt Hospital and Saint Luke's Hospital in New York City, fans were typically run only on still days, when the natural ventilation system needed augmentation.[60]

The more elaborate hospital ventilation systems could provide heating or cooling as well as air flow. At the City Hospital in Boston each duct was divided in half at its delivery point: one half included a steam heating coil, the other did not. By varying the proportion of air that traveled through the hot or the cold half of the duct, the engineer could control the temperature of the air delivered to the room. At other hospitals, long underground supply air ducts tempered the air before delivery. In winter this reduced the heating load; in summer, cooler air could be sent straight to the wards. Some speculated the results might be therapeutic. In 1859, Dr. McKenna in New Orleans suggested that underground chambers beneath wards could create "a supply of air several degrees colder and moister than the outside temperature, by which many an otherwise fatal disease might be effectually checked." At the State Emigrant Hospital in New York City in 1866, one visitor reported an air temperature of seventy degrees in the wards when the outside air was eighty-five degrees in the shade. Not all early combined heating and ventilating systems were as successful. At the Mount Sinai Hospital in New York City only three wards could be kept open in winter because of insufficient heat.[61]

These extensive ventilation systems had aesthetic consequences: hospitals had numerous chimneys, towers, and rooftop ventilators. On the earlier American hospitals these features were often utilitarian structures, added to the building as appurtenances and roof projections (as at the Colored Hospital in New York City). By the 1860s architects turned these functional exhaust towers and chimneys into prominent design features. Decorated towers housed the ventilation equipment but also provided a strong vertical counterpoint to the predominantly horizontally arranged hospitals such as

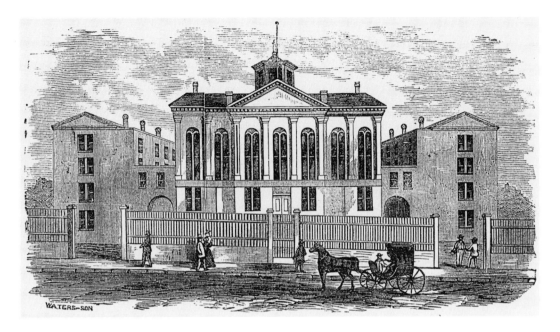

Figure 1.21. Colored Home and Hospital, New York City, view, 1872.

Figure 1.22. Rhode Island Hospital, Providence, exterior, 1868. The prominent towers held risers to ventilate the ward service rooms; the ward was further ventilated by fireplaces in each corner of the ward (marked by the smaller chimneys).

the Hospital of the Protestant Episcopal Church in Philadelphia, the Cincinnati General Hospital, the Rhode Island Hospital in Providence, and the State Emigrant Hospital, Saint Luke's Hospital and the Roosevelt Hospital in New York City.

The Hygienic Requirements of Hospital Materials, Details, and Construction

To meet the requirements of architectural hygiene and efficient care, hospital administrators were early adopters of internal plumbing systems and other efficient building technologies. Hospital designers typically specified hard, nonporous, easily cleaned materials and kept architectural decoration or detail to a minimum. This was a striking contrast to other types of interior spaces such as offices, hotels, and even residences, which were often lavishly decorated and furnished.

Plumbing and Building Technologies

An abundant water supply was critical to a healthy hospital—water was used for bathing patients; cleaning rooms, bedding, and instruments; and removing wastes. The earliest American hospitals occupied sites near a river, stream, pond, or lake; staff at the Smallpox Hospital in New York City were still fetching water by pail from the East River in 1853. Waste disposal before indoor plumbing was usually handled in privies, which were most often located a slight distance from the building but could also be attached to the ward as a means of improving access for nonambulant patients. For his proposed Marine hospital design, Latrobe recommended a "tub room"—a small room with a large vessel that collected the wastes from ambulant and bedridden patients. Once or twice a day the vessel was to be lowered to the ground, carted to a distant corner of the site, emptied, and then returned.[62] All of these approaches were problematic, creating a source of aerial corruption believed to be almost as potent in causing disease as the sick patients themselves.

The installation of indoor plumbing offered drastic improvements to hospital sanitary conditions. It was added to existing buildings and included in the original construction of new hospitals as early as the 1820s and 1830s. An 1821 plan of the Massachusetts General Hospital included cubicles that resembled the self-flushing toilets promoted by Charles Sylvester at the Derbyshire Infirmary in England. In 1837 a new building at the New York Hospital included "a powerful forcing pump in the cellar" to fill four rooftop reservoirs, which in turn supplied gravity-fed water to eighteen wa-

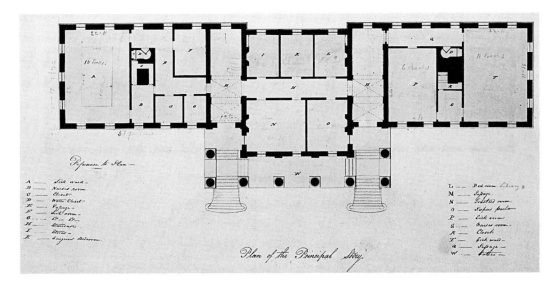

Figure 1.23. Massachusetts General Hospital, Boston, plan of first story, 1821. Bulfinch's interest in accommodating persons from various economic classes led to a design that included a number of smaller wards rather than one large ward.

ter closets and ten bathing rooms. As urban piped water supplies became available, hospitals were quick to connect to them. The New York Hospital governors connected the hospital buildings to the new municipal water supply as soon as the pipelines from the Croton reservoir reached their vicinity, in early 1844.[63]

Internal plumbing and piped water supplies in these early years was a mixed blessing, often contributing to new forms of unsanitary conditions. By May of 1845, shortly after installing Croton water, the governors of the New York Hospital had to order a trench to be dug to relieve their overflowing cesspool. Inside the hospital, imperfect trap designs allowed sewer gas to travel back up through the pipes and imperfect fixture designs did not always completely flush away the wastes from the hopper. Because of the dangers, by the 1860s European pavilion-ward promoters isolated the sanitary fixtures—toilets, baths, sinks, and pipes—in separate sanitary "towers." These structures often included strategically placed windows and air ducts to ensure "a current of air being constantly kept up between the wards and water-closets."[64]

Where to locate the towers in relation to the ward was an unsettled problem. Nightingale's ideal ward designs had located these sanitary towers at the far end of the ward from the nurse's office. This created long travel routes for nurses and ambulatory patients. European pavilion-ward hospital designers typically followed Nightingale's precedent, as did the designers of many postbellum American hospitals (including the Rhode Island Hospital in Providence, and the State Emigrant Hospital and German Hospital in New York City). The designers of the Hospital of the Protestant Episcopal Church in Philadelphia included sanitary "towers" at both ends of the large ward, effectively halving the distance nurses and patients had to travel to use the facilities, though doubling the potential sources of contamination. The Roosevelt Hospital in New York City had the most unusual lavatory arrangement; "instead of placing them against the walls they are placed in the centre of the room and grouped around a shaft" that exhausted the air through all the floors to the roof. Astonishingly complicated hygienic precautions—including steam-injected toilets for disinfection—offset the danger of contamination.[65]

In addition to plumbing, hospital buildings were filled with labor-saving technologies. Civil War barracks hospitals and several postbellum civil hospitals (including the Presbyterian Hospital and German Hospital in New York City and the Hospital of the Protestant Episcopal Church in Philadelphia) made extensive use of small "truck" railways for transporting goods between pavilions. Small utility lifts and dumbwaiters delivered the goods from the lower, service floor to the upper ward floor or floors. At the Roosevelt Hospital, dirty linen chutes delivered soiled bedding to a convenient location and dumbwaiters from the basement delivered the clean linen to the ward linen closet. A glazed pipe flue, with its opening flush with the floor, allowed dust and debris to be swept into the chute, where it landed in an "iron receptacle, whence all can be removed readily to the boiler furnace and burned." In a few facilities, the installation of elevators, even in the low-rise pavilions, eased the movement of bedridden patients between floors. Speaking tubes and call systems facilitated communication, particularly between the wards and the house doctors' rooms. As early as 1858 the City Hospital on Blackwell's Island, designed by James Renwick, incorporated a system of bells and speaking tubes for prompt communication between the wards, doctors' rooms, and main offices.[66] These technologies made the provision of services easier, but at the danger of compromising hygiene. The dangers of contaminated pipes, ducts, and tubes were frequently reported and debated.

Lessons from the Civil War: Temporary vs. Permanent Construction

Fears that years of constant exposure to the aerial poisons emanating from sick patients would saturate the hospital's building materials also promoted an intense American interest in what Dr. John Maynard Woodworth, the first surgeon general of the United States, termed "the simple pavilion of in-

Figure 1.24. Hicks US General Hospital, 1860s. The one-story "barracks" wards, of simple wood construction, were typically arrayed in a layout that allowed simple delivery of goods along a central drive or by a small handtruck.

definite existence." Woodworth recommended hospital pavilions be "constructed with the view of destroying them [as] soon as the peculiar hospital diseases, such as erysipelas, pyaemia, gangrene, &c., are engendered by the cumulated miasma of the buildings." He estimated replacement every ten or fifteen years. A leading surgeon at Bellevue Hospital recommended wooden wards that could be destroyed and rebuilt every five years "or as soon as it was felt that the air in them was becoming poisonous."[67]

Civil War hospital experiences provided corroborating evidence that temporary construction was healthier. A majority of field hospitals for the emergency treatment of injured soldiers had appalling mortality, particularly from "hospital diseases" such as hospital gangrene, septicemia, and other infections. The discussions also revealed that wounded soldiers in drafty barns, shacks, huts, and tents improved in greater numbers and at faster rates than did wounded soldiers in the more permanent commandeered structures such as churches, courthouses, and even hospitals.[68]

By the later years of the Civil War, the idea that cheap, temporary construction might be the best approach to hospital buildings gained wide circulation. The clearest examples were the "barracks" hospitals—an

American variant of pavilion-ward hospital design that kept Nightingale's basic ward layout but included one-story, isolated wooden pavilions or even simple tents, capable of being destroyed at need. The Mower General Hospital outside Philadelphia and the Hicks US General Hospital near Baltimore contained more than a dozen barracks pavilions.

Discussion of the benefits of temporary ward construction continued in publications well into the 1890s. Immediately after the war a few hospitals, like the Presbyterian Hospital in Philadelphia and the Lakeside Hospital in Cleveland, experimented with wards of temporary construction. Though built to be destroyed, most such "temporary" hospital pavilions were in service for decades. American hospitals rarely used such temporary construction for the primary ward structures. The danger of fire was a harsh reality that counteracted the hygienic benefits of the impermanent structures. A competing desire for hospitals, as public institutions, to be built to last and to express their civic presence architecturally led to the creation of durable structures. Temporary structures—tents and cheap wooden pavilions— were most often used to house overflow patients and specific vulnerable patient categories.

The American Civil War hospitals and their barracks construction impressed European observers. By the early 1870s during the Siege of Paris in the Franco-Prussian war, the French (who were losing enormous numbers of soldiers to hospital diseases in permanent buildings) resorted to "putting up tents after the American model, for it is proved beyond a doubt that they are the only safeguard against what is termed hospital rot or gangrene." Rudolf Virchow praised the American Civil War hospitals, and the City Hospital in Moabit, Berlin, was patterned after the Civil War Mower General Hospital outside of Philadelphia. It was "built of inexpensive materials as a temporary hospital for infectious diseases" although in nonepidemic times it would serve as a general hospital for the city. Designers of German hospitals continued to build hospitals reminiscent of this barracks style throughout the nineteenth century, though constructed of stone rather than wood.[69]

The Establishment of Hospital Finishes

The requirements of architectural hygiene also differentiated hospitals aesthetically from other building types. Hospital buildings were designed for cure and reform, and only contingently for beauty. At a time when public and civic buildings were encrusted with stylistic historical ornament, hospital practitioners looked on ornament as a dirt-trap, a hindrance to air flow, an unnecessary expense, and a moral pitfall for an institution that had

Figure 1.25. City Hospital, Boston, view. Though the hospital as built included far less classical detail than was depicted in Gridley Bryant's competition-winning drawings (or included on other contemporaneous public buildings), the hospital buildings received criticism for aesthetic extravagance.

to model restraint. According to James Beekman, "architectural display in a hospital [was] a crime." Stephen Smith criticized several hospitals, including Gridley Bryant's neoclassical design for the Boston City Hospital and John W. Ritch's design for the State Emigrant Hospital in New York City for the use of expensive "architectural accessories, most of which are positively injurious."[70]

On the other hand, as the visible symbol of philanthropy a hospital needed to be respectable and create a civic presence. Rosner notes that hospitals "resembled a home, a church, or a prison, depending upon the underlying purposes of those organizing the facility." For most kinds of hospitals, a subdued exterior architectural aesthetic, the result of massing and proportion, not stylistic details, was considered appropriate. A writer for the *New York Times* lauded Saint Luke's Hospital, which had "gone to no outlay in mere architectural ornament—relying for any beauty of structure on symmetry and proportion." Beaux-Arts-trained architect Richard Morris Hunt stated that for hospitals the best approach was one that obtained architectural effect "by accentuating certain prominent features existing in the plan, in a quiet, unpretending manner."[71] His design for the Presbyterian Hospital in New York was decorated, but more by material patterns and massing than by the layered excess of historic ornament common to his other buildings. In comparison to their other designs, Frank Furness and George E. Hewitt's design for the Jewish Hospital in Philadelphia was bare of ornament.

This austerity continued on the interior of hospitals, primarily as a result of hygienic necessity. At the New England Hospital for Women and Children in Roxbury, Massachusetts, there were "no cornices or ornaments

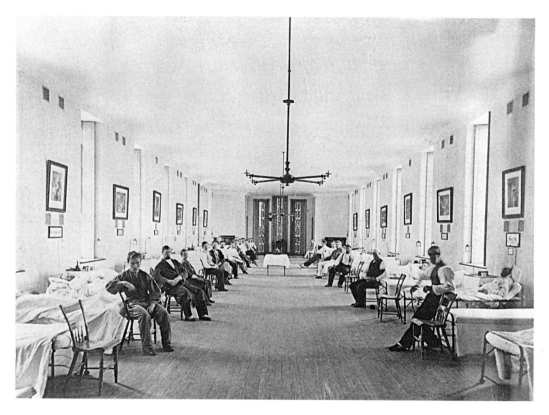

Figure 1.26. Hospital of the Protestant Episcopal Church in Philadelphia, view of male ward, 1869. Exhaust registers are visible on the wall just below the large pictures and close to the ceiling. There were also floor registers under the beds. All corners are rounded, all surfaces undecorated and seamless. The decorative treatment of the south-facing windows would have given the ward the ambience of a chapel, appropriate to the spiritual as well as physiological healing the founders intended to impart. The picture is posed to suggest that religious services are just about to start, the table in the middle of the ward serving as a makeshift altar.

to hold dust or bad air." Corners were rounded to facilitate air flow and cleaning. Cracks, where dirt could hide, were likewise minimized, and materials were joined as seamlessly as possible. Ward finishes and furnishings were white: colors hid dirt. Woodwork was typically natural or light-finished. There was no superfluous ornament, few furnishings, no knickknacks, minimal materials, and an abundance of sunlight and fresh air.[72]

Because of universal fears "that the miasms of hospitals would cling to the walls if they were composed of permeable material," hospital floors, walls, and ceilings had to be "incapable of absorbing the exhalations of the sick." Opinion as to what constituted the best impermeable material varied. Parian cement, glazed tile, stucco, and materials "like glass" all had their champions. If properly sealed, however, common but permeable building materials like hard-finished plaster or wood were acceptable and far more affordable. The designers of the Roosevelt Hospital gave their walls and floors four coats of oil paint before opening "so as to present a surface which cannot absorb impurities and which can be washed with soap and water." Hunt's design of the Presbyterian Hospital in New York City used wood hard-sanded to a perfect finish and then waxed "to prevent the absorption of elements inseparable from hospitals, and which, otherwise, render them unhealthy."[73]

Though impermeable, hospital materials were rarely wet-washed. Concurrent fears that "vapor in a ward tends to suspend the miasmatic emanations and diffuse them more widely" led to the development of unusual cleaning strategies for hospitals. Dry-rubbing (what Nightingale called *frottage*) was preferable to wet-washing, because it did not dampen the ward surfaces. The rules of operation of the Mower United States Army General Hospital in Chestnut Hill, Pennsylvania, required orderlies to request permission from the chief executive officer to wet-scrub a floor and ordered surgeons "to see that water is not thrown on the ward floors."[74]

The hospital ward was a stark, almost abstract space. The white walls and ceiling, often joined by a rounded or coved intersection that effaced any sense of a corner, appeared almost immaterial; the monolithic floor appeared like an abstract plane. Within this featureless architecture, the patients, a few wall-hung paintings, and the building technologies (ventilation grilles, lighting fixtures) stood out in stark contrast.

Fitting Function into a Pneumatic Machine

In 1866 Dr. Stephen Smith stated that there were only two kinds of hospital pavilions—administration and wards.[75] The necessity of all other spaces was debatable and their inclusion in hospital buildings was largely outside the pavilion-ward guidelines. How spaces devoted to religion or to medical practice, research, or education were inserted into hospital buildings thus reveals much about the limits of pavilions and the forces competing for a stake in hospital work.

Medical Spaces in the Hospital

Spaces devoted to specific medical procedures were minimal in early American hospitals. The most common early nineteenth-century medical treatments (bloodletting, purging, wound care, dosing, and basic nursing) required little equipment. In most hospitals, examinations, treatments and care occurred within the ward itself, regardless of the effect on other patients.[76] In the first decades of the nineteenth century, as American medical practices began to alter (with the adoption of the European "clinical" medicine, the integration of dispensaries and hospitals, and the transformation of surgery resulting from the use of anesthesia), the inclusion of medical spaces within the hospital increased.

Examination Rooms, Operating Rooms, and Amphitheaters

The hospital was a public institution; the provision of "privacy" for medical examination of a patient was a luxury, not a necessity. Rosenberg considers the lack of separate rooms for medical examinations in early American hospitals a reflection of the admission process for hospital patients, which involved social as much as medical scrutiny. Indeed, admission to a hospital often required a letter of application, the provision of letters or notes of recommendation, and an interview with the governors to establish "worthiness." After passing this assessment, the patient might have to undergo a medical examination by hospital doctors somewhere in the hospital (for example, the board room, a "receiving" room, or an office) before final admission to a ward. Alternatively, the patient might be admitted directly to a ward bed where the hospital doctors would perform the examination.[77]

The distress caused to other patients by medical actions occurring in the wards was regularly mentioned by hospital practitioners but rarely addressed by the creation of separate spaces. Rooms devoted to medical examinations did begin to show up in hospital plans in the mid-nineteenth century. When located near the hospital entrance (as in the Massachusetts General Hospital or the New York Hospital), these rooms functioned as part of the admission process. When located adjacent to the wards (as in the City Hospital in Boston and the German Hospital in New York City), these rooms offered privacy, for examinations but also potentially for simple medical treatments, saving the ward from the disruptions. Saint Luke's Hospital in New York City included examination rooms at the entrance and off each ward. Many hospitals included no such spaces.

In the same vein, operating rooms, so crucial to modern hospital practice, were not considered essential spaces in the earliest American hospitals. Doctors performed most surgeries within the wards. Before anesthesia, disruptions were intense but brief. A surgeon's skill was directly correlated to speed, and operations were timed in minutes. Dr. James Rushmore Wood was even known to have amputated a thigh in nine seconds! More complicated procedures were infrequent. Between 1821 and 1822, the Mas-

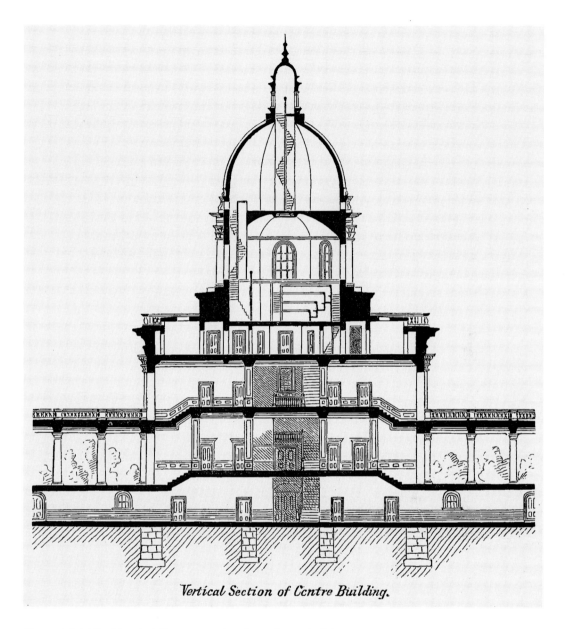

Vertical Section of Centre Building.

Figure 1.27. City Hospital, Boston, section through surgical theater, 1865.

sachusetts General Hospital's records show a regular occurrence of minor surgeries, but an average of only four major surgeries undertaken each month.[78] Such major operations were the procedures of greatest interest to other medical practitioners and of greatest distress to other patients within the ward. A separate space for them thus served two interests—preserving the ward's order and facilitating medical education.

The inclusion of operating amphitheaters—a separate room for major surgeries with a number of seats for an audience—was common in hospitals by the early nineteenth century, though by no means universal. The New York Hospital added an amphitheater in 1801; the Pennsylvania Hospital in 1802; and the Massachusetts General Hospital included an amphitheater in its original 1821 building. To accommodate tiers of seating, amphitheaters were frequently double-height spaces. Surgery required copious lighting from above with no cast shadows; before gas light and electric light, that meant daylighting, from large windows and skylights, domes, or cupolas. This put most amphitheaters on the top floor, a location that created some difficulty in transporting bedridden patients to the amphitheater (particularly if the patient had to be carted up winding narrow stairs). The City Hospital in Boston was an early adopter of elevator technologies to solve this problem. It included lifts in each two-story ward, but to get patients from the wards to the operating room, "patients were transported by an elevator from the basement to the third floor, then shifted to another elevator and raised to the operating-room. As both of these elevators were operated by hand power, some idea may be formed as to the great amount of work required to get the patients to and from the cupola."[79]

The advent of anesthesia in the 1840s transformed surgery and surgical spaces. From a treatment of last resort, surgery became an "elective" procedure—something a person might willingly choose to undergo. Surgeries became more complex, delving into areas of the body that had once been sacrosanct, and of much longer duration—timed in hours rather than minutes. These changes increased the trauma of surgery in the ward for other patients and dramatically increased the demand for separate operating rooms.[80]

Anesthesia also increased demand for pre- and postoperative spaces. Although early hospital practice called for administering the anesthetic to the patient immediately before the procedure in the location of surgery, it was clear that preoperative patients found the presence of medical students and surgical equipment traumatic. By the 1860s and 1870s small separate rooms for administering anesthetics were common. Postoperative recovery rooms, which further improved patient experiences and provided a well-monitored space in which the patient could safely come out from under the anesthetic, also appeared. The Rhode Island Hospital in Providence included a private ward adjacent to the operating room "where patients can be left after undergoing serious operations, until they are able to be removed to the general wards."[81] At times the same room functioned for both before and after operative care.

By no means did the inclusion of separate operating rooms or amphitheaters in some hospitals mean that all surgical procedures were
performed in them or that all hospitals included operating rooms. Many
procedures were still carried out in the wards. One visitor to Bellevue in
1872 described a ward where "at one cot the surgeon was operating upon
a patient whose cries of anguish were distressing, but every one seemed
oblivious." At Saint Mary's Hospital in Philadelphia, which had no operating room, their "method was simply to surround the patient with one or
more screens and operate in the ward." Charles C. Haight designed the
Hospital for the Ruptured and Crippled in New York City with no operating room—its founding doctor believed in mechanical therapy rather than
surgical correction.[82]

Where to locate an operating room within a hospital was a difficult
choice. They were inherently unhygienic and believed capable of infecting
patients in adjacent wards. There were also worries that the ward "air" would
generate hospital disease in the vulnerable surgical patients. By the 1860s
and 1870s, at the Woman's Hospital, Bellevue Hospital, and the City Hospital in New York City, surgery occurred in a tent or a wooden outbuilding.[83]
Many hospitals located the operating room or theater in the administration
building. However, locating the operating room distant from the wards
required transporting patients between buildings—a tedious chore that
potentially exposed persons of delicate health to weather extremes and jos-
tling. A couple of hospitals reportedly located their operating rooms near
the pathological facilities (as at the Mount Sinai and Presbyterian Hospitals in New York City). This supported medical research, but at a time when
the surgeon typically washed his hands *after* the operation, this proximity
could prove dangerous to the patients.

Inevitably, the increase in surgeries and the changing nature of surgery
altered hospital practice. It increased the prominence and prevalence of
interventions rather than restorative care, emphasizing the provision of
medical rather than social assistance. It also increased the number of patients with open wounds in the hospital, and that increased the problem of
hospital diseases.[84]

Space for Clinical Education and Pathological Research

Medical advancement was a valued by-product of philanthropic hospital
care, and a hospital that included spaces relevant to medical education had
a competitive advantage in attracting the most eminent doctors. Nevertheless, most early American hospitals held few spaces devoted to medical education or research. In the early nineteenth century, formal medical schools

were few in the United States, and medical education was largely by personal arrangement—an established doctor would take on students as a form of apprenticeship. Medical students attended lectures and completed a series of readings; they might become doctors without ever touching a patient. Many American medical practitioners finished their education in the hospitals of Paris, which practiced "clinical medicine," whereby the patients were grouped by specific ailment as well as gender and doctors learned through hands-on experience at the bedside and in the morgue. Upon their return to the United States, the young American doctors advocated the adoption of clinical medicine in American hospitals; this presumed the addition of medical research and education facilities to the hospital. Dr. John Watson, a New York surgeon, outlined the necessary conditions for such a medical "clinic": enough patients (living and dead) to study; convenient apartments for examining and treating those patients; special apartments for conferences, consultations, and operations; and a room for postmortems and pathological investigation.[85]

The wards could readily accommodate bedside instruction, since where there was enough "air space" for patients, there was room for a doctor and a number of medical students around a bed. Spaces for conferences and consultations were less available. The common practice of assigning all the patients in a given ward to one doctor (to minimize the doctor's travel time on rounds) made hospitals into places where a number of medical practitioners practiced but did not necessarily interact or collaborate. The students' hospital experience often consisted of watching one doctor treating a number of patients with a wide variety of ailments. It showed medicine as an individual practice. This territoriality was not absolute, and collegial interactions did occur. At the Boston City Hospital, many of the hospital's doctors met on Sundays and visited the patients together.[86] Neutral hospital spaces in which doctors could interact without this territoriality were sparse; medical conferences and consultations were at best held in borrowed boardrooms or in the surgical amphitheater (if available).

With the growing demands of clinical medical education, amphitheaters grew much larger and more spatially complex. The Pennsylvania Hospital's amphitheater could seat more than five hundred; in 1870 the Cincinnati General Hospital's could seat six hundred; in 1873 the University of Pennsylvania Hospital's could seat seven hundred. Bellevue Hospital's new amphitheater in 1871 reportedly provided eight hundred seats and included adjacent rooms for consultation and studies. The administrators of the much smaller Hahnemann Hospital and Medical College of Chicago planned to erect an amphitheater in 1873 that would seat roughly three hundred students and contain "separate ante-rooms, cloak- and dissecting-

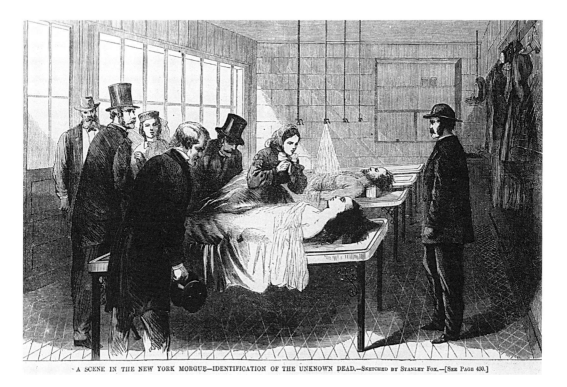

A SCENE IN THE NEW YORK MORGUE—IDENTIFICATION OF THE UNKNOWN DEAD.—Sketched by Stanley Fox.—[See Page 430.]

Figure 1.28. Bellevue Hospital, New York City, view of morgue, 1866. The morgue or dead house was a part of every hospital but rarely depicted either on plans or in drawings. In this view, the bodies are arrayed for viewing and identification, but the space would also have served for pathological dissections, and included overhead water fixtures and hygienic materials to facilitate cleaning afterward.

rooms for male and female students" as well as a laboratory, museum, library, lecture room, and offices.[87]

Clinical medicine also made pathological research a crucial component of medical study and advancement. Hospitals were one of the few places where such study was possible—the unclaimed hospital dead were subjects for dissection. Given the strong public antipathy to dissection (and the graverobbing with which it was associated), a dedicated space for pathological examination was a rarity for the earliest American hospitals. Most hospitals did contain a "dead" house for the temporary storage of bodies (claimed and unclaimed). In the earliest American hospitals these were cramped facilities, usually outbuildings of rough structure and few amenities. They were not conducive to the pathological research suggested by clinical medicine.

After regular pressure from the doctors, hospital administrators did begin to build more elaborate pathological facilities—morgues, autopsy rooms, pathological museums, and laboratories—for research. The New

York Hospital's governors added a separate dead house with pathological facilities in 1840, and Bellevue Hospital's directors added a separate structure to house Dr. James Rushmore Wood's pathological museum as well as pathological facilities. These were still typically separate outbuildings, but they could include airtight cooled storage space, extensive ventilation, easily cleaned and waterproof finishes, dissection tables, pathological museums, and laboratory research space. Most hospitals added such pathological facilities in separate structures, unattached to a ward.[88] Even when included in hospital buildings, these spaces for medical education and research remained a minor spatial component of the hospital. Wards still constituted the majority of a hospital's floor area.

Dispensaries

Dispensaries, which provided routine "outpatient" medical care at minimal cost, first appeared as standalone institutions, an alternative to hospitals. The most successful dispensaries served hundreds of patients per day, and inevitably many dispensary patients presented ailments that were not routine or that required more extensive or more elaborate treatments than could be provided by outpatient visits. These patients were ideal candidates for hospital treatment. Many dispensaries, however, had no space for beds. In those cases, the dispensary physicians (often volunteers and medical students) might refer the nonroutine patient to a nearby hospital. After sufficient interaction, that practice might become a formal affiliation between the institutions. As the benefits of a steady supply of preselected medically appropriate patients became obvious, dispensaries became integral components of hospital practice by the mid-nineteenth century.[89] The attachment of dispensaries to hospitals also altered the admission practices of many hospitals—placing greater emphasis on the applicant's medical conditions and reducing the influence of personal interviews with administrators.

Dispensaries had minimal interior spatial requirements—a large waiting room, perhaps a few consulting and examination rooms opening from it.[90] Clearly, a small nearby operating or procedure room was beneficial, but in many dispensaries small partitions within a single large space were all that separated the patient undergoing examination and treatment from the rest of the patients waiting their turn.

Where to locate a dispensary in the hospital facility was complicated. By their very nature, dispensaries attracted large numbers of persons with a wide variety of ailments. This constituted a real danger of infection for the hospital's patients and meant that dispensaries could not simply be inserted in one of the ward pavilions. The volume of traffic to and from the dispen-

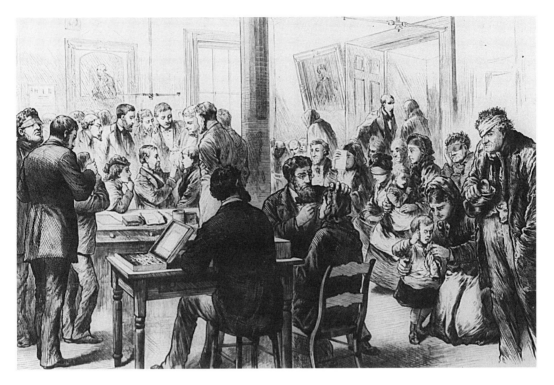

Figure 1.29. New York Eye and Ear Infirmary, New York City, dispensary waiting room, 1875. The dispensary was waiting room, examination room, and treatment room all in one.

sary, as well as its role in generating patients for admission to the hospital, also made a location near the entrance, and if possible, just outside the hospital's walls, desirable.[91]

Spaces of Religion and Reform

At a time when a hospital's charitable role in providing moral reform to its patients was as important as its role in physiological healing, religious spaces in hospitals could be as elaborate and prominent as medical spaces. In the 1860s Saint Vincent's Hospital in New York City had no operating room or pathological research facility, but even its severely overcrowded facilities held a small chapel. Saint Luke's Hospital in New York City initially included two hundred beds, but no operating rooms, amphitheater, or pathological space. Its chapel, on the other hand, could accommodate 350 persons. While denominational hospitals were the most likely to include religious facilities, even municipal hospitals made space for religion—Bellevue Hospital in New York City and Charity Hospital in New Orleans had chapels, for example.

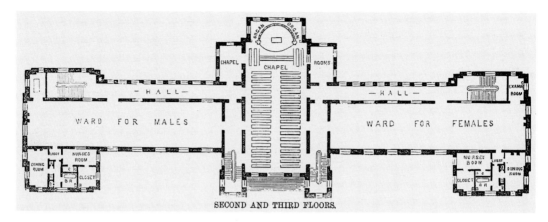

Figure 1.30. Saint Luke's Hospital, New York City, third-floor plan, 1860. The enclosed halls that led from the chapel to the wards allowed patients in bed to hear the services, but were later criticized for their interference with natural ventilation.

The wards themselves were, to a certain extent, conceived as "religious" locations, where reform was as likely to happen as cure. The founders of the Hospital of the Protestant Episcopal Church in Philadelphia hoped that the hospital would be remembered not just for bodily relief "and a record of 'discharged cured[,]' in the common phrase," but also for sending patients home with religion, virtue, and an awareness of the value of health. At Saint Luke's Hospital in New York City, reading of scriptures occurred in the wards every morning and, in a flashback to medieval and Renaissance hospital designs, the building was "so arranged that the wards could open, by means of doors or windows at their termination, into the chapel" so that all patients could hear the service from their beds.[92]

Not all of the hospital's potential for reform was didactic; some was built into the hospital environment. A common assumption of the time was that the quality of an inhabited space and the health of its inhabitants were linked. Poor neighborhoods, where the inhabitants lived in dark, crowded, and often dirty or rundown dwellings, often experienced the greatest incidence of illness in the waves of early nineteenth-century epidemics— yellow fever, cholera, typhus, typhoid fever. The wealthier neighborhoods, with sparsely inhabited buildings on large landscaped lots, were less often overtaken by illness. The hope, at least for hospital founders and designers, was that removing the sick poor from their impoverished (cramped, chaotic, dirty) surroundings and placing them in a well-designed (spacious, orderly, clean) hospital ward, would itself be an active reformative influence.

One observer's description of Roosevelt Hospital is telling:

> When we speak of cleanliness, we do not mean that order of cleanliness which satisfies us in a well-kept house, but that peculiar kind which never rests, where floors are polished, as if waxed, walls without a fly-speck, windows which look as if they were paneless, from the perfect transparency of the glass, where the sunbeams slant toward the floor in long bars of light through an atmosphere too pure to contribute gyrating atoms of floating matter large enough to catch the eye—a painful sort of cleanliness, which makes a visitor feel uncomfortable, regret that he didn't rub his boots better on the mat, that there should be dust on his hat and coat, and which makes him walk daintily and noiselessly, as if he were in a church and knew how to behave himself there, as a great many people don't.[93]

This complex interweaving of architecture, faith, and health defined the nature of the ward.

The Social and Medical Shape of Patient Spaces

The hospital ward was the most distinctive space within any early American hospital. It was also the most standardized. From the eighteenth century to the mid-twentieth century, whether in a hospital of ten beds or a thousand, a ward was a narrow, rectilinear, well-ventilated room with lots of windows and two rows of widely separated beds facing each other across a central aisle. Up to the 1850s ward shape could vary from square to exceedingly narrow rectangles. By the 1860s, with the solidification of pavilion-ward standards, variations diminished and the difference between a ward in a large municipal hospital and one in a small, voluntary hospital might be perceptible only in ceiling treatment or light fixture design.

The standardized ward was the result of architectural hygiene but also of efficient "moral" nursing care. The large open room provided the necessary cubic air volume and free flow of air but also allowed direct nurse oversight of each patient. The narrow width and long walls full of windows maximized natural architectural ventilation and left no dark corners where patients could hide illicit behaviors. Having the patients face into the ward put the patient's head adjacent to the supply of fresh air but also facilitated nurse supervision, allowed direct physical access to the patient on both sides for examination or treatment, and prevented the patient's exhalations and excretions from coating the adjacent walls. To minimize the chance of one ward sharing air with other rooms in the hospital, there was only one

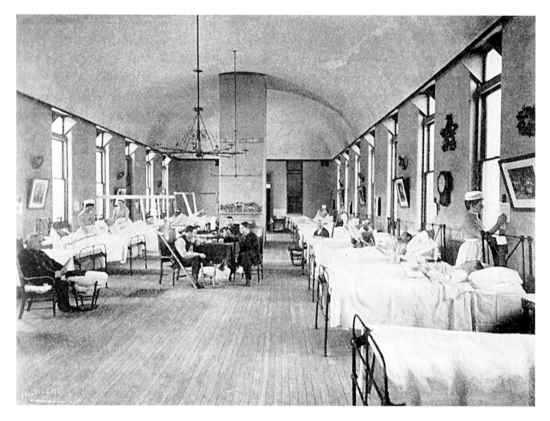

Figure 1.31. Bellevue Hospital, New York City, ward interior of Sturges Pavilion, 1893.

entrance into the ward; this typically passed by the nursing service rooms (scullery, office, diet kitchen, etc.), giving the nurse immediate awareness of the comings and goings on the ward.[94]

A ward designed for efficient nursing was not always efficient for the hospital's social or medical structure. Optimum ward size was determined by the number of patients one nurse could oversee—in the mid-nineteenth century that was roughly twenty to thirty. These large wards were inefficiently sized for medical and social categorization. The ideal was to house one patient category per ward, but it was rare for any hospital to have twenty or thirty patients of exactly the same category at any given time. Empty beds were inefficient and costly and many hospital administrators regularly assigned patients to beds based on availability rather than ward categories. "Mixing" patients of different categories in one ward created social disorganization, complicated medical assignments, and increased the likelihood of cross-infections.[95]

Compounding the problem, hospital patient categories grew increasingly numerous and specific. According to John Green in 1861, in addition to the four primary patient categories (male medical, male surgical, female medical, female surgical), hospitals also required wards for infectious diseases, venereal diseases, ophthalmic cases, ward patients requiring exclusion (delirious or dying patients), "foul" wards (for patients with unsavory symptoms), and wards for lying-in women.[96] Wards for burn victims, syphilitics, delirium tremens sufferers, accident (emergency) cases, dermatology sufferers, and convalescents also occurred. Many of these new categories were for patients with socially stigmatized ailments (venereal diseases) or medically unpalatable ailments (skin diseases); putting these patients in separate wards served to maintain the moral tenor of the large ward. Only the largest hospitals, typically the municipal hospitals, included enough large wards to accommodate such extensive categorization.

Hospitals of all sizes could accommodate more numerous patient categories, however, if the wards were smaller. Nightingale had promoted the provision of a small room adjacent to a large ward that could house dying or disruptive patients. By the 1860s most American general hospitals included, in addition to such accessory wards, at least a few small wards; specialized hospitals might include mostly smaller wards. The Presbyterian Hospital in New York City included a mixture of ward sizes, including twenty-eight-bed wards, twelve-bed wards, two-bed wards, and one-bed rooms. The New York Eye Infirmary in 1856 held a mix of twelve- and four-bed wards.

In smaller wards the ward design could be tailored to the needs of the specific patients. In this way, smaller wards often deviated slightly from the standardized rules of pavilion-ward design. For example, children benefited from the provision of play space and more cheerful ward finishes than the omnipresent white, while eye patients needed "to be kept in a darkened room." These "special" wards could also accommodate special accessory spaces. At the City Hospital in Boston, the eye ward had an ophthalmoscope room, physicians' examining room, and several "private" rooms and wards adjacent. These special wards were also valuable for nosological studies and the advancement of medical specialties—they created an opportunity for the doctors and nurses to study a single ailment as it occurred in a number of patients and to provide more disease-specific care and treatment.[97]

Which categories of patients occupied exactly which wards within any given hospital was the result of a complex social and medical spatial calculus. Typically, the larger, more general categories occupied the large wards; smaller, more specialized categories occupied the smaller wards. Accident wards were typically on the ground floor, near the hospital's entrance, for ease of emergency patient delivery. Ophthalmic cases in general hospitals often occupied a basement ward because the rooms were easier to darken. Socially marginal patient categories frequently occupied spatially marginal wards within the hospital. Delirium tremens or "insane" cases often occupied basements, as the solid foundation walls blocked the sounds of agitated patients and the remote location minimized others' awareness of their disturbing behaviors. Patients of color, if admitted to a hospital, were typically assigned to the most remote or least desirable ward space in a facility. All of these ward categories were typically interchangeable. The New York Hospital regularly reassigned wards to different services based on the number of patients admitted and the number of doctors requiring a ward of their own. As early as the late eighteenth century, however, two categories of patients—those requiring isolation and those paying for all or part of their stay—were regularly assigned to separate, specially designed wards that could not be reassigned to other patient categories.

Isolation Wards

Isolation wards served two different purposes—to protect vulnerable patients from the hospital diseases of the general wards and to separate patients with infectious diseases from the rest of the hospital. Removing the patients most prone to hospital diseases (lying-in patients, surgical patients, fracture victims, and amputees) from the suspected infectious air of the main hospitals was a preventive strategy. Wards for these patients ranged from the "maternity cottage" at the New England Hospital for Women and Children in Boston to the Osborne Pavilion at Bellevue Hospital—an elaborately ventilated, one-story isolation ward for "cases in danger of septic poisoning or infection."[98] These separate pavilions were typically of traditional pavilion-ward layout, but built with extra ventilation technologies or features that maximized the inflow of fresh air.

The removal of patients with known infectious diseases from the general wards into separate infectious wards was crucial to limiting disease within the main building. Because most voluntary general hospitals had rules excluding patients suffering from infectious diseases, a majority of hospital facility plans included no initial provision for separate infectious disease wards. In practice, patients often entered the hospital with latent infectious diseases that manifested only after admission, or acquired an infectious disease during their stay. If left in the general wards, these patients could infect the entire building and its occupants.

Typically, soon after the opening of a new hospital facility, ad hoc "isolation" facilities—tents, huts, shacks, and simple outbuildings—were added to the grounds. These structures could be surprisingly complex. In 1876, the directors of the Presbyterian Hospital in New York City built a one-room, twenty-foot-square structure that came to be called the "Hut." It had room for

Figure 1.32. Isolation Ward, Henry Greenaway, 1875. The section shows the underfloor supply ducts to the individual cubicles and the individual exhaust ducts from the ceiling. The shared bathrooms and common sculleries reveal the minimal concern about daily physical objects (plates, utensils, linens) as carriers of disease.

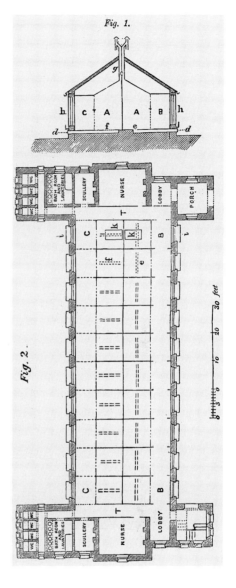

two patients and a nurse but had an elaborate structure consisting of a double wooden wall, an air space between the floor and the ground, and air ducts running beneath the floor.[99]

Within these isolation facilities, patients with various infectious ailments might be intermixed. This was a known problem, but typically isolation structures were built with extra ventilation that was expected to dilute the air sufficiently to prevent cross-infections. In 1872 Henry Greenway proposed an alternate isolation ward design to eliminate this danger. In plan, his ward appears startlingly modern—it comprises numerous separate glass cubicles within a large, traditional pavilion ward. Greenway, however, intended the cubicles to maintain aerial (rather than physical) isolation between patients. Individual supply and exhaust ducts to each cubicle ensured that there would be no sharing of air.[100] The patients would even be allowed visitors, as they could remain in the hallway and see and talk to the patient without breathing the same air.

Sufferers of the most feared infectious diseases (e.g., smallpox or cholera) often were sent to separate, disease-specific "isolation" hospitals. Cholera hospitals were linked to the incidence of the disease; they appeared during epidemics and disappeared as incidence waned. Smallpox had a more constant rate of incidence, and consequently smallpox hospitals were often permanent institutions. These isolation hospitals could include complex precautions to keep the disease from escaping. In New York City, worries that "the hot and poisoned air" of the Reception Hospital for smallpox victims (which was in the densely inhabited Lower East Side) "passed away unrefined and deadly, endangering any citizen who might inhale it," prompted the city to construct a new facility that included extensive aerial containment and purification mechanisms. Sealed wagons drove directly into the building's hallway, where the smallpox victim could be unloaded behind closed doors with no escape of air. In the wards, the windows remained closed and "air-tight"; yet each patient received 1,800 cubic feet of fresh air hourly through "holes in the wainscoting near the floor" next to each bed. The air was then drawn into a huge central furnace set on perforated iron plates above the floor, where it was "burnt up and purified, and once more enters the general atmosphere, perfectly harmless and uninfectious."[101] This system controlled not only the flow of the air within the room but the quality of the air returned to the larger environment as well.

Housing Paying Patients in a Charitable Institution

If the separation of patients into various medical categories supported variant ward designs, the admission of paying patients (a distinctively American innovation in hospital practice) created a whole new set of spatial problems. While European hospitals were almost entirely charitable institutions, the founders of even the earliest eighteenth-century American hospitals conceived of them as flexible aid institutions, not full charities. Every patient was expected to pay what he or she could afford, and noncharity patients were welcome to apply for admission. Even as early as 1754, the organizers of the Pennsylvania Hospital noted that after the hospital had accommodated all the charity patients it could afford, "the Managers shall have the Liberty of taking in other Patients, at such reasonable Rates as they can agree for."[102] The admission of part-charity patients and "private" patients (those who paid the full cost of their care and at times more for luxuries) altered the very nature of the institution, and accordingly its architecture.

In a study on hospital design commissioned by the managers of the Massachusetts General Hospital, Charles Bulfinch commented that hospitals might attract not just the poor or those without families but also "persons from the country who are able to pay, and who are afflicted with maladies which require the attention of the best medical or surgical practitioner and such advice as cannot be obtained at their homes." In 1865 the directors of the Jews' Hospital in New York City similarly observed that their paying patients were "induced to enter the Hospital by the desire of being treated by the medical and surgical staff of the Institution."[103] This foregrounded the hospital as a location of expert medical treatment, not just philanthropic care.

Starr has observed that the location of medical care influenced the relative power of patient, doctor, and other parties. In the late eighteenth and early nineteenth centuries, the norm was for doctors to make house calls to their "private" patients. The doctor was a service provider, performing his examinations in an environment completely controlled by the patient. The provision of medical care in the hospital, however, made the patient a seeker of, or even applicant for, a doctor's attention in an environment controlled by the doctor.[104] This shift has been much discussed in modern times as a factor in the medicalization of society, but in the mid-nineteenth century the question this change raised for hospital designers was how to house "private" patients in a charitable institution.

European hospital design precedents were predicated on housing poor sick persons. The light, clean, spacious, orderly ward was a class-specific design; it offered the architectural antidote to the dark, dirty, crowded, disorderly tenements. With Nightingale's addition of a respectable professional "lady" nurse in charge, the charity ward became a premier location of moral, social, and religious as well as physiological improvement. The administrators of Saint Luke's Hospital in New York City noted how "an atmosphere of propriety settles on a man after he has received his first dose of medicine from the hand of a lady, which does not come before, nor leave him while there. Men bring to light the tatters and shreds of a gentility almost lost. Those who were filthy, somehow become neat; those who were boorish, acquire a tinge of the gentleman." Martin Pernick points out that this expectation of "environmental-moral therapy also played a major role in promoting the growth of hospital care, especially for those patients judged to be medically, economically, or morally incapable of improving their living conditions themselves." The large ward was thus an environment meant to promote the adoption of specific socio-moral habits—cleanliness, order, respectability, and obedience—by the poor, unfortunate, or dissipated.[105] Reform-minded visitors (clergy, society ladies, philanthropic individuals) regularly mined the patients for possible listeners and converts. This made the large ward a socially inappropriate space for the care of people of means.

Bringing private patients into the hospital entailed developing a new patient space. If private patients were "unwilling to be associated with the promiscuous classes, that are found in the Public Ward" they were "willing to pay a higher rate of board for the privilege of entering" smaller rooms or wards. Charles Bulfinch's plans for the Massachusetts General Hospital included just such a number of smaller wards.[106]

Private rooms quickly proved even more appealing than small wards. By 1843 the Pennsylvania Hospital had twenty-six private rooms and several larger apartments in a separate wing. By 1851 the Massachusetts General Hospital's governors were contemplating adding a new wing exclusively for paying patients with separate rooms rather than wards. In 1859

SERVICE OF SONG AND PRAYER IN THE MEN'S WARD, CONVALESCENT HOSPITAL.

NEW YORK CITY.—METROPOLITAN CHARITIES—THE BIBLE AND FRUIT MISSION TO THE PUBLIC HOSPITALS—MINISTERING TO THE CONVALESCENT PATIENTS
ON HART'S ISLAND. *Les Mays, 1879*

N.Y. PUBLIC LIBRARY.
PICTURE COLLECTION

Figure 1.33. Bible and Fruit Mission to the Public Hospitals, New York City, 1879.

the administrators of Saint Vincent's Hospital in New York City, in debt from recent building alterations and enlargements, provided a number of private rooms in some nearby recently purchased houses as a means of generating some income. Private patients flocked to Saint Vincent's houses, and the hospital managers soon found themselves solvent. The success was at least partially due to the unusual physical arrangement. The separate private patient houses meant that the wealthier patients did not have to endure the "social odium" that "ever attaches itself to the beneficiaries of such an institution, however virtuous and estimable the afflicted may be."[107] It also put them in surroundings of domestic scale and detail, making the private hospital patient's experiences a closer approximation to home care.

The financial success of Saint Vincent's private patient rooms was widely known in hospital circles, and widely coveted. In the 1860s administrators of existing hospitals without private patient rooms struggled to find space for them; administrators of hospitals with private rooms struggled to make them more attractive. A majority of the newly built American voluntary hospitals in the 1860s and 1870s included facilities specifically designed for private patients. Some were luxurious. The new Mount Sinai Hospital in New York City included nine private wards with "closets, bath-rooms, lavatories and nurses rooms" and four private wards

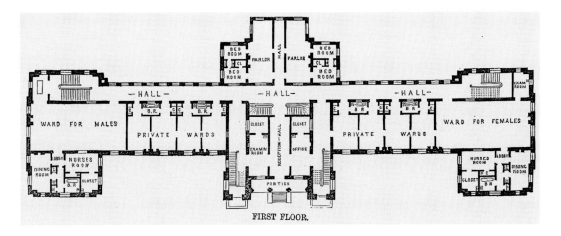

Figure 1.34. Saint Luke's Hospital, New York City, first-floor plan, 1860. The varying ward sizes—private rooms (with private bathrooms) and small wards on the first floor and large wards on the upper floor—provided a range of spaces to correspond with the ability of the patients to pay for all or part of their stay. This plan also reveals the two kinds of examining room—one immediately off the ward to provide privacy and one off the main entrance to accommodate the interviews and diagnostic exams necessary for applicants to prove worthiness for admission.

with bathrooms. Even municipal hospitals, such as the City Hospital in Boston and the Cincinnati General Hospital, included separate rooms for paying patients.[108]

A number of hospitals even developed a three-tier sociospatial division of patient rooms. At the Cincinnati General Hospital, the paying rooms were divided into large wards for the poor, a few smaller wards for the moderately wealthy, and private rooms for those "who may prefer to be entirely isolated from all other patients, and who are able to pay for the extra accommodation." Carl Pfeiffer's design for the Roosevelt Hospital and German Hospital in New York City and Otto H. Matz's design for the Alexian Brothers Hospital in Chicago included a similar three-tier system. At the Woman's Hospital in New York City, free patients occupied the fourth floor, part-pay patients the second and third floors, and full-pay patients the first floor.[109]

Ongoing large-scale urban transformations fueled this rapid increase in private patient facilities. The general economic prosperity of the 1860s gave more people the ability to pay for a hospital stay. Urban growth and density made for smaller houses and an increasing proportion of renters rather than owners; this left little room for home care for the sick, and some uncertainty of tenure for tenants with long illnesses. Diminishing household size left fewer available family members or servants to provide the necessary home care. At the same time, hospitals were gaining a reputation as an "affordable" location for getting top-shelf medical care, since doctors did not charge medical fees to hospital patients.[110]

Hospital historians such as Charles Rosenberg, Annmarie Adams, and David Rosner have emphasized the early twentieth century as the turning point in the private patient revolution and the transformation of hospitals into all-class institutions. While private patient service clearly constituted a very small proportion of hospital care in the early to mid-nineteenth century, the architectural record of the availability and growth of such private patient facilities in hospitals indicates that the timing of the transformation might be more complex. Whether these private patient facilities were built to meet demand or to create demand is unclear. Similarly, the availability of private patient facilities did not guarantee use by paying patients. In Saint Luke's Hospital, the first-floor private patient rooms remained empty and were quickly turned over to house the sisters who provided the nursing in the hospital. In general, evidence indicates that private rooms in hospitals in the 1860s were well used. The private rooms in the Cincinnati General Hospital were in such demand that in 1871 the hospital directors turned two large wards into twenty-four private rooms and by 1873 had opened an entire pay department of thirty rooms "comfortably and neatly furnished" in which "each patient is at liberty to employ any physician he or she may choose."[111]

Private patient facilities were always an economic gamble. Even with the common expectation that paying patients provided income that could subsidize charitable care, for a charitable institution to spend its limited funds on facilities for the well-off was risky. Saint Vincent's Hospital's initial success was the shining example, but it was a fleeting success. The supply of private patient rooms soon outpaced demand. After the economic panic of 1873, fewer people had disposable income—Bellevue was full to the brim with charity patients while private patient rooms and voluntary hospitals that required all patients to pay something for their stay had empty beds.[112]

Given the common belief that bad air caused disease, early American hospital building designs emphasized ventilation and air space over functional adjacencies and patient density. The earliest of American hospitals occupied facilities with multiple, interconnected wings that housed a variety of spaces in a variety of arrangements. By 1861 Thomas C. Amory, the chairman of the committee of the City Council on the Free City Hospital of Boston, could state that the pavilion-ward plan was "universally conceded to be the true basis of a successful arrangement of any large or general hospital."[113] Thousands of Americans of all classes experienced hospital care for the first time in Civil War military hospitals, which were pavilion-ward plans. After the war, pavilion-ward hospitals were founded, built, and operated in cities across America even though the distance between pavilions caused exorbitant construction costs, made it difficult to deliver warm food to the patients, reduced the chance of informal medical interactions, and forced staff to walk miles each day. Hospital administrators and medical practitioners tolerated these difficulties because they believed that the open space between pavilions was crucial to reducing the spread and incidence of airborne hospital diseases. The building itself was understood to be therapeutic.

The mid-nineteenth-century American pavilion-ward hospital facility enclosed an unresolved conflict. Whether a hospital was a philanthropic, reformative institution or a pay-what-you-can medical institution was legible in the extent to which its buildings did or did not include non-ward spaces. A hospital comprising large wards and little else was an efficient location of charitable, reformative, and medical care. A hospital with private patient rooms and facilities for medical education and practice had the potential to become an all-class location for the efficient practice of elite medicine.

Most mid-nineteenth-century hospital designers initially planned facilities with an administration building and several large ward pavilions. The architecture of the wards was an established certainty, a standardized structure determined by hygienic necessity. A ward in New York City might be nearly indistinguishable in interior plan and details from one in Cincinnati. Soon after construction, however, hospital administrators often acceded to the demands of their medical practitioners, nurses, and prospective private patients and added non-ward spaces in unplanned wings, additional stories, or separate pavilions. The location and design of these ancillary spaces was an open question, requiring constant innovation. That innovation occurred in the shadow of fears that poor design decisions would increase disease rates, and had to fit within the physical limitations of the pavilion-ward envelope of low-rise, narrow, widely separated buildings.

CHAPTER 2

The Transformative Potential and Conservative Reality of Germ Theory and Antisepsis, 1874–1877

> Germs. Of so-called "germs" we say nothing, save that, whatever they may prove to be, they must be least numerous and least dangerous in proportion as the ventilation is most complete.
> — *American Architect and Building News,* 1877

> If the constructors and conductors of hospitals were acquainted with or would adopt these hygienic rules on which hospitals should be built and managed, if hospitals were not overcrowded, if the system of ventilation were perfect, if there was a continuous water-supply, a proper isolation of wards and distribution of patients, the causes of septic diseases would not be generated. Those foul and filth-begotten diseases, pyaemia and hospital gangrene, would disappear, and antiseptics, in the absence of septic influences, would become unnecessary.
>
> — Eric Erichsen, 1874

Pavilion-ward hospitals were designed to prevent "hospital diseases." They did not. In 1875 noted surgeon and hospital expert Dr. John Shaw Billings pointed out that "the 'pavilion plan,' which for a time was supposed to be a perfect panacea against all evil, has been found, by sad experience, to furnish no security against the evils" of hospital disease. In New York City, Dr. Robert F. Weir noted that "septicaemia and pyaemia began to develop in the wards of Roosevelt Hospital" despite its being "a comparatively new institution, and well fitted with all the modern acquirements for the care of the sick." Five years after the German Hospital in New York City opened, "the uninterrupted use of the surgical ward was impossible for any length of time. Especially those operated on or wounded were, in spite of the most painstaking attention, frequently seized with hospital gangrene, erysipelas, etc., which in many cases retarded or even jeopardized the healing process."[1]

Hospital officials in newly designed and built pavilion-ward facilities regularly explained away unexpectedly high mortality or morbidity rates as a result of overcrowding in the wards or of the desperate conditions of the patients upon admission. Hospital practitioners in buildings that were not up to pavilion-ward standards continued to blame the buildings for outbreaks. Despite the disappointing results, pavilion-ward design continued to dominate hospital construction and a focus on air quality was pervasive in hospital practice. In the words of Charles Rosenberg, "the maintenance of health reduced itself to the placement of beds and windows, the arrangement of flues and ventilators, the proper design of heating systems."[2]

In the early 1860s Dr. Joseph Lister practiced in large wards that were "among the unhealthiest in the whole surgical division of the Glasgow Royal Infirmary." Though the blame for the incidence of hospital disease in Lister's wards was officially placed upon the building conditions, Lister stated that he "felt ashamed when recording the results of my practice, to have so often to allude to hospital gangrene or pyaemia."[3] Unable to alter the ward conditions to the hygienic standards required for disease prevention, Lister came up with a new strategy based on a new theory.

Hospital diseases were classified as "septic" diseases because the symptoms and progress of the disease imitated decomposition. Inspired by the laboratory experiments of Louis Pasteur that had proven that airborne microorganisms caused decomposition, Lister developed the theory that these microorganisms, the floating particles in the air, and not some chemical (or imperceptible) quality of the air itself, caused the hospital disease. He undertook his own experiments based on this theory, but unlike Pasteur he performed them in the troubled septic environment of his hospital ward rather than in the controlled conditions of a scientific laboratory.

To kill the germs before or even after they entered a wound, Lister experimented with various ways of applying "antiseptics"—"some material capable of destroying the life of the floating particles." His experiments were so successful that by the time of his initial 1867 publication on the antiseptic principle, Lister could state that "during the last nine months not a single instance of pyaemia, hospital gangrene, or erysipelas has occurred in them." He attributed this success not just to the localized killing of germs by his antiseptics in the actual wound, but by the reduction of the

THE REAR OF THE MAIN BUILDINGS FROM THE PARK.

THE JOHNS HOPKINS HOSPITAL, BALTIMORE.—From Photographs.

Figure 2.1. Johns Hopkins Hospital, Baltimore, view of complex, 1880s. John R. Niernsee and Cabot and Chandler, architects; John Shaw Billings, consulting surgeon.

New York Hospital 15th St., New York

Figure 2.2. New York Hospital, New York City, second building, 1880s. George B. Post, architect.

load of airborne particles from sick patients, because after antiseptic treatment "wounds and abscesses no longer poison the atmosphere with putrid exhalations."[4]

Lister's new germ theory and antiseptic surgical practices quickly became a matter of medical and public excitement and debate. Other historians have investigated the dissemination, adoption, and even rejection of early germ theory, and what it meant for medicine, surgery, or even everyday behaviors and expectations.[5] This book asks a different question: what did this mean for hospital architecture? Although construction of new hospital facilities came to a near standstill across the United States in the years following the devastating economic panic of 1873, the two most well-known nineteenth-century American hospitals—the Johns Hopkins Hospital in Baltimore and the second building of the New York Hospital in New York City—were designed in this period. The former was horizontal in layout; the latter was vertical. Both had persons well aware of germ theory involved in their design. The design differences thus reveal the early difficulties of interpreting germ theory's implications for hospital design.[6]

Designing the Johns Hopkins Hospital

In 1873 the members of the Johns Hopkins Hospital Building Committee were charged with building an ideal hospital and medical school facility on a large open site well outside of town. The committee members were businessmen, with little or no experience in hospital administration or construction. They read the available literature on hospital design (largely pavilion-ward tracts), visited numerous recently built American hospitals, and hired John R. Niernsee, a prominent Baltimore architect, as advisor. Niernsee was not known for hospital design but he was familiar with the literature on hospital construction and was well known by the trustees, having done projects for the president of the board as well as for Johns Hopkins. By mid-November 1874, the committee, fully aware of the mortal consequences attributed to faulty hospital design, could reach no consensus as to exactly what form an ideal hospital would take. In March 1875, to resolve the lingering uncertainty, they sought the expert advice of five doctors with practical experience in hospital medicine and design.[7]

The doctors were not asked to reconsider hospital design *in toto*. The building committee assumed that the experts would all adhere to "the now very general method of a central administration building, with wards for the treatment of the sick as carefully separated therefrom and from each other as practicable." The design question posed to the essayists was whether the intended pavilion-ward hospital should be a "barracks" hospital; that is, a one-story temporary construction, or a "pavilion" hospital, a two-story permanent construction.[8]

All five doctors were eminent practitioners, aware of Lister's controversial new theory. Billings and Smith explicitly discussed germs and germ theory; the other essayists referred more to miasmas and contagions. All of the doctors proposed hospitals that were based on pavilion-ward guidelines but that also reflected their experiences in assisting in the design of structures at their home institutions.[9]

Niernsee reviewed the submitted plans, pointing out strengths and weaknesses of the various suggestions, and the building committee members awarded the essay prize to Billings. They also hired Billings to collaborate with Niernsee in the design of the hospital, requiring "the architect of their hospital to prepare his plans in consultation with and under the supervision of a surgeon who is a recognized authority in hospital construction."[10]

The trustees published the five essays in a well-illustrated volume that soon ranked as the authoritative American text on hospital design. Throughout its decade-long planning and construction, every aspect of the design development of the Johns Hopkins Hospital appeared in professional periodicals and separate publications. Billings undertook an extensive tour of European hospitals to learn more about hospital design; this trip also served to make European practitioners aware of the project. Long before it opened, it was the most internationally well-known American hospital and was pivotal in American hospital planning.[11]

Designing the New York Hospital

In contrast to the highly public and publicized design of the Johns Hopkins Hospital, the design of the second building for the New York Hospital occurred largely behind closed doors. Between 1868 and 1872, the New York Hospital's governors and doctors had disagreed, publicly and privately, over the 1869 closure of the original hospital facility and over a sequence of unrealized plans for a new facility. In the late 1860s, after a series of deadly internal hospital disease outbreaks (attributed largely to their outdated facility) and a series of extreme budget shortfalls, the governors decided to cease operations. The doctors protested the closure; the governors refused to build an expensive replacement facility championed by the doctors.[12] For a couple of years, the New York Hospital existed only in name.

In early 1874, when the hospital governors resumed planning a new facility, they did so without official medical input. They quietly bought a small midtown site that already had an existing structure—the well-known Thorn Mansion and its outbuildings. It was only eight New York

City lots—far too small to hold a pavilion-ward facility. The governors were planning to build only a twelve-bed emergency facility—called a house of relief—that would be more than a dispensary but less than a general hospital. This was in direct contrast to the hospital doctors' continuing opinion that "a General Hospital should be established with a capacity of at least two hundred and fifty beds." This first house of relief, however, was to be a "Central Establishment," from which the governors could coordinate the numerous other planned houses of relief.[13] The existing Thorn Mansion could comfortably accommodate the central administrative and executive functions while a new, three-story building on Fifteenth Street would hold a slightly larger than normal (fifty- to ninety-bed) "central" house of relief.

In June of 1874 the governors invited a select list of architects to submit plans to a design competition for the small hospital. Of the invited architects, only one—John W. Ritch—had any prior experience designing hospitals. The governors' building program was so detailed, however, that there was little room for architectural creativity. George B. Post, one of the invited competitors, observed that in the end the jurors would be comparing the competition projects based on the arrangement of lighting, elevator and service areas, ventilation, and facade design.[14]

The building committee members themselves judged the competition entries and selected Post's as the winning design, though it would be "subject to modifications, as to external construction and internal arrangements consistent with the views of the Committee." Those modifications were extensive and detailed; the governors were more than passive clients waiting for architectural input. In September they invited ventilation expert Lewis Leeds to consult with them on general principles of ventilation applicable to hospital buildings. A few days later, J. J. Smith, a manufacturer of steam warming and ventilating apparatus, talked to them on the subject of thermal ventilation. Their investigations competed with Post's role as hired expert on just these subjects. When they communicated their findings to Post, he replied that he knew as much about ventilation as any so-called ventilation experts (who typically promoted their own systems without considering the merits of all available options).[15]

It was only in late 1874, when the plans were well advanced and the site excavations already well under way, that the governors formally informed the medical board of their intention "to erect a hospital Building." The doctors made numerous suggestions "as to matters of detail." The result of these suggestions was the addition of facilities for medical education, research, and practice. With construction already underway, Post revised the plans to accommodate these additions. By the middle of 1875, after more enlargements, the "small" hospital had become a multistory building that held 155 ward patients, a small number of private patient rooms, a large recreation room for convalescents, a small nurse training school, a laboratory, autopsy room, lecture room, room for microscopy, a room for photography, and "all the improvements suggested by the latest and most enlightened experience in hospital construction and organization."[16]

Germ Theory, Antisepsis, and Hospital Design

With these additions on a limited site, the building grew to a startling height—a reported seven or eight stories.[17] This height was unprecedented. At the time, most authorities on hospital design condemned pavilions over three stories. The Johns Hopkins Hospital Building Committee members had worried that even two stories was one story too many.[18] Actual hospital construction in US cities in the 1870s generally ranged from one-story to four-story construction. The taller hospitals typically held only two (at most three) superimposed stories of wards. The new building design for the New York Hospital not only had seven stories, it had five superimposed stories of wards.

Citing miasmatic fears that bad air could spread upward between floors, numerous critics pointed out the potentially deadly consequences of the New York Hospital's building. One philanthropist warned that "large and intricate structures, of several stories, including under one roof any considerable number of wards, are promotive of imperfect ventilation, pyaemia, and as a consequence, of a greatly enhanced death-rate among the patients who are treated in them." The author of an article in the *New York Times* added the opinion that "it would seem to be a result of the latest science in this matter that it is impossible to build a many-storied hospital which shall continue for many years free from infections." The unprecedented height made one architectural critic "shudder at the risks to which some hundreds of helpless wretches are needlessly exposed."[19] The New York Hospital governors defended their design, stating that "no effort on their part or that of the architect has been wanting to make [the plans] express the most advanced principles of Hospital construction, arrangement and convenience." They were confident enough about its medical safety that they could assert "that hospital gangrene, erysipelas and pyaemia will never be developed in the building."[20]

If "advanced" principles of hospital construction were justifying seven stories, those principles were based on something other than established pavilion-ward guidelines. Was the unconventional design of the New York Hospital, undertaken largely by the governors and Post, based on the promise of germ theory? Conversely, why had the Johns Hopkins Hospital,

Table 2.1. Heights of Hospital Buildings in the 1860s and 1870s United States

Hospital Name	Year	Total Number of Floors (including attics)	Number of Floors of Superposed Wards
University of Nashville Hospital	1875	2–3	2
Saint Elizabeth's, Utica, NY	1875	2	2
City Hospital, Boston	1875	2	2
State Emigrant Hospital, Ward's Island, New York City	1868	3	2
Rhode Island Hospital, Providence	1868	3	2
Jewish Hospital, Philadelphia	1873	3	2, 3
Cincinnati General Hospital	1870	3	2
Cleveland City Hospital	1877	3	3
German Hospital, New York City	1869	3	2
Johns Hopkins Hospital	1875–85	1, 2	2
Hahnemann Hospital and Medical School, Chicago	1880	3	2
Mount Sinai, New York City	1872	4	2
New England Hospital for Women and Children, Boston	1876	4	3
Hospital of the Protestant Episcopal Church, Philadelphia	1870	4	2
University Hospital, Philadelphia	1874	4	3
Woman's, New York City	1869	4	3
Presbyterian Hospital, New York City	1872	4	2
Soldier's Home, Washington, DC	1875	4	2
Saint Mary's Hospital, Philadelphia	1868	4	unknown
Mercy Hospital, Chicago	1869	4	3
Cook County Hospital, Chicago	1876	4	3
Hospital for the Ruptured and Crippled, New York City	1874	4	3
Saint Agnes Catholic Hospital, Baltimore	1875	4	unknown
Roosevelt Hospital, New York City	1871	1, 4	1, 3
Hahnemann Hospital, New York City	1876	5	3
Saint Francis, New York City	1865	5	4
New York Ophthalmic	1871	5	3
Jefferson Medical College and Hospital	1876	5	3
New York Hospital	1877	7	5

designed and overseen by John Shaw Billings, a medical practitioner who was well aware of germ theory, taken such a conservative architectural form? Answering those questions requires a brief assessment of the details of germ theory and antiseptic practice in the late 1860s and early 1870s in America.

Practical Requirements of Early Antisepsis

By the early 1870s American medical practitioners were aware of Joseph Lister's germ theory and experimenting with his "antiseptic" surgery. By the autumn of 1876, when Lister himself visited the United States, Dr. William Van Buren could assure him that the students in New York City were already "indoctrinated in the principles of antiseptic surgery." On the whole, American experiences were similar to what J. T. H. Connor has described in Canada: early germ theory and antisepsis found as many detractors as supporters in the medical community. Thomas Gariepy considered Americans in general as far readier to dabble in antiseptic procedures than to adopt, wholesale, the underlying germ theory.[21]

Adopting antiseptic procedures, which used antiseptic solutions (most commonly carbolic acid) as a means of killing any germs that came in contact with a wound, changed what happened in the location of surgery but altered little of the spatial design of the rooms themselves. To make this clear requires some idea of the practical changes wrought by antisepsis. According to Dr. David Bryson Delavan, in the preantiseptic surgery of the early 1870s "patients were brought in for operation without the slightest attempt at washing the parts in any way. The knives had been washed in soap and water and wiped upon a towel after the previous operation. The operator put on an old frock coat which he kept in the operating room for the purpose, and which he buttoned to his chin to protect his clothing from being spattered. It was encrusted with the remains of several years of former operations. Its odor was that of the dissecting room. None of the assistants paid attention to washing their hands."[22]

In contrast was Dr. James Pratt Marr's description of standard "antiseptic" procedures at the Woman's Hospital in New York City in the late nineteenth century:

> The surgeon and others assisting at the operation washed their hands and arms thoroughly with soap and water, scrubbing their closely clipped fingernails with a stiff brush. The hands were then dipped into a solution of bichloride of mercury (1:2000). When time permitted, the resident physician customarily took a full bath shortly before the operation. The nurse, too,

had to comply with these rules. All instruments and the silver-wire sutures were left for one hour prior to operation in a carbolic acid solution (1:20) to which had been added an equal amount of sterile hot water. . . . The walls, floors and furnishings of the operating room were rubbed down with a cloth impregnated with a solution of bichloride of mercury (1:10) and all doors and windows were left open to insure a free circulation of fresh air, considered the best antiseptic of all. Two spray apparatuses saturated the operating room air with a solution of carbolic acid (1:40) for 1 1/2 hours before surgery took place. A roped-off area three feet from the operating table was supposed to guard against contamination from spectators. The abdomen of the patient was shaved, washed with soap and water, and covered with a towel impregnated with a bichloride of mercury solution (1:1000) until the incision was made. This antiseptic operating room was barred to anyone who had attended a case of scarlet fever, diphtheria or erysipelas within 24 hours."[23]

The overall procedural transformation was startling, but it required little from the surrounding architecture except some additional plumbing fixtures and easily cleanable materials. Hospital architecture had for decades been designed for maximum cleaning and cleanliness (rounded corners, no ledges or cracks, minimal ornament, hard materials, and few spatial subdivisions). The practical hygienic changes of antisepsis thus registered in the ancillary spaces—in demand for larger, more up-to date laundry and sterilization facilities; more storage space for antiseptic tools, supplies, and equipment; more sinks, tubs, and cleansing apparatus; better bathing facilities.

The Unsettling, but Minor, Spatial Implications of Germ Theory

If simply adopting antiseptic practices required minimal changes to surgical spaces and wards, adopting the germ theory underpinning those practices reinforced but subtly shifted the focus of existing hospital design. At its simplest, germ theory posited that microorganisms (germs), not air, caused disease. However, Lister and other early germ theorists considered germs to be "atmospheric" entities that floated on dust or wafted individually through the air currents. Nancy Tomes observes, "Early understandings of the germ, which emphasized its ubiquitous presence in air and water and its hardiness outside the body, neatly harmonized with already accepted modes of protection against zymotic disease." The result was "a surprisingly successful marriage between the old sanitary science and the new germ theory." Attention simply shifted from immaterial influences, such as "miasms," "effluvia," or "septic influences," to material agents, such as germs, "disease-dust," or the "floating matter" of the air. In the words of Billings, "the dangerous thing in a hospital is a dust, an excessively fine, organic dust, which is almost omnipresent, which is in the air, the bedding, the hair, and the clothes of all occupants of the building."[24]

With the focus on "disease-dust," open windows—which admitted dust-laden air—were potential sources of contamination. A common assumption was that fresh, natural air (from well-landscaped surroundings) contained a low content of pathogenic particulates. This led at least one Virginia surgeon to consider the air in his state "clean enough" not to require the use of antiseptics during surgery.[25] This assumption reinforced the role of large, open, "natural" sites as a critically important supply of pure (low particulate content) air. Hospital designers in dusty, crowded cities developed strategies to minimize the danger of particulate matter from the outside. After scientific research proved that dust was more concentrated near street level, hospital intake registers moved from ground level to the upper floors to capture the cleaner, upper-level air. Filtering the air supply intakes (by stretching cloths or wire mesh screens across them) also reduced dust content.

Not all dust was the same, however. Billings classified dust into two categories: "microzymes," which were ordinary, unharmful dust particles, and "contagium," which arose "only in diseased men and animals" and caused disease. That meant that hospitals, filled with diseased persons, were already filled with "contagium." According to Billings, spatial ventilation strategies did not work for these "organic living particles of contagium" that did not equally diffuse in the air and which he considered so potent that contact with a single particle could generate disease. Diluting "bad air" had been considered an effective strategy; diluting germ-laden air simply meant "the probability of infection for one exposure may be diminished, but when the small particle does happen to be present, its effects will be the same as though no dilution had been attempted." To control airborne germs in hospitals, then, required a more precise approach to ventilation, one in which "a man shall inhale no air or suspended particle which has previously been in his own body or in those of his companions." It also required safe removal of any accumulated disease-dust. Airborne particulate matter eventually settled on a ward's material surfaces—coating them with potentially disease-causing germs. This prompted worries that porous materials were dangerous dust repositories. As Billings put it, "one stuffed chair or baize screen, or soiled woolen blouse is more dangerous as a means of causing disease, than many square feet of plastered wall."[26] Wood, inherently porous no matter how many coats of varnish, fell into disfavor as a hospital material; harder and smoother building materials like cements, tiles, and glass increased in popularity.

These hard materials repelled dust and withstood the increasingly caustic antiseptic cleansers and disinfectants. Before germ theory, cleaning solutions simply had to dissolve dirt; after germ theory they had to be antiseptic—antagonistic to the viability of microorganisms. Antiseptic cleaners were typically toxic and corrosive, causing heavy wear to less durable surfaces. For example, Lister's preference for carbolic acid made it the "king of disinfectants." Griffeth's Enamel, a glaze washed over existing wall surfaces, reportedly resisted carbolic acid etching and for decades it was a standard hospital finish, particularly in operating rooms and surgical wards.[27]

The idea of germ specificity—that one given kind of germ caused one specific disease—also altered the spatial treatment of patients with contagious diseases. Patients and their germs were hazards—infective agents— requiring antiseptic control. To minimize the germ load in the ward, hospital administrators developed "disinfective" admission procedures, requiring new patients to undergo a good bath and lots of scrubbing. This often led to the installation of "reception" wards that included well-equipped bathing facilities. Germ specificity also shifted the role of isolation from protecting the air to containing the germ, typically by increasingly detailed categorization of patients based on the specific microorganisms they contained. The goal was a facility in which "each malady has its appropriate and designated wards"; to achieve that goal, hospital designers included expanded isolation facilities or a larger proportion of smaller wards.[28]

The Revolutionary Potential

This analysis of the immediate effects of germ theory and antisepsis on hospital architecture has so far revealed minimal architectural changes; this finding runs counter to a strong historical expectation that germ theory engendered sweeping transformations. As Guenter Risse expresses it, "Following acceptance of the germ theory of disease, there was no further need for pavilion-type hospitals." Others, such as Nikolaus Pevsner, Adrian Forty, and Lindsay Prior have expressed similar assumptions that germ theory either invalidated pavilion-ward design or "changed medicine and therefore also hospital design." The visible transformation of American hospitals from the low-rise pavilions of the 1860s to the compact, multiple-storied "stacked pavilions" of the early twentieth century supports this expectation, but as David Charles Sloane and Beverlie Conant Sloane note, "the pavilion had lasted long after bacteriology had proven its basis incorrect."[29] Why? What is missing from the historical debate is a close analysis of the "messy" decades between the 1870s and 1900s, when germ theory was being argued, tested, and refined; hospital designers had to react to the unsettled and constantly changing developments; and pavilions continued to be built.[30]

In an excellent analysis of how architects could innovate within pavilion-ward guidelines, Jeremy Taylor reveals in greater detail the transformation of type that was possible. According to Taylor, while the pavilion-ward system remained dominant in publications and in exemplary hospital construction, smaller-scale innovations—influenced by germ theory as well as other forces—created constant transformative refinements and adjustments, particularly in a switch from natural to mechanical ventilation and in an increasingly compact layout. Taylor's focus on English hospitals, which remained predominantly low-rise structures with large, open wards well into the twentieth century, colors the extent of the transformation he can trace.

In the last decades of the nineteenth century, American hospital designers, engaging with the same process of transformation of type described by Taylor, also developed "pavilion-ward" hospitals that were mechanically ventilated and had minimal space between pavilions (or wings) but also rose to multiple stories, included a greater proportion of non-ward spaces, and included a greater variety of ward sizes. Clearly, more than germ theory was involved in the development of the "modern" hospital (and the next chapters will discuss those other influences). The salient argument was not whether germs or miasmas caused disease but whether the distinction changed anything. The pavilion-ward hospital was structured to create a noninfective pattern of air flow, and it would remain a relevant hospital design strategy as long as disease was considered to be airborne. Lister himself observed that

> if it were true that the air does not contain the causes of putrefaction, then it would not be necessary for me, in carrying out the antiseptic system of treatment, to provide an antiseptic atmosphere. All that would be needful would be to purify the surface of the skin of the part to be operated upon by means of some efficient antiseptic, to have my own hands, and those of my assistants, and also the instruments, similarly purified; and then the operation might be performed without the antiseptic spray which we now use, and no one would rejoice more than myself to be able to dispense with it.

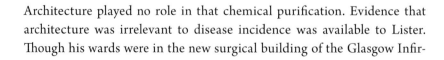

Architecture played no role in that chemical purification. Evidence that architecture was irrelevant to disease incidence was available to Lister. Though his wards were in the new surgical building of the Glasgow Infirmary mortality rates from hospital disease in the ground-floor wards (including his male surgical ward) were alarming. Excavations undertaken to seek the source of the hospital disease revealed that the building had been built adjacent to a mass grave for cholera victims and adjoined the pauper pit graves of the adjacent cathedral. Despite these severely unhygienic influences and even despite overcrowding, after Lister instituted antiseptic practices the incidence of hospital disease and mortality in the very same wards virtually disappeared.[31]

This was the revolutionary potential of germ theory for hospital design —it implied that the details of a person's physical surroundings did not matter to the incidence of infectious diseases. Hospitals could be any shape and be healthy. Jeremy Taylor has shown that by the 1900s prominent medical practitioners did indeed believe that "a modern hospital could be built to a plan other than the pavilion format."[32] In the last decades of the nineteenth century, however, this was an extreme interpretation and one that few were willing to make. Though Lister acknowledged the potential and provided anecdotal and statistical evidence to support it, in the 1880s and 1890s he continued to combat airborne germs in his antiseptic refinements. In these early decades, germ theory not only could support pavilion-ward requirements, it could intensify them. The continuation of pavilion-ward hospital design in the 1880s and 1890s thus does not necessarily indicate a continued adherence by the designers to the miasmatic theory of contagion.

Conservative and Liberal Architectural Interpretations of Germ Theory

Assessed conservatively, germ theory could reaffirm pavilion-ward design and its treatment of hospital architecture as a self-purifying apparatus. Assessed more liberally, germs could justify alternate designs and alternate roles for hospital architecture. The stakes were high, and wrong moves were tallied in mortality statistics. But the tantalizing potential—that hospitals could be any shape, anywhere—made the gamble irresistible.

The Antiseptic Pavilions—The Johns Hopkins Hospital

John Shaw Billings was well aware of germ theory and its implications for hospital design, and he consciously incorporated new strategies of germ control into the buildings of the Johns Hopkins Hospital. The result was not a revolutionary new hospital form, however; it was a mix of tradition and new refinements—what might be termed a post–germ theory pavilion-ward hospital. The difference was that the design details were structured to control germs (whether in patients or in airborne particulate matter), not "bad" air.

In the designs for the Johns Hopkins Hospital, ventilation in the large wards provided for complete aerial separation of patients within a single space, focusing on the patient's exhalations as the source of contamination. Air entered through either windows or supply ducts located between the beds. The air then flowed over the patients and to the center of the room, where it was exhausted through air ducts running the length of the ward above the ceiling and under the floor. These exhaust ducts separated the ward lengthwise into two distinct air spaces, eliminating the spread of germs from one side of the ward to the other. This flow pattern created individualized air "spaces" around each patient, keeping their germs to themselves. The provision of a separate isolation pavilion allowed patients with specific identified diseases (and the germs they harbored) to be removed from the large ward.[33]

Ward details minimized dust and particulate matter. For example, Billings planned no dust flues or clothes chutes, which were labor-saving technological conveniences common in other hospitals. The chutes could never be fully decontaminated and using them stirred up dust. In the Johns Hopkins Hospital, waste and soiled linens would be loaded onto "galvanized iron boxes with tight-fitting covers to be moved about the ward on cars with large, rubber-tired wheels."[34]

One aspect of the Johns Hopkins Hospital facility design was indeed revolutionary, but it was a different revolution than the one offered by germ theory. As described by Alistair Fair, the Johns Hopkins Hospital was a tool for scientific research. Billings intended the hospital facility to function as an experimental environmental research laboratory that would provide the objective data necessary to prove or disprove the long-accepted but scientifically unproven assumptions about design and health. Instead of a "standard" pavilion-ward layout, the master plan for the Johns Hopkins Hospital included rectangular ward pavilions, octagonal ward pavilions, private patient pavilions, isolation pavilions, and tents. Even the seemingly repetitive rectangular ward buildings were part of the experiment—Billings intended for them to have slightly different ventilation system designs. These controlled variations, coupled with a detailed system of hospital record keeping that would "show not only the history of each patient, but of each ward and each bed" would allow doctors to correlate disease incidence to architectural details such as room shape or ventilation design. This correlation would yield knowledge, not speculation or theory, of what effect the physical surroundings had on health, and of what was the "best" ward ventilation or layout.[35] Turning the hospital buildings into an

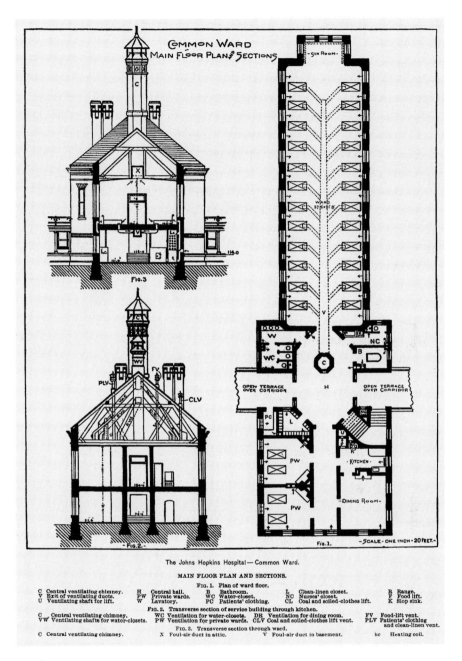

The Johns Hopkins Hospital — Common Ward.

MAIN FLOOR PLAN AND SECTIONS.

FIG. 1. Plan of ward floor.

C Central ventilating chimney.	H Central hall.	B Bathroom.	L Clean-linen closet.	R Range.
V Exit of ventilating ducts.	PW Private wards.	WC Water-closet.	NC Nurses' closet.	F Food lift.
U Ventilating shaft for lift.	W Lavatory.	PC Patients' clothing.	CL Coal and soiled-clothes lift.	K Slop sink.

FIG. 2. Transverse section of service building through kitchen.

C Central ventilating chimney,	WC Ventilation for water-closets.	DR Ventilation for dining room.	FV Food-lift vent.
VW Ventilating shafts for water-closets.	PW Ventilation for private wards.	CLV Coal and soiled-clothes lift vent.	PLV Patients' clothing and clean-linen vent.

FIG. 3. Transverse section through ward.

C Central ventilating chimney.	X Foul-air duct in attic.	V Foul-air duct in basement.	hc Heating coil.

Figure 2.3. Johns Hopkins Hospital, Baltimore, plan and sections of common ward, 1893. Arrows on the plan show that inflow is from the windows and in-wall ducts (one on each side of the patient). Exhaust ducts run from an intake register under the bed to a main duct running under the middle of the ward that fed straight into the central ventilating tower. A similar exhaust vent ran down the center ceiling of the ward. These ducts prevented air from passing from one side of the ward to the other. The tower provided constant updraft for continuous exhaust.

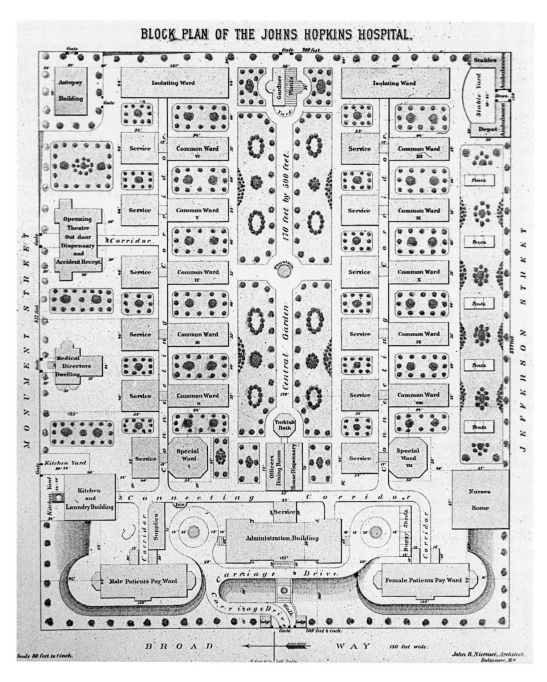

Figure 2.4. Johns Hopkins Hospital, Baltimore, plot plan, 1875. This plan was from the early design stages, and it reveals the varied ward shapes, sizes, and structures, and the location of the medical school, administrative, and service buildings that ring the block.

experimental laboratory was radically innovative in architectural terms; in medical terms, it was inherently conservative in its premise. It embodied the assumption that architectural design was relevant to disease incidence.

The Antiseptic Skyscraper—The New York Hospital

In contrast, the New York Hospital's governors were experimenting with the radical potential of germ theory in the design of their new building. That the governors were well aware of and influenced by germ theory is certain—they disagreed on its implications for the new building design. James Beekman considered "poisonous dust wafted from older and suppurating wounds, or from the walls of long over-crowded wards" to be the cause of hospital disease. He advocated for a pavilion-ward hospital in the country, as it would have less dust than any building in the dirty, congested city. In contrast, Frederic Conkling saw the radical promise of antisepsis in justifying hospitals within the city. He believed that the antiseptic system, "if properly carried out, will remove all danger of septicaemia even in the most crowded and neglected hospitals."[36] Inevitably, the architect played a role in resolving this disagreement. George B. Post did not write explicitly about germs or antisepsis; the best evidence that his views coincided with Conk-ling's rather than Beekman's is found in the building itself, which opened on March 17, 1877, to much fanfare.

The new New York Hospital building was a "germ-proof" structure. Post and the hospital superintendent participated in extensive testing of various building materials to isolate the least absorptive, which would "decrease the danger of the retention of infectious matter."[37] Hard-troweled lime and white sand mortar proved the least absorptive materials for the walls, terrazzo for the floors. Wood was minimized. The wards could also be hosed down (which would facilitate removal of particulate matter—dust and germs—not bad air). Traditional fears that dampness contributed to foul air had promoted dry cleaning strategies for at least a decade. An elaborate mechanical ventilation system was designed to minimize germs. Basement fans drew air into the building from a point twenty-eight feet above the ground—where the air would have a reduced dust content. Then, "before it is admitted to the pipes, the air is passed through gauge screens, and arrangements are made to spray these screens with fresh water in warm weather."[38] These screens provided cooling in summer and humidification in winter but most importantly they filtered out residual particulate matter—germs and dust.

Air flow within the ward was constant and completely choreographed. Though there was a window between each bed, they were to be kept closed.

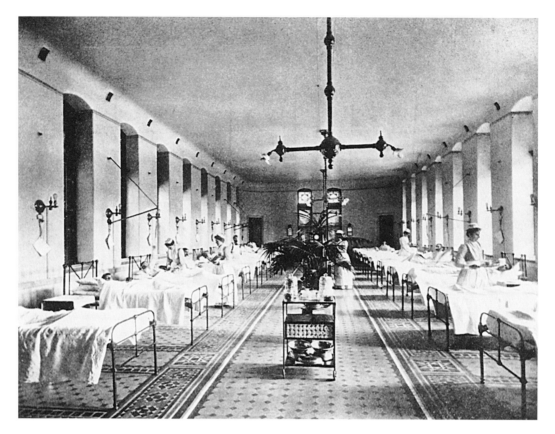

Figure 2.5. New York Hospital, second building, view of male ward, 1895. The hard impermeable surfaces, rounded corners, and simple furniture facilitated cleaning; the floor pattern reinforced bed placement to ensure that each patient stayed in their own air space. Compared to earlier ward designs, the lack of fireplaces either in the corners or the center of the ward is conspicuous and indicates that air movement was entirely mechanically induced.

Post had decided "to remove the system from the disturbing action of the winds and external temperature." In the piers behind each bed, ducts supplied tempered air to a vent that blew the air upward in a fan shape across the windowpanes on each side of the bed (eliminating cold winter drafts). This located the air supply on both sides of the patient's head. Expired air was drawn through an exhaust duct in the floor immediately under each patient's bed. With sufficient air speed, Post guaranteed that rather than just diluting the air, "this system would isolate each bed as far as spreading contagion to adjacent beds."[39] Post also isolated the most contaminated spaces in the hospital (toilets, morgue, pathology) into sanitary "towers" with separate, exhaust-only ventilation. Those towers connected to the main building by an airlock that ensured no air (or germs) bridged the distance.

Figure 2.6. New York Hospital, second building, ground- and ward-floor plans, 1894 (based on 1877 plan). The plan on the top shows a typical ward floor, with rounded corners even in plan. The sanitary facilities were the projections on each end of the ward, separated by an air lock from the ward itself. The plan on the bottom shows the basement floor with the pathology facilities in the projection on the left-hand side of the plan; the isolation facilities on the bottom left-hand corner of the plan; the apothecary to the left of the central staircase; the dispensary to the right of the central staircase; the night receiving wards and delirium wards in the projection above the central staircase; and the stables in the projection on the right-hand side of the plan.

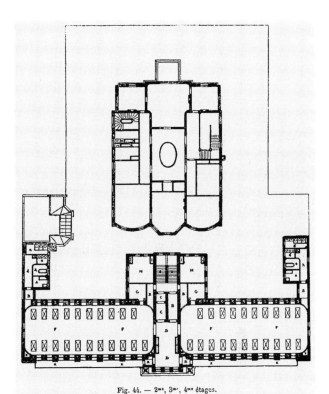

Fig. 44. — 2ᵐᵉ, 3ᵐᵉ, 4ᵐᵉ étages.

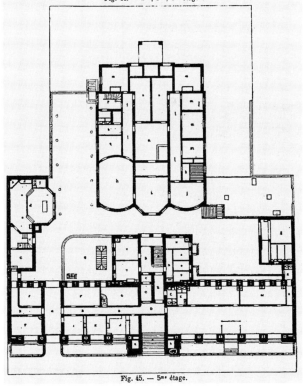

Fig. 45. — 5ᵐᵉ étage.

The New York Hospital was thus a mixture of tradition and innovation. The individual wards followed pavilion-ward guidelines but rather than occupying discrete aerially distinct buildings they occupied a single building that integrated all the different functions of the hospital. The hospital's height was a clear break from tradition, justified by germ theory and antisepsis. At the opening celebration for the new building, Dr. William Van Buren even quoted Joseph Lister's statement that "it is immaterial how many stories of wards there may be in a hospital, provided that the details of the antiseptic method are accurately carried out in all of them."[40] The design of the New York Hospital was thus a demonstration of the freedom that a radical interpretation of germ theory could give to hospital design.

Forces for Tradition or for Innovation

The Johns Hopkins Hospital took a decade to plan and build, but it was internationally recognized as a model of medical-architectural collaboration in hospital design, as a new model of medical school, and as an "improved" model of pavilion-ward design.[41] Its far-reaching influence on the design of hospitals in the United States and in Europe extended well into the twentieth century.

The New York Hospital received mixed reviews. At best it was considered an intriguing innovation or a tolerable example of urban hospital design. At worst it was considered too luxurious, egregiously expensive, and downright dangerous. Billings considered it a bold experiment and noted that "the results obtained, if carefully observed and accurately reported, cannot fail to be of interest."[42]

While the varied reception of these two hospital building projects reveals something of the general status of innovation in hospital design during this period, there is an even thornier question begging to be asked. Why was the most unusual hospital building of the period the one designed by governors and an architect, and not the one designed by an eminent doctor conversant with the latest medical theory in all its detail?

The Inclusion of Space for Medical Education in the Hospital

Simple spatial economies were obvious and important factors in the differences in the two projects.[43] The smaller, more expensive city site inevitably meant the New York Hospital needed to fit a lot of building onto a relatively small area; this necessity pushed the building upward. But was real estate pressure enough to explain the New York Hospital's unusual height? Not entirely—other city hospitals on downtown sites, of similar size and under similar pressure, did not rise so high. While downtown hospitals categorically rose higher than those on the city's outskirts, even the most landlocked city hospitals rarely broke the four-story limit and rarely held more than two or at most three ward floors.

I have encountered four exceptions to that height limit before 1879: the Jefferson Medical College and Hospital in Philadelphia and the Saint Francis Hospital, Hahnemann Hospital, and New York Ophthalmic Hospital in New York City. Two of these were the product of relatively prosaic issues with hospital construction sequence. The sisters of Saint Francis Hospital in New York initially bought an existing five-story tenement building and altered it for hospital uses. They then added a new adjoining building to match the initial tenement structure. Similarly, the Hahnemann Hospital initially built only the five-story central administrative building of a planned facility that also included two flanking, more traditional three-story pavilion wings. For its early years, that single administrative building had to contain all functions, including wards.[44] The other two tall hospital buildings were unusual in that they included facilities for teaching. Was the integration of medical education and hospitals a factor raising hospitals above the four-story limit?

While clinical instruction occurred in hospital wards and surgical amphitheaters in the 1870s and 1880s, medical schools typically maintained separate facilities in immediate proximity to a hospital. Municipal hospitals in particular tended to be surrounded by medical schools on adjacent blocks. Even hospitals that were adjuncts to medical schools maintained this separation of facilities. For example, the University of Pennsylvania Medical College was immediately across the street from the University Hospital in Philadelphia. Even the Johns Hopkins Hospital, which would become known for elevating the medical school from proprietary workshop to university-based education, would include the medical school on an adjacent site, in separate buildings.[45]

The Jefferson Medical College and Hospital and the New York Hospital broke this mold and incorporated spaces for hospital service and medical education "under one roof." How that integration occurred varied. The five-story Jefferson Medical College and Hospital, designed by prominent Philadelphia architects Frank Furness and George E. Hewitt, was, in essence, a three-story pavilion hospital stacked on top of a two-story medical school.[46] Spatial overlap between school and college was minimal: students entered the hospital floors for bedside instruction and patient treatment; patients visited the admission offices by the front door before being ushered to the elevator and up to the wards. This maintained the hygienic separation required by pavilion-ward guidelines. Situating the wards on the upper floors raised them above the street dust and into the sunlight and purer air.

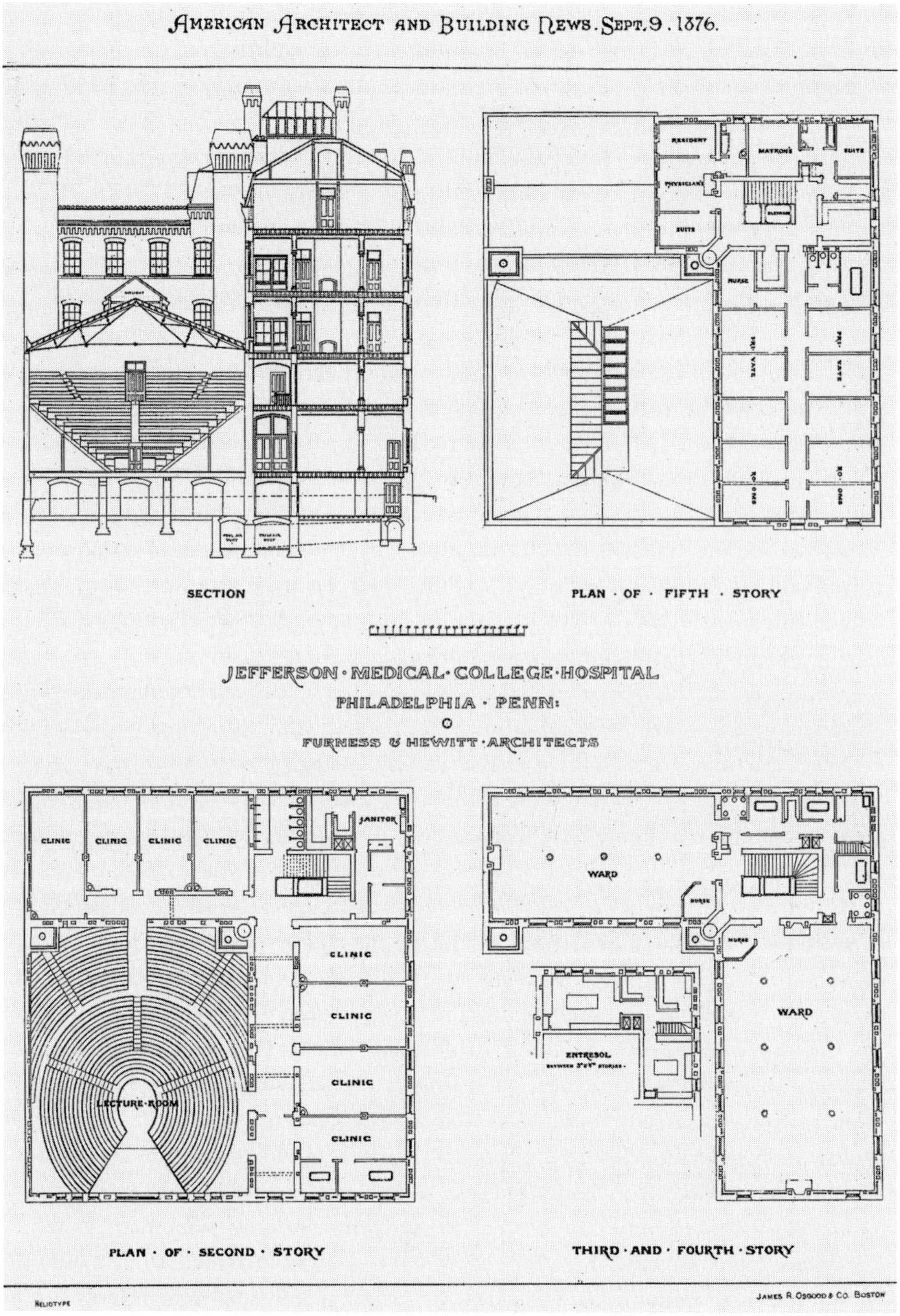

Figure 2.7. Jefferson Medical College and Hospital, Philadelphia, plans and section, 1876. The drawings show the vertical differentiation of the building into medical treatment and education spaces on the lower floors and patient rooms (wards and private rooms) on the upper floors.

The New York Hospital did not have a formal medical school, however. Teaching in the hospital occurred according to the old practice—individual doctors took on students. Access to the hospital was a privilege of the doctor's appointment to the hospital. There was no justification for a separate building for the medical college or teaching facilities. The spaces for education and research were dispersed throughout the New York Hospital building. The surgical amphitheater occupied the top floor, the dispensary was in the basement, medical staff housing was on the first floor, the library was in the Administration Building (the Thorn Mansion), and the pathological laboratory and classroom were in the ground floor of the westernmost sanitary tower. Though each individual space was distinct, getting to any of them required traversing all of the hospital's corridors and connections; the students permeated the building. The complex mechanical ventilation system provided the necessary control of air flow that would keep each space within the hospital "separate."

Combining spaces for medical education and spaces for hospital care within a single facility clearly was a factor in higher hospital design. At the very least it increased the demand for space, often on limited sites. The design of the Jefferson Medical College and Hospital, however, proved that pavilion-ward guidelines could be largely maintained in such a facility. The New York Hospital's innovative shape was not the result of a simple problem of too much program for too small a site.

The Varying Design Personnel on Hospital Projects

The varying personnel involved in the design of the different projects, and their roles, offers one more point of contrast. Doctors and architects both had a claim to hospital design expertise. Carl Pfeiffer wrote in 1874 that architects adapted hospital buildings to their locality while adhering to "the fixed principles which should govern all [hospital] designs. It is for the hygienist to determine upon these principles."[47] In this formulation, since pavilion-ward guidelines were well established, the doctor's role in hospital design was to refine and police the existing rules. This was an inherently conservative role. There was also a third group involved in hospital design. Hospital administrators clearly had a strong influence. They controlled the budget, chose the site, established the program, hired the doctors and architects, and established the exact nature of any medical-architectural collaboration. It was thus in the interaction of all three groups that the conservative or innovative approach to hospital architecture could play out.

The trustees of the Johns Hopkins Hospital chose Niernsee, a well-established architect deep into his career whose practice included large, technically challenging projects, but no high-rises. Niernsee was also knowledgeable of the current (pavilion-ward) standard of hospital design, and of the reputed dangers of deviating from them. This knowledge might have limited the options that Niernsee thought were allowable. The trustees further limited the architectural options. They did not ask the doctors to consider what shape a hospital could be; they asked them to decide whether to build a pavilion-ward hospital of temporary or permanent construction and of one or two stories.[48] In his role in the resultant design, Billings expanded the building program to accommodate a variety of pavilion shapes, but each pavilion was still low-rise, and still largely faithful to pavilion-ward interior requirements.

In contrast, the New York Hospital governors' willingness to plan the building without medical input reveals not only the rift between the governors and the doctors but the governors' confidence that they had sufficient expertise in hospital construction standards to see the project through with Post. Their initial intentions were conservative—to build a four-story building with two floors of wards. Yet they chose to include only relatively young architects with little or no prior hospital design experience in their competition. Post, though early in his career, was already developing a reputation for tall, technologically complex buildings.[49] Post's expertise provided the possibility of a new hospital shape—one that was efficient, centralized, full of building technologies, and hygienic according to a new standard. The governors were flexible enough to entertain the idea of a tall hospital, and committed enough to investigate architectural construction and germ theory to the point where they were comfortable that such an unusual building would not simply be a disease-breeding death-trap. The extra spaces were a factor in pushing the building higher, but only because Post and the governors integrated them into the hospital building rather than housing them in a separate but nearby structure (as was more normal).

The majority of doctors, however, interpreted the New York Hospital's unprecedented height as the errant product of insufficient medical input into the design. In December 1875, at a meeting of over three hundred of New York City's medical practitioners, Dr. C. R. Agnew stated "that it would be wise for the builders of hospitals to consult doctors before they built. If they did New-York would not be treated to the spectacle of a hospital seven or eight stories high whose foundations were laid upon the oozy sedges of a bog. This hit at the new hospital on Fifteenth Street, between Fifth and Sixth avenues, was vigorously applauded."[50] While at one level the doctors were clearly expressing their discontent over the lay control of the hospital, the overwhelming implication was that even the doctors saw their role in hospital design as conservative—keeping the buildings in accordance with pavilion-ward principles.

Architects vs. Doctors on the Role of Buildings in Disease

Why would physicians and surgeons, the practitioners most likely to have personal experience with the liberating effects of antisepsis and germ theory, cling to pavilion-ward guidelines? Perhaps because they had the most at stake. For a building type that linked design details to health, innovation came with the potential risk of life and death. Architects experienced that connection intellectually; doctors experienced it viscerally, professionally, and personally. An architect who designed an innovative but unhealthy hospital often received criticism but, as Post's experience would prove, architects could deflect blame for hospital mortality.

In the early 1880s, at the first incidence of hospital disease in the new New York Hospital building, the governors demanded that Post find the environmental source of the outbreak (the doctors suspected sewer gas). Post's representative and a city health official inspected the plumbing and found only "a couple cracked pipes [and] a couple imperfect joints" (which were promptly fixed). Since the building had been in use for several years without trouble, Post declared himself confirmed in his "opinion that the building is now perfectly protected from gas generated in the sewer" and that if sewer gas was the cause, it was either through the hairline cracks in the interior piping (which was highly unlikely) or due to problems in use and maintenance.[51] For Post, the incident was a nuisance, not a professional roadblock.

For the hospital doctors, who could lose not only hospital patients but potentially their reputations, the stakes were higher. Doctors had blamed building design for hospital disease outbreaks for more than a century. British surgeon Eric Erichsen noted that all surgeons had runs of good and bad luck. Good luck was "usually attributed by the operator himself to superior skill or care—by his colleagues and friends to 'chance.'" Runs of bad luck were explained differently—not as the product of personal skill or luck, but of environmental influence, whether seasonal, or architectural. According to Michael Worboys, "when single patients were affected, sepsis was regarded as just another complication that surgeons had to manage, like blood loss and shock. When septic fevers affected a ward or wing of a hospital, the problem was as much political as medical, requiring decisions on closing wards and halting admissions."[52] If hospital architecture was a scapegoat for hospital disease, protecting doctors from full responsibility for professionally devastating clinical results, it was also a blinder. As long as doctors saw the building conditions as a significant factor in disease, they did not see other factors so clearly.

If the link between hospital design and disease were broken, doctors (and their patients) would have to find some other explanation for how disease spread so rapidly through hospitals; this would inevitably bring up questions about the role of the practitioners themselves in transporting germs. Some doctors clearly did pose those questions—Ignaz Semmelweis and Oliver Wendell Holmes are the most famous of them in this time period. But they posed their questions to a profession who largely could not see disease separate from the physical environment. The inference to be drawn is that in the 1870s medical involvement in hospital design perhaps played a role in suppressing rather than encouraging large-scale innovation, not because the doctors were less innovative but because the stakes for them were more highly charged and they were trained to see hospitals one way.

The first hospital building design that departed from the established pavilion-ward model and yet did not experience hospital disease would potentially be a destabilizing event, challenging the underlying expectation that hospital design played a role in disease incidence. The New York Hospital's Fifteenth Street building, though novel, did not prove to be that turning point. It was neither an abysmal failure nor a glowing success. Experiences in its wards were similar to those in other hospital wards; occasional cases, and sometimes outbreaks of cross-infections, plagued its statistics. This did not prove that bad design caused disease, or the reverse, but it was not a clear enough success to disprove it.

The true proof that bad design was not responsible for disease came not in new hospital designs, but in old ones. In 1875, Lister himself reported the drastic reduction of pyemia, erysipelas, and hospital gangrene in hospitals in Copenhagen, Munich, Leipzig, Halle, Berlin, and Bonn, in wards of less than perfect hygienic conditions where doctors operated under perfect antiseptic precautions. In 1878, in a report on conditions at Bellevue Hospital, a doctor called it "a matter for unfeigned thankfulness, in view of the defective construction of Bellevue Hospital, that the antiseptic method of dressing wounds . . . has so materially diminished the percentage of mortality in surgical cases."[53] If antisepsis could make Bellevue, notoriously the worst hospital facility in New York City (if not the country) healthy, it could make any building healthy. Design did not cause disease. For a few decades more at least, however, saying was not quite believing.

∷ CHAPTER 3 ∷

The Post–Germ Theory Pavilion in the Dawn of Asepsis, 1878–1897

> For to plan a hospital properly, even a simple one, is a matter of special skill and knowledge, and it is a hazardous thing for anybody to attempt who has not acquired these by special study.
>
> — *American Architect and Building News,* 1878

> Dirt must think for once that it has met a foe worthy of its steel; it must feel like hiding its diminished head in some old cellar or garret beyond the reach of the tireless scrubbers of the Presbyterian Hospital. Purity reigns.
>
> — *New York Times,* 1892

Between the 1870s and 1890s drastic medical transformations occurred in hospitals across the country. In operating rooms, surgeons focused on controlling microorganisms. Surgical survival rates increased; infection rates decreased. Medical researchers identified specific pathogenic microorganisms, transforming the basis of diagnosis from analysis of symptoms and external influences to the clinically proven presence or absence of these pathogens. Medical practitioners began to shift from hygienic approaches (which adjusted externalities in order to effect a change in the sick person's condition) to experimental science (which adjusted internalities through drugs or surgery in order to effect a change in the sick person's condition).[1]

As Philadelphia architect and hospital designer Addison Hutton explained, by the 1890s *hospital* had two meanings. The older meaning was "a place of shelter for the poor and helpless only." The newer meaning was a place for "treatment and restoration."[2] The new hospital held different spatial practices. In the old version of hospital practice, patients stayed in their assigned ward beds for the duration of their stay, nursing care was a large

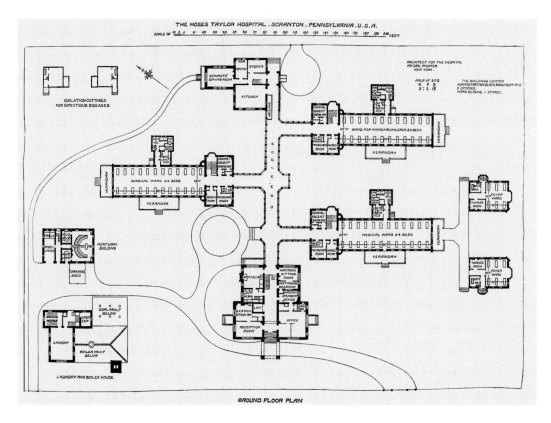

Figure 3.1. Moses Taylor Hospital, Scranton, Pennsylvania, plans, 1892. The Moses Taylor Hospital, designed by Carl Pfeiffer, was much admired by Europeans, and is a strong example of pavilion-ward design. The facility comprised independent buildings widely separated by open ground. The wards were one story; the administration building was three stories.

part of their "treatment," and one attending doctor was assigned to provide medical treatment to all patients within a given ward. In the new version of hospital practice, active "treatment and restoration" often required the movement of patients and practitioners between an increasing variety of specialized spaces—labs, surgical facilities, sterilization and decontamination facilities, wards, and administrative facilities.

The new medicine developed in structures based on the traditional pavilion-ward guidelines, which remained the established and accepted model of hospital design into the early twentieth cenuty. This continuity was not simply the result of architectural inertia. Hospital designers were well aware of the transformative practical, medical, and social issues occurring within pavilion-ward walls, and yet, after weighing all the requirements and options, they almost universally concluded that pavilion-ward design remained the best approach for hospitals, despite its inefficiencies.

What justified the continued success of the pavilion-ward layout? And what differentiated the post–germ theory pavilion hospital from the traditional pavilion hospital? The pavilion-ward hospital was designed to be a self-purifying structure that maintained air purity as a means of preventing airborne disease. As long as the air was assigned a role in disease, the pavilion-ward structure remained valid. Early germ theorists had clearly considered germs to be airborne, but by 1878 prominent researchers like Burdon Sanderson believed that airborne germs were too few and too delicate to cause widespread infection and that there had to be another means of transfer. In that same year, Robert Koch graphically and convincingly demonstrated that germs resided in diseased organisms and could be transferred directly through physical contact. By the 1880s, according to Michael Worboys, "it was increasingly accepted that the atmosphere was not full of pathogenic germs regularly raining down on the body. Rather, septic germs were concentrated in and on diseased people and were part of the ordinary fauna and flora of human skin."[3]

Logically, the theory of transmission by direct contact could have provided the basis for an alternate architectural model of hospital design, one that focused on controlling the movement and condition of persons and objects. The shift from air to contact was neither instantaneous nor simple, however. Many hospital practitioners who were trained before the development of germ theory accepted that germs spread by contact and yet continued to look to the air when things went wrong or could not be explained by direct contact. In an 1894 lecture Dr. Abraham Jacobi could refute the role of sewer gas in disease causation, acknowledge the role of physical contact in transferring disease, and still conclude that "the atmospheric air always contains bacteria, mostly, it is true, dead, and mineral parts. The presence of pathogenic germs has been denied; but there *must* be some in the air, and living ones too, for contagion, unless it result[s] from immediate physical contact of the sick and the well, must take place through the air."[4]

The replacement of antiseptic procedures with aseptic procedures—which created germ-free conditions as a means of eliminating the transfer of germs through direct contact—revealed similar difficulties in completely removing the architectural surroundings from the equation. Asepsis grew from the work of Robert Koch, who achieved his stunning results in the controlled environment of the laboratory and its sterile conditions that eliminated the variable role of the air and architectural surroundings in the transfer of microorganisms. As Thomas Schlich has discussed, aseptic surgical practices were an importation of these controlled methods and conditions into the operating room.[5] They required complete disinfection of all instruments, objects, persons, and materials that would potentially come into contact with the patient during surgery.

This importation enabled a surgical revolution, but operating rooms were not entirely controllable locations and determining the boundaries of asepsis within them was a shifting target. What were the limits of what had to be sterilized? Clearly, instruments, hands, and equipment proximate to the patient had to be sterile or scrupulously clean. What of the room? Bacteriologic research had in fact shown that pathogenic germs resided on (and could be cultured from) the material surfaces of a room that had held a person sick from a contagious disease. In the last decades of the nineteenth century many hospital practitioners saw germs everywhere. Even doctors who practiced asepsis feared "the presence of insidious disease germs or bacteria lurking in the surroundings of operating rooms." If microorganisms clung to the walls, the floors, the furniture, even the ceiling, then asepsis had to encompass a person's total surroundings, not just the moveable objects and inhabitants.[6]

J. T. H. Connor discussed how the shift from antisepsis (dead germs) to asepsis (no germs) created an emphasis on cleanliness that allowed a synthesis between earlier ideas of hygiene and the new germ theory. In this model, new concerns about "germ-filled" surroundings replaced old abstract worries about bad air. Some practitioners, however, simply conflated the theories—implicating both aerial quality and microorganisms when blaming an infected wound on "noxious and germ-laden gases" or worrying about the "noxious vapors and organic impurities" that impregnated porous bricks.[7]

Rather than breaking the traditional connection between architectural surroundings and disease incidence, germ theory and asepsis briefly strengthened the existing hygienic imperative of hospital materials, practice, and design in the last decades of the nineteenth century. If patients were the source of germs and germs could cling to walls or furniture, then adding more walls (such as individual cubicles around each patient) was a potential hazard. If air was not the means of transmission of germs, then separating patients by a sea of air was in fact a safe and effective means of isolation. That natural conditions (fresh air and sunlight) were "antagonistic to many forms of microbic life," made the traditional fresh air–filled, sunlight-maximizing ward design an effective germicidal structure. The pavilion-ward hospital was thus an appropriate design for the new aseptic practice. In fact, as Robert Bruegmann observed, many pavilion hospitals built after antisepsis and germ theory were "even more rigorous with pavilions further apart on larger sites."[8]

The post–germ theory pavilion was not exactly the same as its precursor, however. The difference was in the details. European hospital designers

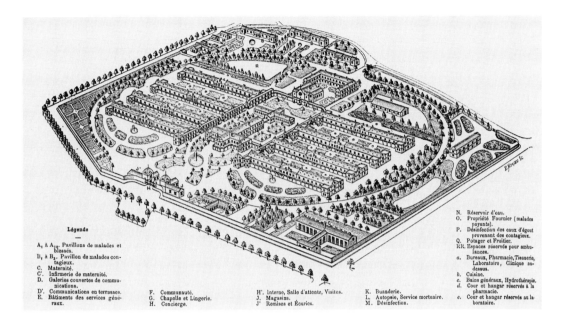

Légende
—
A₁ à A₁₈. Pavillons de malades et
blessés.
B₁ à B₂. Pavillon de malades con-
tagieux.
C. Maternité.
C'. Infirmerie de maternité.
D. Galeries couvertes de commu-
nications.
D'. Communications en terrasses.
E. Bâtiments des services géne-
raux.

F. Communauté.
G. Chapelle et Lingerie.
H. Concierge.

H'. Interne, Salle d'attente, Visites.
J. Magasins.
J' Remises et Écuries.

K. Buanderie.
L. Autopsie, Service mortuaire.
M. Désinfection.

N. Réservoir d'eau.
O. Propriété Fournier (malades
payants).
P. Désinfection des eaux d'égout
provenant des contagieux.
Q. Potager et Fruitier.
RR. Espaces réservés pour ambulances.
a. Bureaux, Pharmacie, Tisanerie,
Laboratoire, Clinique au-
dessus.
b. Cuisine.
c. Bains généraux, Hydrothérapie.
d. Cour et hangar réservés à la
pharmacie.
e. Cour et hangar réservés au laboratoire.

Figure 3.2. Saint Eloi Hospital, Montpelier, France, axonometric, 1892. Casimir Tollet's ward designs were only one story tall, with ogival ceilings; they sat upon an extensive open-air foundation that provided maximum air flow on all sides of the ward. The longer pavilion length, compared to American hospitals, reveals the continuation of larger wards (at times thirty or more beds) in Europe.

interpreted the new aseptic requirements into extreme pavilion-ward structures. Hospitals like the Eppendorf Hospital in Hamburg, Saint Eloi Hospital in Montpellier, Rudolf Virchow Hospital in Berlin, Saint Georg Hospital in Hamburg, and Nouvelle Pitié Hospital in Paris provided greater separation between pavilions, increased air space per patient, and fewer stories of wards than hospitals built before germ theory and asepsis. These refinements were not the result of a reactionary defense of traditional pavilion-ward design strategies; they targeted germs. For example, French engineer Casimir Tollet, developed a "healthy" ward structure with a twenty-five-foot ogival roof (intended to facilitate air flow) that was constructed of wrought iron ribs filled in with bricks, tiles, and cement, and then coated on the interior with plaster. The structures were fireproof and did not "absorb disease-germs," and it was "possible to cleanse the inside surfaces with flames of burning gas, or flush them with streams of water."[9] In essence, this "sterilized" the architectural surfaces, making the building itself aseptic. It also made it clear that the post–germ theory pavilion was not just a miasmatic holdover; it was a structure adapted to the needs of the new theories.

American hospital designers admired the European hospitals of the 1880s, 1890s, and 1900s in the same way that American medical practi-

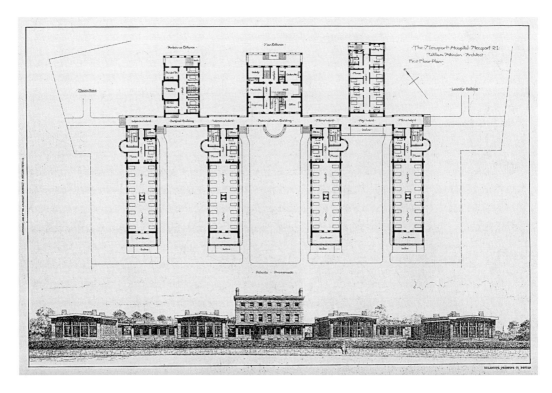

Figure 3.3. Newport Hospital, Rhode Island, plan and elevation, 1895. William Atkinson's staggered placement of pavilions north and south of the corridor allowed maximum air flow. The bow window on the ward buildings was the fresh air passage (air lock) that separated the ward from the sanitary facilities. The small wards in the large ward pavilions were likely to separate ward patients requiring seclusion. A separate pay ward was located north of the corridor, east of the administration building.

tioners admired the medical advances the European medical practitioners made within their walls. American hospital designers imitated some of the details and material finishes of the European post–germ theory pavilions, but for the most part they did not adopt the extreme spacing between pavilions. By the late 1890s American hospital designs, while still pavilion ward, differed extensively from the "extreme" pavilion-ward structures of Europe. This difference showed up in where hospitals were located, who designed them, how they were constructed, and how they accommodated an increasing variety of spaces, practices, and patients.

Sites: Explaining Clumps and Voids across the City

By the late nineteenth century, hospitals sprang up in American cities, small towns, even rural areas—wherever there was an available population

Figure 3.4. Cook County Hospital, Chicago, exterior view, 1880s. The Cook County Hospital, when built, was clearly on the city's outskirts. Visible in the photo are two new ward pavillions, a connecting corridor, and the prominent chimney that created a constant exhaust air flow for specific rooms.

of persons in need of care. In Newport, Rhode Island, the municipal hospital provided care for sailors and mariners. The Sheltering Arms Hospital in Hansford, West Virginia, and the Miners' Hospital near Hazleton, Pennsylvania, provided proximate care for injured miners and their families. In larger cities the socially fragmented turn-of-the-century city held a variety of populations, and a variety of hospitals—general, specialized, large, small—to accommodate them.

For all of these hospitals, no matter the surroundings, hospital publications and hospital experts continued to recommend that "every hospital, wherever placed, should be surrounded by a zone of aeration, unencumbered with buildings or any other cause of obstruction of light and air, to a distance of at least double the height of the buildings."[10] This typically meant a site outside the built-up city. In smaller cities, peripheral sites were still within easy reach of the city center. Rapid urban growth in the largest cities made open sites increasingly distant from the population centers; this complicated the provision of open surroundings.

Some hospital administrators opted for larger peripheral sites, often near a rail or streetcar station to maintain accessibility. Given the growth

Figure 3.5. New York Hospital, New York City, second building, view of hospital complex and surroundings, 1880s. The rapid high-rise development of the surrounding blocks posed a challenge to the hospital's access to sunlight and fresh air for decades.

of American cities, an increasing number of hospitals inevitably occupied sites within built-up neighborhoods, making the acquisition of "open" space a matter of real estate ingenuity rather than initial site size. Canny building committee members regularly chose sites adjacent to parks, rivers, lakes, or wide streets. Proximity to unbuilt lots offered similar advantages, but unregulated urban growth meant that a hospital initially surrounded by open lots or low buildings could soon be surrounded by buildings of twenty stories. Hospital administrators often had to resort to buying up nearby lots at high prices to prevent such undesirable development.[11]

A hospital's accessibility depended as much on the social nature of its surroundings as on actual geographical distance from the city center. Improved public transportation diminished the burden of travel but increased the social consequences of crossing between neighborhoods. While the majority of hospital patients continued to come from poor neighborhoods, the medical staff, administrators, donors, and private patients came from wealthier neighborhoods. Hospitals in poor neighborhoods could make wealthier patrons and practitioners feel uncomfortably conspicuous. In 1890, "a large number of wealthy and fashionable people, friends of home-opathy," attended the opening of the Flower Hospital, which was in a neigh-borhood that "had never before seen so many carriages and so much livery. The result was that the crowd outside the buildings was almost as large as that within." More often, simply getting to a hospital located in or near a tenement neighborhood could pose safety threats to the staff. Doctors at the Roosevelt Hospital recounted many stories about the rough character of the surrounding neighborhood and the threats they experienced when traveling into the adjacent blocks. Administrators of Gouverneur Hospital in New York City received complaints about "gangs of toughs who congre-gate about the home for sick people."[12]

Conversely, impoverished patients might experience social discomfort when traveling to a hospital located too deep within a prosperous neighbor-hood. A trip to the original facility of Saint Luke's Hospital, deep within the fashionable Fifth Avenue district, added an element of social publicity to the difficulties of the many injured and sick tenement dwellers who went there for care. Proximity to a wealthy district was beneficial to donations, however. The governors of Saint Luke's Hospital considered the location "a quiet but powerful witness to the sufferings of the poor and a plea for their relief," and hoped "that the daily sight of these walls causes many, who are living in luxury, to think of the distress of those less favored than them-selves." Conversely, the managers of the cash-strapped Colored Home and Hospital noted that their buildings were unfortunately "comparatively out of sight of the well to do charitable class of our citizens."[13]

Sites near a neighborhood boundary finessed this problem. As the ad-ministrators of the Manhattan Eye and Ear Hospital noted, their "ideal" site was "easily reached from the quarters of the poor," but on a healthy rise (Murray Hill) and close to "a quarter where the population is not so dense, nor so indifferent to the laws of health as to create local causes of disease." Many hospitals occupied sites just outside a poor neighborhood. Some in-stitutions, particularly those offering a charitable service to a specific poor population, were located in the heart of the tenements. Few hospitals were built in the middle of an established well-to-do residential neighborhood—if not because of the cost of real estate then because of organized neighbor-hood opposition.[14]

Even if they were feared as such, hospitals were not vehicles for neigh-borhood degradation or contamination. Their open space and greenery at times made them small natural oases in an urban desert. Attractively land-scaped hospital grounds could encourage other, high-quality development.

Figure 3.6. Pennsylvania Hospital, Philadelphia, bird's-eye view with additions, 1904. The original building with all its additions is in the foreground, with new additional pavilion-style wards (reportedly designed by Dr. Edward W. Cowles of Boston) along the back of the block.

Hospital trustees and administrators, typically well-placed businessmen, policed the tenor of the surrounding neighborhood by tenaciously opposing adverse surrounding developments such as abattoirs or railway tracks.[15]

Late nineteenth-century building committee members also seemingly preferred, rather than avoided, sites that were proximate to other medical institutions. Within a roughly ten-block radius from Stuyvesant Square in New York City were nearly twenty hospital institutions. This list included a handful of general hospitals, several facilities for women, a couple of postgraduate hospitals, contagious disease hospitals, and several specialized medical hospitals. These hospitals were adjacent to the densely populated East Side tenement district but also easily accessible to the wealthier residents of the row houses surrounding Gramercy Square, Madison Square, and Union Square. Each serviced a specific fraction of the demand. The hospital practitioners did not complain about competition or about empty wards. If, as Annmarie Adams and Stacie Burke observe of Toronto at the time, doctors also located their offices in proximity to hospitals and other medical institutions, the neighborhood would have offered extensive private as well as charitable medical services.[16]

In 1891, after the nearby construction of the College of Physicians and Surgeons, the Vanderbilt Clinic, and the Sloane Maternity Hospital, the managers of Roosevelt Hospital proudly referred to their neighborhood as a "medical centre."[17] This idea of a medical center—a group of institutions (hospitals, medical schools, dispensaries, and even private practices) that created a medical district the same way a number of stores with the same variety of goods created a shopping district—implied that clumping increased patronage rather than competition. This expectation did little to forward the idea that hospital facilities should be equitably distributed throughout the city. It also reconfigured site priorities—providing a social as well as hygienic range of acceptability. The ideal site was a compromise between the two.

Designing the Hospital: Reasons for and against the Development of Hospital Architects

In 1894 Philadelphia architect Addison Hutton suggested "the possibility of an improvement in hospital building, which would spring up if the architect should so find himself by early and careful training for the special work of designing and constructing hospitals." In Europe, hospital architects like H. Saxon Snell and Keith Young were centering their practice on and serving as authoritative experts on hospital design in their native countries and even internationally.[18] However, this period developed no convincing specialization in hospital architecture in the United States either as an import or as a local development. Although Americans were aware of the European hospital experts—and studied their publications and exemplary designs—building committees did not directly hire European experts to design US hospital buildings. No American architects focused their practices on hospital design. Several American architects designed a few hospitals; few did so in more than one city. None of the American architects who designed US hospitals (even those who designed a number of hospitals) were known for their hospitals more than other buildings. For example, Charles C. Haight, J. Cleveland Cady (of Cady, Berg, and See), and Addison Hutton each designed a number of hospitals, but they and their firms were far better known for their educational, ecclesiastic, and domestic structures. Publications by American architects on hospital design were few and relatively short.[19]

In fact, doctors were the authors of the most comprehensive American publications on hospital design. The continued strength of medical input may have differentiated American hospital design from European. According to Adams, European hospital designers treated hospital design as similar to other building types such as poor houses and orphanages. This allowed them to develop their hospital expertise from within existing design traditions.[20] In contrast, American practice continued to link hospital design expertise to medicine. The existing professional structure continued: doctors established and policed the requirements of architectural hygiene, while architects implemented those requirements. This left the question of whether doctors or architects should design hospitals unresolved.

Collaboration offered one solution to this conundrum, but the structure of that collaboration in the United States proved critical to hospital architecture and architects. American architects, including Hutton, Carl Pfeiffer, and M. Carey Lea, recommended the collaboration as one between equals—the doctor established the principles; the architect followed them. Medical practitioners like John Shaw Billings and Stephen Smith preferred the model offered by the Johns Hopkins Hospital, where the medical specialist not only consulted but supervised the architect, the preparation of plans, and even the construction. As long as expertise remained divided, the possibility of either profession developing a convincing specialization was diminished.[21]

Without that collaborative interaction, architects had little access to the most current medical theories and practices. Jeremy Taylor cites visits to other hospitals, correspondence with Florence Nightingale or other experts, books, journals, meetings, and lectures as the primary sources of hospital expertise in Britain.[22] In America, publications and visits to existing exemplary hospital facilities were not sufficient to provide the medical knowledge necessary to hospital design. The most often referenced and most lavishly illustrated comprehensive publications on hospital design of the time were penned by European authors, promoted European "extreme" pavilion-ward design, and cited European examples. These publications equivocated on the exact medical theory being fulfilled, promoting the expectation that pavilion-ward design was adequate to meet the needs of all theories—whether germs, living organisms, putrefaction, fermentation, putrefactive fermentation, or some "morbific agency" were to blame.[23] At a time of intense medical controversy between the new and the old theories, this approach would have appealed to the broadest possible audience.

Such equivocation was equally common in American publications on hospital design, but a few, those written by doctors, included brief discussions of the broader implications of germs. In 1877 Dr. Walker Gill Wylie speculated as to whether germs would require a different design approach, such as the stacking of ward floors rather than separating them by outdoor space, or requiring temporary construction as the only means of truly decontaminating an infected hospital. Without mentioning germs, the Cincinnati architect George F. Hammond found higher hospital buildings, if required by tighter city lots, acceptable and safe because of the improvements of antisepsis. By 1894 Drs. John Shaw Billings and Henry M. Hurd's edited volume included articles, particularly on isolation hospitals, that included the new aseptic understanding of the spread of germs by direct contact as well as articles that continued to focus on the role of the air or building materials.[24] None, however, offered a sufficiently detailed understanding of the changing medical requirements for an architect to make the necessary medical decisions independently.

The rapidly changing status of medical theories also made informational site visits to existing hospitals (which were often hygienically out of date by the time of their opening) of unpredictable benefit. In 1891, a committee from Lakeside Hospital in Cleveland traveled the country to visit "leading hospitals" in Baltimore, Philadelphia, Boston, and New York City as a means of deciding what was the best plan of hospital construction. In the end, they concluded that only the Johns Hopkins Hospital and the newly renovated Presbyterian Hospital in New York City were worth emulating.[25]

Even if an architect could have developed independent expertise, specialization was no guarantee of future projects or of a good commission. The continuing popularity of architectural competitions continued to keep the playing field open even to new practitioners. Judges of competitions were rarely hospital design specialists and did not always award the prize based on the most hygienically accomplished design but often according to cost, aesthetics, or personal connections. One frustrated architect bemoaned the problems caused by such well-meaning but ignorant building committee members who usually "have not sufficient knowledge to understand that they know nothing about" hospital design.[26] As charitable institutions, hospital projects also continued to be offered with the expectation that the architect would accept a reduced commission.

If specialization in hospital design did not yet offer competitive advantages, hospital projects did offer an alternative for more pragmatic, technically oriented practitioners. Hutton suggested that students "who have a certain combination of mechanical with artistic genius," were good candidates for hospital design.[27] There is no proof that technically proficient practitioners gained more hospital commissions, but there is clear proof that hospital commissions remained far more elaborate in their ventilation systems than in their ornamentation, and would consequently appeal to a different kind of practitioner.

Figure 3.7. New York Cancer Hospital, New York City, view, 1880s.

The Architect and the Hospital Aesthetic

One constant in hospital design was the expectation that "all unnecessary embellishment or architectural adornments . . . should be avoided." This did not mean hospitals were undecorated. Taylor emphasizes the fine line between simple hygienic design and design that had enough civic presence to aid fundraising. Administration buildings in particular could be lavish, even if the pavilions were simpler. Ernest Flagg's Beaux-Arts masterpiece of Saint Luke's Hospital and Charles C. Haight's much-admired New York Cancer Hospital show the extent to which ornament could still be considered necessary for hospitals. Still, none of these buildings matched the extensive ornament displayed in other prominent buildings or projects of the time. Many hospital buildings were not just minimally decorated, they were unusually aesthetically restrained. Hutton noted that at the Johns Hopkins Hospital, "architecture as an art seems to have been subordinated to the demands of hospital science." A *New York Times* reviewer tactfully described the even plainer buildings of J. Cleveland

Figure 3.8. Presbyterian Hospital, New York City, view from street, 1890s. The plain facades of J. Cleveland Cady's redesigned buildings stand out in stark contrast to Richard M. Hunt's patterned administration building.

Cady's Presbyterian Hospital in New York City as "somewhat severe in its simplicity."[28]

This more utilitarian aesthetic was influenced not only by a deemphasis of ornament but by a fundamental shift in design process. For offices, houses, apartments, hotels, public buildings, libraries, and other civic building types, nineteenth-century architects emphasized facade; for hospitals, designers began with the plan. Adams has posed plan-based design (rather than the ventilation-based design of nineteenth-century hospitals or the facade-based design of other building types) as a hallmark of the early twentieth-century hospital; the shift was clearly well underway in the last decades of the nineteenth century. For the two most admired American hospitals of the time—the Johns Hopkins Hospital and the Presbyterian Hospital in New York after its 1891 renovations—"development of the plans . . . were very fully determined upon for utilitarian reasons before the external effect was considered." According to Hutton, this design approach meant that hospitals inevitably had "certain irregularities of plans and arrangement of openings, because the wants of the interior are dominant, and interfere with the symmetry" of traditional historic architecture. At one level, this meant that rather than using formal, symmetrical classical styles, hospitals were more frequently given stripped-down versions of less inflexible historic styles, like gothic or Romanesque, which could tolerate asymmetry and some minimization of detail. At another level, this meant that hospital exteriors were the product of utility, not aesthetics.[29]

Architects of hospitals made concerted efforts to pose this aesthetic minimalism as a new kind of beauty, one resulting from massing, scale, and pattern. Hutton stated, "Granted that a hospital is a machine, if you will, it seems reasonable that it may be and ought to be an agreeable looking machine." At about the same time, Louis Sullivan's very similar mantra—that "form ever follows function"—was entering American architectural debate. Hutton thought the functional machine could be made beautiful; Sullivan considered the machine shaped by function inherently beautiful. The difference is subtle, but important. Hospital designers were modern in their design strategy, but not in their formal expectations.[30]

Building the Hospital: Germs, Building Technologies, and Wall Structures

Instead of nullifying the aerially focused pavilion-ward material design requirements, germ theory intensified them. Rounded corners, minimal cracks and projections, and impermeable materials minimized germs as readily as foul air. An examination of the changing understanding of "impermeable" materials, the rejection of hollow-wall construction, and the adoption of mechanical rather than natural ventilation in hospital designs in this era reveals how the existing strategies of architectural hygiene were refined rather than replaced by the new medical theories.

How Impermeable Is Impermeable?

Scientific testing altered expectations of what constituted an impermeable material. For example, Dr. Max von Pettenkofer did some experiments in the 1880s that involved blowing out a candle through several of the most common building materials (including brick and wood). This proved that many wall materials that had been considered impermeable (hard, smooth, damp-repellant) were porous and could function as germ sponges. Practitioners worried that "the internal lining of the walls, if it is of a porous nature, must become saturated with the matter floating in the air, and such matter will in the parts occupied by patients be very largely composed of organic particles, epithelium, pus-cells, and the like."[31] This research prompted drastic reappraisals of materials appropriate for hospital use.

When wood was proven to be porous and to retain moisture, it was nearly banished from use in wards. In 1882, less than ten years after the Mount Sinai Hospital moved to a brand-new pavilion-ward facility, the medical board considered "that the wooden moldings, framework and other absorptive material in the wards, so jeopardized the lives of the inmates by rendering them subject to erysipelas and other contagious diseases that it was unsafe to perform any capital operations in the Hospital." The hospital governors tore out all "absorptive" materials and installed impervious walls, thereby providing "every possible protection against hospital infection." In 1880, Dr. Edward H. Janes of the New York Board of Health warned of the dangers of using unglazed brick in interior walls, as the bricks were "porous enough to absorb and filter out from the air they enclose the noxious vapors and organic impurities it contains, and to give them up when fresh air is supplied." When analyzed, a sample of old plaster from a hospital ward with a high rate of septicemia proved to "contain forty per cent of its weight of a sort of offensive mud, deposited from the air which had passed through its pores."[32] Bricks, wood, and common plaster were essentially removed from use in hospitals.

Post–germ theory hospital designers sought a material that presented "an absolutely impervious surface capable of being washed down and thoroughly cleansed without its impermeability being affected." The Presbyterian Hospital in New York City had walls with eight-foot high wainscots of "cream-colored English tile, the surface of which is as hard and smooth as a piece of flint glass." Varnishes, enamels, and resins sealed less impervious materials. In 1882 the directors of Mount Sinai Hospital in New York City even coated their floors "with asphalt, to make them as impervious to taint of disease as the ceilings and walls." Other hospitals also experimented with asphalt floors.[33]

The new impermeable materials did not perform so happily during temperature and humidity fluctuations. One observer described how in cool weather interior moisture began to condense on the impermeable walls and ceilings and coalesce into "drops of very foul liquid" that trickled down to the floor, where they deposited their foul residue.[34] However, material choices had to serve social as well as hygienic functions in the hospital. For example, between the 1880s and the early 1900s, a large number of high-end surgical facilities in American hospitals were marble palaces. Roosevelt Hospital's world-famous Syms Operating Theater had walls, floors, and even some ceilings of white marble. The Presbyterian Hospital's rebuilt

Figure 3.9. Presbyterian Hospital, New York City, view of operating theater looking south, 1898. The operating theater was a marble palace. The hard white surfaces of walls, floor, ceiling and fixtures were inevitably reflective and, coupled with the large skylights and windows, created an intensely brilliant, glare-inducing space.

modern surgical facility had floors, wainscoting, and even doors of marble.[35] Marble was white, beautiful, prestigious, and presumably hygienic, but it was porous. It retained liquids and was difficult to clean. Marble operating rooms were impressive, however, glorifying the surgeons and surgery that were vaulting the hospital into a loftier social position. Thus, hospitals retained their marble surgical palaces well into the twentieth century, in order to attract doctors, patients, and donors.

The Problems with Hollow-Wall Construction and Pipes

By the late nineteenth century, standard construction practices increasingly used skeletal, or hollow-wall, construction. If not entirely constructed of hollow walls, mid-nineteenth-century pavilion wards had been riddled with ducts, air spaces, ventilators, and other wall cavities for improved air flow and quality. This was unacceptable for post–germ theory pavilion-ward hospital design. Hollow walls created a dark, stagnant, inaccessible space that could not be easily cleaned and allowed air to travel from room to room, which tended "to equalize the foulness of each room." According to Hutton, "a principle to be followed as carefully as possible in hospital building is to leave as few cavities in the construction as consistent with the conditions of integrity and endurance."[36]

Solid walls offered the added advantage of greater fireproofing. Hollow walls provided excellent conduits for fire as well as air. The fire that destroyed much of the Presbyterian Hospital in New York City in 1889 began in an air space under the mansard roof (part of the exhaust ventilation system) and spread rapidly in the interstitial spaces. Hospital fires were regular occurrences; estimates ranged from one to two hospitals per month destroyed by fire across the United States. The bedridden condition of many hospital inhabitants made such fires deadly. By the 1880s fireproof construction—comprising solid walls of noncombustible material—was a crucial aspect of hospital design and one increasingly controlled by outside regulation in the form of early fire codes. The rebuilt buildings of the Presbyterian Hospital were of masonry and iron throughout; the wards of the Mary Hitchcock Memorial Hospital in Hanover, New Hampshire, were constructed of fireproof (and impermeable) Guastavino tile domes.[37]

Solid-wall construction precluded hiding the abundant new building technologies—water pipes, gas pipes, air ducts, pneumatic tubes, speaking tubes, laundry chutes, dumbwaiters, and electrical wiring—in wall cavities. Exposed piping and wiring was common in hospital construction, and this also permitted "the easy detection and repair of defects." The rebuilt buildings of the Presbyterian Hospital managers included a state-of-the-art electrical system, which, among other things, powered electric lights and a bell service with 112 stations throughout the hospital buildings. Every private room had a push button to call a nurse; an associated annunciator in the hallway indicated to the nurse where the call had originated. The wires were all exposed. According to one observer, "the wires, covered with rubber and tinted the colors of the ceilings and walls, are strung in lines so narrow and regular that they look like some delicate and novel style of ornament."[38]

Complex design precautions were deployed for building technologies that were considered hygienically dangerous. Plumbing provides a good example, for it posed what was perceived as an extreme sanitary hazard. Pipes often leaked. What they leaked could pose either an inconvenience (water damage) or a health hazard (a reservoir of foul, germ-filled waste). At the time, fears that sewage or sewer gas was the culprit in infectious disease were widespread. These fears conflated concerns about bad air and microorganisms; sewage was considered a source not just of "emanations" and foul

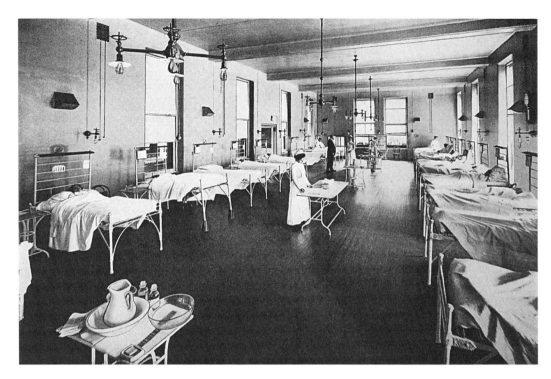

Figure 3.10. Presbyterian Hospital, New York City, view of women's surgical ward, 1903. The electric wires are visible running up the wall from the light fixtures above each bed, and then traveling across the ceiling to the hanging light fixtures in the center of the ward. There were also pull chains hanging from the upper registers to allow the nurse to open or close the ventilation. The oddly shaped wall fixtures were air supply vents.

gases (methane, ammonia, carbon monoxide) but of "microbian organisms of disease" that "[infected] the soil and created 'death-germs.'" This made pipes that contained waste water "biohazards," and faulty plumbing often took the blame for internal incidence of infection. Outbreaks of hospital disease in the 1880s were traced to an obstructed drain at Saint Luke's Hospital in New York City, to rat-damaged sewer pipes at the City Hospital in Boston, and to "sewer" gas (in rooms that had no plumbing) in Bellevue Hospital.[39]

The development of special "hospital" fixtures was an obvious further reaction to this danger. Nancy Tomes has described the growth of "entrepreneurs of the germ"—manufacturers and services that used germ theory to develop and market new items, such as white porcelain toilets or the sanitary trap. The architectural treatment of pipes as contaminated elements within the hospital was a less obvious reaction. Some designers suggested that hollow walls for pipe runs were allowable if the space between the walls could sporadically be filled with an antiseptic or fumigant, thereby rendering it pure. Others, considering fresh air a decontaminant, ventilated the pipes as carefully as they ventilated the wards. Hutton suggested that pipes required "special artificial ventilation separate from the Ward ventilation." The Presbyterian Hospital's pipes occupied separate rooms that were well separated from the wards and independently "ventilated by the suction-ducts." To a lesser extent, air ducts received similar design consideration. Wylie suggested that air ducts be exposed and made of transparent glass, on the grounds that it was impermeable, it allowed sunlight to "purify" the air within the duct, and it made any accumulating contaminating debris visible.[40]

Mechanical Ventilation and the Closed Hospital Environment

With the development of germ theory, "pure" air no longer unequivocally meant "fresh" air; it meant "freedom from, or at least a minimum number of, microscopic germs floating in it." The quality of air supplied by open-window ventilation depended on the quality of the surroundings; mechanical ventilation systems could incorporate particulate filtration or disinfection (typically cloth, mesh screens, or even sheets or sprays of water) to control particulate matter at either air intake or exhaust.[41]

Traditional pavilion-ward design guidelines had advocated natural ventilation as a therapeutic and reformative influence as well as a means of disease prevention. Switching pavilions to mechanical ventilation was thus a socially and politically as well as hygienically determined decision. Taylor provides a detailed account of the nature of the debates over natural and mechanical ventilation in England; the arguments were similar in the United States. Natural ventilation remained common, but a number of late nineteenth-century American hospitals (including the Wesley Hospital in Chicago and the rebuilt Presbyterian Hospital in New York City) included elaborate mechanical ventilation systems. After decades of dogma about fresh air in hospitals, the new controlled ventilation systems, which typically required closed windows for efficient operation, often met with abrupt practical opposition. Stories of ward windows being opened against orders or of inoperable windows being broken to let in fresh air were countered by reports of administrators who locked the windows shut.[42]

Mechanical ventilation systems offered other transformations, including the possibility of making hospitals more compact. Providing a specific minimum air volume per patient remained a crucial aspect of hospital ventilation design; germs even pushed the minimum upward. While 1,200 cubic feet of air per person remained a relatively standard minimum for

Figure 3.11. Royal Victoria Hospital, Belfast, Ireland, view, 1900s. William Henman's design for this building, which abutted each pavilion against the other without any intervening air space, was a radical reinterpretation of hospital design enabled by mechanical ventilation.

ward design, some experts (fearing airborne germs) gave estimates that crept inexorably higher—from two thousand to even four thousand cubic feet per person. If that volume of air had to be provided by open floor space, these upper estimates would have doubled or tripled the size of a ward without increasing the number of patients it could hold. Fan-driven ventilation could provide a requisite cubic air volume by rate of flow, not by size of space. Some hospital designers speculated that mechanical ventilation might lower cubic space requirements in wards by a third. To reduce floor area, however, was to bring the patients into greater physical proximity. Whatever the cubic volume, to prevent patients from rebreathing air, three feet of open space between beds remained a common minimum standard.[43]

Mechanical ventilation systems that relied on closed windows also allowed pavilions to be physically closer without aerial cross-contamination. William Henman's Royal Victoria Hospital in Belfast (1903), which arranged traditional pavilions with no spatial separation (the wards shared long walls) provides the extreme realization of this freedom. A less extreme example of such a compact, mechanically ventilated plan was the original

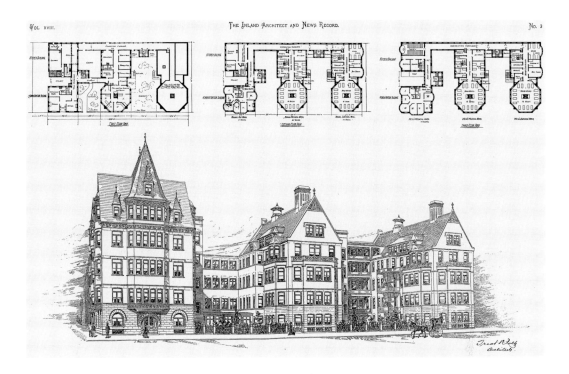

Figure 3.12. Proposed design for Wesley Hospital, Chicago, plans and view, 1894. Although the hospital as built did not include the octagonal wards, this early design envisioned by Treat and Foltz utilized the centralized ward as a means of making a relatively tight urban site functional.

design for the Wesley Hospital in Chicago by architects Treat and Foltz. The hospital being sited on a tight urban lot, in order to prevent the air of one ward from infiltrating the adjacent wards despite their proximity the designers proposed an extensive mechanical ventilation system with closed windows. Theoretically, mechanical ventilation could also enable the superposing of wards in a multistory structure without the danger of air passing vertically from one ward to another.[44]

Mechanical ventilation systems in late nineteenth-century American hospitals were typically combined systems, using both propulsion (fans) to push the air in and extraction (constant suction created by a central chimney) to pull the air out. These systems could offer extensive air purification (for exhaust as well as supply). At the rebuilt Presbyterian Hospital, the central boilers provided hot water for the laundry but also generated the energy needed to run the washing equipment and to operate a "large battery" of steam-driven fans. The supply air could be cleaned and humidified (passed through a sheet of water "cleansing it from all dust and impurities"), warmed (passing it across the boilers), or even cooled (passing

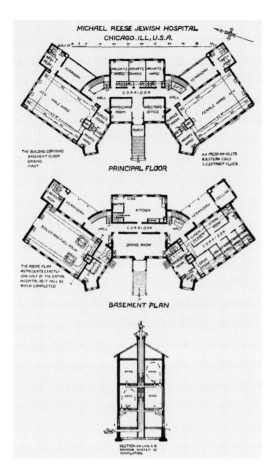

Figure 3.13. Michael Reese Hospital, Chicago, plans and section, 1893. Although the angle of the ward wings was determined by the site, John H. Cochrane used the angles to maximize air flow to the wards. The section reveals the building to be a three-dimensional air flow diagram.

it through a "chilled" sheet of water) before delivery. Specially designed and independently adjustable diffusers in the wards dispersed the flow into the room, making the air motion imperceptible. A tall chimney above the laundry building accommodated the exhaust from the boilers and created a strong suction in numerous exhaust ducts packed around it. The air drawn from "contaminated" areas of the hospital—the isolation building, mortuary, and pathological departments—was passed through "the fires under the steam-boilers" before discharge, thereby disinfecting it.[45] The hospital remained an extensive, self-purifying ventilating machine but it relied on mechanical and induced rather than natural propulsion.

A hospital was also no longer a uniform ventilating structure. Positive ventilation—pumping air into a space—prevented the invasion of unwanted air from other locales of the hospital. Operating suites and wards were positively ventilated. Negative ventilation—drawing air out of a space—prevented any potentially infected air from seeping into other areas of the hospital. Bathrooms, kitchens, isolation facilities, morgues, and laboratories were negatively ventilated. This turned the hospital into a number of separate air spaces, even if those spaces were physically adjacent.

These complex systems could create an internal climate remarkably distinct from the external climate—in air quality, odor, and humidity as well as temperature. After his visit to the rebuilt Presbyterian Hospital, a journalist noted, "To a visitor in the hospital the equitable temperature and the freshness and stillness of the air are very noticeable. Even in wintry weather the patients live in the atmosphere of a mild and gentle Summer's day." According to Dr. Morrill Wyman, the new climatic controls also created the possibility of tailoring a room's conditions, including heat or humidity, to the needs of the patients inhabiting it. Surrounding a bed with a cool atmosphere (as was done for dying President Garfield in 1881 by blowing air over cloths saturated with melted ice water) was one of the earliest examples of this. At the Johns Hopkins Hospital, the heating and ventilation system was reportedly sufficiently elaborate to make it possible "to give one pair of beds a temperature of 70° and another pair in the same room at a little distance a temperature of 60° Fahrenheit, to suit the needs of the different cases."[46]

Mechanical ventilation was not an unmitigated success, however. It was expensive, requiring extensive equipment, miles of ducts, intelligent management by an engineer, and a constant fuel supply. That the blossoming of fan ventilation largely coincided with the development of electricity was no coincidence. Inducing air movement remained an inexact science; debates over the benefits of pushing or pulling the air or whether upward flow was better than downward continued. Many mechanical system designers hedged their bets and installed registers at floor, midway up a wall, and at ceiling. Many systems did not perform as hoped. In the New York Hospital, the forced-air heat of the elaborate ventilation system proved insufficient for the coldest days of the winter, and several rooms (notedly the morgue, autopsy room, and water closets) developed stuffiness or retained odors. The hospital governors regularly asked George B. Post, the architect, to explain the failures and provide solutions.[47] Some administrators of hospitals with unsuccessful mechanical ventilation systems simply turned off the fans and opened the windows.

Facility Layouts: Reasons for and against Pavilions

The vast majority of general hospitals built in the 1880s and 1890s in the United States still followed basic pavilion-ward guidelines, but not to the same degree of conformity as in the 1860s and 1870s.[48] In addition to the design changes wrought by new medical theories, aspects of pavilion-ward design were becoming economically unsustainable. At a time of increasing urban real estate prices, maintaining separate pavilions maximized the size of the site required and the overall construction costs for a given amount of interior space. Extensive connecting corridors between pavilions bloated the amount of enclosed floor area without providing programmable space. The decentralized footprint created internal spatial redundancies, required a large staff for simple maintenance and operation, and required extensive runs for the building systems and technologies (plumbing, ventilation, heating, and electricity) between buildings.

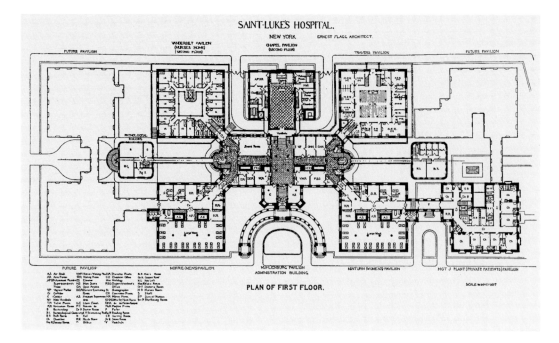

Figure 3.14. Saint Luke's Hospital, New York City, first-floor plan, 1897.

Over the course of the late nineteenth century this costliness compressed American hospital facilities. Whereas hospital administrators of the 1860s had boasted of eighty to one hundred feet of open space between pavilions, by the 1890s there was only sixty feet of space between the pavilions of Saint Luke's Free Hospital in Chicago and only forty feet at Wesley Hospital in Chicago. At the new buildings of Saint Luke's Hospital in New York City, the pavilions and administration building were separated by a roughly ten-foot "open air" knuckle at the corners of the wards.

This compression coincided with a functional shift in hospital practice. In the 1860s and 1870s pavilions in a general hospital had all typically followed the same basic layout—a large open ward with services. Each pavilion functioned as an independent hospital. Patients largely remained in their assigned wards, even for treatment and minor surgeries; doctors and nurses for the most part spent their time within the wards in which their assigned patients were housed. Within those independent ward pavilions, hospitals offered unspecialized care to a broad variety of patients with a wide variety of ailments in large, general wards. In contrast, by the late 1890s general hospitals included pavilions with a variety of layouts, each potentially housing a specific patient category, medical service, or support facility. Special patient and ward categories had increased—including obstetrics, gynecology, pediatrics, nervous diseases, urology, laryngology, otology, ophthalmology, orthopedics, dermatology, and contagious diseases. There were even special wards for new treatments, like Koch's lymph treatment for tuberculosis. Housing a single medical category of patients within a specially designed pavilion not only improved the care offered to that given patient category, it increased the knowledge the physician (and students) could gain from treating and studying the patient group.[49]

These specialized pavilions might include special equipment and specially designed spaces for treatments and unusual patient needs. Rather than one general lying-in ward, maternity departments (like the Hahnemann Hospital in New York City) often included a number of smaller wards and rooms—separating patients by their social class, their degree of infectivity, and their progress in birth (labor, delivery, and postdelivery rooms). Some special wards, like the Roosevelt Hospital's obstetric service, or the Massachusetts General Hospital's Bradlee Ward (designed to provide aseptic care and surgery for patients requiring abdominal or brain surgery) included their own devoted operating facilities. The new Babies' Wards of the Post-Graduate Hospital in New York City included a proprietary operating room, but also a roof garden, sunbeam parlor, space for mothers, and a baby incubator.[50]

Transformation of basic hospital practices also increased the number and complexity of non-ward pavilions required for hospital service. In the 1870s a minimal hospital required large wards, offices, a kitchen, laundry, morgue, pharmacy, staff housing, and perhaps a small operating room. Two decades later, in addition to those spaces even minimal hospitals included dispensaries, extensive surgical facilities, medical departments, therapeutic facilities, examination rooms, laboratories, classrooms, nurse training schools, smaller wards, isolation facilities, and private patient rooms. A number of these spaces required ponderous equipment, or accommodated complicated procedures that required specific room layouts for efficient performance.

These differentiated pavilions could not operate autonomously; they were distinct pieces of a larger, increasingly coordinated whole. Patients, nurses, and doctors as well as staff regularly traveled from one pavilion to another as part of their care and treatment. This supported a new kind of hospital service, offering general care by providing access to a variety of specialized practitioners, spaces, and equipment.

This transformation was not discernible from the general hospital's exterior. Despite the increasing variation in the design of individual pavilions, many hospitals continued to present uniform facades. Ernest Flagg's design for the new Saint Luke's Hospital in New York City projected twelve separate pavilions—two ward buildings, two private patient buildings, a nurses'

Figure 3.15. Saint Luke's Hospital, New York City, exterior view, 1917.

home, a chapel/medical building, a laboratory/medical building, an administration building, and three "future" buildings. Though interior floor plans of each pavilion type varied, and though the buildings to the north held more stories than those to the south, each of the main pavilions filled the same building footprint, occupied the same basic building envelope, and presented a uniform facade to the street.

The construction of medically specialized hospitals, which experienced tremendous growth in the late nineteenth century, was far more revealing of these internal transformations. Whether they offered service to specific types of patients (maternity hospitals, children's hospitals, etc.), to patients with specific ailments (orthopedic patients, eye and ear patients), or to patients and practitioners excluded from general hospitals (chronic disease patients, cancer patients, syphilitics, homeopathists), these institutions offered a flexible and focused medical and spatial alternative to the standardized general hospitals. British hospital expert Henry Burdett considered the growth of special hospitals a sign of "the shortsightedness and conservatism of the authorities of the larger general institutions, who failed to establish special departments until their hands were forced from outside."[51]

By the 1880s and 1890s it was expected that each independent specialty would develop "a building especially constructed to meet [its] particular needs." According to Frederic J. Mouat and H. Saxon Snell, consumptive

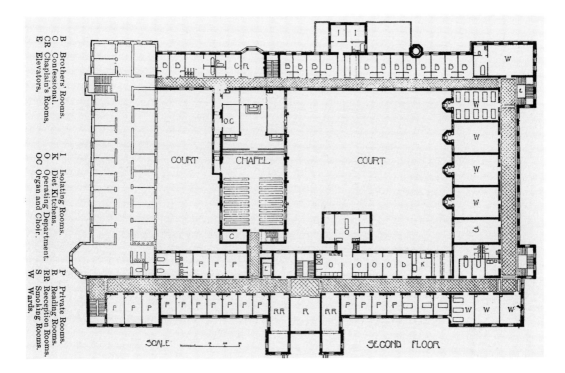

Figure 3.16. Alexian Brothers Hospital, Chicago, plan, 1896. This building was one of Richard E. Schmidt's first hospital designs. Schmidt would go on to become a prominent hospital architect, both in individual practice and then in partnerships. The hospital's unique layout accommodated a wing for separate rooms for private patients, a wing for small wards, and a wing for the brothers and their chapel.

hospitals required "the careful regulation of temperature and artificial means of purifying the air of the wards"; eye wards required "the proper regulation of the light"; and skin disease hospitals required "a complete system of balneological arrangements." These refinements could meet special social as well as medical needs; for example, the cloistered layout and smaller wards of the Alexian Brothers Hospital in Chicago, which was run by a religious order of brothers, suited the religious as well as medical requirements of the hospital. Specialized medical hospitals often rose to more stories than general hospitals, were more likely to occupy a single integrated building rather than a group of pavilions, were often located on smaller sites in the built-up downtown rather than the outskirts, and were more likely to have extensive special equipment or facilities to care for the patients. Of hospitals rising above three stories in height or occupying only one integrated building in this period, a majority were specialized hospitals.[52]

In essence, by catering to only one "category" of patients, specialized hospitals avoided some of the hygienic requirements of pavilion hospital

Figure 3.17. Post-Graduate Hospital, New York City, exterior view, 1890s.

design (that were intended to prevent cross-infections). This becomes clear in the varying critical reactions to tall hospital buildings. Taller general hospitals, such as the New York Hospital and Saint Thomas's Hospital in London (at six and seven stories, respectively), were regularly brought up as negative models of hospital construction. Mouat admired the details of the New York Hospital's design, but refused to reproduce its plans, because he was "satisfied that many-storied hospitals are, and should remain, things of the past." The taller, single-building facilities of specialized institutions did not receive the same criticism. The Hahnemann Hospital in Chicago (seven stories) was depicted in the *American Architect and Building News* as a positive model. Reports that the Post-Graduate Hospital was the tallest hospital in the country made its existence a well-known, and yet uncriticized, fact.[53]

Pieces of the Departmentalized Hospital

To reveal the "invisible" transformation occurring in pavilion hospitals, this section will examine the increasingly varied pieces (dispensaries, sur-

gical facilities, laboratories, nursing spaces, private patient rooms, and specialty wards) of the larger whole.

Medical Spaces in the Hospital

Spaces devoted to medical purposes increased drastically in late nineteenth-century hospitals as dispensaries became crucial elements of hospital practice, surgical suites increased in size and importance, and laboratories became essential adjuncts of both clinical medicine and medical
research.

Dispensaries and Outpatient Departments

Dispensaries were an essential piece of the new general hospital, providing a
large amount of medical care at a small cost to patients, a voluminous experience in treating routine ailments to medical students, and a steady supply
of patients to hospital beds. Dispensaries were also the spatial embodiment
of transformed admission procedures. In the early nineteenth century,
admission to a hospital could involve personal recommendations, personal
interviews by the governors or administrators, and a medical examination,
all of which typically took place somewhere in the administration building.
By the end of the century, medical assessments were increasingly dominant
in admission procedures and they occurred in the dispensary as often as in
the "admission" facilities of the administration building

The dispensary was not, however, a completely medicalized practice:
social assessment of patients persisted. A dispensary had to accommodate
persons with an extreme variety of ailments from a wide variety of cultures,
nations, backgrounds, and classes. As one hospital visitor noted, in the dispensary the patients "appear in their natural state; they are not arrayed in
white gowns and neatly covered with white spreads. They are in all possible
costumes and suffering from all possible complaints, real and imaginary."
In this environment, dispensary practitioners could make broad assessments not just of a patient's symptoms but of their lifestyle, habits, and even
ability to pay.[54]

This variety of visitors with a variety of ailments made dispensaries
a possible reservoir of infection in the larger hospital, and that made
separation from the rest of the hospital crucial. According to Henry
D. Noyes of the New York Eye and Ear Infirmary, the dispensary department could "communicate in the freest manner with the upper portion of the building." He worried about uncontrolled movement of air
and microbes: "How is it possible to maintain effective antisepsis under

these conditions? Up the staircase and through open doors, propelled by out-door currents and by the hot-air furnaces passes into the wards the germ-laden air which we are most anxious to exclude." At Saint Luke's Hospital in Chicago, the ground-floor dispensary was designed with a separate entrance, "making it impossible for patients while there to stroll about the hospital corridors."[55] To effect the necessary separation, dispensaries were often separate buildings, or, if they were part of a mixed-use building, strongly partitioned off from the surrounding spaces, with little to no direct communication with the rest of the building.

In many dispensaries, examinations and even treatments continued to occur in a single large waiting room. "Those who wait, witness the proceedings which occur to every one whom the surgeons treat. That the sights are always trying, are sometimes distressing or even revolting, cannot be avoided." The desire to lessen this distress and maximize the efficiency of treatment and diagnosis inspired more complicated dispensary plans, with more numerous enclosed cubicles. The new Loeb Dispensary of the Jewish Hospital in Philadelphia included a one-and-a-half-story building with a patient waiting room, a physician's room, an apothecary's room, three chambers, and a bathroom. The Vanderbilt Clinic in New York City—adjacent and connected to the College of Physicians and Surgeons and across the street from the Roosevelt Hospital—opened in 1888 in an elaborate building that held laboratories as well as multiple waiting rooms, examination rooms, and treatment rooms. By the 1890s dispensaries like the new, three-story one at Boston City Hospital, might also accommodate multiple medical specialties in spatially distinct facilities. The new dispensary of Saint Luke's Hospital in New York City included "a large waiting-room, four general examining rooms, a gynaecological examining-room, operating-room for slight cases, special room for the treatment of eye, ear, and throat cases, rooms for medicated air, and the general drug-room of the hospital."[56]

As a broad public interface, dispensaries at times received significant aesthetic attention. The directors of the German Hospital in New York City described their new dispensary building in 1884 as "an artistically perfect specimen of the early Italian Renaissance." J. Cleveland Cady's design for the Presbyterian Hospital's Dispensary gained attention from architects as well as medical practitioners as an elegant solution to the problem of a new building type. Cady had patterned its design loosely after a church. The central waiting room functioned as the nave and the smaller examination and treatment rooms running along the sides equated to chapels. The adjacent ventilation tower aided this aesthetic imagery.[57]

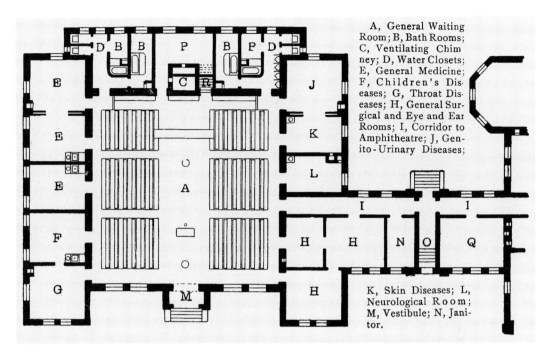

A, General Waiting Room; B, Bath Rooms; C, Ventilating Chimney; D, Water Closets; E, General Medicine; F, Children's Diseases; G, Throat Diseases; H, General Surgical and Eye and Ear Rooms; I, Corridor to Amphitheatre; J, Genito-Urinary Diseases;

K, Skin Diseases; L, Neurological Room; M, Vestibule; N, Janitor.

Figure 3.18. Johns Hopkins Hospital, New York City, plan of outpatient building, 1891. This outpatient building included separate examining rooms for specific categories of ailment. That it also had a direct connection to the amphitheater reveals the critical role of dispensary patients as clinical material for medical education. The enormous ventilating chimney drew the air out of the large, general waiting room as well as the separate clinic rooms.

Figure 3.19. Presbyterian Hospital, New York City, outpatient waiting room, 1904. Though the examination rooms provided a modicum of privacy during diagnosis and treatment, the outpatient building remained a collection of persons of all social strata.

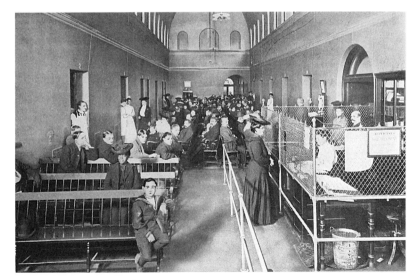

From Rooms to Suites: To Live and Die by the Operating Room

The design of late nineteenth-century operating rooms was drastically influenced by two interrelated developments—aseptic technique and the transformation of surgery in the hospital to a treatment of choice rather than desperation.

In their study of operating rooms as locations of "control," Annmarie Adams and Thomas Schlich have described three stages of early twentieth-century operating room development: the Victorian operating theater, 1893–1916 (modeled after amphitheaters); the interwar surgical suite, 1916–1955 (modeled after classrooms); and the postwar operating room after 1955 (modeled after the laboratory). Their criteria were based on material aspects of the surgical space: size of operating room, number of operating rooms, number of observers accommodated, natural or artificial lighting, integration into a larger building, and separation from direct exterior access).[58] This is a useful categorization of the architectural changes occurring in the design of surgical spaces, but it is based on the facilities of a single hospital—the Royal Victoria Hospital in Montreal.

The history of US hospitals poses a number of challenges to this schema. Based on US designs, the Victorian operating theater's heyday was roughly from 1860 to the mid-1880s, and prominent elements of the interwar surgical suite were already evident by the 1890s. Rather than argue the exact chronology between the stages, or the exact material criteria separating the stages, I will try to expand Adams and Schlich's discussion to include the changing materials and material design acceptable for surgical spaces, a consideration of the interaction of architectural design and the permissible circulation of objects and people within the surgical suite, and an examination of the entire surgical suite (including service spaces and adjunct spaces), not just the space of surgery itself.

Schlich has discussed doctors' strategies to expand the controlled conditions of the laboratory into the operating room as a prime influence on early "aseptic" operating rooms. The desire to make the operating room sterile was impeded by the difficulties inherent in "sterilizing" architectural features—such as floors, walls, and ceilings—that could not easily be boiled, exposed to extreme heat or open flames, or exposed to caustic chemicals for long periods.[59] The inherently "contaminated" state of the patient, of observers, of participants, and even of equipment and supplies posed a further complication. To create aseptic conditions, operating room designers of the late nineteenth century had to eliminate any germs within the operating space and then prevent the further admission of any other germs. Architectural design could facilitate both tasks.

Although "aseptic" materials and finishes were used throughout hospitals, they were inescapable in the operating room. Impermeable materials made it difficult for germs to lodge on or reside in the architecture, but they did not, in and of themselves, make the operating room "germ-free." Designers of operating rooms in Europe and in the United States in the late nineteenth century tried to create rooms that could be sterilized—the building surfaces exposed to steam, or cleaned with caustic chemicals and then hosed down. To this end, the American practitioners followed the examples of German and Austrian hospitals, like Dr. Albin Eder's private sanatorium in Vienna, which included an operating room with steam piping "by which in five minutes the room can be thoroughly disinfected with live steam." The new "septic" operating room of the Walter Garrett Memorial Buildings of the Pennsylvania Hospital in Philadelphia could be turned into a room-sized autoclave. It was "lined throughout with hydraulic cement, and has doors and windows of such character as will permit it to be filled with live steam at a slight pressure." After operations on septic patients (surgical patients who already had an infection or an infected wound), everything remained in the room while "by means of perforated pipes the room [was] sprayed and filled with steam."[60]

This was an unusually thorough aseptic strategy. American hospitals were more likely to include operating room features that enabled them to be hosed down. The much-admired McLane Operating Room for gynecological patients in the Roosevelt Hospital had a "floor of mosaic tile, sloping to the centre, where there is a trap to catch the drainage and keep it perfectly dry." It was noted that the floor had to be completely waterproof and well sloped, and that the drain had to be perfectly trapped and covered when not in use.[61] The impermeable, smooth, featureless aseptic materials and finishes facilitated this cleansing method.

Once an operating room was rendered sterile, preventing the further entrance of "infected" items or persons was critical to maintaining asepsis. This meant that septic patients posed an extreme danger to the aseptic condition of the operating room. German doctor Gustav Adolf Neubuhr's practice of assigning a specific operating room for use on septic cases was influential in American operating suite design.[62] The Syms Operating Building, the new surgical building at the Presbyterian Hospital in New York City, and the new operating suite of the Walter Garrett Memorial Buildings of the Pennsylvania Hospital in Philadelphia each included an operating room assigned to special or septic cases. Similarly, specific "clean" or "aseptic" operating rooms were often reserved for use with patients with no infections and for procedures that opened no "dangerous" cavities.

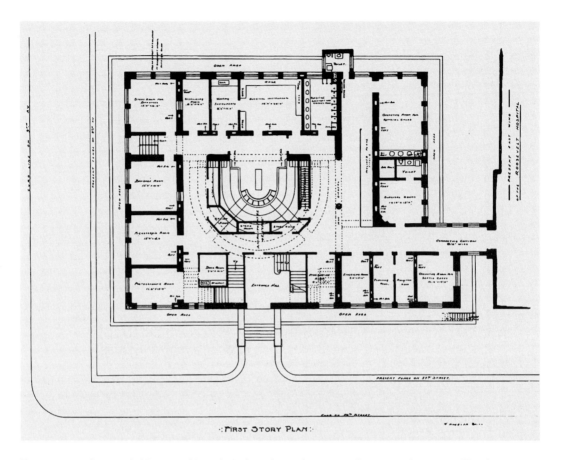

Figure 3.20. Roosevelt Hospital, New York City, Syms Operating Building, plan, 1893. The facility had its own X-ray, laboratory, and microscopy room. Postoperative recovery rooms were on an upper floor, accessible by a long inclined plane. Entrance to the theater seating was from the upper floors, keeping the audience separate from the surgical space. Despite the size and complexity of the facility it held only four operating spaces (the theater, the septic operating room, the special case operating room, and the surgical room).

The provision of facilities for decontamination at the entrance to operating suites prevented the ingress of germs. Special knee-lever- or foot-pedal-operated sinks allowed the surgeons to turn off the water while keeping their hands aseptically clean. The wearing of special garb for operations (like the "antiseptic linen suits" doctors and staff wore at the Syms Operating Theater) was a means of preventing the transport of germs on "street clothes" but it also served as visible proof that the surgeon had, indeed, performed some decontamination before entering the operating room.[63]

These spaces, and the increasingly complicated aseptic presurgical routines they contained (scrubbing, gowning up, and preparing the surgeon and attendants; sterilizing the instruments and supplies; and etherizing and prepping the patient), often were housed in complex spatial sequences. Each item or person that traveled into the operating room had to follow a path that included decontamination and prevented any further contamination afterward. That meant the creation of a separate circulation path for each group of persons or objects within the operating room based on its status as infected or clean. Architectural design—particularly the locations of doors, hallways, and disinfection facilities—could subtly (or not so subtly) encourage movement patterns that would prevent cross-contamination. For example, in the McLane Operating Room of the Roosevelt Hospital, participants in the operation (doctors, attendants, patients) entered through the preparation and etherizing room (fig. 3.21, E). The surgeon and attendants passed into the surgeon's

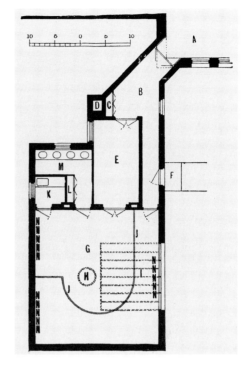

Figure 3.21. Roosevelt Hospital, New York City, McLane Operating Room, plan, 1891.

scrub room and changing room (M and L) and the nurse passed into the sterilizing and prep room, which held the sterile supplies and instruments (K). Students and observers entered through the separate exterior entrance (F) into the operating room without crossing paths with the participants in surgery.

In the 1890s this aseptic spatial choreography was in its infancy, with many breaks in routine and chances for cross-contamination. For example, at the lower floor of the surgical building of the Presbyterian Hospital in New York City, a single elevator provided access for patients before and after surgery, for gowned and ungowned doctors, for gowned and ungowned nurses, and for any other requisite staff. While an amphitheater might have a separate entrance sequence for audience members and participants, the actual separation between audience and operating field might be minimal. A brass rail was all that separated observers from participants in the McLane Operating Room. The Syms Operating Theater could seat 184 students in bleachers that were "so steep that the rear seats are but 28 feet away from the operating table." While there was a steady decrease in the size of audiences, the inclusion of such spectators in the operating room itself

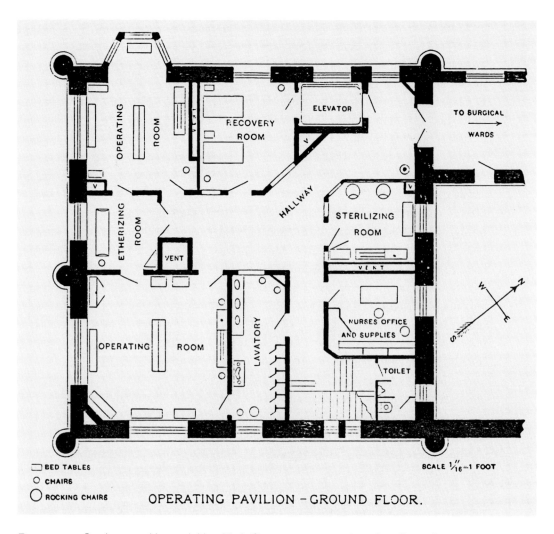

Figure 3.22. Presbyterian Hospital, New York City, operating pavilion, first-floor plan, 1900.

continued until the twentieth century. Gustav Adolf Neubuhr banished spectators from all but the largest of his five operating rooms.[64]

Operating room design was also influenced by the increasing prominence of surgery in the hospital. Just as anesthesia had transformed surgical practices in the 1840s, antisepsis and asepsis changed the frequency, duration, and kind of surgeries being performed. According to Dr. Robert F. Weir, antiseptic treatment "led rapidly to daring boldness of work with such phenomenal success as to astonish everyone. The scalpel and the saw invaded parts of the body hitherto forbidden them." To accommodate the increasing number and complexity of procedures required far more than a single operating amphitheater or room. The directors of the Presbyterian

Hospital in New York City in 1891 boasted that their facility had "almost countless operating rooms" (it had three). In 1893 an addition to the Pennsylvania Hospital in Philadelphia included six new operating rooms. Any given late nineteenth-century hospital might include numerous operating rooms, ranging in size from amphitheaters to small rooms.[65]

In the most up-to-date facilities, operating rooms were often grouped into surgical departments rather than scattered across the hospital. These would often include different sizes and kinds of operating rooms, to accommodate different kinds of patients and procedures. Typically, routine procedures were performed in the smaller, more basically appointed operating rooms; experimental, challenging, or rare procedures were best when performed in the amphitheater or larger operating room, to a larger audience. In Bellevue, the procedure for the daily surgical clinics included preparing all the patients in small operating rooms (closer to the wards). The routine procedures would then be performed in the same small rooms (with the surgeon and ten to twenty students crowded into it). "If, however, the operation is a major operation, the patient is transferred to the Crane operating room on the amphitheater floor" where there were "special provisions for difficult operations" as well as space for more observers.[66]

No matter how rigorously designed, however, the aseptic surgical suite was never a completely technically, practically derived set of spaces. Aseptic details and requirements interacted with social and cultural influences. In the words of Surgeon General Hamilton, an operating room could indeed be "beautiful enough to make one wish to be its inmate." The better-appointed the surgical facility, the more likely the hospital was to attract a wide variety of surgical patients, including those able to pay. The directors of the Roosevelt Hospital expected that the Syms Operating Theater not only would attract "the attention of the medical world," it would attract more patients, particularly paying patients. Immediately after the operating theater opened, the hospital directors had to turn away numerous applicants for surgery simply because the wards and private rooms were full.[67]

While lavish surgical facilities might attract private patients, preferred practices left surgical patients with no conscious memory of the operating room. The superintendent of the Roosevelt Hospital in New York City noted that their surgical patients "have no idea what an operating room is like, and we always take pains to keep it from their sight."[68] Such "amnesia" required the administration of anesthesia and postoperative care in a room other than the operating room. Late nineteenth-century surgical suites regularly included etherizing and recovery rooms nearby or adjacent to the operating room itself. In the Syms Operating Theater these rooms were on the second floor, with ramp access; in the Memorial Wards at the Pennsylvania Hospital, they were on the first floor and the surgical amphitheater was on the floor above. The availability of preoperative and postoperative rooms allowed the maximum scheduling use of the operating room itself, as the "operation" became limited to the time of medical intervention.

Charles Rosenberg observes that the hospital played a role in creating elite medical practitioners, and hospital appointments in the more prominent hospitals were competitively sought. In the 1880s and 1890s a well-appointed surgical suite also attracted eminent practitioners to the hospital's ranks and encouraged more and more daring surgeries. Directors of the J. Hood Wright Hospital in New York City noted a 50 percent increase in surgeries after they simply renovated and refurbished their operating room. In 1894, after remodeling their operating room, the directors of Hahnemann Hospital trumpeted that "the improved facilities of the operating room have enabled our surgeons to perform operations not only of the most difficult nature, but also, in one case at least, to successfully accomplish an operation and secure immediate relief in one of the most intricate cases known to modern surgery, unequaled in any other hospital, if not of a nature unheard of before." Some even speculated that the quality of the operating room facility exercised "a reflex influence upon the surgeon himself."[69] The better the operating facility, it was thought, the better behaved and more careful the doctors were.

Conversely, a poor surgical facility could limit the number and kinds of surgeries undertaken, as doctors, hospital directors, and the public continued to attribute poor patient outcomes to poor operating room conditions. In 1882, despite protests from the doctors, the directors of the Mount Sinai Hospital in New York City outlawed ovariotomies in their facility after a number of poor outcomes that were blamed on their out-of-date surgical facilities. Institutions with inadequate facilities could even draw public censure. The Long Island College Hospital came under serious scrutiny in 1895 when some unsavory details of its antiquated operating theater (absorptive wood finishes and bleachers, stained walls and ceilings, and foul air) came to light. In particular, the comment that the dissecting room overhead filled the operating theater with the "acrid, rancid smell of dissecting room cadavers" caused a ruckus. Upon his return from Germany in 1884, Dr. William Halsted refused to operate "in the tainted old theater at Bellevue." Instead, he erected on the grounds a tent "that featured a hardwood flooring 'laid as fine as any bowling alley,' and was equipped with a gas stove on which to boil instruments." Dr. Robert Roberts requested a similar facility for the run-down City Hospital in New York City in 1886.[70]

The Critical Necessity of Diagnostic and Research Laboratories

Until the 1870s, medical laboratories were largely postmortem research spaces, well separated from the wards and often adjacent to or part of the pathological facilities. Thereafter, doctors across the country used labs to identify microorganisms—both for research and for clinical diagnosis. By 1896 William H. Welch of Johns Hopkins and T. Mitchell Prudden of Columbia University imparted to the governors of Saint Luke's Hospital in New York City "a growing conviction that there is nothing more important connected with hospital work than pathological research by scientists of first rank, devoting their whole time to the subject, in a building constructed for the purpose, furnished with the best equipment that can be produced."[71] Along with this conviction came a mad scramble—at first simply to find space (any space) for labs within the hospital, later to determine where in the hospital labs belonged, and in what kind of facility.

In basic architectural terms, laboratories needed "a well-lighted room, which can be kept moderately free from dust" with access to facilities for animal care. Where to put the lab depended on its intended role in the hospital. In medical research, doctors studied pathological material (the bodies or tissue samples from dead or moribund patients) to research microorganisms and the physiological responses they engendered. Research labs benefited from proximity to the morgue and the operating room (for easy delivery of specimens for study), but needed to be distant from other parts of the hospital in order to minimize the nuisance of odors and the potential for cross-contamination. Research-focused labs, like the lab added above the postmortem room of the City Hospital in Boston in 1894, were thus often placed near the morgue or dead house.[72] In clinical diagnosis, on the other hand, doctors and technicians examined samples taken from living patients to correctly diagnose contagious ailments. Clinical labs therefore benefited from proximity to wards and to operating rooms. Separate clinical labs were rare in the late nineteenth century, but not unheard of. The addition in 1893 of a lab "for the proper examination of living and dead tissues to enable the visiting staff to make their diagnosis complete and thus secure a more thorough treatment of disease" to the Mount Sinai Hospital in New York City is one example.[73] Many hospitals included only one lab that functioned for both research and clinical needs. Any available space in the hospital—whether the small isolation rooms off larger wards or unused offices or storerooms in the basement or other service facilities—might be turned into laboratories.

Given the critical importance of research labs to medical advancement and education, a number of large, elaborate research-focused laboratory facilities were built in this period. In 1884, Andrew Carnegie made a large donation to Bellevue Hospital Medical College for the development of laboratories well equipped enough to keep the talented students in town rather than traveling to the European clinics to finish their education. The resultant Carnegie Laboratory was five floors high, well ventilated, and equipped with state-of-the-art instruments. The new building of the Harvard Medical School in Boston, designed by Ware and Van Brunt, also included extensive laboratory space.[74] Tensions could develop, however, when hospital money (particularly public money) went to future-oriented pure research rather than patient-oriented facilities. In 1892 the directors of the City Hospital in New York City, with an outdated, drastically over-crowded ward building and abysmal surgical facilities, built the elaborate Strecker Memorial Laboratory Building. It contained an autopsy room, morgue, blood bank laboratory, animal house, chemical lab, and serological lab. This addition led Dr. F. H. Wiggins to comment that "we treat a patient all right when he is dead, but the accommodations for the living are awful."[75]

Making Room for a New Kind of Nurse

By the late nineteenth century, nurse training schools were ubiquitous in American hospitals. As well as being an active engine for professionalization, they provided hospitals with cheap labor in the form of nurse trainees, and when these trainees were hired out as professional nurses, could even generate income. The establishment of professional nursing and nurse training schools required new spaces in the hospital, however, particularly improved nurse housing, facilities for nurse education, and a nurses' office in or adjacent to the wards.[76] The status of nurses within a hospital could be read in how these needs were or were not met.

Before the 1870s nurses were housed with the hospital service staff (typically in attics, basements, or unused wards) or occasionally in bedrooms immediately off the wards. Both locations were spatially marginal and subservient. After the 1870s and the movement to professionalize nursing, nurses' rooms were increasingly separated from other staff housing and from the active wards. According to the directors of the Bellevue Hospital Nurse Training School (the first such school in the United States), nurse housing was to be "not a mere lodging, but a comfortable home, where, after their daily labors, they may find relaxation and rest, free from the depressing influences of the hospital." A separate building provided professional autonomy but also "a complete removal from hospital surroundings when off duty," which was considered essential to the health and well-being of the nurses and nurse trainees who were constantly exposed to germs and often on duty for twelve-hour shifts.[77]

The ideal in the 1880s and 1890s was a separate, purpose-designed nurses' building, which both consolidated the nurses in their own space (giving them a sense of professional identity within the hospital) and attracted better candidates. The pleasantness of the nurses' housing was seen as both a reward for the long hours of work and an enticement; "many, who have so far hesitated to devote their services to the sick, will be encouraged by these improved conditions to follow the example of those who have already taken to this noble work."[78]

While a separate nurses' building was appealing, many hospitals lacked either the funds or the space to build one. Nurses and trainees were often housed in repurposed wards or in private rooms, which reduced the available space for patients and limited nurses' ability to develop an autonomous professional identity. For hospitals with residential surroundings (the New England Hospital for Women and Children outside Boston, and Saint Vincent's Hospital and the New York Hospital in New York City, for example) renting, leasing, or purchasing nearby houses and turning them into nurse housing was a relatively cheap and acceptable solution that provided nurses an identifiable space of their own. Many hospital building committees added more nurses' rooms to any and every addition. This mixed-use approach could lead to some unhappy adjacencies. Nurses' rooms were shoehorned into the upper floors of dispensary buildings, private patient buildings, administration buildings, even laboratory buildings. In 1883 the New York Hospital governors commented on "the unpleasant odors which necessarily prevail to some extent on the nurses floor" because of the proximity of the lab.[79] They soon built a separate building just for the nurses in order to remedy the problem.

The provision of a ward office for nurses varied greatly, but its inclusion depended as much on the local status of nurses as on available space and funds. In her plan for an ideal ward, Florence Nightingale gave the supervising nurse a separate room—typically at one of the short ends of the ward—with a window that provided a commanding view down its length. Such a space put the nurse in a position of control over the ward, and founders of the early professional nursing programs saw offices as necessary. Upon the establishment of the Bellevue Hospital Nurse Training School, its directors demanded basic repairs and hygienic alterations in the wards that included the addition of a nurses' room. Other hospital designers followed this example; wards in the San Francisco Marine Hospital included a nurses' room in the ward with a supervisory window "which commands a view of its entire length."[80]

Figure 3.23. New York Hospital, New York City, nurses' home building, 1890s. Although this building was primarily for a nurses' home, given the crowded site the building also included a rooftop isolation facility (visible at the rear roof of the building) for patients with contagious diseases.

Some prominent practitioners were less convinced of the necessity. John R. Niernsee noted that the nurses' room as an adjunct to a ward was "an undecided question as to its use or necessity." According to Billings, the nurse's duties were "to be performed in the ward itself. I consider that to be her room, the absence of which is complained of, and while on duty, her place for rest is in the middle of it." In keeping with this view, some hospital designers simply provided a desk and chair in the central aisle of the ward itself. In truth, nurses and nursing students rarely had time to sit down at a desk, whether it was in the ward or in an office. Nurses' offices were considered luxuries. Even in hospital buildings designed with nurses' offices, the rooms were often repurposed. At the New York Hospital in 1891, the "room formerly occupied by the nurse on duty at night" was turned into a room for "any patient that may need temporary isolation."[81] The lack of official nursing space placed the nurse in a more subservient position—making her an adjunct rather than overseer of the ward.

Ward Design: Germs, Class, and the Challenges of Aggregating Patients

In essentials—windows, cubic volume, openness, and arrangement—the design of the large ward itself remained consistent throughout the last three decades of the nineteenth century. The ward pavilion of the late nineteenth century, however, was recognizably different from that of the midcentury, and not just in the inclusion of aseptic materials. Refinements in ward orientation; changes in the number, location, and arrangement of adjacent ward service areas; and alternate ward shapes and sizes all served to emphasize different aspects of a healthy ward.

Island Wards, Head Houses, and Centralized Wards

By the 1890s sunlight was considered not just a positive influence on patient health but a purifying force on the ward's architectural materials. Experiments showed that sunlight (the ultraviolet radiation in particular) was germicidal. Hospital designers tried to harness this benefit by maximizing sunshine exposure on walls, floors, and building materials. This made a room's solar orientation critical to its hygienic performance. Florence Nightingale had favored wards running east to west to maximize the southern exposure along one of the long walls, and had recommended locating sanitary facilities (toilets, baths, etc.) in projections off one short end wall. In the 1880s and 1890s American hospital designers more regularly opted for a north-south orientation so that "every day of the year in which the sun shines, at least three walls of a rectangular ward will be bathed in sunshine." The design of the rectangular wards of the Johns Hopkins Hospital, which maximized sunlight by leaving the short, south-facing wall open to light and air for a solarium, proved particularly influential.[82]

Niernsee and Billings also recommended the strategy developed by Dr. Stephen Smith in his submission for the Johns Hopkins Hospital, of relocating all the service spaces to a separate structure.[83] This separated ward pavilions into two distinct components—the "island" ward itself and the detached clusters of service spaces, called the "head house." The separation of ward from services provided greater design freedom for both components. The service spaces could be arranged for functional requirements, could accommodate the increasing number of services required for hospital care, and could allow a more compact footprint, unlimited by the

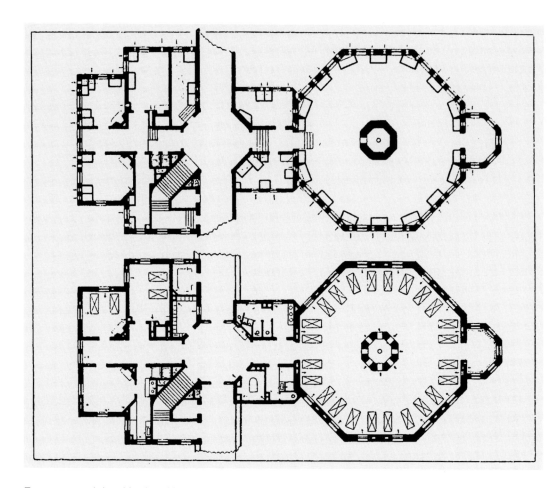

Figure 3.24. Johns Hopkins Hospital, Baltimore, plan of Octagon Ward, 1890s.

ward width. Nightingale's ideal ward of 1859 had included only four accessory ward spaces: toilets, bath, nurses' room, and scullery. Three decades later, head houses in American hospitals regularly included a few "quiet" or "separation" wards (for one or two beds), diet kitchens (with cooking facilities, serving areas, and even convalescent patient dining rooms), linen rooms, patient clothing storage areas, and occasionally examination rooms or small surgical facilities.

Detached head houses also facilitated experiments in novel ward layouts. Centralized wards were the most common variant of the 1880s and 1890s. Jeremy Taylor has discussed in depth the development of the circular ward in Europe, pointing out that circular wards often fit on constricted sites and provided architects an element of design that was not predetermined by pavilion-ward mandates, offering a chance for innovation and aesthetic treatment. Centralized wards offered improved ventilation by eliminating cross-

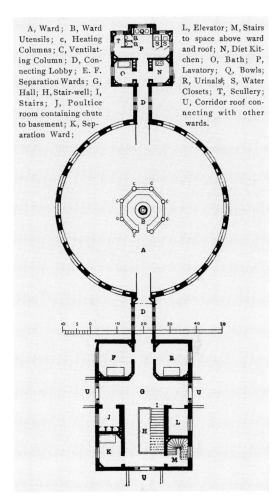

A, Ward ; B, Ward Utensils ; c, Heating Columns ; C, Ventilating Column ; D, Connecting Lobby ; E. F. Separation Wards ; G, Hall ; H, Stair-well ; I, Stairs ; J, Poultice room containing chute to basement ; K, Separation Ward ;

L, Elevator ; M, Stairs to space above ward and roof ; N, Diet Kitchen ; O, Bath ; P, Lavatory ; Q, Bowls ; R, Urinals ; S, Water Closets ; T, Scullery ; U, Corridor roof connecting with other wards.

Figure 3.25. Stuyvenberg Hospital, Antwerp, ward plan, 1872–84. Initial design by F. Baeckelmans, architect.

drafts that could carry germs across a ward from one patient to another. There were two diametrically opposed ventilation patterns for centralized wards. In the octagonal ward of the Johns Hopkins Hospital, designed by John R. Niernsee, air flowed inward from vents in the outer walls to a large, hollow, central exhaust column. This solid center blocked the view across the ward, allowing greater visual privacy but compromising nurse supervision. In contrast, at the Stuyvenberg Hospital in Antwerp air was supplied through a central ring of hollow iron columns and exhausted by registers at the bottom of the perimeter wall next to each bed. The arrangement kept the ward center much more open, and a central, glass-enclosed nurses' station (with a separate air flow) offered complete oversight of the patients. American hospitals that incorporated centralized wards were typically patterned after the Johns Hopkins Hospital model, with an inward air flow and solid centers.[84]

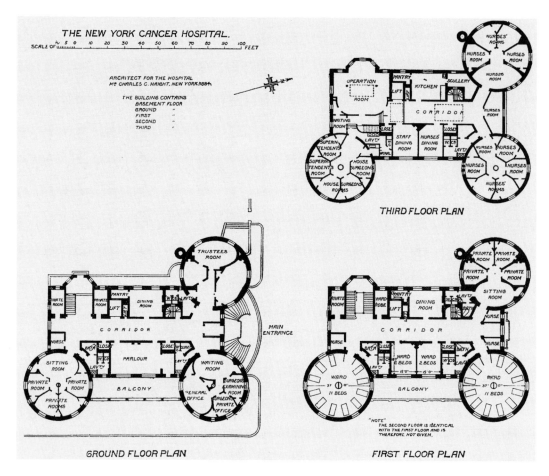

Figure 3.26. New York Cancer Hospital, New York City, plans, 1893. While the centralized wards were rationally laid out, the division of the same centralized floor plan into nurses' rooms and private patient rooms on other floors created some unique design challenges.

While European hospitals continued to include wards of thirty beds or more, by the turn of the century the largest American wards often held fewer than twenty.[85] Many hospitals had a variety of ward sizes, including much smaller ones. Treat and Foltz's design for Wesley Hospital in Chicago included one sixteen-bed, one six-bed, and two one-bed wards per ward floor. Smaller wards also increased efficiency, allowing administrators to assign patients to wards without leaving empty beds and without intermixing patient categories.

Some of the smaller wards were an economic reaction to new public health regulations that required quarantining all the patients in a ward for a specific period of time ranging from several days to several weeks upon the appearance of a contagious disease. The smaller the ward, the fewer patients

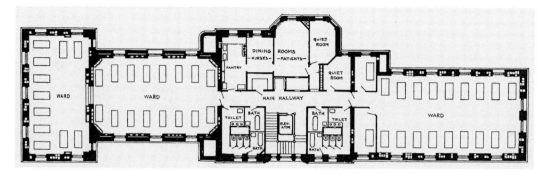

Figure 3.27. Presbyterian Hospital, New York City, plan of medical ward building, 1891. The various ward sizes provided flexibility in categorization. Although the wards included electric lighting and wiring, J. Cleveland Cady banished all plumbing from the wards.

affected by a quarantine, and the less of an impact it had on the hospital's overall efficiency. Smaller wards were particularly appealing for the patient groups most prone to quarantine—children and newly admitted patients.

In fact, quarantine regulations prompted the development of a new category of ward—"reception wards," which categorized patients not by their ailments but by their admission dates. Until the late 1880s standard hospital practice was to take newly admitted patients (and any incipient contagious disease they carried) directly to their assigned large ward. The result was frequent cross-infections. Reception wards provided a mediating space to accommodate newly admitted patients "for a time sufficient to demonstrate whether or not they bring germs of contagious disease with them." After that specified period the patient was reassigned to a "permanent" bed in a large ward. The New York Nursery and Child's Hospital, once plagued by internal epidemics, counted their new "reception" building as a complete success—it allowed them to "keep the general wards of the building free from epidemic disease." Reception wards usually included a handful of small (two- to five-bed) wards but could be much more elaborate, including examination rooms, storage areas, bathing facilities, disinfection facilities, and even small clinical laboratories. They were often located not in a ward pavilion but in the administration or admission building.[86]

Paying Patients and the Spatial Reinforcement of Class

While European hospitals continued to be largely charitable and to provide only one class of accommodations well into the twentieth century, America was "the home of the pay system." According to Rosenberg, the transformation of American hospitals to all-class institutions was essentially complete by the 1920s. The record of hospital buildings corroborates this but also reveals the extent to which this transformation was already underway in the late nineteenth century, and the extent to which it required architectural complicity for true efficiency.[87]

While late nineteenth-century American hospital administrators continued to expect that each patient should pay what he or she could afford, charging patients at different rates when they occupied adjacent beds of the same ward proved unsustainable. The result, as the directors of the German Hospital in New York City noted in 1882, was that when housed in the large wards, patients who could otherwise pay did not.[88] When housed in distinct facilities, with extra space, features, or services, however, the differential was far easier to justify and far more likely to be collected. Socioeconomic divisions correlated to the size of patient rooms: large wards for the poor, small wards for the middle class, private rooms for the wealthy.

Private rooms and small wards also provided a legitimate and easily comprehended boundary for a new kind of hospital charge—doctors' fees. Traditionally, hospital doctors could not charge a fee for their medical service in the hospital, but they were encouraged to send their wealthy patients to the hospital to fill the private rooms and wards and generate income for the hospital. There was little incentive for hospital doctors to recommend a hospital stay to their private patients if by doing so they lost patient fees. In the 1880s many hospital administrators changed their rules to allow hospital doctors to charge fees for their hospital service, but only to paying patients who stayed in a private room in the hospital. Consequently, a hospital with private rooms had a good chance of attracting not only paying patients but more doctors. Hospitals without private patient rooms were at a disadvantage.[89]

The spatial separation of private service from ward service continued to increase in the late nineteenth century. A separate floor or wing was the minimum, a separate pavilion was preferable.[90] On the exterior these private pavilions might resemble all the other standard large-ward pavilions, but on the interior there were increasing spatial and material distinctions. Private patient pavilions typically included single-bed rooms; some might even include private bathrooms and adjoining rooms for a private nurse or family member. Private patient rooms and buildings were also far more luxurious and decorated than wards, but there was a delicate architectural balance between attractiveness and hygienic necessity. The luxury was typically only a veneer added to the initially "hygienically designed" room. Private patients preferred the newest or "best" facility. Hospital administrators with out-of-date facilities often found them underused, and chose to remodel in the hope of maintaining their attractiveness.

Figure 3.28. Roosevelt Hospital, New York City, private room in private patient building, 1898. The hospital directors published a plan of the private patient building, designed by W. Wheeler Smith, in their annual reports, with the cost of one night's stay for each room printed on it. Prospective patients could shop for the room they would stay in. Many rooms had private bathrooms; some were two-room suites—for a family member or private nurse to stay in the adjoining room.

Whether the inclusion of and renovation of private patient rooms was done in the hopes of developing a new clientele or in the interest of wooing an existing clientele remains unclear. The utilization rate of private patient facilities was linked to the state of the broader economy. This meant that private patient income waned at the very times when it was most needed. In the boom years of the 1880s and early 1890s, private patient services were generally successful. The inclusion of private patient buildings in the original master plans of numerous hospital facilities of the time reflected that communal wealth but also put an architectural limit on the proportion of hospital service devoted to private patients during this period. After the panic of 1893 many hospitals suffered a sudden decline in private patient rolls and a sharp increase of charity care. According to David Rosner, in the wake of that economic catastrophe the hospital administrators' desire to attract paying patients (and their income) led them to increase the number of private rooms despite actual demand.[91] My research indicates that this was possible, but not common. After the panic of 1893, the private rooms of many hospitals simply sat empty, adding another economic drain on the hospital's coffers. That strain meant that from the panic of 1897 until the early 1900s rates of new hospital construction (whether new facilities or new buildings), including private patient facilities, waned.

Isolating Germs, Not Just Patients

In the late nineteenth century, one other patient category routinely received accommodation in a single-bed room—those with contagious diseases in a general hospital.

Bacteriological research had established that persons sick from a bacterial disease were themselves the greatest source of pathogenic germs. This made the bodies of patients sick with contagious diseases an element of contamination requiring aseptic control. Given the danger, even with convincing evidence that germs spread by direct contact, designers of isolation facilities continued to install mechanisms to control the particulate content of the air and the germ load on objects and building surfaces. This meant that the standard of isolation remained a separate isolation structure designed "to make sure that nothing goes out which can carry any disease germs of any sort."[92]

To reduce the germ load, isolation facilities received the same aseptic finishes and materials as surgical spaces. This made isolation rooms as austere as private patient rooms were luxurious. Fears of germ potency in isolation facilities even reinvigorated interest in the construction of temporary structures, intended to be burned down sporadically to destroy the accumulated contagions. The Reception Hospital of New York City, for contagious patients, was built so it could be completely purified by fire and still remain standing. Its structure was metal; it had a metal roof and corrugated iron walls. The interior ceiling and floor were of waterproof polished cement, allowing "the unlimited use of disinfecting fluids . . . with no possible injury to the interior." The furniture was of iron and steel and the crockery and plates had a distinctive pattern so it would be recognized if it traveled away from the hospital.[93]

Isolation facility design increasingly controlled the movement of all things (persons, objects, and air) that entered and then exited the room. Complex ventilation systems created separate air flow for each room and typically also sterilized (purified) it before releasing it back into the broader environment. Complex layouts dictated the movement of persons and objects to ensure that germs did not travel casually out of the facility. The

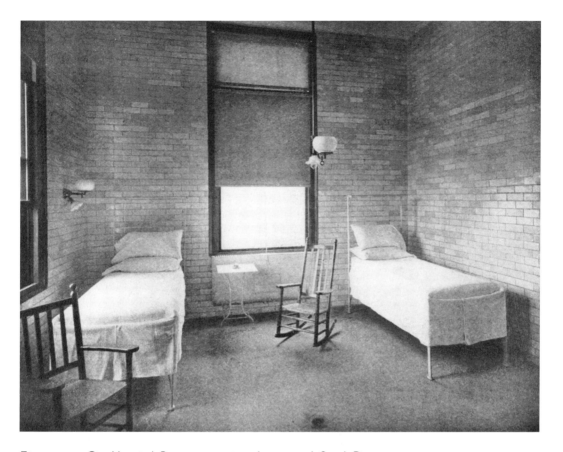

Figure 3.29. City Hospital, Boston, room in isolation ward, South Department, 1906.

design of two isolation units in particular—for the Johns Hopkins Hospital and the Presbyterian Hospital in New York City—reveal the extreme requirements of trying to prevent both material and aerial transfer of germs.

The Johns Hopkins Hospital's isolation building opened in 1885 with well-ventilated single rooms. Although the individual rooms prevented direct contact between patients, the complete separation of each patient's air space was considered equally important. The ventilation system ensured that no air that had been in contact with a patient would then be breathed by another person. Supply air entered each room directly from the exterior through individual basement supply ducts. The air within each room was constantly exhausted through ducts to individual vents along the roof (making the building's roofline a forest of exhaust towers). In most rooms the air was supplied through normal-sized ducts and grilles in the floor; in three "experimental" isolation rooms, room-sized ducts (with heating elements to temper the air) fed the supply air through perforated metal floors under the patient's bed, surrounding the patient with "fresh," germ-free

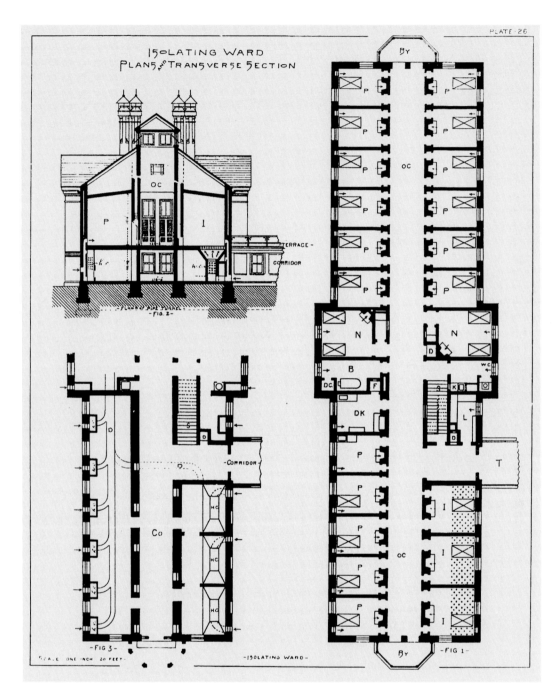

Figure 3.30. Johns Hopkins Hospital, Baltimore, isolation ward, plan and sections, 1880. The three experimental rooms with perforated floors are in the bottom right-hand corner of the plan, shown by the hatched area.

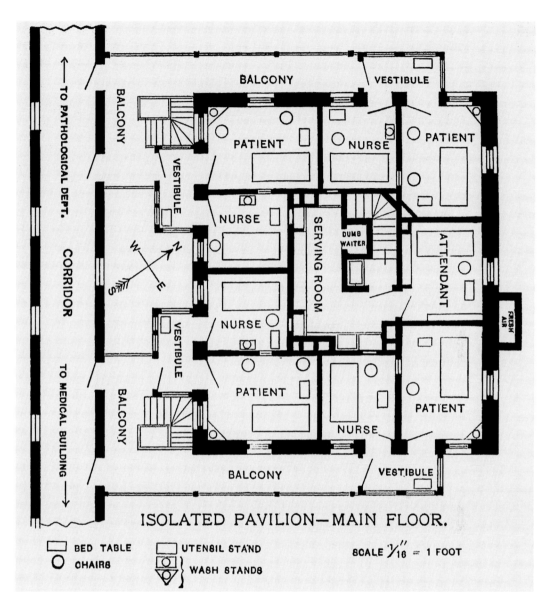

Figure 3.31. Presbyterian Hospital, New York City, isolation building, plan, 1891.

air. Each room had its own metal-lined vertical exhaust duct that could be purified by fire; more than twenty-five separate exhaust flues projected from the roof. Aseptic precautions to prevent material transfer were also in place. The building was to have its own separate nursing staff, and its own bedding and utensils (which were treated differently than those of the rest of the hospital wards). It was an elaborate, expensive building, housing nineteen patients and four nurses on one floor of what was essentially a three-story building (the enclosed attic and basement were part of the ventilation system).[94]

In contrast, the Presbyterian Hospital's isolation building of 1891 housed only four patients, four nurses (each dedicated to one patient), and an attendant. Access to the second-floor facility was via an open-air balcony (fresh air was still considered a purifying influence) to a vestibule that allowed access either to the nurse's room or to the patient's room. Patients remained in the room until they were discharged. Duty shifts for the isolation nurse lasted for a week or more at a time, minimizing the chance of carrying germs out of the facility. The nurse's room had an observation window into the patient's room, but physical access was only through the vestibule, which had a scrub sink for aseptic precautions before and after entry. The attendant entered from the lower floor, by a separate staircase that led into a central compartment with a serving room and sleeping room. The attendant delivered physical goods (meals, medicines, supplies) through a simple pass-through from the serving room into the nurse's room. Dirty items (plates, linens) were sent back through this pass-through and cleaned in the serving area. This ensured that germs did not travel into or out of the building on the plates, utensils, or linens. The isolation building had its own ventilation system, completely disconnected from the central ventilating system. For exhaust air, the isolating building had "a duct of its own, communicating with all its rooms and running to the fires under the steam-boilers, where its air is burned."[95] Like the Johns Hopkins Hospital's isolation building, this design combined complete aerial separation with complete material separation.

Isolation pavilions could be small because the expectation was that general hospitals would only handle contagious disease patients who exhibited symptoms after admission for another (treatable, and noncontagious) ailment. Persons suffering from a contagious disease of public concern (e.g., smallpox, typhus, cholera) were sent not to general hospitals but to separate contagious disease hospitals. These institutions functioned as a means of reducing incidence across the broad population by removing infected individuals from contact with the larger population. Contagious disease hospitals were frequently located well outside the city (such as the Riverside Hospital on North Brothers' Island outside of New York City or the City Hospital well outside Chicago's city limits). These hospitals were the closest American approximations of the extreme post–germ theory pavilions of the European hospitals, with greater space between pavilions and stricter control on pavilion height and size limits. Although the South Department (for contagious cases) of the City Hospital in Boston was located on a block adjacent to the general hospital, the spacing between pavilions was much

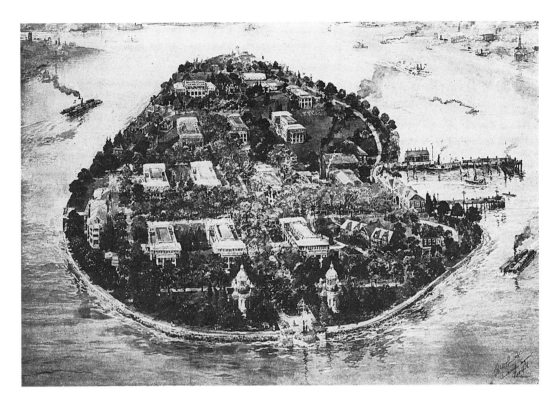

Figure 3.32. Riverside Hospital, New York City, bird's-eye view, 1920. Designed by Westervelt & Austin.

Figure 3.33. Woman's Hospital, New York City, view of hospital and outbuildings, 1898. The original stone structures were designed by Henry G. Harrison.

greater and there was little interaction between the facilities, apart from the transfer of contagious cases from the general service to the contagious service.

Even in general hospitals, the provision of isolation facilities was typically in outbuildings, often of temporary construction. The directors of the Hahnemann Hospital in New York City noted the addition of an Ovariotomy Cottage to their grounds in 1885. The Woman's Hospital in New York City included several wooden outbuildings to hold surgical spaces and for the isolation of the postoperative patients. For landlocked hospitals on small urban sites, like Saint Mary's Hospital for Children, the New York Hospital, and the Wesley Hospital in Chicago, which had no ground space for even a tent, rooftop facilities were the only solution. The roof location still separated the contagious cases from the rest of the hospital and put them in the purest air. Many of these facilities were reachable only through the fresh air "by walking on the roof of the corridor." Saint Luke's Hospital's directors planned rooftop isolation facilities because "they will be more completely cut off from the rest of the establishment than by any other possible arrangement, and at the same time be within easy access for the doctors and nurses."[96]

The 1880s and 1890s saw broad acceptance of the germ theory of disease, proof that germs were transferred by direct contact, and the development of aseptic practices. That these discoveries did not lead directly to a completely new form of hospital architecture and a complete reconsideration of hospital design is obvious—pavilion-ward design remained the standard in America as in Europe throughout the nineteenth century. This seeming continuity was not the product of blind adherence to preexisting standards. It was the result of positive, reasoned decisions made by practitioners deeply involved in interpreting the new theories but also dealing with a complex institution shaped by multiple forces.

Bacteriology at the time was a field with many simultaneous threads of research and discovery. One thread proved that germs were transferred by direct contact from sick organisms to healthy ones. Hospital practitioners, many of whom had lived through the troubling decades of the 1850s, 1860s, and early 1870s when frequent outbreaks of hospital disease were considered the mortal consequence of poor architectural hygiene, believed that germs could be transferred by direct contact. They also believed the findings of the bacteriological research that proved that germs were everywhere (in the air, on material surfaces of objects of daily use, and on floors, walls, and ceilings) and that sunlight and fresh air were antagonistic to germ viability. The rational conclusion was that the pavilion ward's self-purifying design was still relevant to germ reduction. Bacteriology and asepsis were thus interpreted into the existing hospital structure, refining the material requirements of hospital buildings and reconfiguring the spatial design of the portions of the hospital with the greatest bacterial load—operating rooms and isolation facilities.

In many ways pavilion-ward design still suited hospital practice at a time of transition from a place of general charitable care to a place for active specialized medical treatment. The old practices still thrived in the static decentralized layout where each pavilion functioned independently. However, separate pavilions also supported specialization through categorization, minimized physical contact between inhabitants of the various pavilions, and maintained a relationship between patient and ward that held lingering expectations of reform as well as cure. What did not suit the new medicine was the distance between pavilions, which complicated the increasingly requisite movement of patients and practitioners (doctors and nurses) between a variety of increasingly specialized spaces—labs, surgical facilities, sterilization or decontamination facilities, therapeutic facilities, diagnostic facilities, wards, and administration.

Though, from the outside, pavilion-ward hospitals of the 1890s and 1860s looked similar, they were not the same. The pavilion-ward hospital of the 1860s was an array of independent, standardized buildings. The pavilion-ward hospital of the 1890s was a collection of interdependent but physically separate components, each designed to meet the specific functional requirements of the activities it housed—whether private rooms or isolation rooms, surgical facilities or dispensaries, diagnostic or therapeutic facilities, laboratories or centralized services, nurse housing or administration. If the "post–germ theory pavilion" was detectable only in the details, it was still a transformation.

With these shifts, the hospital became a new kind of machine. It was no longer a *machine à guérir* as envisioned in the Enlightenment—a self-purifying structure that would instill health in its occupants; it had become a sorting machine—one that created a vast system of spaces into which the increasingly numerous categories of patients, staff, and activities could be arranged in efficient, economic, and, it was hoped, therapeutic patterns. The machine, however, was not yet up to the complexity of the sorting required. As the hospital began to become all-class; as medical specialization blossomed; as diseases requiring isolation increased; and as medical diagnostic, research, and therapeutic spaces became more in demand the often competing spatial categories to be housed grew far more numerous than pavilions.

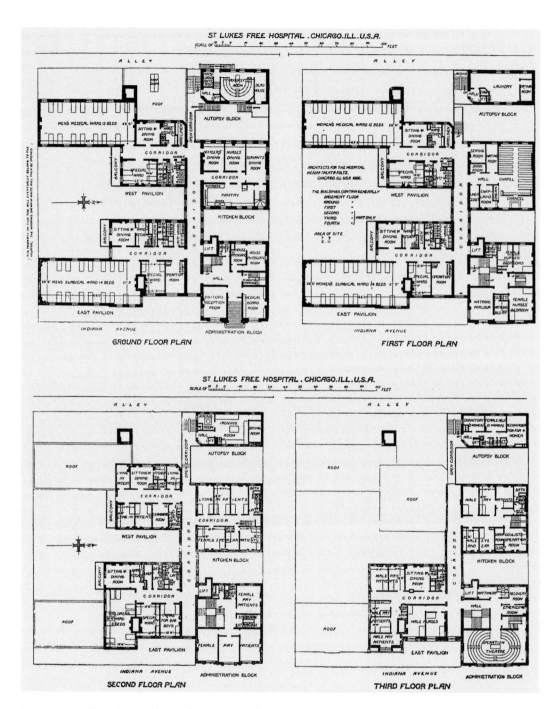

Figure 3.34. Saint Luke's Hospital, Chicago, plans, 1893. The small city lot kept the hospital compact, but Treat and Foltz's design still included a central corridor with five separate pavilions projecting from it. Only two of those pavilions were wards; the others varied in footprint and height according to the specific functions they housed.

By the late nineteenth century, the role of hospital architecture—as a sorting tool or as a hygienic baseline—was an obvious but unresolved question. In that irresolution the old and the new intermingled. New spatial needs were wedged into the traditional structure of pavilions. Traditional requirements for air space between buildings were whittled to vestigial proportions, while *pavilion* came to refer to far more than an independent ward-unit and instead to any number of functionally specific, spatially distinct departments within the larger interdependent hospital. Developments in hospital architecture in the early twentieth century did not resolve this question; they changed it. By the 1900s the largest question for hospital designers was not whether hospital architecture should reinforce hygiene or align architectural boundaries with functional categories; the question of utter importance was how the building could aid efficiency.

CHAPTER 4

Hygienic Decentralization vs. Functional Centralization

Reasons for Continuity and Change, 1898–1917

> If the hospital really is an institution which specializes on changing an invalid into a healthy person, then the hospital is to all intents and purposes a manufacturing plant, and any scheme looking toward its successful management must be similar to the schemes used in other manufacturing establishments of equal size and grade.
>
> — **Frederick D. Keppel, 1916**

> When we bear in mind that during the past thirty years everything in our theories concerning infection, contagion and hygiene has changed, and that scientifically proven facts have taken the place of theories, would it not seem strange that we should still adhere to the same essentials in hospital construction?
>
> — **Albert J. Ochsner, 1907**

By the first decade of the twentieth century the balance between hospitals as medical or charitable institutions had shifted. The discovery of blood types had made transfusions possible, electrocardiograph machines could chart the heart's activity, vitamins had been discovered, X-rays transformed what was visible, heart surgery was performed, and corneas were transplanted. Hospitals housed the clinical material, staff, and facilities crucial to these discoveries. While the provision of basic charitable care remained a central tenet of many hospitals, the provision of medical treatments and research at times eclipsed that role. The promise of modern medicine had even made a stay in the hospital fashionable: according to one society daughter, "One is not quite in the swim nowadays if one has not had an 'operation performed.'"[1]

These shifts altered the basic functional schema of hospitals. They had been a group of separate wards housing patients in beds and providing basic medical care, nursing, and a healthy dose of reform. They were now becoming a group of interdependent specialized spaces that facilitated specific procedural treatments to the increasingly peripatetic patients, nurses, doctors, and staff. At the turn of the century this new hospital for the most part still occupied traditional pavilion-ward facilities. Many practitioners still championed that traditional form. Other practitioners, however, saw the opportunities offered by the new high-rise structures and their centralized building technologies and services. In the first decades of the twentieth century there were strong modern reasons for low-rise decentralized hospital structures, just as there were strong modern reasons for more centralized, compact hospital structures.

Interest in "environmental therapeutics" provided the strongest justification for decentralized low-rise facilities but in a new, modern guise. In the 1900s and 1910s many regular, scientifically trained, practicing doctors used environmental conditions (such as humidity, temperature, or light) as medicaments—scientifically proven direct physiological influences that could be used to counteract pathological physiological symptoms.[2] Decentralized, low-rise facilities—like pavilion-ward hospital design—facilitated environmental therapies by maximizing patient exposure to the therapeutic influence of the outdoors.

The desire for a more efficient and effectual delivery of interactive medical treatment and basic care provided the strongest justifications for centralized high-rise facilities. As described by Joel Howell, the separation of specific technological functions like the operating room from the ward inevitably emphasized circulation in hospital design because it created an increasing movement of people and things throughout the hospital.[3] By the 1900s that "circulation" was beginning to overwhelm hospital practice. Centralization, it was believed, would reduce staff travel time, allow more cost-effective provision of services, and bring all the specialized departments into greater, more convenient proximity.

In 1913 Dr. Samuel Waldron Lambert summarized the resultant architectural dilemma as an irreconcilable tension between hygienic decentralization (putting each distinct unit of hospital operation into a separate building to prevent disease or maximize environmental conditions) and "administrative" or functional centralization (arranging the separate services into an efficient interactive whole "under one roof").[4] This tension destabilized not only the basic understanding of just what hospital architecture was supposed to do but how it was supposed to do it. Was the building a therapy or a tool, its success to be measured in low mortality or low cost? There was not a single answer to this question.

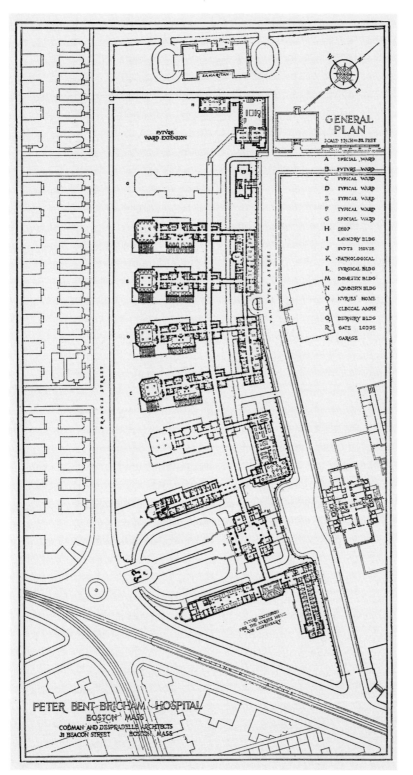

Figure 4.1. Peter Bent Brigham Hospital, Boston, plan, 1913. The program for the design competition called for low-rise wards. Codman and Despradelle's winning design held wards with a highly original layout but had a classically detailed exterior. Harvard Medical School was across the street.

Figure 4.2. Galloway Memorial Hospital, Nashville, bird's-eye view, 1916. On a site that would have supported low-rise pavilions, Samuel Hannaford and Sons designed a relatively compact facility with four-story wards to accommodate medical education and research as well as basic medical care. Only one of the pavilions was completed in initial construction.

The overwhelming result of these competing expectations was increasing variety in hospital designs. Some institutions occupied brand-new, cutting-edge, low-rise decentralized facilities; others thrived in tall, centralized hospital buildings; and many occupied hybrid facilities—with six- or even eight-story pavilions in close proximity to each other. Even hospital experts of the day could not organize the variety. In 1893 Henry Burdett separated hospitals into four main categories: pavilion, block, corridor, and heap of buildings.[5] He considered pavilions generally good, blocks, corridors, and heaps generally bad. Within a decade, even that clarity had broken down. The majority of hospital designs in the 1900s and early 1910s would not clearly fit into one of Burdett's categories. Contemporary descriptions of hospital designs of the early twentieth-century were often compound words: block with corridors, terraced pavilion, low pavilion, high pavilion. Which categories were "good" and which were "bad" was not a matter of established dogma; it was a matter of ongoing concern.

Figure 4.3. Herman Knapp Memorial Hospital, New York City, view, 1917. This specialized hospital treated only patients with eye ailments. Crow, Lewis and Wickenhoefer's vertical arrangement provided more access to light and air than the old low-rise facility that had been surrounded by high-rises and sweatshops.

Despite the variety of hospital building forms, there was sense, and order, beneath the confusion. That order only becomes perceptible, however, when the typological ultimatum of "pavilion-ward" or "not pavilion-ward" is suspended and hospital buildings are examined as individual artifacts designed to solve specific problems in their operation. The pavilion-ward hospital system had posed a universal solution, sufficient for any patient, any doctor, any treatment, any nurse, in any locale. By the 1910s and 1920s, however, most hospitals were in essence specialized hospitals—targeting a specific patient clientele, attracting a specific medical staff, and providing the services and spatial requirements for specific treatments. Chinese hospitals, railroad hospitals, proprietary hospitals, tuberculosis hospitals, sanatoria, cancer hospitals, and chronic disease hospitals joined the existing ranks of lying-in hospitals, eye hospitals, denominational hospitals, and ethnic hospitals. Even general hospitals "specialized." While large-scale general hospitals continued to treat patients of all types from all walks of life; small-scale general hospitals might treat patients with any ailment but serve a specific neighborhood or populace. Much of this specialization reflected the increasingly fragmented nature of urban society and medical practice—each hospital provided care for or by a specific group for specific reasons.[6]

Specialization was also a survival strategy. Historians including Rosemary Stevens, Charles Rosenberg, Paul Starr, and David Rosner have studied the intense fiscal crisis in hospital care of the early twentieth century caused by dwindling donations, increasing costs of care, increasing technological requirements, and unsuccessful attempts to get patients to pay for their care. In this tense economic situation, specialized hospitals, particularly medically specialized hospitals, experienced a number of fiscal benefits.[7] By offering focused, often innovative, treatments they maximized their attractiveness to the "ideal" candidates for hospital care—those who required acute medical treatment, were willing to pay for it, and would not require expensive long-term care. While general hospitals had to provide a wide variety of technologies (to diagnose and treat a wide variety of ailments), specialized hospitals only needed to provide the equipment required for the practice of the specialty. This vastly reduced the material costs of the hospital equipment without compromising care, but created hospital facilities of widely divergent structure and contents.

The broad variety of early twentieth-century hospital designs reflects this institutional specificity, as each distinct "kind" of hospital developed its own typological idiosyncrasy. Hospitals providing environmental therapy typically occupied low-rise, decentralized pavilion-ward facilities, whereas hospitals providing complex procedural treatments were more likely to occupy centralized high-rise buildings. The wide variety of hospital forms in this period was thus the result of abundant specialization in hospitals that rendered the traditional standardized solutions ineffective.

Design Specialists: Hospital Architects and Hospital Consultants

The medicalization of the hospital entailed a medicalization of the hospital designer. Annmarie Adams describes a shift from architects basing hospital designs on existing architectural traditions to hospital architects basing their designs on "their special knowledge of the routines, needs, and procedures of specific departments that enabled them to master the complex programmatic requirements of the modern hospital."[8] Such specialized knowledge supported the development in the first decades of the twentieth century of specialized practitioners—American hospital architects who focused their practices on the building type. Medical practitioners were still assumed within the design process, not only as the means by which hospital architects gained their special "medical" knowledge but as hospital architecture experts in their own right.

In 1902, well-known surgeon Albert J. Ochsner sadly observed that "the work most extensively consulted by architects" when designing hospitals had been published in 1875. This statement reveals the destabilization of traditional hospital design standards (allowing Ochsner to recategorize what had been the American bible of hospital design as a historical document) and the dearth of available comprehensive sources of information on modern hospital design. In the early twentieth century the most detailed and up-to-date information on hospital design was to be found in the increasingly numerous and authoritative professional periodicals. Articles on hospital design appeared in a variety of professional journals catering to architects (the *Brickbuilder*, the *American Architect*, the *Architectural Record*), doctors (the *Medical Record*, *Journal of the American Medical Association*), and nurses (*Trained Nurse and Hospital Review*) until the 1910s. Thereafter, hospital-specific publications like *The Modern Hospital* and *Hospital Management* became the go-to resource. In contrast to the comprehensive information included in pavilion-ward design manuals, distilling a working knowledge of hospital design from often contradictory information from dozens of distinct articles was an exercise in futility.[9]

The increasing variety of existing hospital facilities also made visits to exemplary hospitals more of a challenge than a confirmation of existing published design guidelines. Dr. J. W. Fowler, involved in planning the new City Hospital in Louisville, initially resisted visiting other hospitals because he thought he "had enough experience and data at hand." After visiting several Chicago Hospitals he changed his mind, stating, "I thought I knew from reading and experience something of hospitals and hospital work, but my imagination never painted the things I have witnessed here." He noted the bewildering difficulty of organizing the details of his experiences. Visits provided a broad exposure to a wide variety of individual solutions to the same problem, but, as T. J. Van der Bent observed, they could "result only in an extensive collection of undigestible data." A hospital architect himself, Van der Bent intended to dissuade dilettantes—clearly it was possible to assimilate the information, but only as the result of concerted study such as an expert would undertake. Adams highlights the importance of Edward F. Stevens's tour of European hospitals, with Dr. John Nelson Elliot Brown, between 1905 and 1911 in establishing his expertise in hospital design.[10] Despite the warnings and limitations, architects and doctors—experts and dilettantes—continued to go on tour.

On these trips, the larger, recently built, lavishly appointed hospitals of the bigger cities were the most often visited. In Chicago, Dr. Fowler visited Michael Reese, Saint Luke's, Wesley, Mercy, and Cook County Hospitals—the newest, largest institutions in the city. The newer hospital buildings in New York City (the Presbyterian Hospital, Saint Luke's Hospital, Mount Sinai Hospital, Bellevue, and the Lying-In Hospital) received hundreds of visitors, from as far away as Greece and China. American practitioners also visited hospitals in other countries, particularly those in London, Paris, and Berlin. According to Cameron Logan and Julie Willis, such visits played a role in the development of an early "international hospital network" that brought hospital details and designs from one locale to other, more distant ones. This was obvious in the design of the new Cincinnati General Hospital. Before drawing any plans, an entire commission of specialists (largely medical men) "inspected all the notable modern hospitals in the United States and Europe" and imparted their findings to the architects, Samuel Hannaford and Sons. The result was a design that was based as much on European as on American precedents.[11]

The increasing divergence between European and American hospital design complicated the task of developing a unified design approach based just on informational visits. Early twentieth-century European hospitals (e.g., the Polyclinic in Rome, the Boucicaut Hospital in France and the Berlin General Hospital in Germany) continued the tradition of "extreme" pavilion-ward designs. The Virchow Hospital in Berlin, then considered by many to be the leading hospital in the world, was, according to R. L. Thompson, "a very expensive village" comprising more than fifty buildings and accommodating two thousand patients on sixty-three and a half acres. Each pavilion held a different specialty, with clinics on the ground floor and patient rooms above. The preeminence of German medical research and practice gave rise to a certain reverence for German hospital designs. Dr. W. Gilman Thompson considered the European hospitals "a generation ahead of ours" in their planning.[12]

Some American travelers returned with the compelling hope that to copy the building structure of German hospitals would also be to copy the medical success. The doctors of the Cincinnati General Hospital explicitly instructed Samuel Hannaford and Sons to pattern their new facility designs after the buildings of prominent institutions such as the Virchow Hospital in Berlin, Eppendorf Hospital in Hamburg, and the Johns Hopkins Hospital in America. After its construction, it also became a destination hospital, influencing the design of many other American hospitals. T. J. Van der Bent admired the Cincinnati General Hospital as a faithful European facility design transplanted to America, but complained that disordered findings from visits to multiple hospitals more typically led to poorly designed hospitals that were "fragments of different European and American institutions put together without due consideration to the local conditions or requirements."[13]

While visits were useful, the best means of developing expertise in hospital design was to design a hospital. This catch-22 was compounded by a slow diminishment of open hospital design competitions and an increase in the number of high-profile hospital commissions awarded directly to hospital architects without competition. Unsatisfactory hospital designs were increasingly linked to architectural inexperience. In 1903 architect Bertrand E. Taylor solicited information on the design of small hospitals

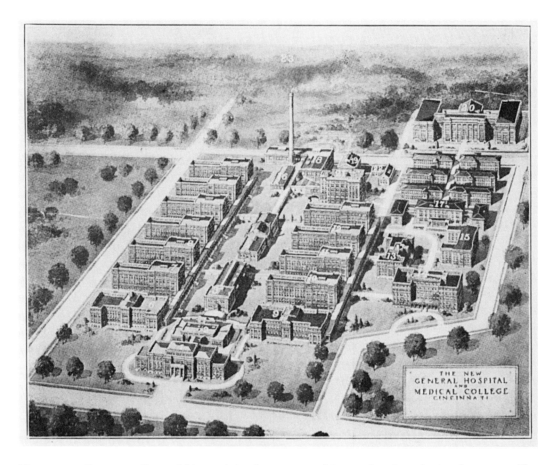

Figure 4.4. Cincinnati General Hospital, bird's-eye view of hospital and medical college, 1911. The widely spread pavilions each held a different clinic or medical specialty. Each individual pavilion was taller than the German examples it copied, but overall the facility was still lower and far more decentralized than many other American hospitals of the time.

across the country, hoping to amass a catalog of useful design details. The responses proved to him that there was little in existing smaller hospitals "worth studying or copying" and that most of the larger facilities had been "designed by an architect of brilliant attainments" who was "totally unfamiliar with even the rudiments of hospital requirements." Dr. Lambert simply stated that too many hospitals had been built by "architects who are studying the problem for the first time," while Charlotte Aikens observed that hiring a less expensive local architect rather than a specialist was as sensible as taking the lowest bidder for performance of a surgical operation.[14]

These shifts supported the specialization of hospital design in the United States. By the early twentieth century a few architects—including

Meyer J. Sturm and Edward F. Stevens—were focusing their practices on hospitals and medical buildings. A number of other architects—including Samuel Hannaford and Sons, York and Sawyer, Ludlow and Peabody, and Kendall, Taylor and Company—continued to take on nonhospital contracts, but did a large percentage of their work in hospital design. Many of these were partnerships, where one of the partners (or associates) was an expert in hospital design—such as J. Cleveland Cady of Cady, Berg, and See; Richard E. Schmidt of Garden, Martin and Schmidt; T. J. Van der Bent of McKim, Mead and White; and Warren C. Hill and Bertrand E. Taylor of Kendall, Taylor and Company, Boston. By the 1910s the more successful hospital design specialists had practices that spanned the country, if not the globe.[15]

These hospital architects actively defended and promoted their specialty. In 1915 Sturm wrote that "a man who has given up the general practice of architecture and who has for years devoted himself to this one class of buildings exclusively, is best qualified to design such buildings." He then offhandedly reckoned that there were fifteen true hospital architects deserving of recognition in the country, only five of whom were truly experts. This exclusivity rubbed some other architectural practitioners the wrong way. One testy respondent, seeing Sturm's writing as thinly veiled self-promotion, asked, "Why this shrinking modesty, why this admission that there are four others?"[16]

The role of medical practitioners in early twentieth-century hospital design experienced similar transformations. Increasing specialization had narrowed the typical medical practitioner's focus. As germ theory replaced traditional theories of disease causation and transfer, doctors' attention shifted from the interaction of patient and surroundings to the reaction of a patient's physiology to germs, drugs, surgery, and other physical interventions. Medical practitioners focused on their medical practices and the functional layout of the spaces in which they practiced, not on the hygienic conditions of the overall facility. Architects complained that doctors only became interested in a new hospital building when the walls were going up, and then only to demand costly changes to adapt a specific space to their individual needs.[17]

Given the increasing complexity of medical practices and the changing demands those practices made on the hospital buildings, however, medical input into hospital design was more necessary than ever, and there were medical practitioners who provided it. Many new hospital buildings were still deeply influenced by at least one of the hospital's doctors who made hospital design a subject of particular study. Dr. Fowler's influence on the City Hospital in Louisville was profound. Drs. D. L. Richardson and John

M. Peters were deeply involved in planning the new isolation facility of the Providence City Hospital, while the Polyclinic Hospital in New York City was "practically designed in every respect by the medical heads." Dr. Henry S. Plummer's role in the design of the influential buildings of the Mayo Clinic was key, and "the architects gratefully acknowledged his leadership." Drs. John M. Markoe and Samuel Waldron Lambert of the Lying-In Hospital of the City of New York played an active role in the design development and even the construction management of their new building. Even these doctors, however, saw their role in design as temporary, an expedient to gain the best building in which they could then continue their medical practice.[18]

Many medical practitioners did not even want a temporary role in the planning and construction of a new hospital. As Morris J. Vogel notes, many times the hospital superintendent (often medically trained) stepped up to fill the role. In 1908 the governing board of Bellevue Hospital sent copies of the preliminary drawings of a planned new surgical wing to the hospital's staff doctors and asked for comments on the design. The busy doctors immediately urged the governing board to hire an outside medical expert on hospital construction who would consult directly with the architects. The board hired S. S. Goldwater, the medically trained superintendent of the Mount Sinai Hospital, who had been deeply involved in the planning of its highly praised new facility as a "hospital consultant"—a neutral medical specialist on hospital design. The design for the new Bellevue Hospital gained international attention and emulation, and over the next decades Goldwater established a successful career as a consultant for hundreds of hospitals across the world.[19] Other medical hospital consultants—such as Charles F. Neergaard, William Henry Walsh, Wiley E. Woodbury, and Louis J. Frank—followed his example.

By the time of the entrance of the United States into World War I, it was widely considered the best practice to hire a hospital architect and a hospital consultant and have them work together. Failing that, it was crucial to involve at least one specialist who could work with a local professional counterpart (a hospital consultant working with a local architect, or a hospital architect working with a local doctor). In fact, such collaborations provided a successful means of entry for newcomers to the specialty. A local architect who worked with a good hospital consultant on the design of one hospital could use that expertise to gain more hospital commissions. The same held for local doctors or superintendents who worked with a hospital architect.

This arrangement provided the medical and architectural expertise necessary to hospital design, but, given the complexity of hospital service, it was far from comprehensive, or neutral. Susan Reverby has noted that "many nursing superintendents argued to nurses and administrators alike that it was nursing's "moral obligation" and "right of experience" to be intimately involved in hospital construction and alterations. Nurses like Annie Goodrich, M. E. McCalmont, and Charlotte Aikens pointed out that nurses knew whether noisy wards kept patients awake at night, whether meals were served cold rather than hot because of long travel distances between kitchen and patient, whether the layout made oversight of patients difficult. These nurses criticized the architect's reliance on doctors for medical design input, because the doctors judged a hospital's efficiency only in relation to their practice within it. According to McCalmont, if a doctor's "operations go smoothly, he thinks he has an ideal operating room and advises all his friends to build one just like it, without at all realizing that perhaps a difference of planning, a better arrangement of plumbing fixtures, etc. might lessen the working force in that department by one or more persons, as well as make the work less exhausting for all."[20]

Nurses were rarely given a voice in the design of new facilities, however. McCalmont complained that "practically every bit of work that is related to or is dependent upon the proper planning of a hospital is done by the women workers—yet that same planning is generally dominated by a group of impractical men." While McCalmont was successful enough in establishing her expertise to be hired to consult on the equipping and furnishing of several new hospital buildings, for the most part, hospitals were designed with little planning input from nurses.[21]

Hygienic Decentralization: Designing for Environmental Therapy and Disease Prevention

In the early twentieth century, the decision to construct a low-rise decentralized hospital facility was in the interest of providing environmental therapy or facilitating disease prevention. This interest was based not on the abstract environmental formulations of the nineteenth century but on scientific research into physiology, germ theory, and asepsis.

Design for Environmental Therapy

In the early twentieth century, medical researchers studied the physiological effects of exposure to environmental conditions (temperature, humidity, air pressure) with as much expectation of positive therapeutic results as from exposure to pharmaceuticals and surgical interventions. This research led to the design of structures that could provide therapeutic environmental conditions naturally (by providing abundant access to sunlight and fresh air) or artificially (by providing technologically induced environmental conditions). The expectation was that the exposure would induce specific curative physiological reactions.

The Low-Rise Decentralized Designs of
Environmentally Therapeutic Facilities

Hospitals that emphasized natural environmental therapies typically served patient categories excluded from general hospitals—particularly patients with contagious or chronic diseases (such as tuberculosis, measles, cancer, heart disease). These were also typically ailments for which "scientific" medicine as practiced in general hospitals had not yet developed successful treatments. For example, although Koch identified the mycobacterium that caused tuberculosis in 1882, an effective pharmaceutical treatment did not appear until the 1940s, with the development of streptomycin. In the decades around the turn of the twentieth century, the only proven beneficial treatment for tuberculosis was the "fresh air cure"—exposure to the outdoors typically coupled with a regimen of rest and fortification. As Annmarie Adams, Kevin Schwartzmann, and David Theodore point out, in the 1900s and 1910s the "architecture (or more generally the patient's immediate environment) served explicitly as an active physical agent in tuberculosis treatment."[22]

While the fresh air cure was most often linked to the treatment of tuberculosis, some considered fresh air a general restorative, able to improve a broad variety of patient conditions. According to practitioners at the Presbyterian Hospital in New York City, "No medicine can compare with pure air, and . . . without an abundance of it medicine may have no efficacy and nursing be of no avail." The physicians and surgeons of Saint Mary's Hospital for Children in New York City believed "that for some of their patients it is more important than medicines or operations."[23]

Facilities designed to maximize natural environmental therapy often resembled the decentralized pavilion-ward structures of earlier decades—both had the same design goal of maximizing exposure to sunlight and fresh air—but there were important differences. Nineteenth-century pavilion-ward designers had maximized the penetration of sunlight and fresh air into the ward as a means of incorporating the abstract (perhaps supernal) healing influence of nature. Doctors of environmentally therapeutic facilities at the turn of the century prescribed exposure to natural conditions as if it were a medicament, to be administered at specific times of the day, for specific lengths of time, with the goal of inducing (or counteracting)

Figure 4.5. Nopeming Hospital for Tuberculosis, Duluth, Minnesota, view, 1917. This hospital, designed by Scopes and Feustmann, offered a range of structures—from a main hospital building to cottages to tents, each providing a variable amount of the fresh air cure. The different facilities also corresponded to the stages of diseases of the inhabitants (acute patients were in the larger building with more nursing care available).

specific physiological conditions. Designers of facilities for natural environmental therapy were designing a medical treatment.

Looking at tuberculosis institutions as representative of facilities designed to provide environmental therapy, most occupied remote sites either in pristine countryside or in well-aired locales outside the city limits. The site was part of the cure, and many tuberculosis hospitals—like the Sea View Hospital on Long Island and the Nopeming Hospital outside of Duluth—occupied sites of natural beauty. After Koch's identification of the tubercle bacillus shifted the understanding of this disease from a common illness to a contagious disease, these distant locations served to isolate tuberculosis from the population centers and the natural surroundings were believed to prevent cross-infections. According to Michael Worboys, even for patients at these institutions, the expectation was that the open air "provided a near-aseptic environment, and hence individual isolation for each patient."[24]

There were social as well as medical distinctions between many of these facilities. Annmarie Adams and Stacie Burke note that the National Sanitarium Association in Canada "tailored sanatoria according to patients' social class (paying or free patients) and disease status (early- or late-stage disease)." Similar distinctions appeared in the United States. The Trudeau Sanitarium at Saranac Lake—a collection of cottages set amidst pristine natural surroundings—stood as the model tuberculosis institution. Its clientele were largely private patients, and the various cottages offered varying levels of amenities, luxury, and privacy. The primary treatment was simple exposure to the outdoors—on balconies, in rooms with floor-to-ceiling operable windows, or in cottages with sunrooms and bedrooms with extensive windows. But the fresh air cure was an adjunct to scientific medicine, not a replacement. Nearby facilities for acute surgical and lab-centered medical treatment picked up where nature left off. Other private sanatoria followed this model, including small-scale open-air facilities, hospital-quality medical facilities, and at times, hotel-level amenities, in often stunningly beautiful natural landscapes. While the design details of early European sanatoria became "intertwined with the clean, linear, functionalist buildings associated with modern architecture," in the United States they tended more toward rustic or resort-style exteriors.[25] The minimalist clean lines of "aseptic" finishes dominated interior design.

Given the extent of the tuberculosis epidemic, such private institutions serviced only a small proportion of the patient load. Faced with the thousands of infected urban dwellers and the acknowledged contagious character of the disease, public health emphasis shifted. According to historians Elizabeth Fee and Dorothy Porter, bacteriology implied that "to control tuberculosis, for example, it was not necessary to improve the living conditions of the one hundred million people in the United States, only to prevent the 200,000 active tuberculosis cases from infecting others."[26] Rather than endorsing broad sanitary reforms, officials of fledgling public health departments encouraged municipalities across the country to build new tuberculosis hospitals—like the Kansas City Tuberculosis Hospital, and the Jasper County Tuberculosis Hospital in Webb City, Missouri—to treat, but also to isolate, the most advanced cases.

Many municipal tuberculosis facilities started as groups of tents, or open-air pavilions hastily erected on the grounds of existing urban municipal general hospitals. By the 1910s it was increasingly common for municipalities to design and build permanent tuberculosis hospitals, at times as separate institutions but also as departments of larger contagious disease facilities. In dealing with patients at varying stages of the disease—from incipient to advanced—the architecture of these facilities varied. Some, like the Sea View Hospital on Long Island (for children), or the Buffalo City Hospital, occupied extensive decentralized facilities. Others, like the Norfolk County Tuberculosis Hospital in Braintree, Massachusetts, or the Kansas City Tuberculosis Hospital, included a larger, central hospital building (with administration and medical services as well as rooms for advanced cases) and extensive outdoor facilities (tents, huts, shelters, cottages) for the open-air treatment of less advanced cases. Adams and Burke have pointed out that the variety of accommodations could correlate to patient conditions. Tents and cottages were typically used by less serious (incipient or recovering) cases, the more hospital-like facilities for patients in the more advanced stages of the disease.[27]

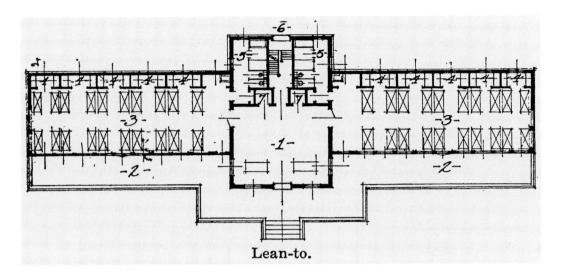

Figure 4.6. Municipal Tuberculosis Hospital, Kansas City, plan of lean-to, 1916. Edgar P. Madorie designed the wings of the lean-to as unheated spaces, with large south-facing openings. Lockers lined the north wall, giving some protection from the cold winds.

The design of the individual open-air structures often rested on scientific studies of the local climate and sunlight. Shelters would be as open as possible, but in colder climates would include a solid north or west wall to block the prevailing winds. More southern facilities might include extensive overhangs to function as sunshades. Indoor sleeping areas were minimal and used only in severely inclement weather; the outdoor balconies, sleeping porches, and shelters were the primary patient spaces. The separation between interior and exterior space was minimal; French doors or even moveable glass panels opened up the building to the outside.[28]

While the fresh air cure was the most well-known environmental therapy, glowing reports of the success of "light" cures in European institutions, particularly in August Rollier's institute in Leysin, Switzerland, interested US practitioners in heliotherapy. Buildings designed to provide the sunshine cure were narrow (sometimes only one room wide) with south-facing balconies wide enough to accommodate beds; roof overhangs were sized and placed so that they blocked the rain, but not the sun. Heliotherapy also influenced the design of hospitals in general. After sunlight was proven to be germicidal, solar orientation and awareness became a critical aspect of the design of any hospital building of any type. Architect William Atkinson recommended that ward buildings be oriented diagonally (northeast to southwest) to ensure that not only every bed but every building surface received the disinfecting force of sunlight. A number of hospitals—like the State Hospital for Consumptives in Tewksbury, Massachusetts, or the Jasper County Tuberculosis Hospital in Webb City, Missouri, developed "sun-trap" plans—angled ward layouts with footprints that resembled a *Y* or *V*—that opened to the south to embrace the sunshine.[29]

Environmental Therapy in the Modern Urban Hospital

Doctors of urban hospitals were also interested in the beneficial influence of environmental therapy, but to deliver "fresh air" in the city required a different, less site-intensive design strategies. The successes of environmental therapy led to a radical reappraisal of the ward's indoor climate. The widespread adoption of mechanical ventilation systems in the late nineteenth century had turned many large wards into highly regulated environments. According to Dr. W. Gilman Thompson, in general hospitals "the greatest evil of all is that the ward is 'ventilated' by a thermometer, a little instrument which, from October to May, is kept steadily at 68 or 70 day and night," regardless of the air's "freshness." As proof, he related that patients in the New York Hospital (a mechanically ventilated and heated building) lingered during convalescence while patients in the much older Bellevue (ventilated by open windows and heated by steam pipes) recovered more quickly. By the 1900s, S. S. Goldwater could state that "the preponderance of present opinion strongly opposes uniformity of temperature, and finds virtue in the natural day-and-night variation."[30]

To garner the beneficial and variable influence of fresh air in the wards, some early twentieth-century hospital designers built brand-new hospital buildings, like the New York Orthopedic Dispensary and Hospital, the Children's Pavilion of Mount Sinai Hospital in New York City, and the Robinson Memorial Pavilion of the Massachusetts General Hospital, with wards that could be completely naturally ventilated, even on urban sites. Administrators of existing hospitals with elaborate mechanical systems chose at times to shut off their boilers, turn off the fans, and open the windows. In terms of air quality, the end results of this resurgence of natural ventilation were not always as satisfactory as hoped. S. S. Goldwater cited a doctor who visited hospitals in sixteen states before entering one that was "tolerably free from objectionable odors." The doctor then wondered why hospitals installed mechanical systems only to leave them idle. Coinciding with this return to natural ventilation was, as Gail Cooper describes, the collapse of the old medical volumetric standards of air quality, with no equivalent replacement standard. Without the requirement of a certain cubic volume of fresh air (whether through rate of flow or air space), the variability of natural ventilation was no longer problematic for hospitals.[31]

Figure 4.7. Presbyterian Hospital, New York City, steel shed of open-air ward, 1908. Although erected on the top of an urban hospital, this shed was similar to the lean-tos of the Kansas City Hospital in figure 4.6.

To gain the full benefits of environmental therapy, however, required more than an open window into an otherwise enclosed space. Bellevue Hospital doctors assigned patients with meningitis to a tent pavilion and experienced "a better percentage of recoveries." Doctors at the Presbyterian Hospital in New York City created open-air roof wards, not just for the tubercular or chronic patient, but for patients with "pneumonia in all stages, post-operation cases of empyema, appendicitis, osteomyelitis, deep perinephritic abscesses, meningitis, burns, fractures, etc." The successes at the Presbyterian Hospital were startling, and widely reported.[32]

By the 1900s even new hospital construction in the city center included extensive fresh air facilities such as roof wards, balconies, patios, solaria, and sun-decks as integral parts of their modern, up-to-date hospital design. The new buildings of Harlem and Fordham Hospitals in New York City had large roof gardens and "wide balconies on which the beds may be rolled directly from the wards, to give patients the benefit of fresh air and sunshine." The design of the new Bellevue Hospital included sun-rooms, open balconies, and roof gardens. Plans for the cutting-edge new Hospital of the Rockefeller Institute gave "particular scope to the open-air treatment" through the provision of extensive balconies and roof wards. Administrators of hospitals occupying existing facilities designed before the 1900s struggled to add fresh air facilities to their often small, densely packed sites deep within the congested (and often polluted) downtown. The addition of open-air balconies—usually light metal structures—off wards was popular where there was sufficient space between pavilions. It was also common to convert outdoor corridors, rooftops, and landings into fresh air facilities, or to erect small pavilions or tents on the hospital grounds, if space permitted. It was not always possible to retrofit fresh air facilities in landlocked urban hospitals. The governors of the New York Hospital regularly cited the inability to make room for fresh air facilities at their densely packed Fifteenth Street facility as one of the main reasons the hospital needed a new facility on a new site.[33] By the end of 1914 fresh air treatment facilities were so prevalent in urban hospitals that one hospital practitioner described the modern urban hospital as "the best possible city substitute for life in the country."[34]

The Spaces of "Artificial" Environmental Therapy

Practitioners also advocated the use of facilities for artificially induced environmental therapies, which could provide specific conditions on demand regardless of the weather. This control allowed practitioners to compensate for undesirable exterior conditions—providing pure air in polluted surroundings, a moderate temperature in an extreme climate, ultraviolet light on cloudy days, or humid air in a dry climate. Increasingly sophisticated artificial climate control capabilities even allowed doctors the ability to tailor room conditions (air flow, temperature, humidity, lighting levels, light quality) to the specific patient. This solved the climatic problem of the large ward, where patients were "gathered without the slightest regard to their individual peculiarities or different requirements of treatment, varied needs as to air, temperature, sunlight, quiet, etc."[35]

The early twentieth-century clinician could prescribe "one atmospheric condition for the pneumonia patient who is in need of respiratory stimulation, and another for the nephritic whose poor circulation and cold extremities suggest a warm and comfortable room, in contradistinction to the cold air, preferably out-of-doors, in which the pneumonia patient thrives." The designers of the Bethesda Maternity Hospital in Cincinnati installed a complex system that washed, filtered, and heated the air before delivery, changed the air in the building eight times an hour, and still kept the temperature of each room within two degrees of its thermostat setting. The designers also noted that "any room may be kept at any temperature desired." The Bethany Hospital in Kansas City included a ventilation sys-

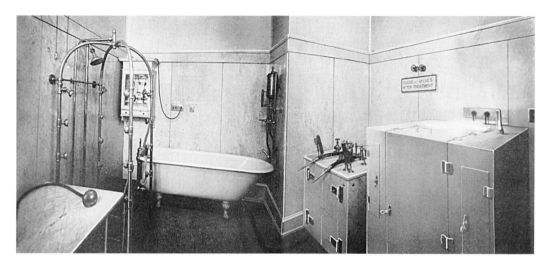

Figure 4.8. Wesley Hospital, Chicago, hydrotherapy room, view in 1912. The Wesley Hospital's hydrotherapy facility was relatively small, but provides a good example of the equipment needed for the various treatments. While European hospitals included far more extensive therapeutic facilities than American, some of the larger hospitals (in imitation of the European facilities) were installing departments that took up entire floors or wings.

tem that could supply "low-temperature air to all rooms utilized for fever patients."[36] Smaller wards and patient rooms facilitated this individualization; the Bethany Hospital in Kansas City had wards of four or fewer beds; the Bethesda Maternity Hospital had rooms of five or fewer patients.

For some artificial environmental therapies—for example, hydrotherapy, physical therapy, heliotherapy, and even electrotherapy—the desired exposure was of shorter duration, and the creation of separate "therapeutic" facilities allowed greater precision in the administration of the treatment. These separate departments required extensive specially designed facilities with complex, often bulky machinery. For example, mechanotherapy (or physiotherapy) included machines made to push, pull, pound, and move different parts of the body, as well as basic exercise equipment.[37]

At the turn of the century, hydrotherapy facilities were included in a wide variety of hospitals. These were often in imitation of European hospitals that included enormous therapeutic departments with a variety of treatments: Turkish baths, Russian baths, electric baths, sitz baths, needle baths, sweat-baths, Nauheim baths, carbonic acid baths, alkaline baths, saline baths, and electro-hydric baths. By the turn of the century, many American hospitals—like the Jewish Hospital in Philadelphia, the Wesley Hospital in Chicago, and the Barnes Hospital in Saint Louis—either added or incorporated similarly expansive hydrotherapeutic facilities.[38]

Artificial heliotherapy or "electric light" therapy blossomed almost overnight after the development of new, high-power electric lights and the reported successes of these "Finsen rays" (ultraviolet rays) in treating lupus in a London hospital. The treatment involved "three arc lamps of 35,000 candle power" with projecting tubes that concentrated the light onto four prone patients on tables for an hour at a time. Practitioners at the New York Skin and Cancer Hospital tried exposing their patients to "lucidescent" light ("ordinary electric light of 500 candle power, focused by parabolic reflectors on two spots") and the Barnes Hospital included "leucodescent" and therapeutic arc lamps.[39]

Artificial environmental therapies incorporated large equipment and often required a sizeable floor area. They were often housed in the basement of a hospital building—where the structure was strong enough to support the equipment and minimize any vibrations from its use, and where the adverse effects of equipment failure (leaks, sparks, small fires) were more easily contained. Treatment thus required the patient to travel from ward to treatment facility and back. To a certain extent, these facilities offered to medical practitioners what the operating room offered to surgeons—a designated space for active treatment filled with technologies and equipment designed to aid the scientific administration of that treatment.

Design for Disease Prevention: Spaital Separation and Aseptic Barriers

Hospitals that contained a heavy germ load (patients suffering from contagious ailments or patients susceptible to infections) also tended to occupy low-rise, decentralized facilities. Hygienic separation of individual pavilions remained standard, but pavilion interior designs were radically transformed. With widespread acceptance that germs spread by contact, physical barriers between infected items proved far more efficacious in prohibiting the spread of germs than open space. Individual isolation pavilions were transformed from large open wards (more space, less building) into an intensely compartmentalized structure (more walls, less open space).[40]

Contact Infection and Aseptic Barriers

The refinement of aseptic procedures gave architecture a new prominence in early twentieth-century isolation design. In the 1910s, according to Dr. D. L. Richardson, superintendent of the Contagious Disease Unit of the Providence City Hospital, a hospital "unit" was "an area which represents a separate and distinct infection; such an area may comprise a single bed or an entire room."[41] In this understanding, regardless of partition place-ment, the hospital was segregated into separate microbial areas that were either free from infection (clean) or infected (contaminated) with a spe-cific pathogen. Walls that reinforced those boundaries could prevent con-tact, but, according to Dr. Richardson, perfect "aseptic" isolation could be achieved even between patients in adjacent beds in large open wards, as long as all persons involved in their care followed aseptic procedures.

These procedures, however, were complex, unforgiving, and difficult to maintain without lapses. Nurses had to be retrained to perform even basic tasks aseptically. For example, "gowning up" for entrance into a contam-inated facility and removing the gown upon exit was a simple precaution to minimize the transfer of germs on clothing. Yet, in proper procedure, gowning up and down included a highly choreographed sequence of mo-tions. Upon exiting, "the nurse scrubs her hands and folds the gown down the middle, clean surface inside, and hangs it on the hook in such a way that it can be slipped on again without contamination." Wendy Madsen's description of the procedures that nurses followed to make and keep the hospital aseptic reveals that over the years many of these tasks became ritualized, but in the early years every step had to be a conscious choice.[42] Any breakdown in procedure meant a corresponding breakdown in aseptic isolation.

Even a minimal barrier could aid asepsis not just by blocking direct contact but by functioning as a procedural reinforcement. Given the high turnover rate of hospital staff, some hospital experts perceived a strategy of providing "the essentials for the prevention of cross-infections in the architecture of the building" as a means of minimizing the aseptic lapses of unskilled staff. The "barrier" nursing of Joseph Grancher, in which move-able screens were erected around infected patients within a larger ward, provides a good example. The barrier itself, a partial-height, moveable, per-meable fence, did not prevent contact; it functioned as a physical reminder of procedural distinctions that the nurses had to make between patients in-side the barrier and outside of it. In the words of hospital architect Richard E. Schmidt, such barriers would "compel the attendants to the performance of certain duties and make the probability of failure to comply with the rules of isolation less likely to occur and also prevent carelessness."[43]

Complete aseptic isolation within the early twentieth-century hospital was thus a balance between structures and procedures. The more open the space, the more rigorous the aseptic technique had to be; the more enclosed the space, the more relaxed the regulations.

The integration of physical barriers and procedures developed into two distinct architectural isolation strategies. Some barriers passively limited

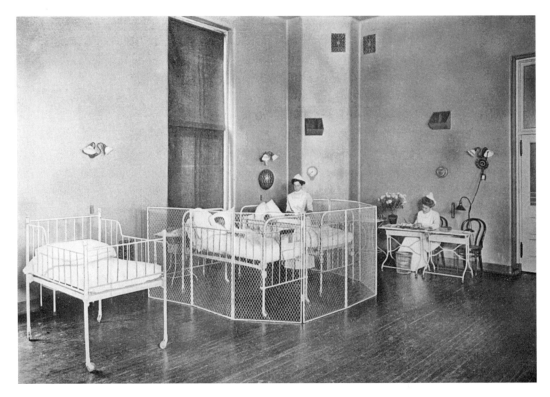

Figure 4.9. Presbyterian Hospital, New York City, barrier nursing in open ward, 1910.

who or what was allowed to cross; others actively altered the contamination status of persons and items as they crossed. Passive aseptic barriers were selective—often allowing air, light, and properly disinfected persons and things to cross, but preventing the passage of infected items or persons. For example, screens in the exterior windows of isolation facilities located in inhabited neighborhoods prevented direct contact between patient and passersby. Gates and partial-height doors to patient rooms provided a sense of openness but limited physical contact. One-way doorknobs were also effective: at the City Isolation Hospital in Minneapolis, "a person enters the soiled room and the door cannot be opened to let him pass back into the ward. He has to go through the whole [decontamination] process and out the other way."[44]

Passive barriers also provided easily policed checkpoints. A nurses' station located at the entrance to a ward provided a means of selecting who or what could enter—the nurse could demand a visitor gown up before entry, ensure that items were properly sterilized before delivery, or demand a practitioner scrub up before or after entry. This control could be personally or technologically administered. At the Evanston General Hospital, "the

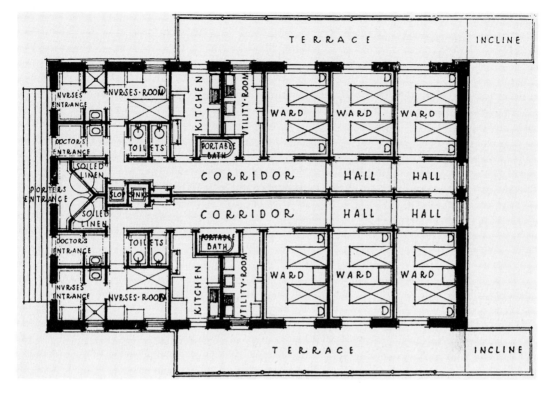

Figure 4.10. Samaritan Hospital, Troy, N.Y., isolation building, first-floor plan, 1915. George B. Post and Sons designed the unit to be expansible—the further wards could be closed off when not in use. Visitors would stand on the terrace and talk to the patient without entering the room.

attendant in the general office [had] control of all the doors on the entire floor through automatic door openers electrically controlled, so that no one can get into any part of the hospital from the public spaces without the consent of the general office attendant."[45]

In contrast, active aseptic barriers allowed free passage, but incorporated architectural and procedural features to ensure decontamination occurred during the crossing. This could be as simple as the conspicuous placement of plumbing fixtures adjacent to doorways to encourage handwashing, or it could be as complex as a multiroom sequence for exit or entry that incorporated elaborate decontamination procedures and equipment. Pass-through sterilizers for objects were highly effective active barriers. At the laundry facility for the Samaritan Hospital in Troy, New York, "the sterilizer is built into the wall between two separate rooms, one designed for the reception of infected articles and the other for the storage of articles after sterilization."[46] The only way for items to get from one side to the other was through the sterilizer.

Active barriers for the passage of persons were more complex. They often accommodated elaborate procedures such as disrobing, washing up (or otherwise disinfecting the body), sterilizing personal objects (such as rings), and dressing in a new set of clothes (perhaps gowns, white suits, or rubber aprons). Early designs tended to create a distinct space for each step in the process. For example, exit from the isolation units of the Ellis Island Contagious Disease Hospital required persons to pass through a series of three rooms—disrobing, decontamination (including a sterilizer and bathtub), and dressing. At the Saint Louis Children's Hospital, the physicians' exit from the isolation unit included a walk-through shower facility (the human equivalent of a pass-through sterilizer). Active barriers required cooperation to be effective: a walk-through shower was of little use if the water was not run.

Aseptic barriers and procedures also relied on multiple circulation paths to keep infected and clean items distinct. In the contagious disease pavilion of the Samaritan Hospital in Troy, New York, designed by George B. Post and Sons, nurses entered and exited through a shower. Doctors entered and exited past an extensive scrub area. The contaminated clothes and soiled linens were dropped into a room with a rotating pass-through—the porter picked up the soiled linens from this facility without entering the building. Kitchen staff and servants could enter the kitchen and utility rooms from a terrace. Visitors were restricted to the exterior terrace and talked through the window.[47]

The New Isolation: Pavilions Filled with Walls, Not Air

Passive and active aseptic barriers began to show up in hospital design wherever "infection" required control, but in isolation and surgical facilities in the first decades of the twentieth century, their use constituted an interior revolution. In 1909 hospital architect Edward F. Stevens glowingly described his 1907 visit to the Pasteur Hospital in Paris, where he "was shown a man ill with African sleeping disease while in the adjoining bed was a man with erysipelas, adjoining this a boy with scarlet fever, all separated by glass partitions but visible and under the eye of the attending nurse." The hospital had a rate of zero cross-infections, and the design contributed to this success. In order to keep the infection "confined to the rooms immediately occupied by the patients," all isolation patients occupied single-bed rooms and were restricted to their cubicles; visitors were limited to an exterior balcony; practitioners had separate circulation paths; and anyone entering or leaving the patient's room had to observe strict decontamination procedures.[48]

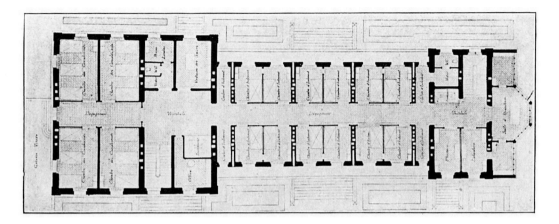

Figure 4.11. Pasteur Hospital, Paris, plan of isolation ward, 1900. The plan shows the proximity of the patient beds in the isolation cubicles, but the physical separation by partitions prevented direct contact. Despite sharing air, the patients did not share germs.

Edward F. Stevens was one of many admirers of this structure; by the 1910s it was widely discussed as a turning point in isolation. Its design incorporated a number of overlapping isolation strategies—the separation of patients into individual cubicles, the inclusion of multiple active and passive aseptic barriers between spaces, and choreographed separate circulation paths for persons and objects based on their state of contamination. None of these individual strategies was original to the Pasteur Hospital. What was original was its effective synthesis of building design and aseptic isolation procedures, which made it the model of a "new" kind of isolation. Its most distinctive architectural feature was the use of individual cubicles, usually of glass. Not everyone was an immediate advocate—some criticized its "imprisonment" of the patients in cubicles, the extensive time nurses and staff spent washing, and the difficulty of teaching and enforcing such complicated aseptic procedures to accompany basic nursing.[49] But for most, the end of hospital disease was worth it.

Within a matter of only a few years, the new isolation became the standard. The tipping point in America was 1910, with the opening of two influential units modeled on the Pasteur Hospital's success. The Contagious Disease Unit of the Providence City Hospital in Rhode Island, designed by Martin and Hall with input from D. L. Richardson and Charles Chapin, was reputedly "the first hospital to be established in this country where contagious diseases are treated on the theory of contact infection." Its design included the same synthesis of aseptic barriers and aseptic procedures as the Pasteur Hospital. In York and Sawyer's design for the Isolation

Figure 4.12. Rockefeller Institute, New York City, view of isolation ward, 1914.

Hospital of the Rockefeller Institute of New York City, the patients were surrounded by glass, and elbow-operated door handles and foot-operated scrub sinks facilitated decontamination before and after entry to a cubicle.[50]

By 1915 new isolation facilities in Europe and the United States were based on the new "cubicle" pattern and administrators of existing hospitals rapidly retrofitted large wards with cubicle partitions. Another indicator of just how quickly the shift occurred is the immediate sense at the time that facilities built just before 1910 were outdated. The Ellis Island Contagious Disease Facility was designed and built in 1907, yet only four years later its doctors considered the numerous separate buildings with large open wards inadequate to the needs of "contact" isolation. They subdivided a number of the large wards into cubicle units with glass windows in their walls to maintain visual control down the length of the ward. By the start of World War I, open multibed wards were virtually obsolete for isolation purposes.[51]

The new isolation involved more than the cubicalization of patients; it involved a highly choreographed and highly controlled circulation of goods and people through the hospital. Different types of personnel or objects had to follow different procedures and might be restricted to specific spaces or required to pass through active barriers for entrance. Doctors and nurses gowned up and washed up upon entry to a cubicle (often in special antechambers), and reversed the process on exit. Visitors had to gown up and often had to remain outside the patient's room (whether on a balcony or in a hallway). Individual pass-through sterilizers for each cubicle often simplified the removal of small items from the patient's room, but larger items (such as sheets, pillows, bedding, even mattresses) required careful transportation to a larger sterilization facility to avoid contamination. At the Providence City Hospital for contagious diseases, service staff sent soiled linens down laundry chutes to fall directly into canvas bags carefully arranged at the bottom of the chute. The bags were carefully tied off to prevent cross-contamination and collected by a gowned attendant. The entire bag, unopened, was thrown into the laundry. After processing, the clean linens were wrapped in clean covers and delivered by gowned attendants to the wards.[52]

The redundant provision of services (e.g., diet kitchens, sanitary facilities, storage areas, even staff housing) within a given isolation unit minimized the need for circulation between units. At the Ellis Island Contagious Disease Hospital each isolation unit had its own separate staff, who were "kept separated from those working in other parts of the hospital." At the Sarah Morris Hospital in Chicago, "in order to keep the nurses in their respective wards as much as possible, many provisions have been made, such as to place separate linen cupboards, medicine cases and bath arrangements either directly in the ward or in an adjoining space separated from the ward by glass partitions."[53] This redundancy essentially made each cubicle (not just every pavilion) its own self-sufficient "unit."

The new isolation, however, was an interior revolution that, for the most part, occupied widely spaced and completely detached pavilions. Isolation facilities (like the Mothers' Aid Pavilion of the Chicago Lying-In Hospital or the Isolation Unit of the Stamford Hospital in Connecticut) typically occupied separate structures in larger facilities. Isolation could also occur at the institutional scale.

The Heyday of Specialized Contagious Disease Hospitals

Increasing awareness that infected persons were germ reservoirs within the community prompted the construction of separate "contagious disease" hospitals—e.g., for victims of smallpox, cholera, measles, or diphtheria—as a "most essential part of the equipment of a city in the battle against contagious diseases." Municipalities across the country established "contagious disease" facilities as crucial aspects of public health; the goal was as much the removal of infected persons from inhabited surroundings as the provision of specialized care.[54] Many occupied facilities with numerous separate pavilions. These typically geographically remote institutions provided a means of keeping the dangerous germs off the streets, out of the general hospitals, and even, theoretically, out of circulation entirely.

The aseptic value of decentralization kept the design of contagious disease hospitals low-rise, decentralized, and pavilion-ward. The strategy of assigning only one germ per building minimized the potential for cross-infections within a pavilion and the separation reduced the number of unnecessary or casual interactions between the staff of the individual structures. Decentralization also functioned as a means of decontamination. Sunlight and fresh air had proven to be germicidal as well as restorative, and exposure to the outdoors remained a form of active aseptic "barrier" between pavilions. Smaller communities often got by with a small facility that might only be opened in need. In the larger cities, or those located along transportation routes—New York City, San Francisco, Boston, or Chicago—these contagious disease hospitals could be on an extensive scale.

The Aseptic Challenges of Building Technologies

Aseptic refinements made material requirements for the early twentieth century hospital even more rigorous. Impermeability remained important. One hospital ward described in 1898 included marble mosaic floors, glass walls, glass ceilings, glass windows, and glass doors, providing "the most complete protection against the growth or entrance of any description of harmful germs." Large slabs of obscure white glass was a preferred wall surface in operating rooms across the country—it was used in the Barnes Hospital in Saint Louis, in the Battle Creek Sanitarium in Michigan, the Jewish Hospital in Philadelphia, and Saint Mary's Hospital in Wisconsin City. In 1906 one architect described a "perfect floor" for a hospital as "non-absorbent, fireproof, germ proof, sound proof, free from liability to crack, uniform in color, non-stainable by acids, easily kept clean and bright and pleasing to the eye." Special hospital fixtures were "characterized by simplicity and by substantial workmanship": "hospital grade" radiators had widely spaced, undecorated fins that could be easily cleaned. At the Lying-In Hospital of the City of New York, designed by Robert H. Robertson with extensive assistance by Lambert and Markoe, all wall-mounted technological features were incorporated as flush, inset pieces; all corners were continuous coved or rounded plaster; all windows had the muntins and mullions on the exterior, and all floors were seamless. The perfectly aseptic hospital interior was a monolithic space—one surface flowing into the next with no corners, joints, cracks, or projections. It was an abstraction.[55]

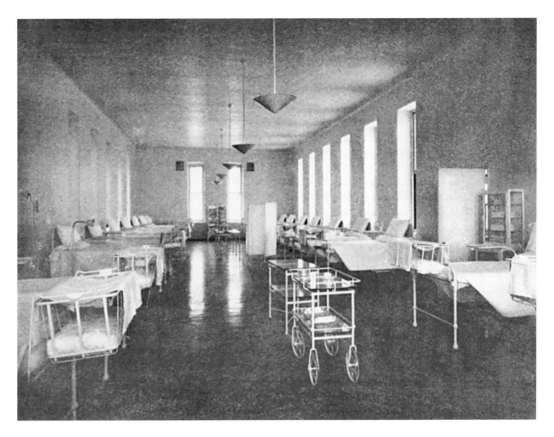

Figure 4.13. Lying-In Hospital of the City of New York, view of ward, 1902.

In the search for more aseptic hospital finishes, many hospital administrators and designers resorted to trying new, even experimental, materials. In 1901 the Mount Sinai Hospital directors installed "antihydrene," a new "antiporous" wall finish, rather than traditional paint. The new Woman's Hospital in New York City and Cook County Hospital in Chicago included a new composite floor material—made of a mixture of magnesium oxide, fine sawdust, asbestos, silicate glass, sand, coloring matter, and magnesium chloride—that was "springy, not slippery," fireproof, and nonabsorptive.[56] Two coats of oil made it impervious.

Manufacturers looking to cash in on the high prices commanded by "hospital grade" materials promoted their hospital products with terms such as "sanitary," "aseptic," or "hygienic." An ad for an artificial marble (made by soaking white sandstone in asphalt and coal tar) described it as weather-resistant, able to "resist acids," and "aseptic." These new materials did not always produce the desired results. The building committee of the Lying-In Hospital of the City of New York chose to finish the floors in lignolith, a manufactured seamless "stone." By 1903, after only a year of use, the doctors reported that "the broken condition of the floors throughout the hospital at the beginning of the year which was due to unforeseen imperfections in the material used, threatened to create a serious and unsanitary state of affairs."[57] During its first years of operations, the floors were constantly being repaired and replaced.

Aseptic design not only required impermeable materials, it required a design that allowed no uncontrolled interaction or movement between spaces; not even of air. According to Markoe and Lambert of the Lying-In Hospital of the City of New York, aseptic design required "absolutely sealing from any possibility of germs, or anything passing up out of" one room into another. Any gap or hole between spaces was a potential conduit for germs. The Providence City Hospital (for contagious diseases) was built so that there were "no communicating or concealed spaces to harbor vermin or in which fire could make its way from floor to floor." To minimize the dangers of pipes, pipe chases, and drains becoming germ conduits throughout the hospital, plumbing expert William Paul Gerhard recommended exposed pipe runs and simplified plumbing layouts for hospitals, with fixtures grouped vertically (in the same location on each floor) and with a minimum of horizontal runs, particularly for drains. To minimize the potential for leaks, pipes and joints for hospital plumbing systems had to be noncorrosive, long-lasting, and smooth. At the Chicago Lying-In Hospital the sterile water pipes were tin-lined galvanized iron and could be sterilized by being flushed with hot water under pressure (at a temperature of about 240 degrees Fahrenheit). Separate towers for sanitary fixtures adjacent to wards and other service areas remained popular despite hospital architect Bertrand E. Taylor's opinion that such separation was unnecessary.[58]

Hospital designers who did utilize hollow-wall construction gave extensive consideration to minimizing the potential for the walls to become infected. Henry Hun, a doctor in Albany, New York, suggested that for disinfection "the darker portion of the plumbing stacks" required "an airshaft with glass in it" to allow the penetration of the germicidal sunlight and fresh air. Ventilation expert D. D. Kimball recommended that the inside of hospital air ducts "should be finished perfectly smooth and should be as accessible as possible, that the interior surfaces may be occasionally cleaned, and that they may not become culture tubes for the propagation of germs." At the new Cincinnati General Hospital each floor had its own dedicated dumbwaiter so there was no cross-contamination by the shared use of items or services between floors.[59]

In-wall technologies that facilitated the disposal or transport of infected items had to be capable of decontamination. Hospital vacuum systems

or dust chutes often fed the refuse straight into the boiler fires for immediate incineration. Henry Hurd recommended laundry chutes that were
"round metal tubes, one, at least for each ward, with smooth interior surfaces, every portion of which can be cleansed and disinfected." The Sarah
Morris Hospital for Children in Chicago had glass-enameled steel clothes
chutes, each with a roof skylight and ventilator, a perforated flushing ring
connected with a hot water supply at the top (for disinfecting the inside
of the chute), and integral drains at the bottom. At the Isolation Building
of the Rockefeller Institute, eminent ventilation specialist Alfred Wolff
designed the ducts to have no dust-collecting elbows. A vertical exhaust
duct ran through the corner of each room directly to the roof, where the
air was sterilized before release. At the bottom of these flues was a steam
radiator that could be opened to release the steam and sterilize the inside of
the ducts. After sterilization, the steam condensed on the inside walls of the
ducts and drained to the bowl-shaped bottom, from which an access panel
allowed it to be sponged out. "It is thus as easy for the nurse to clean out the
whole apparatus with live steam as it is to turn on the heat."[60]

The resultant extreme environment was not universally admired. While
in earlier decades, glaring white materials and constant disinfectant odors
had indicated a reassuring cleanliness, by the 1910s the "sterility" of the
hospital interior was coming in for hard criticism. One patient found the
aseptic spaces—designed around germs, not people—monotonous: "Everything in the little room was of spotless white, white tiled floor, white
iron chair, white rocker, white bed, small white table, not a microbe to be
seen with the best regulated microscope." At a time of intensely colorful
architectural and interior designs in other building types, the monochromatic nature of the hospital offered a convenient aesthetic target. While
some believed that by making dirt more easily visible hospital white instilled better habits of cleanliness, others, like architect Robert J. Reiley,
advocated using colors in the hospital to avoid "the white enamel interior
so repellant [sic] to patients."[61] The critics were in the minority, though. As
M. E. McCalmont asked, "There is a great hue and cry about our 'hospitals looking like hospitals.' What should they look like, pray?"[62] The early
twentieth-century hospital served asepsis first, aesthetics last.

Functional Centralization: Design for Efficiency

If decentralized facilities emphasized the hospital as a collection of independent units, centralized facilities offered the chance to consider the hospital as a whole. S. S. Goldwater believed it was necessary to "regard the
hospital unit as a minor factor in a great correlation of parts which, func-

tionating [sic] together, make up the healthy, growing life of the complete hospital."[63] This holistic conception of the hospital grew out of medical and administrative transformations that increasingly valued integration rather than separation.

The growing need for efficient (lower-cost) provision of basic services made the hospital a tool for facilitating medical treatments—a "factory" "in which broken and diseased persons [were] repaired as far as human ingenuity permits," and a place "in which patients can be treated with proportionately less labor." As with any manufacturing plant, the building design of a hospital could directly influence not only "production" capacity and institutional costs, but the entire production process and its significance.[64]

Group Medical Practice and the Shift from Unitary to Synthetic Design

Interest in the hospital as a functional whole was a reaction against the late nineteenth-century general hospital that had become "a complex of many specialized hospitals." According to historian Harry F. Dowling, in the independent pavilions, each doctor "was an independent peer of the realm, in complete charge of 'his' ward and accountable to no one for his actions." Dr. Will Mayo commented that in these fragmented hospitals, "Man was divided for treatment into parts, as a wagon is divided in the process of manufacture." This division promoted the independent development of specialties, but by the early twentieth century, growing medical awareness of the systemic, holistic nature of many ailments required different practical structures. According to Drs. Philemon E. Truesdale and R. W. French, "Cooperation of medical men, placed in convenient, harmonious, and reciprocal relations, offers the only logical way to make the vast and complicated range of medical knowledge fully serviceable to the individual patient." Collaboration—between specialists and generalists, physicians and surgeons, the lab and the bedside, the clinic and the diagnostic facility—was the new ideal. It offered the potential of improved, holistic treatment, but also economic benefits, as a group of practitioners could more easily afford the increasing spatial and technological requirements for medical practice.[65]

In America, the medical model of this collaboration was the vastly successful "group" medical practice founded by the Doctors Mayo in Rochester, Minnesota, in which numerous specialists consulted on the conditions of each individual patient. Experiences in the Mayo Clinic made it eminently clear that the architectural layout of a medical facility could hinder or facilitate that interaction. When they decided to expand their facilities, the Mayos and other doctors of the Mayo Clinic worked with Minneapolis-based architect Thomas Ellerbe of Ellerbe and Round in the planning of a new medical building that would facilitate collaboration. Dr. Henry S. Plummer, a crucial contributor to the new plans, believed that before "the drawing of plans" it was necessary to "first decide precisely what kind of medicine was to be practiced." The facility design was to be an integral factor in the performance of their innovative medical practice. According to Dr. Richard Olding Beard, "the dominant conception which the building embodies is that of the patient as the subject of a critical, systematic, and exhaustive investigation. The principal parts of the building present a highly co-ordinated mechanism for the pursuit of this investigation by any combination of men and of methods that the particular case may demand."[66]

The new Mayo Clinic building was centralized, with a large waiting room and numerous standardized consultation rooms on the first floor, diagnostic facilities (X-ray, cystoscopy, laboratories) on the second floor, laboratories and a library on the third floor, and pathological facilities on the fourth floor. The slight shift in terminology—from an examination room to a consultation room—reveals a revolutionary change. An examination room allowed a doctor to examine a patient in privacy; consultation rooms (which were combination office and examination rooms) allowed a number of specialists to consult with the patient on diagnosis and treatment. The telltale indicator that a sea change had occurred in spatial allocation within the building was that "the patients did not have [to be] shunted from doctor to doctor and room to room—the medical specialists came to all of them." The consulting room was neutral shared space within an institution that was traditionally territorialized. Rather than dictators within their own pavilion, doctors became itinerant inhabitants of a larger space. The building assisted this transformation. For example, consultation required getting the right doctor to the correct room at the proper time. Within the clinic, "a system of colored signal-lights, ranged along the corridors, announces the presence and whereabouts of each leading clinician."[67]

In the early 1900s patients from across the country, even across the world, flocked to the Mayo Clinic to receive treatment in the new collaborative practice, and American hospital administrators across the country scrambled to reorganize their medical structure to provide a version of this more cooperative, group diagnostic practice. Rewriting existing medical protocols to encourage more collaboration in diagnosis, treatment, and consultation was relatively straightforward; fitting the new procedures into the existing decentralized hospital facilities proved more difficult. The Mayo Clinic's influential 1914 building provided a limited model—it was basically a large outpatient facility. Mayo Clinic patients who required

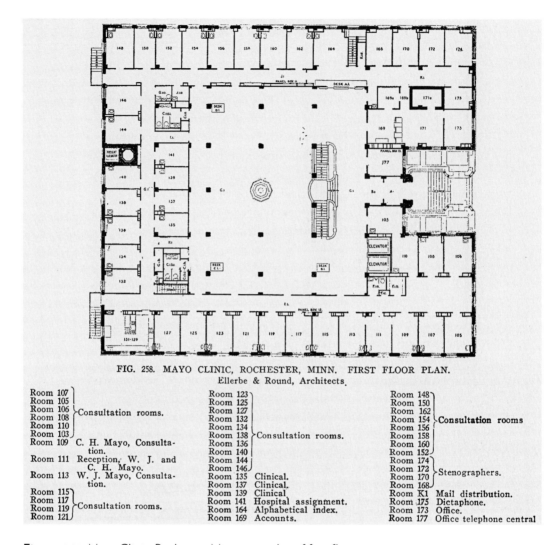

FIG. 258. MAYO CLINIC, ROCHESTER, MINN. FIRST FLOOR PLAN.
Ellerbe & Round, Architects.

Room 107 ⎫
Room 105 ⎬
Room 106 ⎬ Consultation rooms.
Room 108 ⎬
Room 110 ⎬
Room 103 ⎭
Room 109 — C. H. Mayo, Consultation.
Room 111 — Reception, W. J. and C. H. Mayo.
Room 113 — W. J. Mayo, Consultation.
Room 115 ⎫
Room 117 ⎬ Consultation rooms.
Room 119 ⎬
Room 121 ⎭

Room 123 ⎫
Room 125 ⎬
Room 127 ⎬
Room 132 ⎬
Room 134 ⎬
Room 138 ⎬ Consultation rooms.
Room 136 ⎬
Room 140 ⎬
Room 144 ⎬
Room 146 ⎭
Room 135 — Clinical.
Room 137 — Clinical.
Room 139 — Clinical
Room 141 — Hospital assignment.
Room 164 — Alphabetical index.
Room 169 — Accounts.

Room 148 ⎫
Room 150 ⎬
Room 162 ⎬
Room 154 ⎬ Consultation rooms
Room 156 ⎬
Room 158 ⎬
Room 160 ⎬
Room 152 ⎭
Room 174 ⎫
Room 172 ⎬ Stenographers.
Room 170 ⎬
Room 168 ⎭
Room K1 — Mail distribution.
Room 175 — Dictaphone.
Room 173 — Office.
Room 177 — Office telephone central

Figure 4.14. Mayo Clinic, Rochester, Minnesota, plan of first floor, 1914.

hospitalization were typically referred to the nearby Saint Mary's Hospital or one of the nearby hotel-hospitals. How to make an entire hospital, not just a clinic, efficient at promoting interactive medical practice required a reconsideration of hospital design, and in particular an emphasis on the interaction rather than separation of spaces.[68]

In order to foster collaboration, hospitals had to be designed to bring the different specialties and specialists into closer physical proximity. This could be done by centralization (eliminating open land) or by greater density of construction (building higher). Both strategies challenged the hygienic interdiction against tall, interconnected buildings. Even as late as 1908,

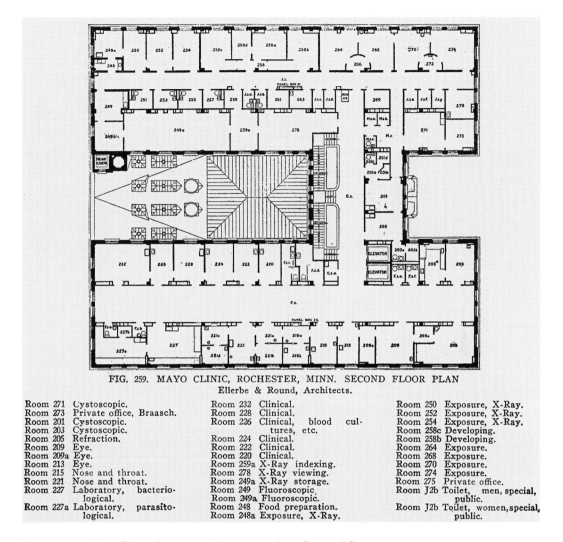

FIG. 259. MAYO CLINIC, ROCHESTER, MINN. SECOND FLOOR PLAN
Ellerbe & Round, Architects.

Room 271 Cystoscopic.	Room 232 Clinical.	Room 250 Exposure, X-Ray.
Room 273 Private office, Braasch.	Room 228 Clinical.	Room 252 Exposure, X-Ray.
Room 201 Cystoscopic.	Room 226 Clinical, blood cul-	Room 254 Exposure, X-Ray.
Room 203 Cystoscopic.	tures, etc.	Room 258c Developing.
Room 205 Refraction.	Room 224 Clinical.	Room 258b Developing.
Room 209 Eye.	Room 222 Clinical.	Room 264 Exposure.
Room 209a Eye.	Room 220 Clinical.	Room 268 Exposure.
Room 213 Eye.	Room 259a X-Ray indexing.	Room 270 Exposure.
Room 215 Nose and throat.	Room 278 X-Ray viewing.	Room 274 Exposure.
Room 221 Nose and throat.	Room 249a X-Ray storage.	Room 275 Private office.
Room 227 Laboratory, bacterio-	Room 249 Fluoroscopic.	Room J2b Toilet, men, special,
logical.	Room 249a Fluoroscopic.	public.
Room 227a Laboratory, parasito-	Room 248 Food preparation.	Room J2b Toilet, women, special,
logical.	Room 248a Exposure, X-Ray.	public.

Figure 4.15. Mayo Clinic, Rochester, Minnesota, plan of second floor, 1914.

the rumored construction of an eleven-story building for the Saint Louis City Hospital led to a loud public outcry from both doctors and citizens.[69]

The tide of opinion was beginning to turn, however, as champions of tall hospital buildings appeared in diverse locations such as Minneapolis and Chicago. In 1902, Dr. Albert J. Ochsner surprised medical audiences when he championed taller, more compact hospital buildings that would reduce wasted travel time for physicians between units and provide better access to sunlight and fresh air to hospitals in the increasingly dense American cities. Ochsner continued to promote the many-storied hospital, in lectures, articles, and his book-length collaborative publication with architect Meyer J.

Sturm. In a series of figure-ground diagrams, Ochsner graphically revealed spatial benefits of ten wards stacked into a ten-story building rather than arranged in ten one-story pavilions. In this discussion, taller hospitals were offering not a more economical use of pricy urban real estate (the justification for the vertical ascent of other building types) but more open space that would provide an uninterrupted supply of sunlight and fresh air flow to the building, no matter how built up the surroundings. In fact, Ochsner considered it "a serious error to build many storied hospitals because of lack of space." The taller hospitals also allowed a more efficient arrangement of spaces—the operating room and kitchen on the top floor for best light and air and to keep smells from permeating the hospital; the administration on the first floor for convenient access; the patient rooms on the upper floors for light and air; each service to occupy a distinct floor—and the easy delivery of goods by dumbwaiter and elevator rather than by handtruck.[70]

European practitioners were also intrigued by the possibilities. William Henman's Royal Victoria Hospital in Belfast had provided a model for greater compactness of plan, but it remained one story. In 1904, A. Beresford Pite's suggestion for a fifteen-story hospital for London appeared in the *Builder*. A perspective rendering showed the building towering above the London skyline. Pite had been inspired by a letter written by Mr. Macalister, Librarian of the Royal Medical and Chirurgical Society, that had been published in the *New York Times*. Macalister had described the illuminating experience in skyscrapers where on the upper floors "the noise of the streets was a pleasant murmur, the rooms were well-windowed and full of sunlight, and would have made ideal wards."[71] But this speculative tower project was not a reorganization of hospital service; it was a means of providing better "hygienic decentralization"—better light and air—even in dense urban surroundings. In plan, the building resembled an arrangement of traditional pavilion-wards in a cross, basically stacking traditional, independent pavilions without providing for increased interaction between them. In practice, European hospitals remained primarily low-rise, decentralized facilities well into the twentieth century.

In America, two divergent architectural strategies for exactly what form a "taller" hospital should take developed in the first decades of the twentieth century. One strategy was simply to make pavilions taller, superimposing or stacking more wards but maintaining the independence of each floor. Such a strategy created hybrid institutions, with traditional ground-level horizontal circulation between identifiably distinct building components and vertical circulation within each of those components. Historians of hospital architecture have categorized such hospital structures as "stacked" pavilions. This term is misleading, as it implies that the decentralization of the

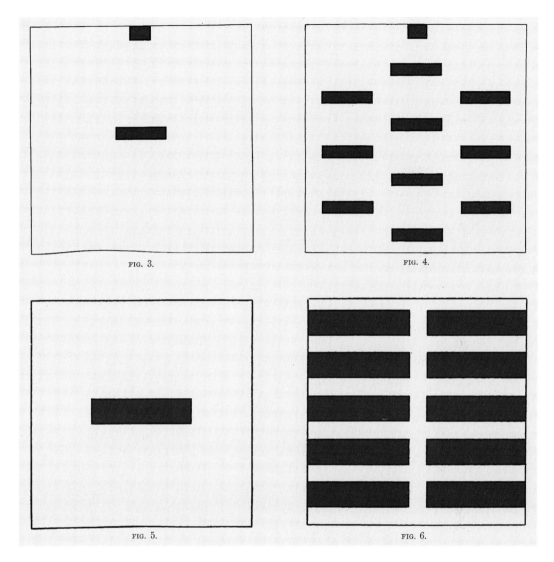

Figure 4.16. Albert J. Ochsner and Meyer J. Sturm, plan diagrams of vertical and horizontal hospitals, 1907. All diagrams show a five-hundred-bed facility using the same building footprint. The upper left-hand diagram shows a ten-story building on a five-acre site. The upper right-hand diagram shows ten one-story buildings on that same five-acre site. The lower diagrams show a ten-story building and ten one-story buildings on a smaller, more urban site of only 520 feet on each side.

pavilions continued unchecked while highlighting the increasing height of hospital facilities.[72] The architectural transformation of hospitals in this period involved far more complexity, however, than the simple multiplication of stories on traditional pavilion-ward designs; it also encompassed exten-

Figure 4.17. Lying-In Hospital of the City of New York, view, 1901.

sive spatial integration and centralization. That integration was far more evident in the second architectural strategy for high-rise hospitals: to integrate all the different hospital functions and requirements in a single, tall, vertically organized, centralized, high-rise structure.

American hospital designers began to build as well as talk about taller, more centralized hospitals in the early twentieth century. Even in decentralized facilities on suburban sites, four to six stories were common; on urban sites, pavilions of six to eight stories were common. Hospitals organized as a single, compact, centralized building pushed even higher. In January 1902 the centralized, nine-story Lying-In Hospital of the City of New York garnered praise rather than censure. The compact layout facilitated a new clinical medical practice (based on German precedents), had shorter circulation patterns, allowed greater spatial integration of disparate departments, and fit a lot of facility on a relatively small site. The aseptic interior design and details meant that all these benefits could occur without risking the health of the patients.[73] This provided a positive model, if not a clear doctrine, for other tall hospitals.

In the 1900s and 1910s different kinds of institutions benefited from different kinds of taller facility. Specialized institutions tended toward more compact plans, and were the most likely to build a single-tower, many-storied hospital building. General hospitals, teaching hospitals, and early medical centers gravitated towards hybrid facilities, with ever taller, denser, and more interconnected separate building components. The reasons for this institution-specific correlation can be found in the varying organizational requirements of the different kinds of institutions.

High-Rise Specialized Hospitals

Specialized hospitals typically served a single kind of patient, provided a focused, specialized medical practice, and were run by a single administrative entity. The need for "hygienic decentralization" of the patients or of different departments was thus minimal. Centralized compact floor plans that organized the practice vertically, by floor (rather than horizontally, by separate building components), were an efficient means of organizing specialized hospital practice. The Herman Knapp Memorial Eye Hospital provides a good example. Its seven floors were divided into service department in the basement, clinic on the first and second floors, wards on the third and fourth floors, private patient rooms on the fifth floor, nurse housing on the sixth floor, and surgical suite, laboratories, X-ray, and staff housing on the seventh floor. The vertical format minimized the "long tramps from ward to ward" that had exhausted doctors, nurses, and staff.[74]

The earliest hospitals to occupy many-storied centralized single buildings were almost all specialized hospitals (e.g., the Babies' Hospital in New York City, the French Hospital in New York City, the Philadelphia Lying-In Hospital, the Philadelphia Polyclinic Hospital, the Augustana Hospital in Chicago, and the Herman Knapp Memorial Eye Hospital in New York City). By 1912 the New York Polyclinic Hospital had opened a new eleven-story building. The following year, the Post-Graduate Hospital pushed to a record height (for hospitals) of thirteen stories. These early many-storied hospitals resembled Ochsner's idealized "tower in a park" but without the park; they typically built to their lot lines.[75] Clearly, Ochsner's combination of open site and tall building was difficult to realize on expensive, congested downtown sites.

These hospitals typically offered a very medicalized service, and in them, the compact, vertically organized plan facilitated the efficient provision of care. That lying-in hospitals—once subject to the most extreme architectural hygiene as a means of preventing postpartum infections—should be numbered among the earliest many-storied hospital structures corroborates this. Though these hospitals might still retain the name of lying-in hospital, they were locations of the new obstetric and gynecological services rather than the more traditional lying-in services. For patients experiencing complications or requiring extra care, the hospital provided the facilities, staff, and aseptic conditions necessary to successful performance

Figure 4.18. Polyclinic Medical School and Hospital, New York City, 1914. The founder, Dr. Wyeth, bought a site in the middle of the block, rather than a corner, because he could get more land for the same price. In compensation, he built taller "for light, air and freedom from noise and dust."

of surgeries and medical interventions.[76] In these many-storied hospitals, operating rooms could outnumber birthing rooms and the experience of delivery was a spatial progression from labor room to delivery room to recovery room—like a factory.

Hybrid Designs: The Stacked Pavilions of General Hospitals, Teaching Hospitals, and Early Medical Centers

The breadth of service performed in general hospitals contributed to the persistent value of horizontal as well as vertical organization of their facilities. Large general hospitals provided for a wide variety of patients, services, and practitioners; this required a great variety of spaces, each with differing requirements for isolation or integration. Traditionally, each hospital department occupied a different building; this allowed each specialty to develop its own efficient internal administration and to maintain a separate identity within the larger whole. This also mimicked the much-admired European model of specialization in which each clinic occupied its own separate building. Although collaboration between specialists was the ideal, the autonomy of each specialty and service within a larger hospital remained strong in the early twentieth century. But decentralization discouraged collaboration. For example, in the planning stages of one new hospital, the various heads of departments (surgical, medical, children's, etc.) "object[ed] to going into another building for demonstration of their cases" and so the hospital designers were faced with requests for five or more amphitheaters.[77]

Whether in the city or in the countryside, many early twentieth-century general hospitals often consisted of a dozen or more buildings, four to eight stories high, in close proximity on a limited site. The spatial complexity of this tight grouping of many-storied pavilions matched the functional complexity of general hospitals, while still providing reduced travel distances. The density of construction also made it possible to fit the growing area of the increasingly large general hospitals (some held two thousand beds or more) onto a city site. McKim, Mead and White's 1904 design for Bellevue Hospital proved a highly influential example of this new dense hybrid hospital. The individual pavilions were taller, and the pavilions were more compactly arranged. The corridors between pavilions had also shifted in design and function. The nineteenth-century hospital's open-air walkways had been sanitary fresh air reservoirs that kept the pavilions hygienically separate. By the 1910s hospital corridors were short, enclosed, continuous, and often contained programmed spaces. They connected the buildings, turning the hospital into the desired functional whole.

The resultant density of building components facilitated service centralization, reduced overall travel distances, and shortened the pipe and duct runs between the pavilions. It also served the functional requirements of an increasingly interactive medical practice. While hospitals on city sites might rise to the most stories, even hospitals with large sites and open natural surroundings, like the Galloway Hospital in Nashville, or the Ohio Val-

Figure 4.19. Bellevue Hospital, New York City, axonometric, 1904. Designed by T. J. Van der Bent (who would go on to design a number of hospitals with McKim, Mead and White) and S. S. Goldwater, this design was well publicized and influential. Given the extensive, widely separated wings and landscaped courtyards, this kind of facility epitomizes the idea of a "stacked" pavilion hospital. The wings are all interconnected into a single, integrated, albeit rambling, facility.

ley General Hospital in Wheeling, West Virginia, built facilities with densely arranged, multistory buildings. Clearly, the hybrid layout was a match to the functional needs of the hospital, not (as for other building types) the direct result of surrounding contextual influence or real estate pressure.

While typically the larger the hospital, the greater the density of its construction, this was not an absolute correlation. Some new large general hospitals maintained the low-rise decentralized pavilion-ward standard. The Cincinnati General Hospital set an alternate model, based on emulation of German hospitals. Other hospitals, like Stratton and Baldwin's design for the Detroit General Hospital and Green and Wicks's design for the Buffalo City Hospital, remained lower-rise and decentralized. The Peter Bent Brigham Hospital in Boston also remained low-rise and decentralized, but it and the Municipal Hospital for the District of Columbia were influenced by a design competition in which the program clearly set requirements for low-rise pavilions.

The transformation of medical education in the early twentieth century, which sought to foster more integral interactions between medical schools and hospitals, also influenced the development of two new types of general hospitals—teaching hospitals and medical centers—both of which provided a new scale of design difficulty. According to Abraham Flexner, the author of a pivotal 1910 report on medical education, "The best hospitals today, and those which accomplish the highest service, are intimately connected with great medical schools. And it is equally true that those medical schools which attain the maximum efficiency are affiliated with properly appointed hospitals." Reactions to Flexner's report transformed medical education, according to Starr and Ludmerer, eventually eliminating proprietary medical schools and creating fewer, but more complete, schools that were linked to a general university education for preclinical studies and to hospitals for clinical studies. The end result was more formalized "affiliations" between fewer, larger, and better-organized medical schools and hospitals. For hospital designers, the question was how to structure that new, more formalized, more integral interaction between the larger, more complex components necessary to clinical studies.[78]

Samuel Waldron Lambert, dean of the College of Physicians and Surgeons of Columbia University in New York City, considered the ideal design for a teaching hospital or a medical center to be immediately adjacent facilities that could operate independently or in unified interaction.[79] The hybrid facility of taller, denser pavilions could provide this combination of independence and interdependence, allowing each institution (not just each ward, department, or service) to occupy distinct building components within an integrated whole. The Barnes Hospital complex in Saint Louis, one of the earliest medical centers, combined the Washington University in Saint Louis's School of Medicine, the new Barnes General Hospital, and the Saint Louis Children's Hospital on one site. In the new facility each institution occupied a wholly independent, custom-designed facility. Horizontal circulation provided interconnection between the different components; vertical circulation provided circulation within a single component. Such hybrid designs, however, kept the medical center functioning as a combination of separate pieces, not as an integrated whole.

By 1916 Lambert diagrammed an ideal teaching hospital and medical center as a low-rise base building with a number of hygienically decentralized towers rising from it. The base held centralized services for efficient administration; the towers (essentially a number of stacked pavilions) held ward units and medical services.[80] Lambert's design fulfilled the competing requirements for hygienic decentralization (keeping everything separate to prevent cross-infections) and functional centralization (keeping everything close to facilitate efficient interactive service). This diagram provided a second, alternate model to Ochsner's single high-rise, one that could accommodate a complex, conglomerate institution.

Figure 4.20. Barnes Hospital and Medical School, Saint Louis, bird's-eye view, 1916. The horseshoe drive leads to the main entrance of the main hospital, with service buildings extending behind it on axis. Behind it on the left-hand edge of the picture is the Children's Hospital; behind it to the right is the Free Clinic and Pathological building. The Washington University Medical School Building is across the street. The plans, all designed by Theodore C. Link, also projected a hospital for African Americans and nurse housing.

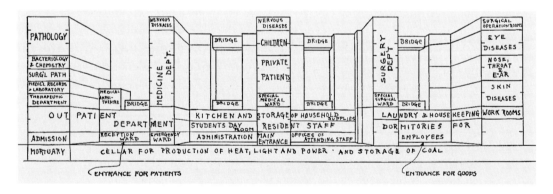

Figure 4.21. Samuel Lambert, diagram of modern hospital, 1916. The diagram shows that each clinic or specialty is still treated as an independent unit, but all the units are arranged into an integrated whole.

The New Interconnected Hospital

Whether in traditional pavilions, a hybrid taller denser pavilion, or a single, centralized structure, daily experiences in the new, interactive hospital were far different from those in the pavilion-ward hospital. Doctors performed a majority of medical procedures somewhere other than in the ward and traveled to laboratories, pathological facilities, libraries, and consultation rooms; meanwhile, patients traveled throughout the hospital for diagnosis, therapy, and recreation; and nurses covered miles and miles of ground between centralized services, wards, medical services, training rooms, supply rooms, and housing. While the increasing interaction between all of these different parts of the hospital promoted taller, denser hospital layouts for the overall facility, each individual department within the hospital—medical services, therapeutic facilities, day spaces—was designed for efficient delivery of a service.

The Medical Services

As the interactive, scientific core of the new collaborative medicine, the hospital's medical services provided a strong centralizing influence. Laboratories as well as X-ray, cystoscopy, and records rooms all needed to be easily accessible to patients, doctors, staff, surgical departments, research departments, records departments, even administrators. These facilities were unstable features within the hospital, however, in that their internal functioning often required extensive equipment that underwent rapid development and required regular replanning and renovation.

The housing of X-ray facilities within early twentieth-century hospitals provides a graphic example of the problems of designing for medical services. The obvious advantages of X-ray photography—being able to "see" inside the body—meant that the adoption of X-ray apparatus in hospitals occurred quickly. Six months after Wilhelm Roentgen's first photographs in November 1895, the governors of the New York Hospital appropriated $300 for the purchase of X-ray apparatus. By 1897, even administrators of small specialized hospitals (like the New York Orthopedic Dispensary and Hospital) were installing X-ray equipment. In Chicago, the Deaconess Hospital's first X-ray machine was installed in 1904, the Provident Hospital's in 1906. By 1911 Edward F. Stevens could comment, "No hospital nowadays is quite complete without its Roentgen or X-Ray room and apparatus." The lack of an in-house facility was considered a severe handicap.[81]

The earliest X-ray installations had to accommodate bulky equipment, and many occupied makeshift spaces in basements and service outbuildings. These marginal locations allayed early fears about the dangers of the rays and the equipment, but also simply indicate where space could be made available. As X-rays quickly became "essential" facilities, some criticized the tendency "to put the X-ray department in the most out-of-the-way, inaccessible, and unsanitary part of the building."[82]

There was in fact no clear best location for an X-ray facility; it was beneficial to too many different parts of the hospital. Proximity to the operating room was clearly desirable, particularly for cases of fractured bones. Since it was a clinical service, to which patients had to be transported, proximity to the wards was also desirable. Outpatients needed it to be accessible, but in a manner that didn't "make it necessary for outdoor and dispensary patients to wander through the halls and ride in the elevators to reach the laboratory." In the mid-1910s, the need for X-rays in multiple departments even prompted experimentation with portable X-ray machines.[83]

By the 1910s, X-ray service in hospitals had developed from a room accommodating equipment into a complex department providing diagnostic but also therapeutic services. The internal spatial requirements of that department were determined by functional necessities. The space needed to be laid out so as to move patients, doctors, nurses, technicians, and staff in and out efficiently, comfortably, safely, and privately, and to accommodate the equipment for efficient use, maintenance, and even replacement. By the late 1910s the development of more lasting plates added the requirement of extensive filing systems and storage. The advent of X-ray therapy increased spatial demands even further. X-ray therapy machines could be large enough to treat numerous patients simultaneously. The increase in volume of patients visiting the X-ray department for therapy required the addition of waiting rooms and sanitary facilities. The establishment of better knowledge of the debilitating effects of long-term exposure to the rays prompted better architectural precautions (with lead-lined walls). Increasingly, this complexity of spatial requirements meant that a well-designed X-ray department required a number of well-protected rooms, arranged into an efficient sequence for the processing of patients, the processing of plates, and of doctors viewing plates.[84] The X-ray department of the new Cook County Hospital in Chicago, designed by Richard E. Schmidt, occupied five thousand square feet of floor space, was divided into fourteen rooms, and included a new zig-zag entrance into the plate rooms and dark rooms that blocked light but allowed free passage.

X-ray facilities thus were not only a functional unit within the larger hospital, they were functional units unto themselves. The success of the design influenced the success of the service. That success, however, was largely measured in throughput—the numbers of patients served; the numbers

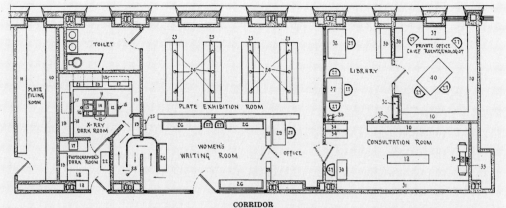

CORRIDOR

SOUTH OF CORRIDOR

10. Plate-filing shelves.
11. Developing tank.
12. Water compartment.
13. Compartment for developer.
14. Compartment for hypo.
15. Inlet and mixing chamber.
16. Outlet.
17. Sink.
18. Work table.

19. Supply shelves.
20. Tray developer.
21. Table with Victor tray-rocker.
22. Supply case.
23. Plate racks for exhibiting plates.
24. Cooper-Hewitt lamps for illuminating plate racks.
25. Clock.
26. Benches.

27. Chairs.
28. Rail.
29. Clerk's desk.
30. Typist's desk.
31. Inspection frame, illuminated by Cooper-Hewitt lamps, with plate files underneath.
32. Victor stereoscope, with plate files underneath.
33. Electric fan.

34. Card index.
35. Coat hooks.
36. Clothes locker.
37. Reference table.
38. Assistant roentgenologist's desk.
39. Bookcase.
40. Chief roentgenologist's desk.
88. Dim red light.
89. Skeleton on stand.

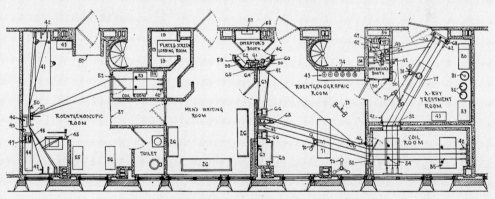

Fig. 2. Plan of new x-ray department at Cook County Hospital.

NORTH OF CORRIDOR

19. Supply shelves.
26. Benches.
41. Victor horizontal roentgenoscope.
42. Insulators.
43. Utility table.
44. Table for lateral recumbent position.
45. Victor vertical roentgenoscope, arranged for orthodiagraphy.
46. Rheostat for interrupterless transformer mounted on wall.
47. Victor Coolidge transformer on insulating shelf.
48. Victor Coolidge ammeter mounted beneath insulating shelf.
49. Victor Coolidge regulator.
50. Victor Coolidge high-tension switch.
51. Milliampere meter mounted on switch.

52. Glass insulator.
53. Victor 2 K.W. interrupterless transformer.
54. Victor Coolidge rotary converter.
55. Bausch & Lomb projector.
56. Bausch & Lomb photomicrograph.
57. Service box containing main switches for entire department.
58. Lead-lined plate box for unexposed plates.
59. Lead-lined plate box for exposed plates.
60. Victor Coolidge battery rheostat.
61. Victor Coolidge battery ammeter.
62. Milliampere meter mounted on wall.
63. Cord from high-tension terminal board to spark-gap indicator and vacuum reducer knob.

64. Spark-gap indicator and vacuum reducer knob.
65. Victor teleflasher.
66. Storage battery on insulated shelf, with special switch arranged so that one battery is on charge while the other is in use.
67. Charging board for storage batteries.
68. High-tension terminal board.
69. Vertical stereoscopic shift.
70. Victor No. 3 radiographic stand.
71. Victor No. 1 radiographic table.
72. Aerial insulators for connecting milliammeter into high-tension line.
73. X-ray protection screen for convenience of visiting roentgenologists.

74. X-ray tube rack.
75. Rheostat for interrupterless transformer on truck.
76. Victor Coolidge ammeter mounted on wall.
77. Treatment table.
78. Victor No. 4 treatment stand.
79. Extra x-ray tube stand, with broad focus Coolidge tube for stomach work.
80. Cystoscopic table.
81. Sterile water tank.
82. Basin.
83. Instrument cabinet.
84. Victor 10 K.V.A. interrupterless transformer.
85. Victor Wantz special interrupterless transformer.
86. Victor therapy flasher.
87. Light-proof curtain.
90. Lead-glass window.

Figure 4.22. Cook County Hospital, Chicago, plan of X-ray department, 1917.

of plates created, analyzed, and stored; the length of time each patient spent in the facility. The design of this medical service was more like the design of an industrial process—it was a factory for medical diagnosis and treatment.

The Functional Operating Suite

Aseptic requirements remained the primary design requirement of early twentieth-century surgical suites, but new medical education practices, the increasing popularity and frequency of surgery as a treatment, and the changing medical organization of surgery in American hospitals influenced the design of surgical spaces.

In operating rooms as well as isolation rooms aseptic barriers and aseptic procedures prevented casual contact between clean and infected items or persons. In the surgical wing of Saint Joseph's Hospital in Chicago, designed by Victor Andre Matteson, a single corridor ran the length of the suite, but only "properly prepared nurses, surgeons in gowns, and the patient" were allowed past the passive barrier (doors) at its midpoint into the clean side of the corridor. Septic cases were banned entirely from the floor, as there was a separate operating room for "pus" cases on the ground floor. Entrance for the surgeon and assistants into the operating room itself was through the active barrier of a "surgeons' final wash-up room." Attendants brought patients to the operating floor by the special surgical elevator, and from there to the preparation room. Three of the four main operating rooms had a dedicated sterilization room (for instruments and supplies) accessed only through the operating room, minimizing the chance of cross-contamination. The swinging double doors that led from the passage straight into the operating room would have been limited to use by the patient on the gurney (and accompanying staff), and by outgoing personnel. The two small viewing areas for audiences to watch an operation were accessed only by small stairways off the "infected" side of the corridor.[85]

Abraham Flexner's call for medical students to receive more hands-on clinical experience and meaningful observation of actual procedures reduced the value of large surgical amphitheaters. As one medical practitioner recalled from his student days, the view from an amphitheater seat was so poor that "it really made no difference what ailed the patient; the professor could use him as text for almost any disease and we would be none the wiser."[86] The inclusion of numbers of observers in the immediate operating space was also problematic for aseptic control.

Amphitheaters dwindled in size. In 1897 the Pennsylvania Hospital's new amphitheater included 204 seats; by 1913 the gargantuan new Cook County Hospital in Chicago held only two amphitheaters of only 120 seats

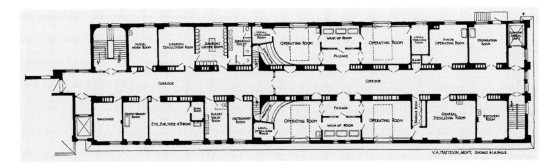

Figure 4.23. Saint Joseph's Hospital, Kansas City, fifth-floor plan, 1916, designed by Victor Andre Matteson.

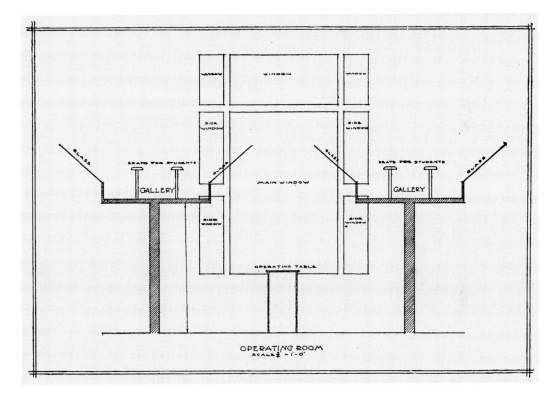

Figure 4.24. Boston Children's Hospital, section of operating rooms, 1913.

each. Newly designed hospital facilities of the 1910s were far more likely to include small-scale viewing platforms in otherwise regular operating rooms; this provided a much more intimate experience for the students. In many hospitals, students were allowed to stand on the operating floor (usually with a simple barrier limiting their proximity) or the administrators installed moveable bleachers along one wall. Since aseptic requirements

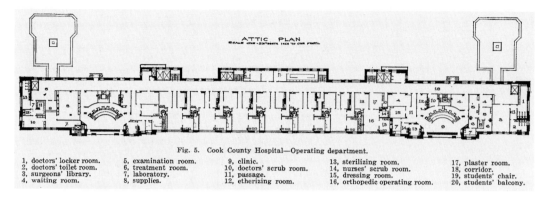

Fig. 5. Cook County Hospital—Operating department.

1, doctors' locker room.	5, examination room.	9, clinic.	13, sterilizing room.	17, plaster room.
2, doctors' toilet room.	6, treatment room.	10, doctors' scrub room.	14, nurses' scrub room.	18, corridor.
3, surgeons' library.	7, laboratory.	11, passage.	15, dressing room.	19, students' chair.
4, waiting room.	8, supplies.	12, etherizing room.	16, orthopedic operating room.	20, students' balcony.

Figure 4.25. Cook County Hospital, Chicago, plan of operating floor, 1913, Richard E. Schmidt.

still had to be met, in these situations student observers might be required to gown up, providing another level of practical experience and precaution. At the Boston Children's Hospital newly designed operating rooms had elevated observation stands, which placed the students nearly directly over the operating table for the best view. Glass barriers allowed visibility but prevented the spread of germs from the students to the patient below. The hospital administrators noted that the angle of the glass was crucial to ensuring that visibility was not impeded by glare or reflections.[87]

The increasing popularity of surgical treatment, however, meant that amphitheaters were the only feature of surgical suites that was shrinking. Hospital designers struggled to accommodate ever-increasing demand for larger, better-equipped, and more numerous operating rooms. The relatively small-scale Wesley Hospital in Chicago held a surgical suite of twenty rooms, while the Cook County Hospital's operating department occupied thirty-one thousand square feet—and that did not include the floor below the operating rooms that was devoted to surgical services. Some of this expansion was simply the result of increasing spatial needs for equipment. Operating rooms were large—sixteen feet square was a common minimum size, but many, like the thirty foot square operating room at the Hahnemann Hospital, were larger. Sterilizing rooms (with through-wall sterilizers) had to accommodate bulky equipment and storage for surgical supplies; scrub-rooms could hold numerous large fixtures and multiple plumbing systems.[88] Having diagnostic facilities—labs, X-ray, cystoscopy—nearby or within the surgical facility was convenient, but further increased the spatial needs and complexity.

American hospitals of the 1900s and 1910s housed far more operating rooms than their nineteenth-century predecessors, but also more than their European counterparts. According to Edward F. Stevens, this was the product of differing organizations of the surgical service in the American and European hospitals: "In the German government hospitals one surgeon will do the majority of the operations, and will naturally need but one or two rooms, while with our hospitals it is not uncommon to see five or six operations going on at once in even a hundred-bed hospital."[89]

The multiplication of operating rooms accommodated a vastly expanding network of practicing surgeons. For years, hospital surgical facilities had been available only to the staff surgeons, who expected (and often lobbied for) cutting-edge facilities, and treated the surgical facilities as their own domains. Dr. John B. Murphy reputedly joined the staff at Mercy Hospital in Chicago only after the nurses agreed to fit up a new operating room according to his requirements. By the early twentieth century, faced with expensive surgical suites that might sit unused for the summer months while the regular staff was on holiday, many hospital administrators extended courtesy access to nearby private practitioners even without a hospital appointment. These "courtesy" surgeons would direct a steady stream of wealthy private patients (who often required and could pay for a couple nights' stay in a private hospital room before and after treatment) to the facility that had the most accessible, best-quality operating rooms.[90] The increasing number of surgeons using the hospital's surgical facilities further increased spatial demands, particularly for more operating rooms and for larger more luxurious locker rooms. At the Barnes Hospital in Saint Louis, the surgical facility housed separate scrub facilities for nurses, doctors, visiting surgeons, and students.

As surgical facilities expanded, whether it was better to provide a number of decentralized operating rooms or to provide a single centralized surgical department remained debatable. Decentralized operating rooms could be specially designed for and proximate to the patient population they served. Septic operating rooms, for patients with septic wounds, served to keep the main surgical suite aseptic. Operating rooms in isolation facilities ensured that the contagious patients would not have to enter the hospital proper. Surgeons of specialties that served vulnerable patients or those with septic tendencies (genito-urinary patients, obstetric patients, and eye patients, for example) continued to request special operating rooms immediately adjacent to the special wards. Decentralized surgical facilities could also foster proprietary usage and could result in underutilized facilities. Many private patient facilities included proprietary operating rooms, to avoid mixing the wealthy patients with the charity patients. To keep the "staff" surgeons happy, and avoid conflicts over assignment of scarce operating rooms, some institutions added separate facilities for the "courtesy" surgeons. Decentralized surgical facilities inevitably meant multiplying the often expensive appliances, equipment, and service areas such as sterilizers, sterile water systems, and scrub-up facilities.

Centralized operating facilities, shared by all hospital staff and departments, could be scheduled effectively for maximum use, benefit from centralized sterilization facilities and sterile supply, keep the operating room separate (isolated) from the other areas of the hospital, and justify the hiring of an experienced specialized operating room nurse or staff to oversee surgeries. (This last development often proved one of the most crucial factors in the reduction of cross-infections.) Such centralized surgical facilities could grow too large for efficient asepsis, however; Richard E. Schmidt pointed out that the mixing of patients within any given operating room was a strong reason for decentralization.[91]

A Matter of Efficiency: Nurse Travel Distances and the Efficient Ward

In the early twentieth century, after decades of stable ward design, a shortage of nurses prompted radical innovations in ward layouts. As an early socially acceptable profession for women, nursing had influenced a redefinition of women's role in society from homemaker and mother to employable labor. By the 1900s working women had more choices of profession. In comparison to work in an office or department store, nursing was arduous. It involved long hours of physically demanding work, with frequent exposure to noxious or noisome materials and difficult patients, doctors, and staff. It also came with the constant danger of being exposed to sickness. While enrollment in nurse training schools remained steady, an increasing number of graduates chose to become private nurses—a more lucrative and less demanding option than hospital service. The resultant hospital nursing shortage had hospital administrators across the country struggling to hire enough ward nurses. This made it critical for hospitals to make the best use of the ward nurses they did have, and to find a way to make nursing attractive to more candidates.

In this difficult labor market, hospital directors reconsidered nursing efficiency not just in terms of spatially reinforced nurse/patient ratios (maximizing the number of patients one nurse could oversee), but in terms of the new efficiency movement overtaking industrial production across the country. In an era of Taylorization, hospital practitioners studied the ward as a place of production with the goal of generating the maximum output of product (healed patients) from the minimum outlay of effort (nurse labor). The result was a new "unit" of measurement of nursing efficiency—namely, "nurse travel distance," or how far a nurse had to walk to respond to basic patient requests. Early studies in nurse kinetics proved the traditional pavilion-ward design to be horrendously inefficient. Nurse and author Charlotte Aikens complained that "miles of unnecessary travel every week are imposed on workers in a hospital in which the nursing conveniences are badly arranged," and wondered "what the pedometer might tell" about hospitals. Studies that put pedometers on nurses "found that a nurse will frequently walk as much as eight miles in a thirty-foot corridor during her tour of duty." Nettie B. Jordan, another nurse and author, called modern hospitals "nurse killers," joked that nurses would benefit from the use of horses on their rounds, and suggested that architects were perhaps unchivalrous for their inefficient designs.[92] Somehow, ward design had to simplify the daily requirements of nursing.

To redesign the ward was to reconceptualize its sociomedical function. In the traditional Nightingale ward, bed placement, window placement, and ward size and shape had functioned to facilitate nursing supervision, to minimize disease transfer by surrounding each patient with abundant therapeutic sunlight and fresh air from a nearby window, and to create an orderly, clean, reformative space that would itself exert a therapeutic influence on the patient. By the early twentieth century it was clear that aseptic procedures could prevent disease transfer in any space. Furthermore, as part of the transformation of the hospital from a charitable to a medical institution, morality and religion were no longer critical elements in the diagnosis, treatment, or prevention of physiological ailments. These shifts freed ward design from the earlier hygienic imperatives and allowed experimentation with new ward layouts for improved efficiencies. While the traditional large ward remained a valid option, deviations from that norm were more frequent and more frequently adopted.[93] To improve nursing efficiency, ward designers rearranged the relation of ward services to the wards and included smaller wards, or groupings of wards of various sizes. In each redesign, interest in reducing the nurse's workload came into conflict with other needs—for centralized services, for minimum care standards, and for detailed patient categorization.

The simplest strategy for reducing nurse travel distances was to reduce the need for them to make trips outside of the ward for basic necessities. Many hospital buildings incorporated labor-saving technologies for this purpose, such as dumbwaiters, paging systems, vacuum tube message delivery systems, and small internal truck railroads for the delivery of materials and supplies. Many of these technologies functioned efficiently only in centralized structures—dumbwaiters required vertical organization and vacuum tube systems were prohibitively expensive in hospitals with widely spaced pavilions. All of them shifted the nature of nursing.

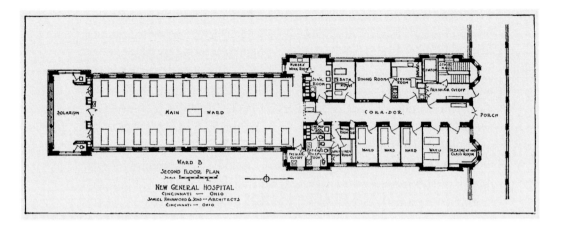

Figure 4.26. Cincinnati General Hospital, ward plan, 1911.

Electric annunciators (nurse call buttons) provide a good example of the complex practical consequences of labor-saving technologies. By the late nineteenth century they were commonly installed in small rooms and wards over which nurses did not have immediate oversight. When the patient pressed a button, a light came on to alert the nurse to the patient's need. These call systems theoretically allowed a small number of nurses to monitor a large number of small wards without compromising patient care. In practice, they put the control in the hands of the patients and still did not necessarily reduce the nurse's daily travel distances. In the earliest call system models, when the patient call was made, the light showed up on a central annunciator board located in the hallway. The nurse had to travel first to the central board to see which patient required aid, then to the patient's room to provide assistance, and then back to the central board to extinguish the call light. Incidents of nurses extinguishing the call light at the central board before paying a visit to the patient were common, if risky. By the 1910s improved annunciator systems mounted individual call lights above the doors to the various patient rooms. This allowed the nurse to go straight to the room requiring service; the call light could only be extinguished at the patient's bedside. Built into the technology was thus not only a given expenditure of effort for all calls (whether necessary or not), but a strategy for ensuring that the proper response occurred. This turned a labor-saving device into a labor-monitoring device. As Susan Reverby so aptly puts it, "the study of the physical structure of the hospital's impact on the nurse's work did not always lead to agreement that the nurse's comfort, or right to determine her own work pace, was an important consideration in hospital efficiency."[94]

Figure 4.27. Stamford Hospital, Connecticut, ward plan, 1911.

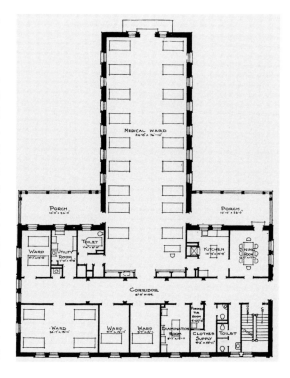

Redesigning the head house, which held the accessory service spaces, also offered the potential to reduce nurse travel distances. Changes in patient care had expanded the head house until it was as large and as long as the ward. The typical arrangement of the head house as a linear extension of the ward exacerbated the problem, lengthening the distance a nurse had to travel to complete even routine tasks. To reduce nurse travel distances, hospital designers experimented with new arrangements of head house and ward.[95]

S. S. Goldwater promoted two variants of T-shaped wards. His plan for a "ward for cities" turned the head house perpendicular to the ward. This arrangement, as exemplified in the wards of the Stamford Hospital in Connecticut, designed by George B. Post and Sons in collaboration with Goldwater, retained the traditional ward layout but reduced travel distance among the service rooms. Alternatively, at the new Mount Sinai Hospital in New York City, Goldwater and Arnold Brunner's collaborative design turned the ward perpendicular to the head house. Another variant was Lindley Murray Franklin's (of York and Sawyer) cruciform design of the New York Orthopedic Hospital, which included four small wards radiating from a central service area—shortening nurse travel distances and allowing wards to share service areas.[96]

Locating the ward services along the long wall of the traditional ward could increase the number of access points to the services and decreased the nurse travel distance accordingly, but it drastically altered the traditional ward layout. This approach appeared in Ernest Flagg's design for the new Saint Luke's Hospital in New York City in 1897, with other versions appearing in George L. Harvey's design for the Gary Hospital in Gary, Indiana, and Kendall, Taylor and Company's design for the Robinson Memorial Building of the Massachusetts Homeopathic Hospital in Boston.[97]

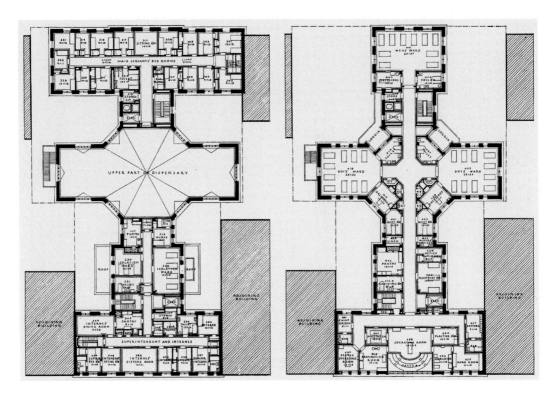

Figure 4.28. New York Orthopedic Hospital, second- and fourth-floor plans, 1916. The cross or X plan would become a particular favorite for urban hospitals, as a way of having centralization but also some separation of the wards.

Smaller wards also affected nurse travel distances. By the 1900s and 1910s, although large wards could still hold twenty or more beds, it was far more common for a hospital to enclose wards of a dozen or fewer beds. Smaller wards, however, typically meant a nurse was responsible for patients in more than one room. This required either more nurses (one per small ward) or for the nurse to make frequent trips to each ward to ensure the patients' safety.[98] A number of innovations in ward designs were tried to solve this problem. One strategy was to group the smaller wards in a way that allowed one nurse to have oversight of all beds from a specific vantage point. In the 1910s and 1920s, this was often more effective in theory than in practice. The designers of the Robert W. Long Hospital in Indianapolis reported that from the crossing point of the corridors a large percentage of the beds on each floor were visible all at once. Impractically, this crossing point was in a hallway outside of both wards and there was no nurses' station at that location so there was little reason for a nurse to occupy the position of maximum supervision within the ward floor. At the Columbia Hospital for Women two larger wards and a num-

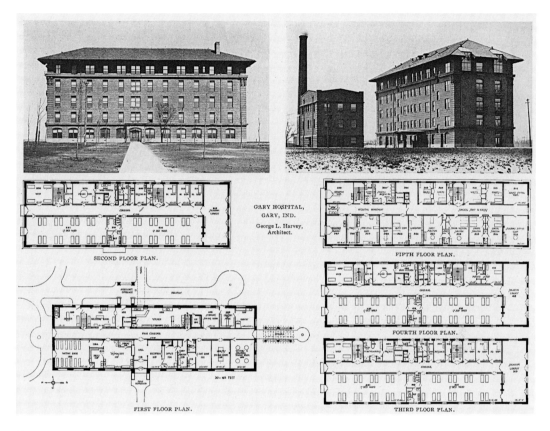

Figure 4.29. Gary Hospital, Gary, Indiana, plans and view, 1912.

ber of smaller wards were grouped around a central anteroom. The nurses' station was located at the point of intersection of these wings, providing the possibility of oversight of all the wards from that one vantage point, but at an acute angle. Installing glass in the walls between wards and corridors could also facilitate nurse oversight of more than one space at a time. At the Peter Bent Brigham Hospital in Boston a glass-walled corridor fronted a number of wards of various sizes. Through this wall, the nurses' station—located in a small alcove—had a commanding view of many of the ward beds.[99]

The popular "Rigs ward" (based on the ward design of the Rigs Hospital in Copenhagen)—offered a compromise between sight lines and the efficiency of smaller wards. The Rigs ward subdivided a large open ward into a series of alcoves, each of which held between two and six beds, arranged parallel rather than perpendicular to the window wall. From the corridor a nurse could oversee the patients in the adjacent alcoves. Each alcove held basic necessary utilities, and larger service/utility rooms were located regularly along the ward corridor. This reduced travel between patients and

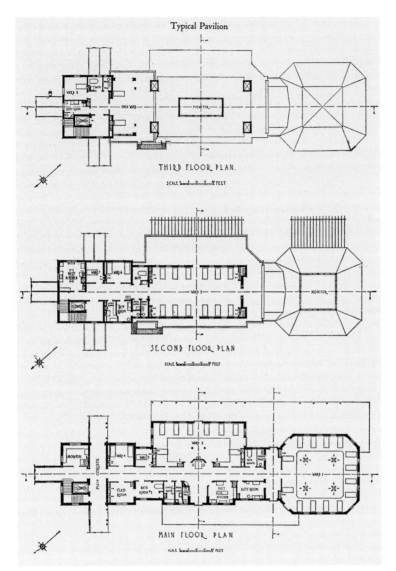

Figure 4.30. Peter Bent Brigham Hospital, Boston, ward plans, 1913. The wards were designed for maximum ventilation including ceiling exhaust, which precluded upper floors.

services. The Rigs ward became common in European and in American hospitals, particularly with the help of Edward F. Stevens, who promoted it in his numerous publications and hospital designs. Many hospitals, like the Galloway Hospital in Nashville and the Mount Sinai Hospital in Cleveland, held a mix of traditional large linear wards, private rooms, and Rigs-style wards of four or six beds. There were, however, social differences between the European and American use of such alcoves and cubicles. In European practice, hospitals still served primarily charity patients, and smaller wards allowed a finer medical categorization. In American hospital practice, small wards and single-bed rooms were the hallmark of private patient service.[100]

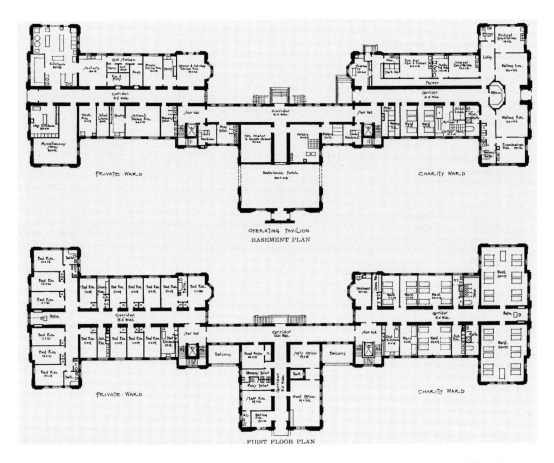

Figure 4.31. Galloway Memorial Hospital, Nashville, basement and first-floor plans, 1916. The left-hand side of the first-floor plan shows the wing arranged into single-bed rooms for private patient service; the right-hand side of the plan shows a wing arranged into a number of smaller wards, including a few Rigs wards.

With the increasing use of smaller wards even for charity and part-pay patients, to maintain the social distinctions among patients, private patient facilities in "charitable" hospitals grew increasingly elaborate and luxurious, approximating hotels rather than an institution concerned with architectural hygienics. Adams points out the development of such attractive accommodations for wealthy patients in the Ross Memorial Pavilion at the Royal Victoria Hospital at Montreal. Many of these private patient services functioned wholly independently of the ward service, even to the extent of including redundant expensive services and facilities, such as operating rooms or X-ray facilities reserved for the use of private patients. Some saw this commodification of hospital facilities and services as a natural progression: "a public, accustomed to a high class of accommodations when they

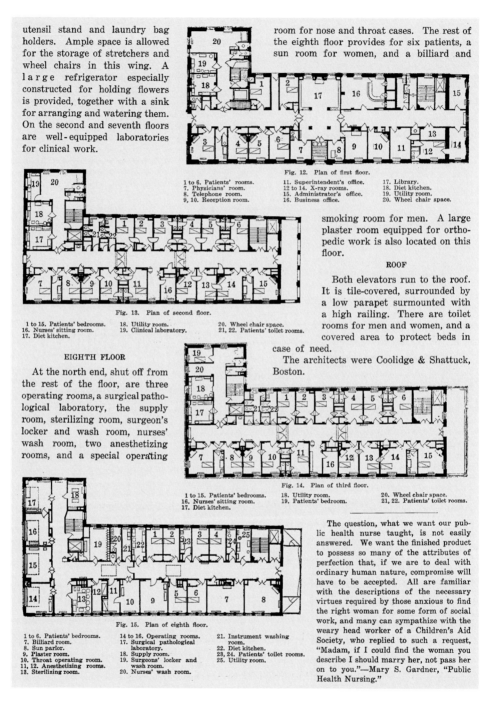

utensil stand and laundry bag holders. Ample space is allowed for the storage of stretchers and wheel chairs in this wing. A large refrigerator especially constructed for holding flowers is provided, together with a sink for arranging and watering them. On the second and seventh floors are well-equipped laboratories for clinical work.

room for nose and throat cases. The rest of the eighth floor provides for six patients, a sun room for women, and a billiard and

Fig. 12. Plan of first floor.

1 to 6. Patients' rooms.	11. Superintendent's office.	17. Library.
7. Physicians' room.	12 to 14. X-ray rooms.	18. Diet kitchen.
8. Telephone room.	15. Administrator's office.	19. Utility room.
9, 10. Reception room.	16. Business office.	20. Wheel chair space.

Fig. 13. Plan of second floor.

1 to 15. Patients' bedrooms.	18. Utility room.	20. Wheel chair space.
16. Nurses' sitting room.	19. Clinical laboratory.	21, 22. Patients' toilet rooms.
17. Diet kitchen.		

smoking room for men. A large plaster room equipped for orthopedic work is also located on this floor.

ROOF

Both elevators run to the roof. It is tile-covered, surrounded by a low parapet surmounted with a high railing. There are toilet rooms for men and women, and a covered area to protect beds in case of need.

The architects were Coolidge & Shattuck, Boston.

EIGHTH FLOOR

At the north end, shut off from the rest of the floor, are three operating rooms, a surgical pathological laboratory, the supply room, sterilizing room, surgeon's locker and wash room, nurses' wash room, two anesthetizing rooms, and a special operating

Fig. 14. Plan of third floor.

1 to 15. Patients' bedrooms.	18. Utility room.	20. Wheel chair space.
16. Nurses' sitting room.	19. Patients' bedroom.	21, 22. Patients' toilet rooms.
17. Diet kitchen.		

The question, what we want our public health nurse taught, is not easily answered. We want the finished product to possess so many of the attributes of perfection that, if we are to deal with ordinary human nature, compromise will have to be accepted. All are familiar with the descriptions of the necessary virtues required by those anxious to find the right woman for some form of social work, and many can sympathize with the weary head worker of a Children's Aid Society, who replied to such a request, "Madam, if I could find the woman you describe I should marry her, not pass her on to you."—Mary S. Gardner, "Public Health Nursing."

Fig. 15. Plan of eighth floor.

1 to 6. Patients' bedrooms.	14 to 16. Operating rooms.	21. Instrument washing
7. Billiard room.	17. Surgical pathological	room.
8. Sun parlor.	laboratory.	22. Diet kitchen.
9. Plaster room.	18. Supply room.	23, 24. Patients' toilet rooms.
10. Throat operating room.	19. Surgeons' locker and	25. Utility room.
11, 12. Anesthetizing rooms.	wash room.	
13. Sterilizing room.	20. Nurses' wash room.	

Figure 4.32. Massachusetts General Hospital, Boston, Private Patient Building, first-, second-, third-, and eighth-floor plans, 1917. The building, designed by Coolidge and Shattuck, was in essence an independent hospital, with its own reception and administration facilities, surgical facilities, clinical laboratory, X-ray, and pathological lab.

are in good health, should expect and be willing to pay for at least as good conditions when they are ill." Others worried that "hotel" service for the wealthy came at the expense of charitable care. One disgusted critic sarcastically observed that there was "a great field of usefulness for a hospital which shall provide expensive suites of rooms for the invalid rich."[101]

Renovating the Existing but Out-of-Date Hospital

The increasing emphasis on interactive and integrated spaces and services, rather than on hygienic decentralization, began a transformation of hospital facilities. That transformation registered in every new facility built. It also registered in every existing facility. As medical practices and hospital practices changed, administrators of hospitals with older facilities did their best to adapt the structures to new requirements. Hospital facilities underwent additions, alterations, and renovations on an almost continual basis; this made hospitals palimpsests. Any given hospital might be built with a coherent, rational master plan based on the understanding of the ideal design requirements for that time. Within a decade, new structures were inevitably added that conformed not to that original master plan but to the current understanding of ideal hospital design. Within two decades the master plan was barely discernible in the actual buildings. Another decade or two and the hospital might look like there had never been an overarching conception of the facility as a rational, organized whole.

The Boston City Hospital in 1904 provides a graphic example of this sequential, and constantly transforming, construction. The original master plan for the facility projected four ward pavilions and an administration building. Two pavilions, the administration building and a boiler house, were initially constructed. Six more ward pavilions were added, each shaped and sized according to the requirements of the decade, not of the original plan. An open field for tents provided additional patient housing. Other, non-ward additions showed up: a medical library behind the administration building, a medical services building interrupting the open-air passages between the administration building and original medical pavilion, and a (much larger) surgical services building that replaced the open-air passage between the administration building and original surgical pavilion. A pathological building, nurses' home, and a complex arrangement of structures for the outpatient department ringed the edges of the site. Service buildings, including ambulance stables, boiler house, and laundry, filled in spaces between wards and extended the hospital across Albany Street. Across Massachusetts Avenue, the South Department, or isolation facilities for contagious disease patients, contained wards and administration and service buildings of its own.

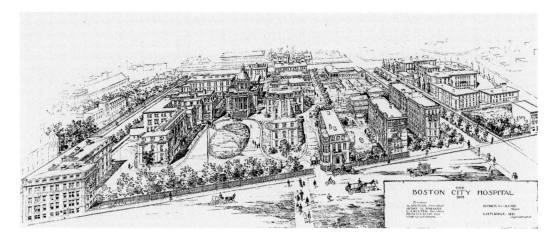

Figure 4.33. City Hospital, Boston, view of hospital, 1904.

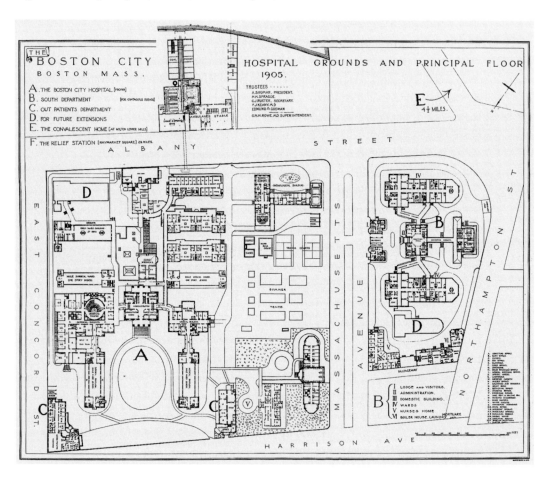

Figure 4.34. City Hospital, Boston, plan of hospital complex, 1904. The original wards and center building flank courtyard A.

The facility detailed in this plan and perspective show a very different facility than what had been projected in 1865. It was also a very different facility than was the ideal of the 1900s and 1910s. Trying to practice interactive medicine in a facility comprising twenty-eight separate buildings, from different eras, was a difficult task indeed.

Hospital Standards and the Spatial Dilemma of Small General Hospitals

The incredible variety of institutions and facilities in existence in the 1900s and 1910s translated into a broad range of hospital experiences for the patient, from negative to positive. A number of public agencies and groups, worried about the detrimental impact of low-quality hospital care, expressed interest in a more rational distribution of hospitals and in establishing minimum hospital standards.

Efforts to coordinate the geographic location of hospitals across an urban area took a new shape in the late 1900s and early 1910s with the development of hospital surveys. A variety of agencies (from municipalities and public agencies to administrative boards of individual hospitals) hired outside experts to analyze and record the state of a specific locale's existing hospitals and synthesize the findings into an area-wide hospital survey. The area hospital survey quickly became a standard planning tool; by the 1920s, it was nearly a prerequisite for any new hospital construction.[102]

Most surveys, however, were more than dry factual accounting. They also compared current conditions to a projected ideal (number of beds in relation to surrounding population, placement of hospitals, variety of hospital types) and offered suggestions for future hospital development. Typically, such a survey identified oversupplied and undersupplied neighborhoods, and regularly revealed that there were not enough hospitals to supply the existing population and that the hospital beds in existence were inequitably and inefficiently distributed. An influential survey could quickly become a developmental agenda rather than simply an informational tool.

For example, New York City was one of the earliest locales to undertake hospital planning surveys. The State Charities Aid Association published one in 1908, and a mayor-appointed municipal commission on hospitals came out with theirs in 1909. Both reports found the city's hospital facilities to be inadequate and inequitably distributed about the city. Both reports concluded that the city was well supplied with smaller institutions but needed a few large, general hospitals, and that while the Upper East Side had become a veritable "Mecca of benevolent enterprises," the West Side was direly undersupplied with hospital beds. The widely read reports influenced hospital development in New York City for more than a decade. The directors of Roosevelt Hospital, already located within the underserved Upper West Side, stated that but for a lack of funds, it was justifiable for Roosevelt Hospital to claim "a manifest destiny and a future development which will make it the large general hospital for the west side of New York."[103] Administrators and benefactors of other existing hospitals, including the New York Hospital, the New York Polyclinic Hospital, and the Presbyterian Hospital, acquired (or considered acquiring) sites for new facilities in the West Side. Clearly, hospital surveys as a means of organizing the disorganized provision of hospital service to a given locale did more than report; they predicted and in some cases influenced development.

The varied quality, kind, and continuity of care provided by the wide variety of institutions was an equally worrisome concern for practitioners at the time. The idea that there should be minimum hospital standards—that all hospital institutions should be able to provide a certain basic quality of care—was a constant talking point in medical and hospital circles in the 1900s and 1910s. The primary goal of setting standards was to be able to control the quality of medical care, but clearly equipment and even facility design influenced the level of care possible. By establishing minimum tolerable levels of technology, spatial arrangement, hygiene, and service, hospital standards held the potential to be highly influential, and also possibly highly limiting, on hospital design. Adams points out that standards would potentially compete with or diminish the expertise of the hospital architect. And yet the possibility of reducing the inconsistencies and inequities between hospital facilities was attractive. Hospital architect Meyer J. Sturm was "unalterably in favor of standardization" as a way of eliminating the endless differences of opinion on all aspects of hospital construction and equipment.[104] Although hospital standardization was at first about setting minimum limits, and not about making hospitals similar, as the rules and guidelines increased in complexity and scope, the standards inevitably made compliant hospitals more alike.

Standards posed particular difficulties for smaller general care institutions. According to Haven Emerson, who compiled numerous hospital surveys in the early decades of the twentieth century, while the larger hospitals had grown much larger than their nineteenth-century counterparts, in 1915 one-third of hospitals in the United States had less than twenty beds, and one-third between twenty and fifty beds. Like the larger, general hospitals, these facilities had to accommodate all kinds of patients, with all kinds of levels of infection, requiring any variety of treatment—from environmental therapy to surgery. They typically had to do so on a small site and with a limited budget. Smaller institutions desperately needed the cost savings of centralized services, but they serviced too varied a patient population to avoid the stricter requirements of hygienically decentralized facilities.[105] Larger hospitals could amortize the costs of X-ray facilities, laboratories, surgical facilities, nurse training facilities, therapeutic facilities, and medical equipment across a large number of patients. Smaller institutions had to offer either reduced facilities or a higher per capita cost for patients. Both were inefficient. Though hospital standards were a regular topic of discussion, effective implementation waited until after 1917.

By the early twentieth century, the simple hospital that consisted of two small separate ward pavilions with a central administration structure (a standard design in the late nineteenth century), was hopelessly inefficient and outdated. Service in small general hospitals that occupied decentralized facilities was often too expensive to maintain. Small general hospitals that occupied single, centralized structures were less costly to operate but often suffered in practice from the extensive internal divisions and compartmentalization necessary to maintain hygienic separation. The constant increase in "necessary" non-ward service spaces such as X-ray, surgical suites, and special facilities for medical specialties exerted a constant pressure on the rest of the hospital. Administrators of small hospitals had to choose between providing basic facilities for more patients or providing better facilities for fewer. Many opted for providing miniature versions of the numerous services and technologies. Each adjacent room might hold a completely separate specialty or service. The Hospital at White Plains, New York, occupied what from the exterior appeared to be a single, centralized structure. Internally, however, each of its floors held from three to six distinct service areas, delimited by corridor breaks and thicker walls.

This need to fit numerous spatially distinct spaces within a small building envelope meant that small general hospitals were often vertically as well as horizontally stratified. Typically, services were located on ground or basement floors and on top or penthouse floors with wards and staff housing on the intervening floors. Operating services were most often located on the top floor, and, if the size of the building footprint permitted, X-ray and other medical services. Some, like the Ithaca City Hospital in New York, held both a small, emergency operating facility at the basement and a more fully equipped suite on the top floor. This vertical rather than horizontal organization was yet another distinction between the nineteenth-century pavilion hospital and the early twentieth-century minimal hospital.

If "modern" hospital care required a certain standard of hospital building and equipment, not all hospitals were up to the new standard. Many charitable institutions walked the baseline of what was needed for a modern

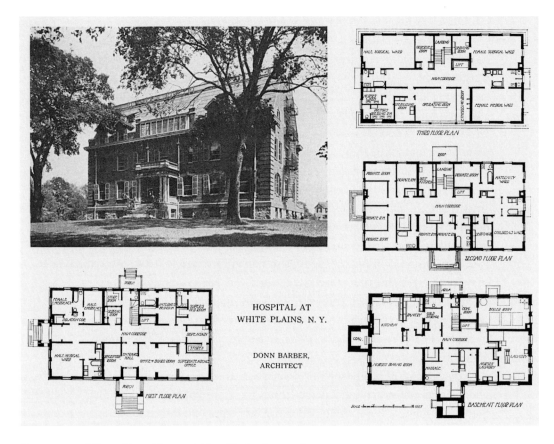

Figure 4.35. White Plains Hospital, New York, plans and view, 1915.

hospital facility but continued to provide primarily basic care to the needy poor. Many medical hospitals struggled to afford the increasing kinds and volumes of facilities and equipment considered necessary. In the 1900s and 1910s, whether the high-tech medical model or the low-tech charitable institutional model was preferable was an open question. The transformation was well underway.

The early twentieth-century hospital was a spatial conundrum: everything needed to be interconnected but nothing was to touch. For best care, doctors promoted group practice, which required all specialties to be in close physical proximity to facilitate consultation, yet each specialty still clearly desired enough dedicated beds, equipment, and space in the hospital to allow independent research and medical advancement. The early twentieth-century modern hospital also encompassed a bewildering array of daily tasks performed by a variety of personnel, ranging from doctors and nurses to patients, interns, orderlies, technicians, laboratory workers, kitchen staff, laundry staff, maintenance personnel, pharmacists, and administrative personnel. These people moved between numerous units, some of which required special layouts or equipment, some of which required critical adjacency to other parts of the hospital, and some of which required absolute isolation. Patient care increasingly required trips from wards to diagnostic and treatment spaces, even from one ward to another. Yet while the hospital's contents and occupants were increasingly in constant motion, hospital practitioners worried that any direct physical interaction was suspect as a possible transfer of germs from one person or thing to another.

Hospital designs varied according to whether the interaction or the separation mattered most to their operation. The distant, decentralized buildings and aseptic cubicles of isolation hospitals emphasized the need to keep things and people from touching. The decentralized but varied structures of early tuberculosis sanatoria and chronic disease and convalescent institutions emphasized the need to provide patients with immediate access to the therapeutic influence of the natural environment. The compact wards, centralized services, and connecting corridors of general hospitals and medically specialized hospitals emphasized the need to make everything interconnected despite the resultant proximities.

According to Minnie Goodnow in 1912, "each section of a hospital, each portion which can be administered as a whole, is, or ought to be, a unit, a single complete thing." In the nineteenth century a "unit" had been a pavilion—its spatial limits coincided with the exterior walls of an individual building. In the early twentieth century, a unit might also be a functional arrangement of spaces within a larger structure—delimited not by exterior walls, but by floors, partitions, doors, windows, or even by nonarchitectural features such as the presence of a specific germ or a level of contamination.[106]

Which was more important, the independence of the unit or the interaction of the units? Was a hospital a single entity? An organismic reassembly of all the various medical specialties across a number of spaces? Or was a hospital a group of individual entities, each operating primarily independently, but connected in a shared administration? Any approach to hospital design that concentrated on the "unit"—some spatial quantity that could be multiplied until the sufficient size for a hospital was reached—compromised the creation of a single, recognizable functioning whole. Any approach to hospital design that focused on the creation of an integrated whole, however, was in danger of collapsing under the complexity of conflicting internal requirements such an institution inevitably housed.

By the 1910s pavilion-ward hospital guidelines were clearly outdated, but there was no single new ideal of hospital design available. Two competing ideals of high-rise hospital design existed and would lead to two very different architectural futures for hospital design. Albert J. Ochsner's 1907 diagram of a single, platonic tower in a large, landscaped site projected a monolithic, organized whole that contained the complexity of hospital functions behind a uniform facade and housed all the different pieces of the hospital under one roof. Circulation within the hospital was vertical, and hygienic decentralization was achieved on a floor-by-floor basis. Conversely, Samuel Waldron Lambert's 1916 diagram of a low base with multiple towers accepted the "complexities and contradictions" of both hygienic decentralization and functional centralization, creating a compartmentalized, yet interconnected whole. At the moment when high-rise hospital design was poised to replace pavilion-ward hospital design as the healthiest way to build an institution, the United States entered World War I, mandating a temporary halt to all nonessential civil construction. When hospital construction resumed in the 1920s, designers of new hospital facilities established a whole new ideal, one that borrowed from Ochsner's proposal and from Lambert's.

CHAPTER 5

The Vertical Hospital as an Attractive Factory, 1917–1929

If only a hospital could be large enough, and command a sufficient clientele, one could imagine a well arranged plan whereby patients would enter, in a continuous stream to the sorting room, thence to the divesting room, the bath, the anesthetizing room, the cutting off room, the assembling room, the finishing room, the seasoning room, and finally to the shipping platform, from which they would be sent to all parts of the world.

— **Arthur Peabody, 1921**

Gloom of aspect of walls inevitably breeds gloom of mind, and unbroken whitened sterility of walls and ceiling produces sterility of thought in the sick mind, which longs to be led out of itself by pleasurable impression from without. Why not think, then, in terms of "home for the sick?"

— **William O. Ludlow, 1919**

During the short period of American involvement in World War I a number of radical modernizations—the expansion of the government and the military, the cultural as well as physical shock of mechanized warfare on an unprecedented scale, the tragedy of thousands of wounded, sick, and poisoned soldiers, and the dawning awareness of American strength and value in the global theater—altered the American experience. The new hospital, a medical workshop rather than a charity, was an integral part of this transformation, experienced by a broad segment of society (including soldiers, journalists, doctors, nurses, technicians, volunteers, and civilians) in the base hospitals of the American Expeditionary Forces as well as in the increasingly numerous civil hospitals of the American cities. More and more, those hospitals occupied facilities designed for efficient provision of medical treatment on a large scale.

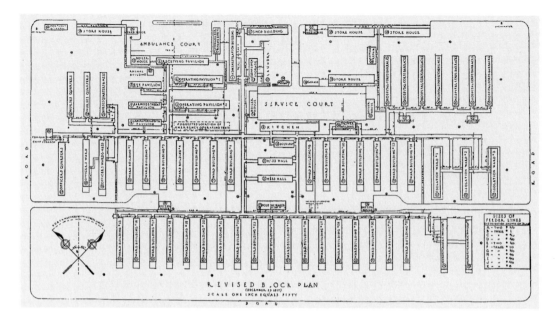

Figure 5.1. US World War I military field hospital, plan, 1919. Wounded soldiers would arrive in the ambulance court, be triaged in the receiving pavilion, then be transported to one of the operating or specialty treatment pavilions, and then to a ward bed. Nurse housing was adjacent to the receiving area and the wards. Officers' wards were set apart, as were isolation wards and neuropsychiatric wards. Services—kitchen, laundry, supplies, shop—were in the center of the complex but accessible to vehicular traffic for delivery of goods.

For war use, the US Army developed a standardized, portable, base hospital "unit"—essentially, a collection of numerous low-rise buildings that strongly resembled a traditional pavilion-plan hospital. It functioned not as a group of independent ward pavilions, however, but as an enormous integrated medical processing facility. Each structure housed a different function or category of occupant; all the different structures working together created a synthetic whole. Patients moved through the pavilions as a Ford automobile moved down its assembly line—from centralized receiving (examination, diagnostics, decontamination) to treatment (operating rooms, procedural rooms, cast rooms, bandaging) and then to recovery (in the various wards). Specially designed pavilions for staff and services occupied positions of maximum efficiency in the delivery of materials and procedures necessary to keep the line flowing.

Efficiency in hospitals (even war hospitals) was tempered by the complicated conditions necessary for the well-being of the human product. For example, in early 1918, the Chief of Engineers' office of the US Army developed a forty-foot-wide ward prototype, which, for nursing efficiency, held upward of one hundred patients in four rows of beds. With these wards already in production, in late 1918 the Assistant Secretary of War asked hospital architects Edward F. Stevens, Charles Butler, and Lindley Murray Franklin (of York and Sawyer) to review the plans for military hospitals. The architects suggested an alternate ward pavilion design of two stories, with fifty beds in two rows on each floor and a partition next to every second bed. Their revised plan still put one hundred patients per pavilion, but provided each patient more direct access to sunlight and fresh air, more privacy, and reduced chances of cross-infection. While this layout required more nurses for a given number of patients, the projected gains in shortened convalescence from more comfortable patients and reduced complications from cross-infections were expected to offset that additional cost. This "Type A" ward unit was put into production and was used in more than fifty base hospitals.[1]

Rosemary Stevens has discussed the extent to which World War I experiences promoted cooperative medicine. In these army base hospitals, medical practitioners from a wide variety of backgrounds and areas—rural general practitioners as well as hospital-seasoned city doctors—experienced the enticing benefits of collaborative practice, access to extensive medical equipment and technologies, and the integration of medical research and medical practice. Whether the military hospital doctors would return to their independent, but isolated, general practices when the war was over was an issue of concern. W. C. Rappleye noted that doctors were growing "dependent upon many of the facilities that well equipped hospitals provide and they come to believe these are necessary for medical practice, for study and for self-development." This dependence tended "to unfit young physicians psychologically to enter into independent practice in smaller communities." Hospitals were seen as a medical amenity that could ease the transition—providing returning doctors a location for access to group practice and all the cutting-edge technologies for diagnosis, treatment, and research. According to architect Emmet E. Bailey, "The physician is entitled to an institution, including the building, which lends itself in every way to his work of ministration to the afflicted."[2]

If military hospital experience taught doctors the benefits of working together, it also revealed that factory-style hospital care was efficient for treating patients but not necessarily for curing them. It did not go unnoticed that soldiers in military hospitals often suffered as much from mental depression as from physical injury. Clearly, shell shock (PTSD) played a complicating role in this depression, but in addition to probing the soldiers' war experiences psychiatrists and doctors considered the role of physical surroundings on patient mental health. Military

wards were invariably large, multibed, spartan rooms—with little privacy, few amenities, and no aesthetic concessions. It was easy to conclude
that the unattractive ward acted as a negative influence on a patient's
mental health, causing longer convalescence and even depression.
The converse, that an attractive ward would exert a positive influence,
seemed equally obvious.[3] Postwar hospital practitioners saw the opportunity that might open up if the institution could be made appealing as
well as efficient.

New Wine, Old Bottles, No Money

These wartime transformations made the postwar civilian hospital a categorically different institution than the prewar hospital. Rather than a
repository of sickness it was to be a source of health—"a community laboratory in the prevention of pain, distress and sickness." From a warehouse
into which sickness flowed, hospitals had become a place of medical production out of which health would flow.[4]

Consensus was that it would not work to fit this new wine into old
bottles. Dr. Asa S. Bacon, superintendent of the Presbyterian Hospital in
Chicago, noted that efficiency studies in industries often led to radical
changes not just in production sequences but "in the abandonment of
present plants and the building of new ones, simply because the physical arrangements of the old were beyond remodeling and hopeless." One
postwar hospital designer admonished himself and his colleagues to
"clear our minds of many fixed ideas based upon experience of the prewar
period." Existing hospital buildings, many of which had been designed to
maximize ward space, suddenly seemed too small and "so constructed,
arranged, and equipped that they are incapable of meeting requirements
that are constantly growing more numerous and more complex."[5]

Changes in hospital practices generated some striking differences in
spatial requirements between the late nineteenth century and the early
twentieth century. The directors of the Mount Sinai Hospital in New
York City estimated that in the 1890s their building had held roughly six
thousand cubic feet of space for each patient treated. Their facilities in
1923 held fourteen thousand cubic feet per patient, and more was desperately needed. Wards, which had once occupied a majority of a hospital's
footprint, were a small part of that larger institution. Myron Hunt, a California architect, estimated that patient spaces (wards and private rooms)
occupied roughly 22–25 percent of the floor space of a hospital. According
to hospital architect Carl A. Erikson, "the other 75 to 80 per cent is seldom seen by either patient or visitor."[6]

Postwar hospital practitioners, full of new ideas, returned to a fertile period of hospital construction. During the years of US involvement in World War I, a national moratorium on new construction had slowed the construction of civilian hospitals to a trickle. After the war, the backlog of delayed projects combined with an avalanche of newly planned "modern" facilities generated a hospital building boom of epic proportions. Editors of the *Architectural Forum* in 1929 predicted that hospitals would account for more than $252,000,000 of new construction across the country, putting it seventh on the list of expenditures by building category.[7] This was a further differentiation between American and European hospitals, as the postwar economy and general rebuilding efforts in Europe limited new hospital construction.

Small communities as well as big cities participated in this construction boom. The tremendous postwar growth of hospitals in smaller locales provided facilities not only for the treatment of patients but for the professional interaction of doctors who had grown used to collaboration during their experiences in the military hospitals. In the more rural locales, the hospital facilities offered access to some of the technologies and specialties that the military hospitals had included as routine. Cutting-edge hospital facilities served as an enticement to medical practitioners in any locale: "No hospital can expect to retain the interest of first class medical and surgical men, unless it provides whatever facilities are needed to enable them to make an intensive study of every case under their care." S. S. Goldwater advocated for open access to hospitals for all doctors to end the stigma of any practitioner operating in professional isolation.[8]

These new hospitals, full of the new architectural requirements of the modern, technological, collaborative facility came with a high price tag. Hospital-grade materials, equipment, and fixtures, which were advertised as more durable, sanitary, or even aseptic were invariably more expensive. The size and complexity of the staff required to keep a modern hospital running increased. Centralized supplies required employees to deliver the goods throughout the hospital. The more complex facilities required a more extensive mechanical staff to keep all the technological services running. Each specialized department required its own operational head and perhaps several technicians. More elaborate patient records required a record-keeping department and staff. Hospital payrolls increased accordingly.

The higher costs of running and building hospitals complicated what was already a precarious financial condition for a majority of American hospitals. If hospitals were essential institutions by the 1920s, they were also largely broke. Hospital income still depended on charitable donations and private patient fees, neither of which were reliable. Many municipal and public funds had dried up. The resultant financial exigencies favored larger institutions, which could benefit from economies of scale—reducing the cost per patient. Richard E. Schmidt noted that one five-hundred-bed facility was cheaper to run than five one-hundred-bed facilities. In 1925, C. Stanley Taylor estimated that current hospital projects were "approximately ten times as large as the average similar structure built fifteen years ago."[9]

The financial exigencies also favored more compact hospital plans, and the combination of larger hospital and more compact layout inevitably pushed hospital facilities higher. A vertically organized layout offered better economical use of (expensive) urban ground space, offered greater access to light and air in crowded urban surroundings, required less material (fewer roofs, foundations, and exterior walls) to build, and relied on reduced travel distances and labor-saving technologies to reduce the personnel load for basic tasks. It also facilitated centralized services, shortened travel distances, and simplified the addition of labor-saving technologies, all of which reportedly reduced staffing requirements. The vertically organized hospital also appealed as an efficient format for the increasingly factory-oriented model of medicine practiced in the hospital, whose advocates demanded that "the dispensary, patients' rooms, operating rooms, etc., should be so located that the maximum number of patients may be visited and treated in the shortest time; otherwise the staff will have to be increased or the patients suffer."[10] While not every new American hospital in the 1920s was a high-rise, the era of the detached pavilion hospital was near its end. Even new low-rise American hospital facilities typically housed all spaces under one roof.

The 1920s hospital had to be more than efficient, however—it had to be attractive. Given the increasing ability of prospective patients to choose between a variety of institutions, an unattractive hospital faced empty rooms and failure. Modern, efficiently planned hospitals might facilitate medical treatment but then suffer from a backlog of depersonalized, depressed patients who lingered in delayed convalescence. The goal for hospital practice was to heal the greatest number of patients in the shortest amount of time for the least amount of expenditure. Was efficient healing to be measured at the point of the successful completion of treatment (patient in recovery) or at the point of successful recovery (patient discharged, cured)? One answer made the hospital a machine to facilitate medical practice, the other made the hospital an environment to encourage healing. Whether a hospital's effectiveness should be measured in throughput (processing the maximum number of patients, doctors, and nurses) or in patient happiness (and the shortened convalescence and increased cures associated with it) created a spatial dilemma: was the hospital a vertical medical factory, or a comfortable, therapeutic vertical home?

Asepsis Trumps Environmental Infection, Frees Building Design

Increasing emphasis on the influence of hospital design on efficiency of treatment was predicated on waning expectations of its influence on the prevention of disease. Wartime experiences had increased confidence in aseptic procedures while reducing traditional worries about the effect of buildings on mortality. By the 1920s it was clear "that acute infectious diseases do not arise from our physical environment." It was also equally accepted that surgical infections, as the product of direct contact, "must always, until it can be proved otherwise, be traced straight back to the surgeon who made the wound." The focus on contact extended beyond the operating room. One practitioner defined aseptic technique as "the separation of patients from each other in a bacteriologic sense."[11]

Asepsis was a product of procedures, not architectural designs or spatial conditions. According to D. L. Richardson, "given a hospital built in every respect along modern lines and let it be under the control of untrained and careless personnel, the results will be disastrous." Lindley Murray Franklin noted that eminent surgeons who observed aseptic procedures "performed critical operations in dirty tenement rooms with perfect success and with no fear of infection." Aseptic procedures, however, were detailed and unforgiving. While the sterile procedures required in surgery and isolation were expected to be complex—even such basic tasks as cleaning bedpans, cleaning linens, managing excretions, and cleaning the ward required complicated, structured strategies for aseptic results.[12] Building design was not irrelevant, though. While aseptic procedures could be maintained in any location, it was far easier to do so in spaces designed to support them.

By the 1920s, aseptic requirements no longer permeated all areas of the hospital. There were areas—surgical suites, isolation facilities, sterilization and decontamination facilities, laundries, and service areas—where the germ load and frequency of contamination still justified aseptic barriers and the impermeable, unornamented details of aseptic design. In less-contaminated or more lightly used areas such as patient rooms, offices, waiting areas, and recreational areas, the hospital finishes became less strictly aseptic and more accepting of porous, soft, or even decorated materials. New cleaning technologies further expanded acceptable material choices for hospital use. C. W. Munger noted, "The vacuum cleaner has

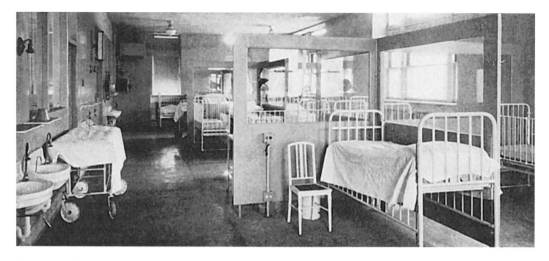

Figure 5.2. Babies and Children's Hospital, Cleveland, typical ward view, 1926. Abram Garfield's design included numerous plumbing fixtures in the ward for ease of decontamination. The partitions allowed the placement of beds in close proximity without danger of cross-contamination by contact, but other hospital administrators would recount that children were known to pass toys beneath partitions.

made it possible for hospitals again to use rugs as floor covering and to use heavier and more decorative hangings for windows."[13]

Earlier fears of building technologies as possible germ conduits faded, and hollow-wall construction in hospitals hid the pipes, wires, annunciators, panels, alarms, tubes, elevators, dumbwaiters, machines, medical equipment, and other building technologies that accompanied fireproof high-rise construction. Plumbing was no longer banished to separate, sanitary towers; it invaded every hospital room, even the once sacrosanct wards. At the Grosse Pointe Hospital in Michigan, "every ward and every patient's room [was] equipped with basins with elbow-acting faucets." This made it "possible to carry out strict surgical technique at every point in the hospital."[14]

Although the bacteriologic separation required by aseptic technique could be effected procedurally, aseptic barriers could still facilitate those techniques. Corridors, once required to be uninterrupted and well aired, were blocked by doorways that not only provided fire breaks between building zones but also marked passage from one aseptic zone to another. Hospital designers developed building layouts that avoided "unnecessary use of parts of the building as thoroughfares by individuals and groups that have no reason for passing through a given department or a part of the hospital."[15] The shift from environmental to contact theories of infection thus transformed the infection-free hospital from a pneumatic engine to a comprehensive circulation diagram.

Hospitals Designed for Germs: Asepsis and Ventilation's Ghost

If aseptic barriers and controlled circulation paths had become as common in modern hospital design as open windows and fresh air corridors had once been, to portray the shift as complete in the 1920s is to give a false impression. In routine practice, strategies to prevent contact infection supplanted strategies to prevent airborne infection, but where there was uncertainty there was still room for the old as well as the new. In particular, any incidence of cross-infection not easily explained by direct contact created an opening for old concerns to return. In 1924, after a rash of cross-infections in postoperative patients at the Truesdale Hospital in Fall River, Massachusetts, the hospital's surgeons scrutinized their aseptic procedures and found a defective autoclave. After fixing the autoclave, infection rates dropped but did not disappear. The surgeons then considered "the possibility of bacteria in the air, agitated by commotion in the operating room." They set out agar plates and grew cultures from the aerial particulates that settled on them. Many bacterial colonies formed. The surgeons covered their instrument table with a linen canopy and placed agar plates under the canopy. Far fewer colonies formed. They then "adopted precautionary measures against infection from dust as a carrier of bacteria" by minimizing any traffic in the operating room, by moving things like blankets, sheets, and towels slowly "so as not to agitate the air in the operating room unnecessarily," and by altering ventilation so that air flowed in and out at slow rates and windows were kept closed.[16] Postoperative infections dwindled further.

This continuing fear of dustborne pathogens strengthened lingering concerns about the aseptic condition of the building materials, furnishings, and air. Administrators of hospitals with natural ventilation installed extensive mechanical ventilation systems with filtration, cooling, and complete control of air flow within operating rooms. Dry cleaning by sweeping or rubbing, which increased the amount of airborne particulate matter in a room, fell out of favor. Administrators of the Sloane Hospital for Women in New York City adopted a cleaning protocol that involved sealing the room for four hours, then slowly wet mopping immediately upon entry to remove the "dust and possibly infectious material" that had settled onto the surfaces and floor.[17]

The design of maternity facilities provides yet another example of the difficulty of completely dismissing the air as a factor in disease. In 1927 Joseph B. De Lee, a well-respected obstetrician and founder of the Chicago Lying-In Hospital, stirred up a veritable medical hornet's nest with the seemingly retardataire suggestion that to prevent puerperal fever and postpartum infections, maternity hospitals should be in "a separate, detached building, a hospital complete in itself." He believed this spatial separation

Figure 5.3. Chicago Lying-In Hospital, view with plan, 1915. The "Mothers' Aid" pavilion (the smaller building at the back of the photo) was used for the immediate isolation of any mother or expectant mother showing any sign of infection.

was required because infection was carried not only by the hospital staff (nurses, interns, doctors) but also "by the air, in swirling air currents laden with dust or dried pulverized pus." He noted that even with rubber gloves, masks, sterilizers, individualization of cases, aseptic technique, and procedural isolation, infections had still invaded the maternity ward in the main building. Thus, he recommended adding architectural isolation—separating infected cases to a physically distinct facility—back into the mix, to complement the other strategies.[18]

The initial response from the medical world ranged from derision to dismissal. J. Whitridge Williams, chief obstetrician at the Johns Hopkins Hospital, discounted air as a carrier of germs, and even suggested that De Lee's "contentions are based upon imperfect appreciation of the possibilities of rigid aseptic technique, and possibly depend upon a lack of personal experience in the intricacies of practical bacteriological technique." A number of other doctors responded more tactfully, suggesting that Dr. De Lee's ideas about "miasmas" were out of date.[19] De Lee had never mentioned miasmas, however. He noted that his articles had been "intended to awaken the profession to the seriousness of the present situation." That situation was that "the reduced percentage of deaths from the accidents of labor is made up by the increase in infection deaths." He cited statistics revealing that childbirth mortality had increased from 1911 to 1921, and that maternity wards remained far more dangerous than home confinements. He told stories of a number of hospital epidemics, and observed that they were rarely reported and often concealed. He recounted his own experiences and the failure of improvements in aseptic technique to quell them. De Lee concluded that "blaming the catgut" was in essence an admission of ignorance—that it meant the doctor didn't know how the infection spread. Within that lingering uncertainty, the air remained a potential player. If air carried germ-laden dust and droplets, then "it must be admitted that ventilating flues and corridors connecting open foci of diseases with susceptible patients are a source of danger." The only way to cut off that potential connection was to have separate buildings. The influence of De Lee's criticism showed up in building designs. By the late 1920s it was common practice for maternity departments in otherwise integrated general hospitals to occupy physically separate facilities.[20] The physical environment thus stood as a marker of the limits of aseptic knowledge—where asepsis failed, or where knowledge of pathogens was incomplete, physical surroundings remained a considered factor in disease and spatial strategies of disease prevention lingered.

Near a Train, by a Road

By the 1920s hospital sites were chosen on the basis of hard evidence that there was a need for a hospital in a given area. Community hospital surveys, which examined hospital accessibility and distribution in relation to population concentrations and transportation networks, were crucial first steps in the planning of any new facility. These surveys mapped existing hospital locations in correlation to population concentrations in order to reveal gaps in coverage—underserved areas in which a new hospital might expect a thriving business. A smaller, congested site in an area with a large demand for hospital beds was far superior to a large site with abundant sunshine and open pastoral surroundings but no patients.

This did not mean environmental quality was no longer considered. Institutional types linked to outdoor environmental therapy maintained their critical relation to natural surroundings; other hospital types required proximities to different site features. According to Isadore Rosenfield and Edgar C. Hayhow, "for tuberculosis sanatoriums, institutions for the mentally ill, and convalescent homes, the country is to be preferred. . . . Hospitals

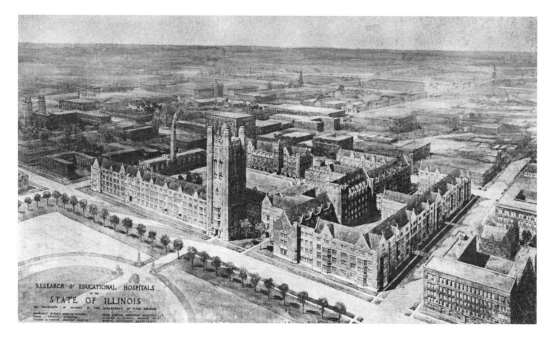

Figure 5.4. Research and Educational Hospitals of the State of Illinois, bird's-eye view, 1920, Schmidt, Garden and Martin.

that cater to a high-paying clientele may be in any quiet, easily accessible neighborhood. A university or teaching hospital must be within reasonable distance of the university, but if the university is in a neighborhood that lacks sufficient clinical material, its hospital must sometimes be in an urban district." The difficulties of unsavory, but populous, surroundings could be finessed by good hospital design. The planners of the Research and Educational Hospitals of the State of Illinois in Chicago noted that the site (the old West Side Ball Park) was "located in a somewhat congested and none too attractive district of the city—a situation having very positive advantages as an assured source of clinical material—the hospital has exercised the privilege of turning its back, as it were, upon its surroundings and making its own beauty within its domain." The cloistered plan, meant to provide the "sheltered seclusion" of Oxford or Cambridge, created a defensive perimeter around its landscaped courtyards.[21]

At a very basic level, the increasing scale of hospitals meant that large sites were still preferable, and, given the growth of cities, these were typically only available and affordable on the urban outskirts. Many of the larger hospitals still occupied peripheral sites, but boundary locations no longer held cultural implications of isolating either the patient from the unhealthy city or the city from the unhealthy patients. Hospital facilities had become part of the "urban furniture" that made modern cities livable, an acceptable interface between abutting neighborhoods of different character. According to Philip W. Foster, a city planner in the Boston area, institutional buildings served as barriers to other developments. If located at the borderline of a residential community, a hospital would "act as a protection against undesirable encroachments, or as a neutral belt dividing sections of different character. A hospital site that stands between a good residence district on one hand and one of lesser character on the other would help both by protecting the better and by adding a desirable open green space adjacent to the more crowded area."[22]

The proximity to traffic arteries and public transportation hubs was a crucial factor in the choice of a hospital site. A hospital located near the terminus of public transportation—a subway, streetcar, or bus line—was accessible to patients from the downtown neighborhoods. A hospital located along major roadways was convenient to the increasing numbers of daily automobile commuters—suburbanites who were likely to be from a wealthier patient base.

Figure 5.5. Columbia-Presbyterian Medical Center, aerial view, ca. 1929. Riverside Drive is visible just beyond the hospital complex. The building included a direct connection to a subway stop, facilitating access from lower Manhattan. This image also gives an idea of the vast scale of the new medical center.

From the Lebanon Hospital in New York City to the Hollywood Hospital in California, peripheral sites placed the hospital at a point of maximum traffic. The administrators of the Northwestern University Hospital complex in Chicago, on a site just north of the downtown Loop, looked forward to a thriving supply of clinical material from the adjacent elevated train station. By its proximity to North Shore Avenue, a main thoroughfare into the city, they also hoped to "be able to serve the North Shore section of Chicago," a wealthier suburb. Appealing to the new individual commuter brought along with it the problem of parking.[23] Clearly, a twentieth-century hospital's location maximized the flow of persons to its doors as much as it did the flow of light and air to the rooms.

Hospital Layouts: A Vertical Alphabet

In early 1923 Goldwater observed that "the ambitions of American hospital planners, which in the past have aimed at the 'greatest hospital' or the 'best equipped hospital' in the world, seem recently to have been diverted into new channels, and the latest boast is that such-and-such a hospital will be the 'tallest in the world.'" All kinds and sizes of hospitals participated in this dream. Julian Goldman, president of the seventy-five-bed Peoples Hospital (formerly the Austro-Hungarian Hospital) of New York City predicted a future twenty-story building. Directors of the Receiving Hospital in Detroit proposed a completed facility of seventeen stories. The planning board for the new Columbia-Presbyterian Medical Center discussed idealized designs of thirty-, forty-, even fifty-story buildings for their new facility.[24]

At a time of great nationalism, high-rises were seen as distinctly American and high-rise hospitals provided a visible and tangible differentiation of American from European development. Experiences in World War I and its aftermath had eroded the long-lived American infatuation with European hospital institutions and their traditional low-rise, decentralized pavilion facilities. Postwar American hospital practitioners were consciously trying to "disentangle our hospital architecture from certain European standards that are not only being discarded by the countries in which they originated, but which never contemplated conditions under which American hospitals must do their work."[25] A high-rise was also a sign of the developing modern, urban, technological culture. Presentation drawings of proposed high-rise hospitals, imitating the dramatic work of Hugh Ferris, showed the buildings at nighttime in dark shadows and light, as beacons of a new, exciting urban future. The high-rise hospital offered a modern hospital for a modern world.

High-rise hospitals became reality as well as dream in the 1920s. Although they set no height records, hospital buildings were no longer the lowest buildings in their neighborhood. The Fifth Avenue Hospital in New York City rose to nine stories (1922); Passavant Hospital in Chicago to eleven (1926); Beth Israel Hospital in New York City to twelve (1929); the Hahnemann Hospital in Philadelphia to seventeen (1929); and Saint Luke's Hospital in Chicago to nineteen (1925). Even hospitals of medium height relied on extensive vertical circulation, divided their services by floors, and functioned as a single, integrated (albeit complex) building.

While the development of other types of buildings into skyscrapers was clearly linked to the rising prices of land in the urban downtown, location was not the determining factor in whether a hospital emphasized horizon-

Figure 5.6. Saint Luke's Hospital, Chicago, proposed addition, 1925. The addition was designed by Charles S. Frost. Though a simple slab building rather than the stepped, set-back buildings of Hugh Ferris's most famous drawings, the dramatic view highlights the hospital as a prominent urban fixture.

tal or vertical organization. Hospitals on downtown sites (like the Broad Street Hospital in downtown New York City, Saint Luke's Hospital in Chicago, or Hahnemann Medical College and Hospital in Philadelphia) inevitably were under pressure for multistory design, but many high-rise hospital facilities (e.g., the Jewish Hospital in Saint Louis, Missouri; the Los Angeles County General Hospital; Tampa Municipal Hospital in Florida; Montefiore Hospital in Pittsburgh; the Syracuse Memorial Hospital in Syracuse, New York; and the Physicians' Hospital in Plattsburgh, New York) were built on large sites well distant from the downtown.

Not all hospitals went vertical. A few of the largest hospitals built in this era (such as Highland Hospital in Oakland, California; the Kingston Hospital in Brooklyn; and the Philadelphia General Hospital) occupied facilities which were clearly horizontally organized. The tide had turned, however, and more new hospitals were arranged vertically than horizontally. A seemingly low-rise hospital building might be simply the base of a future planned tower, with expansion to consist of additional floors rather than buildings. For example, initial construction of the Receiving Hospital in Detroit completed only five stories of a projected seventeen.

This vertical shift served the new operational model of hospitals, which required efficient interaction by numerous departments in the delivery of group medical diagnosis. The increasing interaction of special departments in general hospitals did not by any means reduce the idea that each specialty required its own devoted space and special facilities. This meant that even centralized hospitals were a collection of relatively independent

Figure 5.7. City Hospital, Cleveland, bird's-eye view, early 1920s. Designed by J. H. MacDowell, the wards were angled to maximize the exposure of patient rooms and their balconies to direct sunlight, even though this arrangement ignored the lake view to the east.

Figure 5.8. Isadore Rosenfield, diagram of progressive stages of vertical expansion, 1927.

departments. Goldwater used the term *departmentalized hospital* to describe this approach and noted that one might "with reasonable accuracy appraise the clinical efficiency of a hospital by ascertaining the number of separate departments which contribute to diagnosis and treatment." And yet the goal was not a collection of adjacent independent pieces but a hospital "logically composed, with due regard for its functioning as an organic whole."[26]

The need for constant and efficient interaction between all of these pieces meant that the placement of each department in relation to each other was as important as the efficient design of each department. It was no longer sufficient to simply add a building where there was open space on a site, pack it with all the miscellaneous facilities that needed new quarters, and then let the staff and patients wander their way through the maze. Each new addition required "the preparation of a comprehensive scheme for the contemplated full development." Vertical expansion (adding floors to existing buildings) provided the ability to add more space without constantly reworking circulation routes and departmental adjacencies. It retained existing (presumably efficient) circulation patterns, simply adding more elevator stops.[27]

Unlike other high-rise building types in the 1920s, tall hospitals remained thin buildings. As technological developments such as electric lighting, mechanical heating, and ventilation reduced the need for window access to sunlight for daylighting and air for ventilation, office skyscrapers like the Woolworth Building in New York City or the Tribune Tower in Chicago had block-filling, centralized footprints with extensive interior spaces with no immediate access to an exterior wall. Hospitals of whatever height continued to provide direct window access to light and air to a majority of rooms. Hospitals from this era continued to occupy complex footprints, either rectilinear arrangements, like an *H*, *U*, *E*, or *F*, or, as a result of the continued interest in maximizing sunlight exposure, angled plans, like a *Y*, *X*, or *V*. The cross or *X* plan—which required only one vertical service core and maximized exterior exposure—was particularly popular. The narrow towers often framed landscaped courtyards.[28]

These complex footprints supported horizontal as well as vertical departmentalization. Even in high-rise hospitals, each wing as well as each floor could accommodate a different category of space. The designers of the Allegheny General Hospital in Pittsburgh pointed out that the interplay of vertical and horizontal circulation allowed "unobstructed access from one [department] to the other between those related in service," but segregated unrelated departments from each other while still providing easy access for all departments to the centralized services. Interaction and centralization were more critical than separation. The high-rise hospitals of the 1920s were not the "inflexible" "stacked" pavilion model of the 1900s and 1910s, with separate towers connected only at a common base.[29] Whether comprising multiple wings radiating from a central elevator core (like the Fifth Avenue Hospital and Beth Israel Hospital in New York City and the Hurley Hospital in Flint, Michigan) or multiple elevator cores servicing different portions of a sprawling footprint (such as Children's Hospital in Cincinnati, the Herman Kiefer Hospital in Detroit, or the Ottawa Civic Hospital) the modern hospital was a single, integrated building.

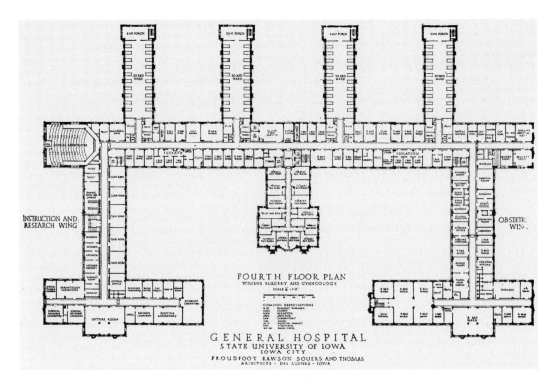

Figure 5.9. State University of Iowa Hospital, Des Moines, fourth-floor plan, 1929. Designed by Proudfoot, Rawson, Soeurs, and Thomas, the rambling footprint gave each unit within the hospital some spatial coherence while still connecting the hospital into a single building.

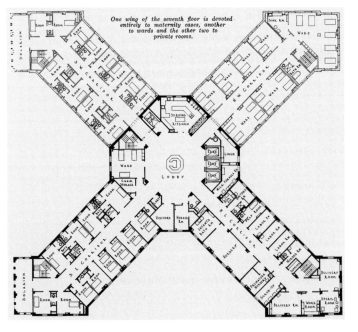

Figure 5.10. Hurley Hospital, Hurley, Michigan, seventh-floor plan, 1929. Designed by Theilbar and Fugard with Paul G. Burt as consultant, this maternity ward floor shows the variety of small wards and private patient rooms offered.

Different Building Types for Different Hospital Types

While vertical design had become the new ideal, the variety of hospital types ensured that there would still be a range of hospital designs. Hospitals that continued to do a large proportion of free or only partial-pay care, like the sprawling, five-story Philadelphia General Hospital (which targeted indigent and middle-class, but not wealthy patients) were more likely to occupy relatively low-rise, decentralized facilities. Tuberculosis hospitals, chronic disease hospitals, and convalescent hospitals, like the Southern Baptist Sanatorium in El Paso, Texas, and the War Mothers' National Memorial Hospital for Tuberculosis in Albuquerque, New Mexico, whose patients still benefited from natural environmental therapy, also remained in more decentralized facilities. As discussed by Annmarie Adams, Kevin Schwartzmann, and David Theodore, as treatment for tuberculosis shifted from fresh air to surgery, the facilities developed to house tubercular patients also shifted away from low-rise decentralized facilities. The special recovery hospitals for polio victims (like the Rainbow Hospital in Euclid, Ohio, or the Shriner's Hospitals in various cities) also tended to be lower-rise and more decentralized. They offered primarily environmental therapies and convalescent care, and they served a patient population with severe mobility issues.[30]

Isolation hospitals and contagious disease hospitals, which had been housed in some of the most decentralized facilities, underwent an extensive transformation during this period. Increased bacteriological understanding of a number of contagious diseases, widespread adoption of contact theories of infection, and improved aseptic procedures made an isolation facility in a general hospital (with all of its available equipment and resources for handling complications) the preferred location for the treatment of many communicable disease patients. By the end of the decade, a survey in New York City by the State Charities Aid Association concluded that "there should be hereafter no separate hospitals established in New York City for communicable diseases; that communicable diseases should be cared for in special and separate buildings in connection with general hospitals." As contagious disease patients moved back into the general hospital, the separate municipal contagious disease hospitals that had blossomed between the 1880s and the 1910s declined. By the 1930s there were few new isolation hospitals being planned or built, and little attention paid to existing ones. Many sat virtually empty, and many would be abandoned or repurposed in the latter decades of the twentieth century.[31]

The rapid adoption of group practice similarly altered the architectural trajectory of specialized hospitals. According to Goldwater, "modern or cooperative medicine predicates the general as against the special hospital.

Figure 5.11. Los Angeles County General Hospital, view, 1930s. Designed by Bergstrom, Hunt, Davis, Hunt and Richards, the hospital was a prominent high-rise building in a city not known for high-rises.

From the standpoint of group practice, the special hospital is not a hospital at all; it is only part of a hospital, a limping thing deprived of essential members, and needing the support of crutches."[32] While standalone specialized institutions (like the Boston Lying-In Hospital, the Babies' Hospital in Philadelphia, or the Children's Hospital in Columbus, Ohio) continued to thrive, this attitude brought many specialties back into the all-encompassing general hospital or into affiliation with a medical center.

The scale of a hospital also influenced the type of facility suited to its practice. Medium-size general hospitals occupied some of the most spatially integrated, vertically organized hospital facilities of the time. The Fifth Avenue Hospital (ten stories) and the Beth Israel Hospital in New York City (fourteen stories), Hurley Hospital in Flint, Michigan (ten stories), and Passavant Hospital in Chicago (thirteen stories) all occupied centralized and spatially integrated single buildings. Other medium-size general hospitals, like the Los Angeles County General Hospital and the Jewish Hospital in Saint Louis) occupied a single structure, but with extensive wings and setbacks.

Instead of creating a singular centralized structure, some hospital designs (like the Beth Israel Hospital in Newark, New Jersey, the Cleveland City Hospital, or the Montefiore Hospital in Pittsburgh) divided

Figure 5.12. Montefiore Hospital, Pittsburgh, view, 1930s. The building, designed by Schmidt, Garden and Erikson in collaboration with S. S. Goldwater, was separated into functional pieces and arranged to take advantage of the height differentials on the site. The lowest building was the dispensary, with its own separate entrance. The tall building highest on the hill held the wards and patient rooms. The connecting wing held the medical services (surgery, diagnostics, X-ray, labs, etc.).

their high-rise facilities into discrete functional units—such as medical services, wards, administration, and nurse housing—that were housed in separate structures. Each component, though part of the larger building, was sized, shaped, and located according to its own spatial requirements and to facilitate the delivery of medical care. Medical service buildings were often lower buildings, but with a central location for maximum connections to other services. Patient rooms were often in the higher buildings, maximizing light and air to the inpatients on upper floors.

The largest general hospitals, teaching hospitals, and medical centers occupied hybrid facilities, with strong horizontal as well as vertical circulation that could facilitate the integration of a number of discrete departments into an interconnected whole. Typically, the stronger the independent identity of a unit, the more likely it was to occupy a separate wing or structure accessible only by horizontal connections.

In teaching hospitals and medical centers that were the result of affiliations of preexisting independent institutions—for example, the Columbia-

Figure 5.13. Lakeside Hospital, in Western Reserve University Hospital Complex, Cleveland, aerial view, mid-twentieth century. From the lower left-hand corner to the upper right-hand corner of the picture the buildings in the complex are: nurses' housing, private patient pavilion, Lakeside Hospital (the largest structure with long cross-wings, designed by Coolidge Shepley Bulfinch and Abbott), the small pathological building along the street, then the Babies' and Children's Hospital (designed by Abram Garfield and S. S. Goldwater) and Maternity Hospital, and the school of medicine buildings.

Presbyterian Medical Center or the Case Western Reserve Medical Center in Cleveland—the separate units housed separate institutions. The resultant facility typically included a number of identifiably distinct structures, in close proximity and with multiple levels of interconnections. The largest medical centers, such as the Columbia-Presbyterian Hospital and the new New York Hospital–Cornell Medical Center, were essentially medicalized high-rise neighborhoods. Each individual department or institution occupied a separate structure, but all of the structures were grouped onto a single campus and expected to function as one interactive whole.[33]

Facilities tended to be more integrated in the larger hospitals that were part of a single administrative identity. The vertically organized A. Montgomery Ward Building of the Northwestern University Medical School was a single high-rise to house a medical school, a dental school, and their associated patient care facilities. A number of teaching hospitals

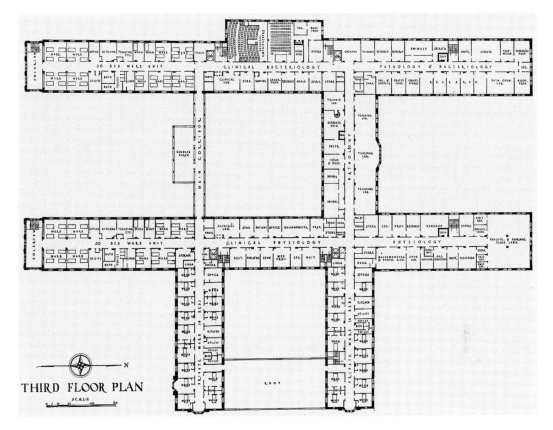

Figure 5.14. Vanderbilt University Medical School and Hospital, Nashville, third-floor plan, 1923. Designed by Coolidge and Shattuck, with extensive input from hospital consultant Winford Smith and medical director G. Canby Robinson, the integrated plan allowed extensive interaction of hospital, university, and research departments. The spiral stairway in the pathology wing led directly up to the operating rooms on the fourth floor. The clinical physiology laboratory was situated between the physiology department and the medical wards.

and medical centers, including the University of Colorado Medical School and Hospital in Denver, Colorado, the Strong Memorial Hospital in Rochester, New York, and the Vanderbilt University Medical School and Hospital in Nashville, Tennessee, occupied sprawling facilities with multiple interconnected wings arranged around internal courtyards rather than going high-rise. Nevertheless, the designers believed that the integration of the facilities "would go far towards eliminating barriers between the preclinical and clinical studies, and will allow all departments to exert a constant influence on the training of the future physician."[34]

While the integrated high-rise facilities of large general hospitals, teaching hospitals, and medical centers stand as the iconic institutional

SKETCH OF COMPLETED REDLANDS COMMUNITY HOSPITAL, REDLANDS, CAL.
MYRON HUNT AND H. C. CHAMBERS, ARCHITECTS

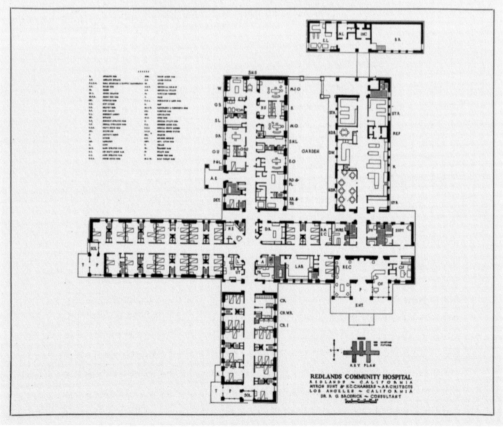

Figure 5.15. Redlands Community Hospital, Redlands, California, plan and bird's-eye view, 1928.

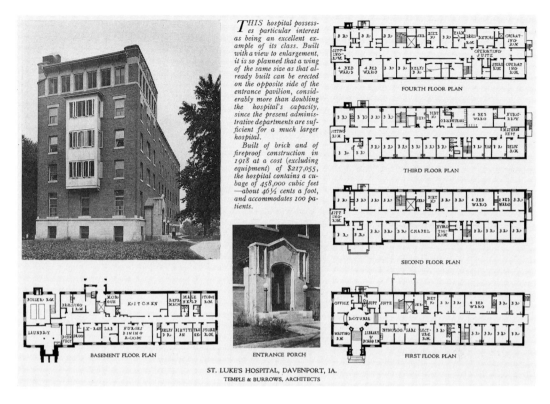

THIS hospital possesses particular interest as being an excellent example of its class. Built with a view to enlargement, it is so planned that a wing of the same size as that already built can be erected on the opposite side of the entrance pavilion, considerably more than doubling the hospital's capacity, since the present administrative departments are sufficient for a much larger hospital.

Built of brick and of fireproof construction in 1918 at a cost (excluding equipment) of $217,055, the hospital contains a cubage of 458,000 cubic feet—about 46½ cents a foot, and accommodates 100 patients.

ST. LUKE'S HOSPITAL, DAVENPORT, IA.
TEMPLE & BURROWS, ARCHITECTS

Figure 5.16. Saint Luke's Hospital, Davenport, Iowa, plans and general view, 1922. Designed by Temple and Burrows, architects, the building as constructed held one hundred beds but had services sized for far more. The addition of a second, ward wing on the other side of the entrance pavilion would more than double the capacity at a relatively low cost.

form of the early twentieth century, their bigness and complexity was neither universally admired nor adopted. According to one critic, "the over-developed medical center . . . often presents such a maze of administrative difficulties—such a physical and hence clinical separation of patients—that the business of treating their interrelated ailments falters because of the lack of timely and efficient unified direction." The majority of American hospitals were small institutions, either targeting a specific underserved patient category or created as a conscious countercurrent to the large, complex institutions. Community hospitals that provided immediate and basic care to the population of a given geographic area were often highly successful. These smaller hospitals offered more personal, less bureaucratic care, provided a location that fostered organized group practice among more rural practitioners, and provided specialized diagnostic, hospital-level care and equipment to all locations.[35]

Designing the small hospital—whether in a large city or a small town—was an exercise in developing the minimum, but efficient, versions of all the necessary services. A number of the more technical departments were difficult to scale down and still function efficiently. Adapting the hospital to local influences—whether cultural or economic—could also pose problems. For example, hospital designers in the South had to figure out how to provide segregated wards, in small footprints with limited budgets. Hospital designers in warmer climates had to adapt available published designs that were often for cold-climate institutions. Despite the prevalent emphasis on centralized, vertical designs, to take advantage of the California climate, Myron Hunt designed the Riverside Community Hospital, San Antonio Community Hospital, and Redlands Community Hospital as sprawling one-story complexes enclosing outdoor spaces with extensive porches.[36]

While a number of small hospitals still occupied structures comprising the traditional central administration building with two ward wings, the more typical and more modern small hospital of the 1920s was a three- to five-story single building, with a central, double-loaded corridor, with different departments on different floors. General services were typically located in the basement; medical services, administration, and diagnostic departments on the ground floor; patient rooms occupied the intervening floors; and remaining medical services and surgery on the top floor, in a penthouse. Isolation was either on the ground floor, on the top floor, or in a separate cottage.[37] Many had either an outbuilding, a separate wing, or a small "bump" for departments (like isolation or pathology) that benefited from the separation.

Hospital Standardization: Large Hospitals vs. Small Hospitals

The differing sizes and types of hospitals in 1920s America inevitably provided a broad variety of care, ranging from approximations of the earlier charitable care to the modern, technology-dependent, diagnostic group medical practice. That range of hospital sizes and types could be perceived as a flexible system capable of accommodating all types of patient and all kinds of treatment, or as a chaos of uncoordinated hospitals all vying for the same patients and doctors, suffering financial hardships from that competition, and not necessarily providing appropriate or even adequate care.[38] For hospital construction, the most influential standards were those developed by the American College of Surgeons (ACS).

In 1918 the ACS established basic minimum requirements for hospital facilities, service, and administration. Doctors set the standards, and as Rosemary Stevens notes, many were based on Abraham Flexner's scathing

1910 report on medical education, which had rejected the traditional proprietary school model and promoted a systematic university-based model
that incorporated hospital experience as an integral aspect of medical
education. Given the variety of existing hospitals, the doctors established
standards that, like the hospitals, were not a one-size-fits-all approach. Seventeen different categories and sizes of hospital—from university hospitals
to small, semipublic hospitals to contagious disease hospitals—were expected to provide different levels of service and facilities. This complexity
eased the transition of existing hospitals into conformance, minimizing the
initial shock of the change, and making it possible for the majority of institutions to meet the ACS standards, if with some effort. Standardization
thus initially did not overtly reduce the diversity of hospitals, it just made
sure that for any given kind of hospital there were minimum services and
facilities. Enforcement of the standards was through simple publicity. Institutions that participated in the standards campaign were given a grade and,
if they passed, were put on a list of approved institutions. Institutions that
refused to participate or participated but did not meet the standards were
not included on the approved list and often saw their patient, practitioner,
and donor base dwindle. As Edward F. Stevens commented, "practically no
hospital is willing to be classed as inefficient."[39]

In practice, however, the burden of meeting the minimum standards
weighed more heavily on smaller hospitals than larger ones. The ACS standards for hospital buildings discouraged minimally equipped institutions
that provided basic care in basic buildings and encouraged facilities that
were of fireproof construction, included numerous building technologies,
and provided advanced medical services such as labs, X-ray, therapeutic
spaces, diagnostics, and extensive operating rooms. Larger institutions
could amortize the cost of such extensive facilities over a large number of
patients; smaller hospitals encountered difficulties in trying to meet the
requirements while still remaining efficient and economical. At a time
when the average American hospital held ninety-eight beds, the ACS's setting of minimum standards thus inevitably resulted in promoting the slow
transition to larger, technologically equipped hospitals over smaller, care-
oriented facilities.[40]

The ACS minimum standards also revealed the design of an efficient
small hospital to be an unsolved problem, worthy of attention by the hospital design community. Dr. John A. Hornsby suggested that small hospitals
were especially prone to poor design because there was rarely anyone with
experience in hospital architecture available during planning and construction.[41] Indeed, the services of either a hospital architect or a hospital
consultant were often beyond the means of smaller institutional budgets.

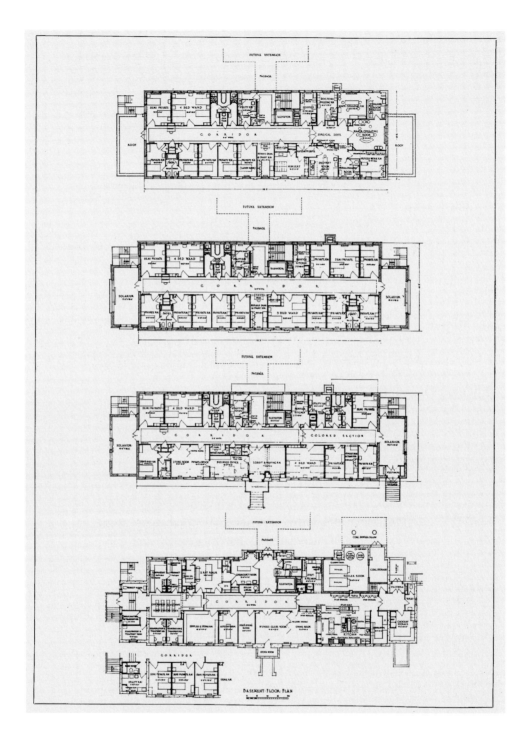

Figure 5.17. Duke Endowment, Charlotte, North Carolina, plans of typical small hospital, 1928. The hospital, designed by Samuel Hannaford and Sons, included various ward sizes, though none were larger than four beds. This allowed fine categorization even in a small hospital.

Figure 5.18. Duke Endowment, Charlotte, North Carolina, view of typical small hospital, 1928. If the interior layout was determined by functional requirements, the hospital exterior was clearly influenced by traditional expectations of the aesthetics of public buildings.

Most publications on hospital design focused on the larger hospitals or on the design of special departments and facilities sized for such larger hospitals.

By the late 1910s the need for publicly available sources on best design practices for smaller hospitals was partially met by the appearance of articles on a few well-designed small institutions, but that information was largely piecemeal and posed single solutions, not general guidelines. In August 1922 the editors of *Modern Hospital* announced an architectural design contest for a small hospital. The contest, which gained international attention, was intended to generate a variety of plans that would be published and function as design aids for local hospital designers across the country.[42]

The Duke Endowment hospitals provided another influential model, particularly in the South. Intended to provide hospital care to the rural communities in the Carolinas, the first hospital of the endowment opened in 1901. A larger hospital opened in 1925. By 1928, with plans to establish more small hospitals in numerous small communities, the Duke Endowment published two versions of an "ideal" plan developed by prominent hospital architectural firm Samuel Hannaford and Sons.[43] Both versions provided a complete hospital in four floors, but one version included a single-loaded corridor with a large porch while the second version was a compact, double-loaded corridor building with little architectural embellishment.

The Attractive Factory

Within these increasingly complex buildings was an ever-growing number of services, departments, technologies, and equipment vying for space, coordination, and use. The ACS committee members who developed the early hospital standards believed that the "vast majority" of American hospitals were "planned without any reference whatever to economy and efficiency in the care of patients." In an age of tight budgets and efficiency experts, administrators of civil hospitals tried to emulate the functional approach of military hospitals, which combined "all the different procedures of operative and postoperative treatment in a complete logical sequence."[44]

A hospital encapsulated multiple, often competing, production paths, which defied any singular optimal solution. Its operation required the regular performance of a vast array of tasks by a variety of personnel. Asa S. Bacon listed seven ideals of hospital efficiency, which included patient care, physician and intern practice, nursing practice, education (of doctors, nurses, and the community), conservation of supplies, full occupancy of beds, and economical construction.[45] While no one worried about the happiness of a Ford automobile as it traversed the assembly line, making the hospital efficient entailed ensuring these varied human products were comfortable on their respective journeys. Designing a hospital that would be attractive to all of these groups at the same time was as impossible as maximizing functional efficiency for all of them simultaneously. Building designers had to choose which tasks or features to facilitate, and how to do so in a pleasing manner. In parts of the hospital devoted to a single use or used by a single group it was possible to develop efficient and attractive solutions. A well-designed laboratory would attract and retain prominent researchers, whereas ample and attractive nurse housing and training school facilities improved matriculation rates of student nurses. Where the tension in efficient hospital design remained the highest was in the parts of the hospital with the greatest amount of interaction of functions and groups—the diagnostic and treatment facilities, the operating facilities, and most of all, the wards and patient rooms.

Hospitals Designed for Technology

As Joel Howell has revealed, the modern hospital building of the 1920s was so full of labor-saving systems and technologies in the interest of efficient provision of service that it was itself a machine. Call buttons improved nursing efficiency. Paging systems simplified communication with the highly mobile medical staff. Telephones and pneumatic tube systems accelerated the requisition and delivery of materials and supplies regardless of the building's footprint. The telautograph could reproduce a handwritten message such as a prescription in a remote location. Automatic temperature controls reduced the number of service personnel needed to regulate the heating and ventilating system. Centralized sterile water supply systems ended the need to sterilize water at multiple locations throughout the building. Centralized services produced economies of scale that could reduce staffing. Dumbwaiters simplified the delivery of food and goods. Centralized vacuum systems simplified cleaning. Laundry chutes and dustbins facilitated the removal of waste. All of these technologies supported new ways of working within the hospital, and influenced the changing nature of care provided.[46]

Not surprisingly, one of the best examples of technologically efficient hospital design was the Henry Ford Hospital in Detroit. It was "organized with attention to business principles," and relied on building technologies to facilitate communication despite its extended footprint. A central hexagonal pavilion, known as the diagnostic building, held administration, executive offices, services, doctors' offices, examination rooms, consultation rooms, lecture rooms, record rooms, and diagnostic and treatment facilities. Leading to and from this centralized nerve center were miles of pipes, ducts, and tunnels for all the labor-saving devices. Doctors could dictate their notes by phone to a stenographer at a central records office or request a report on a previous diagnosis or a case history by phone and quickly receive the records by pneumatic tube. Nurses could phone requests to the various centralized supply departments and the item would be delivered on the automatic elevator. To facilitate this technological dispersal of information, the hospital staff developed standardized medical terminology, reducing complex medical terms "to a system of numerals and decimals which permits of a simple system of cross indexing, making it possible for lay workers to compile reports and records with astonishing rapidity and with absolute accuracy." Its exterior resembled the factories that produced the automobiles, clearly making the reference that the hospital was indeed just another form of factory. The designers considered the Henry Ford Hospital evolutionary, not revolutionary. Other hospital designers soon imitated its innovations.[47]

Figure 5.19. Henry Ford Hospital, Detroit, view, 1920. Albert Kahn, who was also the designer of the Ford Motor Company's factories, approached the hospital design with the same functional approach to the layout and utilitarian aesthetic (using economical concrete frame construction with brick and glass infill).

Artificial Environmental Therapies and the Sealed Hospital

Environmental therapy remained an essential service in the efficient modern hospital. While outdoor facilities for natural environmental therapy, such as sun porches, rooftop wards, gardens, and balconies continued to be included even in urban general hospitals, the use of building technologies to generate controlled conditions for the administration of artificial environmental therapies was increasingly common and elaborate.[48]

General interest in controlling not just the flow of air but also its humidity, temperature, dust content, bacterial load, and odors throughout the hospital prompted the inclusion of increasingly elaborate mechanical ventilation and air-conditioning systems. From a building type once in-

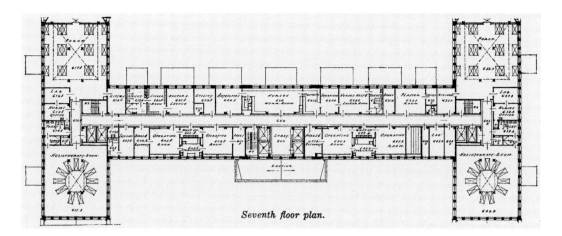

Seventh floor plan.

Figure 5.20. Herman Kiefer Hospital, Detroit, seventh-floor plan, 1929. Designed by Albert Kahn, this hospital for tuberculosis patients included extensive outdoor facilities, but also two heliotherapy rooms with the standard radial layout of beds ringing the ceiling-mounted lamps. The fresh air wings flanked the surgical wing, in essence turning the seventh floor into a treatment facility that offered both environmental cure and medical intervention.

tensely permeable to exterior conditions the hospital became a closed, sealed structure. The shift was so complete that one expert even suggested that hospitals "should avoid placing doors in line with windows, or opposite other doors, so as to avoid draughts." But the sealed hospital did not contain a uniform interior environment.[49]

Research pinpointing physiological responses to specific environmental conditions, including humidity, temperature, oxygen content, and ultraviolet rays, emphasized a more precise control of differentiated conditions. In 1922 W. Dwight Pierce noted that artificial indoor weather was well within the bounds of possibility, and that indoor climate therapy was a distinct option. Warm rooms for the pneumonia patient, dry rooms for the tubercular, oxygen chambers for respiratory ailments, and barometric chambers appeared. The installation of a "climate room" or "health room" provided a form of treatment as well as a popular patient room. Early hospital air-conditioning systems for operating rooms and nurseries reportedly lowered the death rate in postoperative patients and in prematurely delivered babies.[50]

The work of Hess and Ungar on rickets and the discovery that ultraviolet ray exposure was not only "the best germicide we have," but that it "prevents deficiency diseases and is an essential stimulus for protection against infection and toxemia" increased interest in heliotherapy within the hospital. Controlled exposure to therapeutic doses of ultraviolet light was provided through outdoor features—porches, balconies, solaria—but also through increasingly complex indoor heliotherapy facilities. After reports that regular window glass let in light but blocked much of the therapeutic and germicidal ultraviolet rays, many American hospitals installed Vita-Glass (a transparent glass composition that allowed ultraviolet radiation to penetrate) or a competitive variant. Indoor heliotherapy, under full-spectrum, high-intensity lamps, continued to augment the availability of sunlight in troubled climates. By the 1920s such artificial heliotherapy had developed into a relatively common hospital installation that consisted of four full-spectrum arc lamps arranged around a central support that allowed up to thirty prone patients to be treated simultaneously in a room of at least sixteen feet in diameter.[51]

Hospitals Designed for Doctors

Hospitals depended on their doctors, for the provision of treatment to patients, for the referral of private patients, and for the advancement of the institutional reputation (through medical research, publications, and therapeutic advances). Better hospital facilities attracted a better caliber of doctor. On the other hand, medical spatial demands could be extensive. According to Goldwater, many a hospital building program's budget had been derailed by the medical staff who

> understood, of course, that the new hospital would have an abundance of cheap private rooms, a long chain of perfectly appointed operating rooms, laboratories, equal to those of the most famous research centers, a therapeutic institute rivaling the best in Europe, sun parlors as spacious as those of a mammoth resort hotel, cooled air like that of a motion picture house, extensive protected roof spaces for heliotherapy, lecture rooms of university capacity, a medical library to vie with the premier collection of the Surgeon General at Washington, and a hundred other startling features, useful or ornamental.[52]

While few hospital budgets could afford all of those amenities, at a minimum most hospital administrators did their best to keep their outpatient departments and operating rooms current and well equipped.

Outpatient buildings were, as Annmarie Adams points out, the location of continuing charitable care within the increasingly pay-patient hospital, but they were also the easiest means of adding facilities for group practice to an existing hospital. By the 1920s the standalone dispensary that provided a quick medical exam and dispensed a traditional formulary for routine cases was a rarity. In its place stood a modern outpatient clinic that provided group diagnosis, specialists, and surgical facilities, but also a conduit to inpatient

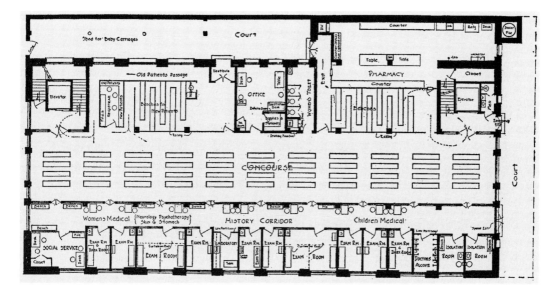

Figure 5.21. S. S. Goldwater, ideal design for outpatient building, first-floor plan, 1921.

beds for unusual (medically interesting) cases. The Mayo Clinic and its diagnostic approach remained the model, whether in a standalone clinic (like the Cleveland Clinic) or in an outpatient department of a larger hospital.[53]

These diagnostic outpatient clinics rose to several stories in height, separated patients into smaller groups to improve patient experience, provided multiple waiting rooms, had subdivisions for clinical specialties, and facilitated group practice. Records departments, extensive filing rooms, and social service and outreach offices allowed practitioners to track outcomes of treatment. The larger outpatient clinics often handled hundreds (if not thousands) of patients on a daily basis. They were designed for efficient flow and maximum throughput of patients. Upon entering, a patient encountered the registration or information desk, then the general waiting room, then a turn at the admission office and records, then to a specialty waiting room, then into a changing room, an exam room, and then a treatment room or an inpatient bed. It was a spatial approximation of a medical assembly line.

If the design of outpatient departments had become a processing sequence, operating rooms remained "the delight of the medical profession." Some practitioners also considered them a delight for patients. At Saint Mary's Hospital in Rochester, Minnesota, (affiliated with the influential Mayo Clinic doctors) there were no anesthetizing rooms—the anesthetic was given in the operating room because "the modern operating room is attractive and interesting, and a view of the surgeon's workshop will be a source of satisfaction to the patient."[54] Operating rooms were one of the

Figure 5.22. University of Michigan Hospital, Ann Arbor, operating room view, 1927. This operating room, in a facility designed by Albert Kahn, with Christopher Parnall as hospital consultant, had green tiles and gray walls. The green was the complementary color to blood red, and was chosen as a means of making the wound more visible. The inclusion of a large window as well as the artificial lights was a more traditional approach to the design.

most regularly updated, renovated, and replaced hospital facilities; the constant updating served to keep the facilities aseptically current, to make them more efficient, to make them more aesthetically appealing, and to make them far more numerous. This made them well-developed examples of Adams and Schlich's category of interwar surgical suite.[55]

In the late 1910s and 1920s the operating room underwent a practical aesthetic revolution. Traditionally, operating rooms had included large windows or skylights and been finished predominantly in high-gloss white materials. This combination produced extensive glare. During an operation, upon glancing from the relatively dark wound to the shiny bright room finishes and back, surgeons suffered from eye fatigue, visual errors, and even momentary loss of vision. To reduce the glare, doctors experimented with colored finishes—such as gray, black, or spinach green. The darker walls reduced contrast, making the room more restful to the surgeon's eyes and improving perception of the surgical wound. Not everyone approved. Dr. William Lee Secor advocated keeping the operating room white, because it showed dirt and was easier to keep clean, but suggested the surgeon and staff could wear dark glasses and beaked caps to combat the glare. Color in the operating room caught on, however, and hospitals across the country soon held green, tan, cream, or other-hued operating rooms. By 1917, "all-white operating rooms [were] no longer the universal rule."[56]

As the operating room colors grew darker, they absorbed more ambient light, and the operating room seemed darker. To compensate, hospital designers like Edward F. Stevens, who advocated natural lighting for operating rooms, designed even larger windows and skylights. Many doctors believed larger skylights simply created larger problems—they created condensation on humid days, provided inconsistent light levels depending on the weather, cast dangerous shadows on the operating field, brought back glare, and created extreme heat loads or cold loss that made the operating room uncomfortable. The development of high-intensity artificial lighting fixtures that could provide constant, shadowless light provided an enticing alternative, but one that was still being perfected. Adams recounts how Stevens's "preference for daylit surgical suites" caused some conflict with doctors in the planning of several hospitals. In the 1920s many hospitals included both artificial lights and natural lighting (with the option to close off the window). By 1929 Goldwater reported that a majority of surgeons preferred to operate under artificial lights. Carl A. Erikson noted in the same year that skylights were waning in operating room designs, and that at least one hospital was building operating rooms without windows at all.[57]

If color and lighting could make the surgeon comfortable; more numerous operating rooms could maximize a surgeon's efficient use of time. According to Stevens, the number of operating rooms in a hospital was to "be governed not by the number of patients in the institution but by the number of the staff who wish to operate at the same time." The common layout of surgical suites, with one sterile supply room between two operating rooms, was a space savings (one set of sterilizers for two operating rooms) but also a means of maximizing an individual surgeon's throughput. While the surgeon operated in one room, the next patient could be prepped in the adjoining operating room. The doctor could go from one operation to the next with little lost time. This multiplication of facilities posed a financial burden to many hospitals, particularly when half of the expensively outfitted rooms might be idle at any one time.[58]

The provision of private offices for doctors within the hospital itself proved a highly attractive feature. The success of the Johns Hopkins Hospi-

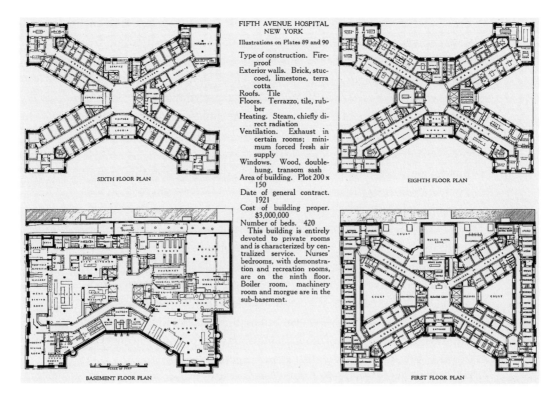

FIFTH AVENUE HOSPITAL
NEW YORK

Illustrations on Plates 89 and 90

Type of construction. Fireproof
Exterior walls. Brick, stuc-
coed, limestone, terra
cotta
Roofs. Tile
Floors. Terrazzo, tile, rubber
Heating. Steam, chiefly direct radiation
Ventilation. Exhaust in
certain rooms; mini-
mum forced fresh air
supply
Windows. Wood, double-
hung, transom sash
Area of building. Plot 200 x
150
Date of general contract.
1921
Cost of building proper.
$3,000,000
Number of beds. 420
This building is entirely
devoted to private rooms
and is characterized by centralized service. Nurses'
bedrooms, with demonstra-
tion and recreation rooms,
are on the ninth floor.
Boiler room, machinery
room and morgue are in the
sub-basement.

SIXTH FLOOR PLAN

EIGHTH FLOOR PLAN

BASEMENT FLOOR PLAN

FIRST FLOOR PLAN

Figure 5.23. Fifth Avenue Hospital, New York City, basement, first-, sixth-, and eighth-floor plans, 1922. Designed by York and Sawyer in collaboration with hospital consultant Wiley E. Woodbury, the hospital was one of the first to be built with all-single-bed rooms. The inclusion of doctors' offices (in the side wings on the right-hand side of the first floor plan) was another innovation. The larger footprint of the lower floors accommodated the larger spaces and bulkier services; the wards were raised into the sunlight and fresh air in narrow wings.

tal's transformation of its medical staff from volunteer, part-time service to salaried, full-time staff (as recommended by Abraham Flexner) proved the turning point in the creation of a new hospital-centered medical service. Many other teaching hospitals and medical centers began to require their practitioners to devote full time to the hospital. Hospital physicians and surgeons (typically eminent practitioners in their field of expertise) could not just give up treating wealthier patients, but neither could they maintain a separate private office while devoting full time to the school and students. The peripheral location of most new medical centers and teaching hospitals added the burden of extensive travel times. The inclusion of private physicians' and surgeons' offices within the hospital facility became a critical feature in attracting eminent practitioners.[59] It also cemented the hospital as the location of all-class medical care.

Inserting private offices in the hospital posed a new design problem; solutions varied between creating a separate building for offices and dispersing the offices throughout the facility. At the University of Iowa Hospital, the private offices of the clinical staff were dispersed "in close proximity to the special services to which its members are assigned." A separate unit was slightly more common, either in a separate corridor, as at the Mercy Hospital in Pittsburgh and the Fifth Avenue Hospital in New York, or in a separate building, as at the Baptist Memorial Hospital in Memphis. When the Columbia-Presbyterian Medical Center opened, it included doctors' offices (with connecting examination rooms) in the Harkness private patient pavilion.[60]

Hospitals Designed for Nurses

Many hospitals continued to experience difficulty filling their nursing staff requirements. With changes in care, more nurses were needed for a given number of patients. Hospitals also continued to compete for women laborers with other, less difficult job opportunities. According to the administrators of Bellevue Hospital, "At the best, hospital work does not appeal to many people. Long hours, contact with disease and limited compensation make it difficult for us to compete successfully with the commercial world for labor." In 1919, the director of Mount Zion Hospital in San Francisco noted that "with the almost unlimited opportunities for women offered today, hospitals must make better inducements for women to take up nursing as a profession than ever before and a modern up-to-date Nurses' Home is of the greatest necessity." Extensive nurse training and housing facilities were lures to attract new laborers and to increase retention of the current employees. Studies for the Columbia-Presbyterian Medical Center indicated that such housing "seems to have considerable importance as bearing upon wage questions and the morale of the personnel and student bodies connected with all of the associated institutions."[61]

In the 1920s, enormous, lavish, and expensive nurse training school buildings were added to existing hospital facilities. The experiences of the administrators of the Henry Ford Hospital in Detroit provide a graphic example. The original facility plan omitted nurse housing facilities because it was "the belief of the Ford organization that after spending eight hours at a hospital, doctors and nurses owe it to themselves and to their patients to get entirely away from the scene of work." In 1924, after only a few years of competing on the open market for scarce nurses, the hospital administrators chose to build a nurse training school building. It was of epic proportions and luxurious detail, rivaling the hospital for size and prominence. Some

Figure 5.24. Saint Luke's Hospital, Chicago, proposed new nurses' home, 1930. This unattributed design for a new nurses' home (on the left), adjacent to the 1920s high-rise hospital additions, demonstrates the attention being paid to nurse housing.

worried about the extravagance of the buildings, and the danger of spoiling the nurses, but the overwhelming majority worried more about how to attract and retain the best nurses and nursing students.[62]

The director of Mount Zion Hospital in San Francisco noted that in addition to a nurses' home, to retain nurses the hospital would have to make the work "much more attractive than in the past." Better nursing conditions within the wards could help. Providing an office could improve the nurse's job and standing, but whether it should be a separate office or a desk in the midst of the ward still remained a matter of debate. In the 1920s nurses were more likely to have a station than either an enclosed office or a mere desk in the ward. These stations were often just outside the ward(s), with a window for oversight of the ward. Goldwater advocated this location to let the nurse and the patients inhabit different climatic conditions. Such a location made the nurse a hall monitor as well as caregiver. "When located opposite the entrance corridor the nurse is enabled to control completely all avenues of communication, supervise the patients and meet members of the staff and visitors upon their entrance to the ward."[63]

A wide variety of designs revealed the wide variety of ideas about how best to design nursing stations. At the Alta Bates Hospital in Berkeley, California, the Jefferson Hospital in Philadelphia, and Saint John's Hospital in New York City, the nurse was in the corridor. At the Jewish Hospital in Saint Louis, the nurse had direct oversight of the patients in their beds. At the Babies' Hospital in Philadelphia, the nurses' station had oversight of the beds and of the corridor. While many of these layouts had been undertaken by the designers in the hopes of increasing the attractiveness of nursing, they were all speculative solutions—at that time, hospital designers were still largely not asking the nurses for their input. In 1921, Louis Frank of the Beth Israel Hospital in New York City noted that when he asked the nurses for their input on the design of the new building, he did so first to get the nurses "interested in the new hospital for propaganda purposes, and secondly, to secure from them information with respect to the proper workings of the new hospital." That the interest was more in creating excitement for the project than in gaining input into the design is clear—he called the meeting with the alumni of their nurse training school, not with the nurses employed in the hospital who would be working in the new building. There was also no attempt to get patient input on design decisions, which, according to Robert Sommer and Robert DeWar, was a lacunae well into the late twentieth century. Even in the 1930s Annie Goodrich would attribute "errors in construction" to "the failure to seek advice from those who, through their daily usage of departments could well direct the plan."[64]

The Multiple Requirements of Ward Design

The competing spatial requirements of different groups was most clear in ward design.[65] What made a patient happy often made a nurse exhausted or an administrator anxious. What pleased a doctor or nurse might worry or annoy a patient. The design of the wards and patient rooms thus reveals the difficulties of truly making the hospital operate like a factory, even an attractive factory.

Environmental Psychology and the Aesthetically Efficient Patient Room

To please patients, hospital wards underwent an aesthetic overhaul in the 1920s. This transformation was one of the ways to differentiate the older meaning of hospital, as a place of charity, from the new, modern meaning of hospital, as a place of efficient scientific medical treatment. Part of that efficiency of treatment required happy, or at least comfortable, patients. According to architect William O. Ludlow, wartime research showed that patients improved more often and more quickly in inviting restful surroundings, and that the "sterile," hyperaseptic hospital room generated harmful psychological effects that lengthened convalescence. In response, the new ideal in hospital interior design was to make sure that there was a "complete absence of anything that might suggest a hospital atmosphere." Postwar designers described wards in terms like "colorful," "home-like," and "private." These were words that had little to do with the institution's history, but if beauty could shorten convalescence (and free up beds to allow the hospital to treat more patients), it was worth it.[66] Beautification of the hospital was predicated on advances in asepsis that reduced the need for the entire room to be maintained in an aseptic state. If the building materials did not have to be sterile or capable of being sterilized, the hospital room could be anything. This shift opened the door to a reconsideration of the hospital patient room as an interior design problem.

Color was the first revolution. White, once associated with purity, cleanliness, and order, had developed negative associations as sterile or off-putting. Coloring the hospital was a simple, inexpensive beautification—it was as easy to order colored paint or tile as it was to order white. Soft tans, creams, and greens started the trend, but by the end of the decade pinks, yellows, and other more intense colors differentiated rooms and wards. At a time of intensive color research, designers discussed the inclusion of color, and the choice of color, as a question of science, not art. The colors chosen were often "restful" shades, usually of the cooler blues, greens, and yellows that were expected to facilitate a proper mental state for healing. A ward at the Columbia-Presbyterian Medical Center painted in "cheerful" green proved highly successful. Passavant Hospital in Chicago had different color combinations for different floors—two were in yellow, three in pink, one in blue, two in green.[67] Administrators of older hospitals, with their white, aseptic finishes, could make their rooms more colorful with simple furnishing choices.

Softening the hospital's color went hand in hand with softening its noise. Annmarie Adams has pointed out Edward F. Stevens's concern with designs, materials, and technologies that quieted the hospital, inside and out. According to Charles F. Neergaard, "the conventional hospital room and its furnishings could hardly be worse if deliberately designed to intensify noise. Rigid walls, bare floors and uncovered furniture offer no check." New technologies increased the problem: elevator doors clanged, motors whirred, call bells rang, food carts rattled, nurses' shoes squeaked. Many hospital administrators added sound-absorbing acoustic material to their hallway ceilings. To limit the noise, elevators migrated from the middle of long hallways into small, contained vestibules. Quiet, self-leveling elevator doors made a huge improvement, and in many areas call bells were replaced with call lights.[68]

Many believed that making the hospital attractive would not only improve patient morale and shorten convalescence, it would improve the hospital's clientele by removing "that great deterrent to entering hospital

Figure 5.25. Wesley Hospital, Chicago, private room, 1923. This private patient room appears more like a hotel room than a hospital room.

care—the time-honored, let me say traditional, dread of that grim and austere place where sickness, misery, and death seem to so many to reign supreme."[69] The modern hospital of the 1920s was intended to be as attractive as the traditional hospital had been off-putting. The monochromatic, hard-surfaced, echo chamber of aseptic hospital design gave way to the colored, softened, noiseless comfort of the patient-focused institution. If the older approach to the hospital ward as a place that encouraged order, induced natural healing, and instilled social reform was lost in this shift, that too was part of the transformation of the hospital to a modern institution.

Private Rooms for All Patients

The comfort revolution for patient accommodations encompassed more than interior design and finishes; it reconfigured the social structure of the patient room. Hospital designers advocated for hospitals with all private rooms as a means of meeting a perceived need for privacy. Edward F. Stevens thought that patients should be treated as if they were guests in a private home, and that meant not sharing a room. According to Louis J. Frank, superintendent of Beth Israel Hospital and budding hospital consultant, "If an individual of ordinary intelligence were asked, when he was ill, whether he would prefer to be in a private room in the hospital or in a bed in the ward, he would invariably choose the private room." Frank and the other promoters of all-private-room hospitals in the 1920s had not actually solicited patient opinions. The hue and cry for privacy thus has to be seen in interaction with other anticipated collateral benefits, such as improved medical treatment, more efficient nursing service, reduced cross-infections, and flexible assignment of patients to rooms. These would benefit efficiency and potential income streams as much as patient happiness.[70]

That private rooms would improve medical treatment seemed obvious. According to Dr. William Everett Musgrave, "the confidential relations that should exist between doctor and patient are not and cannot be maintained in an open ward." In the privacy of an individual room, in contrast, thorough examinations and histories could be taken without embarrassment or polite prevarication. According to Asa S. Bacon, they could happen at any time, even "at odd hours which might otherwise disturb others." This could be to the patient's benefit (the doctor came when needed or called) or to the doctor's benefit (the patient was available for examination whenever convenient for the doctor). Hospital architect Perry W. Swern noted that the small private room eliminated the time wasted in large wards on "arranging bed screens and retiring rooms for consultation," with the end result of "more time for the doctors with their patients, better examinations, histories, and consultation." Bacon observed that the private room could facilitate environmental therapy: "the room temperature can be kept at the degree best suited for each patient, or the room can be turned into a solarium if desired."[71]

The all-private-room hospital was also promoted as a means of reducing the distance nurses traveled daily in their provision of care, as demonstrated by Bacon and Swern in a comparative study of a large ward and a group of private rooms. In this study, Bacon presumed each private room would include all necessary utilities (bathroom, sink, utility closet), reducing travel time for the fulfillment of routine requests. At the all-single-room Beth Israel Hospital in New York City, each room was also "wired for X-ray, electrocardiograph, physical therapy, radio, telephone, nurse's signal, and is piped for a portable bathtub. The section adjacent to each room will provide for food preparation, ice bags, hot water bottles, sterilization, cold running drinking water and other needs of the patients."[72] The multiplication of supplies and services was cheaper than the extra nursing effort spent fetching them from ward service rooms.

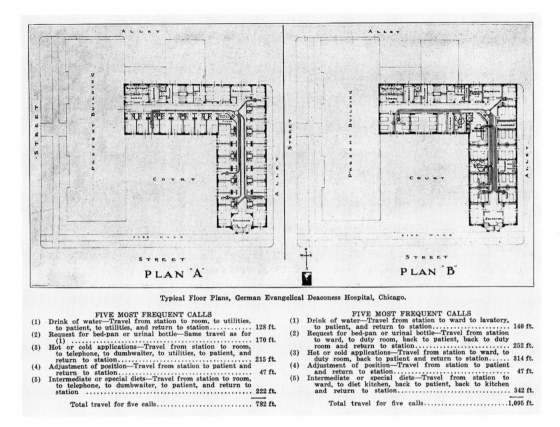

Typical Floor Plans, German Evangelical Deaconess Hospital, Chicago.

FIVE MOST FREQUENT CALLS		FIVE MOST FREQUENT CALLS	
(1)	Drink of water—Travel from station to room, to utilities, to patient, to utilities, and return to station............. 128 ft.	(1)	Drink of water—Travel from station to ward to lavatory, to patient, and return to station......................... 140 ft.
(2)	Request for bed-pan or urinal bottle—Same travel as for (1) .... 170 ft.	(2)	Request for bed-pan or urinal bottle—Travel from station to ward, to duty room, back to patient, back to duty room and return to station......................... 252 ft.
(3)	Hot or cold applications—Travel from station to room, to telephone, to dumbwaiter, to utilities, to patient, and return to station...................................... 215 ft.	(3)	Hot or cold applications—Travel from station to ward, to duty room, back to patient and return to station...... 314 ft.
(4)	Adjustment of position—Travel from station to patient and return to station...................................... 47 ft.	(4)	Adjustment of position—Travel from station to patient and return to station............................... 47 ft.
(5)	Intermediate or special diets—Travel from station to room, to telephone, to dumbwaiter, to patient, and return to station .... 222 ft.	(5)	Intermediate or special diets—Travel from station to ward, to diet kitchen, back to patient, back to kitchen and return to station............................... 342 ft.
	Total travel for five calls........................... 782 ft.		Total travel for five calls......................1,095 ft.

Figure 5.26. Nurse Travel Diagrams, 1921. The study was undertaken by the architect Perry W. Swern in collaboration with Asa S. Bacon. In the diagrams, the location of utilities was clearly as influential on the nurse travel radius as the size and shape of the rooms, but Swern and Bacon emphasized the layout rather than the multiplication of fixtures and storage areas.

This efficiency came at the expense of traditional nursing roles in the ward. In the large ward, direct supervision of the patient had encompassed behavioral as well as medical corrections. Single-bed patient rooms precluded direct oversight, removing the patient from the nurse's moral responsibility. Call buttons, which often substituted for direct oversight, made the nurse into a servant, called at the patient's whim. Technologies (like vacuum tube systems and dumbwaiters) that were intended to save steps inevitably increased the nurse's interaction with building technologies and decreased interaction with patients and other hospital staff.[73] Administrators and doctors, not nurses, were by far the loudest advocates for all private rooms as a means of improving nursing efficiency.

The potential to prevent direct contact and thus eliminate cross-infections was a highly desirable collateral benefit of the all-private-room hos-

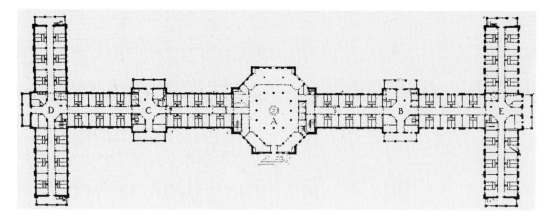

Figure 5.27. Henry Ford Hospital, Detroit, general plan, 1920. The repetitive nature of the plan is a product of the repetitive nature of the patient room. The hospital was essentially four pavilions consisting of a central service area with two patient room wings (B, C, D, and E) arranged into an elongated, interconnected H. The central services occupied the hexagonal central pavilion (A).

pital. After the devastating hospital experiences during the Great Influenza of 1918 and ongoing problems of internal outbreaks of cross-infections, disease prevention still had a visceral importance that resonated in building design. In June of 1919, Dr. Simon Flexner noted that "the lesson derived from the severe experience of the recent pneumonia epidemic is to the effect that such patients are not to be assembled into large groups or kept in open wards." He recommended that for the prevention of droplet infection (coughs and sneezes), beds in wards would have to be at least ten feet apart. At that scale, separate rooms were far more efficient. Furthermore, in hospitals with all single-bed rooms, "each room, having its own equipment, lavatory and toilet, is an isolation unit. Danger of infection and contagion is absolutely eliminated."[74]

One of the greatest boosts to hospital efficiency offered by the all-private-room hospital was "the occupancy of all the beds at all times." With large wards, administrators always had to choose between maintaining a ward's patient category or filling empty beds at the expense of mixing patient groups. In the all-single-bed hospital any patient could be assigned to any room. Many practitioners believed that "the elimination of sex and disease classification . . . [would] allow maximum use of the entire hospital at all times." It would also allow operational savings during emptier periods. At the Henry Ford Hospital, Albert Kahn designed the building so that unused blocks of rooms could be closed off, saving on heat and light expenditures during fluctuating periods of demand. It was also argued that any increased construction costs for the extra plumbing and materials for the single rooms would be offset by the increased bed utilization rates and energy savings over time.[75]

Figure 5.28. Presbyterian Hospital, Chicago, typical floor plan of all-private-patient Bacon unit, 1925. Perry W. Swern of Berlin and Swern, in collaboration with Asa S. Bacon (superintendent of the Presbyterian Hospital in Chicago), drew the plans for this minimal single-bed patient room. Each room took up very little more floor space than had been allotted to a bed in a pavilion-plan.

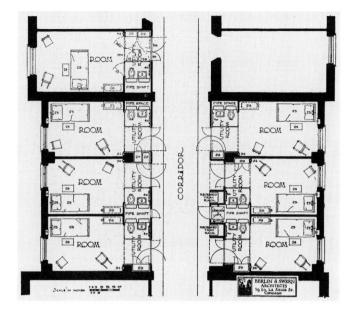

The ideal of the all-single-bed-room hospital was, in essence, an evocation of the hospital as an all-class, socially neutral, attractive factory. It would democratize hospital care, providing every patient with the comfort of privacy and "the best possible service irrespective of race, creed or color." This would make it a new, all-inclusive institution.[76] Given the longstanding equation of wards with free care, small wards with part-pay care, and single-bed rooms with full-pay care, the shift to all individual rooms also had the strong potential to advance the transformation of the hospital to an all-pay institution. The exact shape of the all-single-bed-room building would prove critical in determining whether the hospital would be "democratized" or "monetized" by the shift.

The all-private-room hospital began as an experiment in minimal accommodation. Albert Kahn's 1910 designs for single-bed rooms in the Henry Ford Hospital were designed for efficiency and economy, not luxury. All rooms were identical. The repetitive nature of the units allowed a savings in construction costs, equalized patient amenities, and made a compact plan. The seemingly extravagant inclusion of private bathrooms for each room was justified as a means of increasing nurse efficiency. An addition to the Presbyterian Hospital in Chicago included an addition of an all-private-room wing comprising the minimal rooms of the Bacon plan, which included a toilet and sink, utility room, bed, chair, and all technologies and amenities within roughly 150 square feet. The Fifth Avenue Hospital in New York City (1920–1922) and the Beth Israel Hospital in New York City (1914–1929) were both examples of this new model modern hospital—a high-rise structure with centralized services and all private rooms. Frank expected the Beth Israel Hospital's building to "be a pattern for all hospitals," and that soon patients would refuse to enter any other kind.[77]

The all-private-room hospital was not socially neutral; it was intended for middle-class patients. Directors of the Fifth Avenue Hospital expected to admit a few charity patients or full-pay patients, but their aim was "primarily to take care of the great middle class who desire private rooms but who cannot afford to pay expensive rates." As hospital care had grown more attractive to paying patients, hospital practitioners had observed that hospitals served the very poor and the very rich, but that there was "no medium accommodation for the great middle class," who were in fact the majority of the population.[78] This was a vast underserved market, and how to house the middle-class hospital patient was a topic of intense interest. The all-private-room hospital was one architectural solution, but it was not universally adopted.

Some practitioners opposed the fundamental assumption that all patients desired privacy. Although Erikson was of the opinion that the large multibed hospital ward was "almost as obsolete as the one-horse shay," large wards continued to be included purposefully in brand-new facility designs. Clark Souers, of Proudfoot, Rawson, Souers and Thomas, designers of the twenty-bed wards in the University of Iowa Hospital, noted that "the patients come largely from rural sections and are more contented in the large wards." According to Albert Kahn and Christopher G. Parnall, the designers of the University Hospital of the University of Michigan, Ann Arbor, which had eighteen-bed wards, "patients preferred the larger wards when not acutely ill." In 1935, R. H. Creel noted that sailors in Marine hospitals considered assignment to a private room rather than the large ward a punishment. Regardless of what designers stated patients wanted, the large ward remained far more common in three general hospital categories: large municipal hospitals, which had low budgets and high demand for free care; hospitals for patients requiring long-term care such as orthopedic patients, chronic patients, and convalescents; and teaching hospitals, which required open space at the bedside to accommodate the doctors and students for clinical bedside education.[79] The clinical advantages of large wards extended beyond simple available space. Historically, charity patients in the larger wards could be used for clinical education; private patients in private rooms could not. The boundaries of the large ward thus determined the boundaries of clinical education.

Other practitioners did not see the efficiency of the all-private-room hospital. Goldwater considered them impractical, worrying that the rooms were inconvenient for nursing and (citing a number of patient accidents

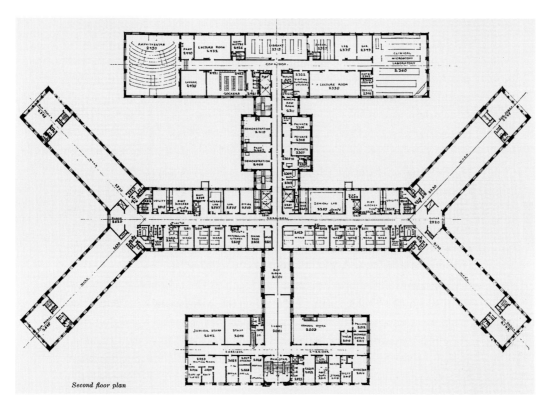

Figure 5.29. University of Michigan Hospital, Ann Arbor, second-floor plan, 1927. The large wards projected at angles to catch the sun; the small wards (arranged like Rigs wards) and private rooms were sandwiched between the administration building and the laboratory/university teaching wing.

in private rooms) even unsafe. Others believed that regardless of absolute travel distance for any given nursing task, the immediate oversight of patients possible in large wards saved nurses thousands of steps. The all-private-room hospital also had the potential to make the doctor's experiences chaotic and inefficient. The assignment of patients to any available room altered the distribution of any given doctor's patients throughout the hospital. Dr. Samuel Kopetzky of the Beth Israel Hospital complained that his patients would "be scattered throughout the house and not concentrated in one section of the building. . . . To run through a fifteen story building to see patients scattered on the different floors is a waste of time and energy."[80]

This flexible assignment of patients to rooms inhibited the territoriality of doctors over specific wards or beds. Some saw this particular loss as a step toward efficiency, emphasizing cooperative medical care and consultation rather than personal aggrandizement. Many saw the inability to group patients by ailment as a hindrance to medical research and the development of new specialties. Flexible assignment of patients to rooms also undermined the ability to place patients requiring special treatments near the necessary facilities—labor and delivery rooms for maternity patients, for example, or schoolrooms and playrooms for pediatrics. All-single-bed institutions with maternity service or pediatrics departments inevitably ended up permanently assigning a number of rooms to each specialty.

The Private Patient Building Is for Doctors

Despite the idealism of all-private-room hospital projects, the far more common pattern in hospital designs continued to be the provision of a segregated multiclass facility providing private rooms for the wealthy, large wards for the poor, and small, multibed wards for the semiprivate service or the middle class. In the 1910s, patient rooms of from two- to eight-beds were considered within the realm of semiprivate facilities.[81]

The traditional approach was to keep each distinct class of service physically separate. The separation of paying (or part-paying) patients from charity patients was still the strongest demarcation. For example, while early plans for the Columbia-Presbyterian Medical Center had included private rooms as part of the general hospital building, the builder, Marc Eidlitz and Sons, argued strongly and successfully that a separate building was required for the maintenance of the proper level of privacy for the private patients. This class separation extended beyond the ward and private room and into the hospital's other services. Early twentieth-century private patient buildings often had a separate entrance, a separate kitchen, separate nursing staffs, separate recreation areas, and even separate waiting rooms. The Albany Hospital had separate X-ray services for private and public patients. The Rhode Island Hospital in Providence included luxurious operating suites in a new private patient building "for the exclusive use" of the private patients and their doctors.[82]

Initially, it was unclear whether a semiprivate service should best be included as a part of the ward service, as part of the private service, or as a third, separate service. Opinion soon landed on separate facilities for each of the three classes of service. This meant that an all-class hospital was essentially running three hospitals simultaneously, each with a different level of service, expected clientele, and protocol for patient treatment. In taller, more centralized hospital structures, private patient facilities often occupied the topmost floors, which offered a better view, were quieter, and had the best light and air, and thus the most prestige. Semiprivate patient facilities, if provided, were in the middle floors, and ward patients were on the lowest patient floors. For example, the Hahnemann Hospital in Philadelphia provided six private patient floors, one semiprivate patient floor,

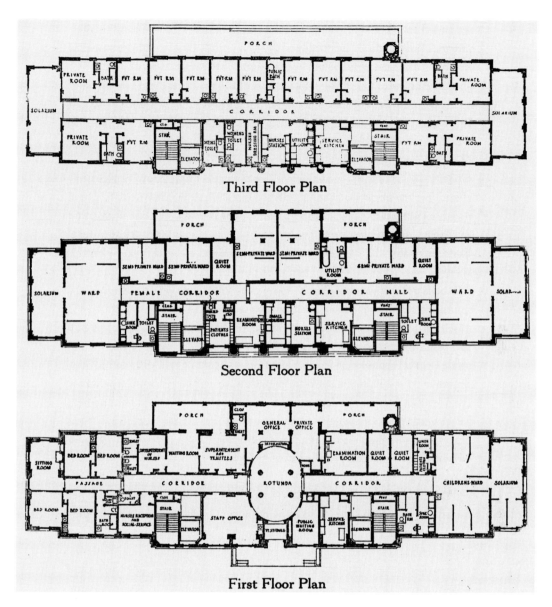

Figure 5.30. Carson C. Peck Memorial Hospital, Brooklyn, first-, second-, and third-floor plans, 1919. This hospital, designed by Ludlow and Peabody (with input from Charles Neergaard), was much admired as an early and elegant solution to the problem of providing hospital accommodations for the middle class with its variety of patient room sizes, but also with its attempt to humanize the building by tempering the aseptic designs of the interiors.

and five floors for public patients. The planners of the Lenox Hill Hospital in New York City described a similar vertical differentiation in their projected new complex.[83] In hospitals with greater horizontal separation, the different classes of service were often located in different wings, or in separate buildings of an interconnected facility. The all-class general hospital in the 1920s was thus all-class but not integrated.

Some hospital practitioners argued that the paying patient (private and semiprivate) would be better served in a wholly separate institution, which could provide "the medical efficiency of the thoroughly modern hospital with the comforts, conveniences, individual service, and genial atmosphere of the thoroughly modern hotel or club." The Carson C. Peck Memorial Hospital in Brooklyn, lauded for its hotel-grade luxury and services, included patient rooms of varying sizes—from small wards to small, single rooms—all targeted to a middle-class clientele. The Kahler Hotel-Hospital in Rochester, Minnesota, adjacent to the new nineteen-story Plummer Building of the Mayo Clinic facilities, served as a model of the new "hotel-hospital." In it, the top floors were for hospital care, the middle floors for convalescent care, and the lower floors were a hotel for family members; all floors had only private rooms with private baths.[84]

Regardless of how the separate services were accommodated, statistics revealed that the overall shift from charitable care to paying service in hospitals was well underway. An increasing proportion of general hospital beds occupied private and semiprivate rooms. A survey of thirty-five hospitals (with a total of 3,500 beds) revealed that in 1908, 8 percent of wards held ten or more beds; by 1928, less than 1 percent did. At the same time, two-, three-, and four-bed wards increased from roughly 8.5 percent of the facilities to 28 percent, and private rooms from 14.5 percent of all hospital beds to 61 percent.[85]

Clearly, the increasing use of the hospital by paying patients signaled the increasing role of the hospital as a medical facility rather than a charity. As private patient care shifted from home care to hospital care and office visits, it was also evident that private rooms were not just for the private patients, they were for the hospital's doctors. With the shift in medical staffing of hospitals from volunteer to full-time, the private patient facilities in many hospitals were, in essence, the stomping grounds of the hospital's medical staff. According to the doctors of the Columbia-Presbyterian Medical Center, "since the center was geographically disadvantageous . . . the Hospital should assure them adequate private patient facilities at reasonable rates." The directors of Saint Luke's Hospital in New York City noted that because of their limited private patient facilities, their medical staff members had been treating their private patients in other institutions. "This works to the disadvantage of the Hospital as the attention of the staff is divided and much time is lost in their going from place to place. It should be our aim to have the attention of the entire Staff concentrated upon Saint Luke's and upon Saint Luke's alone."[86] A new private patient building (the Plant Pavilion) opened at Saint Luke's in 1927.

As privileges for the courtesy medical staff expanded into semiprivate as well as private rooms, it became clear that the different levels of private facilities not only served the different classes but matched the different requirements of practitioners in their various career stages. Luxurious private patient accommodations served the wealthiest patients, who typically booked the services of the most eminent practitioners. In the words of the administrators of the Woman's Hospital in New York City, "It should be appreciated that the younger men on the staff, whom we are endeavoring to develop and whom we wish to encourage and give every opportunity for advancement for the future credit of the Hospital, must have the facilities of the less expensive accommodations for private patients at their disposal, if we are to expect to keep them."[87] Private patient rooms were as much for the doctors as for the patients.

Mixed-Ward Nursing Units

A hospital divided into three distinct services inevitably duplicated some equipment, facilities, staff, and spaces, and (unless the right mix of patients of the correct social class and ailment was in constant supply) held empty beds. In most hospital facilities, the different classes of service still occupied structures based on the traditional narrow, linear pavilion—of roughly 35 feet wide by 70 to 150 feet long. Private service essentially converted the open ward into a series of individual rooms; semiprivate service converted it into a series of small wards. This linear arrangement required extensive nurse travel distances and made privacy and oversight mutually exclusive. This was not an efficient institution. While the all-single-bed hospital (which reduced the hospital to providing only one level of service) had posed one solution to the problem, other hospital designers struggled to develop a more efficient spatial pattern for arranging hospital service while maintaining the social and medical distinctions of the patients.[88]

In the early twentieth century a slow transformation of wards into "nursing units" offered some experiments in more efficient provision of multiclass services. Both terms—*ward* and *nursing unit*—referred to a complex, autonomous, physical space that included patient rooms, adjunct service areas, and circulation; both terms also assumed an efficient size based on the number of patients one head nurse could effectively oversee.[89] The difference was simple—the ward assumed the majority of beds were in one room or arranged in a long, narrow footprint; in a nursing unit the beds could be divided among a number of rooms of varying sizes and bed occupancy.

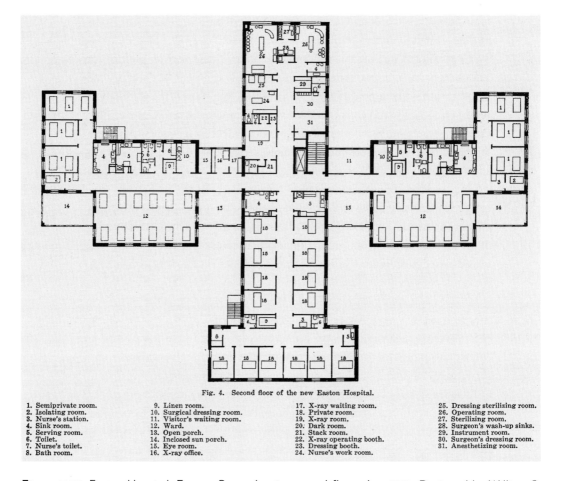

Fig. 4. Second floor of the new Easton Hospital.

1. Semiprivate room.	9. Linen room.	17. X-ray waiting room.	25. Dressing sterilizing room.
2. Isolating room.	10. Surgical dressing room.	18. Private room.	26. Operating room.
3. Nurse's station.	11. Visitor's waiting room.	19. X-ray room.	27. Sterilizing room.
4. Sink room.	12. Ward.	20. Dark room.	28. Surgeon's wash-up sinks.
5. Serving room.	13. Open porch.	21. Stack room.	29. Instrument room.
6. Toilet.	14. Inclosed sun porch.	22. X-ray operating booth.	30. Surgeon's dressing room.
7. Nurse's toilet.	15. Eye room.	23. Dressing booth.	31. Anesthetizing room.
8. Bath room.	16. X-ray office.	24. Nurse's work room.	

Figure 5.31. Easton Hospital, Easton, Pennsylvania, second-floor plan, 1918. Designed by William S. Michler in collaboration with S. S. Goldwater, the design separated the private rooms from the wards, but mixed the small, semiprivate wards and the larger wards in one wing.

By the 1920s there were two basic spatial strategies for arranging a group of varying-sized patient rooms for most efficient nurse access and supervision. One strategy was to put the nurse at the crossing point of a number of short, radiating corridor wings, providing oversight of the beds but also circulation control. This strategy had been used in the 1900s and 1910s, but had typically only grouped patient rooms of the same size and service around any given nursing station. At the New York Orthopedic Hospital of 1916, the central nurses' station overlooked three wards of ten beds each. In the 1920s, the nurse might overlook a number of patient rooms of varying size and services. At the Easton Hospital in Easton, Pennsylvania, the nurses' station for one nursing unit was at a corridor crossing connecting a twelve-bed ward, two two-bed wards, a three-bed ward, and a single-bed room.

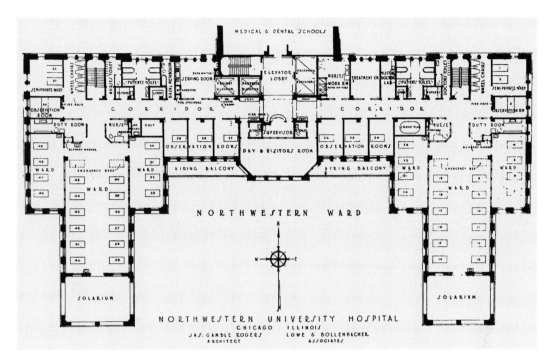

Figure 5.32. Northwestern University Hospital, Chicago, ward plan, 1924. The glassed-in nurses' office had oversight of the two four-bed wards and the large twelve-bed wards, and partial oversight of the two-bed, semiprivate ward and one single-bed room. The four single-bed observation wards were outside of immediate supervision. Located across from the elevator, the supervising nurse also served as hall monitor for visitors and staff.

From the nurse's desk, there was no direct oversight of any of the patients. The single-bed room was for isolation, the smaller wards for semiprivate patients, and the large ward for public patients. Thus the nurse had to provide varying levels of service to patients within the same unit.

Another, more radically transformative arrangement of a nursing unit arrayed the patient rooms around a central nurses' station. This provided clear oversight of a majority of the beds and reduced nurse travel distances, but could accommodate a variety of patient classes in a small area. The "Northwestern ward," designed by James Gamble Rogers for the Northwestern University Hospital, provides a good example of an early version of this arrangement. The nurses' station had oversight of two four-bed wards, a twelve-bed ward, one two-bed semiprivate ward, and a number of single-bed observation rooms. The use of glass windows in the nurses' office or along the corridor allowed some direct supervision of patients, even when they occupied separate rooms. At the Strong Memorial Hospital in Rochester, New York, patients occupied four-bed rooms but the nurse had immediate oversight of sixteen patients through a series of glass windows. The City Hospital of Cleveland designed a nursing unit of thirty-two beds that included a sixteen-bed ward (which could be cubicalized as needed), and several side wards of one to four beds. While occupying a traditional linear plan, this nursing unit had spaces that suited any class of patient (charity to full-pay) and yet at need any of the rooms could be appropriated to a different class or medical category. According to Frank Chapman, however, the combination of ward, semiprivate, and private patients in one nursing unit complicated the nursing service. Each room occupant expected a different level of service, requiring the nurse to allocate time based on patient standing, not patient need.[90] The provision of extra luxuries and private nurses to private patients, in sight of semiprivate and ward patients, inevitably generated dissatisfaction.

These architectural changes had a profound impact upon the daily experience of hospital patients. Rosemary Stevens has pointed out that the loss of the large open ward entailed a loss of the original idea that the ward (and its patients) was the heart of the hospital. "While the old ward was a bustling center of attention, where something was always going on, the private or semiprivate room was peripheral to the more dramatic events happening elsewhere: the appendectomy in the operating suite, the birth in the delivery room, the baby in the newborn nursery."[91] The hotel-hospital lost something of its soul in the transition.

Designing the Efficient Hospital: The Triumph of Specialists

Because of its programmatic and technical complexity, modern hospital design was "the most difficult problem that can be offered the architect." According to C. Stanley Taylor, by the 1920s even the design of small community hospitals was "beyond the individual capacities of the average architect." Similarly, medically trained hospital consultants eclipsed the general practitioner as the source of medical knowledge for hospital designs. Hospital consultants, architects, and architectural firms specializing in hospital designs increased in number, prominence, and distribution. The different individuals even demonstrated distinct patterns of design. Some, like James Gamble Rogers and York and Sawyer, or hospital consultant Wiley E. Woodbury, were more likely to design high-rises; others, like Stevens and Lee; Kendall, Taylor and Company; or hospital consultant S. S. Goldwater, were more likely to design hospitals of more moderate height.[92]

The increasing importance of personal expertise in hospital design shifted the traditional patterns of dissemination of knowledge. Publications became less influential. Books were never current enough or comprehensive enough, and, given the extensive specialization of institutions, universal design principles were no longer relevant. Published articles in professional periodicals were helpful, but their tight focus emphasized details over how to structure those details into a coherent whole.

Information-gathering trips to existing hospitals remained common, but as Isadore Rosenfield and Edgar C. Hayhow noted, trips of inspection as a means of gaining knowledge of hospital design was "fast losing favor because a committee of laymen can learn little of practical value by flying visits here and there." Hospital architect Perry W. Swern also warned hospital designers not to "travel around visiting other hospitals collecting a lot of ideas and expect to secure an efficient arrangement by patching the various ideas together."[93] These hospital specialists suggested that the best source of knowledge for hospital design was a good community survey implemented by an educated building committee that then hired a hospital consultant and hospital architect. The hospital consultant and architect provided the special knowledge that "flying visits" used to provide.

This made hospital design a closed specialty—the best way to gain a hospital design commission was to have designed other hospitals. This complicated the establishment of new practitioners. With no school programs in hospital design, a formal or informal apprenticeship was the primary means for young designers to gain the necessary expertise. Architecture had long been based on the apprenticeship model—young architects worked in a firm before branching out on their own. For budding hospital architects, the only difference was the selection of a firm that designed hospitals. After their apprenticeship was over, young practitioners could either establish their own independent hospital architecture practice or stay within the original firm, rising to prominence if not partnership. For example, for years Carl A. Erikson worked on hospital projects for the firm Garden, Martin and Schmidt. In 1925, with the departure of Martin, the firm made Erikson a new partner in the newly named firm Schmidt, Garden and Erikson. In this manner, several of the most prominent hospital architecture firms became very long-lived, spanning decades of successful specialized practice. Similarly, a number of hospital consultants—including Henry C. Wright and Wiley E. Woodbury—worked as assistants to other consultants before establishing their own consultancies. Others, such as Louis J. Frank, became consultants after their individual experiences as a hospital superintendent involved in the design of a new building. From that initial project, the superintendent would expand practice to a consultancy by advising on other projects, penning articles, and giving lectures on hospital design. Collaboration of a hospital specialist with a local practitioner continued to provide a path for gaining expertise in hospital design for both architects and consultants.

The Changing Nature of Collaboration

The amicable collaboration of hospital architects and consultants depended on clear separation of responsibilities. In terms of design process, consultants were often hired earlier than architects. Hospital consultants aided the building committee (still largely consisting of lay businessmen) in the development of hospital surveys, in the creation of building programs, and in the communication of the committee's desires to the hospital architect once selected. Wright noted how difficult it was for an architect to arrive at an accurate program when the trustees running the building committee often didn't know what the hospital needed and when the medical staff had their own agendas for their department's spatial needs.[94] The consultant provided detailed information on hospital practice to the hospital architect—translating doctors' demands, aseptic requirements, and operational efficiencies into terms the architect could utilize. The consultant might also be involved directly in developing sketch floor plans for individual units, delineating necessary equipment, studying daily operation within a unit to determine efficient layouts, and, at times, even constructing prototypical rooms (particularly for patient housing) for efficiency studies before construction.

Hospital architects formalized the consultant's recommendations for the individual unit layouts and arranged all the distinct units into efficient spatial interactions. The layout was crucial to the hospital's success; as Richard E. Schmidt noted, it was "very difficult, almost impossible, to operate a hospital properly in an unsuitable building." Taken a step further, a good design could positively influence a hospital's organization and administration. Carl A. Ziegler, designer of the Babies' Hospital in Philadelphia, noted that the architect with sufficient information and knowledge might "suggest radical changes in the methods of carrying on the industry he has been asked to house." The hospital architect or consultant could shape the daily experience of the inhabitants.[95]

Collaboration between hospital architects and hospital consultants could be mutually rewarding, but conflict was regular, particularly when there were overlapping responsibilities—as when hospital architects concerned themselves with hospital organization and operation or hospital consultants concerned themselves with formal designs. Frank's perfectionist attention to detail and decided ideas about hospital layouts put him in regular conflict with Louis Allen Abramson on the plans of the Beth Israel Hospital in New York City. Whether the architect or the consultant should be in charge of the design was another frequent bone of contention. Swern warned that if a hospital architect and a medical hospital consultant shared equal responsibility for a design, "the architect will blame the consultant and the consultant the architect, when afterwards your hospital does not prove efficient." The tendency to consider inefficient hospitals as poorly designed (not poorly planned or simply outmoded) remained strong; this often put the architect on the losing end of any controversy. A. L. Bowen, believing that hospitals were "for the most part, the embodiment of the ideas of the architect" and that the majority were not models of stellar design, called for more and better involvement of hospital administrators in the planning of hospitals. In particular, he suggested that "the direction should emanate from the administrator to the architect and not from the architect to the administrator." Frank went further, stating that the hospital architect should "be instructed exactly as to what we [the hospital administration] desire, rather than that we should be compelled to mould ourselves into quarters which he may think suitable for us." Schmidt considered this statement (and several others of Frank's) to be unjust, wrong and ignorant. He concluded that "Mr. Frank [failed] to grasp the real function of the Architect."[96] Collaboration was a delicate balance.

The Dream of the Modern Hospital

In the interest of efficiency and attractiveness, American hospital practitioners of the 1920s built high-rises and vertically arranged structures filled with single-bed rooms, small wards, and a few larger wards. These compact structures facilitated interactive medical practices, provided flexible patient housing to accommodate a wider variety of patient classes, and provided efficient economical nursing and services. They also provided a new form for a new kind of institution—a modern American hospital rather than a traditional European-influenced hospital. "The typical American construction represents not only a different plan but a distinct conception of the hospital itself in organization and function."[97]

The American high-rise hospital was no depository for the sick poor, no dispenser of basic unspecialized care, no symbol of pure philanthropy. It was instead an expression of technological and economic prowess wedded to modern medicine and egalitarian aspirations. The difference between the old hospital, with its "dingy, smelly, unattractive buildings that inspire fear and distrust, situated in noisy, slumlike surroundings," and the new hospital "that one might readily imagine as a modern hotel or apartment house, or a millionaire's country club, or anything magnificent and comfortable, anything but a hospital" was the difference between a "relic of the Dark Ages" and the hospital of the future.[98]

Figure 5.33. Fifth Avenue Hospital, New York City, view from Central Park, 1922.

Modern American hospitals walked a delicate balance, however. Their concentration of medical facilities and practitioners accommodated research and interactive medicine, but made basic healing and recovery quite costly and secondary to treatment. This posed an ominous precedent for future development of an affordable hospital system. As Goldwater observed, "It is the hospitals that will eventually determine, to a large extent, the relations between the medical profession, the taxpayer and the public. Their control of clinical, laboratory and teaching resources, of machinery for the treatment of millions of rich and poor, is potent either for good or ill." That the hospital could be put to more selfish, less universally idealistic uses than its philanthropic tradition was perceptible even then. In 1920, Louis J. Frank worried that "the hospitals, which were erected for the sick, are really built and managed for the convenience of those that are in attendance—the doctors and their entourage."[99] Others worried that the shift from a nonprofit to a profit model for hospitals would make the miracle of modern hospital medicine unavailable to all but the wealthiest.

In the 1920s optimism won out and the modern high-rise hospital stood as an iconic model of the expectation that how one built might influence how one lived. The modern American hospital would be far more than "a workshop for the reconstruction and repair of the human body."[100] It would extend its healing force through social services, visiting nurses, and outreach programs. It was a health factory, in the broadest sense of the term, and the tension between a facility designed to attract more patients, doctors, and nurses and one designed to process more patients, doctors, and nurses was constant. If some dreamed that the hospital could be an attractive factory—appealing and efficient at the same time—the reality was far more fluid. October 24, 1929, Black Thursday, shattered that particular golden dream of the future, elevating economic concerns above all others in hospital design.

:: CHAPTER 6 ::

The "Meadow Monument to Medicine and Science," 1930–1945

> You ride along in the naval dispensary wagon, a gob with a toothache in front of you, an ensign with a patched eye beside you—rolling through the gentle Maryland countryside with nothing more startling to meet the eye than the white cottages and brick bungalows which house some of the overflow from wartime Washington. Then you top a little rise in the road and all of a sudden, out in the middle of nowhere, a massive, eighteen-story skyscraper, towering 270 feet into the air, with solid, sprawling, gleaming white extensions at its feet, stares you in the face. It looks like metropolis in the sheep pasture, and you say to yourself: "What is this—Radio City?"
>
> — **Sidney Shalett, 1943**

The hospital construction boom of the 1920s ground to a rapid halt in the 1930s, and the financial exigencies of the Great Depression proved a severe test of existing hospital design assumptions and strategies. As charity wards overflowed and private rooms sat empty, 1930s hospital practitioners drastically reassessed what was really a necessity in hospital practice and hospital designers scrutinized the influence of the building design on the bottom line. With the success of aseptic practices in reducing cross-infections, this scrutiny finally transformed open space (between buildings or between patients) from a hygienic necessity to a costly, inefficient luxury. In 1931, German hospital architect Hermann Distel stated that in the new "factory of health," "the larger the number of beds an architect is able to provide within a certain range of building expenditure, the more highly rank his service and the social usefulness of his work."[1]

From the last resort of the sick poor, the hospital had become the place where all classes went to get medical treatment. Hospitals of the 1930s no longer offered long-term general care for general ailments; they offered often expensive treatments and short-term care for specific, treatable ailments. Hospital care no longer presumed charity—indeed, it was an equally common expectation that hospital treatment came with a price to the individual patient rather than to a philanthropic group or to the municipality. The development of health insurance in the 1930s increased the ability of participating patients to pay for their hospital stay, but it reinforced expectations that payment was the patient's responsibility—whether to the hospital itself or through a prepayment group insurance plan—and that the hospital provided a chargeable service.[2]

The promise of the modern hospital counterbalanced the grim realities of crowded wards, long waiting lists for rooms, unpaid bills, and deficits. Hospital-based practice and research had changed the shape of disease and recovery: there were vaccines for typhus, yellow fever, and whooping cough; antibacterial sulfa drugs promised cures for infections of all kinds; diabetics could be treated with insulin; severely injured persons could be supplied with blood from a blood bank. As hospitals increased the healthiness of the nation, many saw hospitals as "an opportunity for strengthening from within the democracy of American life in a time of international stress." By 1943, according to journalist Sidney Shalett, the hospital had become a "symbol of the new and greater America that the war is bringing into being."[3]

It was, however, the "modern" hospital—a medical, technological health factory—rather than the traditional hospital—a charitable, environmentally therapeutic, reformative waystation—that provided this hope. The new, high-rise, centralized hospital buildings were so integral to this cultural promise that they were built where they had no economic, urban, or structural justification. The National Naval Medical Center in Bethesda was a "metropolis in the sheep pasture," a glowing tower in a farm field, miles from other buildings, patients, doctors, nurses, staff, or even services. The new New Orleans Charity Hospital was an eighteen-story building on a site with soil conditions that could not support it.[4] Cracks appeared in the foundation within the first year.

Yet the dream of the modern hospital existed in a time of little new hospital construction. Projects begun in the late 1920s were completed in the 1930s, but often only after protracted construction periods due to financial difficulties. Government funds did support construction of some prominent new facilities, but as Rosemary Stevens makes clear, "voluntary hospitals were not by any stretch of the imagination major economic beneficiaries of the early New Deal." With the entrance of the United States into World War II, only vital hospital construction projects were given any consideration in the allocation of scarce materials, and even those projects often had to be simplified to reduce crucial material usage. Large-scale plans were shelved and hospital administrators turned to short-term alter-

Figure 6.1. National Naval Medical Center, Bethesda, aerial view, 1940s. Franklin D. Roosevelt's admiration of the Nebraska State Capitol building inspired the form of the building. Roosevelt also selected the site.

ations and renovations to increase flexibility of space usage (to make the maximum efficient use of the available space) and increase attractiveness (to ensure the maximum patronage by persons capable of paying at least something for their care).[5]

Flexible Design: Dealing with Constant Change

Hospitals of the 1930s had to accommodate drastic and rapid fluctuations in usage. Changing urban neighborhoods and urban growth patterns could alter a hospital's surroundings, and the nature and scale of service it provided, within a matter of years. New scientific discoveries and technological equipment "assure[d] the beginning of obsolescence almost on the day that it is occupied." Shifting patient demand could alter the optimum arrangement of ward spaces and patient rooms seemingly overnight. By the 1930s estimates of the average functional life of a hospital building were between twenty-five and fifty years.[6] Constant rebuilding from the ground up was, however, a very costly means of adapting to constant change.

Flexibility became the catchword of the day in hospital design. Annmarie Adams has described Edward F. Stevens's understanding of flexibility as "far more than simple alterations, but rather the potential of a building to adapt to a total change in function." A flexible hospital would be able to house medical practices in a department one day and surgical practices the next, be able to accept all paying patients one day and all charity patients the next, without leaving empty beds or improperly assigning patients to the wrong category of ward. It would also be able to adjust gracefully to technological and medical change while maintaining efficient functional layouts. Exactly how a permanent building, of tremendous scale and complexity, could accommodate this degree of change was a design problem of epic proportion.[7]

The Mobile and Changing Patient Population

The most critical design choices the planners of a new institution could make were how large to build and where to build. Size determined whether a hospital could take advantage of economies of scale; location determined whether a hospital had a steady supply of patients or sat empty. Planning studies for the Allegheny General Hospital suggested that a hospital of six hundred beds was the minimum size to include all necessary departments and still be efficiently run. Small hospitals (a hundred beds or fewer) remained numerous, but to survive the Depression many effectively became larger-scale institutions through affiliations or mergers with other institutions. Small hospitals (both specialized and general) that served a well-defined and stable patient base could remain successfully independent. For example, the Midtown Hospital of Manhattan was designed to meet the needs of the neighborhood but not to aspire beyond that. Similarly, the Lutheran Hospital of Manhattan, which was only blocks away from the Columbia-Presbyterian Medical Center, thrived as a small community hospital.[8]

The most successful institutions of any size were those that offered new treatments for previously untreatable conditions. For example, after the development of deep radiation therapy for cancer, the New York Cancer Hospital merged with several other hospitals, became the Memorial Hospital for the Treatment of Cancer and Allied Diseases, and moved into a new twelve-story, state-of-the-art building with 160 beds and a million-volt X-ray therapy machine. Similarly, the shift in care of chronic disease cases from custodial to therapeutic saw the creation of new well-equipped, research-centered facilities, like the Neurological Institute of the Columbia-Presbyterian Medical Center or the Goldwater Memorial Hospital in New York City.[9]

In the choice of a site for any new hospital construction, it had become clear that sunlight and fresh air were available anywhere, but patients were not. Planners of smaller, community-focused hospitals chose small sites near underserved neighborhoods, while planners of larger hospitals and medical centers (and of their affiliated institutions) chose large sites that were proximate to transportation routes that could draw from a number of neighborhoods. For smaller, community hospitals that drew the majority of their patients from their immediate surroundings, neighborhood stability—"where the probability of change in physical and social character is remote"—proved essential, yet 1930s urban neighborhoods, particularly impoverished ones, were volatile and changeable. That volatility could create a safety risk, as at the Mercy Hospital in Chicago, where the increasingly crime-riddled surroundings posed safety concerns for the employees. Neighborhood change could also simply shift the nature of the hospital's clientele. C. F. Tenney, the medical director of the Fifth Avenue Hospital in New York City, noted in 1930 that the surrounding neighborhood was changing from predominantly Jewish and Irish to increasingly Latin American. He hoped "that the population will soon again stabilize itself in order that we may be able to hold our old patients, and at the same time count on a definite nucleus for a source of new material."[10] Wealthier neighborhoods proved far less volatile, and smaller community hospitals continued to gravitate to sites within or just on the boundaries of a wealthy neighborhood.

Larger general hospitals and medical centers drew patients from well beyond their local surroundings, relying on an increasingly mobile urban populace. Data suggested that people who could choose often went out of their way to a more distant hospital. According to hospital consultant Charles F. Neergaard, "the reasons for this exodus may be attributed, variously, to the prestige of metropolitan specialists and medical centers, convenience for the commuter and in many instances the desire of the patient to avoid embarrassing gossip."[11] The peripheral sites of medical centers, which created their own neighborhoods rather than being embedded in one, facilitated this anonymity.

By the 1930s the idea that a hospital could alter, even control, its immediate surroundings was obvious. Medical centers might start out as insular medical communities, but they often became the nucleus of a new city. With the prospect of business from numerous staff and patients, hotels, restaurants, retail, and services soon surrounded them. Similarly, while neighborhood opposition to a proposed new hospital in an established locale was still common, some hospital projects achieved such scale and importance that their planners altered the surroundings to suit the hospital. The preferred site for the new Bellevue–New York University Medical Center was just north of the existing hospital—from East 30th to 34th Streets at the East River—a densely inhabited poor neighborhood. That site was available only as the result of one of Robert Moses's enormous slum clearance projects, which also included the construction of several adjacent high-density public housing projects. Sources suggest, but do not explicitly corroborate the idea, that these dense, poor neighborhoods would supply the planned medical center with clinical material.[12]

The Flexible Master Plan—Arranging the Veins, not the Organs

The need for adaptability in hospital design threatened to make master plans, which registered the ultimate development of a hospital decades into the future, an exercise in futility. Pavilion-ward master plans had projected a systematic expansion based on the addition of known, standardized elements (pavilions). By the twentieth century, master plans had to accommodate the constantly changing spatial requirements of scientific medicine and a constantly fluctuating patient load while maintaining efficient patterns of circulation between all the components of the institution.

Additions to hospital facilities were rarely in accordance with the original master plans. As Cameron Logan, Philip Goad, and Julie Willis express it, "Expansion of hospital buildings and campuses according to an underlying architectural order has not been the norm." Hospitals that occupied facilities more than a couple decades old were often an ad hoc mixture of building styles, heights, shapes, and layouts, all wedged onto an increasingly congested site with little to no coherent means of moving anything between them efficiently. When first built, the Barnes Hospital and Medical Center in Saint Louis had occupied dispersed buildings of three to four stories and of uniform facade treatment. By the midcentury, high-rises and mid-rises had replaced many of the original buildings and the hospital complex had expanded to fill the site. The once-uniform buildings had become differentiated, each building expressive of the requirements and standards of the time of its construction. Circulation between the separate, vertically arranged buildings was convoluted, and as extensive as it had ever been in the pavilion-ward hospital. Critics observed that even modern hospitals far too often continued to "look like additions of disparate parts" with no "real sense of that organic wholeness which comes from a true grasp of the basic unity behind the entire hospital idea."[13] In response, hospital designers

Figure 6.2. Washington University Medical Center, aerial view, circa 1964. The original 1914 structures are on the left-hand side of the picture; to the right-hand side are the more densely packed, high-rise additional buildings of later decades, including the Jewish Hospital of Saint Louis and the new Queeny Tower (under construction).

reconsidered the nature of the master plan. Rather than a predetermined group of structures that would create a unified whole, they began to project an abstract and flexible interaction of various (some as yet undetermined) pieces.

Whether horizontal or vertical expansion would better accommodate planning for an uncertain future and a complex interaction of discrete departments was debatable. Horizontal expansion strategies created inefficient, lengthy connections between far-flung departments, but allowed for additional structures to take on a different shape than what was already built. Vertical expansion maintained existing efficient circulation patterns, but locked any additions (including new medical equipment that was growing increasingly large in scale) into the limitations of the footprint of the original buildings. In the end, vertical expansion proved best suited to hospitals with limited sites; horizontal expansion to hospitals with more extensive sites. But any site soon proved limited given the amount of building required. Expansion plans that accommodated both vertical and horizontal development, like Isadore Rosenfield's Flexible Hospital Plan of 1932, offered the benefits of both expansion strategies.[14]

In both vertical and horizontal expansion plans, however, the facility planner located the additional *building*. The designers of the New York Hospital–Cornell Medical Center, noting that otherwise sound hospital buildings had become obsolete simply "because of the inadequacy and in-

Figure 6.3. H. Eldridge Hanna-ford, diagram of functional re-lations between departments, 1932.

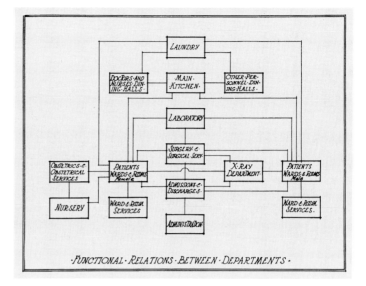

accessibility of the arteries that carry its water, heating, steam, electrical and gas lines," reconceptualized the hospital master plan. Theorizing "that the life of such a building is determined by its 'veins,'" they included drasti-cally oversized service lines and spaces.[15] By designing the interconnections without dictating the location or shape of future building spaces; any indi-vidual section of the building could be reconfigured or even reconstructed without having to rebuild all the technological connections that serviced it. In this approach, the hospital's master plan became not an indication of future blocks of built space, but a complex diagram of corridors, elevators, stairwells, and technology runs (ducts, pipe runs, pneumatic tubes, elec-trical risers). The various departments and facilities were nodes along the circulation pattern.

This abstraction provided flexibility in that the individual pieces (the departments) could be designed according to internal requirements while still being connected in a single, complete, efficient whole. New features could be added, not just in relation to where there was space (whether open land or room for more floors) but in relation to the optimum position along the circulatory arteries. It was hoped that such a hospital would remain effi-cient despite the rapid change in spatial needs and resources.

Early Compact Layouts and Inefficient Skyscrapers

That efficiency had replaced light and air as the foundational requirement for hospital design became clear in the promotion of more compact layouts and in the reconsideration of the benefits of vertical arrangement.[16] In 1934,

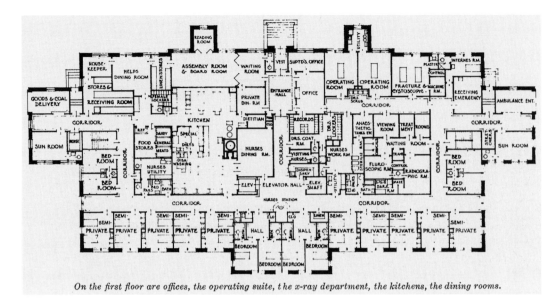

On the first floor are offices, the operating suite, the x-ray department, the kitchens, the dining rooms.

Figure 6.4. Prince Edward Island Hospital, first-floor plan, 1934.

Neergaard stated that it was "axiomatic that the more nearly square a build-ing can be made, to enclose the required space, the more economically it can be built." More compact hospital layouts needed less exterior wall surface; shorter runs for ducts, pipes, wires, and building technologies; and less fuel for heating, lighting, administration, and operation. It also shortened the distances traveled in the performance of basic tasks, reducing the personnel necessary for them. The narrow wings and complex footprints of buildings designed for light and air did not immediately disappear, though. With the increasing vertical differentiation of services and departments in the modern hospital, the lower service floors could be centralized and compact, while the upper, patient-centered floors were more rambling. This was true even in low-rise facilities. In the new building of the Prince Edward Island Hospital, de-signed in collaboration between Neergaard and architects Govan and Fergu-son, the lower stories held multiple corridors maximizing usable space over the given footprint, while the second story, devoted exclusively to patient rooms, was a more typical double-loaded corridor of much narrower building width. Neergaard noted that this "deep" plan, which created large areas of wholly interior space, had required some "courage and resourcefulness" on the part of the architects in "adopting measures which, although they had proved sound elsewhere, were entirely new to the hospital field."[17] That cour-age was required to break decades of hygienic tradition in hospital practice. Other building types had long since adopted far deeper building widths, re-lying on building technologies to compensate for the loss of window walls.

Figure 6.5. Memorial Hospital, New York City, view, 1940s. Designed by James Gamble Rogers, in association with Henry C. Pelton, Architects, the Memorial Hospital was one of the first high-rise hospitals to incorporate a modern, streamlined aesthetic to accompany its modern layout. Adjacent to the New York Hospital–Cornell Medical Center, the building also located the patient tower in the middle of the block, on top of a broad service base. This would guarantee light and air no matter what was built on surrounding blocks.

This division of the hospital into separate upper and lower spatial logics was to some extent a realization of the approach advocated by Samuel Waldron Lambert in 1916. It was a functional solution to disparate practical problems, raising the patient floors above the constant circulation and traffic of the lower floors and providing larger footprints to accommodate the extensive circulation and greater floor area required by many service departments. In the hospitals of post–World War I America, this separation of the lower and upper stories would be given abrupt architectural emphasis and a modernistic treatment—creating the "matchbox on a muffin" model described by Jonathan Hughes. In the 1930s, while the base might be discernible, the upper floors rose in stepped pyramidal blocks above it, emphasizing the overall unity of the institution. These setbacks were clearly influenced by zoning laws, but hospital designers turned them into rooftop balconies for fresh air treatment.[18]

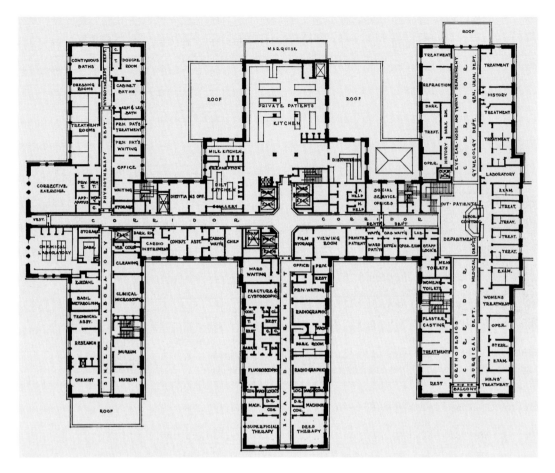

Figure 6.6. Allegheny General Hospital, Pittsburgh, second-floor plan, 1931. Designed by York and Sawyer in collaboration with S. S. Goldwater. The staff elevator opened onto the cross-corridor, the private patient elevators opened onto the stub corridor leading into the X-ray department, the ward elevators opened onto the stub corridor adjacent to the private patients' kitchen, and the service elevator opened into that kitchen. There was also an elevator devoted to outpatient department use and two unassigned elevators opening onto the laboratory corridors. This floor plan, which documents one of the lower floors, also shows the extent of space required by the therapeutic facilities, the X-ray, the labs, the outpatient department, and the special kitchen for private patients.

While the benefits of compact plans were being assimilated into hospital design, the benefits of vertical arrangement were being questioned. There was a growing evidence of "an unpleasant relation between number of stories, building costs and operating efficiency." Tall hospitals were more expensive to build. Waiting for an elevator was as time consuming as walking between pavilions had once been. According to hospital architect Perry W. Swern, the placement, number, and sizing of elevators in hospital build-

Figure 6.7. Meadowbrook Hospital, Long Island, view 1930s. Designed by John Russell Pope and William F. McCulloch in collaboration with S. S. Goldwater, the hospital was a rambling, low-rise structure housing a modern functional plan and clothed in streamlined modernist exterior details.

ings was "more or less guesswork." He advocated more conscious planning of vertical travel routes to increase efficiency, diminish wait time, improve control of access to the various parts of the hospital, and end the overlap of incompatible traffic categories, which could be as benign as a ward patient and a private patient sharing an elevator ride, or as horrifying as a newly admitted patient sharing an elevator ride with an orderly removing a dead body. The designers of the Allegheny General Hospital grouped all of the building's elevators into one central area (a cost-effective construction strategy because it required only one elevator tower) but arranged them to create four different elevator lobbies to accommodate different kinds of circulation (private patients, ward patients, service, staff). The new addition at the Lenox Hill Hospital in New York City had eight elevators: "two for interfloor traffic for nurses and doctors, two for food, two for private patients and two for ward patients."[19]

Given this criticism of tall buildings, low-rise hospital facilities remained a viable option, even for a modern hospital. The streamlined design of the Meadowbrook Hospital in Long Island occupied three-story buildings on a sprawling site. Future additions were planned for horizontal rather than vertical expansion. Carl A. Erikson argued that small hospitals could be only one story—thereby eliminating redundant utility rooms and expensive elevators and stairwells.[20]

The Search for the Efficient Flexible Nursing Unit

Hospital administrators had spent the 1920s adding semiprivate and private patient facilities to the new all-class modern hospital; they spent the 1930s trying to figure out how to use them. In the economic downturn, demand for charitable care increased drastically while paying patients were few and far between. Hospital administrators had to choose between leaving the paying patient rooms empty or turning the smaller rooms over to the insatiable demand for charitable care. Some blamed the problem on the overbuilding of private patient facilities at the expense of ward beds in the 1920s. With the development of healthcare insurance in the 1930s and 1940s (which typically covered the costs of a shared room but not a private room) insured patients soon filled the available semiprivate facilities, but single-bed private rooms often remained vacant.[21]

A more flexible nursing unit—one that would be easy and inexpensive to reconfigure for different patient categories—would clearly be advantageous. Such flexibility thrived in large open spaces with moveable partitions, but foundered in the heavily divided modern hospital. Aseptic hospital details further decreased flexibility: "Built-in coves, floor patterns, window arrangements, heating, plumbing and wiring discourage alteration." Ironically, hospitals with obsolete large open wards found themselves at an advantage over hospitals with an all-private-room layout. An open ward could be easily subdivided by impermanent partitions—whether curtains, glass dividers, or even temporary walls. These partitions could also be rearranged with minimum effort as patient demand shifted. Fred G. Carter considered the benefits for hospitals of the open-plan modern office buildings, where "space is divided to suit the needs and desires of tenants even on short-term leases."[22] Treating the hospital like an office or factory, with a flexible open plan and moveable partitions, was appealing, but given the dangers of too much flexibility—i.e., cross-infections—hospitals largely remained full of solid partitions.

Another, more controversial option for making nursing units more flexible was to make patient rooms more adaptable. Neergaard presented such an approach in his controversial "Flexible Plan" for hospitals at the Construction Section of the 1937 meeting of the American Hospital Association. Neergaard's goal was to make hospitals capable of housing the ceaseless variety of patients with minimal bed vacancy and maximal categorization. This was not a new goal—the proponents of all-private-room hospitals had tried to solve the same problem. In architectural terms, Neergaard suggested the provision of convertible rooms that could accommodate a variable number of patients—single-bed rooms that could accommodate two beds (allowing them to house either private or semiprivate patients), or four-bed wards convertible to five- or six-bed occupancy.[23] This convertibility was in many ways already being practiced, out of necessity rather than planning. In many hospitals, single-bed rooms that were large enough to hold a second bed often did.

Eminent hospital architects Edward F. Stevens and Carl A. Erikson resigned from the conference planning committee in protest of Neergaard's report, which they considered "misleading, inaccurate, and immature." The point of contention was not the number of beds allotted to a room, but Neergaard's scathing critique of existing hospital construction and the designers and administrators who had provided beds "for different kinds of patients out of all proportion to the needs" and had created "restrictive and inelastic" building plans and medical policies.[24] Neergaard was in essence challenging the established and inflexible social distinctions attached to the private building, the semiprivate facility, and the charity wards.

The rigid social compartmentalization of existing patient facilities served the belief that "each type of service should have a separate and largely self-contained unit" occupying its own floor, wing, or even building. By the 1930s that social categorization was excessive. While patients with different ailments might in need be housed in adjacent rooms or even in the same ward, patients of different social categories were typically not intermixed. In the South, black patients were not interspersed with white patients, regardless of demand. In the North, rooms for charity patients were not interspersed with rooms for private patients. According to Erikson, the separation had been taken to extremes: "Generally speaking, hospitals here endeavor to separate the private patients from the ward and semiprivate patients sometimes going to such absurd lengths that the basic philosophy would seem to be a Hindu-like cast[e] system, expensive and absurdly un-American."[25]

It was this rigidity that Neergaard had considered an obstacle to flexibility, and the most radical and controversial part of Neergaard's Flexible Plan Report was its suggestion to break down these moribund social categories and establish new, functional ones. Neergaard suggested that patients be assigned to a ward not based on who they were, but on their varying nursing requirements. He proposed three basic nursing categories: acute, recovery, and convalescent. Acute wards would be small and have more nurses, while convalescent wards would be large and have fewer nurses.[26] This, in essence, treated the hospital like a factory and the patient (of any race, class, or gender) as a product. It would have made the hospital a democratic institution, treating all patients equally, not by changing the architecture per se but by changing the sociospatial limitations placed on it. It was economically cheap, but in the 1930s it proved culturally too dear to implement.

Designing for Group Nursing and Semiprivate Patients

The final adoption by many states of laws limiting nursing positions to eight-hour days had profound implications for hospitals and hospital design. In adding a third nursing shift, hospitals increased the total number of nurses in their employ. This created an immediate need for more nurse locker rooms, more nurse housing, and more dining room facilities for the additional staff. It also increased expenditures on nurse salaries, forcing hospital administrators to examine ways of making nursing more efficient—either by using fewer nurses for a given number of patients or having the patients pay more for the nursing. Research into ward designs that would minimize nurse travel distances, maximize direct nurse supervision, and hold the maximum number of patients one nurse could oversee continued. At the very least, many hospitals of the 1930s included shorter, wider wings that reduced nurse travel distances.[27] Another means of generating efficiencies in nursing, particularly for semiprivate patients, involved redesigning not just the ward but the nursing service along with it.

Traditionally, two kinds of nursing service were provided in the hospital: the ward service, in which a few trained head nurses oversaw a number of student nurses who cared for the charity patients, and the private service, in which private (graduate) nurses, often affiliates of the hospital, were hired directly by the patient. Both were economically viable. Ward nursing was typically far more economical: oversight was easier and student nurses received no salary. On the other hand, the ability to shift nursing charges to patients was fiscally attractive. Which kind of nursing service semiprivate patients should receive was unclear, and, given the increased attention to and demand for semiprivate patient rooms in the 1930s, was a central issue of ward design.

Administrators could not expect a semiprivate patient to be able to afford to hire a private nurse, but ward nursing was not as efficient in the smaller wards and semiprivate rooms. The ad hoc nature of semiprivate patient facilities, as hospitals across the country subdivided large wards into smaller wards or added beds to large private rooms, complicated the problem. Even the world-renowned Columbia-Presbyterian Medical Center, which was built just as interest in semiprivate patients took off, had to scramble to provide facilities for middle-class patients, turning empty rooms in the Harkness Private Patient Pavilion into "group private" service.[28] Consensus was that ad hoc modifications of a large ward or private rooms were inadequate solutions to the problem.

Administrators at a number of hospitals experimented with a new organization of the semiprivate nursing service. In group nursing, a small number of patients within a given space (such as in a small, semiprivate ward) would share the services (and the cost) of a privately hired graduate nurse. The hospital did not bear the nursing charges, and yet "the patients obtain the equivalent of a private nurse service at a greatly lower cost." However, "to be really effective," group nursing "must be arranged for patients housed in groups conveniently placed and conveniently served."[29] It would not work in a large ward, as it would require creating subgroups of patients within a larger group and might create conflict between the ward nurses and the group nurses over specific responsibilities. It would not work on a floor of all single rooms because it would be too difficult for a small number of nurses to keep all the patients in the group under proper supervision and care.

Group nursing was being tried as early as 1922 at the Los Angeles County General Hospital and in the late 1920s at the Grace Hospital in Detroit. Other hospitals reportedly tried it in the 1920s with "discouraging results." Joseph Turner, director of the Mount Sinai Hospital in New York City, believed that the failures were "due not so much to any fault in group nursing as such, but to faulty planning; most of the rooms or buildings in which group nursing has been tried were not built for this purpose, nor were they designed or equipped in such a way as to assist in making group nursing acceptable to patients or workable for nurses." In 1932, Robert Kohn and Charles Butler, working with Turner and hospital consultant S. S. Goldwater, designed a new semiprivate patient building for the Mount Sinai Hospital that was "planned to make a group nursing service possible." The building had three- to four-bed cubicle wards arranged in pairs. Between each pair of wards was a nurses' substation that held the utility fixtures and closets but also provided enough desk space for two nurses, plus a chart rack, bulletin board, signal lights for the call systems, and supply drawers. The layout provided nursing flexibility—offering the necessary support space for group nursing (a consistent group of graduate nurses for patients in one ward or both wards), for special nursing (one graduate nurse per patient), and floor nursing (student nurses shared by all patients on the floor).[30]

In all of these redesigns of wards and nursing service, the one constant remnant of pavilion design was the maintenance of the patient floor as no more than a double-loaded corridor, with patient accommodations in the

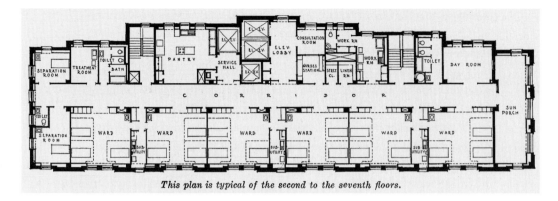

This plan is typical of the second to the seventh floors.

Figure 6.8. Mount Sinai Hospital, New York City, Semiprivate Patient Building, typical floor plan, 1930.

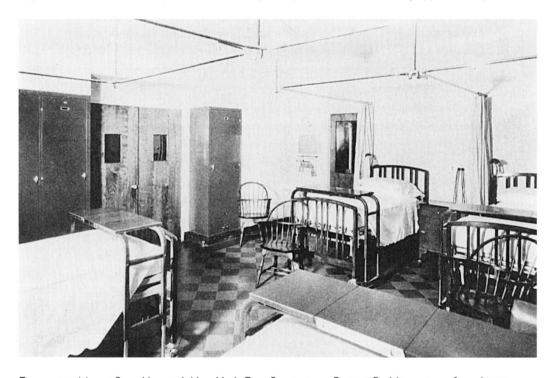

Figure 6.9. Mount Sinai Hospital, New York City, Semiprivate Patient Building, view of ward, 1932.

long linear wings and services at one end of it. By the 1930s and early 1940s, interest in a more efficient patient floor design prompted experiments with double-corridor layouts that allowed more compact building plans, shorter nurse travel distances, better ward ambience, facilitation of centralized services, and reduced construction costs. This layout created an interior service area cut off from direct sunlight and fresh air. Early experiments often involved short stub corridors to isolate the service areas. In the new

Figure 6.10. Chicago Lying-In Hospital, third-floor plan, 1931. Designed by Carl A. Erikson of Schmidt, Garden and Erikson, the building was functionally planned for patient comfort and efficient provision of cutting-edge obstetric and gynecologic treatments. The separate smaller building on the right side of the plan provided isolation for any patient suspected of harboring an infection. Dr. De Lee continued to consider this spatial isolation essential to the prevention of puerperal fever and postpartum infections.

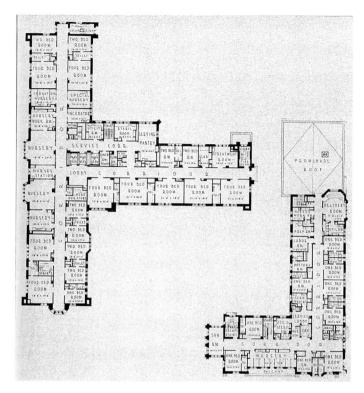

building of the Chicago Lying-In Hospital, to reduce noise and activity in the patient rooms the designers included a short, secondary service corridor off the main one.[31]

A more fully developed, and controversial, version of this deeper ward plan appeared in 1942, when Neergaard presented his "double pavilion plan," which included exterior patient rooms off two internal corridors that surrounded a wholly interior service area. Neergaard calculated that the double pavilion plan layout would provide eleven more beds, yet occupy 150,000 fewer cubic feet and cost an estimated $195,000 less to build than a traditional layout in the same footprint. It also minimized nurse travel distances, maintained exterior access for all patient-occupied spaces, and provided greater spatial flexibility in housing larger spaces or accommodating more complex layouts. Criticism centered on the dark, windowless, center rooms that had no access to the germicidal and health-giving properties of sunlight and turned the service area into "essentially a slum because it condemns nurses and attendants to almost eternal artificial light, poor ventilation and slop and smells resulting from double use of fixtures."[32] The use of the service areas from both sides of the corridor also offered increased potential of cross-contamination from shared supplies.

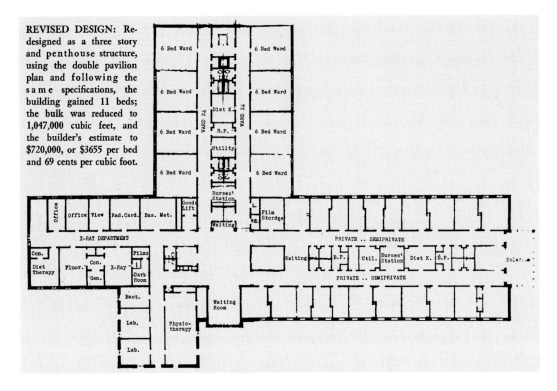

REVISED DESIGN: Redesigned as a three story and penthouse structure, using the double pavilion plan and following the same specifications, the building gained 11 beds; the bulk was reduced to 1,047,000 cubic feet, and the builder's estimate to $720,000, or $3655 per bed and 69 cents per cubic foot.

Figure 6.11. Charles F. Neergaard, double pavilion plan, 1942.

Beauty and Comfort Matter but Asepsis Is Still Essential

These redesigns of the overall nursing unit layout were done in the name of efficiency, and they treated the ward layout as a tool—a means of increasing human efficiency. Healing was the product of interaction with practitioners (doctors, nurses, therapists, technicians) and equipment (diagnostic technologies, surgical facilities), not with the quality of surroundings. The expectation that the building itself could exert a therapeutic influence was not gone; it was simply confined to the patient rooms.

According to eminent architectural historian and educator Talbot F. Hamlin, "the quality of the surroundings of the sick person may be as important in the cure as the specific therapeutic measures themselves." The vast majority of hospital projects in the 1930s included extensive color schemes, an attention to pleasant surroundings, domestic comforts where possible, and a room with a view. An article on the Little Traverse Hospital in Petoskey, Michigan, stated, "Probably the biggest step forward in hospital design in recent years has been the abandonment of the aseptic interiors formerly considered necessary in favor of a more homelike atmosphere."

Figure 6.12. Little Traverse Hospital, Petoskey, Michigan, view of patient room, 1939. Designed by Skidmore and Owings, architects, the hospital included patient rooms that struck a balance between aseptic finishes and features, domestic comforts, and modern functional aesthetics.

While Goldwater might wonder what was wrong with a hospital looking like and acting like a hospital, David Charles Sloane and Beverlie Conant Sloane describe the reactions against the medicalized aseptic environment as a factor in the late twentieth-century movement of treatment from hospitals to the "mall."[33]

The bottom line in this beautification was that these changes were as much a means of attracting patients as of directly aiding their recovery. Redecorating was a cost-effective means of making the old seem new, an important consideration and sometimes the only option in the Depression Era. Rugs and furnishings could brighten a room. Colored paint was cheap and could be applied by the existing hospital maintenance staff. The New York Hospital–Cornell Medical Center building was painted gray on the medical floors, green on the surgical floors, blue on the operating floors,

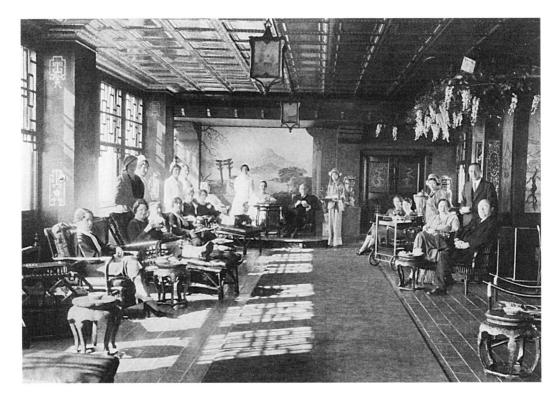

Figure 6.13. Polyclinic Hospital, New York City, solarium of Chinese Lounge, 1933.

and the medical college in red. "In an effort to make it look less like the conventional hospital," the new Lenox Hill Hospital building used "six combinations of color" for walls and ceilings, and varied the color chosen on a room-by-room basis. This would certainly have varied the experience of the nurse as she worked the ward, but as Mabel Binner, a nurse and superintendent, noted, there was no reason for every patient room to have a different color, since patients only occupied one room at a time.[34]

Some patient spaces received full interior decorative treatment, not just a spot of color and a rug. Children's rooms, wards, and departments were given murals and details that made them more like a "fairyland" than a ward. Recreation rooms for adult patients were turned into exotic spaces that were an extreme contrast to the grim aseptic plainness of the utilitarian hospital. The administrators of the Polyclinic Hospital in New York City turned their roof deck into a nautically themed outdoor lounge. It was so popular that they soon thereafter redecorated their solarium, turning it into a "Chinese lounge" with rustic bridge, brooklet trickling from rocks to a crystal pool, and two Chinese girls in traditional garb to serve tea every afternoon.[35]

Humanizing the hospital was not just about beauty, it was about experience. New communication and entertainment technologies even in patient rooms served as amenities to make the patient experience more pleasant. Telephones in patient rooms allowed them to keep in touch with friends and family and eased the isolation. Radio systems with earphones or even radio pillows provided a distraction that improved patient happiness and thus facilitated healing.[36] The hospital patient in a room decorated to look like anything but a hospital room, surrounded by the latest technological diversions, could forget they were in a hospital.

The Tenaciousness of Environmental Contamination

No matter how much interior decoration was applied to patient rooms and lounges, aseptic hospital finishes and details continued to predominate in other areas of the hospital. Despite the triumph of aseptic technique, the longevity of these aseptic finishes was linked to the longevity of the problem of cross-infections. Even in the 1930s, in departments designed to reinforce aseptic procedures and staffed by persons well versed in up-to-date aseptic techniques, hospital cross-infection rates stubbornly refused to disappear. In the end, "every hospital [was] a communicable disease hospital, whether it [recognized] the fact or not." When a study in 1939 made it clear that, despite aseptic practices, nursing and medical students were the largest category of young adults contaminated in large numbers with tuberculosis, worries that the hospital itself was spreading the disease became palpable once again.[37]

Given these disappointing results, worries about contamination of the building materials or of airborne germs experienced a resurgence that even scientific research could not dispel. Researchers at the Yale bacteriological labs set out to prove that the porous, noise-reducing, acoustic materials becoming popular in hospitals were not in fact harboring germs. They did a series of tests on how bacteria penetrated various materials and how long they survived under various cleaning regimens. The researchers concluded that porous materials posed no real danger in harboring germs, but that hospitals should choose materials that could stand up to heavy cleaning. Hospital architect James Govan and two Canadian professors used this research as proof that it did "not follow that because a surface is rough in texture, that it must of necessity provide a good medium for the development of bacteria."[38]

Laboratory evidence seemed to acquire different results than field experience, however. In 1931, after incidence of puerperal fever "practically disappeared" in a lying-in hospital after the walls were painted, a Wash-

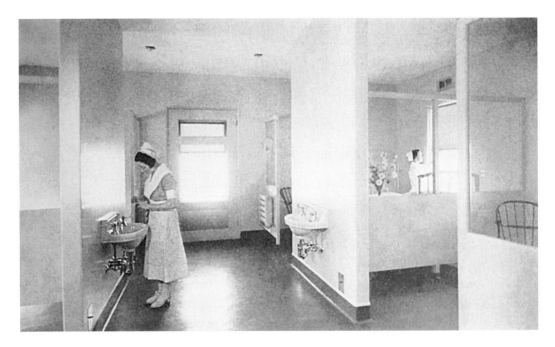

Figure 6.14. Burbank Hospital, Fitchburg, Massachusetts, photo of ward cubicles, 1936. Designed by James Purdon, this isolation facility included fixtures at entrance points to each cubicle and aseptic materials and details.

ington hospital pathologist did some experiments that showed that "in the preparation of vaccines and antitoxins in an unpainted room the cultures became contaminated. When the walls were painted, results were successful." His conclusion was that the paint "was effective in combating disease" because it rendered the porous surfaces (which collected organic matter that facilitated the growth of bacteria) safely impermeable. The discrepancies were enough to ensure that hard, impermeable materials remained ubiquitous in hospitals, particularly in the spaces requiring the most aseptic conditions—operating rooms, laboratories, and isolation facilities. For example, the state-of-the-art isolation building of the Burbank Hospital in Fitchburg, Massachusetts, was finished with concrete floors "top-coated with magnesite germ-proof composition, jointless and with rounded corners everywhere." New materials like plastics, plywood, rubber, and glass block continued to be evaluated on the old criteria of porosity and used accordingly.[39]

New difficulties with increasingly complex plumbing systems made it graphically clear that contamination in the centralized, interconnected, technology-riddled, high-rise building was an insidious problem, difficult to eliminate. Back-siphonage in plumbing posed a challenging and potentially deadly problem, compounded by the high-rise construction of modern hospitals. During the cooling process, sterilizers developed an internal vacuum that could suck water back up from the wastewater drain pipe. Administrators of one hospital attributed several infant deaths to faulty sterilization of bottles due to such back-siphonage.[40]

Even more troubling, the water pressure in many of the taller hospitals was insufficient, and when there was enough draw on the lower floors, water could be siphoned from almost any pipe on the upper floors back into the general plumbing system. In one experiment, Major Joel I. Connelly of the Chicago Public Health Department added red dye to an instrument sterilizer on an upper floor of a brand-new hospital. Under conditions of too much demand on lower floors, when the sterilizer supply was opened, instead of potable water running into the sterilizer, the red dyed water ran from the sterilizer back into the supply pipes. After enough time, "the entire water supply of the hospital was tinged with red, indicating the extent to which the dye traveled from the sterilizer through the water pipes. Wherever the dye appeared at the faucets, drinking fountains or in kitchens, it was apparent that pathogenic micro-organisms from infected materials could also be carried by the water." In the same vein, water from supposedly sterile water supply systems rarely tested as germ-free.[41]

Fixing the piping was not impossible, but it was costly and required extensive attention to detail. One of the underlying problems, however, was in the construction process that separated plumbing installation and hospital equipment installation. While master plumbers could build a system that did not have cross-connections, plumbers were "seldom, if ever, given a job of installing sterilizers, even when they have the general plumbing contract for a hospital." The plumbing was roughed in, then months later, after the sterilizing equipment was delivered, someone else connected the pipes to the equipment. The Master Plumbers' Association created a "plumbing research lab" to test fixtures and see what solutions could be developed. As health inspections of hospital plumbing grew more detailed, many a well-respected hospital underwent a quiet plumbing overhaul.[42]

Active Environmental Purification Technologies

Faced with ongoing outbreaks of internal cross-infections, hospital practitioners once again found renewed interest in the potential role of air in spreading disease. According to William Firth Wells, research into "the bacteriologic behavior of air" had proven that the "hospital air carries a bacterial load enormously in excess of the air outside the hospital." These new studies revealed "a mechanism which not only permits a theory of air-

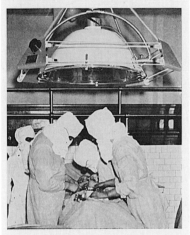

Figure 6.15. Sterilamp Advertisement, 1938.

borne infection but which proves beyond reasonable doubt that we are exchanging within our
enclosed rooms respiratory flora." This explained
the relative effectiveness of pavilion-ward design
in lowering cross-infection rates—"the dilution
of the [infective] droplets by air space or change
of air" had provided a form of an aseptic barrier.
The new bacteriological research revealed that
to create an effective spatial barrier required far
more space between beds than was economically
feasible in the modern hospital, and far more air
exchange than could be economically provided
at tempered levels.[43]

For aerial separation, isolation and maternity
departments continued to be housed in separate structures or separate wings from the main
hospital building. According to Joseph T. Smith,
"general hospital wards are natural sources of infecting agents of all sorts. A maternity hospital,
to be safe, must have absolutely no connection
of any kind with wards for diseased patients."[44]
New technologies offered the possibility of a
more active approach to air purification through
artificial lights and air conditioning. In 1936, Dr.
Deryl Hart of Duke Hospital, in association with
Westinghouse, developed a light fixture that
could kill bacteria with "Bactericidal Radiant
Energy," or ultraviolet light. The initial expectation was that these lights could reduce the bacterial load within the operating room during surgery. Unfortunately, the developers of the light
had difficulty making the light strong enough to
kill bacteria but not so strong that it gave the surgeons, nurses, and patients a sunburn. In early
uses of the bactericidal lights, the surgical staff
resorted to wearing goggles and headgear during the surgery. Hart noted
that "this mode of protection is rather warm and uncomfortable but can
be improved if suction tubes are placed beneath the goggles to keep them
clean."[45]

George F. Dick suggested the use of similar bactericidal (UV) lights as
a means of disinfecting a patient room after occupation by a patient with

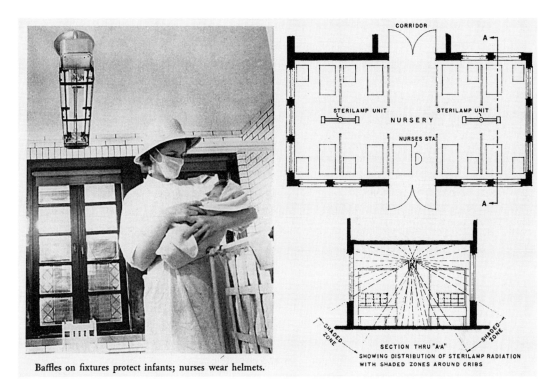

Baffles on fixtures protect infants; nurses wear helmets.

Figure 6.16. Lenox Hill Hospital, New York City, photo, plan and section of UV protection in nursery, 1940.

a contagious disease or an infection. Studies of the efficacy of ultraviolet light air purification were inconclusive, leading one expert, Thomas Byrd Magath, to suggest that "while tests of the air in the room" after bactericidal ultraviolet light exposure "seem to offer interesting suggestions, the whole matter of the importance of these bacteria of the air to operating room infections is too problematic to justify the wholesale installation of ultraviolet air treatment in hospitals." He called for more study and experimentation. Wells, a firm believer in the air as a mechanism of germ transfer, promoted the use of ultraviolet lights not only in the operating room but in the nursing unit, as germicidal barriers between patient spaces. Ultraviolet disinfection screens were installed in a number of hospitals; for example, in 1940 the directors of the Lenox Hill Hospital in New York City installed UV lights in the nursery, with baffles to prevent the light shining directly onto the cribs. The nurses and visitors wore pith helmets.[46]

If germs were spread through the air, then the chance of airborne cross-infection ended when patients were furnished with "individual supplies of air." The centralized ventilation systems installed in many hospitals could become a means of spreading infected air throughout a building in the same way that plumbing spread infected water. The individual room-unit air conditioner proved an extremely attractive solution to creating such separate room ventilation. When Drs. Constantin P. Yaglou and Kenneth D. Blackfan reported "a spectacular reduction in acute and chronic infection of premature infants, chiefly respiratory, by the installation of a separately conditioned air supply for their ward," air conditioning became one of the hottest topics in hospital design, particularly for isolation and surgical spaces.[47]

In spaces housing particularly vulnerable patient populations, all available aseptic strategies—UV light, air conditioning, barriers, spatial separation—might be deployed simultaneously. As illnesses among newborns increased in frequency in the 1930s and 1940s, nursery design underwent intense reconfiguration. By 1939 it was common to put infants in cubicles rather than in group nurseries. The cubicles were a passive barrier, reinforcing aseptic nursing procedures, but some also incorporated individual air supplies and exhausts to eliminate the chance of airborne cross-contamination. Asa S. Bacon described the new nursery of the Presbyterian Hospital in Chicago, in which "each infant in the nursery is housed in a completely enclosed air conditioned cubicle . . . made of steel and shatter-proof glass. Individual equipment is provided in each cubicle for full care of the infant and no infant need ever be removed from a cubicle until it is ready to go home."[48] Some of the cubicles included germicidal ultraviolet lights within the air ducts and over the doorways to provide an active aseptic barrier between the cubicle and the larger room during entrance and exit.

At the Cradle, an institution for infants in Chicago, a fatal and long-lived enteritis epidemic among the infants prompted an overhaul of the nursery facilities to install partial cubicles that reinforced aseptic nursing techniques. The infection rates were drastically reduced, but the infants still caught colds and even pneumonia. To bring the cross-infection rate to zero, the administrators "decided to experiment with controlling air-borne infection." They installed three different infant units: one had open-fronted cubicles; one had open-fronted cubicles with an ultraviolet light installed over the cubicle opening; one had completely enclosed cubicles (with their own separate air-conditioning system) and excessive aseptic procedures for entry and exit. The hope was that experience in the different units would prove which approach to isolation was the most effective at curtailing cross-infection.[49] The results were inconclusive.

Air conditioning might have been initially justified in hospitals as a means of asepsis, but the added benefits of climate control soon became obvious and enticing. By the 1930s, after new studies had shown that prolonged exposure to high heat and humidity or to excessive fluctuations in heat and humidity resulted in lowered resistance to infection, opinion on the healthy hospital environment reversed again. A constant temperature of 68–71 degrees Fahrenheit and relative humidity of 50 percent was forwarded as the zone of maximum human comfort.[50] Air conditioning offered the possibility of providing this ideal comfort zone, or any other indoor weather condition desired by a doctor.

Experiments with indoor climate therapy continued. Administrators of the Montefiore Hospital in Pittsburgh and the Chicago Lying-In Hospital, among others, installed what were termed "weather rooms," which combined the benefits of temperature and humidity control and particulate filtration with the functions of an oxygen chamber. At the Corey Hill Hospital, one young doctor studied the effects of air conditioning (varying the temperature and humidity) on rheumatic patients; it was an example of the creation of a medical "specialty" that required environmental control. Favorable results in air conditioning treatment of asthma, respiratory infections, sinusitis, cardiac, prematurity, and postoperative cases were reported. With individual room controls, a practitioner could theoretically tailor a room's climate to the patient's physiological needs—providing desertlike conditions in one room, and in the adjacent room a veritable jungle.[51]

Air-conditioning systems were expensive. Many hospitals started small—targeting specific spaces. In 1934, Mount Sinai Hospital included air conditioning in the operating rooms of the new semiprivate patient building. The doctors of Saint Vincent's Infirmary in Little Rock, Arkansas, convinced the skeptical sisters to install air conditioning in the surgical and obstetrical wards to great success—the patients were happier and more comfortable and slept better, and there were no postoperative pneumonia cases. The Denver Children's Hospital's new Tammen wing was fully air conditioned in 1936. Of hospitals installing air conditioning by 1935, only three had installed a system to handle an entire wing or building, nineteen had installed them in operating rooms, four in delivery rooms, nine in newborn nurseries, and eight in private rooms. For obvious reasons, southern hospitals were quicker to adopt whole-hospital air-conditioning systems. By 1949 the Florida Agricultural and Mechanical College—largely a black institution—reportedly built a new hospital that included three hundred air-conditioned rooms.[52]

In 1939 Bacon called the open window an "archaic means of ventilation" and believed "the hospital of the future will be hermetically sealed." The sealed building was most economical to mechanically ventilate and cool; it was also a consequence of the changing nature of the outside air. Increasing levels of pollution and dirt in urban surroundings meant that fresh air

Figure 6.17. Chicago Lying-In Hospital, Climate Room, view, 1949. The door to this ward was like that of an industrial refrigerator and served to preserve the environmental differentials within the room. The cabinets above the door held the extensive equipment necessary for the complete control of temperature, humidity, and even oxygen content of the air. The room held three or four beds, implying that at least that number of patients would benefit from the same environmental conditions.

was no longer necessarily attainable through an open window. Some cities recorded days when even at high noon the sun did not reach the streets through the particulate haze. The US Public Health Service in 1936 found a 21.5 percent loss of light in a smoky district of New York City, and 14.1 percent average light loss in Baltimore, neither of which was known for its air pollution. From pure, health-inducing, fresh air, outside air had become suspect as the bearer of "disturbing noises, odors, germs, dust, pollen, and dirt."[53]

The Sealed Operating Room

While even patient rooms were becoming sealed environments, mature aseptic understanding made the operating room sacrosanct—"a holy of holies, not to be entered unnecessarily, and then only under certain conditions." In the interest of asepsis, medical students were completely separated from the operating field, often by a glass window. This diminished what the student could learn. Surgery, at its best, required the surgeon to utilize all senses. The increasing physical separation of surgical audiences thus affected medical education—the observers could no longer hear (or smell) what was going on in the operation, and unless they were perfectly placed, the glass screens could cause glare, reflections, or distortions that interfered with the view.[54]

In James Gamble Rogers's operating room design for the Columbia-Presbyterian Medical center the observation room was on the floor above the operating room. Glass windows in the ceiling of the operating room provided a view onto the operating table immediately below. A radiophone in the operating room allowed the audience to hear the patient's heartbeat. This design was soon imitated; a similar layout, with a microphone from the surgeon to the observers, appeared in the Henrotin Hospital in Chicago by Holabird and Root/Berlin and Swern in 1935.[55]

Erikson pushed operating room design to a new extreme, noting that the goal was "to eliminate the observer from the operating room yet to permit him to see and hear better than is ordinarily possible," To achieve this, he designed an operating room that was a hermetically sealed, multistory, multimedia demonstration facility. His "Model Operating Room" design for the Century of Progress Exhibition at Chicago in 1933 provided two stories of seating with every seat a front-row seat commanding an excellent view of the operating table. The model was part of the Electric Light and Power Industry exhibit, and fittingly, the operating room was wired for sound and vision. The observers were in radio communication with the operating surgeon. A television camera mounted directly above the surgical

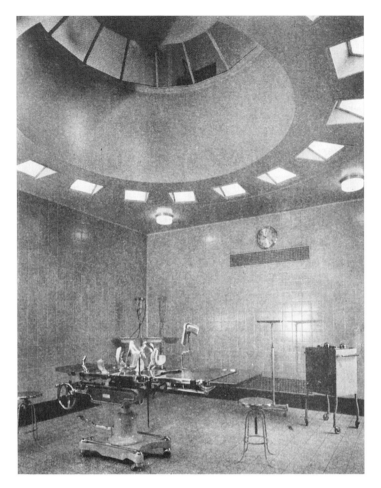

Figure 6.18. Henrotin Hospital, Chicago, operating room, 1935. This completely modern operating room also included extensive artificial lights and colored finishes to reduce glare.

field allowed an image of the operation to be "projected onto the end wall" and provide the optimum view to all observers. Erikson even speculated that "if and when television becomes practical it may be possible to allow the students to remain in their classrooms and thus transfer the operation to the classroom."[56]

Erikson's belief that if the windows could be opened someone would open them prompted him to design his model operating room without windows or skylights at all. The exclusion of windows reportedly improved the lighting, eliminated the problems of dirty, dripping skylights, and reduced the heat load, making operating rooms a much more comfortable space for the doctors. While the trend was clear, the shift was not total: Harold L. Foss and Edward F. Stevens still included skylights and windows in their "Ideal Operating Suite of 1935."[57]

The climate control in the sealed, air-conditioned operating room also provided a simple solution to some new and very real dangers. Anesthetics,

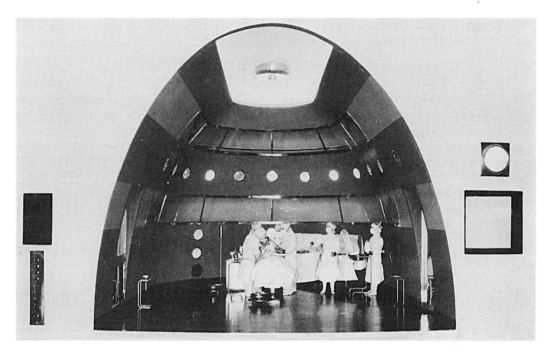

Figure 6.19. Carl A. Erikson, Model Operating Room, view of model, 1933.

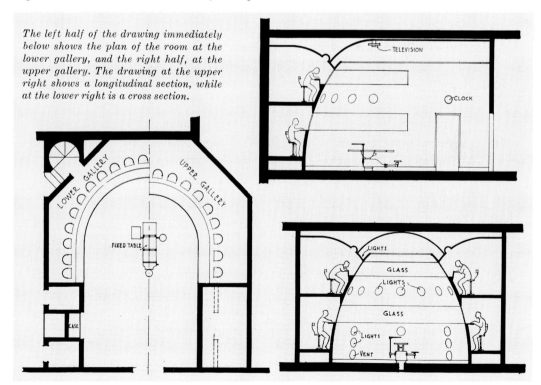

The left half of the drawing immediately below shows the plan of the room at the lower gallery, and the right half, at the upper gallery. The drawing at the upper right shows a longitudinal section, while at the lower right is a cross section.

Figure 6.20. Carl A. Erikson, Model Operating Room, plans and section, 1933.

including ether, were typically volatile substances. As new, even more volatile chemicals (like cyclopropane) replaced ether, the need for a ventilation system that could contain the gas leaks to prevent unintended inhalation or even explosions became critically important. Intensive study of the problem revealed that the environmental design of the operating room was critical to preventing explosions. While cauterizing tools and sparks from electric equipment were dangerous, the majority of operating room explosions were traced back to casual static electric sparks from the movement of persons and equipment in the space. While the initial reaction was to use less-flammable anesthetics, alterations to the materials of the operating room also occurred. Wiring systems and outlets became grounded, non-sparking systems. Metal equipment and furniture was grounded by adding drag chains. Operating room personnel were required to wear conductive shoes. There were also experiments in preventing static sparks by grounding the entire operating room, typically by including metal strips within the flooring, such as grounded brass strips in terrazzo, as at the Huron Road Hospital in Cleveland. Air conditioning offered a solution without changing all the material details of the operating room. Greater room humidity reduced the buildup of static electric sparks; an air-conditioning system that controlled humidity as well as temperature in the operating room greatly reduced the danger.[58]

Expertise, Modern Hospitals, and Modernist Architecture

The 1930s hospital occupied a changing architectural world. The modernist, functionalist architecture of the European avant-garde was migrating (along with many modernist architects) to the United States, beginning a slow transformation of architectural practice and design. Houses, office buildings, civic buildings, and industrial buildings of modernist design appeared across the United States in the 1930s, but American hospital designs remained remarkably unaffected. According to Annmarie Adams, "medicine of the interwar period inspired modernist plans, but these remained embedded in historicist and classicizing exteriors that might easily have been mistaken for hotels, schools, or even town halls."[59]

This stylistic resistance further differentiated American from European hospital designs. While Paul Nelson, an American architect practicing in Europe, designed a hospital complex for Lille, France, that was a small modernist ensemble, in New York City architect Henry Shepley drew several studies of different stylistic treatments for the already functionally determined building mass of the New York Hospital–Cornell Medical Center. For the new Chicago Lying-In Hospital, Erikson designed a state-

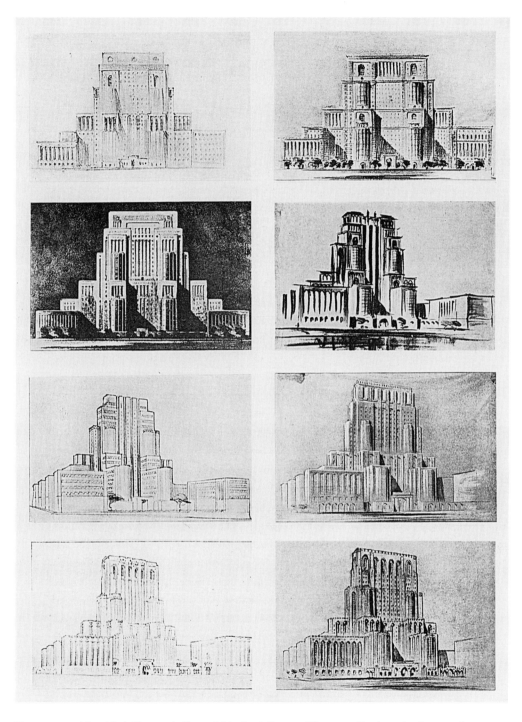

Figure 6.21. New York Hospital–Cornell Medical Center, Elevation Studies. As discussed in a 1933 article in *Architectural Forum*, the various elevation studies were given telltale labels like "Italian Palace," "Graybar," "Swiss Chalet," "Chrysler," "Piranesi," the "Richardson," and "Avignon."

Figure 6.22. Chicago Lying-In Hospital, photo of facility, 1933.

of-the-art modern hospital plan with semiprivate ward facilities, multiple nurseries, separate service corridors, a separate isolation building, and all the advanced functions necessary to modern surgical obstetrics, but he clothed it in gothic details. US hospital designers at best treated modernist architecture as another style, to be applied to existing traditions of functionally derived hospital plans. They approved of the simplicity and minimal stylistic details of modernism, which provided "greater elasticity in meeting the exigencies of modern hospital planning than do the less flexible styles, whether these be Roman, French Renaissance or colonial." That the modernist "international style" was economical to build was a further recommendation.[60]

If American hospital designers treated modernism as a style, Richard Neutra, an American architect known for his early modernist designs, noted that "contemporary architecture, in general, borrowed significant features from projects designed to serve the sick." A number of historians, observing the overlapping emphasis on "minimalist, undecorated, planar surfaces," have connected the dots between aseptic design and modernist architectural designs. Nancy Tomes considers the first decades of the twentieth century as the beginning of "antisepticonsciousness," and "a marked preference for a stripped-down aesthetic." Adrian Forty discusses the related hygienic transformation of manufactured objects as "the basis for

Figure 6.23. Denver Children's Hospital, Denver, Colorado, 1930s. Designed by Mr. Hoyt, this addition held the heliotherapy, hydrotherapy, and physiotherapy facilities.

an entirely new standard of judgement about environments, artefacts and clothing: hygiene rivaled comfort, utility and taste in people's assessment of what they saw." Margaret Campbell has traced the debt modernist designers owed to the design of tuberculosis facilities.[61]

This book has shown that the movement toward a stripped-down aesthetic and emphasis of the plan over the facade appeared in hospital designs as early as the late nineteenth century, but as a hygienic rather than aesthetic strategy that remained largely contained to hospital design until the early twentieth century. What is important to me in this overlap is the realization that the movement for architectural minimalism—a stripped-down, functional approach to building design—had a much longer germination and a much more diverse foundation than is typically discussed in histories of modernist architecture and architects. When reexamined with this complexity in mind, the traditional historical narrative of twentieth-century modernism and of the modern hospital become less clear but also more profound.

By focusing on buildings that express this minimalism externally, scholars of modernist architecture have elevated the European institutions that were modernist in exterior details to the status of iconic examples of the modern hospital. Magnificent modernist healthcare institutions, such

as Alvar Aalto's Paimio Sanatorium, August Rollier's institution at Leysin, or Duiker and Bijvoet's Zonnestraal, are conundrums in the history
of modern hospital design. As institutions specializing in environmental
cures, they reveal the hospital design traditions of the late nineteenth century, characterized by sunlight, fresh air, spatial isolation, passive patients,
and architectural hygiene, rather than of the early twentieth century, which
featured closed windows, functionally differentiated and interconnected
spaces, patients circulating throughout the hospital, and aseptic details.
These sanatoria are stunning examples of modernist architecture, but they
were "of modest significance in the world of medicine and in terms of hospital planning."[62] In stronger terms, they were traditional hygienic hospital
plans clothed in modernist garb.

In the 1930s, the differences between architectural modernists and modern hospital designers were expressed professionally as well as formally.
American hospital architects and modernist architects had different expectations of their own roles in society and of the building's role in promoting
health (or illness). The most vocal of European modernist architects promoted their new designs not just as an expression of the new, enlightened,
industrial urban society, but as a generator of it. In transforming architectural design, European modernist architects hoped to transform society—
politically, socially, physiologically. They published manifestoes, treatises,
and tracts that called for "architecture or revolution," when in fact for them
architecture *was* the revolution, a bloodless means of creating a new order
for an enlightened industrial capitalism or socialism. To achieve this new
order, modernist European architects worked to disseminate their designs
and their approach to design, to make it a universal socioarchitectural form
as well as to generate demand for their services.[63] Like mid-nineteenth-
century pavilion-ward design advocates who had promoted a standardized,
universal, healthy design to be built in any locale, any environment, modernist architects were offering more than a new style. They were offering an
architecturally induced sociopolitical transformation. American hospital
architects, on the other hand, saw the building as promoting or preventing
disease, facilitating medical practice, and facilitating healthy recovery for
sick and wounded persons. If the nineteenth-century hospital had been designed to transform the sick poor into healthy, morally upstanding, solvent
citizens, the twentieth-century hospital was a cutting-edge medical workshop designed to facilitate the repair of the bodies of the sick, ill, injured,
and broken of all classes.[64] This new role as medical workshop was largely divested of the traditional expectation that the hospital environment
would itself exert a sociomoral influence. If the buildings that the hospital
architects designed served as a generator of communal health, it was in-

Figure 6.24. Peru Maternity Hospital, Lima, bird's-eye view, 1939. Stevens, Curtin and Mason of Boston were collaborating architects on this design; Stevens's hospital design practice spanned the globe.

creasingly a product of what happened in the building, not a consequence of interaction with the building itself.

Designing a building that could provide these medical interventions efficiently to a large number of sick people while also preventing the transfer of contagious diseases between them, required extensive specialized information—medical, hygienic, technical, technological. That specialization had kept the hygienically minimalist architecture of late nineteenth- and early twentieth-century American hospital design on the periphery of professional American architectural consciousness. By the 1920s, as hospital construction became a growth industry, architects in general paid more attention to hospital design as a lucrative specialty. The modern hospital architect's practice was founded on focused expertise in specific conditions, however, not a broad dissemination of a new, universal, architectural strategy for appropriate healthy design. By the early twentieth century hospital design was considered nonstandardizable. According to William Henry Walsh, "because of the many diverse conditions existing in different

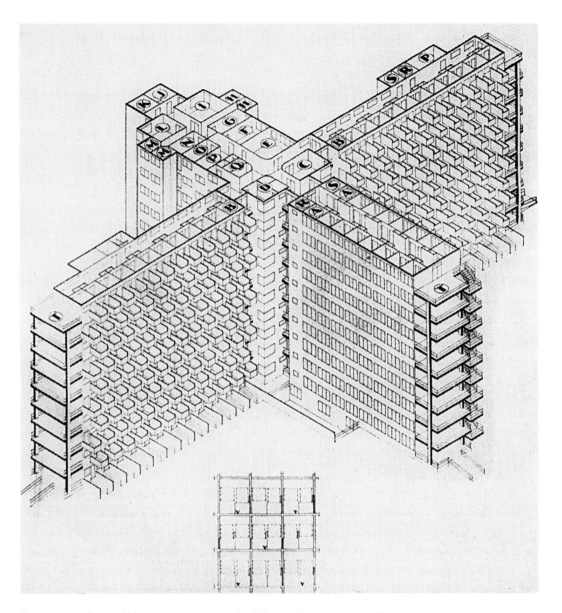

Figure 6.25. Richard Neutra, 400- to 500-bed Hospital, axonometric plan, 1938.

communities which affect the type of hospital required, it has never been possible to design one institution that would completely meet the needs of another location, and so every attempt to standardize hospital planning, even in one city or state, has met with dismal failure."[65]

There were no twentieth-century hospital design manuals, no treatises to give local architects or doctors a clear idea of the requirements. American hospital designers promoted their individualized functional solutions

Figure 6.26. Richard Neutra, 400- to 500-bed Hospital, perspective, 1938.

as the closed and well-defended province of an elite cadre of specialists. According to Charles F. Neergaard, even when regular architects worked with a hospital consultant, they erred on the side of overconfidence and developed designs that achieved "only the 'monumental glorification' of the designer." Medical personnel alone were also no longer sufficient to undertake hospital design. In Walsh's view, local doctors were concerned only about the planning of "their own particular specialties" and they "seldom appreciate the problems of administration and nursing." At a time when the role of architecture in facilitating asepsis and efficient nursing meant that good technique was "built into the structure," an architect who relied only on a regular doctor for information too often designed "a monstrosity, difficult to operate and costly to maintain." Since the hospital architect and hospital consultant were the means of acquiring the modern hospital, the spread of modern hospital design required the dissemination of the specialists. In the 1930s, the most prominent American hospital architects and consultants had international practices, traveling far and wide to design American-style hospitals in distant locales.[66]

Two idealized modernist hospital designs published in the twenty-fifth anniversary issue of the *Modern Hospital* reveal the different architectural modernisms represented by these varying approaches. Influential American modernist architect Richard Neutra presented a five-hundred-bed California Hospital with four ten-story wings extending out into a landscaped site. The northern wing held the ward services; the southern wing held a double-loaded corridor of patient rooms with a communal south-facing balcony; the east and west wings held single-loaded corridors with rooms with private, south-facing balconies. Although the building was a high-rise, there was no demarcated space for the diagnostic, treatment, and service facilities that had become so necessary to interactive medical practice. Patient rooms occupied more than three-quarters of the building's floor area. The extensive balconies and proportion of space devoted to patient rooms indicate that Neutra was likely intending it as a fresh air cure facility. Health was a product of interaction with the external environment. The individual patient in the individual hospital room would receive maximum exposure to sunshine and fresh air rather than maximum exposure to medical practitioners, practices, and technologies. A pavilion and landscape water feature provided wider options for interacting with the outdoors—enticements for the patients in their rooms to improve. The building itself—the commingling of modern design and healing nature—was the therapy.

The modern hospital envisaged by Coolidge Shepley Bulfinch and Abbott, the architects of the New York Hospital–Cornell Medical Center, was also a facility comprising four wings, but the wings were of varying lengths and heights. The building rose to twenty stories at its center, making it much larger than Neutra's design. That extra space did not necessarily house twice the number of patients. While the facade treatment of the building is uniform across the structure, the stepped massing provided floors with varying footprints. As in the New York Hospital–Cornell Medical Center design, the more extensive footprint of the lower floors might house services with bulky technologies while the more limited upper floors might provide reduced nurse travel distances and immediate access to windows for patients. While the building is studded with balconies, it stands remote from its surroundings, with little indication that there would be interaction between interior and exterior environments. Health was a product of the activities occurring within its walls. The building was a tool, to facilitate social and medical practices within it.

Modernist architects of the 1920s and 1930s dreamed that their buildings were a therapy. Full of sunshine, fresh air, and labor-saving technologies, the new architecture would generate a new, modern, politically liberated society, full of healthy citizens, leading happy lives in the new industrial world order. The new designs would create this new world, transforming the inhabitants into virile members of an alternate modern world order. There was no going back. Hospital architects of the same period designed modern American centralized high-rise hospitals and medical

Figure 6.27. Coolidge Shepley Bulfinch and Abbott, Design of 500-bed Hospital, perspective, 1938.

centers as tools to facilitate medicine. The tenants were not the healthy, virile, urban citizens envisaged by the modernist architects; they were sick, diseased, perhaps bedridden, and undergoing physiological revision. The modern hospital was conceptualized as a corrective, a tool to fix those broken by the existing world order.

CHAPTER 7

Postwar Hospital Design Trends

> Ask the man in the street, "Why do you go to a hospital?" He will
> answer, "To get medical care in serious sickness," or words to that
> effect. In common parlance, medical care is the purpose of a hospital.
> — **Michael M. Davis, 1938**

By 1945 hospitals were seen as necessary medical institutions, and there were far too many communities (particularly smaller towns) without access to that necessity. This perceived shortage ensured that after the war there would be an intense increase in hospital construction, but what form the new construction would take was an open question. Wartime developments transformed medicine, urban society, and architectural design, but the urgency of postwar hospital needs left little time for abstract considerations of new, possibly more effective hospital layouts. Much of the postwar hospital construction boom thus relied on the prewar design trajectory. In 1945, the administrators of Bellevue Hospital in New York City abandoned the (still unfinished) 1904 master plan of McKim, Mead and White's "stacked" pavilion facility, and published a pamphlet projecting a new postwar ideal facility. Although the Bellevue Hospital pamphlet was labeled "Medicine's Tomorrow" it was clearly based on hospital design's yesterday: the proposed project depicted high-rise facilities like those built in the late 1920s, with a few modernist flourishes in the siting and the exterior treatment.[1] The postwar hospital design picked up where the prewar hospital left off.

The implementation of the Hospital Survey and Construction Act (known as the Hill-Burton Act) in 1946, which made federal monies available to communities of all sizes to build hospitals, ensured that postwar

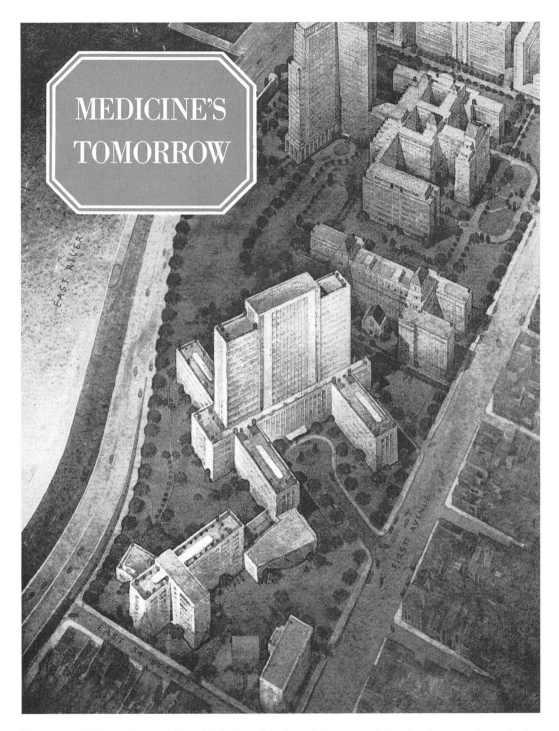

Figure 7.1. Bellevue Hospital, New York City, "Medicine's Tomorrow," sketch of proposed new facility by SOM architects, 1945, © SOM. Remnants of buildings from the 1904 master plan are visible in the upper right-hand corner of the drawing.

hospital construction would be based on prewar designs. The law was intended to remedy the shortage of hospital beds, particularly in rural areas and small communities. It provided money to improve existing hospitals, to build new hospitals, and to add hospitals to all states to bring them up to the average of 4.5 beds per 1,000 people. According to Rosemary Stevens, in the first twenty years following the act there were 4,678 projects, about half of them in communities with a population of under ten thousand.[2] To get those monies, however, required adhering to minimum standards and guidelines for the construction of the hospital buildings. Those standards, as put forth in the critical Appendix A of the act, were based on pre-Depression hospital design practices.

The Hill-Burton Act thus became a force not only for the standardization of hospitals across the country and expansion of service to all communities, but for the continuation of existing hospital design practices. Architect Thomas Ellerbe believed that hospitals built according to the Hill-Burton guidelines would "probably be years out-of-date when compared to new designs already on the drawing boards." In order to build a hospital of a more innovative plan, administrators and designers had to be willing to forgo the government funding. A few did, but the vast majority of postwar hospital construction projects elevated access to government money over design innovation. The result, according to historian Paul Starr, was that the hospital act led to an oversupply of functionally obsolete hospitals, since "the standard for hospitals was impervious to changes in medical practice, such as the growing belief in early ambulation instead of extended bed rest after surgery."[3]

Despite Hill-Burton's prolongation of prewar hospital design strategies, postwar hospital buildings finally began to escape the fundamental dictates of hygienic design. The widespread use of antibiotics solved the problem of nosocomial infections (the modern equivalent of hospital diseases), not by disproving the link between the quality and conditions of a person's surroundings and the incidence of infection, but by rendering that link irrelevant. Antibiotics provided an effective treatment rather than an effective prevention. Infections continued to occur, but patients no longer died from them. This freed hospital design from more than a century of design limitations based on preventing internal disease incidence.

The postwar hospital building no longer necessarily maximized the penetration of the "healthy" exterior environment into the interior. Instead, designers, seeking a controlled, comfortable interior environment, sought to recreate desirable conditions artificially. Decontaminating ultraviolet light units replaced the antiseptic influence of abundant sunshine. The individual room-unit air conditioner replaced the individual open window for each patient, and the windows themselves were often inoperable. The natural world became largely a view out of a window.

By the 1950s some hospital designers arranged the hospital building as if it were any other building type—requiring a layout that facilitated what happened within it rather than dictating an integral relationship to sunlight and fresh air. The "donut" or "racetrack" plan hospital building (as in the Archbishop Bergan Mercy Hospital in Omaha by Leo A. Daly or the "Cube" addition to Bellevue Hospital in New York City of 1973 by Feld, Kaminetzky and Cohen) resembled an office building floor plan far more than it resembled earlier hospital buildings.[4] It also contained extensive areas of interior space, with absolutely no access to fresh air or sunlight.

These new, more compact plans were a good match to the ongoing trend toward larger, more complex institutions, which continued unabated in the postwar period. By the 1960s medical centers and their surrounding services might constitute small cities in themselves. Some—like the Columbia-Presbyterian Medical Center or the New York Hospital–Cornell Medical Center—were concentrated vertical neighborhoods within a larger city. In other locales, where the age of the automobile had developed more dispersed urban development, the greater suburbanization rate and the availability of open land led to the creation of medical centers that constituted separate satellite cities of large urban metro areas. The individual hospital buildings within these medical cities, however, were often vertically arranged even when built on open farmland well outside city limits.

The Texas Medical Center is the epitome of such development. The seven-story Hermann Hospital first opened outside of Houston in 1925. It was joined in 1938 by the twelve-story Jefferson Davis Hospital. By 1940 city and county officials worked to create a hospital district; the Texas State Cancer Hospital (named the M. D. Anderson Hospital of Cancer Research of the University of Texas), the Baylor University College of Medicine, and a hundred-bed naval hospital all joined the neighborhood by 1944. In 1945, the grouping of hospitals in the Houston suburbs gained a charter as the Texas Medical Center. Though independently designed as separate institutions rather than as a single conglomerate whole, the hospitals were largely vertically planned and of ten or more stories. The hospitals required thousands of staff members and drew thousands of patients from across the state and even the country. Hotels, restaurants, and other services soon hovered around the hospitals, providing the missing urban services. The medical center became a town; the town became a city. Texas Medical Center is now the largest medical center in the world, and contains a collection of high-rises that rivals downtown Houston for its density. That scale, and the layout of building plans within these centers, rely on designs that cater to

Figure 7.2. Texas Medical Center, outside Houston, aerial view. The modern hospital is a city unto itself.

efficiency rather than to the creation of an environment that plays any role in therapy or prevention.

This period of design freedom was short-lived, however. As had been experienced with earlier disease prevention strategies (like pavilion-ward hospital design, antiseptic surgery, and aseptic procedures), an initial highly successful period of antibiotic treatment of nosocomial infections was followed by a resurgence of incidence, this time the result of the development of antibiotic resistant strains. By the 1970s the incidence of nosocomial infections was so high that a number of hospital administrators considered shutting down their facilities rather than continuing to produce hospital-acquired infections. Desperate to trace the route of infection, hospital practitioners used what Robert Hyde Jacobs described as a shotgun approach to the problem—considering and addressing all possible routes of infection, including direct contact, indirect contact, and the physical environment. This meant stricter asepsis, more intensive decontamination procedures, and a return to the use of improved ventilation as a means of prevention. Sir John Charnley reported reduced wound infection rates in the Wrightington Hospital in the United Kingdom from 9 percent to 1 percent between the 1960s and 1970s partly as a result of an ultraclean air system that reduced airborne pathogens in the surgical field. The problem also led to the creation of an entirely new profession with the formation of the Association of Practitioners of Infection Control (APIC) in 1972.[5]

In the twenty-first century, even though our understanding of disease causation and transmission is far more certain and accurate than it was in the early nineteenth century, and despite antibiotics, asepsis, antiseptics, epidemiology, microbiology, and extensive environmental technologies and controls, hospital-acquired infections and hospital-generated antibiotic-resistant pathogens continue to plague us. Environment is no longer considered either the generating influence or the primary means of disease transmission, but that it is still an influence is clear. Given the scale of the current problem with nosocomial infections, concerns about air quality and movement in hospitals have experienced a resurgence. Ultraviolet air filters are installed in ICUs, studies showing that there is extensive air infiltration between separate zones within the same building have prompted redesigns of ventilation systems, and there has been discussion of setting uniform standards of aerobiological quality for hospitals. Recent research by microbial biologists like James Meadow and his collaborators, however, has proven that the germ landscape is as varied and pervasive as the human landscape. People give off their own individual aerial "plumes" of germs.[6] This inevitably brings concerns about air quality, air movement, and germ reservoirs in the building's interstices or on the materials back to the foreground. This return to a more environmentally inclusive view of hospital cross-infections is not, by any means, the same understanding as was prevalent in the nineteenth century; nor is it expressive of the same idea of a modern hospital as existed in the early twentieth century. But without knowing the past, those differences are mute. This book is a first tentative step toward knowing that past.

Environment and Health

Which creates health—the world we inhabit, or the actions taken within it? If it is the former, then how we build is crucial to our well-being; if the latter, then how we build is crucial to our performance of those actions. This book has revealed the history of American hospital design to be an oscillation between considerations of the building as a therapy or as a tool. Nineteenth-century hospital designers emphasized environmental therapy (and prevention); twentieth-century hospital designers increasingly considered the hospital building as a tool in the performance of sociospatial practices (medical, administrative, social, acculturative). But the shift has never been complete. If the nineteenth-century hospital practitioner valued sunshine and fresh air in overabundance as a means of cure, reform, and disease prevention, the mid-twentieth-century hospital practitioner valued them as emotionally therapeutic influences. The mid-twentieth-century hospital practitioner considered the facilitation of sociospatial practices as the ultimate role of hospital design, yet the nineteenth-century practitioners struggled to make their buildings efficient for the practice of medicine. If hospital designers in the early twenty-first century are returning to an understanding of the possible value of the building materials and details in health, it is not the same as either of the preceding views. Similarly, if modern functional medical practices have become so byzantine as to create a hospital building chaotic and inhuman enough to be seen as inherently unhealthy, rethinking the role of a building in therapy, cure, and healing does not imply a blind return to older hygienic ideas.

Is it possible to rethink hospital design as a product of both medical efficiency and environmental therapy? The answer to that requires examination of the potential interaction of individuals and their physical surroundings in a new way—one that does not shy away from the study of the link between surroundings and well-being, but also one that seeks knowledge rather than the evocation of a universalizing architecture that will induce health as defined by the individual designer or dominant cultural group.

This book has presumed the hospital building (and in fact, all buildings) to be both potential therapy and potential tool. The hospital is both a medical factory and a healing environment. To perceive both aspects as equally important requires fusing two existing but opposing approaches to built structures. Current scholarship on building history and design examines either how people came to conceive, design, and build a specific building form at a specific time or how a built structure limited, altered, or enabled the social structure and functional intentions of its series of inhabitants. The former emphasizes the influence of people on their surroundings; the latter emphasizes the influence of the surroundings on people.

The duality is an illusion. People and their surroundings are fatefully, perhaps even fatally, entwined. This work has tried to understand the history of hospital design not simply as a product of its times or a confining structure on future possibilities, but as both and more. Medicine alone did not make the hospital what it is; the hospital building did not make scientific medicine what it is. Yet the two are connected. To imagine modern scientific medicine is to imagine a spatial pattern for it. Most commonly, what is imagined is a hospital—a building so structured by the functional requirements of medical practice that generations of historians have understood hospital design as contingent on medical practices. It was. But the modern hospital has also been built upon the bones of an older medical practice that presumed that a person's surroundings played an integral role in their physiological as well as mental health. In more concrete terms, the history of hospital buildings is more than a history of changing details, materials, forms, and technologies in service of an increasingly limited physiological definition of health; it is a chronicle of aspirations and disappointments as to the role architecture might play in a more inclusive conception of health.

Notes

Frequently Used Abbreviations

Archives/Repositories/Collections

MCANYPWC	Medical Center Archives New York–Presbyterian/Weill Cornell
STP	Secretary-Treasurer Papers
BGM	Minutes, Board of Governors of the New York Hospital
VCM	Minutes, Visiting Committee, Board of Governors of the New York Hospital
MSHA	Mount Sinai Archives, Levy Library, Icahn School of Medicine at Mount Sinai
HO	Historian's Office, Mount Sinai Hospital Files, 1852-1955
NYAM	New York Academy of Medicine
NYHS	New York Historical Society
NLM	National Library of Medicine

Periodicals

MH	*Modern Hospital*
AA	*American Architect*
AABN	*American Architect and Building News*
BB	*Brickbuilder*
AF	*Architectural Forum*

AREC	*Architectural Record*
AREV	*Architectural Review*
TN	*Trained Nurse*
TN&HR	*Trained Nurse and Hospital Review*
JAMA	*Journal of the American Medical Association*
BMSJ	*Boston Medical and Surgical Journal*
NYT	*New York Times*
AR	*Annual Report* (exact title varies with individual institution).
BHM	*Bulletin of the History of Medicine*
JSAH	*Journal of the Society of Historians*
JHMAS	*Journal of the History of Medicine and Allied Sciences*

Introduction

Epigraphs: "Sanitary Engineering," *American Architect and Building News* 12, no. 359 (11 Nov. 1882), 231; *Oxford English Dictionary* online, s.v. "hospital."

1. See Charles E. Rosenberg, *The Care of Strangers: The Rise of America's Hospital System* (New York: Basic Books, 1987); Paul Starr, *The Social Transformation of American Medicine* (New York: Basic Books, 1982); Rosemary Stevens, *In Sickness and in Wealth: American Hospitals in the Twentieth Century* (New York: Basic Books, 1989); Guenter Risse, *Mending Bodies, Saving Souls: A History of Hospitals* (New York: Oxford University Press, 1999); David Rosner, *A Once Charitable Enterprise: Hospitals and Health Care in Brooklyn and New York, 1885–1915* (New York: Cambridge University Press, 1982); Joel D. Howell, *Technology in the Hospital: Transforming Patient Care in the Early Twentieth Century* (Baltimore: Johns Hopkins University Press, 1995); Kenneth M. Ludmerer, *Learning to Heal: The Development of American Medical Education* (New York: Basic Books, 1985); Kenneth Ludmerer, *Time to Heal: American Medical Education from the Turn of the Century to the Era of Managed Care* (Oxford: Oxford University Press, 1999); John Harley Warner, *The Therapeutic Perspective: Medical Practice, Knowledge, and Identity in America, 1820–1885* (Cambridge, MA: Harvard University Press, 1988); and Morris J. Vogel, *The Invention of the Modern Hospital: Boston, 1870–1930* (Chicago: University of Chicago Press, 1980).

2. Cameron Logan, Philip Goad, and Julie Willis, "Modern Hospitals as Historic Places," *Journal of Architecture* 15, no. 5 (2010), 601–19.

3. Annmarie Adams diagrammed this historical gap as the years 1916–1939; the period of 1870–1916 was equally unconsidered. Adams, "'That was Then, This is Now': Hospital Architecture in the Age(s) of Revolution, 1970–2001," in *The Impact of Hospitals: 300–2000,* ed. John Henderson, Peregrine Horden, and Alessandro Pastore (New York: Peter Lang, 2007), 223–24. Examples of works focusing on hospitals up to the 1850s include: Christine Stevenson, *Medicine and Magnificence: British Hospital and Asylum Architecture, 1660–1815* (New Haven, CT: Yale University Press, 2000); Dieter Jetter, *Geschichte des Hospitals: Westdeutschland von den anfängen bis 1850* (Wiesbaden: Franz Steiner, 1966); Michel Foucault, ed., *Les màchines á guérir: aux origines de l'hôpital moderne* (Brussels: Pierre Mardaga, 1979); and Robert Bruegmann, "Architecture of the Hospital: 1770–1870, Design and Technology" (PhD diss., University of Pennsylvania, 1976). Examples of works focusing on post-1940s hospital design include: Stephen Verderber and David J. Fine, *Healthcare Architecture in an Era of Radical Transformation* (New Haven, CT: Yale University Press, 2000); David Charles Sloane and Beverlie Conant Sloane, *Medicine Moves to the Mall* (Baltimore:

Johns Hopkins University Press, 2003); Cor Wagenaar, ed., *The Architecture of Hospitals* (Rotterdam: NAi, 2006); Stephen Verderber, *Innovations in Hospital Architecture* (New York: Routledge, 2010); Paul James and Tony Noakes, *Hospital Architecture* (New York: Longman, 1994); and Richard Miller and Earl S. Swensson, *Hospital and Healthcare Facility Design*, 3rd ed. (New York: W. W. Norton, 2012).

4. Stone, "Hospitals: The Heroic Years," *Architect's Journal* 50, no. 164 (15 Dec. 1976), 1127. This list of examples is extracted from John D. Thompson and Grace Goldin, *The Hospital: A Social and Architectural History* (New Haven, CT: Yale University Press, 1975), 187–97; Allan M. Brandt and David C. Sloane, "Of Beds and Benches: Building the Modern American Hospital," in *The Architecture of Science*, ed. Peter Galison and Emily Thompson (Cambridge, MA: MIT Press, 1999), 288–92; Cor Wagenaar, "Five Revolutions: A Short History of Hospital Architecture," in Wagenaar, *Architecture of Hospitals*, 29–36; Adrian Forty, "The Modern Hospital in France and England," in *Buildings and Society: Essays on the Social Development of the Built Environment*, ed. Anthony D. King (London: Routledge and Kegan Paul, 1980), 83–88; and Sloane and Sloane, *Medicine Moves to the Mall*, 40–53.

5. Jeremy Taylor, *The Architect and the Pavilion Hospital: Dialogue and Design Creativity in England, 1850–1914* (London: Leicester University Press, 1997); Sven-Olov Wallenstein, *Biopolitics and the Emergence of Modern Architecture* (New York: Princeton Architectural Press, 2009), 63–79; Sloane and Sloane, *Medicine Moves to the Mall*, 30–66; Annmarie Adams, *Medicine by Design: The Architect and the Modern Hospital, 1893–1943* (Minneapolis: University of Minnesota Press, 2008), xxv.

6. Thompson and Goldin, *Hospital*, xxvii; Henry E. Sigerist, "An Outline of the Development of the Hospital," *BHM* 4, no. 7 (1936), 579; Prior, "The Architecture of the Hospital: A Study of Spatial Organization and Medical Knowledge," *British Journal of Sociology* 39, no. 1 (1988), 93.

7. Michel Foucault, *The Birth of the Clinic: An Archaeology of Medical Perception*, trans. A. M. Sheridan Smith (New York: Vintage Books, 1973); Adams, *Medicine by Design*, xix; Annmarie Adams, Kevin Schwartzman, and David Theodore, "Collapse and Expand: Architecture and Tuberculosis Therapy in Montreal, 1909, 1933, 1954," *Technology and Culture* 49, no. 4 (2008), 941; Adams, "Hospital Architecture in the Age(s) of Revolution," 232. See also Foucault, *Les màchines á guérir*; Taylor, *Architect and the Pavilion Hospital*; David Theodore, "'The Fattest Possible Nurse': Architecture, Computers, and Post-War Nursing," in *Hospital Life: Theory and Practice from the Medieval to the Modern*, ed. Laurinda Abreu and Sally Sheard (New York: Peter Lang, 2013).

8. Wallenstein, *Biopolitics*; Michel Foucault, *The Birth of Biopolitics: Lectures at the Collège de France, 1978–1989*, trans. Graham Burchell (Basingstoke, England: Palgrave Macmillan, 2008); Adams, *Medicine by Design*, 50, 71–88; Adams, Schwartzmann, and Theodore, "Collapse and Expand," 936; Annmarie Adams and Stacie Burke, "'Not a Shack in the Woods': Architecture for Tuberculosis in Muskoka and Toronto," *Canadian Bulletin of the History of Medicine* 23, no. 2 (2006), 440; Thomas Schlich, "Surgery, Science and Modernity: Operating Rooms and Laboratories as Spaces of Control," *History of Science* 45, no. 3 (2007), 231–56; Annmarie Adams and Thomas Schlich, "Design for Control: Surgery, Science, and Space at the Royal Victoria Hospital, Montreal, 1893–1956," *Medical History* 50, no. 3 (2006), 303–24; J. T. H. Connor, "Bigger than a Bread Box: Medical Buildings as Museum Artifacts," *Caduceus* 9, no. 2 (1993), 119–30.

9. On the emphasis on plans, see Adams, "Modernism and Medicine: The Hospitals of Stevens and Lee, 1916–1932," *JSAH* 58, no. 1 (1999), 45.

10. Other hospital studies have highlighted this therapeutic expectation. See Brueg-mann, "Architecture of the Hospital"; Foucault, *Les màchines á guérir*; Jeanne Kisacky, "An Architecture of Light and Air," (PhD diss., Cornell University, 2000); Adams, Schwartz-mann, and Theodore, "Collapse and Expand," 912. It is also evident in studies on other kinds of buildings; for example, see David J. Rothman, *The Discovery of the Asylum: Social Order and Disorder in the New Republic* (Boston: Little, Brown, 1971); David Schuyler, *The New Urban Landscape: The Redefinition of City Form in Nineteenth-Century America* (Balti-more: Johns Hopkins University Press, 1986); Paul Boyer, *Urban Masses and Moral Order in America, 1820–1920* (Cambridge, MA: Harvard University Press, 1978); Carla Yanni, *The Architecture of Madness* (Minneapolis: University of Minnesota Press, 2007); James C. Riley, *The Eighteenth-Century Campaign to Avoid Disease* (New York: St. Martin's, 1987); Victoria Ozonoff, "Medicine, Social Reform, and the Built Environment" (PhD diss., Bos-ton University, 1984).

Chapter 1. The Hospital Building as a Means of Disease Prevention, 1700–1873

Epigraphs: Thomas K. Cruse, "The Treatment of Compound Fractures of the Leg, at Bellev-ue Hospital," *Medical Record* 7, no. 4 (15 Apr. 1872), 140; William Hammond, *A Treatise on Hygiene, with Special Reference to the Military Service* (Philadelphia: J. B. Lippincott, 1863), 16.

1. Cruse, "Treatment of Compound Fractures of the Leg," 140. See also the bibliograph-ic essay, section on miasma and environmental medicine.

2. George Hayward, "History of the Erysipelatous Inflammation That Recently Ap-peared in the Massachusetts General Hospital," *New England Medical Review and Journal* 16 (1827), 284–94, 291, 293; Hammond, *Treatise on Hygiene*, 171; "Hospital diseases" would now be considered cross-infections, secondary infections, or nosocomial infections. See also Graham A. J. Ayliffe and Mary P. English, *Hospital Infections: From Miasmas to MRSA* (Cambridge: Cambridge University Press, 2003), 28–90; and Christine Stevenson, *Medi-cine and Magnificence: British Hospital and Asylum Architecture, 1660–1815* (New Haven, CT: Yale University Press, 2000), 155–94. Erysipelas is a bacterial infection that can produce a telltale red rash on the skin. "Hospital gangrene" has most often been equated with necro-tizing fasciitis, a rapidly spreading bacterial infection that consumes flesh.

3. Jail fever plagued Bellevue Hospital in 1825, 1837, and throughout the 1840s (Mc-Cready, "Address," in Alms House, New York City, AR 8 [1856]: 14–15). Erysipelas again closed the Massachusetts General Hospital's doors in 1832 (N. I. Bowditch, *A History of the Massachusetts General Hospital* [Boston: John Wilson and Son, 1851], 101). Hospital gan-grene and typhus plagued the New York Hospital in 1835 and in the 1850s ("Committee to Enquire into the Causes and Prevalence of Erysipelas in the Hospital" and responses, in STP, B1/F2, MCANYPWC; and John H. Griscom, "Hospital Hygiene," *Transactions of the New York Academy of Medicine* 1, no. 2 [1853], 167–78). Pneumonia ravaged the Charity Hospital in New Orleans in 1860 ("Dr. Flint's Cases at the Charity Hospital," *New Orleans Medical News and Hospital Gazette* 7, no. 5 [July 1860], 427–28). See also Edward D. Chur-chill, "The Pandemic of Wound Infection in Hospitals: Studies in the History of Wound Healing," *Journal of the History of Medicine* 20 (Oct. 1965), 390–404.

4. Starr, "Medicine, Economy and Society in Nineteenth-Century America," in *The Medicine Show: Patients, Physicians and the Perplexities of the Health Revolution in Modern Society*, ed. Patricia Branca (New York: Science History Publications, 1977), 51; John Duffy,

The Healers: The Rise of the Medical Establishment (New York: McGraw-Hill, 1976), 57; Elizabeth Blackmar, *Manhattan for Rent, 1785–1850* (Ithaca, NY: Cornell University Press, 1989); Elizabeth Collins Cromley, *Alone Together: A History of New York's Early Apartments* (Ithaca, NY: Cornell University Press, 1999); Herbert G. Gutman, *Work, Culture, and Society in Industrializing America: Essays in American Working-Class and Social History* (New York: Vintage, 1977); and David J. Rothman, *The Discovery of the Asylum: Social Order and Disorder in the New Republic* (Boston: Little, Brown, 1971).

5. Thomas P. Gariepy, "The Introduction and Acceptance of Listerian Antisepsis in the United States," *JHMAS* 49 (1994), 178; John Aikin, *Thoughts on Hospitals* ([London]: 1771), 13; Jacques Tenon, *Mémoires sur les hôpitaux de Paris* (Paris: De l'Imprimerie de Ph.-D. Pierres, 1788); John Roberton, "On the Defects, with Reference to the Plan of Construction and Ventilation, of Most of Our Hospitals for the Reception of the Sick and Wounded," *Transactions of the Manchester Statistical Society* (1855–56), 133–48; John Howard, *An Account of the Principal Lazarettos in Europe with Various Papers Relative to the Plague* (London: J. Johnson, C. Dilly, and T. Cadell, 1789).

6. Henry E. Sigerist, *Landmarks in the History of Hygiene* (New York: Oxford University Press, 1956); Hayward, "History of the Erysipelatous Inflammation," 284–94.

7. John Henderson, *The Renaissance Hospital: Healing the Body and Healing the Soul* (New Haven, CT: Yale University Press, 2006); John D. Thompson and Grace Goldin, *The Hospital: A Social and Architectural History* (New Haven, CT: Yale University Press, 1975), 15–40. See also bibliographic essay: histories of hospital design to the late eighteenth century.

8. See the bibliographic essay: histories of hospital design to the late eighteenth century.

9. David Charles Sloane and Beverlie Conant Sloane, *Medicine Moves to the Mall* (Baltimore: Johns Hopkins University Press, 2003), 33–40; Thompson and Goldin, *Hospital*, 96–104. On comparative European institutions, see Stevenson, *Medicine and Magnificence*; Robert Bruegmann, "Architecture of the Hospital: 1770–1870, Design and Technology" (PhD diss., University of Pennsylvania, 1976).

10. Benjamin Franklin, *Some Account of the Pennsylvania Hospital, From Its First Rise, to the Beginning of the Fifth Month, Called May, 1754* (Philadelphia, 1854), 21; John E. Ransom, "The Beginnings of Hospitals in the United States," *BHM* 13, no. 5 (May 1943), 514–39.

11. Holmes, "Currents and Counter-currents in Medical Science," as quoted in *American Journal of the Medical Sciences* 40 (1860), 467; Morris J. Vogel, *The Invention of the Modern Hospital: Boston, 1870–1930* (Chicago: University of Chicago Press, 1980), 9. See also Charles Rosenberg, "The Practice of Medicine in New York a Century Ago," *BHM* 41, no. 3 (1967), 223–53.

12. Therapeutic nihilism was in vogue in Paris medicine in the early 1800s; it was imported by American medical students and young doctors who studied in French clinics in the 1820s and 1830s—see Richard Harrison Shryock, *The Development of Modern Medicine: An Interpretation of the Social and Scientific Factors Involved* (New York: Alfred A. Knopf, 1947), 211–23; John Harley Warner, "'The Nature-Trusting Heresy': American Physicians and the Concept of the Healing Power of Nature in the 1850's and 1860's," *Perspectives in American History* 11 (1977–78), 291–324; Warner, *The Therapeutic Perspective: Medical Practice, Knowledge, and Identity in America, 1820–1885* (Cambridge, MA: Harvard University Press, 1988), 240–43; Suellen Hoy, *Chasing Dirt: The American Pursuit of Cleanliness* (New York: Oxford University Press, 1995), 23–27.

13. Shryock, *Development of Modern Medicine*, 42. On the involvement of American doctors in founding and determining the spatial requirements of early American hospitals, see, e.g., Samuel Bard, *A Discourse Upon the Duties of a Physician* (New York: A. & J. Rob-

ertson, 1769), 7; *A Brief Account of the New York Hospital* (New York: Isaac Collins and Son, 1804); Drs. Jackson and Warren, "Circular Letter," 3 Aug. 1810, as quoted in Bowditch, *A History of the Massachusetts General Hospital*, 8fn; and Frederic Shephard Dennis, *A Memoir of James R. Wood* (New York: D. Appleton, 1884), 11.

14. Judith Walzer Leavitt, "'A Worrying Profession': The Domestic Environment of Medical Practice in Mid-Nineteenth-Century America," *BHM* 69, no. 1 (1995), 1–29; Starr, *The Social Transformation of American Medicine* (New York: Basic Books, 1982), 20; Waddington, "The Role of the Hospital in the Development of Modern Medicine: A Sociological Analysis," *Sociology* 7, no. 2 (1973), 218.

15. Warner, *Therapeutic Perspective*, 58; Michel Foucault, *The Birth of the Clinic: An Archaeology of Medical Perception*, trans. A. M. Sheridan Smith (New York: Vintage Books, 1973), 1973; Michel Foucault, ed., *Les màchines á guérir: aux origines de l'hôpital moderne* (Brussels: Pierre Mardaga, 1979).

16. Duffy, *Healers*, 190; Jews' Hospital, New York City, *AR* (1856), 12.

17. Rosemary Stevens, *In Sickness and in Wealth: American Hospitals in the Twentieth Century* (New York: Basic Books, 1989), 17–30. A third hospital category, proprietary hospitals, remains largely outside of my research. Founded, funded, and administered by an owner-physician for private patients, these were typically housed in a physician's office or converted building, rarely in buildings just for hospital purposes.

18. By the 1850s the Charity Hospital in New York City was planned for 832 beds (but often held more than 1,200); the Charity Hospital in New Orleans held nearly 1,000 beds; and Bellevue Hospital in New York City held roughly 1,200 beds. On European hospitals at the time, see Thompson and Goldin, *Hospital*, 79–150; Stevenson, *Medicine and Magnificence*; Harriet Richardson, ed., *English Hospitals, 1660–1948: A Survey of Their Architecture and Design* (Swindon: Royal Commission on the Historical Monuments of England, 1998); Foucault, *Les machines à guérir*, 1977; Dieter Jetter, *Das Europäische Hospital: von der Spätantike bis 1800* (Köln: DuMont, 1986); Adrian Forty, "The Modern Hospital in France and England," in *Buildings and Society: Essays on the Social Development of the Built Environment*, ed. Anthony D. King (Boston: Routledge and Kegan Paul, 1980), 61–93.

19. Upon opening, the Jews' Hospital in New York City held fifty beds; Saint Vincent's in New York City started with thirty; Saint Luke's Hospital in New York City opened with two hundred; and by the 1850s, the New York Hospital held roughly four hundred beds. Admission to a voluntary hospital required medical examinations to determine if the candidate's ailment was curable, but also personal interviews by the hospital's administrators to determine if the candidate was morally acceptable (Charles E. Rosenberg, *The Care of Strangers: The Rise of America's Hospital System* [New York: Basic Books, 1987], 22–27).

20. Kraut, *Silent Travelers: Germs, Genes, and the "Immigrant Menace"* (Baltimore: Johns Hopkins University Press, 1994). David Rosner emphasizes the community nature of many of these early hospitals, and describes the ways in which they reflected neighborhood composition but also local needs. Rosner, *A Once Charitable Enterprise: Hospitals and Health Care in Brooklyn and New York, 1885–1915* (New York: Cambridge University Press, 1982), 13–35; Rosner, "Social Control and Social Service: The Changing Use of Space in Charity Hospitals," *Radical History Review* 21 (Fall 1979), 186–87.

21. Lindsay Granshaw, "'Fame and Fortune by Means of Brick and Mortar': The Medical Profession and Specialist Hospitals in Britain, 1800–1948," in *The Hospital in History*, ed. Lindsay Granshaw and Roy Porter (New York: Routledge, 1989), 199–222. See also George Weisz, *Divide and Conquer: A Comparative History of Medical Specialization* (Oxford: Oxford University Press, 2006). Smallpox Hospital in New York City opened in 1837.

The Lying-In Hospital of the City of New York traces its origins to 1798; the New York Asylum for Lying-In Women to 1823; the Boston Lying-In Hospital opened in 1832. The New York Eye Infirmary opened in 1820, and became the New York Eye and Ear Infirmary in 1823. The Massachusetts Eye and Ear Hospital of Boston was founded in 1824; the Wills Eye Hospital in Philadelphia opened in 1834; the New York Ophthalmic Hospital opened in 1852.

22. Richardson, *English Hospitals*, 15, 104–31

23. Population statistics compiled from Jane Allen, "Population," in *The Encyclopedia of New York City*, ed. Kenneth T. Jackson (New York: New-York Historical Society and Yale University Press, 1995) 910–14. Hospital statistics compiled from Theodore Lorenz, "Hospitals and Dispensaries in New York City. Historical Outline" [New York: 1939], NYAM; J. M. Toner, "Statistics of Regular Medical Associations and Hospitals of the United States," *Transactions of the American Medical Association* 24 (1873), 284–333, 314; US Bureau of the Census, *Historical Statistics of the United States, Colonial Times to 1970* (Washington, DC: Department of Commerce, 1975), 78; and Starr, *Social Transformation of American Medicine*, 73. Charles Rosenberg has discussed contextual urban, social, and medical reasons for this hospital growth (including immigration, changing ideas of health, and industrialization. Rosenberg, *Care of Strangers*, 97–114. See also George Rosen, "The Hospital, Historical Sociology of a Community Institution," in *The Hospital in Modern Society*, ed. Eliot Friedson (London: Free Press of Glencoe, 1963), 29; David B. Lovejoy, Jr., "The Hospital and Society: The Growth of Hospitals in Rochester, New York, in the Nineteenth Century," *BHM* 49, no. 4 (1975), 536–55.

24. Cynthia Imogen Hammond, "Reforming Architecture, Defending Empire: Florence Nightingale and the Pavilion Hospital," in *(Un) Healthy Interiors: Contestations at the Intersection of Public Health and Private Space*, ed. Aran S. MacKinnon and Jonathan Ablard, Studies in the Social Sciences University of West Georgia 38 (Carrollton, GA: University of West Georgia, 2005), 1–25; Carol Helmstadter and Judith Godden, *Nursing before Nightingale, 1815–1899* (Burlington, VT: Ashgate, 2011); Christopher J. Gill and Gillian C. Gill, "Nightingale in Scutari: Her Legacy Reexamined," *Clinical Infectious Diseases* 40, no. 12 (2005), 1799–805; Florence Nightingale, *Notes on Hospitals: Being Two Papers . . .* (London: John W. Parker and Son, 1859); Florence Nightingale, *Notes on Hospitals*, 3rd ed. (London: Longman, Green, Longman, Roberts, and Green, 1863), 5–8; Louise C. Selanders, *Florence Nightingale: An Environmental Adaptation Theory* (London: Sage Publications, 1993), 17-18. See also Rosenberg, "Florence Nightingale on Contagion: The Hospital as Moral Universe," in *Healing and History: Essays for George Rosen*, ed. Rosenberg (New York: Science History Publications, 1979), 118; Rosenberg, *Care of Strangers*, 122–41; Anthony King, "Hospital Planning: Revised Thoughts on the Origin of the Pavilion Principle in England," *Medical History* 10 (1966), 360–73; Nancy Boyd, *Three Victorian Women Who Changed Their World: Josephine Butler, Octavia Hill, Florence Nightingale* (New York: Oxford University Press, 1982), 211.

25. Grace Goldin, "Building a Hospital of Air: The Victorian Pavilions of St. Thomas' Hospital, London," *BHM* 49, no. 4 (1975), 516; Jeremy Taylor, *The Architect and the Pavilion Hospital: Dialogue and Design Creativity in England, 1850–1914* (London: Leicester University Press, 1997), 49; King, "Hospital Planning," 360–73; Rosenberg, *Care of Strangers*, 122–41; Thompson and Goldin, *Hospital*, 165; Hammond, "Reforming Architecture," 11–12.

26. Armand Husson, *Étude sur les hôpitaux* (Paris: Paul Dupont, Imprimeur de l'Administration de l'Assistance Publique, 1862); F. Oppert, *Hospitals, Infirmaries and Dispensaries: Their Construction, Interior Arrangement, and Management . . .* (London: John

Churchill and Sons, 1867); C. H. Esse, *Die Krankenhäuser: ihre Einrichtung und Verwaltung* (Berlin: Von Th. Chr. Fr. Enslin, 1868); Douglas Galton, *An Address on the General Principles Which Should Be Observed in the Construction of Hospitals, . . .* (London: Macmillan, 1869); Charles Lee, *Hospital Construction with Notices of Foreign Military Hospitals* (Albany: Steam Press of C. Van Benthuysen, 1863); Stephen Smith, *Principles of Hospital Construction, Being an Abstract of a Report on Hospital Construction Made to the Trustees of the Roosevelt Hospital* (New York: Holman, 1866), Collection of NLM; John Shaw Billings, *A Report on Barracks and Hospitals with Descriptions of Military Posts. Circular No. 4. Surgeon General's Office* (Washington: Government Printing Office, 1870).

27. Hammond, *Treatise on Hygiene*, 343; *An Account of the Proceedings at the Laying of the Corner-Stone of the New York State Emigrant Hospital on Ward's Island* (New York: John F. Trow, 1865), 12. The widespread adoption of pavilion-ward designs in the 1860s and early 1870s in the larger US cities contradicts a later assumption that the pavilion plan was popularized only after the Johns Hopkins Hospital (A. J. Ochsner, quoted in W. Gilman Thompson, "Modern Hospital Construction," *JAMA* 49, no. 12 [1907], 998).

28. Nightingale, *Notes on Hospitals*, 1863, 35; Board of Aldermen, New York City, *Report of the Special Committee upon the Memorial, Remonstrance, &c, of Sundry Physicians, Relative to a New Organization of the Hospital Department of the Almshouse* (New York: T. Snowden, 1837), 345–46.

29. German Hospital, New York City, *AR* (1857), 5; George R. Stuart, *A History of St. Vincent's Hospital in New York City* ([New York]: Private, 1938), 12–13.

30. "Report of board looking into the expediency of moving the asylum to outside the city," New York Hospital, BGM, 3 Dec. 1867, MCANYPWC; John Salvaggio, *New Orleans' Charity Hospital: A Story of Physicians, Politics, and Poverty* (Baton Rouge: Louisiana State University Press, 1992), 36. Reportedly, more than thirty-five thousand corpses were removed from the site of the Woman's Hospital during excavation. *Acts of Incorporation . . . with an Account of the Laying of the Cornerstone of the Women's Hospital*, 23 May 1866, 17. Examples of new hospital facilities built on sites beyond the city limits include the Pennsylvania Hospital, Presbyterian Hospital, Jewish Hospital, and Hospital of the Protestant Episcopal Church in Philadelphia; Massachusetts General Hospital, Boston Lying-In Hospital, City Hospital, and New England Hospital for Women and Children in Boston; Roosevelt Hospital, Woman's Hospital, Mount Sinai Hospital, Saint Luke's, and German Hospital in New York City; Touro Infirmary, the Hôtel-Dieu, and Charity Hospital in New Orleans; the Cincinnati General Hospital in Cincinnati; and City Hospital in Saint Louis.

31. Vogel, *Invention of the Modern Hospital*, 55; Leonard Paul Wershub, *One Hundred Years of Medical Progress. A History of the New York Medical College Flower and Fifth Avenue Hospitals* (Springfield, IL: Charles C. Thomas, 1967), 33; Frederick C. Irving, "Highlights in the History of the Boston Lying-In Hospital," *Canadian Medical Association Journal* 54 (Feb. 1946), 176.

32. Lenox Hill Hospital, New York City, *AR* (1981) 8; City of Boston, "Report of the Committee on a Free City Hospital," (Boston: J. E. Farwell, 1861), 8–9; George H. M. Rowe, "Historical Description of the Buildings and Grounds of the Boston City Hospital," in *A History of the Boston City Hospital from Its Foundation until 1904*, ed. David W. Cheever, A. Lawrence Mason, George W. Gay, and J. Bapst Blake (Boston: Municipal Printing Office, 1906), 6–7.

33. "Historical Notes," from Historian's Office, MSHA; Presbyterian Hospital, New York City, *AR* 5 (1873), 14; David Bryson Delavan, *Early Days of the Presbyterian Hospital in the City of New York* ([New York]: Published privately, 1926), 89–90.

34. Saint Luke's Hospital, New York City, *AR* 13 (1871), 9.

35. Physicians and Surgeons to Governors, New York Hospital, BGM, 1 March 1870, 6 Dec. 1870, MCANYPWC. See also "Necessity of a Public Hospital Down Town," *NYT*, 9 April 1866; "New-York Hospital. Change of Plans for Building—Necessity for a Down-Town Hospital," *NYT*, 30 Oct. 1869; "The Want of a Down-Town Hospital," *NYT*, 9 Dec. 1869.

36. "Want of a Down-Town Hospital."

37. "Bellevue Hospital: The Opinions of Leading Physicians as to the Building's Fitness for Hospital Purposes," *NYT*, 9 June 1873; "Report of the Committee on a Free City Hospital," 9–10. On the history of ambulances, see Ryan Corbett Bell, *The Ambulance: A History* (Jefferson, NC: McFarland, 2008).

38. Annmarie Adams, *Architecture in the Family Way: Doctors, Houses, and Women, 1870–1900* (Buffalo, NY: McGill-Queen's University Press, 1996); Nancy Tomes, *The Gospel of Germs: Men, Women, and the Microbe in American Life* (Cambridge, MA: Harvard University Press, 1998), 9, 58–60.

39. References to the difficulties of smoky chimneys, cold drafts, and poor ventilation abound in the literature of the time. See Sir John Soane, *Lectures on Architecture. As Delivered to the Students of the Royal Academy from 1809 to 1836 . . .* , ed. Arthur T. Bolton (London: Sir John Soane's Museum, No. 14, 1929), 189–90; Milne, "On the Ventilation of Living-Rooms, Domestic Offices," *Architectural Magazine* 1, no. 2 (1834), 64–70; Milne, "Observations on Some of the Causes of Defective Ventilation, and of Smoke in Public Rooms and in Dwelling-Houses," *Architectural Magazine* 2, no. 1 (1835), 27–31; Charles Sylvester, *The Philosophy of Domestic Economy . . .* (Nottingham: H. Barnett, 1819), 2–3, 8–9; Ure, "Official Report . . . Upon Bernhardt's Stove-Furnaces," *Architectural Magazine* 5 (1837), 31–42; and Walter Bernan [Robert Meikleham], *On the History of Warming and Ventilating Rooms and Buildings by Open Fires, Hypocausts . . .* , 1845.

40. John Aikin, *Thoughts on Hospitals* ([London]: n.p., 1771), 13. See also Jean-Baptiste Leroy, "Précis d'un ouvrage sur les hôpitaux," *Mémoires de l'Académie des Sciences* (Paris: 1787), 585–600; Tenon, *Mémoires sur les hôpitaux de Paris*; Roberton, "On the Defects," 133–48; Husson, *Étude sur les hôpitaux*; Oppert, *Hospitals, Infirmaries and Dispensaries*; Esse, *Die Krankenhäuser*; Howard, *Account of the Principal Lazarettos*.

41. John Jones, *Plain, Concise, Practical Remarks on the Treatment of Wounds and Fractures . . .* (New York: John Holt, 1775); William Paul Crillon Barton, *A Treatise, Containing a Plan for the Internal Organization and Government of Marine Hospitals in the United States . . .* (Philadelphia: Howard Parker for the author, 1814); James Tilton, *Economical Observations on Military Hospitals . . .* (Wilmington: Wilson, 1813), 15–53. Other American publications include Griscom, "Hospital Hygiene," 167–78; John Green, *City Hospitals* (Boston: Little, Brown, 1861); Hammond, *Treatise on Hygiene*; Smith, *Principles of Hospital Construction*, NLM; Billings, *Report on Barracks and Hospitals*; and John Maynard Woodworth, *Hospitals and Hospital Construction* (Washington, DC: US Marine Hospital Service, 1874).

42. Latrobe, "Report of B. Henry Latrobe, on His Design for a Marine Hospital," in Barton, *Treatise* (1814), 114.

43. Thomas G. Morton and Frank Woodbury, *The History of the Pennsylvania Hospital; 1751–1895* (Philadelphia: Times Printing House, 1895), 36–37; Sloane and Sloane, *Medicine Moves to the Mall*, 36; Cincinnati General Hospital, *AR* 32 (1892), 7; R. A. Brintnall, "Hospitals of Ohio, Past and Present, with Recommendations for Their Future," *MH* 20, no. 4 (Apr. 1923), 338–40.

44. New York Hospital, BGM, 10 March 1773, MCANYPWC; James William Beek-

man, *Centenary Address Delivered before the Society of the New York Hospital* ([New York]: Society of the New York Hospital, 1871), 41. Ritch designed Saint Luke's Hospital and the New York Nursery and Child's Hospital; Renwick designed a number of municipal hospitals, including the Smallpox Hospital, an addition to Bellevue Hospital and the Charity Hospital on Blackwell's Island. See also Mary Woods, *From Craft to Profession: The Practice of Architecture in Nineteenth-Century America* (Berkeley: University of California Press, 1999).

45. Spec. Committee on New South Building, New York Hospital, BGM, 15 Nov. 1852; 6 Jan. 1853; 21 Jan. 1853; 10 Feb. 1853; 19 Feb. 1853; 22 Feb. 1853; 28 Feb. 1853; 8 Mar. 1853; MCANYPWC; Hospital of the Protestant Episcopal Church, Philadelphia, AR (1860), 9. The prize money varied—from roughly $300 for the Boston Free City Hospital to $1,300 for the Presbyterian Hospital in New York City ("Free City Hospital," *BMSJ* 65, no. 16 [1862], 507–8; John Francis Richmond, *New York and Its Institutions, 1609–1871* [New York: E. B. Treat, 1872], 365).

46. N. S. Davis, "Mercy Hospital," *Chicago Medical Examiner*, 10 Sept. 1869, 531–34; *Report of the Committee on a Free City Hospital* (Boston: J. E. Farwell, 1861), 11–12; *Proceedings at the Dedication of the [Boston] City Hospital* (Boston: J. E. Farwell, 1865), 53; Thomas E. Vermilye, *Address at the Opening of the Roosevelt Hospital, November 2, 1871* (New York: Evening Post Steam Presses, 1871), 8–9; Smith, *Principles of Hospital Construction*, NLM; Pfeiffer, "Sanitary Relations of Health Principles of Architecture," *NYT*, 12 Nov. 1873; Pfeiffer, "Light: Its Sanatory Influence and Importance in Buildings," *American Architect* 2, no. 79 (30 June 1877), 205–8. Pfeiffer went on to design the German Hospital in New York City, the well-regarded Moses Taylor Hospital in Scranton, Pennsylvania, and an unbuilt project for the New York Hospital in 1868.

47. "Obituary—Carl Pfeiffer," *American Architect* 23, no. 648 (26 May 1888), 241.

48. Francis H. Brown, "Hospital Construction," *BMSJ* 65, no. 3 (22 Aug. 1861), 51. See also Hammond, *Treatise on Hygiene*, 322–23; Frank Hastings Hamilton, *A Treatise on Military Surgery and Hygiene* (New York: Bailliere Brothers, 1865), 127–29; Smith, *Principles of Hospital Construction*, NLM, 16–17.

49. "New Buildings," *NYT*, 15 May 1870; "The Hebrews. Laying the Corner-Stone of a New Jewish Hospital," *NYT*, 25 Nov. 1853.

50. Richard Morris Hunt, "General Description," in Presbyterian Hospital, New York City, AR 1 (1869), 31–34.

51. Walker Gill Wylie, *Hospitals: Their History, Organization, and Construction. Boylston Prize Essay of Harvard University, 1876* (New York: D. Appleton, 1877), 206.

52. The Ward's Island Emigrant Hospital provided 1,200 cubic feet of air per bed; the German Hospital, 1,431; Roosevelt, 1,404 to 1,700; Saint Luke's, 1,092; Boston City Hospital, 1,600; Mount Sinai, 1,400; and the Hospital of the Protestant Episcopal Church in Philadelphia, 2,000 cubic feet ("New State Emigrant Hospital, Ward's Island," *NYT*, 11 Aug. 1864; "A German Hospital," *NYT*, 17 July 1866; "The Roosevelt Hospital—Description of the Building," *NYT*, 9 Oct. 1869; "Description of the Building," in *An Account of St. Luke's Hospital . . .* [New York: Robert Craighead, 1860], 57; "New Buildings"; Green, *City Hospitals*, 46fn). See also Richard Harrison Shryock, "The History of Quantification in Medical Science," *Isis* 52, no. 168 (June 1961), 227.

53. See Galton, *Address on the General Principles*, 6–18; and Woodworth, *Hospitals and Hospital Construction*, 8. This emphasis on floor area could have effectively reduced cross-infections by reducing casual contact between patients—they would have had to get out of bed to touch each other.

54. Stevenson, *Medicine and Magnificence*, 155–71; Jeanne Kisacky, "Breathing Room:

Calculating an Architecture of Air," in *Geometrical Objects: Architecture and the Mathematical Sciences 1400–1800*, ed. Anthony Gerbino (New York: Springer, 2014); Warner, "'Nature-Trusting Heresy,'" 289–324. See the bibliographic essay: ventilation and air conditioning.

55. "Architectural Description of the Proposed Hospital Building," in Hospital of the Protestant Episcopal Church, Philadelphia, *AR* (1860), 30; "The New Roosevelt Hospital," *NYT*, 22 Jan. 1872.

56. Nursery and Child's Hospital, New York City, *AR*, 12 (1866), 8; "Architectural Description of the Proposed Hospital Building," 30. See also Hunt, "General Description," 31–34.

57. *Continuation of the Account*, 42–43; "Jew's Hospital of New York," *Occident and American Jewish Advocate* 13, no. 4 (July 1855), 185.

58. Stevenson, *Medicine and Magnificence*, 213–36; and Sylvester, *Philosophy of Domestic Economy*.

59. "Rhode Island Hospital," *BMSJ* 79 (15 Oct. 1868), 170–71, reprinted from *Providence Evening Bulletin*, 1 Oct. 1868; Hunt, "General Description," 31–34; "The Presbyterian Hospital," *NYT*, 28 June 1873.

60. "Specifications for Heating Apparatus," STP B5/f1, [1869], MCANYPWC; "The State Emigrant Hospital" *NYT*, 12 July 1866. See also Smith, *Principles of Hospital Construction*, NLM, 45; "Laying of the Corner-Stone of the Island Hospital," *NYT*, 23 July 1858; "The Roosevelt Hospital," *Medical Record* 6, no. 18 (15 Nov. 1871), 430; *Account of St. Luke's Hospital*, 32. The Hôpital Lariboisière outside Paris generated some of this interest in mechanical ventilation—see "Foreign Intelligence," *Medical News* 20, no. 235 (July 1862), 153; and Stevenson, *Medicine and Magnificence*, 155–71.

61. *Proceedings at the Dedication*, 12–13; "Hygiene—Building of Hospitals," *New Orleans Medical News and Hospital Gazette* 6, no. 2 (Jan. 1859), 869–70; "The State Emigrant Hospital," *NYT*, 12 July 1866; Mount Sinai Hospital, New York City, *AR* (1868), 21–22.

62. "Small-Pox in New York," *NYT*, 18 May 1853; Latrobe, "Report of B. Henry Latrobe," 115.

63. Sylvester, *Philosophy of Domestic Economy*, 48–49, plate 5; Society of the New York Hospital, *Report of the Building Committee of the New York Hospital, To Inquire into the Expediency of Erecting a New Building* (New York: Mahlon Day, 1837), 8–10; James Duffe, Diary, NYHS.

64. New York Hospital, BGM, Visiting Committee Minutes, 27 Feb. 1852, 25 Apr. 1845, 6 May 1845, 12 Feb. 1850, MCANYPWC; "Rats at Bellevue Hospital," *NYT*, 27 Apr. 1860; Smith, *Principles of Hospital Construction*, NLM, 37–38. See the bibliographic essay: plumbing.

65. "Medical Items and News: the Roosevelt Hospital," *Medical Record*, 430.

66. "Medical Items and News: the Roosevelt Hospital," *Medical Record*, 430; "Roosevelt Hospital—Description of the Building," *NYT*, 9 Oct. 1869; "Laying of the Corner-Stone of the Island Hospital," *NYT*, 23 July 1858; "Hygiene—Building of Hospitals," 869–70; Davis, "Mercy Hospital," 531–34.

67. "Marine Hospital Service, Report of the Supervising Surgeon for the Last Fiscal Year," *NYT*, 5 Nov. 1873; "Bellevue Hospital: Meeting of the Medical Board," *NYT*, 18 June 1873. See also Frank R. Freemon, *Gangrene and Glory: Medical Care during the American Civil War* (Madison, NJ: Fairleigh Dickinson University Press, 1998); and Thompson and Goldin, *Hospital*, 170–75.

68. Hammond, *Treatise on Hygiene*, 397–98; Hamilton, *Treatise on Military Surgery and Hygiene*, 132–35.

69. *New York Evening Post*, 7 Feb. 1871, as quoted in Beekman, *Centenary*, 22; Rudolf Virchow, *Über Hospitäler und Lazarette* (Berlin: C. G. Luderitz, 1869), 825–54; Albert Buck, ed. *A Reference Handbook of the Medical Sciences* (New York: William Wood, 1886) s.v. "Hospitals," 3:707.

70. Beekman, *Centenary*, 21; Smith, *Principles of Hospital Construction*, NLM, 10–11.

71. Rosner, "Social Control and Social Service," 183–97, 186; "St. Luke's Hospital. Laying the Corner-Stone—Interesting Ceremonies," *NYT*, 8 May 1854; Hunt, "General Description," 34.

72. Committee of the Board of Directors of the New England Hospital, *History and Description of the New England Hospital* (Boston: W. L. Deland, 1876), 14; Smith, *Principles of Hospital Construction*, NLM, 20–24.

73. Smith, *Principles of Hospital Construction*, NLM, 24; Willard Parker, quoted in Presbyterian Hospital, New York City, *AR* 5 (1873), 69; Hammond, *Treatise on Hygiene*, 309; "Roosevelt Hospital," *Medical Record*, 430; "Presbyterian Hospital," *NYT*.

74. Smith, *Principles of Hospital Construction*, NLM, 25; *Rules and Special Orders of the Mower United States Army General Hospital at Chestnut Hill* (Philadelphia: J. B. Lippincott, 1865), 14.

75. Smith, *Principles of Hospital Construction*, NLM, 12. The Herbert Hospital in England, one of Florence Nightingale's pet projects, included twenty large wards (accommodating more than six hundred patients) but only one small operating theater, and no examination rooms, or laboratories.

76. Rosenberg, "Practice of Medicine," 223–53.

77. Rosenberg, *Care of Strangers*, 24.

78. Dennis, *Memoir of James R. Wood*, 14; *Some Account of the Medical School in Boston: And of the Massachusetts General Hospital* (Boston: Phelps and Farnham, 1824), 10–12.

79. Brown, "Hospital Construction," 80; George W. Gay, "Reminiscences of the Boston City Hospital," in Cheever et al., eds., *History of the Boston City Hospital*, 245.

80. Martin S. Pernick, *A Calculus of Suffering: Pain, Professionalism, and Anesthesia in Nineteenth-Century America* (New York: Columbia University Press, 1985); Guenter Risse, *Mending Bodies, Saving Souls: A History of Hospitals* (New York: Oxford University Press, 1999), 339–61; Owen H. Wangensteen and Sarah D. Wangensteen, *The Rise of Surgery: From Empiric Craft to Scientific Discipline* (Minneapolis: University of Minnesota Press, 1978); and Christoph Mörgeli, *The Surgeon's Stage: A History of the Operating Room* (Basel, Switzerland: Editiones Roche, 1999).

81. "Rhode Island Hospital," *BMSJ* 79, no. 11 (15 Oct. 1868), 171.

82. "Bellevue and Potter's Field," *NYT*, 7 April 1872; W. W. Keen, "Hospitals of Sixty Years Ago," *MH* 32, no. 1 (1929), 49; Fenwick Beekman, *Hospital for the Ruptured and Crippled: A Historical Sketch Written on the Occasion of the Seventy-Fifth Anniversary of the Hospital* ([New York]: Privately printed, 1939), 21.

83. Harold Speert, *Sloane Hospital Chronicle* (Philadelphia: F. A. Davis, 1963), 82; James V. Ricci, "The City Hospital," *The Society of the Alumni of City Hospital, New York* (1952), 68; "Mount Sinai Hospital. Inauguration of the New Buildings," *NYT*, 30 May 1872; Delavan, *Early Days*, 51.

84. Kenneth D. Keele, "Clinical Medicine in the 1860s," in *Medicine and Science in the 1860s*, ed. F. N. L. Poynter (London: Wellcome Institute of the History of Medicine, 1968), 8–10; F. F. Cartwright, "Antiseptic Surgery," in Poynter, *Medicine and Science in the 1860s*, 81–84.

85. Watson, "A Lecture on Practical Education in Medicine, and on the Course of

Instruction at the New York Hospital, Delivered at the Hospital on the 3d of November, 1846," *New York Journal of Medicine and Collateral Sciences* 8, no. 22 (1847), 7–22, 23. On clinical medicine and education, see Warner, *Therapeutic Perspective*, 187; Risse, *Mending Bodies, Saving Souls*, 289–338; Kenneth M. Ludmerer, *Learning to Heal: The Development of American Medical Education* (New York: Basic Books, 1985); Louis S. Greenbaum, "'Measure of Civilization': The Hospital Thought of Jacques Tenon on the Eve of the French Revolution," *BHM* 49, no. 1 (1975), 43–56; Erwin H. Ackerknecht, *Medicine at the Paris Hospital, 1794–1848* (Baltimore: Johns Hopkins University Press, 1967); Foucault, *Birth of the Clinic*; and Phyllis Allen Richmond, "The Hôtel-Dieu of Paris on the Eve of the Revolution," *JHMAS* 16, no. 4 (1961), 335–53.

86. Gay, "Reminiscences of the Boston City Hospital," 243–44.

87. Morton and Woodbury, *History of the Pennsylvania Hospital*, 98; Cincinnati General Hospital *AR* (1892), 7; "University of Pennsylvania: New Buildings," *Medical News* 31, no. 368 (Aug. 1873), 130; "Science of Surgery," *NYT*, 6 Sept. 1871; Hahnemann Medical College and Hospital, *AR*, 12 (1871), 7.

88. Postmortem facilities were added to the New York Hospital in 1840, Bellevue Hospital in 1856. The Roosevelt Hospital in 1871 included pathological facilities in the original design. Watson, "Lecture on Practical Education," 22; Dennis, *Memoir of James R. Wood*, 11; "Bellevue Hospital Improvements," *NYT*, 11 Aug. 1857.

89. Mount Sinai Hospital in New York City added dispensary service in 1872, the Massachusetts General Hospital in 1868, the Cincinnati General Hospital in 1872, the Pennsylvania Hospital in Philadelphia in 1872, and the City Hospital in Boston in the late 1860s.

90. Oppert, *Hospitals, Infirmaries and Dispensaries*, 78–79.

91. A dispensary building was added to Bellevue Hospital adjacent to the gatehouse in 1866; the Pennsylvania Hospital opened a dispensary in their Eighth Street Gate House in 1872.

92. *An Account of the Proceedings at the Laying of the Corner-Stone of the Hospital of the Protestant Episcopal Church in Philadelphia*, (Philadelphia: Henry B. Ashmead, 1860), 82–83; W. A. Muhlenberg, *A Plea for a Church Hospital, in the City of New-York. In Two Lectures, . . .* (New York: Standard and Swords, 1850), 17fn; *Account of St. Luke's Hospital*, 34.

93. "Local Intelligence, Blackwell's Island," *NYT*, 18 July 1866.

94. This spatial analysis has benefited from Cynthia Imogen Hammond's discussion of the Nightingale ward ("Reforming Architecture," 1–25). See also Thompson and Goldin, *Hospital*, 155–69; Rosenberg, *Care of Strangers*, 122–41.

95. New York Hospital, Board of Governors, Visiting Committee Minutes, 29 May 1846, MCANYPWC; Rosenberg, *Care of Strangers*, 169–74. Examples of ward sizes from this period include: the Island Hospital in New York City held twenty-, twenty-four-, and thirty-bed wards; the Colored Home and Hospital in New York City held twenty-eight-bed wards; the newest building of the New York Hospital held twenty- to twenty-five-bed wards; the German Hospital in New York City held thirty-two-bed wards; Mount Sinai Hospital in New York City held twenty-bed wards; and the Presbyterian Hospital in New York City planned "large" wards of twenty-eight beds; the Hospital of the Protestant Episcopal Church in Philadelphia held thirty-bed wards; the Boston Free City Hospital held thirty-two-bed wards; the Presbyterian Hospital in Philadelphia held thirty-four-bed wards; and the Providence Hospital in Rhode Island held twenty-four-bed wards.

96. Green, *City Hospitals*, 18–19.

97. "Eye and Ear Hospitals," *NYT*, 5 Aug. 1869. Children's wards appeared in the New York Hospital in 1856, the German Hospital in New York City in 1857, in Saint Luke's Hos-

pital in 1858, in Roosevelt Hospital in 1869, in the Hospital of the Protestant Episcopal Church in Philadelphia in 1871, and in the Mount Sinai and German Hospitals in New York City in 1873. See also the sections in the bibliographic essay on specialization and on pediatrics and obstetrics.

98. Bellevue Hospital logged mortality rates for amputation cases at 48 percent in 1872 and 1873 and for lying-in patients at 40 percent in May of 1874 (State Charities Aid Association, Visiting Committee, Bellevue Hospital, New York City, *AR* 3 [1875], 10). Surgical mortality rates in Philadelphia hospitals hovered around 25 percent and in the Massachusetts General Hospital at 26 percent (Gariepy, "Introduction and Acceptance of Listerian Antisepsis," 179). Virginia G. Drachman, *Hospital with a Heart: Women Doctors and the Paradox of Separatism at the New England Hospital, 1862–1969* (Ithaca, NY: Cornell University Press, 1984), 74; State Charities Aid Association, Visiting Committee, Bellevue Hospital, New York City, *AR* 8 (1880), 12–13; "Miscellaneous City News. An Experimental Hospital. A Ward Answering the Latest Demands of Sanitary Science—The Osborne Pavilion at Bellevue," *NYT*, 31 Dec. 1878.

99. Eleanor Lee, *History of the School of Nursing of the Presbyterian Hospital, New York 1892–1942* (New York: G. P. Putnam's Sons, 1942), 8; Presbyterian Hospital, New York City, *AR* 8 (1876), 8. A plan of a similar structure is available in Wylie, *Hospitals*, 141. Ad hoc isolation outbuildings were built at Saint Luke's Hospital in New York City in 1861; Mount Sinai Hospital in New York City in 1867; at the Boston City Hospital by 1867; Roosevelt Hospital in 1871 and 1874; and the German Hospital in New York City in 1870.

100. Henry Greenway, "A New Mode of Hospital Construction," *British Medical Journal* 1, no. 593 (11 May 1872), 495–97; "Broadside of the Display at the Paris Universal Exhibition, 1878, British Section, Group ii, Class 14," in [Collection of Broadsides on Hospital Construction], 1872–1879, NLM.

101. "The Small-Pox. Erection of a New Hospital on the River Front—Its Construction and Hygienic Effect," *NYT*, 26 Jan. 1873. Engineer Knapp patented the "air-consuming apparatus."

102. Franklin, *Some Account*, 25. By 1796, the managers of the Pennsylvania Hospital, facing budget deficits, limited the number of full charity patients to thirty (Morton and Woodbury, *History of the Pennsylvania Hospital*, 79).

103. Charles Bulfinch, "Report," in Leonard K. Eaton, "Charles Bulfinch and the Massachusetts General Hospital," *Isis* 41 (1950), 10. Jews' Hospital, New York City, *AR* (1866), 10. At the time, 8 percent of their patients were paying. Hospitals were not targeting the local wealthy "private" patients of private practitioners, but travelers or other persons of means who were caught without adequate private patient care. Hospitals charged private patients for their room and board, but typically, hospital doctors were not allowed to charge hospital patients for their services. This was a bone of contention for decades.

104. Starr, "Medicine, Economy and Society," 55–65.

105. Saint Luke's Hospital, New York City, *AR*, 15 (1873), 20; Pernick, *Calculus of Suffering*, 16; Rosner, "Social Control and Social Service," 183–97. See also Drs. Jackson and Warren, Circular Letter, 3 Aug. 1810, as quoted in Bowditch, *A History of the Massachusetts General Hospital*, 8fn; and Vogel, *Invention of the Modern Hospital*, 40–41.

106. Cincinnati General Hospital, Cincinnati, *AR* 8 (1869), 5; New York Hospital, BGM, 2 July 1867, MCANYPWC, Minutes; Bulfinch, "Report," 10–11; Rosner, "Social Control and Social Service," 192; Rosner, *Once Charitable Enterprise*, 62–71.

107. Edward Hartshorne and Samuel L. Hollingsworth, "Medical Education and Institutions," *Medical News* 1, no. 1 (Jan. 1843), 8; Massachusetts General Hospital, Boston,

AR (1851), 7; Sister Marie Stephen, "Our Catholic Hospitals," *MH* 51, no. 3 (1938), 78–81, 81; Stuart, *History of St. Vincent's Hospital*, 18; Presbyterian Hospital, New York City, *AR* 3 (1871), 20–21.

108. "New Buildings"; Cincinnati General Hospital, Cincinnati, *AR* 8 (1869), 8.

109. Cincinnati General Hospital, Cincinnati, *AR* 8 (1869), 5; Roosevelt Hospital, New York City, *AR* 1 (1872), 7–8; Vermilye, *Address*, 10; German Hospital, New York City, *AR* (1869), 29; Lawrence Davidson, *The Alexian Brothers of Chicago: An Evolutionary Look at the Monastery and Modern Health Care* (New York: Vantage Press, 1990), 40; James Pratt Marr, *Pioneer Surgeons of the Woman's Hospital: The Lives of Sims, Emmet, Peaslee and Thomas* (New York: F. A. Davis, 1957), 38.

110. Starr, "Medicine, Economy and Society," 48; Cromley, *Alone Together*; Blackmar, *Manhattan for Rent*.

111. Rosenberg, *Care of Strangers*, 237–61; Annmarie Adams, *Medicine by Design: The Architect and the Modern Hospital, 1893–1943* (Minneapolis: University of Minnesota Press, 2008), 35–40; Rosner, "Social Control and Social Service," 192; Rosner, *Once Charitable Enterprise*, 62–71; Saint Luke's Hospital, New York City, *AR* 7 (1865), 6; Cincinnati General Hospital, Cincinnati, *AR* 10 (1872), 6; Cincinnati General Hospital, Cincinnati, *AR* 11 (1873), 6. See also "Anniversary of the New-York Woman's Hospital," *NYT*, 28 Jan. 1861; German Hospital, New York City, *AR* (1869), 29.

112. "American Hospitals," *NYT*, 22 Feb. 1873; Saint Luke's Hospital, New York City, *AR* 7 (1865), 9.

113. *Report of the Committee on a Free City Hospital*, 26.

Chapter 2. The Transformative Potential and Conservative Reality of Germ Theory and Antisepsis, 1874–1877

Epigraphs: "The Ventilating and Warming of School-Houses in the Northern United States," *American Architect and Building News* 2, no. 93 (6 Oct. 1877), 318; Eric Erichsen, "Impressions of American Surgery," *Lancet* 104, no. 2673 (21 Nov. 1874), 719.

1. John Shaw Billings, *A Report on the Hygiene of the U. S. Army with Descriptions of Military Posts* (Circular No. 8. Surgeon General's Office, Washington: Government Printing Office, 1875), liv–lv; R. F. Weir, quoted in Stephen Smith, "Some Practical Tests of the Claims of the Antiseptic System," *Transactions of the Medical Society of the State of New York* (1878), 127; German Hospital, New York City, *AR* (1875), 29.

2. Charles E. Rosenberg, *The Care of Strangers: The Rise of America's Hospital System* (New York: Basic Books, 1987), 137. Early mortality at Roosevelt and Saint Luke's Hospitals in New York City was approximately 1 in 7, or 14 percent ("Bellevue Hospital," *NYT*, 18 June 1873). See also Edward D. Churchill, "The Pandemic of Wound Infection in Hospitals: Studies in the History of Wound Healing," *Journal of the History of Medicine* 20 (Oct. 1965), 391–404; Michael Worboys, *Spreading Germs: Disease Theories and Medical Practice in Britain, 1865–1900* (Cambridge: Cambridge University Press, 2000), 73–107.

3. Lister, "On the Antiseptic Principle in the Practice of Surgery," *British Medical Journal* 2, no. 351 (21 Sept. 1867), 248.

4. "On the Antiseptic Principle in the Practice of Surgery," 246, 248.

5. See the bibliographic essay: germ theory, antisepsis, asepsis.

6. These were the two most-cited American hospitals in contemporary publications on hospital design. See Addison Hutton, "The Planning of Hospitals," *AABN* 45, no. 973

(18 Aug. 1894), 64–67; Frederic J. Mouat and Henry Saxon Snell, *Hospital Construction and Management* (London: J. & A. Churchill, 1883), 55; Henry C. Burdett, *Hospitals and Asylums of the World: Their Origin, History, Construction, Administration, Management, and Legislation* (London: J & A Churchill, The Scientific Press, 1891–1893), 3:ix; Antoine Depage, Paul Vandervelde, and Victor Cheval, *La construction des hôpitaux* (Brussels: Misch and Thron, Librairies-Éditeurs, 1909), 121; George F. Hammond, *A Treatise on Hospital and Asylum Construction; with Special Reference to Pavilion Wards* (Cleveland: published by author, 1891); Robert Bruegmann, "Two American Hospitals in 1876," *JSAH* 35, no. 4 (Dec. 1976), 280–83.

7. See Alistair Fair, "'A Laboratory of Heating and Ventilation': The Johns Hopkins Hospital as Experimental Architecture, 1870–90," *Journal of Architecture* 19, no. 3 (2014), 357–81; Gert H. Brieger, "The Original Plans for the Johns Hopkins Hospital and Their Historical Significance," *BHM* 39, no. 6 (Nov./Dec. 1965), 518–28; John Shaw Billings, *Description of the Johns Hopkins Hospital* (Baltimore: Isaac Friedenwald, 1890); Carleton B. Chapman, *Order out of Chaos: John Shaw Billings and America's Coming of Age* (Boston: Boston Medical Library in the Francis A. Countway Library of Medicine, 1994), 518–28; and Guenter Risse, *Mending Bodies, Saving Souls* (New York: Oxford University Press, 1999), 403–7.

8. Johns Hopkins Hospital, *Hospital Plans: Five Essays Relating to the Construction, Organization & Management of Hospitals . . .* (New York: William Wood, 1875), xi.

9. Johns Hopkins Hospital, *Hospital Plans: Five Essays*, 11–15, 285–86. Caspar Morris proposed wards similar to the ones he had helped plan at the Hospital of the Protestant Episcopal Church in Philadelphia; Stephen Smith proposed one-story wards similar to the surgical ward of Roosevelt Hospital in New York City that he had designed in collaboration with Carl Pfeiffer; Norton Folsom proposed square wards, like the one he had helped add to the Massachusetts General Hospital in Boston.

10. John R. Niernsee, *Review of "Hospital Plans,"* (Baltimore, 1876); "The attitude of the officials . . . ," *AABN* 2, no. 93 (6 Oct. 1877), 318; Fair, "Laboratory of Heating and Ventilation," 367. Niernsee resigned the commission in 1877, to return to South Carolina and resume work on the State House (which had been interrupted by the Civil War), although he remained a frequent visitor to the construction site; prominent Boston architects Cabot and Chandler were appointed his replacement.

11. Johns Hopkins Hospital, *Hospital Plans: Five Essays*; Johns Hopkins Hospital, *Reports and Papers Relating to Construction and Organization*, 8 vols. (1876–1878). Positive reviews began appearing for *Hospital Plans* in the first quarter of 1876 (see "Hospital Construction and Organization," *Medical Record* 11, part 1 [22 Jan. 1876], 57–58, part 2 [29 Jan. 1876], 73–76, part 3 [5 Feb. 1876], 89–92, part 4 [12 Feb. 1876], 105–7, part 5 [19 Feb. 1876], 121–26; and "Hospital Plans," *North American Review* 123 (July 1876), 233–38. Billings noted that the ward plans of the new Cook County Hospital took their arrangement of isolation wards "from the plan which I first proposed for the Hopkins Hospital" (John Shaw Billings, "On the Plans for the Johns Hopkins Hospital at Baltimore, pt. II," *Medical Record* 12, no. 3 [Mar. 1877], 146). As late as the 1900s, *Hospital Plans: Five Essays* still stood as the authoritative guide to hospital design in America (Albert J. Ochsner and Meyer J. Sturm, *The Organization, Construction and Management of Hospitals: With Numerous Plans and Details* [Chicago: Cleveland Press, 1907], 25).

12. Report of Special Committee on Retrenchment, 17 Apr. 1866; BGM, 1 Mar. and 8 Mar. 1870, "Report of Physicians and Surgeons on Convertibility of Bloomingdale Asylum Buildings to Hospital Purposes," in STP b4/f6, MCANYPWC; "The Proposed Removal

of the New York Hospital," *NYT*, 4 Jan. 1869; "The New York Hospital," *Medical Record* 4 (1 July 1869), 205–7; Rosenberg, *Care of Strangers*, 142–44; Eric Larrabee, *The Benevolent and Necessary Institution: The New York Hospital, 1771–1971* (Garden City, NY: Doubleday, 1971), 207–45; and Jeanne Kisacky, "Restructuring Isolation: Hospital Architecture, Medicine, and Disease Prevention," *BHM* 79, no. 1 (2005), 1–49. Specifications for an unbuilt new building favored by the doctors and designed by Carl Pfeiffer are in STP B5/f1 MCANYP-WC.

13. See, for example, "Proposed Removal of the New York Hospital"; "The Late New York Hospital," *Medical Record* 7, no. 7 (1 June 1872), 229–30; BGM, New York Hospital, 4 Jan. 1869, 16 Jan. 1869, 1 Mar. 1870, and 3 Feb. 1874 (Report of Committee on House of Relief), MCANYPWC.

14. The program called for an "urban" pavilion plan: a four-story brick building; 32 feet deep by 125 feet long; services in the mostly above-ground "basement"; administration on the first floor; two floors of wards; a kitchen and operating room on the top floor ("Form of Circular to Architects . . . ," 10 June 1874; Cady to Gandy, 8 July 1874; Robertson to Gandy, 29 May 1874; Post to Special Committee, 1 Aug. 1874, all in Minutes, Special Committee on the New Building, in STP, b7/f1, MCANYPWC). Three of the architects—George B. Post, J. Cleveland Cady, and Robert H. Robertson—had opened their offices only within the last five years.

15. "Draft of Report of Special Committee Charged with Reporting a Plan of Hospital Building to Be Erected on 15th Street . . ."; Post to Swan, 23 Sept. 1874, and 21 Sept. 1874, in Minutes, Special Committee on the New Building in STP, b7/f1, MCANYPWC. Post would later express a low opinion of Leeds's ventilation system, saying that not one of the "entire collection of shafts carried off one cubic foot per hour of foul air." Post to Henry B. Hyde, 22 Mar. 1887, Henry B. Hyde Papers, Baker Library, Harvard Business School, as quoted in Sarah Bradford Landau and Carl Condit, *Rise of the New York Skyscraper* (New Haven, CT: Yale University Press, 1996), 68n12.

16. Special Committee on the New Building to Board of Physicians, 18 Nov. 1874; 24 Nov. 1874, in STP, b7/f1, MCANYPWC; New York Hospital, New York City, *AR* (1875), 10; New York Hospital, New York City, *AR* 107 (1876), 7; 22 June 1876, in Minutes, Special Committee on the New Building, in STP b7/f1, MCANYPWC.

17. "A Protest from Doctors," *NYT*, 1 Dec. 1875.

18. Billings, *Report on the Hygiene*, lv–lvi; William Hammond, *A Treatise on Hygiene, with Special Reference to the Military Service* (Philadelphia: J. B. Lippincott, 1863), 322–27, 355; Woodworth, "Marine Hospital Service," *NYT*, 5 Nov. 1873; Sir John Eric Erichsen, *On Hospitalism and the Causes of Death after Operations* (London: Longmans, Green, 1874), 91–93. There were occasional advocates of taller hospital structures; see, e.g., William Repper's comments in "Afternoon Session," *NYT*, 11 Nov. 1874.

19. State Charities Aid Association, New York City, *AR* 2 (1874), 25–26; "A Maternity Hospital," *NYT*, 17 Mar. 1875; "Architecture at the Exhibition of Contemporary Art," *AABN* 5, no. 177 (17 May 1879), 159. See also Frederic J. Mouat in Moaut and Snell, *Hospital Construction and Management*, sect. 1, 51, 55.

20. "Report of Committee on Design for Hospital Building," in BGM 17 Feb. 1875, MCANYPWC.

21. Van Buren, quoted in Joseph Lister, "The Antiseptic Method of Dressing Open Wounds," *Medical Record* 11, no. 43 (21 Oct. 1876), 695; J. T. H. Connor, "Listerism Unmasked: Antisepsis and Asepsis in Victorian Anglo-Canada," *JHMAS* 49, no. 2 (1994), 209–30; Thomas P. Gariepy, "The Introduction and Acceptance of Listerian Antisepsis

in the United States," *JHMAS* 49, no. 2 (1994), 167–206. British surgeon Eric Erichsen commented on the relatively sparse (and unmethodical) use of antiseptics in "Impressions of American Surgery," 719. See also the section on germ theory, antisepsis, asepsis in the bibliographic essay.

22. Delavan, as quoted in "History of the City Hospital," Society of the Alumni of City (Charity) Hospital, New York City *AR* (1904), 84.

23. James Pratt Marr, *Pioneer Surgeons of the Woman's Hospital: The Lives of Sims, Emmet, Peaslee and Thomas* (Philadelphia: F. A. Davis, 1957), 135–36.

24. Lister, "On the Antiseptic Principle," 246–7; Tomes, *The Gospel of Germs: Men, Women, and the Microbe in American Life* (Cambridge, MA: Harvard University Press, 1998), 46; Billings, "On the Plans for the Johns Hopkins Hospital at Baltimore, pt. I," *Medical Record* 12 (24 Feb. 1877), 131; Billings, "On the Plans for the Johns Hopkins . . . pt. II," 146. John Tyndall's experiments on the floating matter in the air and Edmund Parkes's determination of the exact content of airborne particles were influential. Tyndall, "On Dust and Disease," *Fraser's Magazine*, new series 1, no. 3 (Mar. 1870), 302–11; Edmund A. Parkes, *A Manual of Practical Hygiene: Prepared Especially for Use in the Medical Service of the Army*, 2nd ed. (London: John Churchill and Sons, 1866).

25. Hunter McGuire, quoted in Gariepy, "The Introduction and Appearance of Listerian Antisepsis," 179.

26. Billings, "On the Plans for the Johns Hopkins . . . pt. I," 131; "Afternoon Session," *NYT* (11 Nov. 1874); Billings, *Report on the Hygiene*, lx; and Billings, in Johns Hopkins Hospital, *Hospital Plans: Five Essays*, 12–14, 21–22. See also Suellen Hoy, *Chasing Dirt: The American Pursuit of Cleanliness* (New York: Oxford University Press, 1995).

27. Charles McDowell to Doctor Dearborn, in Leonard Paul Wershub, *One Hundred Years of Medical Progress. A History of the New York Medical College Flower and Fifth Avenue Hospitals* (Springfield, IL: Charles C. Thomas, 1967), 118; "Notes and Clippings: Griffith's Enamel," *AABN* 1, no. 10 (26 Feb. 1876), 72; and "Notes and Clippings: Among the Many Devices," *AABN* 1, no. 14 (1 Apr. 1876), 112.

28. "Hospitals Then and Now," *NYT*, 29 Dec. 1878; Stephen Smith, in Johns Hopkins Hospital, *Hospital Plans: Five Essays*, 285.

29. Risse, *Mending Bodies, Saving Souls*, 469; Adrian Forty, "The Modern Hospital in France and England," in *Buildings and Society: Essays on the Social Development of the Built Environment*, ed. Anthony D. King (Boston: Routledge and Kegan Paul, 1980), 83; Pevsner, "Hospitals," in *A History of Building Types* (Princeton, NJ: Princeton University Press, 1976), 158; Lindsay Prior, "The Architecture of the Hospital: A Study of Spatial Organization and Medical Knowledge," *British Journal of Sociology* 39, no. 1 (1988), 93–95; David Charles Sloane and Beverlie Conant Sloane, *Medicine Moves to the Mall* (Baltimore: Johns Hopkins University Press, 2003), 58.

30. Jeremy Taylor, *The Architect and the Pavilion Hospital* (London: Leicester University Press, 1997), 91.

31. Joseph Lister, "A Contribution to the Germ Theory of Putrefaction and Other Fermentative Changes, and to the Natural History of Torulae and Bacteria," *Transactions of the Royal Society of Edinburgh* 27, no. 3 (1875), 315; Joseph Lister, "On the Effects of the Antiseptic System of Treatment upon the Salubrity of a Surgical Hospital," *Lancet* 95, no. 2418 (1 Jan. 1870), 4–5. Risse's account provides a valuable balanced examination of the multiple influences in the reduction of infections in Lister's success (*Mending Bodies, Saving Souls*, 361–98).

32. Taylor, *The Architect and the Pavilion Hospital*, 91.

33. "Johns Hopkins Hospital, Baltimore," *AABN* 1 (16 Dec. 1876), 405–6; A. A. Cox,

"The Johns Hopkins Hospital, Baltimore, Maryland," *AABN* 35, no. 837 (9 Jan. 1892), 24–26; Bruegmann, "Two American Hospitals," 280–28; Fair, "Laboratory of Heating and Ventilation," 358–61.

34. Billings, in Johns Hopkins Hospital, *Hospital Plans: Five Essays*, 26; "Johns Hopkins Hospital, Baltimore," 405–6.

35. Fair, "Laboratory of Heating and Ventilation," 358–61, 372–77; Billings, in Johns Hopkins Hospital, *Hospital Plans: Five Essays*, 4, 9.

36. Beekman, "Report of the Committee on a Village of Cottage Hospitals," in BGM, 24 Feb. 1876; Conkling, "Report in Response to the Report on Village Hospitals," in BGM, 5 July 1876, 79, MCANYPWC. Eric Larrabee recounts that Conkling himself would admit that votes by the Board of Governors "often went twenty-five to one, the one being himself" (*Benevolent and Necessary*, 235).

37. Post, "Description of the Buildings," in *New York Hospital. Report of the Building Committee*, William H. Van Buren (New York: L. W. Lawrence, 1877), 25–28.

38. Post, "Description of the Buildings," 31; Bruegmann, "Two American Hospitals," 280–81.

39. Post, "Description of the Buildings," 30, 32. The use of the word *contagion* was a flag for germs rather than miasma. Walker Gill Wylie described a similar underbed exhaust duct in *Hospitals: Their History, Organization, and Construction. Boylston Prize Essay of Harvard University, 1876* (New York: D. Appleton, 1877), 127–28.

40. Joseph Lister, quoted in Van Buren, *New York Hospital*, 20.

41. Hutton, "Planning of Hospitals," 65–67; Mouat and Snell, *Hospital Construction and Management*, 55; Burdett, *Hospitals and Asylums of the World*, 3:ix; and DePage, Vandervelde, and Cheval, *La construction des hôpitaux*, 121.

42. Billings, "On the Plans for the Johns Hopkins . . . pt. II," 146. For contemporary reviews, see Wylie, *Hospitals*, 198–99; Mouat and Snell, *Hospital Construction and Management*, 51, 55; "Every few months," *AABN* 14, no. 417 (22 Dec. 1883), 289; Hammond, *Treatise on Hospital and Asylum Construction*, 50–52; "New York Hospital," *Medical Record* (1877), 186; "Architecture at the Exhibition of Contemporary Art," 159; "Letter from New York," *BMSJ* 96, no. 20 (17 May 1877), 596–98, and 97, no. 15 (11 Oct. 1877), 432–34; *Sixth Annual Report of the State Charities Aid Association . . .* (New York: 1878), 11–12.

43. That the New York Hospital had to purchase its site while the Johns Hopkins had been the recipient of a large, donated site also factored into the design economies.

44. John Francis Richmond, *New York and Its Institutions, 1609–1871* (New York: E. B. Treat, 1872), 374–75. See also Saint Francis Hospital, New York City, *AR* 1 (1867); "Correspondence. The Hahnemann Hospital. New York." *AABN* 1, no. 43 (21 Oct. 1876), 343. Since administrative pavilions typically did not hold patients, they could rise to more stories than ward pavilions.

45. For example, in 1870, the Chicago Medical College built a new building on the grounds of Mercy Hospital. In the 1880s and 1890s, buildings for the medical department of the University of New York, Cornell University Medical College, and Bellevue Medical College moved to new buildings on sites adjacent to Bellevue Hospital in New York City. The College of Physicians and Surgeons moved to a site across the street from Roosevelt Hospital. The Johns Hopkins Medical School opened in 1893. On medical education of the time, see Kenneth M. Ludmerer, *Learning to Heal: The Development of American Medical Education* (New York: Basic Books, 1985); on medical school design, see Katherine L. Carroll, "Creating the Modern Physician: The Architecture of American Medical Schools in the Era of Medical Education Reform," *JSAH* 75, no. 1 (2016), 48–73.

46. "Jefferson College Hospital," *Medical News* 35, no. 415 (July 1877), 108. Jefferson College was an early adopter of the clinical approach to medical education.

47. Quoted in "Afternoon Session," *NYT*, 11 Nov. 1874.

48. Whether or not any of the five doctors would have proposed taller buildings without these guidelines is unlikely. In his essay, Billings admitted the necessity of taller hospitals in urban locations but still expressed a strong preference for lower buildings, and he advocated the design of Barnes Hospital (four stories) in Washington, DC, as a model of such a taller hospital. Stephen Smith conclusively preferred one-story buildings. Norton Folsom advocated one-story wards. Only Caspar Morris assumed that the operational efficiency of a taller building was worth the hygienic tradeoff of a two- (or even three-) story building.

49. Post figures prominently in Landau and Condit's *Rise of the New York Skyscraper*. Post might also have had access to relevant medical information through his uncle, Alfred Post, an attending surgeon at the New York Hospital.

50. "A Protest from Doctors." See also "Cottage Hospitals," *Medical Record* 11, no. 32 (5 Aug. 1876), 511–12. General medical resentment against lay governor "interference" in medical matters had been simmering for years. For further evidence of the doctors' feelings, see "To the Governors of the New York Hospital," BGM, 1 Mar. 1870, MCANYPWC; and "The Late New York Hospital," *Medical Record* 7, no. 7 (1 June 1872), 229.

51. Report of Geo. B. Post to Henry J. Davison, Chairman, Heat and Ventilation Committee, dated Oct. 2, 1882, STP b12/f1. See also Kisacky, "Restructuring Isolation," 1–49.

52. Erichsen, *On Hospitalism*, 12–15, 26–36; Worboys, *Spreading Germs*, 74–75; Adams, *Architecture in the Family Way*.

53. Lister, "An Address on the Effect of the Antiseptic Treatment upon the General Salubrity of Surgical Hospitals," *British Medical Journal* 2, no. 782 (25 Dec. 1875), 769–71; "Report of the Special Committee on the Erection of a New Bellevue Hospital," as quoted in State Charities Aid Association, Visiting Committee, Bellevue Hospital, New York City, *AR* 6 (1878), 11.

Chapter 3. The Post–Germ Theory Pavilion in the Dawn of Asepsis, 1878–1897

Epigraphs: "Common Councilmen as Architects," *AABN* 3, no. 128 (8 June 1878), 203; "Founded by James Lenox. The Chief Features of the Presbyterian Hospital," *NYT*, 3 July 1892.

1. John Harley Warner, *The Therapeutic Perspective: Medical Practice, Knowledge, and Identity in America, 1820–1885* (Cambridge, MA: Harvard University Press, 1988), 244–50. The list of diseases linked to specific microorganisms in this time includes anthrax, malaria, cholera, diphtheria, typhoid fever, rabies, tetanus, and plague. Not all ailments were or are caused by germs; there were many for which germ theory changed little.

2. Addison Hutton, "The Planning of Hospitals," *AABN* 45, no. 973 (18 Aug. 1894), 64.

3. Koch, *Untersuchungen Über Die Aetiologie Der Wundinfectionskrankheiten* (Leipzig: Vogel, 1878); Worboys, *Spreading Germs: Disease Theories and Medical Practice in Britain, 1865–1900* (Cambridge: Cambridge University Press, 2000), 73–107, 158, 172; Nancy Tomes, *The Gospel of Germs: Men, Women, and the Microbe in American Life* (Cambridge, MA: Harvard University Press, 1998), 92–99.

4. Abraham Jacobi, "The Production of Diseases by Sewer Air," *New York Medical Journal* 60 (28 July 1894), 104. Arpad G. Gerster noted the inherently different attitudes

of students trained after Lister's antisepsis and those trained before it ("The Technique of Antiseptic and Aseptic Surgery," in *System of Surgery*, vol. 1, ed. Frederic S. Dennis and John Shaw Billings [Philadelphia: Lea Brothers, 1895], 677).

5. Thomas Schlich, "Asepsis and Bacteriology: A Realignment of Surgery and Laboratory Science," *Medical History* 56, no. 3 (2012), 332–34. On the shift from antisepsis to asepsis, see also J. T. H. Connor, "Listerism Unmasked: Antisepsis and Asepsis in Victorian Anglo-Canada," *JHMAS* 49, no. 2 (1994), 207–39; J. T. H. Connor, "The Victorian Revolution in Surgery," *Science* 304, no. 5667 (2 Apr. 2004), 54–55; Christoph Mörgeli, *The Surgeon's Stage: A History of the Operating Room* (Basel, Switzerland: Editiones Roche, 1999), 219–46; Thomas P. Gariepy, "The Introduction and Acceptance of Listerian Antisepsis in the United States," *JHMAS*, 49, no. 2 (1994), 167–206; and Tomes, *Gospel of Germs*, 91–111.

6. "For Scientific Surgery. Plans on Which the Syms Operating Theatre Will be Built," *NYT*, 2 Nov. 1890. See also Andrew McClary, "Germs Are Everywhere: The Germ Threat as Seen in Magazine Articles, 1890–1920," *Journal of American Culture* 3 (1980), 33–46; Nancy Tomes, *Gospel of Germs*.

7. Connor, "Listerism Unmasked," 231; "A Report upon the Cases of Erysipelas and Cellulitis Occurring in the Service of Dr. VanderPool & Dr. Thompson from June 1st 1882 until Oct. 22 18[8]2 respectfully submitted to the Visiting Committee of the New York Hospital," [6], in BGM, STP, b12/f4, ANYMCAPWC; "A difficulty," *AABN* 7, no. 213 (24 Jan. 1880), 25.

8. Dr. A. H. Meisenbach, "Our New City Hospital, Where Should It be Located and How Constructed," *Medical Review* (Saint Louis) 34, no. 8 (22 Aug. 1896), 127; Bruegmann, "Architecture of the Hospital: 1770–1870, Design and Technology," (PhD diss., University of Pennsylvania, 1976), 114.

9. Edward Cowles, "Hospitals," in *A Reference Handbook of the Medical Sciences*, ed. Albert H. Buck (New York: William Wood, 1886), 3:707. Cowles was likely quoting from Frederic J. Mouat and Henry Saxon Snell, *Hospital Construction and Management* (London: J. & A. Churchill, 1883), 72, 175. See also Casimir Tollet, *Les hôpitaux modernes au xixe siècle* (Paris: Chez l'auteur, 1894). Similar sterilization strategies were still used in hospitals in the early twentieth century. BettyAnn Kevles, a former lab technician at the Cincinnati General Hospital (1911), describes the procedure of "burning out" a lab counter to ensure sterile conditions: "The old lab tops were of soapstone. We would remove everything off of them, wipe them down with 100-proof alcohol on paper towels to get rid of any debris. Then we would spray the tops with the alcohol, quickly, and then toss down a match. There was not a huge whoosh of flame, like a flambé, but there would be a short blue flame which would quickly burn itself out. Then we would wipe it down again with the alcohol soaked towels. Let it dry and we were good for another week." Personal communication, BettyAnn Kevles to Jeanne Kisacky (28 Aug. 2015).

10. Mouat and Snell, *Hospital Construction and Management*, 1883, 23. See also John Eaton, "Hospital Construction," *AABN* 19, no. 526 (23 Jan. 1886), 43; and Henry C. Burdett, *Hospitals and Asylums of the World: Their Origin, History, Construction, Administration, Management, and Legislation* (London: J & A Churchill, The Scientific Press, 1891–1893), 4:x, 7–8.

11. Saint Mary's Hospital for Children, New York City, *AR* 25 (1894); German Hospital, New York City, *AR* (1888), 9; "Hospital Pays a High Price. A Deal for Mrs. De Peyster's House in Fifteenth Street," *NYT*, 8 May 1897.

12. "All Ready for Patients. The New Flower Hospital Fully Equipped," *NYT*, 8 Jan. 1890; Condict W. Cutler, Alexander T. Martin, and Thomas C. Peightal, *The Roosevelt Hos-

pital 1871–1957 (New York: Roosevelt Hospital, 1957), 96–105, 117–34; "A House Surgeon's Protest. Unsanitary Surroundings of Gouverneur Hospital Set Forth," *NYT*, 3 Sept. 1892; "Great Din about a Hospital. A Goose Market and Boiler-Welting Near Gouverneur," *NYT*, 10 Sept. 1894.

13. Saint Luke's Hospital, New York City, *AR* 23 (1881), 10; Colored Home and Hospital, New York City, *AR* 52 (1891–92), 7.

14. "A Handsome Building. The New Manhattan Eye and Ear Hospital," *NYT*, 3 Sept. 1881. On neighborhood opposition, see "A Hospital as a Nuisance. An Injunction Obtained against an Institution for Babies," *NYT*, 19 June 1888; "Will Be a Noxious Neighbor. Kilmartin's Plea as to a Projected Hospital," *NYT*, 16 Dec. 1892; Morris J. Vogel, *The Invention of the Modern Hospital: Boston, 1870–1930* (Chicago: University of Chicago Press, 1980), 52–55.

15. "Gossip Concerning Realty. The St. Luke's Hospital Property Sale Still Discussed," *NYT*, 4 June 1893; "To Consolidate Nuisances. Serious Dangers to Roosevelt Hospital Contained in a Legislative Bill," *NYT*, 12 Mar. 1881; New York Hospital, BGM, 3 March 1886, MCANYPWC.

16. Adams and Burke, "A Doctor in the House: The Architecture of Home-Offices for Physicians in Toronto, 1885–1930," *Medical History* 52 (2008), 180–83.

17. Roosevelt Hospital, New York City, *AR* 20 (1891), 8.

18. Hutton, "Planning of Hospitals," 64; Jeremy Taylor, *The Architect and the Pavilion Hospital* (London: Leicester University Press, 1997), 1–39; Harriet Richardson, ed. *English Hospitals, 1660–1948* (Swindon: Royal Commission on the Historical Monuments of England, 1998), 11. Annmarie Adams describes H. Saxon Snell's role in the design of the Royal Victoria Hospital in Montreal, in *Medicine by Design: The Architect and the Modern Hospital, 1893–1943* (Minneapolis: University of Minnesota Press, 2008).

19. American "independence" likely would have prevented the consideration of hiring an English hospital architect; Canadian relations with the mother country were far more cordial. Publications on hospital design by American architects include Hutton, "Planning of Hospitals," 64–67; M. Carey Lea, "The Construction of Hospitals," *AABN* 5, no. 171 (1879), 110–11.

20. Walker Gill Wylie, *Hospitals: Their History, Organization, and Construction. Boylston Prize Essay of Harvard University, 1876* (New York: D. Appleton, 1877); George F. Hammond, *A Treatise on Hospital and Asylum Construction; with Special Reference to Pavilion Wards* (Cleveland: published by author, 1891); and John Shaw Billings and Henry M. Hurd, eds., *Hospitals, Dispensaries and Nursing* (Baltimore: Johns Hopkins Press and the Scientific Press, 1894); Adams, *Medicine by Design*, 90.

21. Hutton, "Planning of Hospitals," 64; Pfeiffer, "Sanitary Relations and Health Principles of Architecture," *NYT*, 12 Nov. 1873; Lea, "Construction of Hospitals," 110–11. Harriet Richardson indicated that in Britain, documented examples of collaboration between medical and architectural personnel on hospital designs were relatively rare (*English Hospitals*, 11). Henry Burdett promoted the "American" collaborative model (as exemplified by the Johns Hopkins Hospital) as "a better system" than what prevailed in Europe (*Hospitals and Asylums*, 4:ix).

22. Taylor, *Architect and the Pavilion Hospital*, 40–70.

23. Douglas Galton, *Healthy Hospitals* (Oxford: Clarendon Press, 1893), 31; Mouat and Snell, *Hospital Construction and Management*, 21; Burdett, *Hospitals and Asylums*; Tollet, *Les hôpitaux modernes*. While these European publications discussed and reproduced hundreds of images of European hospitals, in combination they included detailed visual information on only a handful of American hospitals, including the Boston City Hospital,

the Johns Hopkins Hospital, the New York Hospital, the New York Cancer Hospital, the Mary Hitchcock Memorial Hospital, Saint Margaret Memorial Hospital in Pittsburgh, Saint Luke's Free Hospital in Chicago, and the Moses Taylor Hospital in Scranton.

24. Wylie, *Hospitals*, 95–97, 127; Hammond, *Treatise on Hospital and Asylum Construction*, 50–52; Billings and Hurd, *Hospitals, Dispensaries and Nursing.*

25. Lakeside Hospital, Cleveland, *AR* (1891), 10–14. I have used this committee's judgment to color my own emphasis on the Johns Hopkins Hospital and the Presbyterian Hospital as illustrations of model American hospital design in this period.

26. "Common Councilmen as Architects," 203. In contrast, European competitions often limited submissions to invited architects (with some hospital experience) and gave the hospital architect a role as expert judge of the entries (Taylor, *Architect and the Pavilion Hospital*, 72–100).

27. Hutton, "Planning of Hospitals," 66.

28. Eaton, "Hospital Construction," 43–44, 43; Taylor, *Architect and the Pavilion Hospital*, 1, 21; Hutton, "Planning of Hospitals," 65; "Founded by James Lenox."

29. Adams, *Medicine by Design*, 90; "This attitude," *AABN*, 2, no. 93 (6 Oct. 1877), 317–18; "Report of the Building Committee," Presbyterian Hospital, New York City, *AR* 23 (1891), 20–21; Hutton, "Planning of Hospitals," 66.

30. Hutton, "Planning of Hospitals," 66; Sullivan, "The Tall Office Building Artistically Considered," *Lippincott's Magazine*, Mar. 1896, 408.

31. Max von Pettenkofer, *Über den Luftwechsel in Wohngebaüden* (Literarisch-Artistische Anstalt der J. G. Cottaschen Buchhandlung, 1858); Atlee, "Our Clothing and Our Houses," *AABN* 16, no. 470 (27 Dec. 1884), 306; Burdett, *Hospitals and Asylums*, 4:10–11. See also Didem Ekici, "Skin, Clothing, and Dwelling: Max von Pettenkofer, the Science of Hygiene, and Breathing Walls," *JSAH* 75, no. 3 (Sept. 2016), 281–98; and Gail Cooper, *Air-Conditioning America: Engineers and the Controlled Environment, 1900–1960* (Baltimore: Johns Hopkins University Press, 1998), 59–60.

32. Mount Sinai Hospital, New York City, *AR* (1882), 5, 14; "A difficulty," *AABN* 7, no. 213 (24 Jan. 1880), 25; "M. Boussard," *AABN* 26, no. 721 (19 Oct. 1889), 178. See also "The Permeability of Walls as Affecting Ventilation," *AABN* 13, no. 373 (17 Feb. 1883), 78–79 (reprinted from *Builder* 44 [20 Jan. 1883], 65–66); "The Sanitary Aspect of Plastering," *AABN* 8, no. 256 (20 Nov. 1880), 248.

33. Burdett, *Hospitals and Asylums*, 4:10–11; "Founded by James Lenox"; "A New Chicago Hospital," *Inland Architect and News Record* 25, no. 3 (Apr. 1895), 30–31; "More Room for Patients. Improvements to Be Made in the Mount Sinai Hospital," *NYT*, 27 Apr. 1882. American hospitals that installed asphalt flooring include Saint Luke's Hospital, Chicago ("A Model Hospital Addition," *Inland Architect and News Record* 13, no. 4 [Apr. 1889]); Bellevue Hospital, New York City ("Glimpses of Bellevue. What a Visit to the Famous Hospital Discloses," *NYT*, 8 Nov. 1891); and Reception Hospital, New York City ("Health Department's Pride. New Reception Hospital Nearly Ready for Patients," *NYT*, 11 July 1893). An early use of coal tar in Australia was also documented ("A new source of danger," *AABN* 25, no. 697 [4 May 1889], 205).

34. "M. Boussard," 178; "Permeability of Walls as Affecting Ventilation," 78–79.

35. "For Scientific Surgery"; Presbyterian Hospital, New York City, *AR* 23 (1891), 19.

36. "Permeability of Walls as Affecting Ventilation," 78; Hutton, "Planning of Hospitals," 64. See also "Dr. O. W. Wight," *AABN* 21, no. 578 (22 Jan. 1887), 37.

37. David Bryson Delavan, *Early Days of the Presbyterian Hospital in the City of New York* ([New York]: Privately published, 1926), 53; "One-Story Hospitals," editorial, *AABN* 12,

no. 353 (30 Sept. 1882), 161; Edward Atkinson, "Will Someone Answer These Questions?," editorial, *AABN* 24, no. 668 (13 Oct. 1888), 174; "The Mary Hitchcock Memorial Hospital," *AABN* 49, no. 1024 (10 Aug. 1895), 59. See also Hahnemann Hospital, New York City, *AR* (1893), 8. Fireproof construction was a building specialty that architects and engineers controlled and thus an entrée for architects into hospital design. See also Sara Wermiel, *The Fireproof Building: Technology and Public Safety in the Nineteenth-Century City* (Baltimore: Johns Hopkins University Press, 2000).

38. "Founded by James Lenox."

39. "A discussion," *AABN* 14, no. 405 (29 Sept. 1883), 145; Saint Luke's Hospital, New York City, *AR* 22 (1880), 7; George H. M. Rowe, "Historical Description of the Buildings and Grounds of the Boston City Hospital," in *A History of the Boston City Hospital from Its Foundation until 1904*, ed. David W. Cheever, A. Lawrence Mason, George W. Gay, and J. Bapst Blake (Boston: Municipal Printing Office, 1906), 80; "Typhoid in Bellevue: The Hospital Reported to Be in Bad Sanitary Condition," *NYT*, 4 Sept. 1884; "Made Ill by Sewer Gas," *NYT*, 15 Aug. 1885. See bibliographic essay, sections on miasma and environmental medicine and germ theory, antisepsis, asepsis

40. Tomes, *Gospel of Germs*, 68–88; "Hospital Construction and Organization, II," *Medical Record* 11, no. 5 (29 Jan. 1876), 73; Hutton, "Planning of Hospitals," 65; "Report of the Building Committee," 18; "Founded by James Lenox"; Wylie, *Hospitals*, 119–20.

41. *Laying of the Corner-Stone of the New York Eye and Ear Infirmary,* (New York: De Vinne, 1890), 19; "Some very curious observations," *AABN* 13, no. 380 (7 Apr. 1883), 158. Antiseptic-impregnated cloth filters were used at the Birmingham General Hospital in England, sheets of water in the Presbyterian Hospital in New York City. "Ventilation of Hospitals," *AABN* 48, no. 1015 (8 June 1895), 102–3; "Report of the Building Committee," 18; "Founded by James Lenox."

42. Taylor, *Architect and the Pavilion Hospital*, 168–213; "Wesley Hospital, Chicago," *Inland Architect and News Record* 18, no. 3 (Oct. 1891), 32; "Report of the Building Committee," 16; Thompson, "Cooked or Canned Air," editorial, *NYT*, 6 Jan. 1912; Lea, "Construction of Hospitals," 110.

43. On cubic air volume requirements, see "Circular Hospital Wards," *AABN*, 18, no. 512 (17 Oct. 1885), 186; Eaton, "Hospital Construction," 43; Kellogg, "Practical Suggestions Respecting the Ventilation of Buildings," *AABN*, 47, no. 1005 (30 Mar. 1895), 136; "Ventilation of Hospitals," 102.

44. Taylor, *Architect and the Pavilion Hospital*, 168–213; "Wesley Hospital, Chicago," 32; Hammond, *Treatise on Hospital and Asylum Construction*, 52.

45. Presbyterian Hospital, New York City, *AR* 22 (1890), 13–17; "Founded by James Lenox." Other hospitals listed room air changes of three times per hour ("Miners' Hospital," *AABN* 25, no. 703 [15 June 1889], 283) to twelve times per hour for the New York Cancer Hospital (A. A. Cox, "American Construction through English Eyes, II," *AABN*, 33, no. 815 [8 Aug. 1891], 87).

46. "Founded by James Lenox"; "New York Hospital," *NYT*, 22 Nov. 1891; Wyman, "Hospital Ventilation," *AABN* 48, no. 1010 (4 May 1895), 47; A. A. Cox, "The Johns Hopkins Hospital, Baltimore, Maryland," *AABN* 35, no. 837 (9 Jan. 1892), 24–26.

47. See BGM, New York Hospital, Committee on Heating and Ventilation, 1877–1882, MCANYPWC; Hammond, *Treatise on Hospital and Asylum Construction*, 154

48. Examples of pavilion-ward hospitals include the Grady Hospital in Atlanta; the Western Pennsylvania Hospital in Pittsburgh; the Moses Taylor Hospital in Scranton, Pennsylvania; the Miners' Hospital in Hazleton, Pennsylvania; the Newport Hospital in

Rhode Island; Saint Elizabeth's Hospital in Utica, New York; the Mary Hitchcock Hospital in Hanover, New Hampshire; Cook County Hospital and the Michael Reese Hospital in Chicago; and many more.

49. Presbyterian Hospital, New York City, *AR* 24 (1892), 12; German Hospital, New York City, *AR* (1891), 25; George Rosen, *The Structure of American Medical Practice, 1875–1941*, ed. Charles E. Rosenberg (Philadelphia: University of Pennsylvania Press, 1983), 43–50, 47.

50. Hahnemann Hospital, New York City, *AR* (1894), 5; "The Roosevelt Hospital. Where the Sick Are Treated without Money or Price," *NYT*, 6 Dec. 1891; "Sick Infants at Home," *NYT*, 10 Dec. 1892; "Good Care for Infants. Needs of the Babies' Wards of the Post-Graduate Hospital," *NYT*, 19 Jan. 1895.

51. Burdett, *Hospitals and Asylums*, 4:307. See also Richardson, *English Hospitals*, 104–31.

52. Lying-In Hospital, New York City, *AR* (1893), 15; Mouat and Snell, *Hospital Construction and Management*, 59. See also Richardson, *English Hospitals*, 15. General hospitals that rose above three stories include the New York Hospital (7), Saint Luke's Hospital in New York City (5), and Wesley Hospital in Chicago (6). Specialized hospitals over three stories include the Hahnemann Hospital, Chicago (7); the New York Ophthalmic Hospital, New York City (5); Manhattan Eye and Ear Hospital, New York City (4); Post-Graduate Hospital, New York City (6); Saint Mary's Hospital, New York City (5). Hospitals that occupied only one building (rather than separate pavilions) include the Hahnemann Hospital in Chicago, the New York Cancer Hospital, Laura Franklin Hospital for Children, Manhattan Eye, Ear, and Throat Hospital, Saint Mary's Hospital for Children, Sloane Maternity Hospital, and the House of Relief in New York City.

53. Mouat and Snell, *Hospital Construction and Management*, 51, 55; "Architecture at the Exhibition of Contemporary Art," *AABN* 5, no. 177 (17 May 1879), 159.

54. "Roosevelt Hospital," *NYT*.

55. Henry D. Noyes, in *Laying of the Corner-Stone of the New York Eye and Ear Infirmary* (New York: De Vinne, 1890), 19; "A Model Hospital Addition," *Inland Architect and News Record* 13, no. 4 (Apr. 1889), 59.

56. Noyes, in *Laying of the Corner-Stone*, 18; Henry Nathan Wessel, *History of the Jewish Hospital Association of Philadelphia* (Philadelphia: Edward Stern, 1908), 11; Ernest Flagg, "Description of St. Luke's Hospital," in *History of St. Luke's Hospital with a Description of the New Buildings* (New York: Wynkoop and Hallenbeck, 1893), 30.

57. German Hospital, New York City, *AR* (1884), 9; Montgomery Schuyler, "The Works of Cady, Berg, and See," *AREC* 6, no. 4 (June 1897), 531.

58. Adams and Schlich, "Design for Control: Surgery, Science, and Space at the Royal Victoria Hospital, Montreal, 1893–1956," *Medical History* 50, no. 3 (2006), 310. See also the bibliographic essay on operating rooms and surgery.

59. Thomas Schlich, "Surgery, Science and Modernity: Operating Rooms and Laboratories as Spaces of Control," *History of Science* 45, no. 3 (2007), 231–56; Thomas Schlich, "Negotiating Technologies in Surgery: The Controversy about Surgical Gloves in the 1890s," *BHM* 87, no. 2 (2013), 178, 183.

60. John B. Hamilton, "The Hospitals of Europe," *NYT*, 9 Feb. 1891; "Description of the Walter Garrett Memorial Building," in Pennsylvania Hospital, Philadelphia, *AR* (1897), 21–22; Graham A. J. Ayliffe and Mary P. English, *Hospital Infection: From Miasmas to MRSA* (Cambridge: Cambridge University Press, 2003), 103–17; Schlich, "Surgery, Science and Modernity," 231–56.

61. "Roosevelt Hospital." *NYT*. The asphalt floor of Bellevue Hospital's amphitheater also sloped to allow for constant drainage ("Glimpses of Bellevue," 1891).

62. Gustav Adolf Neubuhr, *Die aseptische Wundbehandlung in meinen Privathospital-ern* (Kiel: Lipsius and Tischer, 1886). On Neubuhr, see Mörgeli, *Surgeon's Stage*, 222–24; Schlich, "Negotiating Technologies in Surgery," 188; Schlich, "Asepsis and Bacteriology," 308–34; and Bette J. Clemons, "The First Modern Operating Room in America," *AORN Journal* 71, no. 1 (2000), 164–68, 170.

63. Connor, "Listerism Unmasked," 207–39; "Two Operating Theatres," *NYT*, 27 Apr. 1895.

64. Roosevelt Hospital, New York City, *AR* 19 (1890), 11; Schlich, "Asepsis and Bacteriology," 329.

65. Robert F. Weir, "Personal Reminiscences of the New York Hospital from 1856 to 1900," *General Bulletin of the Society of the New York Hospital* 1, no. 10 (14 June 1917), 1–40, 31; "The Presbyterian Hospital," *NYT*, 20 Dec. 1891; Pennsylvania Hospital, Philadelphia, *AR* (1893), 14. See also Connor, "Victorian Revolution in Surgery," 54–55; Michael Essex-Lopresti, "Operating Theatre Design," *Lancet* 353, no. 9157 (20 Mar. 1999), 1007–10.

66. "Glimpses of Bellevue," 1891. Patient categories that were particularly susceptible to infections were often given their own operating room. The Roosevelt Hospital's McLane Operating Room was devoted to gynecology patients, for example, while the Massachusetts General's Bradlee Ward was for abdominal and cerebral cases (Hammond, *Treatise on Hospital and Asylum Construction*, 93).

67. "The Hospitals of Europe," *NYT*, 9 Feb. 1891; Roosevelt Hospital, New York City, *AR* 22 (1893), 11, 14.

68. "Roosevelt Hospital." On the experience of surgery, see also Martin S. Pernick, *A Calculus of Suffering: Pain, Professionalism, and Anesthesia in Nineteenth-Century America* (New York: Columbia University Press, 1985).

69. Charles E. Rosenberg, *The Care of Strangers: The Rise of America's Hospital System* (New York: Basic Books, 1987), 166–89; J. Hood Wright Memorial Hospital, New York City, *AR* (1895), 13; Hahnemann Hospital, New York City, *AR* (1894), 7; Protestant Episcopal Hospital, Philadelphia, *AR* 1894, 16–17.

70. Medical Board Minutes, 31 Jan. 1882, 21 Feb. 1882, in MSHA; "Regents Interested Now," *NYT*, 28 April 1895; Clemons, "First Modern Operating Room," 170; James V. Ricci, "The City Hospital," *The Society of the Alumni of City Hospital, New York* (1952), 61–71.

71. Saint Luke's Hospital, New York City, *AR* 38 (1896), 11. See also Charles T. Olcott, "Pathology at the New York Hospital, 1810–1932," *BHM* 34, no. 2 (Mar./Apr. 1960), 137–47.

72. Pennsylvania Hospital, Philadelphia, *AR* (1893), 26; Rowe, "Historical Description," 29–30.

73. Medical Board Minutes, 12 Jan. 1893, MSHA. The lab opened in January 1894.

74. "To Aid in Preventing Disease. Mr. Andrew Carnegie's Gift to Bellevue Hospital Medical College," *NYT*, 27 Apr. 1884; "The Carnegie Laboratory," *NYT*, 15 May 1885. Katherine L. Carroll discusses the Harvard Medical School building in "Creating the Modern Physician: The Architecture of American Medical Schools in the Era of Medical Education Reform," *JSAH* 75, no. 1 (Mar. 2016), 50.

75. Ricci, "City Hospital," 61–71; "City's Hapless Wards," *NYT*, 10 Nov. 1895.

76. Susan M. Reverby, *Ordered to Care: The Dilemma of American Nursing, 1850–1945* (New York: Cambridge University Press, 1987), 61. Many other spaces in the hospital (bandage preparation rooms, sterilization rooms) also unofficially skewed towards nurse

"control" because the nurses performed the bulk of the tasks within them but they were added for clinical reasons. See also the bibliographic essay: history of nursing.

77. State Charities Aid Association, *Report of the Committee on Hospitals, 23 Dec. 1872, Training School for Nurses, to Be Attached to Bellevue Hospital* (New York: Cushing, Bardua, [1873]), 25; Presbyterian Hospital, New York City, *AR* 26 (1894), 12.

78. German Hospital, New York City, *AR* (1892), 25; German Hospital, New York City, *AR* (1893), 7. The Boston City Hospital added a separate four-story nurses' home across the street from the hospital in 1885. The Pennsylvania Hospital in Philadelphia opened their new Nurses' House in 1892. The German Hospital in New York City built a five-story structure for their nurse training school in 1894. Saint Luke's Hospital in New York City's new building plan of 1895 assigned two (of a total of eight) pavilions to the nurses' needs; one nurses' pavilion was built in the initial construction phase.

79. George R. Stuart, *A History of St. Vincent's Hospital in New York City* ([New York]: Private, 1938), 22; Virginia G. Drachman, *Hospital with a Heart: Women Doctors and the Paradox of Separatism at the New England Hospital, 1862–1969* (Ithaca, NY: Cornell University Press, 1984), 134; BGM, New York Hospital, 5 Feb. 1889, 6 Mar. 1883, MCANYPWC. The quality of such rented or repurposed building space was sometimes debatable. In 1886, at the City Hospital in New York City, the nurses were moved into the adjacent, recently vacated former Smallpox Hospital building (NYAM, MS. City Hospital, Welfare Island, NY [miscellaneous papers, photos, 1897–1952. Roster of Nursing School alumnae, 1877–1934], folder 2 history, undated [1924–1951]). See also Annmarie Adams, "Rooms of their Own: Nurses' Residences at Montreal's Royal Victoria Hospital," *Material Culture Review* 40 (Fall 1994), 29–41.

80. Dorothy Giles, *A Candle in Her Hand: A Story of the Nursing Schools of Bellevue Hospital* (New York: G. P. Putnam's Sons, 1949), 98–99; John Maynard Woodworth, *Hospitals and Hospital Construction* (Washington, DC: US Marine Hospital Service, 1874), 9.

81. Niernsee, *Review of "Hospital Plans"* (Baltimore: 1876), 7; Billings, "On the Plans for the Johns Hopkins . . . pt. II," *Medical Record* 12, no. 3 (3 Mar. 1877), 146; "New York Hospital."

82. W. B. Hugo Downes and Thomas Porter Blunt, "The Influence of Light upon the Development of Bacteria," *Nature* 16 (1877), 218. Later studies proved this germicidal effect was the result of the UV rays. Hutton, "Planning of Hospitals," 65. John R. Niernsee especially recommended these solaria, which originated with Stephen Smith's essay for the Johns Hopkins Hospital. Niernsee, *Review of "Hospital Plans"*, 5–6; Johns Hopkins Hospital, *Hospital Plans: Five Essays Relating to the Construction, Organization & Management of Hospitals . . .* (New York: William Wood, 1875), 302–4.

83. Smith, in *Hospital Plans: Five Essays,* 302–4; Billings, "On the Plans for the Johns Hopkins . . . pt. II," 146. The service building served two surgical ward pavilions, eliminating some spatial redundancies, but undermining the idea that each ward was a wholly independent unit. The complete absence of plumbing in the ward itself would come to be a hardship in nurse service.

84. Taylor, *Architect and the Pavilion Hospital*, 134–67; Jeremy Taylor, "Circular Hospital Wards: Professor John Marshall's Concept and Its Exploration by the Architectural Profession in the 1880s," *Medical History* 32, no. 4 (1988), 433; C. H. Blackall, "The Stuyvenberg Hospital, Antwerp," *AABN* 19, no. 528 (6 Feb. 1886), 63; Richardson, *English Hospitals*, 7–8, 32. American hospitals incorporating centralized wards included the New York Cancer Hospital, the Mary Hitchcock Memorial Hospital, the Wesley Hospital in Chicago, the Memorial Wards of the Pennsylvania Hospital in Philadelphia, temporary wards at the

Lakeside Hospital in Cleveland, and the Children's Ward of the Presbyterian Hospital in Philadelphia.

85. As late as 1894 a German hospital expert, Herr Boettger, advocated thirty-bed wards as the best size, with twenty-bed wards for those "containing certain classes of patients," ("A lecture," *AABN* 44, no. 956 [21 Apr. 1894], 26).

86. New York Nursery and Child's Hospital, New York City, *AR* 30 (1884), 24. See also "Fever Hospitals. IV," *Architecture and Building* 24, no. 8 (22 Feb. 1896), 92.

87. Burdett, *Hospitals and Asylums*, 3:55; Rosenberg, *Care of Strangers*, 237–61.

88. German Hospital, New York City, *AR* (1882), 15; Rosner, *A Once Charitable Enterprise: Hospitals and Health Care in Brooklyn and New York, 1885–1915* (New York: Cambridge University Press, 1982), 62–93, 65. Physically distinct facilities for paying patients (including full-pay patients) clearly existed well before that point; whether they were used as enticements, used completely by private patients, or used by charity patients who could pay for part of their stay remains an unresolved question.

89. Thomas Addis Emmet, *Incidents of My Life: Professional, Literary, Social. With Services in the Cause of Ireland* (New York: G. P. Putnam's Sons, 1911), 333; Albert R. Lamb, *The Presbyterian Hospital and the Columbia-Presbyterian Medical Center 1868–1943. A History of a Great Medical Adventure* (New York: Columbia University Press, 1955), 57; Rosner, *Once Charitable Enterprise*, 62–121.

90. Hospitals with separate pavilions for paying patients included Saint Elizabeth's Hospital in Utica, New York; the Newport Hospital in Rhode Island, and the new Saint Luke's Hospital in New York City. The New York Cancer Hospital in New York City had to develop unusual layouts for their private patient rooms that occupied the same centralized floor plan as their large open wards.

91. David Rosner, "Social Control and Social Service: The Changing Use of Space in Charity Hospitals," *Radical History Review* 21 (Fall 1979), 189.

92. G. H. M. Rowe, "Isolating Wards and Hospitals for Infectious Diseases," in Billings and Hurd, *Hospitals, Dispensaries and Nursing*, 132–41; and Dr. J. L. Notter, comments on Dr. M. L. Davis's "Hospital for Contagious and Infectious Diseases," in Billings and Hurd, *Hospitals, Dispensaries and Nursing*, 175–83.

93. "Health Department's Pride. New Reception Hospital Nearly Ready for Patients," *NYT*, 11 July 1893. Knowledge of fireproofing was incomplete, and awareness that although iron and steel were noncombustible, they were not fire "proof," was only developing. See also Wermiel, *Fireproof Building*.

94. John Shaw Billings, *Description of the Johns Hopkins Hospital* (Baltimore: Isaac Friedenwald, 1890). Alistair Fair's analysis of this hospital as a "laboratory of heating and ventilation," has illuminated the revolutionary aspect of the design ("'A Laboratory of Heating and Ventilation': The Johns Hopkins Hospital as Experimental Architecture, 1870–90," *Journal of Architecture* 19, no. 3 [2014], 370). My analysis of this isolation building diverges from Fair's on two points. First, Fair describes the perforated plates in the three experimental rooms as exhaust ducts with air flowing downward through them (370). Based on Billings's description, I have discussed them as fresh air-supply grilles, with an upward flow of air around the patient (Billings, *Description of the Johns Hopkins Hospital*, 96). Second, according to Fair, the rooms in this isolation ward were "meant not so much for those patients with particularly infectious conditions as those whose conditions meant that they themselves were deemed 'offensive,' perhaps particularly malodorous" ("A Laboratory of Heating and Ventilation," 369). In traditional pavilion-ward literature, smaller wards adjacent to a large ward were indeed often intended for

the separation of socially or medically offensive patients. In practice, a separate pavilion full of isolation rooms was far more likely to house patients suffering under a specific ailment category known or believed to be transmissible (erysipelas, smallpox, typhus, cholera).

95. Presbyterian Hospital, New York City, *AR* 22 (1890), 14 and *AR* 23 (1891), 17.

96. Hahnemann Hospital, New York City, *AR* (1885–1888), 41; "The Woman's Hospital," *NYT*, 18 Nov. 1881; "New Hospital for Children. Dedication of St. Mary's in Thirty-Fourth-Street Next Week," *NYT*, 17 Dec. 1880; BGM, New York Hospital, 1 Dec. 1892 and MBM, 27 Nov. 1892, MCANYPWC; "Wesley Hospital, Chicago," 32; Flagg, "Description of St. Luke's Hospital," 33–34.

Chapter 4. Hygienic Decentralization vs. Functional Centralization: Reasons for Continuity and Change, 1898–1917

Epigraphs: Frederick D. Keppel, "The Modern Hospital as a Health Factory," *Modern Hospital* 7, no. 4 (Oct. 1916), 304; Albert J. Ochsner, in Ochsner and Meyer J. Sturm, *The Organization, Construction and Management of Hospitals, with Numerous Plans and Details* (Chicago: Cleveland Press, 1907), 26.

1. "Girl's Hospital Experience," *NYT*, 4 June 1899, 20.

2. See John S. Haller, *Kindly Medicine: Physio-Medicalism in America, 1836–1911* (Kent, OH: Kent State University Press, 1997); James C. Whorton, *Nature Cures: The History of Alternative Medicine in America* (Oxford: Oxford University Press, 2002); Roger Cooter, ed., *Studies in the History of Alternative Medicine* (Basingstoke, UK: Macmillan, 1988). While such environmental therapies have long been associated with alternative medicine, that practitioners of "scientific medicine" and allopathy made medicinal use of environmental influence during this period is also undeniable. The study of rickets and the discovery of vitamin D was a convincing demonstration that environmental factors could have immediate physiological effects. The modern-day iteration of this approach, which considers environmental factors immediate influences on health, is also referred to as "clinical ecology" or "environmental medicine." It tends to see environmental factors as contributing to ailments in addition to cures.

3. Howell, *Technology in the Hospital: Transforming Patient Care in the Early Twentieth Century* (Baltimore: Johns Hopkins University Press, 1995), 59.

4. Lambert, "Is Pavilion or Sky-Scraper Hospital Best?" *MH* 1, no. 2 (Oct. 1913), 95–98. Lambert referred to "administrative centralization." I use the phrase "functional centralization" as more expressive to modern readers of the broader spatial intent—to design all the disparate service elements (medical as well as administrative) for efficient, interactive performance of tasks.

5. Henry C. Burdett, *Hospitals and Asylums of the World: Their Origin, History, Construction, Administration, Management, and Legislation* (London: J. & A. Churchill, Scientific Press, 1891–93), 4:98–100.

6. See George Weisz, *Divide and Conquer: A Comparative History of Medical Specialization* (Oxford: Oxford University Press, 2006); David Rosner, *A Once Charitable Enterprise: Hospitals and Health Care in Brooklyn and New York, 1885–1915* (New York: Cambridge University Press, 1982), 13–35; George Rosen, "The Hospital, Historical Sociology of a Community Institution," in *The Hospital in Modern Society*, ed. Eliot Friedson (London: Free Press of Glencoe, 1963), 29; Caroline C. S. Murphy, "From Friedenheim to Hospice:

A Century of Cancer Hospitals," in *The Hospital in History*, ed. Lindsay Granshaw and Roy Porter (New York: Routledge, 1989).

7. Stevens, *In Sickness and in Wealth* (New York: Basic Books, 1989); Rosenberg, *The Care of Strangers: The Rise of America's Hospital System* (New York: Basic Books, 1987); Starr, *The Social Transformation of American Medicine* (New York: Basic Books, 1982); Rosner, *Once Charitable Enterprise*, 36–60. See also David T. Marshall, "Hospital Charity Abused," editorial, *NYT*, 1 Mar. 1903; "Trapping Pseudo-Paupers Who Cheat Free Dispensaries and Clinics," editorial, *NYT*, 19 Mar. 1905; "Financial Problems of the Hospitals," *NYT*, 3 Jan. 1904.

8. Annmarie Adams, *Medicine by Design: The Architect and the Modern Hospital, 1893–1943* (Minneapolis: University of Minnesota Press, 2008), 108.

9. Albert J. Ochsner, "Essentials in the Construction of Hospitals for Large Cities," *JAMA* 39, no. 21 (22 Nov. 1902), 1315. Ochsner was referring to Johns Hopkins Hospital, *Hospital Plans: Five Essays Relating to the Construction, Organization and Management of Hospitals . . .* (New York: William Wood, 1875). Book-length works on hospital design were still published, but they were typically references rather than design manuals. See Albert J. Ochsner and Meyer J. Sturm, *The Organization, Construction and Management of Hospitals: With Numerous Plans and Details* (Chicago: Cleveland Press, 1907); John Allen Hornsby and Richard E. Schmidt, *The Modern Hospital: Its Architecture: Its Equipment: Its Operation* (Philadelphia: W. B. Saunders Company, 1914); and Antoine Depage, Paul Vandervelde, and Victor Cheval, *La construction des hôpitaux* (Brussels: Misch and Thron, 1907).

10. J. W. Fowler, "Poetry and Prose in the Hospital," *MH* 1, no. 2 (Oct. 1913), 105; T. J. Van der Bent, "Causes of and Remedies for Unsatisfactory Hospital Architecture," *MH* 2, no. 2 (Feb. 1914), 84; Adams, *Medicine by Design*, 94–95; Adams, "Modernism and Medicine: The Hospitals of Stevens and Lee, 1916–1932," *JSAH* 58, no. 1 (1999), 45.

11. Fowler, "Poetry and Prose," 104–5. See also Presbyterian Hospital, New York City, *AR* 31 (1899), 10–11; Presbyterian Hospital, New York City, *AR* 32 (1900), 11; Bellevue and Allied Hospitals, New York City, *AR* 2 (1903); Saint Luke's Hospital, New York City, *AR* 47 (1897), 10; "Mr. Morgan's Beneficence," *NYT*, 15 Jan. 1897; Cameron Logan and Julie Willis, "International Travel as Medical Research: Architecture and the Modern Hospital," *Health and History* 12, no. 2 (2010), 116–33; J. R. Schmidt, "The New General Hospital at Cincinnati," *AREC* 37, no. 5 (May 1915), 453.

12. R. L. Thompson, "Berlin Letter," *MH* 1, no. 2 (Oct. 1913), 132; W. Gilman Thompson, quoted in *Report of the Commission on Hospitals Appointed by the Mayor of the City of New York* (New York: Martin B. Brown, 1909), 133; W. Gilman Thompson, "New York's Hospitals Outclassed in Europe," *NYT*, 12 Feb. 1911. See also E. F. Stevens, "The American Hospital Development," *AREC* 38, no. 6 (Dec. 1915), 641–61; "Letter from Vienna. European and American Methods of Building Hospitals Contrasted," *MH* 2, no. 1 (Jan. 1914), 56–57; "How Diseases Are Treated in Europe. Dr. E. F. King Tells What He Saw in Many Hospitals," *NYT*, 27 Oct. 1901; E. F. Stevens, "The Surgical Unit. European and American Architecture Compared—Description of Equipment," *MH* 1, no. 1 (Sept. 1913), 18–21.

13. Schmidt, "New General Hospital at Cincinnati," 453–63; "Finest Hospital in the World in Cincinnati," *NYT*, 1 Dec. 1912; Louis J. Frank to Jos. H. Cohen, 6 Jan. 1916, box 10, 131, Louis Frank Papers 1921–1935, folder 1 of 5, Beth Israel Hospital Archive; Van der Bent, "Causes of and Remedies for Unsatisfactory Hospital Architecture," 84–85; W. Gilman Thompson, "New York's Hospitals Outclassed in Europe," *NYT*, 12 Feb. 1911.

14. Bertrand E. Taylor, "Hospital Planning, III. Suburban Hospitals," *BB* 13, no. 3 (Mar. 1904), 47; Samuel W. Lambert, *Memorandum on the Ideal Development of Hospital and*

Medical School (New York: Privately printed, 1912), 14; Charlotte Aikens, "The Hospital Review," *TN&HR* 48, no. 1 (Jan. 1912), 38. See also Oliver H. Bartine, "Building the Hospital—Organization and Methods," *MH* 4, no. 2 (Feb. 1915), 117; Charlotte A. Aikens, "The Futility of Competitions in Hospital Plans," *TN&HR* 48, no. 3 (Mar. 1912), 148–50. The architectural competition did not end abruptly. Some prominent competitions in this era include the new Mount Sinai Hospital in New York City (1898), the Providence City Hospital of Rhode Island (1907), and the Peter Bent Brigham Hospital in Boston (1904). See also Jeremy Taylor, *The Architect and the Pavilion Hospital: Dialogue and Design Creativity in England, 1850–1914* (London: Leicester University Press, 1997), 72–100.

15. Meyer J. Sturm, "Principles of Hospital Construction," *MH* 5, no. 5 (Nov. 1915), 353–55. By 1915, Sturm had designed dozens of hospital buildings. Adams has discussed the specialized practice of Edward F. Stevens, but there is very little historical information available on the other firms that specialized in hospitals (Adams, *Medicine by Design* and "Modernism and Medicine" 89–108).

16. Sturm, "Recognition of Hospital Architects," *MH* 4, no. 3 (Mar. 1915), 211; E. Stanley Field, "Hospital Architects and Competitions," letter to editor, *MH* 4, no. 4 (Apr. 1915), 284.

17. Meyer J. Sturm, "Practical Idealism in Planning Hospitals," *TN* 45, no. 3 (Sept. 1910), 150–55; Warren C. Hill, "The Hospital Superintendent and the Architect," *Transactions of the American Hospital Association* 17 (1915), 196–201; "Extras in Hospital Architecture," *MH* 4, no. 5 (May 1915), 326–27. See also Gail Cooper, *Air-Conditioning America: Engineers and the Controlled Environment, 1900–1960* (Baltimore: Johns Hopkins University Press, 1998), 61–62.

18. Providence City Hospital, Providence, RI, *AR* 1 (1910), 41; "Physicians Swell New Hospital Fund," *NYT*, 15 May 1910; William J. Mayo, as quoted in Fredrick A. Willius, *Henry Stanley Plummer: A Diversified Genius* (Springfield, IL: Charles C. Thomas, 1960), 39; Bonnie Richter, ed., *The Ellerbe Tradition: Seventy Years of Architecture and Engineering* (Minneapolis: Ellerbe, 1980), 15; Markoe to Lewis Cass Ledyard, 1 Feb. 1901, in Correspondence of Drs. James Markoe and Samuel W. Lambert, v. 2, Medical Board, Society of the Lying-In Hospital of the City of New York, MCANYPWC.

19. Morris J. Vogel, "Managing Medicine: Creating a Profession of Hospital Administration in the United States, 1895–1915," in Granshaw and Porter, *Hospital in History*, 243–60; Bellevue Hospital, New York City, *AR* 7 (1908), 40. On the rise of hospital consultants and professional hospital administrators, see Adams, *Medicine by Design*, 102–4; Stevens, *In Sickness and in Wealth*, 68–74; and S. S. Goldwater, *On Hospitals* (New York: Macmillan, 1947). In the United States, hospital consultants actively worked to develop the new position into a profession.

20. Susan M. Reverby, *Ordered to Care: The Dilemma of American Nursing, 1850–1945* (New York: Cambridge University Press, 1987), 153, 144; Anna Goodrich, "Some Common Points of Weakness in Hospital Construction," *TN* 32, no. 5 (May 1904), 311–15; Charlotte A. Aikens, "What to Avoid in Planning a Hospital," *TN* 50, no. 5 (May 1913), 291; M. E. McCalmont "Practical Details in Hospital Planning and Equipment. Part II—General Continued," *BB* 22, no. 7 (July 1913), 159.

21. M. E. McCalmont, "Practical Details in Hospital Planning and Equipment. Part II," 159; M. E. McCalmont, "Co-Operation in Hospital Planning," *American Architect* 100, no. 1874 (22 Nov. 1911), 208; Mount Zion Hospital, San Francisco, *AR* (1912), 12.

22. Adams, Schwartzman, and Theodore, "Collapse and Expand: Architecture and Tuberculosis Therapy in Montreal, 1909, 1933, 1954," *Technology and Culture* 49, no. 4 (2008), 912. Environmental therapy was also a part of the design of asylums for persons with men-

tal illness. See Carla Yanni, *The Architecture of Madness* (Minneapolis: University of Minnesota Press, 2007). Thomas Mann's novel *The Magic Mountain* (Berlin: S. Fischer, 1924) reveals the collision of cultural, medical, and environmental expectations in sanatoria. On the history of tuberculosis sanatoria, see Annmarie Adams and Stacie Burke, "'Not a Shack in the Woods': Architecture for Tuberculosis in Muskoka and Toronto," *Canadian Bulletin of the History of Medicine* 23, no. 2 (2006), 429–55; Sheila M. Rothman, *Living in the Shadow of Death: Tuberculosis and the Social Experience of Illness in American History* (Baltimore: Johns Hopkins University Press, 1994); David L. Ellison, *Healing Tuberculosis in the Woods: Medicine and Science at the End of the Nineteenth Century* (Westport, CT: Greenwood Press, 1994); Frank Ryan, *The Forgotten Plague: How the Battle against Tuberculosis Was Won and Lost* (Boston: Back Bay Books, 1993); Susan Sontag, *Illness as Metaphor* (New York: Farrar, Straus and Giroux, 1978); Michael Worboys, "The Sanatorium Treatment for Consumption in Britain, 1890–1914," in *Medical Innovations in Historical Perspective*, ed. John V. Pickstone (New York: St. Martin's, 1992), 47–71.

23. Presbyterian Hospital, New York City, *AR* 38 (1906), 15; "Hospital's Strong Ally— An Open Air Roof Ward, Experiment at the Presbyterian Institution a Success," *NYT*, 9 Dec. 1906; Saint Mary's Hospital for Children, New York City, *AR* 36 (1905), 8; W. Gilman Thompson, "The Treatment of Pneumonia, Especially by Outdoor Air," *American Journal of the Medical Sciences* 135, no. 1 (Jan. 1908), 16; "Pneumonia Being Conquered In the Open Air," *NYT*, 26 Jan. 1908; Christian Holmes, "A Suggestive Plan," *JAMA* 50, no. 13 (1908), 1026.

24. Worboys, "Sanatorium Treatment for Consumption," 52.

25. Adams and Burke, "Not a Shack in the Woods," 431; Adams, Schwartzman, and Theodore, "Collapse and Expand," 914; Nancy Tomes, "Tuberculosis Religion," in *The Gospel of Germs: Men, Women, and the Microbe in American Life* (Cambridge, MA: Harvard University Press, 1998), 113–34; Margaret Campbell, "What Tuberculosis Did for Modernism: The Influence of a Curative Environment on Modernist Design and Architecture," *Medical History* 49, no. 4 (2005), 463–88.

26. Elizabeth Fee and Dorothy Porter, "Public Health, Preventive Medicine, and Professionalization: England and America in the Nineteenth Century," in Andrew Wear, ed., *Medicine in Society: Historical Essays* (New York: Cambridge University Press, 1992), 268.

27. "Portable Hospital Ready. Bellevue Ready to Try Open-Air Consumption Treatment," *NYT*, 18 Apr. 1904, 6; Adams and Burke, "Not a Shack in the Woods," 440.

28. The use of these balconies and the fresh air cure continued past the development of antibiotic therapies and surgery. Adams, Schwartzmann, and Theodore, "Collapse and Expand," 912–13.

29. August Rollier, *La cure de soleil* (Paris: Bailliere, 1914); William Atkinson, "The Orientation of Hospital Buildings," *BB* 12, no. 7 (July 1903), 134–40; William Atkinson, *The Orientation of Buildings or Planning for Sunlight* (New York: John Wiley and Sons, 1912). M. Carey Lea suggested angle wings with the point of the *V* facing south for maximum sunlight in 1887. M. C. L., "The Orientation of Hospitals," *AABN* 21, no. 592 (30 Apr. 1887), 215.

30. Thompson, "Fresh Air Treatment in Hospital Wards," in *Medical and Surgical Report of the Presbyterian Hospital* 8, ed. John S. Thatcher and George Woolsey (Dec. 1908), 10–19; S. S. Goldwater, "Notes on Hospital Planning, II," *BB* 21, no. 8 (1912), 207. The works of Leonard Hill in England were highly influential—see *The Science of Ventilation and Open-Air Treatment. Part I.* (Medical Research Committee/National Health Insurance, 1919).

31. Goldwater, "Lost Art of Hospital Ventilation," *MH* 22, no. 3 (Mar. 1924), 249;

Cooper, *Air-Conditioning America*, 61–63; Arnold Brunner and S. S. Goldwater, "New Children's Pavilion of Mount Sinai Hospital, New York," *MH* 20, no. 2 (Feb. 1923), 126; "Robinson Memorial Building," *AA* (10 Jan. 1917), 19. The administrators of Mount Zion Hospital in San Francisco ran their mechanical system only during short periods in day-time ("Where Free Patients Will Fare Well," *MH* 3, no. 1 [July 1914], 6). See also C.-E. A. Winslow, *Fresh Air and Ventilation* (New York: E. P. Dutton, 1926); D. D. Kimball, "Some Essentials of Hospital Heating and Ventilation," *American Architect* 100, no. 1869 (18 Oct. 1911); Frank Sutton, "Is Mechanical Ventilation in Hospitals a Success?" *MH* 6, no. 5 (May 1916), 317–19; W. Gilman Thompson, "Cooked or Canned Air," editorial, *NYT*, 6 Jan. 1912.

32. Bellevue and Allied Hospitals, New York City, *AR* 4 (1905), 25; Presbyterian Hospital, New York City, *AR* 38 (1906), 13. See also "Pneumonia Being Conquered in the Open Air," *NYT*, 26 Jan. 1908, SM6; "Hospital's Strong Ally"; W. P. Northrup, "The Open Air Roof Ward," in Thatcher and Woolsey, *Medical and Surgical Report* 8 (Dec. 1908), 1–9; Thompson, "Fresh Air Treatment in Hospital Wards," 10–19.

33. Bellevue and Allied Hospitals, New York City, *AR* 6 (1907), 24; "Work on New Bellevue Hospital Soon to Begin," *NYT*, 10 July 1905; "Cost of New Bellevue Will be $11,000,000," *NYT*, 23 Apr. 1904; "Rockefeller Gives Another $500,000," *NYT*, 31 May 1908; BGM, New York Hospital, 24 Dec. 1909, MCANYPWC. On the addition of fresh air facilities to existing hospitals, see also Medical Board Minutes, 14 Feb. 1911, MSHA; Roosevelt Hospital, New York City, *AR* 36 (1907), 17–18; Saint Mary's Hospital for Children, New York City, *AR* 38 (1907); Provident Hospital, Chicago, *AR* 22 (1913); "A New Hospital of Many Ideals," *NYT*, 11 Apr. 1915; and A. L. Goodman, "Old Building Reconstructed into an Excellent Children's Hospital," *MH* 5, no. 3 (Sept. 1915), 164–67.

34. "New York Hospital for Ruptured and Crippled," *MH* 3, no. 6 (Dec. 1914), 355.

35. W. Gilman Thompson, "Modern Hospital Construction," *JAMA* 49, no. 12 (21 Sept. 1907), 993.

36. Goldwater, "Notes on Hospital Planning, II," 207; Golder, "The New Bethesda Maternity Hospital in Cincinnati," *MH* 4, no. 3 (1915), 171; "The New Bethany Hospital, Kansas City, Kansas," *MH* 7, no. 4 (Oct. 1916), 293.

37. See "Physical Therapeutics in New York Hospitals," *MH* 7, no. 3 (Sept. 1921), 236–37; "German Hospital Gives Free Massage. Machines Already Extensively in Use in Europe Introduced for the First Time Here," *NYT*, 12 June 1907; Haller, *Kindly Medicine*.

38. John E. Brown, "A Comparison between German and American Hospital Construction," *BB* 22, no. 4 (Apr. 1913), 73–76; Jewish Hospital, Philadelphia, *AR* 41 (1906), 19; Wesley Hospital, Chicago, *AR* 21 (1909), 36; Barnes Hospital, Saint Louis, *AR* 1 (1915–1916), 30–32.

39. "How Diseases Are Treated in Europe"; "Light Cure for Pain. Cancer Hospital Finds 500 Candle Power Electric Rays Helpful," *NYT*, 1 Nov. 1907; Barnes Hospital, Saint Louis, *AR* 1 (1915–1916), 30. See also Daniel Freund, *American Sunshine: Diseases of Darkness and the Quest for Natural Light* (Chicago: University of Chicago Press, 2012), 37–96; Murphy, "From Friedenheim to Hospice," 223–42.

40. Jeanne Kisacky, "Restructuring Isolation: Hospital Architecture, Medicine, and Disease Prevention," *BHM* 79, no. 1 (2005), 1–49.

41. Richardson, "Manual of Aseptic Technique for Providence City Hospital," appended to Providence City Hospital, RI, *AR* 6 (1916), 6. An "infection" did not necessarily mean a specific disease; it could mean a specific level of contamination, as in something or someone that had just come off the street, or an area that contained septic infections of various germs. Richardson's manual was widely quoted and reiterated (for example, Lucile A.

Butler and Virginia Rau, "The Hospital Care of Contagious Diseases," *MH* 10, no. 3 [March 1918], 195). Richardson's view was both a crystallization and a radical reinterpretation of the interactions of germs and buildings (for example, see George H. M. Rowe, "The Hospital 'Unit,'" *BB* 13, no. 8 [1904], 156).

42. Richardson, "Manual of Aseptic Technique," 19; Richardson, "Contagious Group of the Providence City Hospital," *AA* 100, no. 1869 (18 Oct. 1911), 159. Wendy Madsen notes that infection control often conflicted with economy in materials—sterilization and cleaning shortened the lifespan of many supplies, including surgical instruments as well as bedding ("Keeping the Lid on Infection: Infection Control Practices of a Regional Queensland Hospital 1930–50," *Nursing Inquiry* 7, no. 2 [2000], 81–90).

43. John Hornsby, cited in Richard E. Schmidt, "Hospitals for Communicable Diseases," *MH* 10, no. 3 (Mar. 1918), 154; Schmidt, "Hospitals for Communicable Diseases," 156. On Joseph Grancher see Annick Opinel, "The Pasteur Hospital as an Element of Emile Roux's Anti-Diphtheria Apparatus (1890–1914)," *Dynamis* 27 (2007), 83–106; and Toby Gelfand, "11 January 1887, the Day Medicine Changed: Joseph Grancher's Defense of Pasteur's Treatment for Rabies," *BHM* 76 (2002), 698–718.

44. "Screen Suggestions for the Coming Summer," *MH* 16, no. 3 (Mar. 1921), 277; J. G. Wilson, "The Contagious Disease Hospital for Immigrants at Ellis Island, NY," *MH* 9, no. 5 (Nov. 1917), 315; L. A. Lamoreaux, "Architecture of the Modern Hospital," *MH* 1, no. 1 (Sept. 1913), 41–42.

45. Meyer J. Sturm, "The Evanston General Hospital's Contagious Pavilion," *MH* 3, no. 3 (Sept. 1914), 168.

46. James Otis Post and S. S. Goldwater, "The New Samaritan Hospital of Troy, NY," *MH* 4, no. 1 (Jan. 1915), 9–10.

47. *Ellis Island Statue of Liberty National Monument: Historic Structures Report, Units 2, 3, 4* (US Dept of the Interior/National Park Service, 1988), pt 2, exhibit 2, 4; S. S. Goldwater, "The St. Louis Children's Hospital," *MH* 5, no. 6 (Dec. 1915), 387–94 (shower delineated on plan on 393). It is also likely that the shower-bath leading into an operating facility was used after a long operation, not before (Clarence W. King, "The Small Southern Hospital," *MH* 15, no. 4 [Oct. 1920], 263); Post and Goldwater, "The New Samaritan Hospital of Troy, NY," 9–10.

48. Edward F. Stevens, "The Contagious Hospital," *BB* 17, no. 9 (Sept. 1908), 183–84; D. L. Richardson, "Disinfection as Part of the Hospital Administration," *MH* 1, no. 2 (Oct. 1913), 76–77.

49. "On the Use of an Elastic Ward Unit in the Construction of Hospitals for Contagious Diseases," *BB* 19, no. 9 (Sept. 1910), 210; Kisacky, "Restructuring Isolation," 39–45; Adams, *Medicine by Design*, 56–61; Prior, "Architecture of the Hospital," 95–96. Stevens attributed the design of the Pasteur Hospital to Louis Pasteur himself, but the architect involved was Florentin Martin (Stevens, "Contagious Hospital," 183; Opinel, "Pasteur Hospital," 90–92). On aseptic isolation practices and designs before the Pasteur Hospital, see Henry Greenway, "A New Mode of Hospital Construction," *British Medical Journal* 1, no. 593 (11 May 1872), 495–97; M. L. Davis, "Hospital for Contagious and Infectious Diseases," 175–76; G. H. M. Rowe, "Isolating Wards and Hospitals for Infectious Diseases," 132–41; and Dr. Alan Herbert and Dr. W. Douglass Hogg, "Isolation Wards and Hospitals in Paris," 162–74, all in John Shaw Billings and Henry M. Hurd, *Hospitals, Dispensaries and Nursing* (Baltimore: Johns Hopkins University Press and Scientific Press, 1894).

50. "Contagious Group of the Providence City Hospital," 159; "More Rockefeller Millions to Science," *NYT*, 18 Oct. 1910; "Germ-Proof Rooms in Modern Hospital," *NYT*, 13 Oct. 1910.

51. Wilson, "Contagious Disease Hospital for Immigrants at Ellis Island, NY," 313–17; "New Island in the Bay," *NYT*, 18 Dec. 1904; Roosevelt Hospital, New York City, *AR* 43 (1914); A. Levinson, "The Children's Hospital of Vienna," *MH* 4, no. 4 (Apr. 1915), 262–65; "New Hospital of Many Ideals"; Goldman, "Old Building Reconstructed," 164–67. See also Marguerite M. Jackson and Patricia Lynch, "Isolation Practices: A Historical Perspective," *American Journal of Infection Control* 13, no. 1 (1985), 21–31. Isolation hospitals might still have large wards that included only one "germ" per ward (e.g., measles or diphtheria wards) with the understanding that a patient could not be reinfected by the same pathogen while suffering from it.

52. Frederic W. Southworth and Lucius W. Johnson, "Requirements of Modern Contagious Disease Hospitals," *MH* 5, no. 4 (Oct. 1915), 221–24; Providence City Hospital, RI, *AR* 1 (1910), 18.

53. Harlan D. Unrau, *Historic Resource Study (Historical Component). Ellis Island Statue of Liberty National Monument New York-New Jersey* (US Dept. of the Interior/NPS, 1984), 2:646; "The Sarah Morris Hospital for Children, Chicago, Ill.," *AA* 108, no. 2077 (13 Oct. 1915), 248. See also Joseph B. De Lee and Richard E. Schmidt, "The Chicago Lying-In Hospital and Dispensary," *MH* 4, no. 6 (June 1915), 386–88; Herbert E. Davis and Anna M. Schill, "New Isolation Unit, Hurley Hospital, Flint, Michigan," *MH* 6, no. 2 (Feb. 1916), 98–101.

54. Samuel S. Woody, "Municipal Hospitals for Contagious Diseases," *American Journal of Public Health* 2, no. 9 (Sept. 1912), 726. The story of Typhoid Mary highlights some of these issues. See Judith Walzer Leavitt, *Typhoid Mary: Captive to the Public's Health* (Boston: Beacon Press, 1996).

55. "A Glass Hospital Ward," *AABN* 61, no. 1177 (16 July 1898), 24; Henry Carleton, "Materials for Hospital Floors," *BB* 15, no. 11 (Nov. 1906), 236; William Paul Gerhard, "Hospital Sanitation—I," *AABN* 87, no. 1530 (22 Apr. 1905), 128; Jeanne Kisacky, "Germs Are in the Details: Aseptic Design and General Contractors at the Lying-in Hospital of the City of New York, 1897–1901," *Construction History* 28, no. 1 (2013), 83–106. See also Bartine, "Hospital Construction. The Viewpoint of a Hospital Superintendent," *AABN* 108, no. 2077 (13 Oct. 1915), 241; Charles L. Hubbard, "The Question of Heat & Ventilation," *AREC* 34, no. 3 (Sept. 1913), 250; Wm. Paul Gerhard, "Hospital Sanitation—II," *AABN* 87, no. 1531 (29 Apr. 1905), 135–37. On the adoption of technologies in other building types, see Reyner Banham, *The Architecture of the Well-Tempered Environment* (London: Architectural Press, 1969).

56. Mount Sinai Hospital Building Committee, Minutes, 27 Dec. 1901, MSHA; "Tile Floors and Walls for Hospitals," *AA* 111, no. 2142 (10 Jan. 1917), 32; Allen and Collens, "The New Woman's Hospital, New York," *AREC* 21, no. 4 (Apr. 1907), 281–94; "Cook County Hospital, Chicago, Ill.," *AA* 108, no. 2077 (13 Oct. 1915), 247.

57. "Artificial Black Marble," *AA* 58, no. 146 (11 Dec. 1897) 91. The black color of the material was a detriment to its widespread use in hospitals. The Society of the Lying-In Hospital of the City of New York, *Description of Building and Floor Plans* [n.p., n.d.], Pamphlet, MCANYPWC; Lying-In Hospital, New York City, *AR* 105 (1903), 21.

58. 26 Feb. 1901, Correspondence of Drs. James Markoe and Samuel W. Lambert, vol. 2, Society of the Lying-In Hospital, Medical Board, MCANYPWC; Providence City Hospital, RI, *AR* 1 (1910), 4; William Paul Gerhard, "The Plumbing, Water Supply and Drainage of Hospitals, III," *Architecture and Building* 28, no. 25 (18 June 1898), 188; Gerhard, "Hospital Sanitation—I," 1905, 127–30; "Chicago Lying-In Hospital," *AA* 108, no. 2079 (27 Oct. 1915), 283; Bertrand E. Taylor, "Hospital Planning. V," *BB* 13, no. 5 (May 1904), 91.

59. Henry Hun, "A Study of a Hospital Plan," *Albany Medical Annals* 18, no. 9 (Sept.

1897), 448. See also Kimball, "Some Essentials of Hospital Heating and Ventilation"; H. E. Hannaford, "Architecture and Equipment of the New Cincinnati General Hospital," *MH* 2, no. 1 (Jan. 1914), 1–8.

60. E. F. Stevens, "Vacuum Cleaning Systems a Desirable Feature in Modern Hospitals," *AA* 100, no. 1868 (11 Oct. 1911), 148; Henry M. Hurd, "Hospital Construction from a Medical Standpoint," *BB* 9, no. 12 (Dec. 1900), 250; "Sarah Morris Hospital for Children," 248. See also "The Hospital Laundry Chute," *AA* 108, no. 2067 (4 Aug. 1915), 80; "Cook County Hospital, Chicago, Ill," 247; "Germ-Proof Rooms in Modern Hospital"; "More Rockefeller Millions to Science." On Alfred Wolff, see also Cooper, *Air-Conditioning America*, 9–23; and Bernard Nagengast, "Alfred Wolff—HVAC Pioneer," *ASHRAE Journal* 32, no. 1 (Jan. 1990), S66–S83.

61. "One Night in a Great City Hospital: From the Patient's Point of View," *TN&HR* 29, no. 6 (Dec. 1902), 332–33; "All-White Operating Rooms," *MH* 2, no. 1 (Jan. 1914), 45–46; Reiley, "The New Hospital of the House of Calvary," *MH* 3, no. 2 (Aug. 1914), 82. See also "Beauty as a Curative Agent," *MH* 6, no. 2 (Feb. 1916), 112–13; Victor C. Twiss, "Interior Decorations in Hospitals," *MH* 7, no. 4 (Oct. 1916), 337; Jeanne Kisacky, "Blood Red, Soothing Green, and Pure White: What Color Is Your Operating Room?," in *Color and Design*, ed. Marilyn Delong and Barbara Martinson (London: Berg, 2013), 118–24.

62. M. E. McCalmont, "Practical Details in Hospital Planning, Part II," 161.

63. S. S. Goldwater, "The Passing of the 'Hospital Unit,'" *MH* 1, no. 1 (Sept. 1913), 15.

64. Keppel, "The Modern Hospital as a Health Factory," *MH* 7, no. 4 (Oct. 1916), 304; Robert H. Greene, "Report of Medical Board," in French Hospital, New York City, *AR* (1901), 31. See also McCalmont, "Co-Operation in Hospital Planning" 208; Charlotte A. Aikens, "Hospital Planning and Hospital Efficiency," *TN* 49, no. 2 (Aug. 1912), 91–93; Meyer J. Sturm, "The Economic Principles of Efficiency in Hospitals," *AA* 102 (14 Aug. 1912) 58–61; Minnie Goodnow, "Conservation—The Waste of Human Energy in Hospitals," *TN* 52, no. 1 (Jan. 1914), 14–17. See also Howell, *Technology in the Hospital*; Edward T. Morman, ed., *Efficiency, Scientific Management, and Hospital Standardization* (New York: Garland Publishing, 1989); David A. Hounshell, *From the American System to Mass Production, 1800–1932: The Development of Manufacturing in the United States* (Baltimore: Johns Hopkins University Press, 1984); Alfred D. Chandler, *The Visible Hand: The Managerial Revolution in American Business* (Cambridge, MA: Belknap Press of Harvard University Press, 1977).

65. Dr. A. Jacobi, "Address," in *The Mount Sinai Hospital Buildings* (New York: Isaac Goldman, 1901), 28–29; Harry F. Dowling, *City Hospitals: The Undercare of the Underprivileged* (Cambridge, MA: Harvard University Press, 1982), 120; Will Mayo, "Commencement Address," in *Collected Papers by the Staff of St. Mary's Hospital Mayo Clinic* (Philadelphia: W. B. Saunders Company, 1911), 561; Truesdale and French, "Grouping of Medical Men for Office and Hospital Practice," *MH* 3, no. 6 (Dec. 1914), 381; S. S. Goldwater, "Hospital Construction: 1918 and After," *MH* 12, no. 1 (Jan. 1919), 5. See also "Special Diseases in General Hospitals," editorial, *MH* 4, no. 5 (May 1915), 325–26; Lloyd B. Whitman, "The Relation of the Ophthalmic Department to the General Hospital," *MH* 4, no. 5 (May 1915), 304–6.

66. Harry J. Harwick on Plummer, quoted in Willius, *Henry Stanley Plummer*, 38; Beard, "The Mayo Clinic Building at Rochester," *Journal-Lancet: The Journal of the Minnesota State Medical Association* 34, no. 16 (15 Aug. 1914), 425. See also "Team Work," editorial, *MH* 4, no. 5 (May 1915), 324–25; "Marvels of Surgery in a Minnesota Hospital," *NYT*, 8 Dec. 1907; John A. Hornsby, "How a Great Clinic Works," *MH* 10, no. 5 (May 1918), 333–35. The rapid growth of the clinic had resulted in chaotic facility expansion; their spaces were so

scattered across several blocks of the downtown that "guides were needed to help patients find their way through the Mayo maze" (Richter, *Ellerbe Tradition*, 15). On the Mayos, see W. Bruce Fye, *Caring for the Heart: Mayo Clinic and the Rise of Specialization* (New York: Oxford University Press, 2015); W. Bruce Fye, "The Origins and Evolution of the Mayo Clinic from 1864 to 1919: A Minnesota Family Practice Becomes an International 'Medical Mecca,'" *BHM* 84, no. 3 (2010), 323–57; George Rosen, *The Structure of American Medical Practice*, ed. Charles E. Rosenberg (Philadelphia: University of Pennsylvania Press, 1983), 53–61.

67. Richter, *Ellerbe Tradition*, 15; Beard, "Mayo Clinic Building at Rochester," 430.

68. The extent to which the Mayo brothers were the direct influence on this scramble is hard to overestimate. As just one example, a meeting between Dr. William Mayo and Henry Ford in late 1915 changed Ford's ideas about hospital design for the new Henry Ford Hospital in Detroit (http://www.henryford.com/body.cfm?id=47713). Annmarie Adams and Stacie Burke note the influence of the Mayo Clinic as a model for group practice and the challenge that it posed to the independence of the private practitioner. The development of medical office buildings, where a number of specialized private practitioners could interact in a form of "private" collaboration, was one architectural response. Adams and Burke, "A Doctor in the House: The Architecture of Home-Offices for Physicians in Toronto, 1885–1930," *Medical History* 52 (2008), 191–92.

69. "Against Tall Buildings for Hospitals," *AABN* 93, no. 1695 (17 June 1908), 16. See also Max Junghaendel, "Axioms and Principles of Modern Hospital Construction," *AABN* 67, no. 1263 (10 Mar. 1900) 75–77; Hurd, "Hospital Construction from a Medical Standpoint," 248–9; Rowe, "The Hospital 'Unit,'" 156–57. See also John D. Thompson and Grace Goldin, *The Hospital: A Social and Architectural History* (New Haven, CT: Yale University Press, 1975), 187–99.

70. Lamoreaux, "Architecture of the Modern Hospital," *MH* 1, no. 1 (Sept. 1913), 41–42; Ochsner, "Essentials in the Construction of Hospitals for Large Cities," 1315; Ochsner and Sturm, *Organization, Construction and Management of Hospitals*; "Discussion on the Papers of Drs. Thompson and Ochsner," *JAMA* 49, no. 12 (1907), 999. The graphic similarities between these diagrams and some of the early light/shadow diagrams of *zeilenbau* housing in Europe by modernist architects such as Walter Gropius and Hannes Meyer is notable. It does not mean Gropius and Meyer studied Ochsner but more likely that designing for maximum light and air came with clear architectural implications.

71. Pite also noted the sharp difference between this novel hospital form and William Henman's startling one-story hospital with wards "in close formation" for the Royal Victoria Hospital in Belfast. Pite, "A City Tower of Healing," *Builder*, 11 June 1904, 636–37.

72. Nikolaus Pevsner, *A History of Building Types* (Princeton, NJ: Princeton University Press, 1976); Thompson and Goldin, *Hospital*; Guenter Risse, *Mending Bodies, Saving Souls: A History of Hospitals* (New York: Oxford University Press, 1999), 469–70; Robert Bruegmann, "Architecture of the Hospital: 1770–1870, Design and Technology" (PhD diss., University of Pennsylvania, 1976), 114; David Theodore, Stacie D. Burke, and Annmarie Adams, "Tower of Power: The Drummond Medical Building and the Interwar Centralization of Medical Practice," *Scientia Canadensis* 32, no. 1 (2009), 62–65; Sloane and Sloane, *Medicine Moves to the Mall*, 57–59.

73. Correspondence of Drs. James Markoe and Samuel W. Lambert, vol. 2, Society of the Lying-In Hospital, Medical Board, MCANYPWC. See also Kisacky, "Germs Are in the Details," 83–106; "Mr. Morgan's Beneficence"; "Lying-In Hospital," *Harper's Weekly*, 15 Feb. 1902, 195; "This Busy World," *Harper's Weekly*, 23 Jan. 1897, 79; and Robert L. Dickin-

son, "The New Lying-In Hospital in New York," *American Monthly Review of Reviews* 25, no. 4 (Apr. 1902), 445. These hospitals correspond in many ways to the spatial strategies described in Katherine L. Carroll's account of "single-building facilities for preclinical studies," "Creating the Modern Physician: The Architecture of American Medical Schools in the Era of Medical Education Reform," *JSAH* 75, no. 1 (Mar. 2016), 58–61.

74. Hun, "Study of a Hospital Plan," 438. See also "Block or Pavilion Type Hospital?," *MH* 4, no. 4 (Apr. 1915), 289.

75. W. Morgan Hartshorn, *New York Polyclinic Medical School and Hospital* (New York: Private, 1942) 28–29; "Hospital Review," *TN* 47, no. 3 (Sept. 1911), 169–70; "Unique Features of Our First Skyscraper Hospital," *NYT*, 14 Jan. 1912. I have encountered only one early high-rise hospital that even approximated Ochsner's recommended open landscaped site—the hospital of the very well-funded Rockefeller Institute in New York City.

76. Annmarie Adams has analyzed the transformations of the maternity service in E. F. Stevens's design for the Royal Victoria Montreal Maternity Hospital in 1926 (Adams, *Medicine by Design*, 42–52). Both the Lying-In Hospital of the City of New York and the Chicago Lying-In Hospital were affiliated with extensive dispensary service and home delivery services. Hospital care was reserved for the complicated cases or for the private patients who paid for the hospital care as a "luxury" service as well as a medical treatment.

77. Brown, "Comparison between German and American Hospital Construction," 73; "Block or Pavilion Type Hospital?," *MH* 4, no. 4 (Apr. 1915), 289. There were many conflicting spatial requirements in hospital planning. Research spaces, pathology, labs, and mortuaries required physical separation from the wards. Surgical facilities needed to be separate, but easily accessible. Diagnostic equipment and therapeutic facilities had to be easily accessible to the wards. Vulnerable, infectious, and chronic patients still required separation from the general wards; surgical patients, acute patients, and patients with complicated ailments benefited from proximity to diagnostic and therapeutic facilities.

78. Abraham Flexner, *Medical Education in the United States and Canada: A Report to the Carnegie Foundation for the Advancement of Teaching* (New York: Carnegie Foundation for the Advancement of Teaching, 1910); Starr, *Social Transformation of American Medicine*, 118–22; Kenneth Ludmerer, *Time to Heal: American Medical Education from the Turn of the Century to the Era of Managed Care* (Oxford: Oxford University Press, 1999); Stevens, *In Sickness and in Wealth*, 57–67. Carroll categorizes medical school design into three types: "institute design," "pre-clinical studies in a single building," and the "unified medical-school hospital." Carroll, "Modernizing the American Medical School, 1893–1940: Architecture, Pedagogy, Professionalization, and Philanthropy" (PhD diss., Boston University, 2012); and "Creating the Modern Physician," 50–67. Carroll's third category, for which I have used the alternate term "teaching hospital," overlaps with this study of hospital design.

79. Lambert, *Memorandum on the Ideal Development*, 1912, 2–3. The use of the term *medical center* had started in the late nineteenth century, but it had referred to a group of institutionally separate hospitals in casual geographic proximity. By the 1910s *medical center* referred to a number of formally affiliated institutions, with the implicit expectation that they occupied (or would occupy) an integrated or at least coordinated facility.

80. Samuel W. Lambert, "Study of the Plans for a Large Modern Hospital," *MH* 6, no. 3 (Mar. 1916), 164–70.

81. BGM, New York Hospital, 4 May 1896, MCANYPWC; Smith, *New York Orthopaedic Hospital*, 16; Stevens, "Details and Equipment of Hospitals," 140. The Mississippi State Charity Hospital in Vicksburg had to transport cases to nearby private hospitals for X-ray

diagnoses (*AR* (1912–1913). On the changing use of the X-ray machine and the changing social meaning of X-ray images, see Howell, *Technology in the Hospital*, 103–68.

82. I. Seth Hirsch, "The Hospital X-Ray Laboratory—Its Scope and Limitations. Part II," *MH* 4, no. 2 (Feb. 1915), 95.

83. Cutler, *Roosevelt Hospital*, 21; Bellevue and Allied Hospital, New York City, *AR* 11 (1912), 75; "Cook County Hospital, Chicago, Ill," 247; I. Seth Hirsch, "The Hospital X-Ray Laboratory—Its Place in the Hospital," *MH* 4, no. 1 (Jan. 1915), 11; I. Seth Hirsch, "The Hospital X-Ray Laboratory. Part II," 92–97; MBM, New York Hospital, 11 Apr. 1911, MCANYPWC. Directors of the German Hospital installed electrical outlets behind each bed so that "ophthalmoscopes, X-ray or other electrical appliances" might be used at the bedside ("New Hospital of Many Ideals").

84. Edward S. Blaine, "The X-Ray Department of Cook County Hospital," *MH* 8, no. 5 (May 1917), 321–28; New York Skin and Cancer Hospital, *AR* (1908), 19.

85. Hugh McKenna and Victor Andre Matteson, "Hospital of High-Grade Construction Built at a Very Low Cost," *MH* 6, no. 1 (Jan. 1916), 17–19.

86. D. Riesman, quoted in Robert P. Hudson, "Abraham Flexner in Perspective: American Medical Education 1865–1910," *BHM* 46, no. 6 (Nov./Dec. 1972), 550.

87. Stevens, "Details and Equipment of Hospitals," 139–40; "Description of the Walter Garrett Memorial Building," in Pennsylvania Hospital, Philadelphia, *AR* (1897), 21–22; Member of the Executive Committee of the Hospital, "Boston New Children's Hospital Has Novel Features," *MH* 1, no. 2 (Oct. 1913), 94. These facilities largely correspond to and corroborate the Type II Classroom model described by Adams and Schlich, but the transformations predated the corresponding construction at the Royal Victoria Hospital in Montreal by more than a decade ("Design for Control: Surgery, Science, and Space at the Royal Victoria Hospital, Montreal, 1893–1956," *Medical History* 50, no. 3 [2006], 310).

88. Wesley Hospital, Chicago, *AR* 21 (1909), 35; Richard E. Schmidt, "Some Special Features of the New Cook County Hospital," *MH* 1, no. 4 (Dec. 1913), 214; Hahnemann Hospital, Chicago, *AR* (1900), 12–13; Henry N. Wessel, *History of the Jewish Hospital Association of Philadelphia* (Philadelphia: Edward Stern, 1908), 19.

89. Stevens, "Surgical Unit," 18. See also Adams and Schlich, "Design for Control," 315.

90. Joy Clough, *In Service to Chicago: The History of Mercy Hospital* (Chicago: Mercy Hospital and Medical Center, 1979), 48; Provident Hospital, Chicago, *AR* 6 (1897), 9; Lenox Hill Hospital, New York City, *AR* (1927), 27; Lenox Hill Hospital, New York City, *AR* (1928), 15.

91. Richard E. Schmidt, "Architecture of the Great Charity Hospital," *MH* 1, no. 1 (Sept. 1913), 41; Stevens, "Surgical Unit," 18–21. See also Bartine, "Hospital Construction," 68.

92. Charlotte A. Aikens, "The Futility of Competitions," *TN&HR* 48, no. 3 (Mar. 1912), 150; Charlotte A. Aikens, "What the Pedometer Might Tell," *TN* 51, no. 1 (July 1913), 37; W. Gilman Thompson, "Efficiency in Nursing," *JAMA* 61, no. 24 (13 Dec. 1913), 2146–49; and Nettie B. Jordan, "Comparative Service in the Community Hospital," *MH* 6, no. 1 (Jan. 1916), 20. See also David Theodore, "'The Fattest Possible Nurse'": Architecture, Computers, and Post-War Nursing," in *Hospital Life: Theory and Practice from the Medieval to the Modern*, ed. Laurinda Abreu and Sally Sheard (New York: Peter Lang, 2013); Edward T. Morman, ed., *Efficiency, Scientific Management, and Hospital Standardization*, 1989; Reverby, *Ordered to Care*, 1987; Thompson and Goldin, *Hospital*, 1975; Frederick Winslow Taylor, *The Principles of Scientific Management* (New York: Harper and Bros., 1911); Daniel Nelson, *Frederick W. Taylor and the Rise of Scientific Management* (Madison: University of Wisconsin Press, 1980).

93. Hospitals as diverse in size, layout, and location as the Cincinnati General Hospital, the Cook County Hospital in Chicago; Robert W. Long Hospital in Indianapolis; Barnes Hospital in Saint Louis; Freedmen's Hospital in Washington, DC; Harper Hospital in Detroit; Bellevue Hospital and Lying-In Hospital of the City of New York; and the Samaritan Hospital in Troy, New York, continued to include the traditional large ward.

94. Reverby, *Ordered to Care*, 154.

95. Head houses could include, for example, numerous isolation/quiet rooms, clinical laboratories, examination and treatment rooms, utility rooms, dayrooms, convalescent dining rooms, open-air balconies and porches, flower rooms, serving rooms, expanded bathing facilities, and sterilization facilities. At many hospitals, including the Louisville Hospital, Cook County Hospital, Cincinnati General Hospital, San Francisco Hospital, and Harper Hospital, the head house was as long as the ward.

96. S. S. Goldwater, "A Plan for the Construction of Ward Buildings in Crowded Cities," *TN* 45, no. 5 (Nov. 1910), 285–90; Goldwater, "Notes on Hospital Planning," 207–10; Lindley M. Franklin, "The New York Orthopaedic Dispensary and Hospital," *BB* 25, no. 2 (1916), 62–64; Franklin, "New York Orthopedic Hospital Has New Home," *MH* 6, no. 5 (May 1916), 311–16. Several influential European hospitals adopted the X or cross-plan, including Alfred Waterhouse's University College Hospital (1897–1906) and Alfred Pite's "Tower of Healing." See also Harriet Richardson, ed., *English Hospitals, 1660–1948: A Survey of Their Architecture and Design* (Swindon: Royal Commission on the Historical Monuments of England, 1998), 34.

97. Ernest Flagg, "Description of St. Luke's Hospital as It Will Be When Completed," in *History of St. Luke's Hospital with a Description of the New Buildings* (New York: Wynkoop and Hallenbeck, 1893); "Gary Hospital, Gary, Ind.," *BB* 21, no. 7 (July 1912), 182; Warren C. Hill, "Robinson Memorial of the Massachusetts Homeopathic Hospital," *MH* 7, no. 1 (July 1916), 4–8.

98. Examples of hospitals with wards of around a dozen beds include the Watts Hospital in Durham, North Carolina; the Galloway Hospital in Nashville, Tennessee; the French Hospital in New York City; Saint Luke's Hospital in Jacksonville, Florida; and Barnard Skin and Cancer Hospital in Saint Louis. Private patients could either hire individual private nurses or be charged enough to cover the extra salary for the additional nurses required to adequately monitor the numerous rooms and small wards. In isolation facilities, the extra nursing was part of the isolation.

99. Charles P. Emerson, "New Robert W. Long Hospital, of Indianapolis," *MH* 2, no. 6 (June 1914) 333; Herbert B. Howard, "Peter Bent Brigham Hospital. Arrangement of Wards for Purposes of Efficiency and Economy of Administration," *MH* 1, no. 1 (Sept. 1913), 23.

100. E. F. Stevens, "The Ward and Operating Units of the General Hospital, *MH* 1, no. 1 (Sept. 1913), 40. See also Thompson and Goldin, *Hospital*, 216; Taylor, "Hospital Planning. V," 90–95; Schmidt, trans., "Arrangement of the New Munich-Schwabing Hospital," *MH* 1, no. 3 (Nov. 1913), 190–91.

101. Adams, *Medicine by Design*, 35–40; "The New York Hospitals. A Boon Not Only to the Poor, but to the Well-to-Do. Many Wealthy Persons Now Take Advantage of Conveniences of the Private Wards," *NYT*, 31 Dec. 1900; "Comfort in a Hospital. Elaborate Are the Furnishings Required by Whealthy [*sic*] Patients," *NYT*, 24 May 1908. See also Thompson and Goldin, *Hospital*, 207–10; Rosner, *Once Charitable Enterprise*, 75–95; Saint Luke's Hospital, Chicago, *AR* 41 (1904) 11; "How to Build Hospitals," *AABN* 90, no. 1609 (27 Oct. 1906), 134; S. S. Goldwater, "Planning for Private Patients. Hospitals for Paying Patients

Exclusively Not Desirable—The Consideration Due to Private Patients—Architectural and Administrative Requirements," *MH* 2, no. 1 (Jan. 1914), 9–18.

102. See Cleveland Hospital Council, *Cleveland Hospital and Health Survey* (Cleveland, 1920); E. H. L. Corwin, *The Hospital Situation in Greater New York* (New York, 1924); George Elihu Bellows, *Health and Hospital Survey, Kansas City, Missouri* (Kansas City, 1931). See also Haven Emerson and Anna C. Phillips, *Hospitals and Health Agencies of Louisville, Ky.* (Louisville, KY: 1925); Emerson, *Health and Hospital Survey of Bethlehem, Pa.* (1925); Emerson, *Philadelphia Hospital and Health Survey* (Philadelphia, 1929).

103. Resident of Nineteenth Ward, "Unequal Hospital Distribution," Editorial, *NYT*, 9 Feb. 1902; State Charities Aid Association, *New Hospitals Needed in Greater New York. Recommendations by the Standing Committee on Hospitals of the State Charities Aid Association with a Report on Present Conditions and Future Needs by Mr. Phil P. Jacobs* (New York: State Charities Aid Association, 1908); City of New York, *Report of the Commission on Hospitals Appointed by the Mayor of the City of New York January 31, 1906* (New York: Martin B. Brown, 1909); "Hospital Reform Urged by Commission," *NYT*, 9 Aug. 1908; Resident of Nineteenth Ward, "Unequal Hospital Distribution," editorial, *NYT*, 9 Feb. 1902; "West Side in Need of a New Hospital," *NYT*, 14 Nov. 1909; Samuel W. Lambert, *Hospitals and Medical Education* (New York: 1908), 5–6.

104. Adams, *Medicine by Design*, 120–21; Sturm, "Artificial Illumination in Hospitals," *MH* 3, no. 3 (Sept. 1914), 154. Sturm suggested that architects should be included in any committees on hospital standardization. See Morman, *Efficiency, Scientific Management, and Hospital Standardization*; Stevens, *In Sickness and in Wealth*; American College of Surgeons, *Manual of Hospital Standardization: A History, Development and Progress of Hospital Standardization* (Chicago: American College of Surgeons, 1946).

105. Emerson, quoted in Stevens, "American Hospital Development," 641. Mount Sinai Hospital in New York City's new 1904 facility held over five hundred beds; the newly planned Bellevue held over one thousand. Many small general hospitals provided the only hospital service for a large geographical area and consequently accepted patients with any ailment.

106. Minnie Goodnow, "The Complete Ward Unit," *TN* 49, no. 4 (Oct. 1912), 221; Richardson, "Manual of Aseptic Technique for Providence City Hospital," 5.

Chapter 5. The Vertical Hospital as an Attractive Factory, 1917–1929

Epigraphs: Arthur Peabody, "The Human Side of the Modern Hospital," *MH* 17, no. 4 (Oct. 1921), 269; William O. Ludlow, "Some Lessons the War Has Taught," *MH* 12, no. 4 (Apr. 1919), 283.

1. Edward F. Stevens, "Development of the Hospital Ward Unit of the United States Army," *MH* 12, no. 6 (June 1919), 408–16; http://www.worldwar1.com/dbc/basehosp.htm.

2. Stevens, *In Sickness and in Wealth: American Hospitals in the Twentieth Century* (New York: Basic Books, 1989), 80–104; Rappleye, "Fifteen Years of Hospital and Medical Coordination," *MH* 31, no. 2 (Aug. 1928), 63; Bailey, "How to Build an Efficient General Hospital for a Small Community," *MH* 11, no. 3 (Sept. 1918), 165.

3. See Thomas W. Salmon, MD, *The Care and Treatment of Mental Diseases and War Neuroses ("Shell Shock") in the British Army* (New York: War Work Committee of the National Committee for Mental Hygiene, 1917); Katherine Metcalf Roof, "What Place Has

NOTES TO PAGES 238–242

Art in Modern Hospital Therapy?," *TN&HR* 23, no. 4 (Oct. 1924), 329; Ludlow, "Some Lessons the War Has Taught," 283.

4. "The Hospital and the Art of Living," editorial, *MH* 23, no. 4 (Nov. 1924), 338. See also A. C. Bachmeyer, "Hospital Administration during 1924," *MH* 24, no. 1 (Jan. 1925), 8; E. H. Lewinski-Corwin, "Community Responsibility of Hospitals," *MH* 26, no. 2 (Feb. 1926), 109–14; Amy Beers, "The County Hospital in Iowa," *MH* 22, no. 2 (Feb. 1924), 119–20.

5. Asa Bacon, "The New Efficient Hospital," *Presbyterian Hospital Bulletin* 39 (Apr. 1919), 2; "Building New Hospitals," *MH* 12, no. 1 (Jan. 1919), 62. The sentiment was echoed by Continental authors as well—see "The Construction of Hospitals," *Lancet* 208, no. 5378 (25 Sept. 1926), 660–61.

6. Mount Sinai Hospital, New York City, *AR* 71 (1923), 24–25; Myron Hunt, "One-Story Hospitals in California," *MH* 22, no. 3 (Mar. 1924), 240; Mother M. Catharine and Carl A. Erikson, "St. Catharine's Hospital—An Example of Flexibility in Planning," *MH* 31, no. 6 (Dec. 1928), 58; Frank E. Chapman, "Hospital Planning and Its Trend," *AF* 49, no. 6 (Dec. 1928), 831.

7. Hospitals came in behind apartments, offices, schools, public buildings, industrial construction, and hotels. *AF* cited in "$252,527,000 to Go for Hospital Construction This Year," *MH* 32, no. 2 (Feb. 1929), 120.

8. "The Parting of the Ways," editorial, *MH* 16, no. 1 (Jan. 1921), 32; Goldwater, "The Extension of Hospital Privileges to All Practitioners of Medicine," *MH* 24, no. 4 (Apr. 1925), 303–6; "The Influence of the War on Hospital Development," *TN&HR* 64, no. 1 (Jan. 1920), 39.

9. Schmidt, "Modern Hospital Design," *AF* 37, no. 6 (Dec. 1922), 254; Taylor, "Hospital Building in 1925: A Forecast," *MH* 24, no. 3 (Mar. 1925), 201.

10. Lindley Murray Franklin, "Hospital Design: The Relation of Initial Cost to the Expense of Operation and Maintenance," *AF* 30, no. 6 (June 1919), 171.

11. Richardson, "The Care of Infectious Diseases in Hospitals," *MH* 12, no. 4 (Apr. 1919), 245; Urban Maes and Frederick Fitzherbert Boyce, "The Aseptic Ritual and the Surgeon," *MH* 40, no. 6 (June 1933), 42; "Preventing Hospital Infections," *MH* 31, no. 6 (Dec. 1928), 97.

12. Richardson, "Management of Contagious Disease Hospitals," *MH* 13, no. 3 (Sept. 1919), 190; Franklin, "Hospital Design," 172. Wendy Madsen describes the maddening precision demanded by infection control practices in this time period. Madsen, "Keeping the Lid on Infection: Infection Control Practices of a Regional Queensland Hospital 1930–50," *Nursing Inquiry* 7, no. 2 (2000), 81–90. The idea that asepsis made clean surgery possible anywhere, given adequately trained personnel, provides an interesting counterpoint to the common assumption that aseptic practices required the controlled environment of the operating room. J. T. H. Connor, "Bigger Than a Bread Box: Medical Buildings as Museum Artifacts," *Caduceus* 9, no. 2 (1993), 120; and Annmarie Adams and Thomas Schlich, "Design for Control: Surgery, Science, and Space at the Royal Victoria Hospital, Montreal, 1893–1956," *Medical History* 50, no. 3 (2006), 308.

13. C. W. Munger, "The Development of Hospital Housekeeping," *MH* 24, no. 1 (Jan. 1925), 30; Janet Peterkin, "Capitalizing Color Appeal by Means of the Interior Decorator's Art," *MH* 33, no. 1 (July 1929), 64–73.

14. Edward F. Stevens, "Planning a Fifty Bed Hospital for Beauty as Well as Utility," *MH* 30, no. 2 (Feb. 1928), 64. See also A. R. McGonegal, "Modern Hospital Sanitary Installations," *AF* 49, no. 6 (Dec. 1928), 939–42; S. S. Goldwater, "Tendencies in Hospital Planning and Construction," *MH* 26, no. 1 (Jan. 1926), 6. Harriet Richardson dates the

migration of plumbing from sanitary towers and into wards in English hospitals to the mid-1910s. *English Hospitals, 1660–1948* (Swindon: Royal Commission on the Historical Monuments of England, 1998), 11.

15. H. J. Gerstenberger, Abram Garfield, S. S. Goldwater, "Babies' and Children's Hospital of Cleveland," *MH* 17, no. 3 (Sept. 1921), 188. See also Asa S. Bacon, "Routing of Patients, Doctors, and Visitors," *MH* 17, no. 3 (Sept. 1921), 179–83; John Hornsby, "Standardization of Hospitals—Class XVII, Infectious-Disease Hospitals," *MH* 10, no. 4 (Apr. 1918), 246.

16. Philemon E. Truesdale, "Operating Room Safeguards," *MH* 23, no. 1 (July 1924), 20–21.

17. Harold Speert, *The Sloane Hospital Chronicle* (Philadelphia: F. A. Davis Company, 1963), 188. See also A. Wayne Clark, Gustave S. Math Ey, "Dust and Postoperative Tetanus in Hospitals," *MH* 16, no. 6 (June 1921), 546–48; W. Gilman Thompson, "Fresh Air Treatment in Hospital Wards," *Medical and Surgical Report of the Presbyterian Hospital* 8 (Dec. 1908), 13.

18. Joseph B. De Lee, "What Are the Special Needs of the Modern Maternity?," *MH* 28, no. 3 (Mar. 1927), 59. See also Judith W. Leavitt, *Brought to Bed: Childbearing in America, 1750–1950* (New York: Oxford University Press, 1986), 171–89. On the history of obstetrics please refer to the bibliographic essay on pediatrics and obstetrics.

19. J. Whitridge Williams, "Is an Architecturally Isolated Building Essential for a Lying-In Hospital?" *MH* 28, no. 4 (Apr. 1927), 58–59; "Separate Building or Department for the Maternity?" *MH* 28, no. 5 (May 1926), 103–5.

20. Joseph B. De Lee," How Should the Maternity Be Isolated?" *MH* 29, no. 3 (Sept. 1927), 65, 71. On separate maternity facilities, see Demetrius Tillotson, "Some Special Features of the Presbyterian Hospital of Colorado," *MH* 28, no. 4 (Apr. 1927), 55–58; Tilden, Register and Pepper and S. S. Goldwater, "Abington Hospital Broadens Its Service to Humanity," *MH* 32, no. 4 (Apr. 1929), 52–58; "Preventing Hospital Infections," 96.

21. Rosenfield and Hayhow, "Planning, Building, and Equipping a Hospital," *MH* 29, no. 6 (Dec. 1927), 90; Edgar Martin, "From the Standpoint of the Architects," *MH* 15, no. 6 (Dec. 1920), 452, 453. See also Richard E. Schmidt, "The Research and Educational Hospitals of the State of Illinois," *AA* 119, no. 2358 (2 Mar. 1921), 225–30; Richard Resler, "Sunlight Factor in Purchasing Property for Urban Hospitals," *MH* 18, no. 3 (Mar. 1922), 241–42.

22. Philip W. Foster, "The Modern Hospital in the City Plan," *MH* 20, no. 3 (Mar. 1923), 207–8.

23. "Lebanon Hospital to Overlook River," *NYT*, 11 May 1924; T. R. Ponton, "Hollywood Hospital—the Nucleus of a Future Health Center," *MH* 27, no. 2 (Aug. 1926), 63–67; "Northwestern University Plans New Hospital and Medical Campus," *MH* 22, no. 1 (Jan. 1924), 72. David Theodore, Stacie Burke, and Annmarie Adams note the increasing emphasis on private parking in the design and location of medical office buildings of private practitioners; see Theodore, Burke, and Adams, "Tower of Power: The Drummond Medical Building and the Interwar Centralization of Medical Practice," *Scientia Canadensis* 32, no. 1 (2009), 65–67. See also David Rosner, "Social Control and Social Service: The Changing Use of Space in Charity Hospitals," *Radical History Review* 21 (Fall 1979), 192.

24. Goldwater, "Hospital Planning and Construction in 1922," *MH* 20, no. 1 (Jan. 1923), 1; "$1,000,000 Hospital for the East Side," *NYT*, 18 Jan. 1921; "People's Hospital Expands Its Work among the Needy," *NYT*, 25 Jan. 1925; Albert R. Lamb, *The Presbyterian Hospital and the Columbia-Presbyterian Medical Center 1868–1943. A History of a Great Medical Adventure* (New York: Columbia University Press, 1955), 182.

25. "Dr. Lambert's Paper," editorial, *MH* 6, no. 3 (Mar. 1916), 186. See also Michael M. Davis, "Impressions of a Hospital Visitor in Europe," *MH* 28, no. 4 (Apr. 1927), 50.

26. Goldwater, "The Search for the Ideal in Hospital Organization," *MH* 18, no. 2 (Feb. 1922), 110; Goldwater, "Hospital Construction: 1918 and After," *MH* 12, no. 1 (Jan. 1919), 5.

27. York and Sawyer and S. S. Goldwater, "New Surgical Pavilion," *MH* 21, no. 6 (Dec. 1923), 580. See also Edward Stotz, "High Hospital Building Proves a Success," *MH* 14, no. 1 (Jan. 1920), 9; Goldwater, "Basic Ideas in Hospital Planning," *MH* 16, no. 4 (Apr. 1921), 305–9; Isadore Rosenfield, "Planning for Future Expansion," *MH* 28, no. 4 (Apr. 1927), 63–67; Frank E. Chapman, "Economical Hospital Planning," *MH* 31, no. 1 (July 1928), 49–53. For some criticism of vertical expansion, see S. S. Goldwater, "Hospital Planning and Construction in 1924," *MH* 24, no. 1 (Jan. 1925), 2–3.

28. On building technologies related to high-rise development see Reyner Banham, *The Architecture of the Well-Tempered Environment* (London: Architectural Press, 1969). See the bibliographic essay section on skyscrapers.

29. G. Walter Zulauf, "Fifty Years A-Growing," *MH* 48, no. 3 (Mar. 1937), 50; Goldwater, "Hospital Planning and Construction in 1922," 3.

30. Philip H. Johnson and Joseph C. Doane, "An Example of Flexibility in Planning a Large Institution," *MH* 30, no. 3 (Mar. 1928), 77–83; H. F. Vermillion, "Southern Baptists Construct Well Planned Sanatorium," *MH* 16, no. 2 (Feb. 1921), 97–99; Adams, Schwartzman, and Theodore, "Collapse and Expand: Architecture and Tuberculosis Therapy in Montreal, 1909, 1933, 1954," *Technology and Culture* 49, no. 4 (2008), 908–42; Hal F. Hentz, "The Building Program of the Shriners' Hospitals for Crippled Children, part I," *MH* 23, no. 1 (July 1924), 22; Hal F. Hentz, "The Building Program of the Shriners' Hospitals for Crippled Children, part II," *MH* 23, no. 2 (Aug. 1924), 136–42.

31. "Survey Finds Separate Contagious Hospitals Not Needed," *MH* 39, no. 5 (Nov. 1932), 114. See also Palmer and Hornbostel and S. S. Goldwater, "The Contagious Ward of the Morristown Memorial Hospital, Morristown, N.J.," *MH* 10, no. 3 (Mar. 1918), 171–73; D. L. Richardson, "Aseptic Nursing in American Hospitals," *MH* 13, no. 1 (July 1919), 10–13; D. L. Richardson, "Hospitalization of Infectious Diseases: A Problem for Every Institution," *TN&HR*, 74, no. 1 (Jan. 1925), 48–49; *Public Health and Hospitals in the St. Louis Area: A Mid-Century Appraisal* (New York: American Public Health Association, 1957), 5; F. G. Carter, "Fitting the Contagious Unit into Its Proper Niche," *MH* 34, no. 4 (Apr. 1930), 71–73.

32. Goldwater, "Hospital Construction: 1918 and After," 5.

33. See Janet Peterkin, "Manhattan's Colossus of Medical Centers," *MH* 31, no. 1 (1928), 55–65; "The Hospitals of Western Reserve University," *MH* 37, no. 3 (Sept. 1931); suppl. 11–22; Sloan, "Vast New Medical Center Guards New York's Health," *MH* 40, no. 3 (Mar. 1933), 48–57; Katherine Carroll, "Creating the Modern Physician: The Architecture of American Medical Schools in the Era of Medical Education Reform," *JSAH* 75, no. 1 (Mar. 2016), 48–73; and Katherine Carroll, "Modernizing the American Medical School, 1893–1940: Architecture, Pedagogy, Professionalization, and Philanthropy" (PhD diss., Boston University, 2012).

34. Coolidge and Shattuck, Winford H. Smith, and G. Canby Robinson, "The New Plant of the Vanderbilt University Medical School and Hospital," *MH* 20, no. 2 (Feb. 1923), 109.

35. "The Specialist and the Hospital," editorial, *MH* 29, no. 1 (Aug. 1927), 93. See also "More Small Hospitals Favored for New York City," *MH* 32, no. 3 (Mar. 1929), 60; "Why Large Hospitals Are Criticized," *MH* 32, no. 1 (Jan. 1929), 87–95; "The Influence of the War on Hospital Development," *TN&HR* 64, no. 1 (Jan. 1920), 38; Roswell T. Pettit, "The Diagnostic Hospital of a Small Community," *MH* 17, no. 3 (Sept. 1921), 195–99; Olof Z. Cervin,

"The Small Community Hospital," *MH* 18, no. 5 (May 1922), 415–18; Frank G. Nifong, "The A B C Movement for Hospitalization in the Counties of Missouri," *MH* 19, no. 3 (Sept. 1922), 193–98.

36. Edward F. Stevens, "The Planning of the Small Hospital," *MH* 19, no. 6 (Dec. 1922), 497–502; H. Eldridge Hannaford and Brigadier V. R. Post, "New Ideas in Small Hospital Construction," *MH* 27, no. 5 (Nov. 1926), 61–66; "The Chamberlain Memorial Hospital Serves Industrial Community," *MH* 16, no. 1 (Jan. 1921), 42–43; Clarence W. King, "The Small Southern Hospital," *MH* 15, no. 4 (Oct. 1920), 260–63; Hunt, "One-Story Hospitals in California," 235–40; Carline Vermilye, "Providing for Six Towns in a One-Story Community Hospital," *MH* 26, no. 2 (Feb. 1926), 129–31; H. Eldridge Hannaford, "General Considerations in Planning a Small Hospital," *AF* 49, no. 6 (Dec. 1928), 873–81.

37. Examples of small hospitals include Saint Luke's Hospital in Davenport, Iowa; Mary Francis Skiff Hospital, Newton, Iowa; Engelwood Hospital, Engelwood, New Jersey; the Methodist Hospital in Dallas, Texas; Brookville General Hospital, Brookville, Pennsylvania; Chester County Hospital, Westchester, Pennsylvania; Benjamin Stickney Cable Memorial Hospital in Ipswich, Massachusetts; Kenosha Hospital, Kenosha, Wisconsin; Barre City Hospital, Barre, Vermont; and Saint Joseph's Hospital, Mitchell, South Dakota.

38. Rosemary Stevens's examination of the variety of regulatory strategies deployed by various groups gives a picture of the difficulties and complexities surrounding any attempt to control hospital practices or development. Stevens, *In Sickness and in Wealth*, 68–79, 82–89, 114–39.

39. Abraham Flexner, *Medical Education in the United States and Canada: A Report to the Carnegie Foundation for the Advancement of Teaching* (New York: Carnegie Foundation for the Advancement of Teaching, 1910); Stevens, *In Sickness and in Wealth*, 52–53; Edward F. Stevens, "What the Past Fifteen Years Have Taught Us in Hospital Construction and Design," *AA* 132, no. 2534 (5 Dec. 1927), 701–8. John Hornsby wrote a series of articles in the *Modern Hospital* outlining the proposed classes of hospitals and some of the issues of standardization; see Hornsby, "Standardization of Hospitals," *MH* 8, no. 4 (Apr. 1917), 256–58; 9, no. 2 (Aug. 1917), 103–12; 9, no. 3 (Sept. 1917), 180–82; 9, no. 4 (Oct. 1917), 253–62; 9, no. 5 (Nov. 1917), 341–49; 9, no. 6 (Dec. 1917), 409–12; 10, no. 1 (Jan. 1918), 41; and 10, no. 2 (Feb. 1918), 95–100.

40. Edward F. Stevens, "Will the Consolidated Hospital Supplant the Small Hospital?," *MH* 33, no. 2 (Sept. 1929), 92–4; "The Growth of the Hospital Idea," *MH* 13, no. 2 (Aug. 1919), 124–25. The report cited the average hospital in 1873 as having 238 beds, and noted that the ninety-eight-bed average for hospitals was without including the really large general hospitals of several thousand beds of the 1910s.

41. John A. Hornsby et al., "Standardization of Hospitals—Class V," *MH* 9, no. 5 (Nov. 1917), 341–49. The committee was equally disparaging of large municipal hospitals where politics could curtail medical efficiencies. Edward F. Stevens, "The Small Hospital," *AF* 45, no. 4 (Oct. 1926), 229.

42. "An Announcement," *MH* 19, no. 1 (Aug. 1922), 129; "Modern Hospital's Contest for Small Hospital Plans Announced," *MH* 19, no. 4 (Oct. 1922), 313–15; "Small Hospital Architectural Contest Awakens International Interest," *MH* 19, no. 5 (Nov. 1922), 423–24; "200 Architects Plan Ideal Small Hospital," *MH* 20, no. 1 (Jan. 1923), 69. "Five Prize-Winning Plans in Small General Hospital Contest," *MH* 20, no. 5 (May 1923), 453–76. See Edward F. Stevens, "The Benjamin Stickney Cable Memorial Hospital, Ipswich, Mass.," *MH* 12, no. 3 (Mar. 1919), 157–60; Bailey, "How to Build an Efficient General Hospital," 165–68; "Chamberlain Memorial Hospital Serves Industrial Community," 42–43; G. R.

Egeland, "An Economically Built Small Hospital," *MH* 19, no. 5 (Nov. 1922), 387–90; Carl A. Erikson, "Planning the Small Community Hospital," *AF* 37, no. 6 (Dec. 1922), 310–14.

43. C. H. Shepard, "Reducing the Mortality of the Negro," *MH* 27, no. 1 (July 1926), 55–57; "Architects Chosen for Duke Endowment Program," *MH* 28, no. 3 (Mar. 1927), 138; H. Eldridge Hannaford, "General Considerations in Planning a Small Hospital," 873–77; H. Eldridge Hannaford, "Outlining the Standards for the Duke Hospital Program," *MH* 30, no. 3 (Mar. 1928), 71–76.

44. Hornsby et al., "Standardization of Hospitals—Class IV," *MH* 9, no. 4 (Oct. 1917), 259; Robert Stuart, "The Reconstruction Hospital: A Heritage from the World War," *MH* 19, no. 4 (Oct. 1922), 284. See also Frederick D. Keppel, "The Modern Hospital as a Health Factory," *MH* 7, no. 4 (Oct. 1916), 303–6. Albert Kahn's designs for factories (like the Ford Motor Company facilities at Highland Park and later at River Rouge) exemplify the role of building design in industrial production—a well-designed factory could increase output and decrease costs. See Grant Hildebrand, *Designing for Industry: The Architecture of Albert Kahn* (Cambridge, MA: MIT Press, 1974).

45. Bacon, "New Efficient Hospital," 2–3.

46. Howell, *Technology in the Hospital: Transforming Patient Care in the Early Twentieth Century* (Baltimore: Johns Hopkins University Press, 1995); Annmarie Adams, *Medicine by Design: The Architect and the Modern Hospital, 1893–1943* (Minneapolis: University of Minnesota Press, 2008), 121–26; Franklin, "Hospital Design," 171–72; Albert E. Sawyer, "A Machine That Helps Solve the Patient Traffic Problem," *MH* 31, no. 6 (Dec. 1928), 67–72.

47. D. D. Martin, "Henry Ford Hospital in Time of Peace," *MH* 14, no. 4 (Apr. 1920), 268, 269. The hospital was completed just before WWI, used by the military during the war, then returned to civilian purposes at its end. See also Bassett Jones, "The Modern Building Is a Machine," *AA* 125, no. 2438 (2 Jan. 1924), 93–98.

48. As one example, Myron Hunt calculated that porches occupied nearly 10 percent of the floor area for a California hospital he designed. "One-Story Hospitals in California," 240.

49. R. G. Brodrick, "Hospital Planning in Relation to Efficiency in Professional Service," *MH* 24, no. 3 (Mar. 1925), 218. See also C.-E. A. Winslow, "Sanitary Survey of Institutions," *MH* 12, no. 5 (May 1919), 363–65; "Ventilation in Health and Disease," *TN&HR* 70, no. 6 (June 1923), 525; John R. Allen, "Hospital Ventilation and Heating," *MH* 15, no. 1 (July 1920), 22–24; New York State Commission on Ventilation, *Report of the New York State Commission on Ventilation* (New York: E. P. Dutton, 1923).

50. W. Dwight Pierce, "Bringing Climate to the Patient," *MH* 19, no. 3 (Sept. 1922), 199–202; Alvan L. Barach, "Keeping Patients Comfortable by Means of the Health Room," *MH* 33, no. 6 (1929), 89–91; "Air Control: The Next Great Step in Hospital practice," *MH* 13, no. 3 (Sept. 1919), 201–2; Ellsworth Huntington, "Air Control and the Reduction of the Death Rate after Operations," *MH* 14, no. 1 (Jan. 1920), 10–15. Konrad Meier pointed out that correlating external climate to internal statistics might not be statistically accurate. "Hospital Ventilation," *MH* 15, no. 4 (Oct. 1920), 273.

51. De Lee, "What Are the Special Needs of the Modern Maternity?," 62; R. Plato Schwartz, "Supplying the Equivalent of Sunlight for Treating Chronic Diseases," *MH* 28, no. 3 (Mar. 1927), 162; A. F. Hess and L. J. Unger, "The Cure of Infantile Rickets by Artificial Light and by Sunlight," *Proceedings of the Society for Experimental Biology and Medicine* 18 (1921), 298; J. C. Elsom, "Is Artificial Light Therapy an Essential Form of Treatment?," *MH* 28, no. 5 (May 1927), 101–2; George E. Phillips, "Detroit's New Tuberculosis Unit," *MH* 32, no. 3 (Mar. 1929), 93–97. On Vita-Glass and its competitors, see Daniel Freund, *American*

Sunshine: Diseases of Darkness and the Quest for Natural Light (Chicago: University of Chicago Press, 2012), 55–61, 80–88, 109–11.

52. S. S. Goldwater, "Introducing the Chairman of the Building Committee," *MH* 28, no. 1 (Jan. 1927), 50–51.

53. Adams, "'That was Then, This is Now': Hospital Architecture in the Age(s) of Revolution," in *The Impact of Hospitals: 300–2000*, ed. John Henderson, Peregrine Horden, and Alessandro Pastore (New York: Peter Lang, 2007), 226–27; "Parting of the Ways," 32. See also "General Principles in Planning Dispensaries," *MH* 20, no. 3 (Mar. 1923), 221–27; Michael M. Davis, "Planning Buildings for Out-Patient Service; General Principles," *MH* 26, no. 3 (Mar. 1926), 219–27. Hospitals with "diagnostic" model outpatient clinics included the Long Island Medical College and Hospital in New York, the University of Michigan Hospital in Ann Arbor, and the Boston City Hospital. The Cleveland Clinic was a diagnostic clinic that later added hospital service.

54. C. W. Dickey and R. G. Brodrick, "Modern Structure Replaces Old Queen's Hospital, Honolulu," *MH* 24, no. 6 (June 1925), 515; Paul N. Jepson, "Planning the Surgical Service," *MH* 26, no. 3 (Mar. 1926), 202.

55. Adams and Schlich, "Design for Control," 310.

56. William Lee Secor, "The White Operating Room," *MH* 9, no. 3 (Sept. 1917), 170–71; "Operating Room Floors," *MH* 8, no. 2 (Feb. 1917), 148. See also Lindley M. [Franklin], "The New York Orthopaedic Dispensary and Hospital," *BB* 25, no. 3 (Mar. 1916), 62–64; Paluel J. Flagg, "A Scientific Basis for the Use of Color in the Operating Room," *MH* 22, no. 6 (June 1924), 555–59; "Operating Room Decoration and Surgical Efficiency," *MH* 22, no. 6 (June 1924), 577–78; "Hospital Bans White as Color Scheme," *NYT*, 4 Nov. 1923; Charles G. Mixter and Harold Field Kellogg, "Architecture and Equipment of the Jordan Hospital, Plymouth, Mass.," *MH* 8, no. 4 (Apr. 1917), 265; "Green and Black Operating Colors," *MH* 3, no. 1 (July 1914), 67–68; "The Green Operating Room at St. Luke's Hospital, San Francisco," *MH* 11, no. 2 (Aug. 1918), 97–98. See also Kisacky, "Blood Red, Soothing Green, and Pure White: What Color Is Your Operating Room?," in *Color and Design*, ed. Marilyn Delong and Barbara Martinson (London: Berg, 2012), 118–24.

57. Adams, *Medicine by Design*, 104–8; Goldwater cited the preference as roughly two-thirds of the operations occurring under artificial light ("Hospital Planning and Construction in 1924," *MH* 24, no. 1 [Jan. 1925], 4); Carl A. Erikson, "When You Build, Consider—The Changing Hospital World," *MH* 32, no. 3 (Mar. 1929), 51–52; Herbert O. Collins, "The Operating Room," *MH* 5, no. 3 (Sept. 1915), 181–83; Howell posited that the availability of good artificial illumination was a factor in shifting surgery from the home to the hospital (*Technology in the Hospital*, 58–59). See also Meyer J. Sturm, "Artificial Illumination in Hospitals," *MH* 3, no. 3 (Sept. 1914), 154–59; Oliver H. Bartine, "Artificial Illumination in Hospital, Discussion of Mr. Meyer J. Sturm's Paper on Artificial Illumination in Hospitals . . . ," *MH* 4, no. 1 (Jan. 1915), 46–48; Kirk M. Reid, "The Lighting of Hospitals," *AF*, 49, no. 6 part 2 (Dec. 1928), 917.

58. Edward F. Stevens, "Details of Planning General Hospitals," *AF* 37, no. 6 (Dec. 1922), 266; Jepson, "Planning the Surgical Service," 201–4. At the Presbyterian Hospital in New York City, chief surgeon George E. Brewer resorted to a scheduled rotation—one half of the attending doctors operated in the morning, the other in the afternoons (Adrian V. S. Lambert, "Report," in Presbyterian Hospital, New York City, *AR* 52 [1920], 63). Many thought that "the use of the same operating room and nurses by more than one surgeon and his assistants [was] not good practice." Philemon E. Truesdale, "Regulating Operating Room Traffic," *MH* 29, no. 1 (July 1927), 85.

59. "Private Rooms Only in This Hospital," *Hospital Management* 10, no. 6 (Dec. 1920), 42; Wiley E. Woodbury, "New Fifth Ave. Hospital," *MH* 19, no. 3 (Sept. 1922), 188; Lamb, *Presbyterian Hospital*, 198; Kenneth Ludmerer, *Time to Heal: American Medical Education from the Turn of the Century to the Era of Managed Care* (Oxford: Oxford University Press, 1999); David Theodore, Stacie D. Burke, and Annmarie Adams, "Tower of Power: The Drummond Medical Building and the Interwar Centralization of Medical Practice," *Scientia Canadensis* 32, no. 1 (2009), 51–68.

60. Clark Souers and Christopher G. Parnall, "The New Medical Unit at the University of Iowa," *MH* 33, no. 4 (Oct. 1927), 77; Stotz, "High Hospital Building Proves a Success," 4–5; "Private Rooms Only in This Hospital," 42; Peterkin, "Manhattan's Colossus," 60–61.

61. Bellevue and Allied Hospitals, New York City, *AR* 21 (1922), 35; Mount Zion Hospital, San Francisco, *AR* (1919), 11; Minutes, Joint Administrative Board, 1 Mar. 1927, Archives Augustus C. Long Medical Library Columbia-Presbyterian Medical Center. By 1925, assuming a twenty-four-hour staffing service, recommendations were that one nurse was needed for every two beds, yet most hospitals were providing one nurse to every three to five beds (Brodrick, "Hospital Planning in Relation to Efficiency," 215). See also Department of Hospitals, New York City, *AR* 1 (1929), 112–14; Susan M. Reverby, *Ordered to Care: The Dilemma of American Nursing, 1850–1945* (New York: Cambridge University Press, 1987), 77–94; Adams, *Medicine by Design*, 72–88; and Adams, "Rooms of Their Own: Nurses' Residences at the Montreal Royal Victoria Hospital," *Material History Review* 40 (1994), 29–41.

62. Martin, "Henry Ford Hospital in Time of Peace," 266–70; W. L. Graham, "Plans for Ford Hospital School Conform to New Ideas," *MH* 23, no. 1 (July 1924), 15–18; "Luxurious Nurses' Homes Are of Questionable Benefit," editorial, *MH* 19, no. 2 (Aug. 1922), 127.

63. Mount Zion Hospital, San Francisco, *AR* (1919), 11; Arnold Brunner and S. S. Goldwater, "New Children's Pavilion of Mount Sinai Hospital, New York," *MH* 20, no. 2 (Feb. 1923), 128. See also S. S. Goldwater, "The Lost Art of Hospital Ventilation," *MH* 22, no. 3 (Mar. 1924), 252; Goldwater, "Hospital Planning and Construction in 1924," 2; R. G. Brodrick, "Planning an Efficient Ward Unit," *MH* 18, no. 3 (Mar. 1922), 208. On where to locate the nurse, see also Roosevelt Hospital, New York City, *AR* 48 (1919), 19; Perry W. Swern, "The Interior Arrangement of Hospitals," *MH* 17, no. 2 (Aug. 1921), 104–8; William D. Crow, "Essential Equipment for the General Hospital," *AF* 37, no. 6 (Dec. 1922), 277; Richard Resler, "Locating and Organizing the Nurses' Station," *MH* 24, no. 3 (Mar. 1925), 257–59.

64. Beth Israel Hospital, New York City, Board of Directors Meeting Minutes, box 1, 1915–1924, 15 May 1921, report of Louis J. Frank, pdf p401; Robert Sommer and Robert DeWar, "The Physical Environment of the Ward," in *The Hospital in Modern Society*, ed. Eliot Friedson (London: Free Press of Glencoe, 1963), 319–35; Annie Warburton Goodrich, *The Social and Ethical Significance of Nursing: A Series of Addresses* (New York: Macmillan, 1932), 95.

65. Charles E. Rosenberg, *The Care of Strangers: The Rise of America's Hospital System* (New York: Basic Books, 1987), 286–309.

66. Ludlow, "Some Lessons the War Has Taught," 283; Woodbury, "New Fifth Ave. Hospital," 188. See also William O. Ludlow, "Making the Hospital a Place of Beauty for the Patient," *MH* 13, no. 5 (Nov. 1919), 365–68; Henry J. Davison, "An Argument for Beauty in a Hospital," *MH* 10, no. 4 (Apr. 1918), 277; Chapman, "Hospital Planning and Its Trend," 829.

67. Ludlow, "Some Lessons the War Has Taught," 283; Peterkin, "Manhattan's Colossus," 59; Peterkin, "Capitalizing Color Appeal," 69–71. See also William O. Ludlow, "Color

in the Hospital," *AA* 118, no. 2330 (18 Aug. 1920), 227; Sm. B. Stratton, "Hospital Finish and Decoration," *AF* 37, no. 6 (Dec. 1922), 283–85; "Hospital Bans White as Color Scheme"; M. Rea Paul, "How Color Affects the Mental Attitude and Physical Condition of Patients," *MH* 22, no. 3 (Mar. 1924), 260–65; Flagg, "Scientific Basis for the Use of Color," 555–59; Roof, "What Place Has Art," 329–38; M. Luckiesh and A. J. Pacini, *Light and Health: A Discussion of Light and Other Radiations in Relation to Life and to Health* (Baltimore: Williams and Wilkins, 1926); and Faber Birren, "The Psychologic Value of Color," *MH* 31, no. 6 (Dec. 1928), 85–88.

68. Adams, *Medicine by Design*, 112–13; Annmarie Adams, "Modernism and Medicine: The Hospitals of Stevens and Lee, 1916–1932," *JSAH* 58, no. 1 (1999), 46; Charles F. Neergaard, "Sound Proofing the Hospital," *AREC* 66, no. 2 (Aug. 1929), 176; Harold J. Seymour, "Eliminating Noise from the Hospital," *MH* 21, no. 3 (Sept. 1923), 264; George C. Hannam, "Noise Problems in the Modern Hospital," *MH* 22, no. 3 (Mar. 1924), 258–59. See also Edward F. Stevens, "Hospital Noises and How to Minimize Them," *MH* 24, no. 6 (June 1925), 511–13; M. Adele Oliver, "How to Create a Home-like Atmosphere in the Hospital," *MH* 25, no. 3 (Oct. 1925), 287–90.

69. Ludlow, "Making the Hospital a Place of Beauty for the Patient," 365–68.

70. Stevens, "Small Hospital," 229–48; Louis J. Frank, "The Spirit of Beth Israel," *MH* 15, no. 2 (Aug. 1920), 110; Louis J. Frank, "The Individual Room Hospital—The Hospital of the Future," *MH* 17, no. 6 (Dec. 1921), 475; Thompson and Grace Goldin, *The Hospital: A Social and Architectural History* (New Haven, CT: Yale University Press, 1975), 206–30.

71. William Everett Musgrave, "We Should Not Herd Our Sick," *MH* 27, no. 5 (Nov. 1926), 70; Swern, "Interior Arrangement of Hospitals," 106; Bacon, "New Efficient Hospital," 4.

72. Swern, "Interior Arrangement of Hospitals," 106; "Presbyterian Hospital, Chicago, Adds New Unit of 'Bacon Plan' Rooms," *MH* 24, no. 3 (Mar. 1925), 203–4, 241; "Beth Israel Opens with 40 Patients," *NYT*, 13 Mar. 1929; "OPEN $3,500,00 Hospital," *NYT*, 29 Sept. 1922; Helen Bain, "Nurse-Saving Arrangements at the Fifth Avenue Hospital," *TN* 71, no. 4 (Oct. 1923), 336–38; Brodrick, "Hospital Planning in Relation to Efficiency," 216; Alice Shephard Gilman, "Considering the Nurse in Hospital Construction," *MH* 30, no. 1 (Jan. 1928), 120–30.

73. Swern, "Interior Arrangement of Hospitals," 104–8; Bacon, "New Efficient Hospital," 4.

74. Simon Flexner quoted in Frank, "Individual Room Hospital," 478; "Private Rooms Only in This Hospital," 41.

75. Bacon, "New Efficient Hospital," 4; "Private Rooms Only in This Hospital," 42; Martin, "Henry Ford Hospital in Time of Peace," 268. See also E. H. Lewinski-Corwin, "The Relation of the Private Pavilion to the Hospital Ward," *MH* 18, no. 2 (Feb. 1922), 151–52.

76. "Open $3,500,000 Hospital," *NYT*, 29 Sept. 1922.

77. Martin, "Henry Ford Hospital in Time of Peace," 266–70; Beth Israel Hospital, Building Committee Meeting Minutes, 8 May 1919, 19 June 1919; L. Frank, "Report of Superintendent," Beth Israel Hospital Board of Directors, Meeting Minutes, 16 Mar. 1919, pdf p269 in Beth Israel Hospital Archives; "Presbyterian Hospital, Chicago, Adds New Unit," 241; Richard Resler, "Technique in Planning Private Rooms," *MH* 19, no. 6 (Dec. 1922), 485.

78. Wiley E. Woodbury, quoted in "New 5th Avenue Hospital," *NYT*, 12 June 1920; Bacon, "New Efficient Hospital," 2.

79. Erikson, "When You Build, Consider," 49; Souers and Parnall, "New Medical

Unit at the University of Iowa," 74; Albert Kahn and Christopher G. Parnall, "A Teaching Hospital That Incorporates New Ideas," *MH* 28, no. 5 (May 1927), 63–69; R. H. Creel, "A Seaman's Hospital—Built at Low Cost, Compact in Design," *MH* 45, no. 2 (Aug. 1935), 43. Hospitals with larger wards include Brockton Hospital, Brockton, Massachusetts; Chester County Hospital, Westchester, Pennsylvania; Cadet Hospital, West Point, New York; Saint Joseph's Hospital, Far Rockaway, New Jersey; SoleMar Hospital, South Dartmouth, Massachusetts; Tampa Municipal Hospital, Tampa Bay, Florida; Jewish Hospital, Brooklyn, New York; Abington Memorial Hospital, Abington, Pennsylvania; Masonic Soldiers and Sailors Hospital, Utica, New York; City Hospital, Cleveland, Ohio; Beth Israel Hospital, Newark, New Jersey; and the Philadelphia General Hospital.

80. S. S. Goldwater, "The Single Room Hospital: A Commentary," editorial, *MH* 18, no. 3 (Mar. 1922), 256–58; Samuel J. Kopetzky to Louis J. Frank, 13 Feb. 1929, box 10, 129; Louis Frank Paper Subject Files, 1924–1936, Beth Israel Hospital Archives; Morris J. Vogel, *The Invention of the Modern Hospital: Boston, 1870–1930* (Chicago: University of Chicago Press, 1980), 97–104.

81. Henry C. Wright, "Wards or Semi-Private Rooms: Report of a Symposium," *MH* 24, no. 3 (Mar. 1925), 228–32; S. S. Goldwater and E. M. Bluestone, "How Many Ward Patients Need Separate Rooms?," *MH* 24, no. 3 (Mar. 1925), 197–200; Edward F. Stevens, "The Open Ward vs. Single Rooms," *MH* 18, no. 3 (Mar. 1922), 233–34.

82. Minutes, Committee on Plans, 4 May 1923, Columbia-Presbyterian Medical Center Archives; John M. Berry, "The New X-ray Laboratory at the Albany Hospital," *MH* 15, no. 4 (Oct. 1920), 264–66; "New Hospital Addition to Care for Private Patients Exclusively," *MH* 13, no. 6 (Dec. 1919), 502. Examples of luxurious private patient buildings include the Meyer House of the Michael Reese Hospital in Chicago (1927) and the Private Patient Building (1922) and Semi-Private Patient Pavilion (1929) of the Mount Sinai Hospital in New York City.

83. "New Structure to Be Erected for Hahnemann Hospital," *MH* 28, no. 6 (June 1927), 106; "Lenox Hill Plans $6,000,000 Hospital," *NYT*, 20 Dec. 1928.

84. Roswell T. Pettit, "The Application of Hotel Service to the Hospital," *MH* 12, no. 4 (Apr. 1919), 238; Charles F. Neergaard, "The Carson C. Peck Memorial Hospital," *MH* 14, no. 5 (May 1920), 341–48; J. J. Drummond, "'The Kahler' Offers Triple Service," *Hospital Management* 12, no. 6 (Dec. 1921), 36–38; David Hadden, "A Hospital as a Hotel for the Sick," *MH* 19, no. 2 (Aug. 1922), 123–25.

85. Erikson, "When You Build, Consider."

86. Lamb, *Presbyterian Hospital*, 198; Saint Luke's Hospital, New York City, *AR* 28 (1926), 21. See also "Private Rooms Only in This Hospital," 42; Woodbury, "New Fifth Ave. Hospital," 188; Paul Starr, "Medicine, Economy and Society in Nineteenth-Century America," in *The Medicine Show: Patients, Physicians and the Perplexities of the Health Revolution in Modern Society*, ed. Patricia Branca (New York: Science History Publications, 1977), 47–65; Starr, *The Social Transformation of American Medicine* (New York: Basic Books, 1982).

87. Woman's Hospital, New York City, *AR* 71 (1926), 44; Alan DeForest Smith, *The New York Orthopaedic Hospital: A Century of Progress in Orthopaedic Surgery* (New York: New York Orthopaedic Hospital, 1966), 43.

88. See, for example, Brodrick, "Hospital Planning in Relation to Efficiency in Professional Service," 215–18; Swern, "Interior Arrangement of Hospitals," 104–8; Gilman, "Considering the Nurse in Hospital Construction," 120–30; J. J. Golub, "The Tired Nurse—What Can We Do for Her?" *MH* 31, no. 4 (Oct. 1928), 77–81.

89. The earliest use of the term *nursing unit* I have encountered was in descriptions of

the new ideal designs for isolation facilities (as described in chapter 4), which by the 1910s comprised single-bed rooms and small wards to limit cross-infections. By the 1920s, however, the phrase was commonly used to describe the variety of ward sizes and arrangements that were in use for even general patient categories. Estimates for how many patients one head nurse (and her subordinate student nurses and staff) could oversee effectively ranged from roughly twenty-four to thirty-seven (Chapman, "Hospital Planning and Its Trend," 828; Henry C. Wright, "Some Fundamentals in Hospital Planning," part 2, *AA* 120, no. 2383 [Dec. 1921], 472; and De Lee, "What Are the Special Needs of the Modern Maternity?," 59–69). See also Stevens, *In Sickness and in Wealth*, 106–13.

90. James Gamble Rogers, "The 'Northwestern Ward,'" *MH* 22, no. 4 (Apr. 1924), 348–49; Nathanial W. Faxon, "Rochester's New Medical Group—An Example of Progress," *MH* 29, no. 5 (Nov. 1927), 56, 59; J. H. Macdowell and S. S. Goldwater, "The New City Hospital of Cleveland," *MH* 18, no. 5 (May 1922), 399–400; Chapman, "Hospital Planning and Its Trend," 828. See also Maurice B. Biscoe, "The University of Colorado School of Medicine and Hospital at Denver," *MH* 20, no. 4 (Apr. 1923), 323.

91. Stevens, *In Sickness and in Wealth*, 113.

92. Howell Taylor, "How Not to Select the Architect," *MH* 24, no. 3 (Mar. 1925), 206; C. Stanley Taylor, "Modern Trends in Hospital Construction," *MH* 30, no. 3 (Mar. 1927), 61; "Where Is the Science of Medicine in Hospital Planning?," editorial, *MH* 24, no. 3 (Mar. 1925), 246. See also N. V. Perry, "Details of Hospital Construction," *MH* 11, no. 6 (Dec. 1918), 470. Prominent hospital design firms across the country included Stevens and Lee; York and Sawyer; Kendall, Taylor, and Company; Garden, Martin and Erikson; Samuel Hannaford and Sons; Crow, Lewis, and Wick; Ludlow and Peabody; Cervin and Horn; James Gamble Rogers; Myron Hunt; and Shepley, Bulfinch, Richardson, and Abbot.

93. Rosenfield and Hayhow, "Planning, Building, and Equipping a Hospital," 89; Swern, "Interior Arrangement of Hospitals," 108. Such trips were still common; see "Seeks New Construction Ideas," *NYT*, 17 July 1921.

94. Henry C. Wright, "Some Fundamentals in Hospital Planning," part 1, *AA* 120, no. 2382 (7 Dec. 1921), 424–27; Henry H. Kendall, "The Architect and His Employers," *MH* 18, no. 3 (Mar. 1922), 211; S. S. Goldwater, "Preliminary Survey for Hospital Design," *AF* 37, no. 6 (Dec. 1922), 255–56.

95. Schmidt, "Modern Hospital Design," 245; Ziegler, "The Babies' Hospital of Philadelphia," *AA* 123, no. 2412 (31 Jan. 1923), 93.

96. Beth Israel Hospital Archives, Louis Frank Paper Subject Files, 1923–1925, box 10, 129, entries for March through May, 1923; Swern, "Interior Arrangement of Hospitals," 108; Bowen, "The Administrator's Part in Hospital Planning," *MH* 18, no. 3 (Mar. 1922), 229; Frank, "Planning a Hospital Synthetically," 101; Richard E. Schmidt, "Practical Problems in Architectural Practice," *AA* 120, no. 2382 (7 Dec. 1921), 429–30. It is telling that Frank's comment appeared in the *Modern Hospital*, a journal for hospital managers and consultants, while Schmidt's appeared in the *American Architect*.

97. Davis, "Impressions of a Hospital Visitor in Europe," 50.

98. Russell B. Porter, "The Fifth Avenue Hospital," *NYT*, 19 Nov. 1922.

99. S. S. Goldwater, "An International View of Hospital Problems," *MH* 32, no. 5 (May 1929), 50; Frank, "Spirit of Beth Israel," 110. It is at this point that Adrian Forty's formulation of the modern hospital as the product of medical demands after the loss of its hygienic requirements becomes telling. Forty, "The Modern Hospital in France and England," in *Buildings and Society: Essays on the Development of the Built Environment*, ed. Anthony D. King (Boston: Routledge and Kegan Paul, 1980), 61–93.

100. Will G. Corlett and R. G. Brodrick, "Peralta Hospital Emphasizes the Hospital's Human Side," *MH* 31, no. 5 (Nov. 1928), 61–70.

Chapter 6. The "Meadow Monument to Medicine and Science," 1930–1945

Epigraph: Sidney Shalett, "Citadel of Navy Medicine," *NYT*, 18 Apr. 1943.

1. Distel, "Calculating Building Costs to Protect the Hospital," *MH* 36, no. 5 (May 1931), 83.

2. John E. Murray, *Origins of American Health Insurance: A History of Industrial Sickness Funds* (New Haven, CT: Yale University Press, 2007); Paul Starr, *The Social Transformation of American Medicine* (New York: Basic Books, 1982), 235–334; Rosemary Stevens, *In Sickness and in Wealth: American Hospitals in the Twentieth Century* (New York: Basic Books, 1989), 182–99.

3. "Hospital Presses Plea for $2,965,000," *NYT*, 28 Sept. 1939; Shalett, "Citadel of Navy Medicine." See also Michael Bliss, *The Discovery of Insulin* (Chicago: University of Chicago Press, 1982); Douglas P. Starr, *Blood: An Epic History of Medicine and Commerce* (New York: Alfred A. Knopf, 1998); John E. Lesch, *The First Miracle Drugs: How the Sulfa Drugs Transformed Medicine* (Oxford: Oxford University Press, 2007).

4. Shalett, "Citadel of Navy Medicine"; Raymond P. Schmidt, "A Tower in Nebraska," *Prologue* 41, no. 4 (2009), 44–49; John Salvaggio, *New Orleans' Charity Hospital: A Story of Physicians, Politics, and Poverty* (Baton Rouge: Louisiana State University Press, 1992), 141–42.

5. Stevens, *In Sickness and in Wealth*, 170; Ruth Hill Zimmerman, "Vital Hospitals Can Be Built," *MH* 58, no. 3 (Mar. 1942), 47–48; H. Eldridge Hannaford, "Remodeling the Hospital to Meet Today's Requirements," *MH* 41, no. 1 (July 1933), 55–58; Rev. John G. Martin, "Old Hospital Undergoes Rejuvenation," *MH* 41, no. 1 (July 1933), 64–68; H. Eldridge Hannaford, "Low Building Costs Offer Rare Chance to Remodel the Hospital," *MH* 42, no. 4 (Apr. 1934), 82–84; John H. Hayes, "Rehabilitation instead of Replacement," *MH* 44, no. 3 (Mar. 1935), 70–75; Raymond Sloan, "New Buildings for Old," *MH* 47, no. 3 (Sept. 1936), 44–48; Charles H. Lench, "Once a Tenement—Now a Modern Clinic," *MH* 40, no. 5 (May 1933), 81–84.

6. Fred G. Carter, "Should the Building Last Forever?," *MH* 60, no. 3 (Mar. 1943), 50; Veronica Miller, "The Superintendent Takes a Lesson in Hospital Planning," *MH* 34, no. 6 (June 1930), 93.

7. Annmarie Adams, "Modernism and Medicine: The Hospitals of Stevens and Lee, 1916–1932," *Journal of the Society of Architectural Historians* 58, no. 1 (1999), 51; Isadore Rosenfield, "Planning the Flexible Hospital," *AF* 57, no. 5 (Nov. 1932), 424–26. Cameron Logan, Philip Goad, and Julie Willis have noted that this "functionally specific planning and technical servicing has proven a great practical challenge for hospital modification, and attempts to reuse hospital buildings adaptively." "Modern Hospitals as Historic Places," *Journal of Architecture* 15, no. 5 (2010), 613.

8. S. S. Goldwater and G. Walter Zulauf, "Pittsburgh's Latest Achievement in Hospital Planning," *MH* 37, no. 3 (Sept. 1931), 61; David H. McAlpin Pyle, "Looking Ahead a Few Years," *MH* 52, no. 4 (Apr. 1939), 76–77; Carl A. Erikson, "The Small Hospital's Home and How It Should Be Arranged," *MH* 44, no. 3 (Mar. 1935), 76–79; Edward S. Pope, "A Specially Planned Hospital for Special Needs," *MH* 36, no. 5 (May 1931), 66–72; Raymond Sloan, "A Hospital Gets Down to Business," *MH* 46, no. 5 (May 1936), 43.

9. Edwin A. Salmon, "New Battleground in Cancer War," *MH* 55, no. 3 (Sept. 1940), 58; Isadore Rosenfield, "The Fruit of Research," *MH* 48, no. 3 (Mar. 1937), 58–64; Charles Neergaard, "A Hospital That Provides a Unique Service for the Nervously Ill," *MH* 35, no. 1 (July 1930), 79–86. Other new treatments included insulin for diabetics, sulfa drugs, salvarsan for syphilitics, and improved physiotherapies for injured patients.

10. H. Eldridge Hannaford, "Planning the General Hospital," *AF* 57, no. 5 (Nov. 1932), 392; Joy Clough, *In Service to Chicago: The History of Mercy Hospital* (Chicago: Mercy Hospital and Medical Center, 1979), 76. It was the transitional nature of the population, not the shifting ethnicities, that caused the friction. Fifth Avenue Hospital, New York City, *AR* 7–8 (1929–1930), 33–34.

11. Neergaard, "Metropolitan vs. Suburban Care," *MH* 47, no. 4 (Oct. 1936), 65.

12. "Medicine's Tomorrow," ([New York]: 1945), 22, in Bellevue Hospital, New York, NY, Miscellaneous Papers . . . 1845–1948, Manuscript Collection, NYAM; Richard H. Parke, "N.Y.U.-Bellevue Plan Grows, with Cost at $32,744,000," *NYT*, 17 Jan. 1949.

13. Logan, Goad, and Willis, "Modern Hospitals as Historic Places," 606; Talbot Hamlin, "Architecture of Hospitals," *Pencil Points* 21, no. 11 (1940), 711; Frank E. Chapman, "Planning the Initial and Future Building Program," *MH* 35, no. 4 (Oct. 1930), 49–54.

14. Rosenfield, "Planning the Flexible Hospital," 424–26.

15. "Central Structure of Newest Medical Center in New York Is Begun," *MH* 35, no. 2 (Aug. 1930), 126; Logan, Goad, and Willis, "Modern Hospitals as Historic Places," 606–8.

16. On the emphasis on efficiency, see Malcolm T. MacEachern, "Factors that Influence Ratio of Personnel to Patients," *MH* 35, no. 4 (Oct. 1930), 73–78; Sloan, "Hospital Gets Down to Business," 43; Raymond Sloan, "Beekman Street Answers Call of Downtown New York," *MH* 43, no. 1 (July 1934), 40–44; Wilber C. McLin, "If Your Personnel Needs a Lift: Motion and Time Studies Are in Order," *MH* 59, no. 4 (Oct. 1942), 54–56; R. H. Creel, "A Seaman's Hospital—Built at Low Cost, Compact in Design," *MH* 45, no. 2 (Aug. 1935), 43.

17. Neergaard, "Stretching the Community Dollar," *MH* 42, no. 3 (Mar. 1934), 59.

18. Samuel W. Lambert, "Study of the Plans for a Large Modern Hospital," *MH* 6, no. 3 (Mar. 1916), 164–70; Jonathan Hughes, "The 'Matchbox on a Muffin': The Design of Hospitals in the Early NHS," *Medical History* 44, no. 1 (Jan. 2000), 21–56; "The Memorial Hospital for the Treatment of Cancer and Allied Diseases, New York City," *AF* 71 (1939), 379–83. On zoning, see Keith D. Revell, "Regulating the Landscape: Real Estate Values, City Planning, and the 1916 Zoning Ordinance," in *The Landscape of Modernity*, ed. David Ward and Olivier Zunz (New York: Russell Sage Foundation, 1992); and Carol Willis, "Zoning and 'Zeitgeist': The Skyscraper City in the 1920s," *Journal of the Society of Architectural Historians* 45, no. 1 (Mar. 1986), 47–59.

19. "Architects Answer the Question: What about Postwar Planning?," *MH* 60, no. 3 (Mar. 1943), 58; Perry W. Swern, "Vertical Transportation in Hospitals," *Hospitals* 16, no. 2 (Feb. 1939), 13; Joseph Ellner, "A Hospital That Is a Credit to Its Park Avenue Surroundings," *MH* 38, no. 3 (Mar. 1932), 78; J. Govan, "Advantages of Vertical over Horizontal in Hospital Construction," *Transactions of the American Hospital Association* 40 (1938), 688–694.

20. John Russell Pope, William F. McCulloch, and S. S. Goldwater, "A County Hospital That Will Serve Also as a Health Center," *MH* 38, no. 5 (May 1932), 61–66; Erikson, "Small Hospital's Home," 77. See also Charles Butler and L. M. Franklin, "Chronic Disease Patients: Housing Them, Large Scale," *MH* 54, no. 1 (Jan. 1940), 67–73; M. Pollak, "Skyscraper Sanatoriums Provoke Argument at Lively Meeting of Tuberculosis Section," *MH* 49, no. 4 (Oct. 1937), 82.

21. "Hospital Crowding Grave City Problem," *NYT*, 17 July 1932; Carl A. Erikson, "Let's Fill Those Empty Beds," *MH* 43, no. 3 (Sept. 1934), 93–97; "Hospital Building Held Inopportune," *NYT*, 7 May 1932; "Architects Answer the Question," 55–58; Saint Luke's Hospital, New York City, *AR* 79 (1937), 52; Saint Luke's Hospital, New York City, *AR* 80 (1938), 29. See also Guenter Risse, *Mending Bodies, Saving Souls: A History of Hospitals* (New York: Oxford University Press, 1999), 482–90; Stevens, *In Sickness and in Wealth*, 171–200; Starr, *Social Transformation of American Medicine*, 290–335. Annmarie Adams has suggested that the separate private patient buildings were a phenomenon of short duration in Canadian hospital experience, with an abrupt end following the economic depression of 1929. *Medicine by Design: The Architect and the Modern Hospital, 1893–1943* (Minneapolis: University of Minnesota Press, 2008). Separate private patient buildings continue in US hospital practice today.

22. Rosenfield, "Planning the Flexible Hospital," 424; Carter, "Should the Building Last Forever?," 50–52.

23. "'Flexible Plan' Touches off Fireworks at Meeting of Construction Section," *MH* 49, no. 4 (Oct. 1937), 75; Goldwater, "Current Hospital Trends," *AF* 57, no. 5 (Nov. 1932), 390. There was some practical criticism of this approach—as a single-bed room "converted" to double-bed occupancy might not leave enough space between bed and wall for access by nurse or doctor (S. S. Goldwater, "Corner Bunks or Island Beds? A Plea for Comfort and Efficiency," *MH* 34, no. 1 [Jan. 1930], 75–76). See also Louis J. Frank, "Where Each Patient Has Room to Himself at Modest Cost," *MH* 26, no. 1 (Jan. 1931), 76; A. T. North, "The St. Cloud Hospital: Planned as Complete Unit, It Combines Both General and Special Facilities," *AF* 54, no. 1 (Jan. 1931), 105–14.

24. "'Flexible Plan' Touches off Fireworks," 75.

25. Mr. Sage, "Report on the Semi-Private Situation at the Presbyterian Hospital," undated [1938], 7, in Albert R. Lamb, Records, Materials Collected for The Presbyterian Hospital & the CPMC, 1858–1943, Archives of the Cornell Presbyterian Medical Center, Augustus Long Library; Carl A. Erikson, "What Germany Does and What Germany Doesn't," *MH* 36, no. 4 (Apr. 1931), 78.

26. "'Flexible Plan' Touches off Fireworks," 75.

27. Mary Lee Mitchell, "The Eight-Hour Day for the Private Duty Nurse," *American Journal of Nursing* 34, no. 5 (May 1934), 443; Mary Ellen Manley, "Shifting to an Eight-Hour Nursing Day," *MH* 50, no. 4 (Apr. 1938), 54–55; Joseph C. Doane, "Shortening Nurse Travel Lanes," *MH* 52, no. 3 (Mar. 1939), 62–63.

28. Sage, "Report on the Semi-Private Situation." See also Goldwater, "Current Hospital Trends," 387–90; Carl A. Erikson, "Remodeling—The Next Best Thing," *MH* 42, no. 4 (Apr. 1934), 56; Evan Parry, "Design for Saving," *MH* 46, no. 3 (Mar. 1936), 51; Robert D. Kohn, Charles Butler, S. S. Goldwater, and Joseph Turner, "Mt. Sinai Provides Comforts for Patients of Moderate Means," *MH* 35, no. 4 (Oct. 1930), 67–72.

29. Ellner, "Hospital That Is a Credit," 77–78; Joseph Turner, "An Experiment with Group Nursing that Augurs Success," *MH* 39, no. 1 (July 1932), 54. See also Susan M. Reverby, *Ordered to Care: The Dilemma of American Nursing, 1850–1945* (New York: Cambridge University Press, 1987), 184–87.

30. Alden B. Mills, "Milestones in Hospital History—1913–1938," *MH* 51, no. 3 (Sept. 1938), 152; Ellner, "Hospital That Is a Credit," 75–82; Turner, "Experiment with Group Nursing," 49–50; Kohn, Butler, Goldwater, and Turner, "Mt. Sinai Provides Comforts for Patients of Moderate Means," 67–72.

31. Carl A. Erikson, "The New Hospital Reflects Seventeen Years of Progress," *MH*

36, no. 3 (Mar. 1931), 72–77; Janet Peterkin, "Latest Equipment, Efficient Layout Feature Chicago Hospital," *MH* 40, no. 6 (June 1933), 67; Joseph B. De Lee, "Safeguarding Motherhood at the Chicago Lying-In Hospital," *MH* 36, no. 3 (Mar. 1931), 66–67; Adams, "Modernism and Medicine," 46.

32. Charles F. Neergaard, "Double Pavilion Plan," *MH* 58, no. 3 (Mar. 1942), 70; Isadore Rosenfield, "The Double Pavilion Plan Is Essentially a Slum," *MH* 58, no. 5 (May 1942), 56.

33. Hamlin, "Architecture of Hospitals," 712; "Little Traverse Hospital, Petoskey, Michigan," *AF* 71 (Nov. 1939), 384–87; S. S. Goldwater, "The Enthronement of Beauty in the Hospital," *MH* 34, no. 3 (Mar. 1930), 75–76; David Charles Sloane and Beverlie Conant Sloane, *Medicine Moves to the Mall* (Baltimore: Johns Hopkins University Press, 2003). See also Rev. John G. Benson, "Humanizing the Hospital," *MH* 43, no. 5 (Nov. 1934), 41–43; Sister M. Therese, "Making the Hospital Human," *TN&HR* 92, no. 4 (Oct. 1934), 349–51.

34. D. B. Edmonston, "The Value of Color in the Hospital," *TN&HR* 92, no. 1 (Jan. 1934), 44–47; "The Designing Procedure of Coolidge, Shepley, Bulfinch & Abbot, Architects of the New York Hospital–Cornell Medical College Buildings," *AF* 58, no. 2 (Feb. 1933), 92; Raymond P. Sloan, "Vast New Medical Center Guards New York's Health," *MH* 40, no. 3 (Mar. 1933), 56; Ellner, "Hospital That Is a Credit," 79; Mabel W. Binner, "How a Hospital Housekeeper Should Keep House," *MH* 39, no. 6 (Dec. 1932), 92. See also Raymond P. Sloan, "A Hospital that Features Hospitality," *MH* 40, no. 1 (Jan. 1933), 51–54: Faber Birren, "Functional Color in Hospitals," *MH* 53, no. 5 (Nov. 1939), 65–66.

35. "Children's Ward Speaks Patient's Language," *MH* 44, no. 3 (Mar. 1935), 90; Sloan, "Hospital That Features Hospitality," 51–54.

36. Victor J. Klutho, "St. Mary's Marks Golden Anniversary with a New Plant," *MH* 41, no. 6 (Dec. 1933), 53–58; G. Walter Zulauf, "Fifty Years a-Growing," *MH* 48, no. 3 (Mar. 1937), 54. That these amenities were likely offered in private and semiprivate patient rooms, but not larger wards, was understood.

37. James E. Perkins, "Isolating Communicable Disease," *MH* 55, no. 4 (Oct. 1940), 85. See also F. G. Carter, "Strict Aseptic Technique Is Required in the Contagious Unit," *MH* 41, no. 3 (Sept. 1933), 67–69; "Built without Corners," *MH* 47, no. 6 (Dec. 1936), 63–66; H. P. Von Arsdall and J. S. Baird, "Contagion Succumbs to Science," *MH* 59, no. 1 (July 1942), 52–54; M. Pollak, "Do Our Hospitals Actually Spread Tuberculosis?," *MH* 53, no. 2 (Aug. 1939), 44–45. On the role of architecture in asepsis, see Joseph C. Doane, "Asepsis and Architecture," *MH* 51, no. 5 (Nov. 1938), 69–70; Mary W. Northrop, "A Housekeeper's View of Asepsis," *MH* 52, no. 1 (Jan. 1939), 84–88; T. B. Magath, "Asepsis in the Operating Room," *MH* 52, no. 2 (Feb. 1939), 55–58; William Firth Wells, "Air-Borne Infections," *MH* 51, no. 1 (July 1938), 66. Aseptic improvements included the use of gloves and masks during operations and improved sterilization techniques. See Capt. Charles A. Rockwood, Jr. and Don H. O'Donoghue, "The Surgical Mask: Its Development, Usage, and Efficiency," *AMA Archives of Surgery* 80 (June 1960), 103–11; "Precision Sterilization Made Possible by Installation of Temperature Measuring Devices," *Hospitals* 10, no. 1 (Jan. 1936), 130–32.

38. Charles Neergaard, "Are Acoustical Materials a Menace in the Hospital?" *MH* 35, no. 2 (Aug. 1930), 72–74; James Govan, G. R. Anderson, and H. E. Reilley, "Twin Problems in Construction—Insulation and Acoustics," *MH* 42, no. 3 (Mar. 1934), 56.

39. "Why the Painted Wall Is Popular in Hospitals," *MH* 36, no. 3 (Mar. 1931), 103; "Built without Corners," 63; "Architects Answer the Question," 55–58.

40. Herman N. Bundesen, "Health Hazards in Plumbing," *MH* 44, no. 4 (Apr. 1935), 72.

41. Bundesen, "Health Hazards in Plumbing," 71; Joel I. Connelly, "Safeguarding the Sterile Water Supply," *MH* 45, no. 1 (July 1935), 63.

42. Connelly, "Safeguarding the Sterile Water Supply," 62; "Plumbing Hazard in Hospitals," *Hospitals* 10, no. 1 (Jan. 1936), 132, 135. See W. Scott Johnson, "Plumbing the Situation," *MH* 47, no. 4 (Oct. 1936), 94, 96, 98; F. M. Dawson, "Pollution in the Plumbing," *MH* 53, no. 6 (Dec. 1939), 80–84.

43. Wells, "Air-Borne Infections," 66, 69; J. J. Golub, "Infections Challenge Planning," *MH* 52, no. 3 (Mar. 1939), 67.

44. "Infections in the Nursery," *MH* 50, no. 2 (Feb. 1938), 55; "Guarding against Infection in Maternity Cases," *MH* 36, no. 2 (Feb. 1931), 83–84; "Layout for Lying-In," *MH* 50, no. 3 (Mar. 1938), 50–53. The Mothers' Aid Pavilion recreated the separate isolation facility that De Lee had championed at the earlier building complex. De Lee credited immediate isolation of infected cases to the separate building in their low rate of postpartum infection, whether or not scientific proof of its efficacy existed to reinforce that belief (De Lee, "Safeguarding Motherhood," 65–66).

45. "Control of Air-Borne Pathogenic Bacteria by Bactericidal Radiant Energy," *MH* 46, no. 6 (June 1936), 80. See also Magath, "Asepsis in the Operating Room," 55–58.

46. George F. Dick, "Disinfection by Radiation," *MH* 53, no. 5 (Nov. 1939), 53–55; Magath, "Asepsis in the Operating Room," 55–58; Wells, "Air-Borne Infections," 68; John H. Hayes, "Light Rays Baffle Bacteria," *MH* 55, no. 2 (Aug. 1940), 86.

47. Wells, "Air-Borne Infections," 167; Blackfan and Yaglou, "The Premature Infant: A Study of the Effects of Atmospheric Conditions on Growth and Development," *American Journal of Diseases of Children* 46, no. 5, part 2 (Nov. 1933), 1175–236.

48. Bacon, "Designed for Premature Infants," *MH* 52, no. 1 (Jan. 1939), 61.

49. Carl A. Erikson and Louis W. Sauer, "Control of Infection Begins in the Cradle," *MH* 55, no. 4 (Oct. 1940), 54.

50. Goldwater, "Current Hospital Trends," 390. On the history of air conditioning, see Marsha E. Ackerman, *Cool Comfort: America's Romance with Air Conditioning* (Washington, DC: Smithsonian Institution Press, 2002); Gail Cooper, *Air-Conditioning America: Engineers and the Controlled Environment, 1900–1960* (Baltimore: Johns Hopkins University Press, 1998); Reyner Banham, *The Architecture of the Well-Tempered Environment* (London: Architectural Press, 1969).

51. Abraham Oseroff, "The Weather Rooms—A Step forward in Oxygen Therapy," *MH* 46, no. 4 (Apr. 1936), 60–62; A. G. Young, "Nice Weather They're Having," *MH* 48, no. 6 (June 1937), 81–83; Lucius R. Wilson, "Allergy Room Is Appreciated," *MH* 53, no. 1 (July 1939), 64; C. P. Yaglou, "Advantages and Limitations of Hospital Air Conditioning," *MH* 53, no. 1 (July 1939), 50–51. See also C. A. Mills, "Hospitals Can Do Something about the Weather," *MH* 42, no. 4 (Apr. 1934), 69–70; C. A. Mills, "Artificial Climate—A New Service to Hospital Patients," *MH* 43, no. 4 (Oct. 1934), 57–59; John Paul Jones and Victor B. Phillips, "Air Conditioning for Hospitals," *MH* 47, no. 5 (Nov. 1936), 76–83; M. B. Ferderber, A. A. Rosenberg, and F. C. Houghten, "Physiological Aspects of Air Conditioning," *MH* 53, no. 1 (July 1939), 63; C. W. Munger, Mary V. Stephenson, Perry W. Swern, and Lucius R. Wilson, "Report of Committee on Air Conditioning," *Transactions of the American Hospital Association* 39 (1936), 176–83; William J. Overton, "The Coming Era of Air Conditioning," *MH* 36, no. 1 (Jan. 1936), 90, 92.

52. John Mannix and R. C. Buerki, "The Case for Air Conditioning," *MH* 50, no. 4 (Apr. 1938), 81–84; Mount Sinai Hospital, New York City, *AR* 82 (1933), 7; Sister Michaella, "Air Conditioning and Modernization," *MH* 46, no. 3 (Mar. 1936), 100; Munger, Stephenson, Swern, and Wilson, "Report of Committee on Air Conditioning," 176–83; "Big Negro Hospital Is Begun in Florida," *NYT*, 10 Feb. 1949. See also John Paul Jones and Victor B.

Phillips, "Air Conditioning for Hospitals," *MH* 47, no. 5 (Nov. 1936), 76–83; Alden B. Mills, "Air Conditioning at Slight Expense," *MH* 47, no. 6 (Dec. 1936), 83–84; A. J. Hockett, "Air Conditioning Operating Rooms," *MH* 48, no. 5 (May 1937), 83–85.

53. Asa S. Bacon, "Doing Away with the Open Window in the Hospital," *MH* 39, no. 2 (Aug. 1939), 37–38; "Air Pollution and the Power Engineer," *MH* 46, no. 1 (Jan. 1936), 120; "Purifying and Tempering Indoor Air," *MH* 41, no. 1 (July 1933), 77–78. See also Salmon, "New Battleground in Cancer War," 56–59; David Stradling, *Smokestacks and Progressives: Environmentalists, Engineers, and Air Quality in America, 1881–1951* (Baltimore: John Hopkins University Press, 1999); Daniel Freund, *American Sunshine: Diseases of Darkness and the Quest for Natural Light* (Chicago: University of Chicago Press, 2012).

54. A. Wayne Clark; Gustave S. Math Ey, "Dust and Postoperative Tetanus in Hospitals," *MH* 16, no. 6 (June 1921), 548; Woman's Hospital, New York City, *AR* 64 (1919), 42. See also Philemon E. Truesdale, "Regulating Operating Room Traffic," *MH* 29, no. 1 (July 1927), 84–85; Abner A. Richter, Howard Irvin Eiler, and S. S. Goldwater, "The Administration Building of the New Reading Hospital," *MH* 24, no. 4 (Apr. 1925), 322–28.

55. Jane Peterkin, "Manhattan's Colossus," *MH* 31, no. 1 (July 1928), 55–66; Veronica Miller, "Henrotin Blends Beauty and Service," *MH* 44, no. 5 (May 1935), 52. Other such operating rooms could be found at the Eye Institute of the Columbia Presbyterian Medical Center and the Robinson Memorial Hospital in Boston ("New Eye Institute Opened to the Public," *NYT*, 11 Jan. 1933; "Air Conditioned Operating Rooms," *MH* 47, no. 2 [Aug. 1936]: 120).

56. Carl A. Erikson, "Model Operating Room Is Feature at A Century of Progress," *MH* 40, no. 6 (June 1933), 87–90. The projection of images of an operation onto a screen developed as early as the 1920s; see Christoph Mörgeli, *The Surgeon's Stage: A History of the Operating Room* (Basel, Switzerland: Editions Roche, 1999), 241. Paul Nelson's ovoid operating room in the project at Saint-Lo, France, continued this exploration into domical surgical structures, but without the viewing windows. Terence Riley, *The Filter of Reason: Work of Paul Nelson* (New York: Rizzoli, 1990).

57. Erikson, "Model Operating Room," 87–90; A. G. Stephenson, "A Tramp Abroad in the Hospital Field," *MH* 44, no. 1 (Jan. 1935), 74; Foss and Stevens, "An Ideal Operating Suite," *MH* 44, no. 2 (Feb. 1935), 65–69. See also Francis J. Eisenman, "Protecting Patients through Air Conditioning," *MH* 46, no. 5 (May 1936), 62–64; Louis Allen Abramson, "Why Windows," *MH* 61, no. 1 (July 1943), 57–58; A. T. Bazin, "It's the Wound Not the Room That Needs Careful Lighting," *MH* 42, no. 3 (Mar. 1934), 75–79; "Walls of Glass," *MH* 48, no. 5 (May 1937), 82.

58. Overton, "Coming Era of Air Conditioning," 90; P. L. Hoover and E. C. Cutler, "Eliminating the Explosion Hazard in Operating Rooms," *MH* 35, no. 1 (July 1930), 49–54; Margaret H. McCurdie, "Anesthesia Explosion Hazards: Some Methods of Control," *American Journal of Nursing* 41, no. 3 (Mar. 1941), 261–64; Raymond G. Bodwell, "Building from the Inside Out," *MH* 47, no. 4 (Oct. 1936), 61; Eisenman, "Protecting Patients through Air Conditioning," 62–64; Victor B. Phillips, "Safeguarding the Operating Room against Explosions," *MH* 46, no. 4 (Apr. 1938), 81–82, 84, 86, 88; Jones and Phillips, "Air Conditioning for Hospitals," 76–83; Yaglou, "Advantages and Limitations of Hospital Air Conditioning," 50–55; "Air Conditioned Operating Rooms," 120.

59. Adams, *Medicine by Design*, 129.

60. Riley, *Filter of Reason*; J. G. William Greeff, LeRoy P. Ward, and S. S. Goldwater, "Novel Design for Brooklyn's Municipal Hospital," *MH* 34, no. 5 (May 1930), 73–78, 74; Raymond P. Sloan, "Styling the Postwar Hospital," *MH* 60, no. 3 (Mar. 1943), 52–54.

61. Richard Neutra, quoted in "Hospitals of Tomorrow," *MH* 51, no. 3 (Sept. 1938), 91; Nancy Tomes, *The Gospel of Germs: Men, Women, and the Microbe in American Life* (Cambridge, MA: Harvard University Press, 1998), 159; Adrian Forty, *Objects of Desire* (New York: Pantheon Books, 1986), 171–72; Margaret Campbell, "What Tuberculosis Did for Modernism: The Influence of a Curative Environment on Modernist Design and Architecture," *Medical History* 49, no. 4 (Oct. 2005), 463–88. See also Annmarie Adams, *Architecture in the Family Way: Doctors, Houses, and Women, 1870–1900* (Buffalo: McGill-Queen's University Press, 1996); Adams and Burke, "Not a Shack in the Woods," 437; Gwendolyn Wright, *Moralism and the Model Home: Domestic Architecture and Cultural Conflict in Chicago, 1873–1913* (Chicago: University of Chicago Press, 1980); Beatriz Colomina, "The Medical Body in Modern Architecture," *Daidalos* 65 (June 1997), 60–71.

62. As Logan, Goad, and Willis note, the selection of these modernist facilities as icons of the modern hospital "has skewed the preserved sample in ways that are quite problematic." Logan, Goad, and Willis, "Modern Hospitals as Historic Places," 602, 605.

63. Le Corbusier, *Vers une Architecture* (Paris: G. Cres, 1923). For an introduction to the numerous writings of modernist architects, see Ulrich Conrads, *Programs and Manifestoes on 20th-Century Architecture* (Cambridge, MA: MIT Press, 1987).

64. Logan, Goad, and Willis, "Modern Hospitals as Historic Places," 603.

65. American architectural periodicals between the 1870s and 1910s were filled with houses, offices, government buildings, churches, libraries, even high-rises, but typically illustrated fewer than a dozen hospitals per year. If the early twentieth century had finally seen more professional architectural attention paid to hospitals, that attention had coincided with the rapid increase in hospital construction (it was a lucrative market) and with the increasing specialization of hospital design. William Henry Walsh, "The Function of the Nurse in Hospital Planning," *TN&HR* 88, no. 1 (Jan. 1932), 68.

66. Joseph C. Doane, "Toward That Utopian Building," *MH* 48, no. 3 (Mar. 1937), 75; Charles F. Neergaard, "Report of the Committee on Hospital Planning and Equipment," *Hospitals* 10, no. 2 (Feb. 1936), 98; Walsh, "Function of the Nurse," 68–70; Cameron Logan and Julie Willis, "International Travel as Medical Research: Architecture and the Modern Hospital," *Health and History* 12, no. 2 (2010), 116–33. Hospital architects and consultants had also settled into their roles with less competition and more collaboration. This showed up in less acrimonious planning processes, but also in mutual professional recognition. Numerous professional articles in periodicals such as the *Modern Hospital*, *Hospitals*, and *Architectural Forum* were penned by architect and consultant in collaboration; in 1930, S. S. Goldwater received an honorary membership in the American Institute of Architects for his years of influential service in hospital consultation.

Chapter 7. Postwar Hospital Design Trends

Epigraph: Michael M. Davis, "Hospitals Provide Medical Care," *Modern Hospital* 51, no. 1 (July 1938), 57.

1. "Medicine's Tomorrow," ([New York]: 1945), in Bellevue Hospital, New York, NY. Miscellaneous Papers . . . 1845–1948, Manuscript Collection, NYAM.

2. Rosemary Stevens, *In Sickness and in Wealth: American Hospitals in the Twentieth Century* (New York: Basic Books, 1989), 200–224.

3. Thomas Ellerbe, quoted in Bonnie Richter, ed., *The Ellerbe Tradition: Seventy Years of Architecture and Engineering, From the Papers of Thomas Farr Ellerbe* (Minneapolis: Eller-

be, 1980), 77; Paul Starr, *The Social Transformation of American Medicine* (New York: Basic Books, 1982), 350. The consequences of the Hill-Burton Act were far-reaching and are only beginning to undergo historical assessment. See Joy Knoblauch, "The Work of Diagrams, from Factory to Hospital in Postwar America," *Manifest: A Journal of American Architecture and Urbanism* 1 (Oct. 2013), 154–63; N. McLaughlin, "Tough Act to Follow. Hill-Burton Reshaped Healthcare and Showed What Government Can Accomplish," *Modern Healthcare* 15, no. 35 (2005), 32; J. Mantone, "The Big Bang. The Hill-Burton Act Put Hospitals in Thousands of Communities and Launched Today's Continuing Healthcare Building Boom," *Modern Healthcare* 15, no. 35 (2005), 6–7; J. M. Brown, "South Carolina and Hill-Burton," *Journal of the South Carolina Medical Association* 96, no. 3 (2000), 126–30; C. Scarborough, "The Legacy of Hill-Burton," *Healthcare Alabama* 7, no. 4 (1994), 8–10, 27; Judith R. Lave and Lester B. Lave, *The Hospital Construction Act: An Evaluation of the Hill-Burton Program, 1948–1973* (Washington: American Enterprise for Public Policy Research, 1974).

4. On hospital design and construction in the late twentieth century, see the bibliographic essay section on twentieth-century hospital architecture.

5. Robert Hyde Jacobs, Jr., "The Architect's Guide to Surgical Infection," *AORN Journal* 1, no. 3 (1963), 47–63; Richard P. Gaulin, *Design Features Affecting Asepsis in the Hospital* (Washington, DC: US Department of Health, Education, and Welfare, 1960); Charnley cited in Graham Ayliffe and Mary P. English, *Hospital Infection: From Miasmas to MRSA* (Cambridge: Cambridge University Press, 2003), 176. See also Dennis R. Schaberg, David H. Culver, and Robert P. Gaynes, "Major Trends in the Microbial Etiology of Nosocomial Infection," supplement, *American Journal of Medicine* 91, no. 3B (16 Sept. 1991), 72S–75S; Robert W. Haley, David H. Culver, John W. White, W. Meade Morgan, T. Grace Emori, Van P. Munn, and Thomas M. Hooton, "The Efficacy of Infection Surveillance and Control Programs in Preventing Nosocomial Infections in US Hospitals," *American Journal of Epidemiology* 121, no. 2 (1985), 182–205; Richard E. Dixon, "Control of Health-Care-Associated Infections, 1961–2011," supplement, *Morbidity and Mortality Weekly Report* 60, no. S4 (7 Oct. 2011), 58–63.

6. Wladyslow J. Kowalski, "Air Treatment Systems for Controlling Hospital-Acquired Infections: The Epidemiology and Aerobiological Pathways of Airborne Nosocomial Infections and Methods of Air and Surface Disinfection," *HPAC Engineering* 79, no. 1 (2007). See also the various articles in "Section III: Clean Air" in *The Architecture of Hospitals*, ed. Cor Wagenaar (Rotterdam: NAi, 2006), 156–99; James F. Meadow, Adam E. Altrichter, Ashley C. Bateman, Jason Stenson, GZ Brown, Jessica L. Green, and Brendan J. M. Bohannan, "Humans Differ in Their Personal Microbial Cloud," *PeerJ* (22 Sept. 2015), doi:10.7717/peerj.1258.

Bibliographic Essay

This work has focused on changing understandings of the role of the built environment in cure, prevention, and health, as revealed by hospital design in the United States from the eighteenth century to the mid-twentieth century. Accordingly, key elements of its argument and information have come from a variety of historical disciplines—particularly the history of architecture, the history of medicine, the history of design, institutional histories, and urban and social histories. The following bibliographic essay, which includes key secondary works in a selected group of historical disciplines, is intended to be a broad introduction to the concepts and historical discussions that have influenced this work and its conclusions. It is broken into four main sections: hospital history from an architectural viewpoint; hospital history from a medical viewpoint; architectural histories relevant to hospital design; and medical histories relevant to hospital design. The focus has been on the development of hospital and healthcare spaces in the Western world, primarily the United States or places that were influential on the development of hospital design in the United States.

Hospital History from an Architectural Viewpoint

Surveys

John D. Thompson and Grace Goldin's survey of Western hospital design from antiquity to the early twentieth century, *The Hospital: A Social and Architectural History* (New Haven, CT: Yale University Press, 1975), has stood for four decades as the standard history of hospital architecture. Its strength lies in its breadth of coverage and its consideration of the many forces that influenced the shape of hospital design. Thompson and Goldin's focus on ward design as a record of the changing social role of the hospital within different eras and societies, and their selection of which times and places to focus on (and which not to) have been continued by later scholars of hospital design. Nikolaus Pevsner's *A History of Building Types* (Princeton, NJ: Princeton University Press, 1976) offers a concise historical survey of hospital design from a traditional architectural historical approach, which focuses on the formal transformation of hospitals largely as the product of specific influential persons (architects, doctors, reformers). Surveys of hospital design in specific places, like Dieter Jetter's works on German hospital history, such as *Das Europäische Hospital: von der Spätantike bis 1800* (Köln: DuMont, 1986) and *Geschichte Des Hospitals: Westdeutschland Von Den Anfängen bis 1850* (Wiesbaden: Franz Steiner, 1966), have also proven fruitful in revealing deep historical trends and local variations. Harriet Richardson's edited volume, *English Hospitals, 1660–1948: A Survey of Their Architecture and Design* (Swindon: Royal Commission on the Historical Monuments of England, 1998) provides a wealth of documentation of hospital buildings across a number of periods in hospital development. Allan Brandt and David Charles Sloane's article, "Of Beds and Benches: Building the Modern American Hospital," in *The Architecture of Science*, edited by Peter Galison and Emily Thompson (Cambridge, MA: MIT Press, 1999), examines the history of American hospital design as a means of understanding more recent "humanizing" trends in the design of medical care facilities located in shopping centers and malls.

Histories of Hospital Design to the Late Eighteenth Century

Scholarship on Renaissance hospital design, including John Henderson's *The Renaissance Hospital: Healing the Body and Healing the Soul* (New Haven, CT: Yale University Press, 2006) and Katharine Park's "Healing the

Poor: Hospitals and Medical Assistance in Renaissance Florence," in *Medicine and Charity before the Welfare State*, edited by Jonathan Barry and Colin Jones, 26–45 (New York: Routledge, 1991), as well as Jesko V. Steynitz's *Mittelalterlich hospitaler der orden und Stadte als Einrichtungen der sozialen sicherung* (Berlin: Duncker and Humblot, 1970), reveals the religious as well as the medical function of the hospital. The shift from hospital design as a location of spiritual/medical practice to a scientific/medical practice has made the late eighteenth century, and the ideal hospital designs promoted in Europe, a period of historical interest. Christine Stevenson's *Medicine and Magnificence: British Hospital and Asylum Architecture, 1660–1815* (New Haven, CT: Yale University Press, 2000) bridges the period between the baroque hospital as a religious institution to the early Enlightenment hospital as a sociomedical institution. Notable works that focus on the late eighteenth-century development of the "scientific" hospital include Robert Bruegmann's "Architecture of the Hospital: 1770–1870, Design and Technology" (PhD diss., University of Pennsylvania, 1976), and Anthony Vidler's "Confinement and Cure: Reforming the Hospital, 1770–1789," in *The Writing of the Walls: Architectural Theory in the Late Enlightenment* (Princeton, NJ: Princeton Architectural Press, 1987).

Histories of Hospital Designs Focusing on Biopolitics or Control

The politically, socially, and medically charged space of the hospital in the last two centuries has enabled an outgrowth of scholarship that examines hospital designs as a means of revealing the interactions of designed space and political intention. Michel Foucault's edited work, *Les machines à guèrir: aux origines de l'hôpital moderne* (Brussels: Pierre Mardaga, 1979), focused attention on the hospital as revelatory of the medicalization of society and as an example of biopolitics—the use of environmental design for political control. Sven-Olov Wallenstein's *Biopolitics and the Emergence of Modern Architecture* (New York: Princeton Architectural Press, 2009) continued this biopolitical examination of hospital design and extended it with selected examples of hospitals from the late eighteenth century to the present day. Thomas A. Markus examined the spatial expression of power hierarchies in eighteenth-century hospital design in *Buildings and Power: Freedom and Control in the Origin of Modern Building Types* (London: Routledge, 1993). Joy Knoblauch extends the biopolitical examination into late twentieth-century sociological spatial studies in her dissertation, "Going Soft: Architecture and the Human Sciences in Search of New Institutional Forms" (PhD diss., Princeton University, 2012).

Nineteenth-Century Hospital Design—Pavilion Wards

The influence of Florence Nightingale and her followers in developing, standardizing, and disseminating the pavilion-ward system of hospital design has permeated most discussions of nineteenth-century Western hospital design. Many works tweak this standard story, filling in gaps in time or geographic coverage in the history of the development and spread of pavilion-ward design. In "Hospital Planning: Revised Thoughts on the Origin of the Pavilion Principle in England," *Medical History* 10 (1966): 360–73, Anthony D. King pushes the beginning of the pavilion-ward plan earlier, with a discussion of the contributions of John Roberton's writings. In *The Architect and the Pavilion Hospital: Dialogue and Design Creativity in England, 1850–1914* (London: Leicester University Press, 1997), Jeremy Taylor examines the impact of the standard pavilion-ward system on the role of architects and the form of the design process for hospitals.

Late Nineteenth Century to Early or Mid-Twentieth Century

Though generally understudied, the transitional period between pavilion wards and early twentieth-century hospital designs is addressed by a few historical works. Annmarie Adams's *Medicine by Design: The Architect and the Modern Hospital, 1893–1943* (Minneapolis: University of Minnesota Press, 2008) examines hospital design in this volatile period from a material culture approach, and emphasizes the interaction of the buildings with different groups who experienced the designs—nurses, doctors, architects. David Charles Sloane and Beverlie Conant Sloane's *Medicine Moves to the Mall* (Baltimore: Johns Hopkins University Press, 2003) gives a brief history of American hospital design that establishes the relocation of medical care from homelike spaces to more institutional facilities as a means of understanding the late twentieth-century reaction that moved treatment spaces to shopping malls as a means of "civilizing the machine." David Charles Sloane provides a more concise version of his argument regarding the move of hospitals from homelike spaces to scientific institutional settings and then to malls in "Scientific Paragon to Hospital Mall," *JAE* 48, no. 2 (1994): 82–98. Adrian Forty's "The Modern Hospital in France and England," in *Buildings and Society: Essays on the Development of the Built Environment*, edited by Anthony D. King (Boston: Routledge and Kegan Paul, 1980), notes the extreme formal transition of hospitals from pavilions to high-rises and examines theoretical and social influences on that transition. Robert Bruegmann's "Two American Hospitals in 1876," *JSAH* 35, no.

4 (1976): 280–83, compares the designs of the New York Hospital and Johns Hopkins Hospital at a critical turning point in hospital architecture.

Twentieth-Century Hospital Architecture

There has been a recent increase in detailed, comprehensive, and informative publications on late twentieth-century hospital design. Stephen Verderber and David J. Fine's *Healthcare Architecture in an Era of Radical Transformation* (New Haven, CT: Yale University Press, 2000) intended to pick up where Thompson and Goldin's work left off. In this and later works, like *Innovations in Hospital Architecture* (New York: Routledge, 2010), Verderber's focus on the interaction of ideas of health and hospital design has proven particularly evocative. Cor Wagenaar's edited volume *The Architecture of Hospitals* (Rotterdam: NAi, 2006) provides a good topical introduction to current issues in hospital design. The work *50 Years of Ideas in Health Care Buildings* (London: Nuffield Trust, 1999) by Susan Francis, Rosemary Glanville, Ann Noble, and Peter Scher provides a good overview of changing design in England after the 1930s. Jonathan Hughes's "Hospital-City," *Architectural History* 40 (1997): 266–88, is a good introduction to postwar hospital design in England.

In addition to historical and theoretical treatments of hospital design, a number of hospital design sourcebooks, which provide design information and guidelines for designers of hospitals in the current day, are informative. Richard Miller and Earl S. Swensson's *Hospital and Healthcare Facility Design*, 3rd ed. (New York: W. W. Norton, 2012), has been successful enough to earn three revised editions. Robin Guenther and Gail Vittori's *Sustainable Healthcare Architecture*, 2nd ed. (Hoboken, NJ: John Wiley, 2013), promotes designs that are healthy for inhabitants and for the larger environment. Paul James and Tony Noakes's *Hospital Architecture* (New York: Longman, 1994), intended as a design sourcebook, now also offers a record of the status of hospital design in the 1980s and 1990s.

Despite the recent increase in scholarly attention given to this period of hospital architecture, there has still been very little research on the influence of the Hill-Burton Act. For some initial studies, see C. Scarborough, "The Legacy of Hill-Burton," *Healthcare Alabama* 7, no. 4 (1994): 8–10, 27; J. M. Brown, "South Carolina and Hill-Burton," *Journal of the South Carolina Medical Association* 96, no. 3 (2000): 126–30; and Joy Knoblauch, "The Work of Diagrams, from Factory to Hospital in Postwar America," *Manifest: A Journal of American Architecture and Urbanism* 1 (Oct. 2013): 154–63.

Hospital History from a Medical Viewpoint

Surveys

Several surveys of hospital history from a medical viewpoint have posited an interaction between hospital design and the medical practices within the hospital, but few have discussed building design in specifics. Henry E. Sigerist's "An Outline of the Development of the Hospital," *BHM* 4, no. 7 (1936): 573–81, provides a concise outline of three developmental stages of European hospitals—early medieval/Christian institutions, urban charitable institutions, and medical institutions—and ties American hospital development to the same three-part sequence—poorhouses/guesthouses, real hospitals, the modern hospital. Guenter Risse's *Mending Bodies, Saving Souls: A History of Hospitals* (New York: Oxford University Press, 1999) uses case studies to cover specific periods in great depth, examining the social and spiritual as well as the medical role of the hospital in its specific context at different places and times. In many cases he gives close attention to the hospital designs. Mary Risley's *House of Healing: The Story of the Hospital* (Garden City, NY: Doubleday, 1961) provides a more accessible but less detailed history of hospitals in Western society. Lindsay Prior's short but influential article, "The Architecture of the Hospital: A Study of Spatial Organization and Medical Knowledge," *British Journal of Sociology* 39, no. 1 (1988): 86–113, argues that hospital architecture is critically influenced by the medical theories and practice it housed, and cannot be understood without them.

Edited volumes have broadened historical understanding of hospital history by bringing a variety of viewpoints into the discussion. Essays in *The Hospital in History* (New York: Routledge, 1989), edited by Lindsay Granshaw and Roy Porter, illuminate key topics of hospital history from the Middle Ages to the twentieth century. Essays in *Hospital Life: Theory and Practice from the Medieval to the Modern* (New York: Peter Lang, 2013), edited by Laurinda Abreu and Sally Sheard, shed light on various aspects of daily existence and strategies for nurses, doctors, patients, and visitors in a variety of places and times. In *The American General Hospital: Communities and Social Contexts* (Ithaca, NY: Cornell University Press, 1989), edited by Diana Elizabeth Long and Janet Golden, the essays reveal the changing interaction between hospitals and their larger context, but also changing interactions between hospital institutions and the communities they served.

Medical Histories of American Hospitals

Of works that focus on American hospital development, Charles E. Rosenberg's *The Care of Strangers: The Rise of America's Hospital System* (New York: Basic Books, 1987) is the standard for a comprehensive study of the social, institutional, and medical transformation of American hospitals from charitable to all-class medical institutions. Rosemary Stevens's *In Sickness and in Wealth: American Hospitals in the Twentieth Century* (New York: Basic Books, 1989) provides an incredibly detailed and well-documented accounting of the financial repercussions of that social transformation. David J. Rothman's *The Discovery of the Asylum: Social Order and Disorder in the New Republic* (Boston: Little, Brown, 1971) studies the development of institutions (prisons, hospitals, asylums, schools) as the primary strategy for Americans to deal with social problems, with special attention to the role that the physical plant of the institutional buildings played in the cure of the inmates.

Medical Histories of Individual Institutions, Locations, or Themes

More focused studies of hospital development have concentrated on specific times, specific places, or specific populations. For example, John E. Ransom's "The Beginnings of Hospitals in the United States," *BHM* 13, no. 5 (1943): 514–39, recounts the founding of the earliest of American hospitals. Morris J. Vogel's *The Invention of the Modern Hospital: Boston, 1870–1930* (Chicago: University of Chicago Press, 1980) and David Rosner's *A Once Charitable Enterprise: Hospitals and Health Care in Brooklyn and New York, 1885–1915* (New York: Cambridge University Press, 1982) study the development of hospitals in a single city to illuminate the interaction between urban growth as well as medical change with hospital development. Other histories study the provision (or underprovision) of hospital care to specific social groups. See, for example, Harry F. Dowling's *City Hospitals: The Undercare of the Underprivileged* (Cambridge, MA: Harvard University Press, 1982) and Vanessa Northington Gamble's *Making a Place for Ourselves: The Black Hospital Movement, 1920–1945* (New York: Oxford University Press, 1995).

Other focused studies examine specific aspects of hospital history that relate to medical practice and development. Joel D. Howell's *Technology in the Hospital: Transforming Patient Care in the Early Twentieth Century* (Baltimore: Johns Hopkins University Press, 1995) discusses the transformative effect of administrative and medical equipment as it infiltrated hospital practice. There have also been a few illuminating sociological studies that attempt to reveal the interaction between hospital practices, hospital spaces, and existing social hierarchies and divisions; see, for example, Eliot Friedson's *The Hospital in Modern Society* (London: Free Press of Glencoe, 1963) and Ivan Waddington's "The Role of the Hospital in the Development of Modern Medicine: A Sociological Analysis," *Sociology* 7, no. 2 (1973): 211–24.

Architectural Histories Relevant to Hospital Design

Modernism and Health

The expectation that environmental design would have a direct effect on the health of occupants was influential not just in hospital design but in architectural modernism. Social and urban historians have examined such attitudes on the urban scale. Paul Boyer's *Urban Masses and Moral Order in America, 1820–1920* (Cambridge, MA: Harvard University Press, 1978) and Roy Lubove's *The Progressives and the Slums: Tenement House Reform in New York City, 1890–1917* (Pittsburgh: University of Pittsburgh Press, 1962) both brought to light the expectation that an improved urban or group housing design would generate an improved urban populace.

A number of more recent studies in architectural history have also begun to examine the role of environmental engineering in modernist designs and expectations. Some, like Margaret Campbell's "What Tuberculosis Did for Modernism: The Influence of a Curative Environment on Modernist Design and Architecture," *Medical History* 49, no. 4 (2005): 463–88, and Ken Butti and John Perlin's *A Golden Thread: 2500 Years of Solar Architecture and Technology* (Palo Alto, CA: Cheshire Books, 1954) approached the topic via issues of the delivery of sunlight and fresh air as environmental therapies. Others, like Paul Overy's *Light, Air & Openness: Modern Architecture between the Wars* (London: Thames & Hudson, 2007) and Peder Anker's *From Bauhaus to Ecohouse: A History of Ecological Design*, have examined these curative expectations not as related to specific ailments and their cure or prevention, but as a broad theoretical approach to the environment. Annmarie Adams's *Architecture in the Family Way: Doctors, Houses, and Women, 1870–1900* (Buffalo: McGill-Queen's University Press, 1996) examines these expectations as revealed by prescriptions by doctors, homemakers, and reformers in the design of "healthy" houses. Christine Nickl-Weller and Hans Nickl's *Healing Architecture* (Salenstein, Switzerland: Braun, 2013) provides an interesting insight into twenty-first-century forays into "healthy" architectural designs.

Ventilation and Air Conditioning

Long-lived medical expectations that fresh air and sunlight caused health and darkness and stagnation caused disease made ventilation and lighting design critical to hospital performance. The development of environmental systems and technologies has been largely neglected by architectural historians. Reyner Banham's *The Architecture of the Well-Tempered Environment* (London: Architectural Press, 1969) is still the most comprehensive examination of the influence of these new technological systems on modern and modernist designs. John E. Crowley's *The Invention of Comfort: Sensibilities & Design in Early Modern Britain & Early America* (Baltimore: Johns Hopkins University Press, 2001) examines an earlier period of adoption of environmental systems, revealing a shifting understanding of what was comfortable. John Hix's *The Glass House* (Cambridge, MA: MIT Press, 1974) examines how the demands for making usable greenhouses fueled the development of better systems of heating and ventilation.

On combined heating and ventilation systems, Barry Donaldson and Bernard Nagengast's *Heat and Cold: Mastering the Great Indoors: A Selective History of Heating, Ventilation, Air-Conditioning and Refrigeration from the Ancients to the 1930s* (Atlanta: ASHRAE, 1994) provides a detailed introduction to the development of systems for delivering tempered air to specific spaces. Robert Bruegmann's "Central Heating and Forced Ventilation: Origins and Effects on Architectural Design," *JSAH* 37, no. 3 (1978): 143–60; Eugene S. Ferguson's "An Historical Sketch of Central Heating: 1800–1860," in *Building Early America: Contributions toward the History of a Great Industry*, edited by Charles E. Peterson, 165–85 (Radnor, PA: Chilton, 1976), and Benjamin W. Walbert's "The Infancy of Central Heating in the United States: 1803 to 1845," *Association for Preservation Technology* 3, no. 4 (1971): 76–87, describe the changes wrought by central heating on architectural designs.

Gail Cooper's *Air-Conditioning America: Engineers and the Controlled Environment, 1900–1960* (Baltimore: Johns Hopkins University Press, 1998) and Marsha E. Ackerman's *Cool Comfort: America's Romance with Air Conditioning* (Washington, DC: Smithsonian Institution Press, 2002) provide good introductions to the adoption of air conditioning into buildings. T. A. Heppenheimer's "Cold Comfort: It Took Half a Century for Air Conditioning to Become Accepted and Decades More for It to Become Universal," *American Heritage* 20, no. 4 (2005): 26–37, reveals its slow rate of adoption.

Plumbing

The critical role of fresh water and the absolute necessity of disposing of wastewater safely made plumbing critical to hospital performance. As with environmental systems, the history of plumbing has been largely neglected. Maureen Ogle has been blazing the trail with works such as *All the Modern Conveniences: American Household Plumbing, 1840–1890* (Baltimore: Johns Hopkins University Press, 1996); "Water Supply, Waste Disposal, and the Culture of Privatism in the Mid-Nineteenth-Century American City," *Journal of Urban History* 25, no. 3 Mar. (1999): 321–47; and "Domestic Reform and American Household Plumbing, 1840–1870," *Winterthur Portfolio* 28, no. 1 (1993): 33–58. May N. Stone examined the issues around the adoption of early plumbing systems in "The Plumbing Paradox: American Attitudes toward Late Nineteenth-Century Domestic Sanitary Arrangements," *Winterthur Portfolio* 14, no. 3 (1979): 283–309. Ellen Lupton and J. Abbott Miller's *The Bathroom, the Kitchen and the Aesthetics of Waste: A Process of Elimination* (New York: Kiosk, 1992) examines the ways in which twentieth-century architects and designers tried to make plumbing aesthetically pleasing. Mark Girouard's "Country House Plumbing," *Country Life* 164, no. 4250 (1978): 2130–32; and 164, no. 4251 (1978): 2218–20, provides a revealing look at early plumbing systems.

Skyscrapers

As hospitals went high-rise, they encountered many of the design difficulties of taller buildings that are described in histories of skyscraper design. Carl Condit's *The Rise of the Skyscraper* (Chicago: University of Chicago Press, 1952) emphasizes technological development and economic necessity in the development of tall buildings. Thomas Leslie's *Chicago Skyscrapers, 1871–1934* (Urbana: University of Illinois Press, 2013) continues the examination of skyscrapers from a technological viewpoint. Sarah Bradford Landau and Carl Condit's *Rise of the New York Skyscraper* (New Haven, CT: Yale University Press, 1996) puts the Chicago story into a larger context. Carol Willis's *Form Follows Finance: Skyscrapers and Skylines in New York and Chicago* (New York: Princeton Architectural Press, 1995) emphasizes the role of real estate markets and finance in the shape and height of urban buildings. The essays in *The American Skyscraper: Cultural Histories*, edited by Roberta Moudry (New York: Cambridge University Press, 2005) illuminate various aspects of the larger urban and cultural context of skyscraper development.

Professionalization

The development of hospital architecture as a specialized field of design is embroiled with the professionalization of both architects and doctors. Samuel Haber's *The Quest for Authority and Honor in the American Professions, 1750–1900* (Chicago: University of Chicago Press, 1991), Magali Sarfatti Larson's *The Rise of Professionalism: A Sociological Analysis* (Berkeley: University of California Press, 1977) and Burton J. Bledstein's *The Culture of Professionalism: The Middle Class and the Development of Higher Education in America* (New York: W. W. Norton, 1976) provide a good background in the larger movement to professionalize a number of crafts. Robert Gutman's *Architectural Practice: A Critical View* (Princeton, NJ: Princeton Architectural Press, 1988) and Mary Woods's *From Craft to Profession: The Practice of Architecture in Nineteenth-Century America* (Berkeley: University of California Press, 1999) provide the historical details of the professionalization of architects. Cameron Logan and Julie Willis's "International Travel as Medical Research: Architecture and the MH," *Health and History* 12, no. 2 (2010): 116–33, offers an illuminating study of how travel played a role in professionalizing hospital design.

For medical professionalization, Joseph F. Kett's *The Formation of the American Medical Profession: The Role of Institutions, 1780–1860* (New Haven, CT: Yale University Press, 1968) provides a good introduction. Morris J. Vogel's "Managing Medicine: Creating a Profession of Hospital Administration in the United States, 1895–1915," in *The Hospital in History*, edited by Lindsay Granshaw and Roy Porter (New York: Routledge, 1989), examines the professionalization of hospital administrators.

Medical Histories Relevant to Hospital Design

Hospitals house medicine and medical practices, and they are inevitably colored by what they house. The eighteenth to the twentieth century in America was a volatile period in American medical history. To understand varying hospital designs (even as an architectural practitioner) thus inevitably requires knowledge of underlying medical theories and practices. For this, a number of social histories of American medicine are particularly helpful.

History of Medical Theories and Practice
Informative to Hospital Design History

John Harley Warner's *The Therapeutic Perspective: Medical Practice, Knowledge, and Identity in America, 1820–1885* (Cambridge, MA: Harvard University Press, 1988) reveals a shift in medical attention from considering each individual patient and their symptoms as a unique unit to considering the constellation of symptoms caused by a pathogen as a unique unit. This inspired the question of how such a shift might have affected a medical consideration of an individual's physical surroundings on health. Michel Foucault's *The Birth of the Clinic: An Archaeology of Medical Perception*, translated by A. M. Sheridan Smith (New York: Vintage Books, 1973) examines the shifting spatial as well as social structure of medicine as hospital doctors examined groups of patients with similar ailments in a ward or clinic setting rather than individual patients in their homes.

Paul Starr's *The Social Transformation of American Medicine* (New York: Basic Books, 1982) reveals the transformation of social interactions between doctors, patients, and other players in the practice of medicine. Steve Sturdy and Roger Cooter's "Science, Scientific Management, and the Transformation of Medicine in Britain c. 1870–1950," *History of Science* 36, no. 4 (1998): 421–66, illuminates the role of efficiency in hospital practice and hospital design in an era of shrinking budgets and increasing expenditures. John Duffy's *A History of Public Health in New York City, 1625–1866* (New York: Russell Sage Foundation, 1968) demonstrates how the new medical ideas interacted with older environmental ideas in the creation of a broader, public view of health that encompassed not just hospital rooms but entire cities.

Miasma Theory and Environmental Medicine

The most succinct introduction to the concepts and ideas of the aerial or miasmatic theory of disease is Caroline Hannaway's "Environment and Miasmata," in the *Companion Encyclopedia of the History of Medicine*, vol. 1, edited by W. F. Bynum and Roy Porter, 292–308 (London: Routledge, 1993). Phyllis Allen Richmond's "Some Variant Theories in Opposition to the Germ Theory of Disease," *Journal of the History of Medicine and Allied Sciences* 9 (1954): 290–303, reveals the complexity of theories of infection. Frederick Sargent's *Hippocratic Heritage: A History of Ideas about Weather and Human Health* (New York: Pergamon, 1982) presents a survey of the Western understanding of environment and health.

A number of histories examine the eighteenth- and nineteenth-century understandings of the physical environment as a direct influence on individual health in various locations. See Andrew Wear, "Making Sense of Health and the Environment in Early Modern England," in *Medicine in Society: Historical Essays*, edited by Andrew Wear (New York: Cambridge University Press, 1992); Conevery Bolton Valenčius, *The Health of the Country: How American Settlers Understood Themselves and Their Land* (New York: Basic Books, 2002); Simon Schaffer, "Measuring Virtue: Eudiometry, Enlightenment, and Pneumatic Medicine," in *The Medical Enlightenment of the Eighteenth Century*, edited by Andrew Cunningham and Roger French, 280–318 (Cambridge: Cambridge University Press, 1990); Jacqueline Karnell Corn, *Environment and Health in Nineteenth Century America: Two Case Studies* (New York: Peter Lang, 1989); and James C. Riley, *The Eighteenth-Century Campaign to Avoid Disease* (New York: St. Martin's, 1987).

Alternative Medicine in the Nineteenth and Early Twentieth Centuries

Works in the history of medicine provide a crucial guide to alternative medicines, such as the nature cure or hydrotherapy, which nineteenth-century hospital designers tried to house. See, for example, Roger Cooter, ed., *Studies in the History of Alternative Medicine* (Basingstoke, UK: Macmillan, 1988); James C. Whorton, *Nature Cures: The History of Alternative Medicine in America* (Oxford: Oxford University Press, 2002); John S. Haller, *Kindly Medicine: Physio-Medicalism in America, 1836–1911* (Kent, OH: Kent State University Press, 1997); and Kelvin Rees, "Water as a Commodity: Hydropathy in Matlock," in Cooter, *Studies in the History of Alternative Medicine*.

The rest cure for tuberculosis was inherently an environmental therapy, and is examined in a number of histories, all of which consider the sanatorium environment to varying degrees. See, for example, Annmarie Adams and Stacie Burke, "'Not a Shack in the Woods': Architecture for Tuberculosis in Muskoka and Toronto," *Canadian Bulletin of the History of Medicine* 23, no. 2 (2006): 429–55; Sheila M. Rothman, *Living in the Shadow of Death: Tuberculosis and the Social Experience of Illness in American History* (Baltimore: Johns Hopkins University Press, 1994); David L. Ellison, *Healing Tuberculosis in the Woods: Medicine and Science at the End of the Nineteenth Century* (Westport, CT: Greenwood Press, 1994); Frank Ryan, *The Forgotten Plague: How the Battle against Tuberculosis Was Won and Lost*

(Boston: Back Bay Books, 1993); Susan Sontag, *Illness as Metaphor* (New York: Farrar, Straus and Giroux, 1978); Michael Worboys, "The Sanatorium Treatment for Consumption in Britain, 1890-1914," in *Medical Innovations in Historical Perspective*, edited by John V. Pickstone (New York: St. Martin's Press, 1992), 47–71. Environmental therapy was also a part of the design of asylums for persons with mental illness. See, e.g., Carla Yanni, *The Architecture of Madness* (Minneapolis: University of Minnesota Press, 2007).

Germ Theory, Antisepsis, Asepsis

The secondary literature on the development, adoption, and dissemination of germ theory, antisepsis, and asepsis is vast. Margaret Pelling's "Contagion/Germ Theory/Specificity," in *Companion Encyclopedia of the History of Medicine*, vol. 1, edited by W. F. Bynum and Roy Porter, 309–34 (London: Routledge, 1993), provides a succinct and compelling introduction to the topic. Several works, including Michael Worboys, *Spreading Germs: Disease Theories and Medical Practice in Britain, 1865–1900* (Cambridge: Cambridge University Press, 2000); Jerry L. Gaw, *"A Time to Heal": The Diffusion of Listerism in Victorian Britain* (Philadelphia: American Philosophical Society, 1999); and Lindsay Granshaw, "'Upon This Principle I Have Based a Practice': The Development and Reception of Antisepsis in Britain, 1867–90," in *Medical Innovations in Historical Perspective*, edited by John V. Pickstone, 17–46 (New York: St. Martin's, 1992), provide a detailed account of the dissemination in England. Thomas P. Gariepy's "The Introduction and Acceptance of Listerian Antisepsis in the United States," *Journal of the History of Medicine and Allied Sciences* 49, no. 2 (1994): 167–206, has proven invaluable in developing a chronology of adoption in the United States, and J. T. H. Connor's "Listerism Unmasked: Antisepsis and Asepsis in Victorian Anglo-Canada," *Journal of the History of Medicine and Allied Sciences* 49, no. 2 (1994): 207–39, does the same for Canadian adoption. Phyllis Allen Richmond's "American Attitudes toward the Germ Theory of Disease (1860–1880)," *Journal of the History of Medicine and Allied Sciences* 9, no. 4 (1954): 428–54, reveals that American doctors picked and chose what aspects of germ theory/antiseptic practices to adopt. Toby Gelfand's "11 January 1887, the Day Medicine Changed: Joseph Grancher's Defense of Pasteur's Treatment for Rabies," *BHM* 76 (Winter 2002): 698–718, details the development of barrier nursing and aseptic practices in the prevention of cross-infections even in confined spaces.

A number of works, including Nancy Tomes's *The Gospel of Germs: Men, Women, and the Microbe in American Life* (Cambridge, MA: Harvard University Press, 1998) and Suellen Hoy's *Chasing Dirt: The American Pursuit of Cleanliness* (New York: Oxford University Press, 1995) reveal the influence of the adoption of germ theory on everyday people and practices.

Hospital Disease and Nosocomial Infections

It is hard to underestimate the influence that hospital-acquired infections had upon the success or failure of hospitals, and consequently on the design of hospital buildings to facilitate prevention. Edward D. Churchill's "The Pandemic of Wound Infection in Hospitals: Studies in the History of Wound Healing," *Journal of the History of Medicine* 20 (Oct. 1965): 391–404, reveals that the difficult hygienic state of early hospitals, coupled with increasingly daring medical procedures, may have contributed to the development of early forms of resistant or virulent strains. Graham A. J. Ayliffe and Mary P. English, *Hospital Infection: From Miasmas to MRSA* (Cambridge: Cambridge University Press, 2003), and Jean-Marie Galmiche, *Hygiène et médecine: Histoire et actualité des maladies nosocomiales* (Paris: Louis Pariente, 1999), provide a historical survey of hospital-acquired infections across the *longue durée*. Modern manuals for avoiding cross-infections, like John V. Bennett and Philip S. Brachman, eds., *Hospital Infections* (Philadelphia: Lippincott-Raven, 1998) provide a register of current practices that are helpful in assessing the historical approaches to prevention.

Childbed fever has received particular attention, particularly given the experiences of Ignaz Semmelweis. See Sherwin B. Nuland, *The Doctor's Plague: Germs, Childbed Fever, and the Strange Story of Ignác Semmelweis* (New York: W. W. Norton, 2003). Other studies, like W. F. Bynum, and Vivian Nutton, eds., *Theories of Fever from Antiquity to the Enlightenment* (London: Wellcome Institute for the History of Medicine, 1981), examine the problems of prevention for specific high-risk populations. John M. Eyler's "Scarlet Fever and Confinement: The Edwardian Debate over Isolation Hospitals," *BHM* 61, no. 1 (1987): 1–24, examines the problem in relation to specific spatial reactions to infections. Elizabeth Lomax's "The Control of Contagious Disease in Nineteenth-Century British Paediatric Hospitals," *Social History of Medicine* 7, no. 3 (1994): 383–400, focuses on similar problems in children's hospitals.

History of Nursing

Nurses have always been critical to hospital practice, but their role underwent a sea change between the late eighteenth and the early twentieth centuries. Lavinia L. Dock and M. Adelaide Nutting's four-volume *History of Nursing* (New York: G. P. Putnam's Sons, 1907–1912) remains the most comprehensive history of nursing, although it was written at the height of professionalization. Numerous other studies have emphasized the influence of professionalization, particularly as promoted by Florence Nightingale, on the nurse's role and presence within the hospital. Notable among these works for the history of nursing in American hospitals are Patricia D'Antonio, *American Nursing: A History of Knowledge, Authority, and the Meaning of Work* (Baltimore: Johns Hopkins University Press, 2010); Susan Reverby, *Ordered to Care: The Dilemma of American Nursing, 1850–1945* (New York: Cambridge University Press, 1987); Dorothy A. Sheahan, "The Social Origins of American Nursing and Its Movement into the University: A Microcosmic Approach" (PhD diss., New York University, 1980); and Jane E. Mottus, *New York Nightingales: The Emergence of the Nursing Profession at Bellevue and New York Hospital, 1850–1920* (Ann Arbor, MI: UMI Research Press, 1981). Carol Helmstadter and Judith Godden's recent work, *Nursing before Nightingale, 1815–1899* (Burlington, VT: Ashgate, 2011) provides a good counterpoint, emphasizing instead the transformative influence of the increasing demands changing medical practices placed upon nurses and nursing.

A number of more institutional histories that document the development of individual nursing schools at particular hospitals also offer a wealth of information regarding the transformation of American nursing in the late nineteenth and early twentieth centuries. For example, see Abby Howland Woolsey, *A Century of Nursing, with Hints toward the Organization of a Training School . . .* (New York: G. P. Putnam's Sons, 1950); Dorothy Giles, *A Candle in Her Hand: A Story of the Nursing Schools of Bellevue Hospital* (New York: G. P. Putnam's Sons, 1949); Eleanor Lee, *History of the School of Nursing of the Presbyterian Hospital, New York 1892–1942* (New York: G. P. Putnam's Sons, 1942); and Annie Warburton Goodrich, *The Social and Ethical Significance of Nursing: A Series of Addresses* (New York: Macmillan, 1932).

Operating Rooms and Surgery

On the history of operating room designs and practices, see Christoph Mörgeli, *The Surgeon's Stage: A History of the Operating Room* (Basel, Switzerland: Editiones Roche, 1999); Thomas Schlich, "Surgery, Science and Modernity: Operating Rooms and Laboratories as Spaces of Control," *History of Science* 45, no. 3 (2007): 231–56; Annmarie Adams and Thomas Schlich, "Design for Control: Surgery, Science, and Space at the Royal Victoria Hospital, Montreal, 1893–1956," *Medical History* 50, no. 3 (2006): 303–24; and Thomas Schlich, "Asepsis and Bacteriology: A Realignment of Surgery and Laboratory Science," *Medical History* 56, no. 3 (2012): 308–34.

Much information on operating room design can also be found in histories of surgery and surgical practice; see, for example, Owen H. Wangensteen and Sarah D. Wangensteen, *The Rise of Surgery: From Empiric Craft to Scientific Discipline* (Minneapolis: University of Minnesota Press, 1978), and Harold Ellis, ed., *The Cambridge Illustrated History of Surgery*, 2nd ed. (Cambridge: Cambridge University Press, 2009). Martin S. Pernick's *A Calculus of Suffering: Pain, Professionalism, and Anesthesia in Nineteenth-Century America* (New York: Columbia University Press, 1985) reveals the role of anesthesia in increasing the complexity, duration, and invasiveness of surgery, a critical influence on the changing design and size of operating suites.

Specialization and Group Medical Practice

The increasing specialization of medicine and hospitals played a crucial role in hospital design. George Weisz, *Divide and Conquer: A Comparative History of Medical Specialization* (New York: Oxford University Press, 2006), is the first work to focus on specialization in American hospital practice. Lindsay Granshaw's, "'Fame and Fortune by Means of Brick and Mortar': The Medical Profession and Specialist Hospitals in Britain, 1800–1948," in *The Hospital in History*, ed. Lindsay A. Granshaw and Roy Porter, 199–220 (New York: Routledge, 1989), examines the development of specialization in London.

Group practice was a product of medical specialization but also a transformative reaction to it. W. Bruce Fye reveals the critical role of the Mayo Clinic in the development of group medical practice and specialization in *Caring for the Heart* (New York: Oxford University Press, 2015) and in "The Origins and Evolution of the Mayo Clinic from 1864 to 1939: A Minnesota Family Practice Becomes an International 'Medical Mecca,'" *BHM* 84, no. 3 (2010): 323–57. George Rosen discusses group practice in *The Structure of American Medical Practice*, edited by Charles E. Rosenberg (Philadelphia: University of Pennsylvania Press, 1983), 53–61. *The Handbook of Group Research and Practice*, edited by Susan A. Wheelan (Thousand Oaks, CA: Sage

Publications, 2005), includes a number of essays that consider the historical development of the practice, including Donelson R. Forsyth and Jeni L. Burnette, "The History of Group Research"; and Sally H. Barlow, Gary M. Burlingame, and Addie J. Fuhrlman, "The History of Group Practice: A Century of Knowledge."

Pediatrics and Obstetrics

Pediatrics and obstetrics have received more historical attention than other specialties. Medical histories of the development of pediatrics include Eduard Seidler, "An Historical Survey of Children's Hospitals," in *The Hospital in History*, edited by Lindsay Granshaw and Roy Porter (New York: Routledge, 1989); Buford L. Nichols, Angel Ballabriga, and Norman Kretchmer, *History of Pediatrics, 1850–1950* (New York: Raven, 1991); and Thomas E. Cone, *History of American Pediatrics* (Boston: Little, Brown, 1979). Architectural historians focusing on the design of children's institutions or facilities include Annmarie Adams and David Theodore, "Designing for 'the Little Convalescents': Children's Hospitals in Toronto and Montreal, 1875–2006," *Canadian Bulletin of the History of Medicine* 19, no. 1 (2002): 201–43; Annmarie Adams, *Medicine by Design: The Architect and the Modern Hospital, 1893–1943* (Minneapolis: University of Minnesota Press, 2008); Lindsay Prior, "The Architecture of the Hospital: A Study of Spatial Organization and Medical Knowledge," *British Journal of Sociology* 39, no. 1 (1988): 86–113; and David Charles Sloane and Beverlie Conant Sloane, *Medicine Moves to the Mall* (Baltimore: Johns Hopkins University Press, 2003).

Histories of the development of obstetrics, gynecology, and childbirth include Raymond De Vries, Sirpa Wrede, Edwin van Teijlingen, and Cecilia Benoit, eds., *Birth by Design: Pregnancy, Maternity Care, and Midwifery in North America and Europe* (New York: Routledge, 2001); Judith W. Leavitt, *Brought to Bed: Childbearing in America, 1750–1950* (New York: Oxford University Press, 1986); Richard W. Wertz and Dorothy C. Wertz, *Lying-In: A History of Childbirth in America* (New York: Free Press, 1977); and Margaret Marsh and Wanda Ronner, *The Empty Cradle: Infertility in America from Colonial Times to the Present* (Baltimore: Johns Hopkins University Press, 1996). Studies that begin to examine spatial practices accompanying the medicalization of childbirth include William R. Rosengren and Spencer DeVault, "The Sociology of Time and Space in an Obstetrical Hospital," in *The Hospital in Modern Society*, edited by Eliot Friedson, 266–92 (London: Free Press of Glencoe, 1963); and Leslie Kanes

Weisman, *Discrimination by Design: A Feminist Critique of the Man-Made Environment* (Urbana: University of Illinois Press, 1992).

Medical Education

With the integration of hospital practice and medical education, the history of the development of medical education became crucial to hospital design. I have only touched lightly on the topic; Katherine Carroll's recent work on the architecture of medical schools goes into much greater depth. See "Creating the Modern Physician: The Architecture of American Medical Schools in the Era of Medical Education Reform," *JSAH* 75, no. 1 (March 2016): 48–73; and "Modernizing the American Medical School, 1893–1940: Architecture, Pedagogy, Professionalization, and Philanthropy" (PhD diss., Boston University, 2012). Several excellent histories from medical viewpoints include William G. Rothstein, *American Medical Schools and the Practice of Medicine: A History* (New York: Oxford University Press, 1987), and Kenneth M. Ludmerer, *Learning to Heal: The Development of American Medical Education* (New York: Basic Books, 1985) and *Time to Heal: American Medical Education from the Turn of the Century to the Era of Managed Care* (Oxford: Oxford University Press, 1999).

Figure Sources and Credits

Introduction

I.1. Howard Cox, artist, in Malcolm MacEachern, *Hospital Organization and Management* (Chicago: Physician's Record Press, 1935), fp29. Courtesy Physician's Record Press.

Chapter 1

1.1. Image no. V0013990, Wellcome Images Online Database, Wellcome Library, London.

1.2. Robert Carlisle, *An Account of Bellevue Hospital* (1893), 77.

1.3. Online Image Collection, Image no. A013036, National Library of Medicine.

1.4. Wills Eye Hospital, Philadelphia, *Annual Report* (1881), cover.

1.5. State Emigrant Hospital, New York City, *Annual Report* (1865), 42–43.

1.6. Online Image Collection, Image no. C05695, National Library of Medicine.

1.7. Massachusetts General Hospital, view, Bowditch, *A History of the Massachusetts General Hospital* (1851), frontispiece.

1.8. New York Hospital from Broadway, 1854, "Hospital," Image no. 800632, Picture Collection, New York Public Library, Astor, Lenox and Tilden Foundations.

1.9. Online Image Collection, Image no. 2001698958, Library of Congress.

1.10. *Proceedings at the Dedication of the [Boston] City Hospital* (1865), endplate 3.

1.11. Mount Sinai Hospital, New York, *Annual Report* (1874), back cover.

1.12. Saint Luke's Hospital, from Ed Sears, *Story of the Greatest Nations: From the Dawn of History to the Present* (1896), Image no. 805179 Picture Collection, New York Public Library, Astor, Lenox and Tilden Foundations.

1.13. Cleveland City Hospital, *Annual Report* (1876), frontispiece.

1.14. Protestant Episcopal Hospital, *Annual Report* (1859), Online Image Collection, Image no. pao835, HABS PA-1764, Library of Congress.

1.15. *Campbell's Gazeteer* (1874), loose print.

1.16. Presbyterian Hospital, New York City, *Annual Report* (1872), 2d frontispiece.

1.17. Stephen Smith, *Principles of Hospital Construction* (1866), fp52, National Library of Medicine copy.

1.18. Roosevelt Hospital, New York City, *Annual Report* 22 (1893), fp35.

1.19. Joseph Smith, "Address Delivered on the Occasion of the Inauguration of the New South Building of the New York Hospital," 1855, insert.

1.20. Online Image Collection, Image no. A010617, National Library of Medicine.

1.21. John Francis Richmond, *New York and Its Institutions* (1872), fp35.

1.22. Rhode Island Hospital, Providence, *Proceedings* (1868), frontispiece.

1.23. Plans and Elevations of Massachusetts General Hospital, built under the superintendence of Alexander Parris, architect, Boston, 1823, "Plan of the Principal Story," courtesy Boston Athenaeum.

1.24. Online Image Collection, Image no. 92506174, Library of Congress.

1.25. David Cheever, A. Lawrence Mason, George Gay, and J. Bapst Blake, eds., *A History of the Boston City Hospital* (1906), frontispiece.

1.26. Online Image Collection, Image no. pao835, HABS PA-1764, Library of Congress.

1.27. *Proceedings at the Dedication of the [Boston] City Hospital* (1865), endplate 1.

1.28. *Harper's* 10, no. 429 (July 1866) in Online Image Collection, Image no. a013027, National Library of Medicine.

1.29. Online Image Collection, Image no. a01727, National Library of Medicine.

1.30. Saint Luke's Hospital, New York City, *Annual Report* (1860), 54.

1.31. Robert Carlisle, *An Account of Bellevue Hospital* (1893), fp92.

1.32. Broadsheet, in archival collection, National Library of Medicine.

1.33. New York City—Metropolitan Charities—The Bible and Fruit Mission to the Public Hospitals—Ministering to the Convalescent Patients on Hart's Island, May 5, 1879, Image no. 805188, Picture Collection, New York Public Library, Astor, Lenox and Tilden Foundations.

1.34. Saint Luke's Hospital, New York City, *Annual Report* (1860), 53.

Chapter 2

2.1. Online Image Collection, Image no. a012896, National Library of Medicine.

2.2. Postcard, author's collection.

2.3. John Shaw Billings and Henry M. Hurd, eds., *Hospitals, Dispensaries, Nursing* (1893), fp442.

2.4. Online Image Collection, Image no. a01875, National Library of Medicine.

2.5. Courtesy of Medical Center Archives of New York-Presbyterian/Weill Cornell.

2.6. Casimir Tollet, *Les Hopitaux Modernes au XIXe Siecle* (1894), figs. 44 and 45, 68.

2.7. *American Architect and Building News* (9 Sept. 1876), plate, Bird Library, Fine Arts Collection, Syracuse University.

Chapter 3

3.1. Burdett, *Hospitals and Asylums of the World* (1893), courtesy Cornell University Rare Book Room.

3.2. Tollet, *les Edifices Hospitaliers depuis leur origine . . .* (1892), fig 256, 268.

3.3. *American Architect and Building News*, (6 July 1895), plate, Bird Library, Fine Arts Collection, Syracuse University.

3.4. Image no. V0030941, Wellcome Library London.

3.5. Courtesy of Medical Center Archives of New York–Presbyterian/Weill Cornell.

3.6. Pennsylvania Hospital, Philadelphia, *Annual Report* 153 (1904), frontispiece.

3.7. Online Image Collection, Image no. A012784, National Library of Medicine.

3.8. Walsh, *History of Medicine in New York*, v3 (1919) fp770.

3.9. Presbyterian Hospital, New York City, *Annual Report* 30 (1898), frontispiece. Operating Theater Looking South.

3.10. Presbyterian Hospital, New York City, *Annual Report* 35 (1903), frontispiece.

3.11. National Library of Ireland on the Commons, Royal_Victoria_Hospital_in_Belfast .jpg, Wikimedia Commons.

3.12. *Inland Architect* 8, no. 3 (1894).

3.13. Henry Burdett, *Hospitals and Asylums of the World* (1893), portfolio, plate, Cornell University Rare Book Room.

3.14. Saint Luke's Hospital, New York City, *Annual Report* 59 (1917) pullout insert, fp42.

3.15. Saint Luke's Hospital, New York City, *Annual Report* 59 (1917), frontispiece.

3.16. Alexian Hospital, Chicago, *Annual Report* 30 (1896), 42.

3.17. Online Image Collection, Image no. a01842, National Library of Medicine.

3.18. George Hammond, *Treatise on Hospital and Asylum Construction* (1891), 61.

3.19. Presbyterian Hospital, New York City, *Annual Report* 36 (1904), frontispiece.

3.20. John Shaw Billings and Henry M. Hurd, eds., *Hospitals, Dispensaries, Nursing* (1893), fp428.

3.21. George Hammond, *Treatise on Hospital and Asylum Construction* (1891), 89.

3.22. Presbyterian Hospital, New York City, *Annual Report* 32 (1900), insert after title page.

3.23. Medical Center Archives of the New York-Presbyterian/Weill Cornell.

3.24. Antoine Depage, Paul Vandervelde, and Victor Cheval, *La construction des hôpitaux* (1909), 159.

3.25. George Hammond, *Treatise on Hospital and Asylum Construction* (1891), 15.

3.26. Henry Burdett, *Hospitals and Asylums of the World* (1893), portfolio, 89.

3.27. Presbyterian Hospital, New York City, in *Annual Report* 23 (1891), frontispiece.

3.28. Roosevelt Hospital, New York City, *Annual Report* 27 (1898), facing 24.

3.29. David Cheever, A. Lawrence Mason, George Gay, and J. Bapst Blake, eds., *A History of the Boston City Hospital* (1906), 38.

3.30. John Shaw Billings, *Description of the Johns Hopkins Hospital* (1880), plate 26.

3.31. Presbyterian Hospital, New York City, in *Annual Report* 33 (1901).

3.32. Riverside Hospital, New York City, in Leavitt, "The Landscape Treatment of Hospital Grounds," *Modern Hospital* 14, no. 3 (Mar. 1920), 229.

3.33. Woman's Hospital, New York City, *Annual Report* 43 (1898), frontispiece.

3.34. Henry Burdett, *Hospitals and Asylums of the World* (1893), portfolio, 11.

Chapter 4

4.1. Edward F. Stevens, *American Hospital of the Twentieth Century* (1921), figs. 8, 9.

4.2. Samuel Hannaford and Sons, "The Galloway Memorial Hospital at Nashville, Tenn.," *American Architect and Building News* 110, no. 2122 (23 Aug. 1916), plates.

4.3. Arnold Knapp, "The Herman Knapp Memorial Eye Hospital, New York City," *Modern Hospital* 9, no. 3 (Mar. 1917), 153.

4.4. R. A. Brintnall, "Hospitals of Ohio, Past and Present, with Recommendations for the Future," *Modern Hospital* 20, no. 4 (Apr. 1923), 340.

4.5. Arthur T. Laird and W. L. Sullivan, "Nopeming Hospital for Tuberculosis at Duluth, Minn.," *Modern Hospital* 8, no. 3 (Mar. 1917), 189.

4.6. Edgar P. Madorie, "The Municipal Tuberculosis Hospital of Kansas City," *Modern Hospital* 6, no. 4 (Apr. 1916), 252.

4.7. W. P. Northrup, "The Open Air Roof-Ward," in Thatcher and Woolsey, eds., *Medical and Surgical Report of the Presbyterian Hospital in the City of New York*, 8 (1908), inserts before 1, fig. 6.

4.8. Wesley Hospital, Chicago, *Annual Report* 24 (1912), 24.

4.9. Presbyterian Hospital, New York City, in *Annual Report* 42 (1910), fp81.

4.10. James Otis Post and S. S. Goldwater, "The New Samaritan Hospital of Troy, N.Y.," *Modern Hospital* 4, no. 1 (Jan. 1915), 7.

4.11. E. F. Stevens, *The American Hospital of the Twentieth Century* (1921), fig. 198, 170.

4.12. *Marc Eidlitz & Son, 1854–1914* (New York: 1914), n.p.

4.13. Lying-In Hospital of the City of New York, *Annual Report* (1902), fp58.

4.14. Edward F. Stevens, *The American Hospital of the Twentieth Century* (1921), fig. 258, 220.

4.15. Edward F. Stevens, *The American Hospital of the Twentieth Century* (1921), fig. 259, 221.

4.16. Albert J. Ochsner and Meyer J. Sturm, *The Organization, Construction and Management of Hospitals* (1907), figs. 3–6, 117–20.

4.17. Lying-In Hospital of the City of New York, *Annual Report* (1901), frontispiece.

4.18. John A. Wyeth, *With Sabre and Scalpel: The Autobiography of a Soldier and Surgeon* (1914), 462a, Cornell University Rare Book Room.

4.19. McKim, Mead and White, Architects, "The New Bellevue Hospital," *American Architect* 100, no. 1868 (11 Oct. 1911), plate.

4.20. *Western Architect* 23, no. 6 (23 June 1916), 85.

4.21. Samuel Lambert, "Study of the Plans for a Large Modern Hospital," *Modern Hospital* 6, no. 3 (Mar. 1916), 166, fig. 6.

4.22. Edward S. Blaine, "The X-Ray Dept. of Cook County Hospital," *Modern Hospital* 8, no. 5 (June 1917), 323, fig 2.

4.23. C. Hugh McKenna and Victor Andre Matteson, "Hospital of High-Grade Construction Built at a Very Low Cost," *Modern Hospital* 6, no. 1 (Jan. 1916), 19, fig. 5.

4.24. "Boston New Children's Hospital Has Novel Features," *Modern Hospital* 1, no. 2 (Oct. 1913), 94, plate 2.

4.25. Richard E. Schmidt, "Some Special Features of the New Cook County Hospital," *Modern Hospital* 1, no. 4 (Dec. 1913), 213, fig. 5.

4.26. Edward F. Stevens, *The American Hospital of the Twentieth Century* (1921), fig. 44, 36.

4.27. Plan of Stamford Hospital, CT, by George B. Post and Sons, *American Architect* 100, no. 1869 (18 Oct. 1911), 153.

4.28. L. M. Franklin and York and Sawyer, "New York Orthopedic Hospital Has New Home," *Modern Hospital* 6, no. 5 (May 1916), 315, figs. 5–6.

4.29. *Brickbuilder* 21 (July 1912), 178.

4.30. Edward F. Stevens, *The American Hospital of the Twentieth Century* (1921), fig. 40, 34.

4.31. Samuel Hannaford and Sons, "The Galloway Memorial Hospital at Nashville, Tenn.,", *American Architect* 110, no. 2122 (23 Aug. 1916), plate.

4.32. Joseph B. Howland, "The Private Ward of the Massachusetts General Hospital," *Modern Hospital* 9, no. 6 (Dec. 1917), 389–92, figs. 12, 13, 14, 15.

4.33. David Cheever, A. Lawrence Mason, George Gay, and J. Bapst Blake, eds., *A History of the Boston City Hospital* (1906), front insert pullouts.

4.34. David Cheever, A. Lawrence Mason, George Gay, and J. Bapst Blake, eds., *A History of the Boston City Hospital* (1906), front insert pullouts.

4.35. "White Plains Hospital, White Plains, NY," *Brickbuilder* 24 (1915), 69.

Chapter 5

5.1. Edward F. Stevens, *The American Hospital of the Twentieth Century* (1921), appendix, fig. 4, 369.

5.2. "Three Different Types of Wards," *Modern Hospital* 27, no. 3 (Sept. 1926), 76.

5.3. "Chicago Lying-In Hospital, Chicago, IL. Richard E. Schmidt, Garden and Martin, Hospital and Mothers' Aid Pavilion," *American Architect* 108, no. 2079 (27 Oct. 1915), plate.

5.4. Dr. Albert C. Eycleshymer, "The Research and Educational Hospitals of the State of Illinois," *Modern Hospital* 15, no. 6 (Dec. 1920), 448.

5.5. Presbyterian Hospital, New York City, *Annual Report* 61 (1929), frontispiece.

5.6. A. C. Bachmeyer, "Hospital Administration during 1924," *Modern Hospital* 24, no. 1 (Jan. 1925), 7.

5.7. Online Image Collection, Image no. D02329, National Library of Medicine.

5.8. Isadore Rosenfield, "Planning for Future Expansion," *MH* 28, no. 4 (Apr. 1927), 66, fig. 4. Courtesy NBBJ Architects.

5.9. Clark Souers and Christopher G. Parnall, "The New Medical Unit at the University of Iowa," *Modern Hospital* 33, no. 4 (1929), 73–78.

5.10. Paul G. Burt, "A Hospital Design that Ensures Advantages of Light and Air," *Modern Hospital* 32, no. 1 (Jan. 1929), 71.

5.11. Postcard, author's collection.

5.12. Postcard, author's collection.

5.13. Courtesy: Images from the Collections of Shepley Bulfinch Richardson and Abbott, Architects.

5.14. Coolidge and Shattuck, Winford H. Smith, and G. Canby Robinson, "The New Plant of the Vanderbilt University Medical School and Hospital," *Modern Hospital* 20, no. 2 (Feb. 1923), 115.

5.15. Myron Hunt, "Hospital Construction in Warm Climates," *Architectural Forum* 49, no. 6 (Dec. 1928), part 2, 902.

5.16. *Architectural Forum* 37, no. 6 (Dec. 1922), 270.

5.17. H. Eldridge Hannaford, "General Considerations in Planning a Small Hospital," *Architectural Forum* 49, no. 6 (Dec. 1928), 875.

5.18. H. Eldridge Hannaford, "General Considerations in Planning a Small Hospital," *Architectural Forum* 49, no. 6 (Dec. 1928), 876.

5.19. Alexander T. Cooper, "The Henry Ford Hospital in Time of War," *Modern Hospital* 14, no. 4 (Apr. 1920), 260.

5.20. George E. Phillips, "Detroit's New Tuberculosis Unit," *Modern Hospital* 32, no. 3 (Mar. 1929), 96. Courtesy Albert Kahn Associates, Inc.

5.21. Edward F. Stevens, *The American Hospital of the Twentieth Century* (1921), fig. 272, 232.

5.22. Albert Kahn, Christopher G. Parnall, "A Teaching Hospital that Incorporates New Ideas," *Modern Hospital* 28, no. 5 (May 1927), 66. Courtesy: Albert Kahn Associates, Inc.

5.23. York and Sawyer, Wiley E. Woodbury, "Fifth Avenue Hospital, New York," *Architectural Forum* 37, no. 6 (Dec. 1922), between plates 89 and 90.

5.24. "New Nurses' Home to Cut Illness Costs at Saint Luke's, Chicago," *Modern Hospital* 35, no. 5 (Nov. 1930), 142.

5.25. Wesley Hospital, Chicago, *Annual Report* (1923), 111.

5.26. Perry W. Swern, "The Interior Arrangement of Hospitals," *Modern Hospital* 17, no. 2 (Aug. 1921), 106.

5.27. D. D. Martin, "Henry Ford Hospital in Time of Peace," *Modern Hospital* 14, no. 4 (Apr. 1920), 268.

5.28. "Presbyterian Hospital, Chicago, Adds New Unit of 'Bacon Plan' Rooms," *Modern Hospital* 24, no. 3 (Mar. 1925), 203.

5.29. Albert Kahn, Christopher G. Parnall, "A Teaching Hospital that Incorporates New Ideas," *Modern Hospital* 28, no. 5 (May 1927), 65. Courtesy: Albert Kahn Associates, Inc.

5.30. Ludlow and Peabody, "The Carson C. Peck Memorial Hospital, Brooklyn, N.Y.," *Architectural Forum* 30, no. 6 (June 1919), 178.

5.31. William S. Michler, S. S. Goldwater, "The New Building for Easton Hospital, Easton, PA," *Modern Hospital* 10, no. 5 (May 1918), 320.

5.32. James Gamble Rogers, "The 'Northwestern Ward,'" *Modern Hospital* 22, no. 4 (Apr. 1924), 349.

5.33. York and Sawyer, Wiley E. Woodbury, Fifth Avenue Hospital, New York, *Architectural Forum* 37, no. 6 (Dec. 1922), plate 89.

Chapter 6

6.1. Slide 80-GK-13801, National Archives.

6.2. Aerial Photograph of the Washington University Medical Center with a view east of the City of Saint Louis, circa 1964 (Image no. VC30we69), Becker Medical Library, Washington University School of Medicine.

6.3. H. Eldridge Hannaford, "Planning the General Hospital," *Architectural Forum* 57, no. 5 (Nov. 1932), 394, fig. 6.

6.4. Charles F. Neergaard, "Stretching the Community Dollar," *Modern Hospital* 42, no. 3 (Mar. 1934), 58.

6.5. National Cancer Institute, ID 1744, Memorial_sloan-kettering_cancer_center.jpg, Wikimedia Commons.

6.6. York and Sawyer, S. S. Goldwater, G. Walter Zulauf, "Pittsburgh's Latest Achievement in Hospital Planning," *Modern Hospital* 37, no. 3 (Sept. 1931), 65.

6.7. Postcard, author's collection.

6.8. Robert D. Kohn and Charles Butler, S. S. Goldwater, Joseph Turner, "Mt. Sinai Provides Comforts for Patients of Moderate Means," *Modern Hospital* 35, no. 4 (Oct. 1930), 69.

6.9. Joseph Turner, "An Experiment with Group Nursing That Augurs Success," *Modern Hospital* 39, no. 1 (July 1932), 49.

6.10. Joseph B. De Lee, "Safeguarding Motherhood at the Chicago Lying-In Hospital," *Modern Hospital* 36, no. 3 (Mar. 1931), 71.

6.11. Charles F. Neergaard, "Double Pavilion Plan," *Modern Hospital* 58, no. 3 (Mar. 1942), 70.

6.12. Room for occupancy at the Little Traverse Hospital, Petoskey (Mich.), Sept. 27, 1939; Photographer—Hedrich Blessing, Film Negative HB-05447-O. Courtesy Chicago History Museum.

6.13. Raymond P. Sloan, "A Hospital that Features Hospitality," *Modern Hospital* 40, no. 1 (Jan. 1933), 54.

6.14. "Built without Corners," *Modern Hospital* 47, no. 6 (Dec. 1936), 63.

6.15. Wocher's and Sons, advertisement for Sterilamp, *Modern Hospital* 51, no. 2 (Aug. 1938), 110.

6.16. John H. Hayes, "Light Rays Baffle Bacteria," *Modern Hospital* 55, no. 2 (Aug. 1940), 86.

6.17. Climate Room, at the Chicago Lying-in Hospital, Chicago (Ill.), Aug. 23, 1949, Photographer—Hedrich-Blessing, Film negative, HB-12537-B, photo courtesy of Special Collections Research Center, University of Chicago Library. Copyright permission granted from Chicago History Museum.

6.18. Veronica Miller, "Henrotin Blends Beauty and Service," *Modern Hospital* 44, no. 5 (May 1935), 49.

6.19. Carl A. Erikson, "Model Operating Room Is Feature at A Century of Progress," *Modern Hospital* 40, no. 6 (June 1933), 89.

6.20. Carl A. Erikson, "Model Operating Room is Feature at A Century of Progress," *Modern Hospital* 40, no. 6 (June 1933), 87.

6.21. "Preliminary Elevation Studies, New York Hospital–Cornell Medical School." Courtesy: Images from the Collections of Shepley Bulfinch Richardson and Abbott, Architects.

6.22. Janet Peterkin, "Latest Equipment, Efficient Layout Feature Chicago Hospital," *Modern Hospital* 40, no. 6 (June 1933), 63.

6.23. Postcard, author's collection.

6.24. *Modern Hospital* 53, no. 3 (Sept. 1939), 64.

6.25. "Hospitals of Tomorrow," *Modern Hospital* 51, no. 3 (Sept. 1938), 91. Courtesy Dion Neutra, Architect, © 2016.

6.26. "Hospitals of Tomorrow," *Modern Hospital* 51, no. 3 (Sept. 1938), 91. Courtesy Dion Neutra, Architect, © 2016.

6.27. "Hospitals of Tomorrow," *Modern Hospital* 51, no. 3 (Sept. 1938), 90. Courtesy: Images from the Collections of Shepley Bulfinch Richardson and Abbott, Architects.

Chapter 7

7.1. Courtesy of the New York Academy of Medicine Library, © SOM.

7.2. Aerial view of Texas Medical Center, from Image file titled "aerial-UTMSH-DSC 1985_5388x2848.jpg" available on the following webpage: http://uth.tmc.edu/med/comm /downloads/index.html. Courtesy of the University of Texas Medical School at Houston, Dwight C. Andrews.

Index

Note: Page references in *italics* refer to figures.